CONTENTS

PREFACE   xiii

PART 1 ETHICAL THEORY

Introduction   1

Conventional Morality   11

THE MYTH OF THE CAVE   11
Plato

A DEFENSE OF CULTURAL RELATIVISM   17
William Graham Sumner

A CRITIQUE OF CULTURAL RELATIVISM   23
Carl Wellman

Moral Psychology   32

MAN'S SELF-INTERESTED NATURE   32
Thomas Hobbes

MORAL DEVELOPMENT: A MODERN STATEMENT
OF THE PLATONIC VIEW   36
Lawrence Kohlberg

Basic Approaches to Ethical Theory   45

NICOMACHEAN ETHICS   45
Aristotle

FOUNDATIONS OF THE METAPHYSICS OF MORALS   54
Immanuel Kant

UTILITARIANISM   64
John Stuart Mill

Justice   76

DISTRIBUTIVE JUSTICE   76
John Rawls

JUSTICE AS ENTITLEMENT   86
Robert Nozick

MORALITY AND THE LIBERAL IDEAL   95
Michael J. Sandel

Morality and the Law   100

MORALITY AND THE CRIMINAL LAW   100
Patrick Devlin

IMMORALITY AND TREASON   109
H.L.A. Hart

PART 2   CENSORSHIP AND SEXUAL ETHICS

Introduction   115

Case Study: 118
PARIS ADULT THEATRE I. V. SLATON

DEMOCRACY, CENSORSHIP, AND THE ARTS   123
Walter Berns

PORNOGRAPHY AND RESPECT FOR WOMEN   127
Ann Garry

FREEDOM AND THE OFFENSE PRINCIPLE   137
Joel Feinberg

NATURAL LAW AND UNNATURAL ACTS   146
John M. Finnis

HOMOSEXUALITY AND NATURAL LAW   152
Burton Leiser

ISSUES
IN MORAL
PHILOSOPHY

ISSUES IN MORAL PHILOSOPHY

Thomas Donaldson

Loyola University of Chicago

McGRAW-HILL BOOK COMPANY

New York   St. Louis   San Francisco   Auckland   Bogotá
Hamburg   Johannesburg   London   Madrid   Mexico   Montreal   New Delhi
Panama   Paris   São Paulo   Singapore   Sydney   Tokyo   Toronto

This book was set in Optima by Publication Services.
The editor was Emily G. Barrosse;
the production supervisor was Diane Renda;
the cover was designed by Carla Bauer.
Project supervision was done by Publication Services.
R. R. Donnelley & Sons Company was printer and binder.

ISSUES IN MORAL PHILOSOPHY

2 3 4 5 6 7 8 9 0   DOCDOC   8 9 8 7 6

ISBN 0-07-017534-9

Library of Congress Cataloging-in-Publication Data
Main entry under title:

Issues in moral philosophy.

   1. Ethics—Addresses, essays, lectures.   2. Social ethics—Addresses, essays, lectures.   I. Donaldson, Thomas, date
BJ1012.I88   1986   170   85-18047
ISBN 0-07-017534-9

To Jane Donaldson Baldwin

PART 3   PREJUDICE AND EQUALITY

Introduction   **161**

Case Study: **165**
FREIDA MAE JONES

THE EQUAL RIGHTS AMENDMENT   **169**

STATEMENT ON THE EQUAL RIGHTS AMENDMENT   **169**
U.S. Commission on Civil Rights

THE INEVITABILITY OF PATRIARCHY   **172**
Steven Goldberg

ON BEING A WOMAN   **177**
Simone de Beauvoir

SEXUAL BLINDNESS AND SEXUAL EQUALITY   **181**
Bernard Boxill

REVERSE DISCRIMINATION AS UNJUSTIFIED   **190**
Lisa Newton

A DEFENSE OF PROGRAMS OF PREFERENTIAL TREATMENT   **194**
Richard Wasserstrom

PART 4   ABORTION

Introduction   **201**

Case Studies: **205**
SUSAN CRENSHAW
KIMBERLY WILSON
SARAH FEINBERG
DIANA LUDLOW

AKRON CENTER FOR REPRODUCTIVE HEALTH
V. CITY OF AKRON   **208**

AN ALMOST ABSOLUTE VALUE IN HISTORY   **215**
John T. Noonan, Jr.

ABORTION AND INFANTICIDE   **220**
Michael Tooley

A THIRD WAY   **231**
Wayne Sumner

ABORTION AND THE CONCEPT OF A PERSON   **248**
Jane English

PART 5   EUTHANASIA

Introduction   **259**

Case Studies: **262**
DONALD COWART
TYSON FAULKS

SUMMARY: *SUPERINTENDENT OF BELCHERTOWN*
STATE SCHOOL V. SAIKEWICZ   **264**

SOME NONRELIGIOUS VIEWS AGAINST PROPOSED
"MERCY-KILLING" LEGISLATION   **264**
Yale Kamisar

"MERCY-KILLING" LEGISLATION—A REJOINDER   **277**
Glanville Williams

ACTIVE AND PASSIVE EUTHANASIA   **284**
James Rachels

EUTHANASIA   **290**
Philippa Foot

PART 6   PUNISHMENT AND THE DEATH PENALTY

Introduction   **307**

Case Study: **313**
GREGG V. GEORGIA (1976)

THE CRIME OF PUNISHMENT   **320**
Karl Menninger

THE PROBLEM WITH REHABILITATION   **330**
American Friends Service Committee

JUSTIFYING PUNISHMENT   **339**
R.S. Downie

THE RIGHT TO PUNISH 346
Immanuel Kant

THE DEATH SENTENCE 348
Sidney Hook

CAPITAL PUNISHMENT 350
Hugo Adam Bedau

**PART 7 ECONOMIC RESPONSIBILITIES:
CORPORATE AND SOCIAL**

Introduction 363

Case Study: 367
PLASMA INTERNATIONAL

THE SOCIAL RESPONSIBILITY OF BUSINESS IS
TO INCREASE ITS PROFITS 369
Milton Friedman

CAN A CORPORATION HAVE A CONSCIENCE? 374
Kenneth E. Goodpaster and John B. Matthews, Jr.

THE NEW PROPERTY 388
George C. Lodge

THE CASE AGAINST HELPING THE POOR 395
Garrett Hardin

RICH AND POOR 404
Peter Singer

BASIC RIGHTS 412
Henry Shue

PART 8 NUCLEAR WAR

Introduction 421

Case Study: 423
THE FREEZE REFERENDUM

A BRIEF HISTORY OF THE ARMS RACE 425
Solly Zuckerman

SCIENTISTS DESCRIBE "NUCLEAR WINTER"   431
Constance Holden

A RATIONAL APPROACH TO DISARMAMENT   433
Caspar W. Weinberger

NUCLEAR DETERRENCE AND SELF-DEFENSE   439
Thomas Donaldson

A CONTRACTUAL DEFENSE OF NUCLEAR DETERRENCE   450
Christopher Morris

THE CHALLENGE OF PEACE: GOD'S PROMISE
AND OUR RESPONSE   461

APPENDIX: THE HUMAN LIFE BILL   473

PREFACE

Ethics exhibits two divergent approaches: the first focuses on issues of contemporary interest, and the second on more abstract issues of theoretical and
historical significance. Having examined the stacks of ethics textbooks available
for use in college classrooms, I found that only a few attempt an examination of
both, and many fail to integrate the two kinds of subject matter successfully.
This polarization is regrettable because ethics traditionally has reflected a mix
of classical and contemporary issues. Some topics must be examined now, for
it is *now* that answers are needed. Other topics, while less urgent, deserve
examination because they display a relevance that seems as permanent as the
human condition.

This anthology attempts to harmonize these two critical aspects of ethics.
The book's aim is to serve as a basic text for an introductory course in ethics
that will shortchange neither the instructor's desire for conceptual sophistication
nor the students' demand for relevance. The first section takes up fundamental
issues of broad significance: the authority of conventional morality, moral
psychology, basic approaches to ethical theory, justice, and morality and the
law. The remaining sections explore topics of special contemporary relevance:
censorship and sexual ethics, abortion, euthanasia, punishment and the death
penalty, prejudice and equality, economic responsibilities, and nuclear
deterrence.

Topics are arranged to allow for a step-by-step progression in concepts for
the student, and the theoretical issues introduced in Part One are re-
encountered in the discussions of applied issues in later sections. For example,
the relationship between law and morality discussed in Part One is followed
immediately by the discussion of morality and censorship in Part Two, and the
same question of law and morality re-emerges in the sections on capital
punishment and economic responsibilities. Furthermore, I have attempted to
arrange the articles within parts in a logical sequence that first highlights key
aspects of the issue being disputed and then displays an increasing sophistication
to which the issue's analysis is subject. Finally, like issues are arranged with
like; for example, all three topics centering on life-death decisions—abortion,
euthanasia, and the death penalty—are collected together.

The book also utilizes a device that has gained increasing acceptance in philosophical circles: the case method. Once used exclusively in schools of business or law, the case study has shown itself to have successful application to a wide range of ethical issues. Seven of the book's eight parts begin with a case study, and the instructor may engage students in the discussion of a concrete problem typical of those encountered in the real world. For most instructors the primary role of the case study is to reveal ethical issues as they occur in context and to whet the students' appetites for the theoretical discussions that follow.

Critics of abortion will note that Part Four includes more articles defending the permissibility of abortions (and in one instance, infanticide) than criticizing it. This is not a disguised attempt to promote abortion (indeed, my own views happen to lie in the opposite direction; rather it is an acknowledgment that, wherever truth happens to lie, the variety of kinds of pro-abortion justifications commonly offered is greater than the variety of pro-life justifications. In order to provide the student with an accurate conceptual map from which to judge the issues, it was necesary in this instance for the princple of equal time to give way to that of fair coverage. However, no inference about the relative strength of any point of view should be drawn.

The book has benefited enormously from the patient evaluation of others. I am especially indebted to the reviewers who accepted McGraw-Hill's invitation to critique the first draft: Robert T. Radford, Oklahoma State University; Robert J. Mulvaney, University of South Carolina; Richard Voight, Northampton Area Community College; and Thomas Auxter, University of Florida. Their painstaking attention to the philosophical and organizational aspects of the book was responsible for the dramatic improvement made between the first and final drafts. I want also to acknowledge a number of people who contributed directly or indirectly to the task of creating the book: Richard DeGeorge, Gerald Dworkin, Russell Hardin, Jeffrey MacMahon, Eric Park, Henry Shue, Manuel Velasquez, and Patricia Werhane. My research assistants, Dennis Keenan and Marcia Lehe, deserve substantial credit not only for handling many technical aspects of manuscript preparation, but also for making suggestions about material to include. Terri Gitler and Frances Stickney Newman, both of Publication Services, did a first-rate job of copy editing and page proof production. Thanks finally should go to Emily Barrosse, my editor at McGraw-Hill, whose careful questions and comments sparked my editorial imagination.

Thomas Donaldson

ISSUES
IN MORAL
PHILOSOPHY

PART ONE

ETHICAL THEORY

INTRODUCTION

In the classic tragedy by Sophocles, *Antigone,* a woman agonizes over the fate of her brother who was killed while opposing the king of Thebes. Her grief is more acute because of the new decree promulgated by the king demanding that her brother's body be left to rot beyond the city's walls, deprived of the burial required by ancient custom. Violation of the decree carries the penalty of death. Thus, not to bury her brother means flouting family duty and defying the will of the gods; but burying him means defying the law of the state and bringing death upon herself. In the end, she disobeys the decree.

Retold for over two thousand years, this simple story draws its power from its ability to dramatize a difficult moral dilemma. Each of us must at some point confront one of the key issues of *Antigone*—whether to obey the law of the land, or our own conscience. Moreover, different, but equally difficult, moral questions can intrude in our lives with a direct demand for answers. Is it acceptable to secure an abortion? Should my conscience bother me if I kill an enemy soldier? Should I work for a nuclear freeze? Is business bluffing ethical? Am I bound to send some of my food or money to starving people in the far corners of the world?

A major aim of this anthology is to aid moral reflection by illustrating the connection between ethical theory and practice. In this section the emphasis is on ethical theory, or, in other words, on the basic issues dominating the conceptual background against which ethical decisions must be made. These issues include the authority of custom, the major modes of ethical reasoning, the nature of justice, and the relationship between law and morality. However

1

cold and abstract they may sound, such issues have a critical relationship to practical problems.

We shall be using the words "ethics" and "morality" interchangeably, although differences between the two exist in ordinary language. The word "ethics" evolved from the Greek words, "ethos," denoting personal character and "ta ethika," used to refer to philosophical inquiries into the nature of good and evil. The word "morality," in contrast, has its origins in the same Latin stem as the word "mores," meaning social customs or habits. In turn, common parlance distinguishes between "ethics" and "morality" as it distinguishes matters of individual character from those of custom. Yet despite this, modern philosophers use the words almost interchangeably, and mean by them the inquiry into, or substance of, whatever is good and right for human beings.

One can think about ethics, or one can think *about thinking* about ethics, and sometimes it helps to note the difference. In this vein, modern philosophers separate *normative* ethics from *non-normative* ethics. *Normative* ethics is what most persons think of when hearing the word "ethics"; it attempts to isolate and justify ethical principles, precepts, and positions. In other words, it purports to tell us something about how we ought to behave. *Non-normative* ethics, on the other hand, consists either of (1) *metaethics*, which is the analysis of the meaning and use of moral concepts and of the nature of moral reasoning; or of (2) *descriptive ethics*, which is the description and recording of ethical practices. Although most of the articles in this book are normative rather than non-normative, issues of metaethics and descriptive ethics are interwoven throughout.

Many philosophers take pains to distinguish normative ethics from science. Put in its simplest form, the distinction they wish to draw is between "is" and "ought," or between that which ought to be done or ought to exist, and that which is done, or is the case. Science tells us that cancer kills, not that it should kill. Ethics, on the other hand, tells us that people ought not to murder, not that they do not murder. The distinction is apt in many ways, for it highlights the differences in methodology needed for ethical versus scientific investigations. The painstaking survey that illuminates public preferences for soft drinks or political candidates (and is helpful to pollsters and manufacturers of soft drinks) may say nothing about which candidates or soft drinks people *ought* to pick.

Nevertheless, the simple distinction between fact and value breaks down in important ways. To begin with, sophisticated theories exist which attempt to bridge the gap between "is" and "ought." Aristotle and Spinoza, for example, both identify the good with an underlying reality in nature. Second, the gap suggests something false about moral belief; namely, that facts are irrelevant. Often, agreement about the facts will generate agreement about ethics. The woman who disagrees with U.S. policy in Central American, or the man who objects to welfare payments made to the poor, usually maintains factual beliefs about these issues—say, that the Soviets are not orchestrating national revolutions, or that welfare recipients would prefer not to work—that are crucial to her or his moral views. Clear up factual disputes and, in many cases, the ethical disputes will likewise vanish.

The issue of the fact-value distinction has confused and divided generations of philosophers. Spinning off from the nucleus of this issue are a few specific, unresolved questions:

1 Are ethical judgments *true* or *false*?
2 Is genuine ethical knowledge, whether factual or nonfactual, possible?
3 Can values be derived from facts? (Can one derive an *ought* from an *is*?)

Those who answer questions (1) and (2) with a "no" are *non-cognitivists* because of their belief that moral judgments do not *refer* to anything, but instead are merely expressions either of attitudes or of emotions. Those, on the other hand, who answer (1) and (2) with a "yes" are "cognitivists" and fall into two separate subcategories depending on how they answer question (3). If they believe that an "is" can be used to derive an "ought," or in other words that ethical knowledge can be derived from empirical truths (facts about the world), then they are "naturalists." But if, on the other hand, they deny that facts underlie values, preferring to view moral knowledge as the product of moral intuition, they are classified as *intuitionists*. As should be obvious, there is no simple answer to the question of the relationship between facts and values, and one's perspective on the issue will be strongly influenced by one's answer to subsidiary questions such as factual derivability, moral knowledge, and the status of ethical judgments.

It is tempting to by-pass the moral theory of the present section and turn immediately to the problems of practice that come later. Yet patience with theory is a prerequisite for practical success. Only an acquaintance with moral basics can untangle and clarify background assumptions that frequently determine moral attitudes. One word of encouragement: despite the fact that philosophy is notorious for disagreement, most philosophers do agree that people can come to think better and more clearly about ethics, just as they can come to think more clearly about law or biology. Indeed students are usually amazed to discover how much agreement exists among moral philosophers, and how much headway has been made in resolving stubborn moral problems.

CONVENTIONAL MORALITY

When studying ethics, one is forced to begin in the middle. We all bring to our study a host of beliefs, experiences, and attitudes, and many of these are remnants of the morality of our friends, teachers, and family. Thus, it makes sense to inquire early in one's study about the status of conventional morality, of, in other words, the moral views that are accepted by ordinary members of society, and of the authority, if any, such views possess.

Those lucky few who depart from ordinary ways of thinking and attain true moral knowledge, says Plato, are like people who once were chained to rocks in a dark cave and who mistook shadows on the wall for reality. Once free, they are bedazzled by the light of the sun but will never again settle for the illusions and half-truths of their former existence. In the selection that begins this section, we read the classic allegory of the cave from Plato's *Republic,* a story that underscores Plato's own conviction of the value of philosophical knowledge. In the section that precedes the allegory, Plato clarifies his own vision of what insight into the "Good" (an expression he uses to represent the highest object of philosophical knowledge) ultimately means.

In sharp contrast to Plato, the anthropologist William Graham Sumner argues in "A Defense of Cultural Relativism" that mores are, and ought to be, relative to culture. In certain South Sea societies a young woman's attractiveness as a prospective marriage partner is enhanced by proving her fertility by having a child out of wedlock. In ours just the reverse is true. How, asks Sumner, are we to say that one culture is objectively "right" and the other "wrong?" If Sumner is correct, the implications for ethics are staggering. If he is, then ethics should doubtlessly be reduced to a branch of anthropology or to what earlier we called "descriptive ethics," and the ethicist should hope at best to explain and describe existing moral customs. Yet in a fascinating reply to the relativist, the contemporary philosopher Carl Wellman makes use of the distinction already noted between "is" and "ought." The mere existence of differences in moral attitudes among cultures, he points out, does not entail moral relativity. Indeed, it entails relativity no more than differences in factual attitudes among cultures would entail factual relativity. A disagreement between two cultures about the shape of the earth—one culture believing it to be round and the other flat—would not entail that the shape of the earth is a matter of taste. Wellman next considers more sophisticated versions of relativism, including those that derive relativity from cultural differences in moral reasoning. Although stopping short of claiming to have proven a universal, objective ethical truth, he concludes that the cultural relativism has offered no persuasive reason for accepting its assertions.

MORAL PSYCHOLOGY

Anyone seriously wishing to understand ethics must eventually confront not only the issue of how people *ought* to think and behave, but of how they *do* think and behave, and the latter issue falls under the heading of moral psychology. Two diametrically opposed views about the nature of moral psychology are presented in the readings from Hobbes and Kohlberg. In one, the seventeenth-century philosopher, Thomas Hobbes, defends his view that people are inherently, and unalterably, self-interested. Sometimes called "psychological egoism," this view sees all actions, however well disguised by apparent benevolence, as motivated by selfish interests. Even the hero who jumps on a grenade, apparently sacrificing his life for the lives of his friends, is doing so in order to satisfy some internal and ultimately self-interested urge. Peace and harmony among such self-interested creatures, Hobbes concludes, can only be secured by arranging human affairs in a manner where obedience to the demands of peace, in this instance imposed by the will of a sovereign, harmonizes with the self-interest of each.

Here it is important not to confuse Hobbe's theory of *psychological* egoism with that of *ethical* egoism. The former presumes to say nothing about how people *should* behave, only about how they *do* behave. Thus, if Hobbes is correct, we cannot help acting always on the basis of our own self-interest. *Ethical* egoism, on the other hand, disregards the underlying question of whether our psychology is inevitably self-interested; it claims instead that, however the psychological question is resolved, we *should* act on the basis of our own self-interest.

At sharp odds with the psychological egoism of Hobbes, the psychologist Lawrence Kohlberg defends what he labels a "Platonic" approach to moral psychology. According to him, moral development among children occurs in stages. A child with little if any sense of morality beyond the desire to obey rules for his or her own interests, can progress to higher stages in which universal values and the superiority of conscience over law prevail. Thus, Kohlberg emphatically rejects the Hobbesian vision of human nature as inherently selfish.

BASIC APPROACHES TO ETHICS

From one perspective the history of moral philosophy is the history of attempts to discover concepts sufficiently basic to ground all true moral propositions; to discover, in other words, the ultimate foundations of ethics. The history of that search is too lengthy to repeat but begins at least with the first systematic philosophy of the Ancient Greeks and perhaps even earlier.[1]

In this book we can hope at most to distill the complexities of this search into a small group of recurrent principles and methods. In this section three historical readings are presented that represent three distinct styles of moral reasoning.

In excerpts from the *Nicomachean Ethics* we find Aristotle defending a mode of ethical reasoning ultimately based on the function of things in nature. Aristotle asserts that we must ask about the natural *function* of the human species, individual and collective. Just as an acorn naturally grows into a strong and healthy oak tree—if it is not racked by disease or drought—so too human beings are disposed to develop their unique strengths and virtues. According to Aristotle, the uniqueness of the human species lies in its capacity for rational activity, and hence human flourishing (also translated as "happiness") necessarily involves activity in accordance with a rational principle. Aristotle believes that the study of ethics is inseparable from the study of what constitutes human flourishing in general, and virtue in the human species includes the develop-

[1]Archaeological evidence suggests that attempts to formulate concepts of social equality and universal rights were underway as early as the Middle Kingdom of Ancient Egypt, or about 2,000 B.C.; see John Wilson, *The Burden of Egypt* (Chicago: University of Chicago Press, 1953).

ment of both the "intellectual" and the "moral" virtues. Because Aristotle understands the good for humankind in terms of its end or "telos," his theory is often called *teleological.* Aristotle straightforwardly identifies the good of any thing, human or not, with its inherent nature, and it is through this inherent nature that we understand its telos. In at least one sense then, for Aristotle, what *is* also is what *ought to be.* This feature of his philosophy has prompted some philosophers to label Aristotle's ethics a philosophy of "human nature."

Unfortunately Aristotle couples this last premise with his own belief—shared by most Greeks of his day—that people are fundamentally different by nature, to yield the conclusion that the nature of virtue varies depending on the kind of person possessing it. Thus, slaves, women, and free men are all fundamentally different and capable only of their respective virtues. Of course Aristotle reserved the highest and most complete virtue for free, white males, a conclusion that has drawn a swarm of criticism in the more egalitarian nineteenth and twentieth centuries. One should note, however, that it is possible to retain the main lines of Aristotle's moral theory while dropping the questionable factual assumption that there are naturally distinct kinds of moral beings.

The eighteenth-century German philosopher, Immanuel Kant, views ethics not in terms of human nature but in terms of human reason. Already famous for his inquiries into the nature of human reason, in which he argued that all rational beings have access to certain "pure concepts of the understanding," Kant in his ethical writings identifies an equally pure and fundamental concept of morality. This concept, he tells us, belongs not to theoretical reason which possesses the power to draw rational conclusions, but to practical reason which generates actions. All of us are able to recognize this concept's validity, and we need no empirical or factual knowledge to verify its claims upon us. He calls this fundamental concept the "categorical imperative," and proceeds to offer three formulations of it, two of which are highlighted in the current selection:

1 Act so that you can will the principle of your action to be a universal law.
2 Treat other rational beings as ends in themselves (i.e., as having value in themselves) and never merely as means to ends.

The question of whether these two formulations, as Kant believed, are different ways of saying the same thing, cannot be discussed here. But this much is certain: Kant believed that recognition of the truth of the categorical imperative (sometimes also called the "moral law") was the cornerstone of ethical behavior. Kant's famous distinction between acting for the sake of "duty" and acting from "inclination" is ultimately resolved into a distinction between action prompted by mere desire or impulse (inclination) and action prompted by a genuine respect for the moral law (duty). A "good will," writes Kant, is the only thing in or out of the world that is unconditionally good. It is the only thing, in other words, that needs the accompaniment of no other thing to make it good.

And the good will, for Kant, was without doubt a will guided by reason, guided by the acknowledgment of the validity of the categorical imperative.

Because Kant focuses on moral principles and precepts, and not on consequences or human nature, he is called a "deontologist," and his style of philosophy "deontology." "Deontology" has come increasingly to refer to any brand of moral philosophy that emphasizes principles over consequences and that is "rule oriented." Kant's approach certainly jibes with this general picture, insofar as he denounces attempts to ground ethics in facts, whether present or future, and insofar as he focuses not on the consequences of acts but on their principles and motives. But "role oriented," like any blanket classification, is imperfect. Probably just as important as Kant's emphasis on principles and their universalizability is his stress on treating other rational beings as having worth in themselves and not as merely means to achieve some end. Here Kant goes beyond a simple rule-oriented approach.

Many moral philosophers construct normative evaluations not around principles, but consequences. Their approach, for obvious reason, has been dubbed "consequentialism." Consequentialism evaluates moral behavior by weighing its probable consequences through a general interpretation of human good that assesses the probable consequences of alternative acts. One consequentialist theory, entitled "preference-oriented" consequentialism, defines human good in terms of the maximal satisfaction of human preferences. Another, entitled "pluralistic" consequentialism, undertakes the same kind of evaluation but does so not in terms of preference satisfaction, but of the achievement of a particular bundle of specified goods, such as pleasure, knowledge, and friendship.

The most popular form of consequentialism, however, is called "utilitarianism" (or sometimes more specifically "hedonistic utilitarianism"). In utilitarianism, in contrast to pluralistic consequentialism, it is unnecessary to weigh, for example, the value of knowledge alongside that of friendship, for both are cashed into the common currency of pleasure. There may be different kinds of pleasure, or even different grades or levels of pleasure, but in the end, whether in the case of human knowledge or human friendship, it matters simply how much total happiness is generated for how many. The guiding rule of traditional utilitarianism, thus, is simply to bring about the greatest happiness for the greatest number of persons.

The doctrine of utilitarianism is represented in this section by its most famous advocate, John Stuart Mill. Mill, an eighteenth-century English philosopher, believed that paying attention to consequences and, in particular, to their effect on human happiness was the bottom line for ethical reasoning. He also believed, incidentally, that it was a corrective against the rule-bound ethics of traditional philosophy. A close reading of Mill, however, reveals that he is sometimes willing to evaluate rules as well as acts when undertaking utilitarian calculations of happiness. Later utilitarians have developed Mill's insight further and have called their style of philosophy "rule utilitarianism."

For the rule utilitarian, actions that seemingly generate the greatest amount of happiness for the greatest number, such as hanging an innocent man to prevent a mob lynching, can nonetheless be declared immoral on the basis of their violating a rule the general following of which is needed to generate the greatest happiness for the greatest number.

JUSTICE

As one of the first philosophers to discuss justice, Aristotle defined it as "giving equally to equals," or "giving each person his due." But many philosophers have found his definition unsatisfactory, wondering what Aristotle meant by "equals," or by a person's "due." Clearly justice cannot entail a straightforwardly equal distribution in every case, for if so it would follow that giving unequal amounts of medicine to two children (where the sicker of the two children received more medicine) would be unjust.

A society may be just in every respect yet fall short of moral perfection. A completely just society might, for example, exhibit no sense of charity or love. Hence, when speaking of justice we are speaking only of one aspect of morality, an aspect which concerns fairness and consistency of treatment. Although we can speak of justice in family behavior and social practices generally, most philosophical attention in the latter half of the twentieth century has been given to the topic of "distributive justice." Distributive justice deals with the distribution or allocation of goods among society's members. It covers, for example, questions about the distribution of wealth, employment, education, and medical resources and evaluates economic and political systems in accordance with their capacity to distribute such goods fairly.

A remarkable surge of interest in the topic of distributive justice was prompted by the publication of a single book, *A Theory of Justice* (1971), written by the philosopher John Rawls.[2] Although written prior to *A Theory of Justice*, the article by Rawls in this section summarizes many of the basic points in his theory. Rawls argues that competing concepts of justice should be evaluated by asking whether persons behind a "veil of ignorance," ignorant of their personal characteristics and position in society, would accept them. Rawls believes that such persons would accept two particular principles: (1) that persons have an equal right to the most extensive liberty compatible with a like liberty for all; and (2) that inequalities fostered by the institutional structure of society are unfair unless they work to the advantage of all, including those who are worst off. Thus, for Rawls, the presumption in favor of an equal distribution of society's goods should be overridden only when doing otherwise will actually improve the position of those who are worst off.

In a classic rejoinder to Rawls, Robert Nozick begins by questioning the very notion of "distributive justice." If by raising the issue of "distributive justice"

[2]Cambridge, Mass: Harvard University Press, 1971.

we mean to ask how we should divide up society's goods, as if we had a pie waiting to be divided on a table, then surely the question is misplaced. For unlike the pie on the table, society's goods are *already distributed.* What we should be asking, says Nozick, is whether the existing distribution is fair. For Nozick this means asking whether people have acquired their goods by just means. If they have, then it follows that they are entitled to have what they possess. This emphasis on the notion of entitlement has led many to refer to Nozick's interpretation of justice as the "entitlement" view.

According to Nozick, if one focuses not on *how* goods were acquired (a historical approach) but on *what* the distribution should look like (a "patterned" approach) one runs the risk of depriving persons of goods to which they are entitled. It runs the risk of using government intervention and taxation to deprive persons of wealth and other goods they have justly acquired. If people are willing to pay twenty-five cents each to Wilt Chamberlain to watch him play basketball, then is it fair for the government to deprive him of the money, even if it will go to someone "worse off"? Rawls' scheme, Nozick believes, would entail forbidding "capitalistic acts among consenting adults."

The contemporary debate over the interpretation of justice begun in the early 1970s by Rawls and Nozick has been joined in the 1980s by a variety of voices, many of them critical of the very assumptions underlying the Rawls-Nozick dispute. One philosopher in particular, Michael Sandel, has criticized pervasive assumptions currently held about justice. In the article included in this section, "Morality and the Liberal Ideal," he argues that the modern political mind-set is preoccupied with individual liberty and fair procedures at the expense of a fuller and more positive concept of social-personal good.

MORALITY AND THE LAW

Ethics and legality are easily confused. Perhaps this is because so many things that are immoral are also, quite properly, illegal. Or perhaps it is because so many people use legality as a convenient yardstick to measure moral acceptability. And yet preventing issues of legality from thoroughly dissolving into those of ethics and hence avoiding what might be called the "legalistic" fallacy is one of the key ingredients for clear thinking. A person commits the legalistic fallacy when he or she infers that *because* something is immoral it therefore *should* be illegal, or vice versa. I commit the fallacy if I infer from the fact that excessive drinking is immoral that it should therefore be illegal, or if I infer from the fact that slavery was legal in 1860 that it was therefore morally acceptable.

Both Patrick Devlin and H.L.A. Hart are well aware of the need to distinguish legal from moral issues, but they disagree about the relationship of morality to law. As a practical matter, Devlin grants that there should be a realm of privacy beyond the reach of the law. Yet for him the ultimate basis of the law can be nothing other than the morality of society, and hence, given that beliefs about morality can change, it follows that nothing can be absolutely off-limits to the law. If, for example, we altered our moral views about the value of privacy, the law might even be justified in regulating activities once regarded as immoral but off-limits, such as drunkeness in one's own home. The reason for this, he argues, is that moral views constitute the collective conscience of the society, and without law to support our fundamental values of family and propriety, the very fabric of society would unravel.

   H.L.A. Hart finds Devlin's view mistaken and potentially dangerous. With no guiding principle save that of matching the law to moral opinion, he asks, what protects individuals from suffocation by the moral majority? And if the boundaries of law are to be matched finally with those of the law, how can moral reformers make their point without actually breaking the law? Hart recommends, instead, that the connection between law and morality be mediated by a strong recognition of existing human rights, especially the right of individual liberty.

CONVENTIONAL MORALITY

The Myth of the Cave

Plato

...Socrates, what is your own account of the Good? Is it knowledge, or pleasure, or something else?

There you are! I exclaimed; I could see all along that you were not going to be content with what other people think.

Well, Socrates, it does not seem fair that you should be ready to repeat other people's opinions but not to state your own, when you have given so much thought to this subject.

And do you think it fair of anyone to speak as if he knew what he does not know?

No, not as if he knew, but he might give his opinion for what it is worth.

Why, have you never noticed that opinion without knowledge is always a shabby sort of thing? At the best it is blind. One who holds a true belief without intelligence is just like a blind man who happens to take the right road, isn't he?

No doubt.

Well, then, do you want me to produce one of these poor blind cripples, when others could discourse to you with illuminating eloquence?

No, really, Socrates, said Glaucon, you must not give up within sight of the goal. We should be quite content with an account of the Good like the one you gave us of justice and temperance and the other virtues.

So should I be, my dear Glaucon, much more than content! But I am afraid it is beyond my powers; with the best will in the world I should only disgrace myself and be laughed at. No, for the moment let us leave the question of the real meaning of good; to arrive at what I at any rate believe it to be would call for an effort too ambitious for an inquiry like ours. However, I will tell you, though only if you wish it, what I picture to myself as the offspring of the Good and the thing most nearly resembling it.

Well, tell us about the offspring, and you shall remain in our debt for an account of the parent.

I only wish it were within my power to offer, and within yours to receive, a settlement of the whole account. But you must be content now with the interest only; and you must see to it that, in describing this offspring of the Good, I do not inadvertently cheat you with false coin.

We will keep a good eye on you. Go on.

First we must come to an understanding. Let me remind you of the distinction we drew earlier and have often drawn on other occasions, between the

Taken from Books VI and VII of *The Republic of Plato*, translated by F.M. Cornford (Oxford University Press, 1941). Some footnotes omitted. Reprinted by permission of Oxford University Press.

multiplicity of things that we call good or beautiful or whatever it may be and, on the other hand, Goodness itself or Beauty itself and so on. Corresponding to each of these sets of many things, we postulate a single Form or real essence, as we call it.

Yes, that is so.

Further, the many things, we say, can be seen, but are objects of rational thought; whereas the Forms are objects of thought, but invisible.

Yes, certainly.

And we see things with our eyesight, just as we hear sounds with our ears and, to speak generally, perceive any sensible thing with our sense-faculties.

Of course.

Have you noticed, then, that the artificer who designed the senses has been exceptionally lavish of his materials in making the eyes able to see and their objects visible?

That never occurred to me.

Well, look at it in this way. Hearing and sound do not stand in need of any third thing, without which the ear will not hear nor sound be heard;[1] and I think the same is true of most, not to say all, of the other senses. Can you think of one that does require anything of the sort?

No, I cannot.

But there is this need in the case of sight and its objects. You may have the power of vision in your eyes and try to use it, and colour may be there in the objects; but sight will see nothing and the colours will remain invisible in the absence of a third thing peculiarly constituted to serve this very purpose.

By which you mean—?

Naturally I mean what you call light; and if light is a thing of value, the sense of sight and the power of being visible are linked together by a very precious bond, such as unites no other sense with its object.

No one could say that light is not a precious thing.

And of all the divinities in the skies[2] is there one whose light, above all the rest, is responsible for making our eyes see perfectly and making objects perfectly visible?

There can be no two opinions: of course you mean the Sun.

And how is sight related to this deity? Neither sight nor the eye which contains it is the Sun, but of all the sense-organs it is the most sun-like; and further, the power it possesses is dispensed by the Sun, like a stream flooding the eye.[3] And again, the Sun is not vision, but it is the cause of vision and also is seen by the vision it causes.

---

[1]Plato held that the hearing of sound is caused by blows inflicted by the air (*Timaeus* 67 B, 80 A); but the air is hardly analogous to light.

[2]Plato held that the heavenly bodies are immortal living creatures, i.e. gods.

[3]Plato's theory of vision involves three kinds of fire or light: (1) daylight, a body of pure fire diffused in the air by the Sun; (2) the visual current or 'vision,' a pure fire similar to daylight, contained in the eye-ball and capable of issuing out in a stream directed towards the object seen; (3) the colour of the external object, 'a flame streaming off from every body, having particles proportioned to those of the visual current, so as to yield sensation' when the two streams meet and coalesce (*Timaeus*, 45 B, 67 C).

Yes.

It was the Sun, then, that I meant when I spoke of that offspring which the Good has created in the visible world, to stand there in the same relation to vision and visible things as that which the Good itself bears in the intelligible world to intelligence and to intelligible objects.

How is that? You must explain further.

You know what happens when the colours of things are no longer irradiated by the daylight, but only by the fainter luminaries of the night: when you look at them, the eyes are dim and seem almost blind, as if there were no unclouded vision in them. But when you look at things on which the Sun is shining, the same eyes see distinctly and it becomes evident that they do contain the power of vision.

Certainly.

Apply this comparison, then, to the soul. When its gaze is fixed upon an object irradiated by truth and reality, the soul gains understanding and knowledge and is manifestly in possession of intelligence. But when it looks towards that twilight world of things that come into existence and pass away, its sight is dim and it has only opinions and beliefs which shift to and fro, and now it seems like a thing that has no intelligence.

That is true.

This, then, which gives to the objects of knowledge their truth and to him who knows them his power of knowing, is the Form or essential nature of Goodness. It is the cause of knowledge and truth; and so, while you may think of it as an object of knowledge, you will do well to regard it as something beyond truth and knowledge and, precious as these both are, of still higher worth. And, just as in our analogy light and vision were to be thought of as like the Sun, but not identical with it, so here both knowledge and truth are to be regarded as like the Good, but to identify either with the Good is wrong. The Good must hold a yet higher place of honour.

You are giving it a position of extraordinary splendor, if it is the source of knowledge and truth and itself surpasses them in worth. You surely cannot mean that it is pleasure.

Heaven forbid, I exclaimed. But I want to follow up our analogy still further. You will agree that the Sun not only makes the things we see visible, but also brings them into existence and gives them growth and nourishment; yet he is not the same thing as existence. And so with the objects of knowledge: these derive from the Good not only their power of being known, but their very being and reality; and Goodness is not the same thing as being, but even beyond being, surpassing it in dignity and power....

Next, said I, here is a parable to illustrate the degrees in which our nature may be enlightened or unenlightened. Imagine the condition of men living in a sort of cavernous chamber underground, with an entrance open to the light and a long passage all down the cave.[4] Here they have been from childhood,

---

[4] The *length* of the 'way in' (*eisodos*) to the chamber where the prisoners sit is an essential feature, explaining why no daylight reaches them.

chained by the leg and also by the neck, so that they cannot move and can see only what is in front of them, because the chains will not let them turn their heads. At some distance higher up is the light of a fire burning behind them; and between the prisoners and the fire is a track[5] with a parapet built along it, like the screen at a puppet-show, which hides the performers while they show their puppets over the top.

I see, said he.

Now behind this parapet imagine persons carrying along various artificial objects, including figures of men and animals in wood or stone or other materials, which project above the parapet. Naturally, some of these persons will be talking, others silent.[6]

It is a strange picture, he said, and a strange sort of prisoners.

Like ourselves, I replied; for in the first place prisoners so confined would have seen nothing of themselves or of one another, except the shadows thrown by the fire-light on the wall of the Cave facing them, would they?

Not if all their lives they had been prevented from moving their heads.

And they would have seen as little of the objects carried past.

Of course.

Now, if they could talk to one another, would they not suppose that their words referred only to those passing shadows which they saw?[7]

Necessarily.

And suppose their prison had an echo from the wall facing them? When one of the people crossing behind them spoke, they could only suppose that the sound came from the shadow passing before their eyes.

No doubt.

In every way, then, such prisoners would recognize as reality nothing but the shadows of those artificial objects.

Inevitably.

Now consider what would happen if their release from the chains and the healing of their unwisdom should come about in this way. Suppose one of them set free and forced suddenly to stand up, turn his head, and walk with eyes lifted to the light; all these movements would be painful, and he would be too dazzled to make out the object whose shadows he had been used to see. What do you think he would say, if someone told him that what he had formerly seen was meaningless illusion, but now, being somewhat nearer to

[5]The track crosses the passage into the cave at right angles, and is *above* the parapet built along it.

[6]A modern Plato would compare his Cave to an underground cinema, where the audience watch the play of shadows thrown by the film passing before a light at their backs. The film itself is only an image of 'real' things and events in the world outside the cinema. For the film Plato has to substitute the clumsier apparatus of a procession of artificial objects carried on their heads by persons who are merely part of the machinery, providing for the movement of the objects and the sounds whose echo the prisoners hear. The parapet prevents these persons' shadows from being cast on the wall of the Cave.

[7]Adam's text and interpretation. The prisoners, having seen nothing but shadows, cannot think their words refer to the objects carried past behind their backs. For them shadows (images) are the only realities.

reality and turned towards more real objects, he was getting a truer view? Suppose further that he were shown the various objects being carried by and were made to say, in reply to questions, what each of them was. Would he not be perplexed and believe the objects now shown him to be not so real as what he formerly saw?

Yes, not nearly so real.

And if he were forced to look at the fire-light itself, would not his eyes ache, so that he would try to escape and turn back to the things which he could see distinctly, convinced that they really were clearer than these other objects now being shown to him?

Yes.

And suppose someone were to drag him away forcibly up the steep and rugged ascent and not let him go until he had hauled him out into the sunlight, would he not suffer pain and vexation at such treatment, and, when he had come out into the light, find his eyes so full of its radiance that he could not see a single one of the things that he was now told were real?

Certainly he would not see them all at once.

He would need, then, to grow accustomed before he could see things in that upper world. At first it would be easiest to make out shadows, and then the images of men and things reflected in water, and later on the things themselves. After that, it would be easier to watch the heavenly bodies and sky itself by night, looking at the light of the moon and stars rather than the Sun and the Sun's light in the day-time.

Yes, surely.

Last of all, he would be able to look at the Sun and contemplate its nature, not as it appears when reflected in water or any alien medium, but as it is in itself in its own domain.

No doubt.

And now he would begin to draw the conclusion that it is the Sun that produces the seasons and the course of the year and controls everything in the visible world, and moreover is in a way the cause of all that he and his companions used to see.

Clearly he would come at last to that conclusion.

Then if he called to mind his fellow prisoners and what passed for wisdom in his former dwelling-place, he would surely think himself happy in the change and be sorry for them. They may have had a practice of honouring and commending one another, with prizes for the man who had the keenest eye for the passing shadows and the best memory for the order in which they followed or accompanied one another, so that he could make a good guess as to which was going to come next. Would our released prisoner be likely to covet those prizes or to envy the men exalted to honour and power in the Cave? Would he not feel like Homer's Achilles, that he would far sooner 'be on earth as a hired servant in the house of a landless man' or endure anything rather than go back to his old beliefs and live in the old way?

Yes, he would prefer any fate to such a life.

Now imagine what would happen if he went down again to take his former seat in the Cave. Coming suddenly out of the sunlight, his eyes would be filled with darkness. He might be required once more to deliver his opinion on those shadows, in competition with the prisoners who had never been released, while his eyesight was still dim and unsteady; and it might take some time to become used to the darkness. They would laugh at him and say that he had gone up only to come back with his sight ruined; it was worth no one's while even to attempt the ascent. If they could lay hands on the man who was trying to set them free and lead them up, they would kill him.[8]

Yes, they would.

Every feature in this parable, my dear Glaucon, is meant to fit our earlier analysis. The prison dwelling corresponds to the region revealed to us through the sense of sight, and the fire-light within it to the power of the Sun. The ascent to see the things in the upper world you may take as standing for the upward journey of the soul into the region of the intelligible; then you will be in possession of what I surmise, since that is what you wish to be told. Heaven knows whether it is true; but this, at any rate, is how it appears to me. In the world of knowledge, the last thing to be perceived and only with great difficulty is the essential Form of Goodness. Once it is perceived, the conclusion must follow that, for all things, this is the cause of whatever is right and good; in the visible world it gives birth to light and to the lord of light, while it is itself sovereign in the intelligible world and the parent of intelligence and truth. Without having had a vision of this Form no one can act with wisdom, either in his own life or in matters of state.

So far as I can understand, I share your belief.

Then you may also agree that it is no wonder if those who have reached this height are reluctant to manage the affairs of men. Their souls long to spend all their time in that upper world—naturally enough, if here once more our parable hold true. Nor, again, is it at all strange that one who comes from the contemplation of divine things to the miseries of human life should appear awkward and ridiculous when, with eyes still dazed and not yet accustomed to the darkness, he is compelled, in a law-court or elsewhere, to dispute about the shadows of justice or the images that cast those shadows, and to wrangle over the notions of what is right in the minds of men who have never beheld Justice itself.

It is not at all strange.

No; a sensible man will remember that the eyes may be confused in two ways—by a change from light to darkness or from darkness to light; and he will recognize that the same thing happens to the soul. When he sees it troubled and unable to discern anything clearly, instead of laughing thoughtlessly, he will ask whether, coming from a brighter existence, its unaccustomed vision is

---

[8]An allusion to the fate of Socrates.

obscured by the darkness, in which case he will think its condition enviable and its life a happy one; or whether, emerging from the depths of ignorance, it is dazzled by excess of light. If so, he will rather feel sorry for it; or, if he were inclined to laugh, that would be less ridiculous than to laugh at the soul which has come down from the light.

That is a fair statement.

If this is true, then, we must conclude that education is not what it is said to be by some, who profess to put knowledge into a soul which does not possess it, as if they could put sight into blind eyes. On the contrary, our own account signifies that the soul of every man does possess the power of learning the truth and the organ to see it with; and that, just as one might have to turn the whole body round in order that the eye should see light instead of darkness, so the entire soul must be turned away from this changing world, until its eye can bear to contemplate reality and that supreme splendor which we have called the Good. Hence there may well be an art whose aim would be to effect this very thing, the conversion of the soul, in the readiest way; not to put the power of sight into the soul's eye, which already has it, but to ensure that, instead of looking in the wrong direction, it is turned the way it ought to be.

A Defense of Cultural Relativism

William Graham Sumner

The Folkways are "Right." Rights. Morals   The folkways…extend over the whole of life. There is a right way to catch game, to win a wife, to make one's self appear, to cure disease, to honor ghosts, to treat comrades or strangers, to behave when a child is born, on the warpath, in council, and so on in all cases which can arise. The ways are defined on the negative side, that is, by taboos. The "right" way is the way which the ancestors used and which has been handed down. The tradition is its own warrant. It is not held subject to verification by experience. The notion of right is in the folkways. It is not outside of them, of independent origin, and brought to them to test them. In the folkways, whatever is, is right. This is because they are traditional, and therefore contain in themselves the authority of the ancestral ghosts. When we come to the folkways we are at the end of our analysis. The notion of right and ought is the same in regard to all the folkways, but the degree of it varies with the importance of the interest at stake. The obligation of conformable and cooperative action is far greater under ghost fear and war than in other

From William Graham Sumner, *Folkways* (Boston: Ginn and Company, 1907). Pp 28, 29, 36–38, 58–59, 76–78, 231–232. Copyright 1907 by Ginn and Company.

matters, and the social sanctions are severer, because group interests are supposed to be at stake. Some usages contain only a slight element of right and ought. It may well be believed that notions of right and duty, and of social welfare, were first developed in connection with ghost fear and other-worldliness, and therefore that, in that field also, folkways were first raised to mores. "Rights" are the rules of mutual give and take in the competition of life which are imposed on comrades in the in-group, in order that the peace may prevail there which is essential to the group strength. Therefore rights can never be "natural" or "God-given," or absolute in any sense. The morality of a group at a time is the sum of the taboos and prescriptions in the folkways by which right conduct is defined. Therefore morals can never be intuitive. They are historical, institutional, and empirical.

World philosophy, life policy, right, rights, and morality are all products of the folkways. They are reflections on, and generalizations from, the experience of pleasure and pain which is won in efforts to carry on the struggle for existence under actual life conditions. The generalizations are very crude and vague in their germinal forms. They are all embodied in folklore, and all our philosophy and science have been developed out of them.

Integration of the Mores of a Group or Age   In further development of the same interpretation of the phenomena we find that changes in history are primarily due to changes in life conditions. Then the folkways change. The new philosophies and ethical rules are invented to try to justify the new ways. The whole vast body of modern mores has thus been developed out of the philosophy and ethics of the Middle Ages. So the mores which have been developed to suit the system of great secular states, world commerce, credit institutions, contract wages and rent, emigration to outlying continents, etc., have become the norm for the whole body of usages, manners, ideas, faiths, customs, and institutions which embrace the whole life of a society and characterize an historical epoch. Thus India, Chaldea, Assyria, Egypt, Greece, Rome, the Middle Ages, Modern Times, are cases in which the integration of the mores upon different life conditions produced societal states of complete and distinct individuality (ethos). Within any such societal status the great reason for any phenomenon is that it conforms to the mores of the time and place. Historians have always recognized incidentally the operation of such a determining force. What is now maintained is that it is not incidental or subordinate. It is supreme and controlling. Therefore the scientific discussion of a usage, custom, or institution consists in tracing its relation to the mores, and the discussion of societal crises and changes consists in showing their connection with changes in the life conditions, or with the readjustment of the mores to changes in those conditions.

Purpose of the Present Work   "Ethology" would be a convenient term for the study of manners, customs, usages, and mores, including the study of the way in which they are formed, how they grow or decay, and how they affect the interests which it is their purpose to serve. The Greeks applied the term "ethos" to the sum of the characteristic usages, ideas, standards, and codes by which a group was differentiated and individualized in character from other groups. "Ethics" were things which pertained to the ethos and therefore the things which were the standard of right. The Romans used "mores" for customs in the broadest and richest sense of the word, including the notion that customs served welfare, and had traditional and mystic sanction, so that they were properly authoritative and sacred. It is a very surprising fact that modern nations should have lost these words and the significant suggestions which inhere in them. The English language has no derivative noun from "mores," and no equivalent for it. The French *mœurs* is trivial compared with "mores." The German *Sitte* renders "mores" but very imperfectly. The modern peoples have made morals and morality a separate domain, by the side of religion, philosophy, and politics. In that sense, morals is an impossible and unreal category. It has no existence, and can have none. The word "moral" means what belongs or appertains to the mores. Therefore the category of morals can never be defined without reference to something outside of itself. Ethics, having lost connection with the ethos of a people, is an attempt to systematize the current notions of right and wrong upon some basic principle, generally with the purpose of establishing morals on an absolute doctrine, so that it shall be universal, absolute, and everlasting. In a general way also, whenever a thing can be called moral, or connected with some ethical generality, it is thought to be "raised," and disputants whose method is to employ ethical generalities assume especial authority for themselves and their views. These methods of discussion are most employed in treating of social topics, and they are disastrous to sound study of facts. They help to hold the social sciences under the dominion of metaphysics. The abuse has been most developed in connection with political economy, which has been almost robbed of the character of a serious discipline by converting its discussions into ethical disquisitions.

Why Use the Word Mores?   "Ethica," in the Greek sense, or "ethology," as above defined, would be good names for our present work. We aim to study the ethos of groups, in order to see how it arises, its power and influence, the modes of its operation on members of the group, and the various attributes of it (ethica). "Ethology" is a very unfamiliar word. It has been used for the mode of setting forth manners, customs, and mores in satirical comedy. The Latin word "mores" seems to be, on the whole, more practically convenient and available than any other for our purpose, as a name for the folkways with the connotations of right and truth in respect to welfare, embodied in them. The analysis and definition given above show that in the mores we must recognize a dominating force in history, constituting a condition as to what can be done, and as to the methods which can be employed.

Mores Are a Directive Force   Of course the view which has been stated is antagonistic to the view that philosophy and ethics furnish creative and determining forces in society and history. That view comes down to us from the Greek philosophy and it has now prevailed so long that all current discussion conforms to it. Philosophy and ethics are pursued as independent disciplines, and the results are brought to the science of society and to statesmanship and legislation as authoritative dicta. We also have *Volkerpsychologie, Sozialpolitik*, and other intermediate forms which show the struggle of metaphysics to retain control of the science of society. The "historic sense," the *Zeitgeist*, and other terms of similar import are partial recognitions of the mores and their importance in the science of society. We shall see below that philosophy and ethics are products of the folkways. They are taken out of the mores, but are never original and creative; they are secondary and derived. They often interfere in the second stage of the sequence—act, thought, act. Then they produce harm, but some ground is furnished for the claim that they are creative or at least regulative. In fact, the real process in great bodies of men is not one of deduction from any great principle of philosophy or ethics. It is one of minute efforts to live well under existing conditions, which efforts are repeated indefinitely by great numbers, getting strength from habit and from the fellowship of united action. The resultant folkways become coercive. All are forced to conform, and the folkways dominate the societal life. Then they seem true and right, and arise into mores as the norm of welfare. Thence are produced faiths, ideas, doctrines, religions, and philosophies, according to the stage of civilization and the fashions of reflection and generalization.

What Is Goodness or Badness of the Mores?   It is most important to notice that, for the people of a time and place, their own mores are always good, or rather that for them there can be no question of the goodness or badness of their mores. The reason is because the standards of good and right are in the mores. If the life conditions change, the traditional folkways may produce pain and loss, or fail to produce the same good as formerly. Then the loss of comfort and ease brings doubt into the judgment of welfare (causing doubt of the pleasure of the gods, or of war power, or of health), and thus disturbs the unconscious philosophy of the mores. Then a later time will pass judgment on the mores. Another society may also pass judgment on the mores. In our literary and historical study of the mores we want to get from them their educational value, which consists in the stimulus or warning as to what is, in its effects, societally good or bad. This may lead us to reject or neglect a phenomenon like infanticide, slavery, or witchcraft, as an old "abuse" and "evil," or to pass by the crusades as a folly which cannot recur. Such a course would be a great error. Everything in the mores of a time and place must be regarded as justified with regard to that time and place. "Good" mores are those which are well adapted to the situation. "Bad" mores are those which are not so adapted. The mores are not so stereotyped and changeless as might appear, because they are forever moving towards more complete adaption to conditions and interests, and also towards more complete adjustment to each other. People in mass have never made or kept up a custom in order to hurt their own interests. They have made innumerable errors as to what their interests were and how to satisfy them, but they have always aimed to serve their interests as well as they could. This gives the standpoint for the student of the mores. All things in them come before him on the same plane. They all bring instruction and warning. They all have the same relation to power and welfare. The mistakes in them are component parts of them. We do not study them in order to approve some of them and condemn others. They are all equally worthy of attention from the fact that they existed and were used. The chief object of study in them is their adjustment to interests, their relation to welfare, and their coordination in a harmonious system of life policy. For the men of the time there are no "bad" mores. What is traditional and current is the standard of what ought to be. The masses never raise any question about such things. If a few raise doubts and questions, this proves that the folkways have already begun to lose firmness and the regulative element in the mores has begun to lose authority. This indicates that the folkways are on their way to a new adjustment. The extreme of folly, wickedness, and absurdity in the mores is witch persecutions, but the best men of the seventeenth century had no doubt that witches existed, and that they ought to be burned. The religion, statecraft, jurisprudence, philosophy, and social system of that age all contributed to maintain that belief. It was rather a culmination than a contradiction of the current faiths and convictions, just as the dogma that all men are equal and that one ought to have as much political power in the state as another was the culmination of the political dogmatism and social philosophy of the nineteenth century. Hence our judgments of the good or evil consequences of folkways are to be kept separate from our study of the historical phenomena of them, and of their strength and the reasons for it. The judgments have their place in plans and doctrines for the future, not in a retrospect.

The Mores Have the Authority of Facts   The mores come down to us from the past. Each individual is born into them as he is born into the atmosphere, and he does not reflect on them, or criticize them any more than a baby analyzes the atmosphere before he begins to breathe it. Each one is subjected to the influence of the mores, and formed by them, before he is capable of reasoning about them. It may be objected that nowadays, at least, we criticize all traditions, and accept none just because they are handed down to us. If we take up cases of things which are still entirely or almost entirely in the mores, we shall see that this is not so. There are sects of free-lovers amongst us who want to discuss pair marriage. They are not simply people of evil life. They invite us to discuss rationally our inherited customs and ideas as to marriage, which, they say, are by no means so excellent and elevated as we believe. They have never won any serious attention. Some others want to argue in favor of polygamy on grounds of expediency. They fail to obtain a hearing. Others want to discuss property. In spite of some literary activity on their part, no discussion of property, bequest, and inheritance has ever been opened. Property and marriage are in the mores. Nothing can ever change them but the unconscious and imperceptible movement of the mores. Religion was originally a matter of the mores. It became a societal institution and a function of the state. It has now to a great extent been put back into the mores. Since laws with penalties to enforce religious creeds or practices have gone out of use any one may think and act as he pleases about religion. Therefore it is not now "good form" to attack religion. Infidel publications are now tabooed by the mores, and are more effectually repressed than ever before. They produce no controversy. Democracy is in our American mores. It is a product of our physical and economic conditions. It is impossible to discuss or criticize it. It is glorified for popularity, and is a subject of dithyrambic rhetoric. No one treats it with complete candor and sincerity. No one dares to analyze it as he would aristocracy or autocracy. He would get no hearing and would only incur abuse. The thing to be noticed in all these cases is that the masses oppose a deaf ear to every argument against the mores. It is only insofar as things have been transferred from the mores into laws and positive institutions that there is discussion about them or rationalizing upon them. The mores contain the norm by which, if we should discuss the mores, we should have to judge the mores. We learn the mores as unconsciously as we learn to walk and eat and breathe. The masses never learn how we walk, and eat, and breathe, and they never know any reason why the mores are what they are. The justification of them is that when we wake to consciousness of life we find them facts which already hold us in the bonds of tradition, custom, and habit. The mores contain embodied in them notions, doctrines, and maxims, but they are facts. They are in the present tense. They have nothing to do with what ought to be, will be, may be, or once was, if it is not now.

Mores and Morals; Social Code   For everyone the mores give the notion of what ought to be. This includes the notion of what ought to be done, for all should cooperate to bring to pass, in the order of life, what ought to be. All notions of propriety, decency, chastity, politeness, order, duty, right, rights, discipline, respect, reverence, cooperation, and fellowship, especially all things in regard to which good and ill depend entirely on the point at which the line is drawn, are in the mores. The mores can make things seem right and good to one group or one age which to another seem antagonistic to every instinct of human nature. The thirteenth century bred in every heart such a sentiment in regard to heretics that inquisitors had no more misgivings in their proceedings than men would have now if they should attempt to exterminate rattlesnakes. The sixteenth century gave to all such notions about witches that witch persecutors thought they were waging war on enemies of God and man. Of course the inquisitors and witch persecutors constantly developed the notions of heretics and witches. They exaggerated the notions and then gave them back again to the mores, in their expanded form, to inflame the hearts of men with terror and hate and to become, in the next stage, so much more fantastic and ferocious motives. Such is the reaction between the mores and the acts of the living generation. The world philosophy of the age is never anything but the reflection on the mental horizon, which is formed out of the mores, of the ruling ideas which are in the mores themselves. It is from a failure to recognize the to and fro in this reaction that the current notion arises that mores are produced by doctrines. The "morals" of an age are never anything but the consonance between what is done and what the mores of the age require. The whole revolves on itself, in the relation of the specific to the general, within the horizon formed by the mores. Every attempt to win an outside standpoint from which to reduce the whole to an absolute philosophy of truth and right, based on an unalterable principle, is a delusion. New elements are brought in only by new conquests of nature through science and art. The new conquests change the conditions of life and the interests of the members of the society. Then the mores change by adaptation to new conditions and interests. The philosophy and ethics then follow to account for and justify the changes in the mores; often, also, to claim that they have caused the changes. They never do anything but draw new lines of bearing between the parts of the mores and the horizon of thought within which they are inclosed, and which is a deduction from the mores. The horizon is widened by more knowledge, but for one age it is just as much a generalization from the mores as for another. It is always unreal. It is only a product of thought. The ethical philosophers select points on this horizon from which to take their bearings, and they think that they have won some authority for their systems when they travel back again from the generalization to the specific custom out of which it was deduced. The cases of the inquisitors and witch persecutors who toiled arduously and continually for their chosen ends, for little or no reward, show us the relation between mores one the on side and philosophy, ethics, and religion on the other.

A Critique of Cultural Relativism

Carl Wellman

It is often thought that the discoveries of anthropology have revolutionary implications for ethics. Readers of Sumner, Benedict, and Herskovits are apt to come away with the impression that the only moral obligation is to conform to one's society, that polygamy is as good as monogamy, or that no ethical

From Carl Wellman, "The Ethical Implications of Cultural Relativity," *Journal of Philosophy* LX, No. 7 (1963), 169–184. With omissions. Copyright 1963 by Journal of Philosophy. Reprinted by permission of the Journal of Philosophy and Carl Wellman.

judgment can be rationally justified. While these anthropologists might complain that they are being misinterpreted, they would not deny that their real intent is to challenge the traditional view of morals. Even the anthropologist whose scientific training has made him skeptical of sweeping generalities and wary of philosophical entanglements is inclined to believe that the scientific study of cultures has undermined the belief in ethical absolutes of any kind.

Just what has been discovered that forces us to revise our ethics? Science has shown that certain things that were once thought to be absolute are actually relative to culture. Something is relative to culture when it varies with and is causally determined by culture. Clearly, nothing can be both relative to culture and absolute, for to be absolute is to be fixed and invariable, independent of man and the same for all men.

Exactly which things are relative and in what degree is a question still being debated by cultural anthropologists. Important as this question is, I do not propose to discuss it. It is the empirical scientist who must tell us which things vary from culture to culture and to what extent each is causally determined by its culture. It is not for me to question the findings of the anthropologists in this area. Instead, let me turn to the philosophical problem of the implications of cultural relativity. Assuming for the moment that cultural relativity is a fact, what follows for ethics?

What follows depends in part upon just what turns out to be relative. Anthropologists are apt to use the word "values" to refer indiscriminately to the things which have value, the characteristics which give these things their value, the attitudes of the persons who value these things, and the judgments of those people that these things have value. Similarly, one finds it hard to be sure whether "morals" refers to the mores of a people, the set of principles an observer might formulate after observing their conduct, the practical beliefs the people themselves entertain, or the way they feel about certain kinds of conduct. Until such ambiguities are cleared up, one hardly knows what is being asserted when it is claimed that "values" or "morals" are relative.

It seems to me there are...different things of interest to the ethicist that the anthropologist might discover to be relative to culture: mores,...human nature, acts, goals,...moral judgments, and moral reasoning.* Since I can hardly discuss all the ethical conclusions that various writers have tried to draw from these different facts of cultural relativity, what I propose to do is to examine critically the reasoning by which one ethical conclusion might be derived from each of them.

[MORES]

It has long been recognized that mores are relative to culture. Mores are those customs which are enforced by social pressure. They are established patterns

*Editor's note: The original version of Professor Wellman's article discusses four additional items, that is, social institutions, value experiences, moral emotions, and moral concept. For want of space these have been omitted.

of action to which the individual is expected to conform and from which he deviates only at the risk of disapproval and punishment. It seems clear that mores vary from society to society and that the mores of any given society depend upon its culture. What does this imply for ethics?

The conclusion most frequently drawn is that what is right in one society may be wrong in another. For example, although it would be wrong for one of us to kill his aged parents, this very act is right for an Eskimo. This is because our mores are different from those of Eskimo society, and it is the mores that make an act right or wrong.

Let us grant, for the sake of discussion, that different societies do have different mores. Why should we grant that the mores make an act right or wrong? It has been claimed that this is true by definition. "Right" simply means according to the mores, and "wrong" means in violation of the mores. There is something to be said for this analysis of our concepts of right and wrong. It seems to explain both the imperativeness and the impersonality of obligation. The "ought" seems to tell one what to do and yet to be more than the command of any individual; perhaps its bindingness lies in the demands of society. Attractive as this interpretation appears at first glance, I cannot accept it. It can be shown that no naturalistic analysis of the meaning of ethical words is adequate. In addition, this particular analysis is objectionable in that it makes it self-contradictory to say that any customary way of acting is wrong. No doubt social reformers are often confused, but they are not always inconsistent.

If the view that the mores make an act right or wrong is not true by definition, it amounts to the moral principle that one ought always to conform to the mores of his society. None of the ways in which this principle is usually supported is adequate. (a) Any society unconsciously develops those mores which are conducive to survival and well-being under its special circumstances Each individual ought to obey the mores of his society because this is the best way to promote the good life for the members of that society. I admit that there is a tendency for any society to develop those mores which fit its special circumstances, but I doubt that this is more than a tendency. There is room for reform in most societies, and this is particularly true when conditions are changing for one reason or another. (b) One ought to obey the mores of his society because disobedience would tend to destroy those mores. Without mores any society would lapse into a state of anarchy that would be intolerable for its members. It seems to me that this argument deserves to be taken seriously, but it does not prove that one ought always to obey the mores of his society. What it does show is that one ought generally to obey the mores of his society and that whenever he considers disobedience he should give due weight to the effects of his example upon social stability. (c) One ought to obey the mores of his society because disobedience tends to undermine their existence. It is important to preserve the mores, not simply to avoid anarchy, but because it is their mores which give shape and meaning to the life of any people. I grant that the individual does tend to think of his life in terms of the mores of his group and that anything which disrupts those mores tends to rob his life of significance. But once again, all this shows is that one should conform to the mores of his society on the whole. Although there is some obligation to conformity, this is not the only nor the most important obligation on the member of any society.

Therefore, it does not seem to me that one can properly say that the mores make an act right or wrong. One cannot define the meaning of these ethical words in terms of the mores, nor can one maintain the ethical principle that one ought always to obey the mores of his society. If the mores do not make acts right or wrong, the fact that different societies have different mores does not imply that the same kind of act can be right in one society and wrong in another....

[HUMAN NATURE]

Another thing which may be relative to culture is human nature. As soon as one ponders the differences between the Chinese aristocrat and the Australian bushman, the American tycoon and the Indian yogi, one finds it hard to believe that there is anything basic to human nature which is shared by all men. And reflection upon the profound effects of enculturation easily leads one to the conclusion that what a man is depends upon the society in which he has been brought up. Therefore, let us assume that human nature is culturally relative and see what this implies.

This seems to imply that no kind of action, moral character, or social institution is made inevitable by human nature. This conclusion is important because it cuts the ground out from under one popular type of justification in ethics. For example, capitalism is sometimes defended as an ideal on the grounds that this is the only economic system that is possible in the light of man's greedy and competitive nature. Or it might be claimed that adultery is permissible because the ideal of marital fidelity runs counter to man's innate drives or instincts. If there is no fixed human nature, such arguments are left without any basis.

One may wonder, however, whether the only alternatives are an entirely fixed and an entirely plastic human nature. It might be the enculturation could mold a human being but only within certain limits. These limits might exist either because certain parts of human nature are not at all plastic or because all parts are only moderately plastic. For example, it might turn out that the need for food and the tendency to grow in a certain way cannot be modified at all by enculturation, or it might turn out that every element in human nature can be modified in some ways but not in others. In either case, what a man becomes would depend partly upon enculturation and partly upon the nature of the organism being enculturated.

Thus cultural relativity may be a matter of degree. Before we can decide just what follows from the fact that human nature is relative to culture we must know how far and in what ways it is relative. If there are certain limits to the plasticity of human nature, these do rule out some kinds of action, character, or institution. But anthropology indicates that within any such limits a great many alternatives remain. Human nature may make eating inevitable, but what we eat and when we eat and how we eat is up to us. At least we can say that to the degree that human nature is relative to culture no kind of action, moral character, or social institution is made impossible by human nature.

[ACTS]

It has been claimed that acts are also relative to culture. This is to say that the same general type of action may take on specific differences when performed in different societies because those societies have different cultures. For example, it is one thing for one of us to kill his aged parent; it is quite a different thing for an Eskimo to do such an act. One difference lies in the consequences of these two acts. In our society disposing of old and useless parents merely allows one to live in greater luxury; to an Eskimo this act may mean the difference between barely adequate subsistence and malnutrition for himself and his family. What are we to make of this fact that the nature of an act is culturally relative?

One possible conclusion is that the same kind of act may be right in one society and wrong in another. This presupposes that the rightness of an act depends upon its consequences and that its consequences may vary from society to society. Since I accept these presuppositions, I agree that the rightness or wrongness of an act is relative to its social context.

It is important, however, to distinguish this conclusion from two others with which it is often confused. To say that the rightness of an act is relative to the society in which it is performed is not to say that exactly the same sort of act can be both right and wrong. It is because the social context makes the acts different in kind that one can be right while the other is wrong. Compare an act of infanticide in our society with an act of infanticide in some South Seas society. Are these two acts the same or different? They are of the same kind inasmuch as both are acts of killing an infant. On the other hand, they are different in that such an act may be necessary to preserve the balance between family size and food resources in the South Seas while this is not the case in our society. These two acts are generically similar but specifically different; that is, they belong to different species of the same genus. Therefore, the conclusion that the same kind of act may be right in one society and wrong in another does not amount to saying that two acts which are precisely the same in every respect may differ in rightness or wrongness.

Neither is this conclusion to be confused with the view that acts are made right or wrong by the mores of society. No doubt our society disapproves of infanticide and some South Seas societies approve of it, but it is not *this* which makes infanticide wrong for us and right for them. If infanticide is wrong for us and right for them, it is because acts of infanticide have very different consequences in our society and in theirs, not because the practice is discouraged here and customary there.

[GOALS]

The goals that individuals or groups aim for also seem relative to culture. What objects people select as goals vary from society to society depending upon the cultures of those societies. One group may strive for social prestige and the accumulation of great wealth, another may aim at easy comfort and the avoidance of any danger, a third may seek military glory and the conquest of other peoples. What follows from this fact of cultural relativity?

This fact is often taken as a basis for arguing that it is impossible to compare the value of acts, institutions, or total ways of life belonging to different societies. The argument rests on the assumptions that acts, institutions, and ways of life are means directed at certain ends, that means can be evaluated only in terms of their ends, and that ends are incommensurable with respect to value.

Granted these assumptions, the argument seems a good one, but I doubt that ends are really incommensurable. It seems to me that we can recognize that certain ends are more worthwhile than others, for example that pleasure is intrinsically better than pain. I may be mistaken, but until this has been shown, the conclusion that it is impossible to compare the value of acts, institutions, or ways of life belonging to different societies has not been established....

[MORAL JUDGMENTS]

The aspect of cultural relativity most often emphasized is that pertaining to moral judgments. Objects that the members of one society think to be good are considered bad by another group; acts considered wrong in one society are thought of as right in another. Moreover, these differences in judgments of value and obligation seem to reflect cultural differences between the respective societies. There is a great deal of evidence to suggest that ethical judgments are relative to culture.

To many anthropologists and philosophers it is a corollary of this fact that one of a set of contrary ethical judgments is no more valid than another, or, put positively, that all ethical judgments are equally valid. Unfortunately, there is a crucial ambiguity lurking in this epistemological thicket. Ethical judgments might have equal validity either because all are valid or because none are: similarly one ethical judgment might be no more valid than another either because both are equally valid or because both are equally lacking in validity. Since these two interpretations are quite different, let us consider them separately.

On the first interpretation, the conclusion to be drawn from the fact that ethical judgments are relative to culture is that every moral judgment is valid for the society in which it is made. Instead of denying the objective validity of ethical judgments, this view affirms it, but in a qualified form which will allow for the variations in ethical belief.

There seem to be three main ways of defending this position. (a) Ethical judgments have objective validity because it is possible to justify them rationally. However, this validity is limited to a given society because the premises used in such justification are those which are agreed upon in that society. Since there are no universally accepted premises, no universal validity is possible. I would wish to deny that justification is real if it is limited in this way. If all our reasoning really does rest on certain premises which can be rejected by others without error, then we must give up the claim to objective validity. When I claim validity for ethical judgments, I intend to claim more than that it is possible to support them with logical arguments; I also claim that it is incorrect to deny the premises of such arguments. (b) Any ethical judgment is an expression of a total pattern of culture. Hence it is possible to justify any single judgment in terms of its coherence with the total cultural configuration of the judger. But one cannot justify the culture as a whole, for it is not part of a more inclusive pattern. Therefore, ethical judgments have objective validity, but only in terms of a given cultural pattern. I would make the same objection to this view as to the preceding one. Since it allows justification to rest upon an arbitrary foundation, it is inadequate to support any significant claim to objective validity. (c) Any ethical judgment has objective validity because it is an expression of a moral code. The validity of a moral code rests on the fact that without conformity to a common code social cohesion breaks down, leading to disastrous results. Since any given moral code provides cohesion for one and only one society, each ethical judgment has validity for a single society. There are at least two difficulties with this defense of objectivity. Surely one could deny some ethical judgments without destroying the entire moral code they reflect; not every judgment could be shown to be essential to social stability. Moreover, the argument seems to rest on the ethical judgment that one ought not to contribute to the breakdown of social stability. How is this judgment to be shown to be valid? One must either appeal to some other basis of validity or argue in a circle. None of these arguments to show that every moral judgment is valid for the society in which it is made is adequate.

On the second interpretation, the conclusion to be drawn from the fact that moral judgments are relative to culture is that moral judgments have no objective validity. This amounts to saying that the distinction between true and false, correct and incorrect, does not apply to such judgments. This conclusion obviously does not follow simply from the fact that people disagree about ethical questions. We do not deny the objective validity of scientific judgments either on the grounds that different scientists propose alternative theories or on the grounds that the members of some societies hold fast to many unscientific beliefs.

Why, then, does the fact that moral judgments are relative to culture imply that they have no objective validity? (a) Individuals make different ethical judgments because they judge in terms of different frames of reference, and they adopt these frames of reference uncritically from their cultures. Since ethical judgments are the product of enculturation rather than reasoning, they cannot claim rational justification. I do not find this argument convincing, for it seems to confuse the origin of a judgment with its justification. The causes of a judgment are one thing; the reasons for or against it are another. It remains to be shown that any information about what causes us to judge as we do has any bearing on the question of whether or not our judgments are correct. (b) It is impossible to settle ethical questions by using the scientific method. Therefore, there is no objective way to show that one ethical judgment is any more correct than another, and, in the absence of any method of establishing the claim to objective validity, it makes no sense to continue to make the claim. I will concede that, if there is no rational method of establishing ethical judgments, then we might as well give up the claim to objective validity. And if the scientific method is restricted to the testing of hypotheses by checking the predictions they imply against the results of observation and experiment, it does seem to be inapplicable to ethical questions. What I will not concede is the tacit assumption that the scientific method is the only method of establishing the truth. Observation and experimentation do not figure prominently in the method used by mathematicians. I even wonder whether the person who concludes that ethical judgments have no objective validity can establish *this* conclusion by using the scientific method. The fact that ethical judgments cannot be established scientifically does not by itself prove that they cannot be established by any method of reasoning. (c) There might be some method of settling ethical disputes, but it could not be a method of reasoning. Any possible reasoning would have to rest upon certain premises. Since the members of different societies start from different premises, there is no basis for argument that does not beg the question. I suspect, however, that we have been looking for our premises in the wrong place. The model of deduction tempts us to search for very general premises from which all our more specific judgments can be deduced. Unfortunately, it is just in this area of universal moral principles that disagreement seems most frequent and irremedial. But suppose that these ethical generalizations are themselves inductions based upon particular moral judgments. Then we could argue for or against them in terms of relatively specific ethical judgments and the factual judgments that are in turn relevant to these. Until this possibility is explored further, we need not admit that there is no adequate basis for ethical reasoning. Thus it appears that none of these refutations of the objective validity of ethical judgments is really conclusive.

The fact that ethical judgments are relative to culture is often taken to prove that no ethical judgment can claim to be any more valid than any of its contraries. I have tried to show that, on neither of the two possible interpretations of this conclusion, does the conclusion necessarily follow from the fact of cultural relativity.

[MORAL REASONING]

Finally, moral reasoning might turn out to be relative to culture. When some ethical statement is denied or even questioned, the person who made the statement is apt to leap to its defense. He attempts to justify his statement by producing reasons to support it. But speakers from different societies tend to justify their statements in different ways. The difference in their reasoning may be of two kinds. Either their reasoning may rest on different assumptions or they may draw inferences in a different manner. That is, the arguments they advance may either start from different premises or obey different logics. We can ignore the former case here; for it boils down to a difference in their judgments, and we have discussed that at length in the preceding section. Instead let us assume that people who belong to different societies tend to draw their moral conclusions according to different logics depending upon their respective cultures. What difference would it make if moral reasoning were thus culturally relative?

The most interesting conclusion that might be drawn from the fact that moral reasoning is relative to culture is that it has no objective validity. The claim to objective validity is empty where it cannot be substantiated. But how could one justify the claim that any given kind of moral reasoning is valid? To appeal to the same kind of reasoning would be circular. To appeal to some other kind of reasoning would not be sufficient to justify this kind; for each kind of reasoning involves principles of inference which go beyond, and therefore cannot be justified by appealing to, any other kind.

I find this line of argument inconclusive for several reasons. First, it is not clear that a given kind of reasoning cannot be justified by appealing to a different kind of reasoning. In fact, this seems to be a fairly common practice in logic. Various forms of syllogistic argument can be shown to be valid by reducing them to arguments of the form Barbara. Again, a logician will sometimes justify certain rules for natural deduction by an involved logical argument which does not itself use these same rules. Second, in what sense is it impossible to show another person that my moral arguments are valid? I can show him that the various moral arguments I advance conform to the principles of my logic. If he does not accept these principles, he will remain unconvinced. This may show that I cannot persuade him that my arguments are valid, but does it show that I have not proved that they are? It is not obvious that persuading a person and proving a point are identical. Third, is the claim to objective validity always empty in the absence of any justification for it? Perhaps some reasoning is ultimate in that it requires no further justification. To assume the opposite seems to lead to an infinite regress. If every valid justification stands in need of further justification, no amount of justification would ever be sufficient.

I do not claim to have established the objective validity of moral reasoning. I am not even sure how that validity might be established or even whether it needs to be established. All I have been trying to do is to suggest that such validity is not ruled out by the fact, if it is a fact, that moral reasoning is relative to culture....

MORAL PSYCHOLOGY

Man's Self-Interested Nature

Thomas Hobbes

OF THE INTERIOR BEGINNINGS OF VOLUNTARY MOTIONS; COMMONLY CALLED THE PASSIONS

...That which men desire, they are also said to LOVE, and to HATE those things for which they have aversion. So that desire and love are the same thing; save that by desire, we always signify the absence of the object; by love, most commonly the presence of the same. So also by aversion, we signify the absence; and by hate, the presence of the object.

Of appetites and aversions, some are born with men; as appetite of food, appetite of excretion, and exoneration, which may also and more properly be called aversions, from somewhat they feel in their bodies; and some other appetites, not many. The rest, which are appetites of particular things, proceed from experience, and trial of their effects upon themselves or other men. For of things we know not at all, or believe not to be, we can have no further desire than to taste and try. But aversion we have for things, not only which we know have hurt us, but also that we do not know whether they will hurt us, or not.

...Whatsoever is the object of any man's appetite or desire, that is it which he for his part calleth *good*; and the object of his hate and aversion, *vile* and *inconsiderable*. For these words of good, evil, and contemptible, are ever used with relation to the person that useth them; there being nothing simple and absolutely so; nor any common rule of good and evil, to be taken from the nature of the objects themselves; but from the person of the man, where there is no Commonwealth; or, in a Commonwealth, from the person that representeth it; or from an arbitrator or judge, whom men disagreeing shall by consent set up, and make his sentence the rule thereof.

...Of pleasure or delights, some arise from the sense of an object present; and those may be called *pleasures of sense*; the word *sensual*, as it is used by those only that condemn them, having no place till there be laws. Of this kind are all onerations and exonerations of the body; as also all that is pleasant, in the *sight*, *hearing*, *smell*, *taste*, or *touch*. Others arise from the expectation,

From *The Leviathan* (1651; rpt. London: Oxford University Press, 1967), Part I. Chapters VI and XIII, Part II, Chapter XVII.

that proceeds from foresight of the end, or consequence of things; whether those things in the sense please or displease. And these are *pleasures of the mind* of him that draweth those consequences, and are generally called JOY. In the like manner, displeasures are some in the sense, and called PAIN; others in the expectation of consequences, and are called GRIEF....

OF THE NATURAL CONDITION OF MANKIND AS CONCERNING THEIR FELICITY AND MISERY

Nature hath made men so equal, in the faculties of the body, and mind; as that though there be found one man sometimes manifestly stronger in body, or of quicker mind than another, yet when all is reckoned together, the difference between man and man, is not so considerable, as that one man can thereupon claim to himself any benefit to which another may not pretend, as well as he. For as to the strength of body, the weakest has strength enough to kill the strongest, either by secret machination, or by confederacy with others, that are in the same danger with himself.

And as to the faculties of the mind, setting aside the arts grounded upon words, and especially that skill of proceeding upon general and infallible rules, called science; which very few have, and but in few things; as being not a native faculty born with us; nor attained, as prudence, while we look after somewhat else, I find yet a greater equality amongst men than that of strength. For prudence, is but experience; which equal time, equally bestows on all men, in those things they equally apply themselves unto. That which may perhaps make such equality incredible, is but a vain conceit of one's own wisdom, which almost all men think they have in a greater degree than the vulgar; that is, than all men but themselves, and a few others, whom by fame, or for concurring with themselves, they approve. For such is the nature of men, that howsoever they may acknowledge many others to be more witty, or more eloquent, or more learned; yet they will hardly believe there be many so wise as themselves; for they see their own wit at hand, and other men's at a distance. But this proveth rather that men are in that point equal, than unequal. For there is not ordinarily a greater sign of the equal distribution of anything, than that every man is contented with his share.

From this equality of ability, ariseth equality of hope in the attaining of our ends. And therefore if any two men desire the same thing, which nevertheless they cannot both enjoy, they become enemies; and in the way to their end, which is principally their own conservation, and sometimes their delectation only, endeavor to destroy or subdue one another. And from hence it comes to pass, that where an invader hath no more to fear, than another man's single power; if one plant, sow, build, or possess a convenient seat, others may probably be expected to come prepared with forces united, to dispossess, and deprive him, not only of the fruit of his labour, but also of his life or liberty. And the invader again is in the like danger of another.

And from this diffidence of one another, there is no way for any man to secure himself, so reasonable as anticipation; that is, by force, or wiles, to master the persons of all men he can, so long, till he sees no other power great enough to endanger him; and this is no more than his own conservation requireth, and is generally allowed. Also because there be some, that taking pleasure in contemplating their own power in the acts of conquest, which they pursue farther than their security requires; if others, that otherwise would be glad to be at ease within modest bounds, should not by invasion increase their power, they would not be able, long time, by standing only on their defence, to subsist. And by consequence, such augmentation of dominion over men being necessary to a man's conservation, it ought to be allowed him.

Again, men have no pleasure, but on the contrary a great deal of grief, in keeping company, where there is no power able to overawe them all. For every man looketh that his companion should value him, at the same rate he sets upon himself; and upon all signs of contempt, or undervaluing, naturally endeavours as far as he dares (which amongst them that have no common power to keep them in quiet, is far enough to make them destroy each other), to extort a greater value from his contemners, by damage; and from others, by the example.

So that in the nature of man, we find three principal causes of quarrel. First, competition; secondly, diffidence; thirdly, glory.

The first maketh men invade for gain; the second, for safety; and the third, for reputation. The first use violence, to make themselves masters of other men's persons, wives, children, and cattle; the second, to defend them; the third, for trifles, as a word, a smile, a different opinion, and any sign of undervalue, either direct in their persons, or by reflection of their kindred, their friends, their nation, their profession, or their name.

Hereby it is manifest, that during the time men live without a common power to keep them all in awe, they are in that condition which is called WAR; and such a war, as is of every man, against every man. For WAR, consisteth not in battle only, or the act of fighting; but in the tract of time, wherein the will to contend by battle is sufficiently known; and therefore the notion of *time*, is to be considered in the nature of war, as it is in the nature of weather. For as the nature of foul weather, lieth not in a shower or two of rain, but in an inclination thereto of many days together; so the nature of war, consisteth not in actual fighting, but in the known disposition thereto, during all the time there is no assurance to the contrary. All other time is PEACE.

Whatsoever therefore is consequent to a time of war, where every man is enemy to every man, the same is consequent to the time wherein men live without other security, than what their own strength, and their own invention shall furnish them withal. In such condition, there is no place for industry, because the fruit thereof is uncertain, and consequently no culture of the earth; no navigation, nor use of the commodities that may be imported by sea; no commodious building; no instruments of moving, and removing, such things as require much force; no knowledge of the face of the earth; no account of time; no arts; no letters; no society; and, which is worst of all, continual fear, and danger of violent death; and the life of man, solitary, poor, nasty, brutish, and short....

OF THE CAUSES, GENERATION AND DEFINITIONS OF A COMMONWEALTH

The final cause, end, or design of men who naturally love liberty and dominion over others, in the introduction of that restraint upon themselves in which we see them live in commonwealths, is the foresight of their own preservation, and of a more contented life thereby; that is to say, of getting themselves out from that miserable condition of war, which is necessarily consequent...to the natural passions of men, when there is no visible power to keep them in awe, and tie them by fear of punishment to the performance of their covenants and observation of those laws of nature set down [previously].

...The only way to erect such a common power, as may be able to defend them from the invasion of foreigners and the injuries of one another, and thereby to secure them in such sort as that, by their own industry, and by the fruits of the earth, they may nourish themselves and live contentedly; is, to confer all their power and strength upon one man, or upon one assembly of men, that may reduce all their wills, by plurality of voices, unto one will; which is as much as to say, to appoint one man, or assembly of men, to bear their person; and everyone to own and acknowledge himself to be author of whatsoever he that so beareth their person, shall act or cause to be acted in those things which concern the common peace and safety; and therein to submit their wills, everyone to his will, and their judgments, to his judgment. This is more than consent, or concord; it is a real unity of them all, in one and the same person, made by covenant of every man with every man, in such manner as if every man should say to every man, *"I authorize and give up my right of governing myself to this man, or to this assembly of men, on this condition, that thou give up thy right to him, and authorize all his actions in like manner."* This done, the multitude so united in one person, is called a *commonwealth*, in Latin *civitas*. This is the generation of that great LEVIATHAN, or rather, to speak more reverently, of that *mortal god*, to which we owe under the *immortal God*, our peace and defense. For by this authority, given him by every particular man in the commonwealth, he hath the use of so much power and strength conferred on him, that by terror thereof he is enabled to perform the wills of them all, to peace at home and mutual aid against their enemies abroad. And in him consisteth the essence of the commonwealth; which to define it, is *one person, of whose acts a great multitude, by mutual covenants one with another, have made themselves every one the author, to the end he may use the strength and means of them all, as he shall think expedient, for their peace and common defense.*

And he that carrieth this person, is called *sovereign*, and said to have sovereign power; and everyone besides, his *subject*.

The attaining to this sovereign power is by two ways. One, by natural force; as when a man maketh his children to submit themselves and their children to his government, as being able to destroy them if they refuse; or by war subdueth his enemies to his will, giving them their lives on that condition. The other, is when men agree amongst themselves to submit to some man, or assembly of men, voluntarily, on confidence to be protected by him against all others. This latter may be called a political commonwealth, or commonwealth by *institution*; and the former, a commonwealth by *acquisition*....

Moral Development: A Modern Statement of the Platonic View

Lawrence Kohlberg

When I called this essay a Platonic view I hoped it implied a paradox that was more than cute. It is surely a paradox that a modern psychologist should claim as his most relevant source not Freud, Skinner, or Piaget but the ancient believer in the ideal form of the good. Yet as I have tried to trace the stages of development of morality and to use these stages as the basis of a moral education program, I have realized more and more that its implication was the reassertion of the Platonic faith in the power of the rational good....

Because morally mature men are governed by the principle of justice rather than by a set of rules, there are not many moral virtues but one. Let us restate the argument in Plato's terms. Plato's argument is that what makes a virtuous action virtuous is that it is guided by knowledge of the good. A courageous action based on ignorance of danger is not courageous; a just act based on ignorance of justice is not just, etc. If virtuous action is action based on knowledge of the good, then virtue is one, because knowledge of the good is one. We have already claimed that knowledge of the good is one because the good is justice. Let me briefly document these lofty claims by some lowly research findings. Using hypothetical moral situations, we have interviewed children and adults about right and wrong in the United States, Britain, Turkey, Taiwan, and Yucatan. In all cultures we find the same forms of moral thinking. There are six forms of thinking and they constitute an invariant sequence of stages in each culture. These stages are summarized in the table on page 38.

Why do I say existence of culturally universal stages means that knowledge of the good is one? First, because it implies that concepts of the good are culturally universal. Second, because an individual at a given level is pretty much the same in his thinking regardless of the situation he is presented with and regardless of the particular aspect of morality being tapped. There is a general factor of maturity of moral judgment much like the general factor of intelligence in cognitive tasks. If he knows one aspect of the good at a certain level, he knows other aspects of the good at that level. Third, because at each stage there is a single principle of the good, which only approaches a moral principle at the higher levels. At all levels, for instance, there is some reason for regard for law and some reason for regard of rights. Only at the highest stage, however, is regard for law a regard for universal moral law and regard for rights a regard for universal human rights. At this point, both regard for law and regard for human rights are grounded on a clear criterion of justice which was present in confused and obscure form at earlier stages.

Let me describe the stages in terms of the civil disobedience issue in a way that may clarify the argument I have just made. Here's a question we have asked: Before the Civil War, we had laws that allowed slavery. According to the law if a slave escaped, he had to be returned to his owner like a runaway horse. Some people who didn't believe in slavery disobeyed the law and hid the runaway slaves and helped them to escape. Were they doing right or wrong?

A bright, middle-class boy, Johnny, answers the question this way when he is ten: "They were doing wrong because the slave ran away himself. They're being just like slaves themselves trying to keep 'em away." He is asked, "Is slavery right or wrong?" He answers, "Some wrong, but servants aren't so bad because they don't do all that heavy work."

Johnny's response is Stage 1: *Punishment and obedience orientation.* Breaking the law makes it wrong; indeed the badness of being a slave washes off on his rescuer.

Three years later he is asked the same question. His answer is mainly a Stage 2 *instrumental relativism.* He says: "They would help them escape because they were all against slavery. The South was for slavery because they had big plantations and the North was against it because they had big factories and they needed people to work and they'd pay. So the Northerners would think it was right but the Southerners wouldn't."

So early comes Marxist relativism. He goes on: "If a person is against slavery and maybe likes the slave or maybe dislikes the owner, it's OK for him to break the law if he likes, provided he doesn't get caught. If the slaves were in misery and one was a friend he'd do it. It would probably be right if it was someone you really loved."

At the end, his orientation to sympathy and love indicates the same Stage 3, *orientation to approval, affection, and helpfulness....*

At age nineteen, in college, Johnny is Stage 4: *Orientation to maintaining a social order of rules and rights.* He says: "They were right in my point of view. I

LEVELS AND STAGES IN MORAL DEVELOPMENT

Levels	Basis of moral judgment	Stages of development
I	Moral value resides in external, quasi-physical happenings, in bad acts, or in quasi-physical needs rather then in persons and standards.	*Stage 1:* Obediences and punishment orientation. Egocentric deference to superior power or prestige, or a trouble-avoiding set. Objective responsibility.
		Stage 2: Naively egoistic orientation. Right action is that instrumentally satisfying the self's needs and occasionally others'. Awareness of relativism of value to each actor's needs and perspective. Naive egalitarianism and orientation to exchange and reciprocity.
II	Moral value resides in performing good or right roles, in maintaining the conventional order and the expectations of others.	*Stage 3:* Good-boy orientation. Orientation to approval and to pleasing and helping others. Conformity to sterotypical images of majority or natural role behavior, and judgment by intentions.
		Stage 4: Authority and social-order maintaining orientation. Orientation to "doing duty" and to showing respect for authority and maintaining the given social order for its own sake. Regard for earned expectations of others.
III	Moral value resides in conformity by the self to shared or sharable standards, rights, or duties.	*Stage 5:* Contractual legalistic orientation. Recognition of an arbitrary element or starting point in rules

LEVELS AND STAGES IN MORAL DEVELOPMENT *(continued)*

Levels	Basis of moral judgment	Stages of development
		or expectations for the sake of agreement. Duty defined in terms of contract, general avoidance of violation of the will or rights of others, and majority will and welfare.
		Stage 6: Conscience or principle orienta- tion. Orientation not only to actually or- dined social rules but to principles of choice involving appeal to logical universality and consistency. Orien- tation to conscience as a directing agent and to mutual respect and trust.

hate the actual aspect of slavery, the imprisonment of one man ruling over another. They drive them too hard and they don't get anything in return. It's not right to disobey the law, no. Laws are made by the people. But you might do it because you feel it's wrong. If 50,000 people break the law, can you put them all in jail? Can 50,000 people be wrong?"

Johnny here is oriented to the rightness and wrongness of slavery itself and of obedience to law. He doesn't see the wrongness of slavery in terms of equal human rights but in terms of an unfair economic relation, working hard and getting nothing in return. The same view of rights in terms of getting what you worked for leads Johnny to say about school integration: "A lot of colored people are now just living off of civil rights. You only get education as far as you want to learn, as far as you work for it, not being placed with someone else, you don't get it from someone else."

Johnny illustrates for us the distinction between virtue as the development of principles of justice and virtue as being unprejudiced. In one sense Johnny's development has involved increased recognition of the fellow-humanness of the slaves. For thinking of slaves as inferior and bad at age ten he thinks of them as having some sort of rights at age nineteen. He is still not just, however, because his only notions of right are that you should get what you earn, a conception easily used to justify a segregated society. In spite of a high school and college education, he has no real grasp of the conceptions of rights underlying the Constitution or the Supreme Court decisions involved. Johnny's lack of virtue is not that he doesn't want to associate with Negroes, it is that he is not capable of being a participating citizen of our society because he does not understand the principles on which our society is based. His failure to understand these principles cuts both ways. Not only does he fail to ground the rights of Negroes on principles but he fails to ground respect for law on this base. Respect for law is respect for the majority. But if 50,000 people break the law, can 50,000 be wrong? Whether the 50,000 people are breaking the law in the name of rights or of the Ku Klux Klan makes no difference in this line of thought.

It is to be hoped that Johnny may reach our next stage, Stage 5, *social contract legalism*, by his mid-twenties, since some of our subjects continue to develop up until this time. Instead of taking one of our research subjects, however, let us take some statements by Socrates as an example of Stage 5. Socrates is explaining to Crito why he refuses to save his life by taking advantage of the escape arrangements Crito has made:

> Ought one to fulfill all one's agreements?, Socrates asks. Then consider the consequences. Suppose the laws and constitution of Athens were to confront us and ask, Socrates, can you deny that by this act you intend, so far as you have power, to destroy us. Do you image that a city can continue to exist if the legal judgments which are pronounced by it are nullified and destroyed by private persons? At an earlier time, you made a noble show of indifference to the possibility of dying. Now you show no respect for your earlier professions and no regard for us, the laws, trying to run away in spite of the contracts by which you agreed to live as a member of our state. Are we not speaking the truth when we say that you have undertaken in deed, if not in word, to live your life as a citizen in obedience to us? It is a fact, then, that you are breaking convenants made with us under no compulsion or misunderstanding. You had seventy years in which you could have left the country if you were not satisfied with us or felt that the agreements were unfair.

As an example of Stage 6, *orientation to universal moral principles*, let me cite Martin Luther King's letter from a Birmingham jail.

> There is a type of constructive non-violent tension which is necessary for growth. Just as Socrates felt it was necessary to create a tension in the mind so that individuals could rise from the bondage of half-truths, so must we see the need for nonviolent gadflies to create the kind of tension in society that will help men rise from the dark depths of prejudice and racism.
>
> One may well ask, "How can you advocate breaking some laws and obeying others?" The answer lies in the fact that there are two types of laws, just and unjust. One has not only a legal but a moral responsibility to obey just laws. One has a moral responsibility to disobey unjust laws. An unjust law is a human law that is not rooted in eternal law and natural law. Any law that uplifts human personality is just, any law that degrades human personality is unjust. An unjust law is a code that a numerical or power majority group compels a minority group to obey but does not make binding on itself. This is difference made legal.

I do not advocate evading or defying the law as would the rabid segregationist. That would lead to anarchy. One who breaks an unjust law must do so openly, lovingly, and with a willingness to accept the penalty. An individual who breaks a law that conscience tells him is unjust, and willingly accepts the penalty of imprisonment in order to arouse the conscience of the community over its injustice, is in reality expressing the highest respect for law.

King makes it clear that moral disobedience of the law must spring from the same root as moral obedience to law, out of respect for justice. We respect the law because it is based on rights, both in the sense that the law is designed to protect the rights of all and because the law is made by the principle of equal political rights. If civil disobedience is to be Stage 6, it must recognize the contractual respect for law of Stage 5, even to accepting imprisonment. That is why Stage 5 is a way of thinking about the laws which are imposed upon all, while a morality of justice which claims to judge the law can never be anything but a free, personal ideal. It must accept the idea of being put in jail by its enemies, not of putting its enemies in jail. While we classified Socrates' statements to Crito as Stage 5, his statement of his civilly disobedient role as a moral educator quoted earlier was Stage 6, at least in spirit.

Both logic and empirical study indicate there is no shortcut to autonomous morality, no Stage 6 without a previous Stage 5.

We have claimed that knowledge of the moral good is one. We now will try to show that virtue in action is knowledge of the good, as Plato claimed ... Knowledge of the good in terms of what Plato calls opinion or conventional belief is not virtue. An individual may believe that cheating is very bad but that does not predict that he will resist cheating in real life. Espousal of unprejudiced attitudes toward Negroes does not predict action to assure civil rights in an atmosphere where others have some prejudice; however, true knowledge, knowledge of principles of justice, does predict virtuous action. With regard to cheating, the essential elements of justice are understood by both our Stage 5 and our Stage 6 subjects. In cheating, the critical issue is recognition of the element of contract and agreement implicit in the situation, and the recognition that while it doesn't seem so bad if one person cheats, what holds for all must hold for one. In a recent study, 100 sixth-grade children were given experimental cheating tests and our moral judgment interview. The majority of the children were below the principled level in moral judgment; they were at our first four moral stages. Seventy-five percent of these children cheated. In contrast, only 20 percent of the principled subjects, that is, Stage 5 or 6, cheated. In another study conducted at the college level, only 11 percent of the principled subjects cheated, in contrast to 42 percent of the students at lower levels of moral judgment. In the case of cheating, justice and the expectations of conventional authority both dictate the same behavior. What happens when justice and authority are opposed?

An experimental study by Stanley Milgram involved such an opposition. Under the guise of a learning experiment, undergraduate subjects were ordered by an experimenter to administer increasingly more severe electric shock punishment to a stooge victim. In this case, the principles of justice involved in the Stage 5 social contract orientation do not clearly prescribe a decision. The victim had voluntarily agreed to participate in the experiment, and the subject himself had contractualy committed himself to perform the experiment. Only Stage 6 thinking clearly defined the situation as one in which the experimenter did not have the moral right to ask them to inflict pain on another person. Accordingly, 75 percent of those at Stage 6 quit or refused to shock the victim, as compared to only 13 percent of all the subjects at lower stages.

A study of Berkeley students carries the issue into political civil disobedience. Berkeley students were faced with a decision to sit in the Administration building in the name of political freedom of communication. Haan and Smith administered moral judgment interviews to over 200 of these students. The situation was like that in Milgram's study. A Stage 5 social contract interpretation of justice, which was that held by the University administration, could take the position that a student who came to Berkeley came with foreknowledge of the rules and could go elsewhere if he did not like them. About 50 percent of the Stage 5 subjects sat in. For Stage 6 students, the issue was clear cut, and 80 percent of them sat in. For students at the conventional levels, Stages 3 and 4, the issue was also clear cut, and only 10 percent of them sat in. These results will sound very heartwarming to those who have engaged in protest activities. Protesting is a sure sign of being at the most mature moral level; however, there was another group [that] was almost as disposed to sit in as the Stage 6 students. These were our Stage 2 instrumental relativists, of whom about 60 percent sat in. From our longitudinal studies, we know that most Stage 2 college students are in a state of confusion. In high school most were at the conventional level, and in college they kick conventional morality, searching for their thing, for self-chosen values, but cannot tell an autonomous morality of justice from one of egoistic relativism, exchange, and revenge. Our longitudinal studies indicate that all of our middle-class Stage 2 college students grow out of it to become principled adults. If the pressures are greater and you are a Stokely Carmichael, things may take a different course.

I make the point to indicate that protest activities, like other acts, are neither virtuous nor vicious, it is only the knowledge of the good which lies behind them which can give them virtue. As an example, I would take it that a Stage 6 sense of justice would have been rather unlikely to find the Dow Chemical sit-in virtuous. The rules being disobeyed by the protesters were not unjust rules, and the sit-in was depriving individuals of rights, not trying to protect individual rights. Principled civil disobedience is not illegitimate propaganda for worthy political causes, it is the just questioning of injustice.

I hope this last example will indicate the complexity of the behaviors by which knowledge of justice may be manifested and that no trait of virtue in the ordinary sense will describe the behavior of the principled or just man. Having, I hope, shown the validity of the Platonic view of virtue, I will take the little time left to consider the sense in which it may be taught. The Platonic view implies that, in a sense, knowledge of the good is always within but needs to be drawn out like geometric knowledge in Meno's slave. In a series of experimental studies, we have found that children and adolescents rank as "best" the highest level of moral reasoning they can comprehend. Children comprehend all lower stages than their own, and often comprehend the stage one higher than their own and occasionally two stages higher, though they cannot actively express these higher stages of thought. If they comprehend the stage one higher than their own, they tend to prefer it to their own. This fact is basic to moral leadership in our society. While the majority of adults in American society are at a conventional level, Stages 3 and 4, leadership in our society has usually been expressed at the level of Stages 5 and 6, as our example of Martin Luther King suggests. While it may be felt as dangerous, the moral leadership of the Platonic philosopher-ruler is nonetheless naturally felt.

Returning to the teaching of virtue as a drawing out, the child's preference for the next level of thought shows that it is greeted as already familiar, that it is felt to be a more adequate expression of that already within, of that latent in the child's own thought. If the child were responding to fine words and external prestige he would not pick the next stage continuous with his own, but something else.

Let me now suggest a different example in the sense in which moral teaching must be a drawing out of that already within. At the age of four my son joined the pacifist and vegetarian movement and refused to eat meat, because as he said, "it's bad to kill animals." In spite of lengthy Hawk argumentation by his parents about the difference between justified and unjustified killing, he remained a vegetarian for six months. Like most Doves, however, his principles recognized occasions for just or legitimate killing. One night I read to him a book of Eskimo life involving a seal-killing expedition. He got angry during the story and said, "You know, there is one kind of meat I would eat, Eskimo meat. It's bad to kill animals so it's all right to eat Eskimos."

For reasons I won't detail, this eye for an eye, tooth for a tooth concept of justice is Stage 1. You will recognize, however, that it is a very genuine though four-year-old sense of justice and that it contains within it the Stage 6 sense of justice in shadowy form. The problem is to draw the child's perceptions of justice from the shadows of the cave step by step toward the light of justice as an ideal form. This last example indicates another Platonic truth, which is that the child who turns from the dark images of the cave toward the light is at first still convinced that his dark images best represent the truth. Like Meno's slave, the child is initially quite confident of his moral knowledge, of the rationality and efficacy of his moral principles. The notion that the child feels ignorant and is eager to absorb the wisdom of adult authority in the moral domain is one which any teacher or parent will know is nonsense. Let me give another example. Following a developmental timetable, my son moved to an expedient Stage 2 orientation when he was six. He told me at that time, "You know the reason people don't steal is because they're afraid of the police. If there were no police around everyone would steal." Of course I told him that I and most people didn't steal because we thought it wrong, because we wouldn't want other people to take things from us, and so on. My son's reply was, "I just don't see it, it's sort of crazy not to steal if there are no police."

The story indicates, that like most ordinary fathers, I had no great skill in teaching true virtue. My son, of course, has always been virtuous in the conventional sense. Even when he saw no rational reason for being honest, he received the highest marks on his report card on the basis of the bag of virtues of obedience, responsibility, and respect for property. Contrary to what we usually think, it is quite easy to teach conventionally virtuous behavior but very difficult to teach true knowledge of the good.

The first step in teaching virtue, then, is the Socratic step of creating dissatisfaction in the student about his present knowledge of the good. This we do experimentally by exposing the student to moral conflict situations for which his principles have no ready solution. Second, we expose him to disagreement and argument about these situations with his peers. Our Platonic view holds that if we inspire cognitive conflict in the student and point the way to the next step up the divided line, he will tend to see things previously invisible to him.

In practice, then, our experimental efforts at moral education have involved getting students at one level, say Stage 2, to argue with those at the next level, say Stage 3. The teacher would support and clarify the Stage 3 arguments. Then he would pit the Stage 3 students against the Stage 4 students on a new dilemma. Initial results with this method with a junior high school group indicated that 50 percent of the students moved up one stage and 10 percent moved up two stages. In comparison, only 10 percent of a control group moved up one stage in the four-month period involved.

Obviously, the small procedures I have described are only a way station to genuine moral education.... [A] more complete approach implies full student participation in a school in which justice is a living matter. Let me sketch out one Platonic republic with this aim, a boarding school I recently visited. The heart of this school is described in its brochure somewhat as follows:

> The sense of community is most strongly felt in the weekly Meeting, consisting of faculty, their families and students. Decisions are made by consensus rather than by majority rule. This places responsibility on each member to struggle to see through his own desires to the higher needs of others and the community, while witnessing the deepest concerns of his conscience. The results of these decisions are not rules in the traditional sense, but agreements entered into by everyone and recorded as minutes.

The brochure goes on to quote a letter by one of its graduation students:

> The School is an entity surrounded by the rest of the world in which each individual struggles against that which restrains him—himself. It has been said that the School gives too much freedom to its young, often rebellious students. But a film will

darken to a useless mass of chemical if its not developed in time. People change early, too. If they meet a loving atmosphere, they are affected by it profoundly. Growing up is a lonely thing to be doing, but at the Meeting School, it is also a beautiful thing.

All schools need not and cannot be self-contained little Republics in which knowledge of the good is to be brought out through love and community as well as through participation in a just institution. Such schools do stand as a challenge to an educational establishment which makes a pious bow to the bag of virtues while teaching that true goodness is tested on the College Boards. The Platonic view I've been espousing suggests something still revolutionary and frightening to me if not to you, that the schools would be radically different places if they took seriously the teaching of real knowledge of the good.

BASIC APPROACHES TO ETHICAL THEORY

Nicomachean Ethics

Aristotle

BOOK I

[*All human activities aim at some good.*] Every art and every inquiry, and similarly every action and pursuit, is thought to aim at some good; and for this reason the good has rightly been declared to be that at which all things aim. But a certain difference is found among ends; some are activities, others are products apart from the activities that produce them. Where there are ends apart from the actions, it is the nature of the products to be better than the activities. Now, as there are many actions, arts, and sciences, their ends also are many; the end of the medical art is health, that of shipbuilding a vessel, that of strategy victory, that of economics wealth. But where such arts fall under a single capacity—as bridle-making and the other arts concerned with the equipment of horses fall under the art of riding, and this and every military action under strategy, in the same way other arts fall under yet others—in all of these the ends of the master arts are to be preferred to all the subordinate ends; for it is for the sake of the former that the latter are pursued. It makes no difference whether the activities themselves are the ends of the actions, or something else apart from the activities, as in the case of the sciences just mentioned.

From *Ethica Nicomachea*, translated by W.D. Ross for *The Oxford Translation of Aristotle* edited by W.D. Ross, Volume 9 (1925). Books One and Two with omissions. Abridged by the editor.

[*The science of* the *good for man in politics.*] If, then, there is some end of the things we do, which we desire for its own sake (everything else being desired for the sake of this), and if we do not choose everything for the sake of something else (for at that rate the process would go on to infinity, so that our desire would be empty and vain), clearly this must be the good and the chief good. Will not the knowledge of it, then, have a great influence on life? Shall we not, like archers who have a mark to aim at, be more likely to hit upon what is right? If so, we must try, in outline at least, to determine what it is, and of which of the sciences or capacities it is the object. It would seem to belong to the most authoritative art and that which is most truly the master art. And politics appears to be of this nature; for it is this that ordains which of the sciences should be studied in a state, and which each class of citizens should learn and up to what point they should learn them; and we see even the most highly esteemed of capacities to fall under this, e.g., strategy, economics, rhetoric; now, since politics uses the rest of the sciences, and since, again, it legislates as to what we are to do and what we are to abstain from, the end of this science must include those of the others, so that this end must be the good for man. For even if the end is the same for a single man and for a state, that of the state seems at all events something greater and more complete whether to attain or to preserve; though it is worth while to attain the end merely for one man, it is finer and more god-like to attain it for a nation or for city-states. These, then, are the ends at which our inquiry aims, since it is political science, in one sense of that term.

[*We must not expect more precision than the subject matter admits.*] Our discussion will be adequate if it has as much clearness as the subject matter admits of, for precision is not to be sought for alike in all discussions, any more than in all the products of the crafts. Now fine and just actions, which political science investigates, admit of much variety and fluctuation of opinion, so that they may be thought to exist only by convention, and not by nature. And goods also give rise to a similar fluctuation because they bring harm to many people; for before now men have been undone by reason of their wealth, and others by reason of their courage. We must be content, then, in speaking of such subjects and with such premises to indicate the truth roughly and in outline, and in speaking about things which are only for the most part true and with premises of the same kind to reach conclusions that are no better. In the same spirit, therefore, should each type of statement be *received*; for it is the mark of an educated man to look for precision in each class of things just so far as the nature of the subject admits; it is evidently equally foolish to accept probable reasoning from a mathematician and to demand from a rhetorician scientific proofs.

Now each man judges well the things he knows, and of these he is a good judge. And so the man who has been educated in a subject is a good judge of that subject, and the man who has received an all-round education is a good judge in general. Hence a young man is not a proper hearer of lectures on political science; for he is inexperienced in the actions that occur in life, but its discussions start from these and are about these; and, further, since he tends to follow his passions, his study will be vain and unprofitable, because the end aimed at is not knowledge but action. And it makes no difference whether he is young in years or youthful in character; the defect does not depend on time, but on his living, and pursuing each successive object, as passion directs. For to such persons, as to the incontinent, knowledge brings no profit; but to those who desire and act in accordance with a rational principle knowledge about such matters will be of great benefit.

These remarks about the student, the sort of treatment to be expected, and the purpose of the inquiry, may be taken as our preface.

[*The good for man is generally agreed to be happiness.*] Let us resume our inquiry and state, in view of the fact that all knowledge and every pursuit aims at some good, what it is that we say political science aims at and what is the highest of all goods achievable by action. Verbally there is very general agreement; for both the general run of men and people of superior refinement say that it is happiness, and identify living well and doing well with being happy; but with regard to what happiness is they differ, and the many do not give the same account as the wise. For the former think it is some plain and obvious thing, like pleasure, wealth, or honour; they differ, however, from one another—and often even the same man identifies it with different things, with health when he is ill, with wealth when he is poor; but conscious of their ignorance, they admire those who proclaim some great ideal that is above their comprehension. Now some thought that apart from these many goods there is another which is self-subsistent and causes the goodness of all these as well. To examine all the opinions that have been held were perhaps somewhat fruitless; enough to examine those that are most prevalent or that seem to be arguable.

[*The popular views that the good is pleasure, honour, wealth.*] Let us, however, resume our discussion from the point at which we digressed. To judge from the lives that men lead, most men, and men of the most vulgar type, seem (not without some ground) to identify the good, or happiness, with pleasure; which is the reason why they love the life of enjoyment. For there are, we may say, three prominent types of life—that just mentioned, the political, and thirdly the contemplative life. Now the mass of mankind are evidently quite slavish in their tastes, preferring a life suitable to beasts, but they get some ground for their view from the fact that many of those in high places share the tastes of Sardanapallus. A consideration of the prominent types of life shows that people of superior refinement and of active disposition identify happiness with honour; for this is, roughly speaking, the end of the political life. But it seems too superficial to be what we are looking for, since it is thought to depend on those who bestow honour rather than on him who receives it, but the good we divine to be something proper to a man and not easily taken from him. Further, men seem to pursue honour in order that they may be assured of their goodness; at least it is by men of practical wisdom that they seek to be honoured, and among those who know them, and on the ground of their virtue; clearly, then, according to them, at any rate, virtue is better. And perhaps one might even suppose this to be, rather than honour, the end of the political life. But even this appears somewhat incomplete; for possession of virtue seems actually compatible with being asleep, or with lifelong inactivity, and, further, with the greatest sufferings and misfortunes; but a man who was living so no one would call happy, unless he were maintaining a thesis at all costs. But enough of this; for the subject has been sufficiently treated even in the current discussions. Third comes the contemplative life, which we shall consider later.

The life of money-making is one undertaken under compulsion, and wealth is evidently not the good we are seeking; for it is merely useful and for the sake of something else. And so one might rather take the aforenamed objects to be ends; for they are loved for themselves. But it is evident that not even these are ends; yet many arguments have been thrown away in support of them. Let us leave this subject, then.

[*The good must be something final and self-sufficient.*] Let us again return to the good we are seeking, and ask what it can be. It seems different in different actions and arts; it is different in medicine, in strategy, and in the other arts likewise. What then is the good of each? Surely that for whose sake everything else is done. In medicine this is health, in strategy victory, in architecture a house, in any other sphere something else, and in every action and pursuit the end; for it is for the sake of this that all men do whatever else they do. Therefore, if there is an end for all that we do, this will be the good achievable by action, and if there are more than one, these will be the goods achievable by action.

So the argument has by a different course reached the same point; but we must try to state this even more clearly. Since there is evidently more than one end, and we choose some of these (e.g., wealth, flutes, and in general instruments) for the sake of something else, clearly not all ends are final ends; but the chief good is evidently something final. Therefore, if there is only one final end, this will be what we are seeking, and if there are more than one, the most final of these will be what we are seeking. Now we call that which is in itself worthy of pursuit more final than that which is worthy of pursuit for the sake of something else, and that which is never desirable for the sake of something else more final than the things that are desirable both in themselves and for the sake of that other thing, and therefore we call final without qualification that which is always desirable in itself and never for the sake of something else.

Now such a thing happiness, above all else, is held to be; for this we choose always for itself and never for the sake of something else, but honour, pleasure, reason, and every virtue we choose indeed for themselves (for if nothing resulted from them we should still choose each of them), but we choose them also for the sake of happiness, judging that by means of them we shall be happy. Happiness, on the other hand, no one chooses for the sake of these, nor, in general, for anything other than itself.

From the point of view of self-sufficiency the same result seems to follow; for the final good is thought to be self-sufficient. Now by self-sufficient we do not mean that which is sufficient for a man by himself, for one who lives a solitary life, but also for parents, children, wife, and in general for his friends and fellow citizens, since man is born for citizenship. But some limit must be set to this; for if we extend our requirement to ancestors and descendants and friends' friends we are in for an infinite series. Let us examine this question, however, on another occasion; the self-sufficient we now define as that which when isolated makes life desirable and lacking in nothing; and such we think happiness to be; and further we think it most desirable of all things, without being counted as one good thing among others—if it were so counted it would clearly be made more desirable by the addition of even the least of goods; for that which is added becomes an excess of goods, and of goods the greater is always more desirable. Happiness, then, is something final and self-sufficient, and is the end of action.

Presumably, however, to say that happiness is the chief good seems a platitude, and a clearer account of what it is is still desired. This might perhaps be given, if we could first ascertain the function of man. For just as for a flute player, a sculptor, or any artist, and, in general, for all things that have a function or activity, the good and the "well" is thought to reside in the function, so would it seem to be for man, if he has a function. Have the carpenter, then, and the tanner certain functions or activities, and has man none? Is he born without a function? Or as eye, hand, foot, and in general each of the parts evidently has a function, may one lay it down that man similarly has a function apart from all these? What then can this be? Life seems to be common even to plants, but we are seeking what is peculiar to man. Let us exclude, therefore, the life of nutrition and growth. Next there would be a life of perception, but *it* also seems to be common even to the horse, the ox, and every animal. There remains, then, an active life of the element that has a rational principle; of this, one part has such a principle in the sense of being obedient to one, the other in the sense of possessing one and exercising thought. And, as "life of the rational element" also has two meanings, we must state that life in the sense of activity is what we mean; for this seems to be the more proper sense of the term. Now if the function of man is an activity of soul which follows or implies a rational principle, and if we say "a so-and-so" and "a good so-and-so" have a function which is the same in kind, e.g., a lyre player and a good lyre player, and so without qualification in all cases, eminence in respect of goodness being added to the name of the function (for the function of a lyre player is to play the lyre, and that of a good lyre player is to do so well); if this is the case [and we state the function of man to be a certain kind of life, and this to be an activity or actions of the soul implying a rational principle, and the function of a good man to be the good and noble performance of these, and if any action is well performed when it is performed in accordance with the appropriate excellence if this is the case], human good turns out to be activity of soul in accordance with virtue, and if there is more than one virtue, in accordance with the best and most complete.

But we must add "in a complete life." For one swallow does not make a summer, nor does one day; and so too one day, or a short time, does not make a man blessed and happy.

Let this serve as an outline of the good; for we must presumably first sketch it roughly, and then later fill in the details.

[*Current beliefs about happiness.*] With those who identify happiness with virtue or some one virtue our account is in harmony; for to virtue belongs virtuous activity. But it makes, perhaps, no small difference whether we place the chief good in possession or in use, in state of mind or in activity. For the state of mind may exist without producing any good result, as in a man who is asleep or in some other way quite inactive, but the activity cannot; for one who has the activity will of necessity be acting, and acting well. And as in the Olympic Games it is not the most beautiful and the strongest that are crowned but those who compete (for it is some of these that are victorious), so those who act win, and rightly win, the noble and good things in life.

[T]he man who does not rejoice in noble actions is not even good; since no one would call a man just who did not enjoy acting justly, nor any man liberal who did not enjoy liberal actions; and similarly in all other cases. If this is so, virtuous actions must be in themselves pleasant. But they are also *good* and *noble*, and have each of these attributes in the highest degree, since the good man judges well about these attributes; his judgement is such as we have described. Happiness then is the best, noblest, and most pleasant thing in the world, and these attributes are not severed as in the inscription at Delos—

> Most noble is that which is justest, and best is health; But pleasantest is it to win what we love.

For all these properties belong to the best activities; and these, or one—the best—of these, we identify with happiness.

Yet evidently, as we said, it needs the external goods as well; for it is impossible, or not easy, to do noble acts without the proper equipment. In many actions we use friends and riches and political power as instruments; and there are some things the lack of which takes the lustre from happiness, as good birth, goodly children, beauty; for the man who is very ugly in appearance or ill-born or solitary and childless is not very likely to be happy, and perhaps a man would be still less likely if he had thoroughly bad children or friends or had lost good children or friends by death.

[*How happiness is acquired.*] The answer to the question we are asking is plain also from the definition of happiness; for it has been said to be a virtuous activity of soul, of a certain kind. Of the remaining goods, some must necessarily pre-exist as conditions of happiness, and others are naturally co-operative and useful as instruments. And this will be found to agree with what we said at the outset; for we stated the end of political science to be the best end, and political science spends most of its pains on making the citizens to be of a certain character, viz., good and capable of noble acts.

[*Intellectual and moral faculties and virtues.*] Since happiness is an activity of soul in accordance with perfect virtue, we must consider the nature of virtue; for perhaps we shall thus see better the nature of happiness.

Some things are said about it, adequately enough, even in the discussions outside our school, and we must use these; e.g., that one element in the soul is irrational and one has a rational principle. Whether these are separated as the parts of the body or of anything divisible are, or are distinct by definition but by nature inseparable, like convex and concave in the circumference of a circle, does not affect the present question.

Of the irrational element one division seems to be widely distributed, and vegetative in its nature, I mean that which causes nutrition and growth; for it is this kind of power of the soul that one must assign to all nurslings and to embryos, and this same power to full-grown creatures; this is more reasonable than to assign some different power to them. Now the excellence of this seems to be common to all species and not specifically human; for this part or faculty seems to function most in sleep, while goodness and badness are least manifest in sleep (whence comes the saying that the happy are no better off than the wretched for half their lives; and this happens naturally enough, since sleep is an inactivity of the soul in that respect in which it is called good or bad), unless perhaps to a small extent some of the movements actually penetrate to the soul, and in this respect the dreams of good men are better than those of ordinary people. Enough of this subject, however; let us leave the nutritive faculty alone, since it has by its nature no share in human excellence.

There seems to be also another irrational element in the soul—one which in a sense, however, shares in a rational principle. For we praise the rational principle of the continent man and of the incontinent, and the part of their soul that has such a principle, since it urges them aright and towards the best objects; but there is found in them also another element naturally opposed to the rational principle, which fights against and resists that principle. For exactly as paralysed limbs when we intend to move them to the right turn on the contrary to the left, so is it with the soul; the impulses of incontinent people move in contrary directions. But while in the body we see that which moves astray, in the soul we do not.

Therefore the irrational element also appears to be two-fold. For the vegetative element in no way shares in a rational principle, but the appetitive, and in general the desiring element in a sense shares in it, in so far as it listens to and obeys it.

Virtue too is distinguished into kinds in accordance with this difference; for we say that some of the virtues are intellectual and others moral, philosophic wisdom and understanding and practical wisdom being intellectual, liberality and temperance moral. For in speaking about a man's character we do not say that he is wise or has understanding but that he is good-tempered or temperate; yet we praise the wise man also with respect to his state of mind; and of states of mind we call those which merit praise virtues.

BOOK II

[*Moral virtue acquired by practice.*] Virtue, then, being of two kinds, intellectual and moral, intellectual virtue in the main owes both its birth and its growth to teaching (for which reason it requires experience and time), while moral virtue comes about as a result of habit, whence also its name *ethike* is one that is formed by a slight variation from the word *ethos* (habit). From this it is also plain that none of the moral virtues arises in us by nature; for nothing that exists by nature can form a habit contrary to its nature. For instance the stone which by nature moves downward cannot be habituated to move upwards, not even if one tries to train it by throwing it up ten thousand times; nor can fire be habituated to move downwards, nor can anything else that by nature behaves in one way be trained to behave in another. Neither by nature, then, nor contrary to nature do the virtues arise in us; rather we are adapted by nature to receive them, and are made perfect by habit.

Again, of all the things that come to us by nature we first acquire the potentiality and later exhibit the activity (this is plain in the case of the senses; for it was not by often seeing or often hearing that we got these senses, but on the contrary we had them before we used them); but the virtues we get by first exercising them, as also happens in the case of the arts as well. For the things we have to learn before we can do them, we learn by doing them, e.g., men become builders by building and lyre players by playing the lyre; so too we become just by doing just acts, temperate by doing temperate acts, brave by doing brave acts.

[*Moral virtue is a disposition to choose the mean.*]We may remark, then, that every virtue or excellence both brings into good condition the thing of which it is the excellence and makes the work of that thing be done well; e.g., the excellence of the eye makes both the eye and its work good; for it is by the excellence of the eye that we see well. Similarly the excellence of the horse makes a horse both good in itself and good at running and at carrying its rider and at awaiting the attack of the enemy. Therefore, if this is true in every case, the virtue of man also will be the state of character which makes a man good and which makes him do his own work well.

If it is thus, then, that every art does its work well—by looking to the intermediate and judging its works by this standard (so that we often say of good works of art that it is not possible either to take away or to add anything, implying that excess and defect destroy the goodness of works of art, while the mean preserves it; and good artists, as well say, look to this in their work), and if, further, virtue is more exact and better than any art, as nature also is, then virtue must have the quality of aiming at the intermediate. I mean moral virtue; for it is this that is concerned with passions and actions, and in these there is excess, defect, and the intermediate. For instance, both fear and confidence and appetite and anger and pity and in general pleasure and pain may be felt both too much and too little, and in both cases not well; but to feel them at the right times, with reference to the right objects, towards the right people, with the right motive, and in the right way, is what is both intermediate and best, and this is characteristic of virtue. Similarly with regard to actions also there is excess, defect, and the intermediate. Now virtue is concerned with passions and actions, in which excess is a form of failure, and so is defect, while the intermediate is praised and is a form of success; and being praised and being successful are both characteristics of virtue. Therefore virtue is a kind of mean, since, as we have seen, it aims at what is intermediate.

Again, it is possible to fail in many ways (for evil belongs to the class of the unlimited, as the Pythagoreans conjectured, and good to that of the limited), while to succeed is possible only in one way (for which reason also one is easy and the other difficult—to miss the mark easy, to hit it difficult); for these reasons also, then, excess and defect are characteristic of vice, and the mean of virtue;

For men are good in but one way, but bad in many.

Virtue, then, is a state of character concerned with choice, lying in a mean, i.e., the mean relative to us, this being determined by a rational principle, and by that principle by which the man of practical wisdom would determine it. Now it is a mean between two vices, that which depends on excess and that which depends on defect; and again it is a mean because the vices respectively fall short of or exceed what is right in both passions and actions, while virtue both finds and chooses that which is intermediate. Hence in respect of its substance and the definition which states its essence virtue is a mean, with regard to what is best and right an extreme.

But not every action nor every passion admits of a mean; for some have names that already imply badness, e.g., spite, shamelessness, envy, and in the case of actions adultery, theft, murder; for all of these and suchlike things imply by their names that they are themselves bad, and not the excesses or deficiencies of them. It is not possible, then, ever to be right with regard to them; one must always be wrong. Nor does goodness or badness with regard to such things depend on committing adultery with the right woman, at the right time, and in the right way, but simply to do any of them is to go wrong. It would be equally absurd, then, to expect that in unjust, cowardly, and voluptuous action there should be a mean, an excess, and a deficiency; for at that rate there would be a mean of excess and of deficiency, an excess of excess, and a deficiency of deficiency. But as there is no excess and deficiency of temperance and courage because what is intermediate is in a sense an extreme, so too of the actions we have mentioned there is no mean nor any excess and deficiency, but however they are done they are wrong; for in general there is neither a mean of excess and deficiency, nor excess and deficiency of a mean.

Foundations of the Metaphysics of Morals

Immanuel Kant

TRANSITION FROM THE COMMON RATIONAL KNOWLEDGE
OF MORALS TO THE PHILOSOPHICAL

Nothing in the world—indeed nothing beyond the world—can possibly be conceived which could be called good without qualification except a *good will*. Intelligence, wit, judgment, and the other talents of the mind, however they may be named, or courage, resoluteness, and perseverance as qualities of temperament, are doubtless in many respects good and desirable. But they can become extremely bad and harmful if the will, which is to make use of these gifts of nature and which in its special constitution is called character, is not good. It is the same with the gifts of fortune. Power, riches, honor, even health, general well-being, and the contentment with one's condition which is called happiness, make for pride and even arrogance if there is not a good will to correct their influence on the mind and on its principles of action so as to make it universally conformable to its end. It need hardly be mentioned that the sight of a being adorned with no feature of a pure and good will, yet enjoying uninterrupted prosperity, can never give pleasure to a rational impartial observer. Thus the good will seems to constitute the indispensable condition even of worthiness to be happy.

Some qualities seem to be conducive to this good will and can facilitate its action, but, in spite of that, they have no intrinsic unconditional worth. They rather presuppose a good will, which limits the high esteem which one otherwise rightly has for them and prevents their being held to be absolutely good. Moderation in emotions and passions, self-control, and calm deliberation not only are good in many respects but even seem to constitute a part of the inner worth of the person. But however unconditionally they were esteemed by the ancients, they are far from being good without qualification. For without the principle of a good will they can become extremely bad, and the coolness of a villain makes him not only far more dangerous but also more directly abominable in our eyes than he would have seemed without it.

The good will is not good because of what it effects or accomplishes or because of its adequacy to achieve some proposed end; it is good only because of its willing, i.e., it is good of itself. And, regarded for itself, it is to be esteemed incomparably higher than anything which could be brought about by it in favor of any inclination or even of the sum total of all inclinations. Even if it should happen that, by a particularly unfortunate fate or by the niggardly provision of a stepmotherly nature, this will should be wholly lacking in power

From Immanuel Kant, *Foundations of the Metaphysics of Morals* (Indianapolis: Bobbs-Merrill Educational Publishing, Inc.), translated Lewis W. Beck. First and Second sections with omissions. Some footnotes omitted. Pp. 9, 10, 13–20, 24, 25, 29, 31–33, 39–41, 45–47. Abridged by the editor. Copyright 1959 © Bobbs-Merril Educational Publishing, Inc., a subsidiary of ITT. Excerpts reprinted by permission.

to accomplish its purpose, and if even the greatest effort should not avail it to achieve anything of its end, and if there remained only the good will (not as a mere wish but as the summoning of all the means in our power), it would sparkle like a jewel in its own right, as something that had its full worth in itself. Usefulness or fruitlessness can neither diminish nor augment this worth. Its usefulness would be only its setting, as it were, so as to enable us to handle it more conveniently in commerce or to attract the attention of those who are not yet connoisseurs, but not to recommend it to those who are experts or to determine its worth.

I here omit all actions which are recognized as opposed to duty, even though they may be useful in one respect or another, for with these the question does not arise at all as to whether they may be carried out *from* duty, since they conflict with it. I also pass over the actions which are really in accordance with duty and to which one has no direct inclination, rather executing them because impelled to do so by another inclination. For it is easily decided whether an action in accord with duty is performed from duty or for some selfish purpose. It is far more difficult to note this difference when the action is in accordance with duty and, in addition, the subject has a direct inclination to do it. For example, it is in fact in accordance with duty that a dealer should not overcharge an inexperienced customer, and wherever there is much business the prudent merchant does not do so, having a fixed price for everyone, so that a child may buy of him as cheaply as any other. Thus the customer is honestly served. But this is far from sufficient to justify the belief that the merchant has behaved in this way from duty and principles of honesty. His own advantage required this behavior; but it cannot be assumed that over and above that he had a direct inclination to the purchaser and that, out of love, as it were, he gave none an advantage in price over another. Therefore the action was done neither from duty nor from direct inclination but only for a selfish purpose.

On the other hand, it is a duty to preserve one's life, and moreover everyone has a direct inclination to do so. But for that reason the often anxious care which most men take of it has no intrinsic worth, and the maxim of doing so has no moral import. They preserve their lives according to duty, but not from duty. But if adversities and hopeless sorrow completely take away the relish for life, if an unfortunate man, strong in soul, is indignant rather than despondent or dejected over his fate and wishes for death, and yet preserves his life without loving it and from neither inclination nor fear but from duty—then his maxim has a moral import.

To be kind where one can is duty, and there are, moreover, many persons so sympathetically constituted that without any motive of vanity or selfishness they find an inner satisfaction in spreading joy, and rejoice in the contentment of others which they have made possible. But I say that, however dutiful and amiable it may be, that kind of action has no true moral worth. It is on a level with [actions arising from] other inclinations, such as the inclination to honor, which, if fortunately directed to what in fact accords with duty and is generally useful and thus honorable, deserve praise and encouragement but no esteem.

For the maxim lacks the moral import of an action done not from inclination but from duty. But assume that the mind of that friend to mankind was clouded by a sorrow of his own which extinguished all sympathy with the lot of others and that he still had the power to benefit others in distress, but that their need left him untouched because he was preoccupied with his own need. And now suppose him to tear himself, unsolicited by inclination, out of this dead insensibility and to perform this action only from duty and without any inclination—then for the first time his action has genuine moral worth.

It is in this way, undoubtedly, that we should understand those passages of scripture which command us to love our neighbor and even our enemy, for love as an inclination cannot be commanded. But beneficence from duty, when no inclination impels it and even when it is opposed by a natural and unconquerable aversion, is practical love, not pathological love; it resides in the will and not in the propensities of feeling, in principles of action and not in tender sympathy; and it alone can be commanded.

[Thus the first proposition of morality is that to have moral worth an action must be done from duty.] The second proposition is: An action performed from duty does not have its moral worth in the purpose which is to be achieved through it but in the maxim by which it is determined. Its moral value, therefore, does not depend on the realization of the object of the action but merely on the principle of volition by which the action is done, without any regard to the objects of the faculty of desire. From the preceding discussion it is clear that the purposes we may have for our actions and their effects as ends and incentives of the will cannot give the actions any unconditional and moral worth. Wherein, then, can this worth lie, if it is not in the will in relation to its hoped-for effect? It can lie nowhere else than in the principle of the will, irrespective of the ends which can be realized by such action. For the will stands, as it were, at the crossroads halfway between its a priori principle which is formal and its a posteriori incentive which is material. Since it must be determined by something, if it is done from duty it must be determined by the formal principle of volition as such since every material principle has been withdrawn from it.

The third principle, as a consequence of the two preceding, I would express as follows: Duty is the necessity of an action executed from respect for law.

Therefore, the pre-eminent good can consist only in the conception of the law in itself (which can be present only in a rational being) so far as this conception and not the hoped-for effect is the determining ground of the will. This pre-eminent good, which we call moral, is already present in the person who acts according to this conception, and we do not have to look for it first in the result.[1]

---

[1]It might be objected that I seek to take refuge in an obscure feeling behind the word "respect," instead of clearly resolving the question with a concept of reason. But though respect is a feeling, it is not one received through any [outer] influence but is self-wrought by a rational concept; thus it differs specifically from all feelings of the former kind which may be referred to inclination or fear. What I recognize directly as a law for myself I recognize with respect, which means merely the consciousness of the submission of my will to a law without the intervention of

But what kind of a law can that be, the conception of which must determine the will without reference to the expected result? Under this condition alone the will can be called absolutely good without qualification. Since I have robbed the will of all impulses which could come to it from obedience to any law, nothing remains to serve as a principle of the will except universal conformity of its action to law as such. That is, I should never act in such a way that I could not also will that my maxim should be a universal law. Mere conformity to law as such (without assuming any particular law applicable to certain actions) serves as the principle of the will, and it must serve as such a principle if duty is not to be a vain delusion and chimerical concept. The common reason of mankind in its practical judgments is in perfect agreement with this and has this principle constantly in view.

Let the question, for example, be: May I, when in distress, make a promise with the intention not to keep it? I easily distinguish the two meanings which the question can have, viz., whether it is prudent to make a false promise, or whether it conforms to my duty. Undoubtedly the former can often be the case, though I do see clearly that it is not sufficient merely to escape from the present difficulty by this expedient, but that I must consider whether inconveniences much greater than the present one may not later spring from this lie. Even with all my supposed cunning, the consequences cannot be so easily foreseen. Loss of credit might be far more disadvantageous than the misfortune I now seek to avoid, and it is hard to tell whether it might not be more prudent to act according to a universal maxim and to make it a habit not to promise anything without intending to fulfill it. But it is soon clear to me that such a maxim is based only on an apprehensive concern with consequences.

To be truthful from duty, however, is an entirely different thing from being truthful out of fear of disadvantageous consequences, for in the former case the concept of the action itself contains a law for me, while in the latter I must first look about to see what results for me may be connected with it. For to deviate from the principle of duty is certainly bad, but to be unfaithful to my maxim of prudence can sometimes be very advantageous to me, though it is certainly safer to abide by it. The shortest but most infallible way to find the answer to the question as to whether a deceitful promise is consistent with duty is to ask myself: Would I be content that my maxim (of extricating myself from difficulty by a false promise) should hold as a universal law for myself as

---

other influences on my mind. The direct determination of the will by the law and the consciousness of this determination is respect; thus respect can be regarded as the effect of the law on the subject and not as the cause of the law. Respect is properly the conception of a worth which thwarts my self-love. Thus it is regarded as an object neither of inclination nor of fear, though it has something analogous to both. The only object of respect is the law, and indeed only the law which we impose on ourselves and yet recognize as necessary in itself. As a law, we are subject to it without consulting self-love; as imposed on us by ourselves, it is a consequence of our will. In the former respect it is analogous to fear and in the latter to inclination. All respect for a person is only respect for the law (of righteousness, etc.) of which the person provides an example. Because we see the improvement of our talents as a duty, we think of a person of talents as the example of a law, as it were (the law that we should by practice become like him in his talents), and that constitutes our respect. All so-called moral interest consists solely in respect for the law.

well as for others? And could I say to myself that everyone may make a false promise when he is in a difficulty from which he otherwise cannot escape? I immediately see that I could will the lie but not a universal law to lie. For with such a law there would be no promises at all, inasmuch as it would be futile to make a pretense of my intention in regard to future actions to those who would not believe this pretense or—if they overhastily did so—who would pay me back in my own coin. Thus my maxim would necessarily destroy itself as soon as it was made a universal law.

Thus within the moral knowledge of common human reason we have attained its principle. To be sure, common human reason does not think of it abstractly in such a universal form, but it always has it in view and uses it as the standard of its judgments. It would be easy to show how common human reason, with this compass, knows well how to distinguish what is good, what is bad, and what is consistent or inconsistent with duty. Without in the least teaching common reason anything new, we need only to draw its attention to its own principle, in the manner of Socrates, thus showing that neither science nor philosophy is needed in order to know what one has to do in order to be honest and good, and even wise and virtuous.

It is clear that no experience can give occasion for inferring the possibility of such apodictic laws. This is especially clear when we add that, unless we wish to deny all truth to the concept of morality and renounce its application to any possible object, we cannot refuse to admit that the law of this concept is of such broad significance that it holds not merely for men but for all rational beings as such; we must grant that it must be valid with absolute necessity and not merely under contingent conditions and with exceptions. For with what right could we bring into unlimited respect something that might be valid only under contingent human conditions? And how could laws of the determination of our will be held to be laws of the determination of the will of a rational being in general and of ourselves in so far as we are rational beings, if they were merely empirical and did not have their origin completely a priori in pure, but practical, reason?

Nor could one give poorer counsel to morality than to attempt to derive it from examples. For each example of morality which is exhibited to me must itself have been previously judged according to principles of morality to see whether it is worthy to serve as an original example, i.e., as a model. By no means could it authoritatively furnish the concept of morality. Even the Holy One of the Gospel must be compared with our ideal of moral perfection before He is recognized as such; even He says of Himself, "Why call ye Me (whom you see) good? None is good (the archetype of the good) except God only (whom you do not see)." But whence do we have the concept of God as the highest good? Solely from the idea of moral perfection which reason formulates a priori and which it inseparably connects with the concept of a free will. Imitation has no place in moral matters, and examples serve only for encouragement.

Everything in nature works according to laws. Only a rational being has the capacity of acting according to the conception of laws, i.e., according to principles. This capacity is will. Since reason is required for the derivation of actions from laws, will is nothing else than practical reason. If reason infallibly determines the will, the actions which such a being recognizes as objectively necessary are also subjectively necessary. That is, the will is a faculty of choosing only that which reason, independently of inclination, recognizes as practically necessary, i.e., as good. But if reason of itself does not sufficiently determine the will, and if the will is subjugated to subjective conditions (certain incentives) which do not always agree with objective conditions; in a word, if the will is not of itself in complete accord with reason (the actual case of men), then the actions which are recognized as objectively necessary are subjectively contingent, and the determination of such a will according to objective laws is constraint. That is, the relation of objective laws to a will which is not completely good is conceived as the determination of the will of a rational being by principles of reason to which this will is not by nature necessarily obedient.

All imperatives command either hypothetically or categorically. The former present the practical necessity of a possible action as a means to achieving something else which one desires (or which one may possibly desire). The categorical imperative would be one which presented an action as of itself objectively necessary, without regard to any other end.

Since every practical law presents a possible action as good and thus as necessary for a subject practically determinable by reason, all imperatives are formulas of the determination of action which is necessary by the principle of a will which is in any way good. If the action is good only as a means to something else, the imperative is hypothetical; but if it is thought of as good in itself, and hence as necessary in a will which of itself conforms to reason as the principle of this will, the imperative is categorical.

The imperative thus says what action possible to me would be good, and it presents the practical rule in relation to a will which does not forthwith perform an action simply because it is good, in part because the subject does not always know that the action is good and in part (when he does know it) because his maxims can still be opposed to the objective principles of practical reason.

The hypothetical imperative, therefore, says only that the action is good to some purpose, possible or actual. In the former case it is a problematical,[2] in

---

[2][The *First Introduction to the Critique of Judgment* says: "This is the place to correct an error into which I fell in the *Foundations of the Metaphysics of Morals*. After I had stated that the imperatives of prudence commanded only conditionally, and indeed only under the condition of merely possible, i.e., problematic, ends, I called that kind of practical precept 'problematic imperatives.' But there is certainly a contradiction in this expression. I should have called them 'technical imperatives,' i.e., imperatives of art. The pragmatic imperatives, or rules of prudence which command under the condition of an actual and even subjectively necessary end, belong also among the technical imperatives. (For what is prudence but the skill to use free men and even the natural dispositions and inclinations of oneself for one's own designs?) Only the fact that the end to which we submit ourselves and others, namely, our own happiness, does not belong to the merely arbitrary ends [which we may or may not have] justifies a special name for these imperatives because the problem does not require merely a mode of reaching the end as is the case with technical imperatives, but also requires a definition of what constitutes this end itself (happiness). The end must be presupposed as known in the case of technical imperatives" (Akademie ed., XX, 200 n.)]

the latter an assertorical, practical principle. The categorical imperative, which declares the action to be of itself objectively necessary without making any reference to a purpose, i.e., without having any other end, holds as an apodictical (practical) principle.

We can think of that which is possible through the mere powers of some rational being as a possible purpose of any will. As a consequence, the principles of action, in so far as they are thought of as necessary to attain a possible purpose which can be achieved by them, are in reality infinitely numerous. All sciences have some practical part which consists of problems of some end which is possible for us and of imperatives as to how it can be reached. These can therefore generally be called imperatives of skill. Whether the end is reasonable and good is not in question at all, for the question is only of what must be done in order to attain it. The precepts to be followed by a physician in order to cure his patient and by a poisoner in order to bring about certain death are of equal value in so far as each does that which will perfectly accomplish his purpose. Since in early youth we do not know what ends may occur to us in the course of life, parents seek to let their children learn a great many things and provide for skill in the use of means to all sorts of arbitrary ends among which they cannot determine whether any one of them may later become an actual purpose of their pupil, though it is possible that he may some day have it as his actual purpose. And this anxiety is so great that they commonly neglect to form and correct their judgment on the worth of things which they may make their ends.

There is one end, however, which we may presuppose as actual in all rational beings so far as imperatives apply to them, i.e., so far as they are dependent beings; there is one purpose not only which they *can* have but which we can presuppose that they all *do* have by a necessity of nature. This purpose is happiness. The hypothetical imperative which represents the practical necessity of action as means to the promotion of happiness is an assertorical imperative. We may not expound it as merely necessary to an uncertain and a merely possible purpose, but as necessary to a purpose which we can a priori and with assurance assume for everyone because it belongs to his essence. Skill in the choice of means to one's own highest welfare can be called prudence[3] in the narrowest sense. Thus the imperative which refers to the choice of means to one's own happiness, i.e., the precept of prudence, is still only hypothetical; the action is not absolutely commanded but commanded only as a means to another end.

Finally, there is one imperative which directly commands a certain conduct without making its condition some purpose to be reached by it. This imperative

---

[3]The word "prudence" may be taken in two senses, and it may bear the name of prudence with reference to things of the world and private prudence. The former sense means the skill of a man in having an influence on others so as to use them for his own purposes. The latter is the ability to unite all these purposes to his own lasting advantage. The worth of the first is finally reduced to the latter, and of one who is prudent in the former sense but not in the latter we might better say that he is clever and cunning yet, on the whole, imprudent.

is categorical. It concerns not the material of the action and its intended result but the form and the principle from which it results. What is essentially good in it consists in the intention, the result being what it may. This imperative may be called the imperative of morality.

There is…only one categorical imperative. It is: Act only according to that maxim by which you can at the same time will that it should become a universal law.

Now if all imperatives of duty can be derived from this one imperative as a principle, we can at least show what we understand by the concept of duty and what it means, even though it remain undecided whether that which is called duty is an empty concept or not.

The universality of law according to which effects are produced constitutes what is properly called nature in the most general sense (as to form), i.e., the existence of things so far as it is determined by universal laws. [By analogy], then, the universal imperative of duty can be expressed as follows: Act as though the maxim of your action were by your will to become a universal law of nature.

We shall now enumerate some duties, adopting the usual division of them into duties to ourselves and to others and into perfect and imperfect duties.[4]

1 A man who is reduced to despair by a series of evils feels a weariness with life but is still in possession of his reason sufficiently to ask whether it would not be contrary to his duty to himself to take his own life. Now he asks whether the maxim of his action could become a universal law of nature. His maxim, however, is: For love of myself, I make it my principle to shorten my life when by a longer duration it threatens more evil than satisfaction. But it is questionable whether this principle of self-love could become a universal law of nature. One immediately sees a contradiction in a system of nature whose law could be to destroy life by the feeling whose special office is to impel the improvement of life. In this case it would not exist as nature; hence that maxim cannot obtain as a law of nature, and thus it wholly contradicts the supreme principle of all duty.

2 Another man finds himself forced by need to borrow money. He well knows that he will not be able to repay it, but he also sees that nothing will be loaned him if he does not firmly promise to repay it at a certain time. He desires to make such a promise, but he has enough conscience to ask himself whether it is not improper and opposed to duty to relieve his distress in such a way. Now, assuming he does decide to do so, the maxim of his action would be as follows: When I believe myself to be in need of money, I will borrow money

---

[4]It must be noted here that I reserve the division of duties for a future *Metaphysics of Morals* and that the division here stands as only an arbitrary one (chosen in order to arrange my examples). For the rest, by a perfect duty I here understand a duty which permits no exception in the interest of inclination; thus I have not merely outer but also inner perfect duties. This runs contrary to the usage adopted in the schools, but I am not disposed to defend it here because it is all one to my purpose whether this is conceded or not.

and promise to repay it, although I know I shall never do so. Now this principle of self-love or of his own benefit may very well be compatible with his whole future welfare, but the question is whether it is right. He changes the pretension of self-love into a universal law and then puts the question: How would it be if my maxim became a universal law? He immediately sees that it could never hold as a universal law of nature and be consistent with itself; rather it must necessarily contradict itself. For the universality of a law which says that anyone who believes himself to be in need could promise what he pleased with the intention of not fulfilling it would make the promise itself and the end to be accomplished by it impossible; no one would believe what was promised to him but would only laugh at any such assertion as vain pretense.

3 A third finds in himself a talent which could, by means of some cultivation, make him in many respects a useful man. But he finds himself in comfortable circumstances and prefers indulgence in pleasure to troubling himself with broadening and improving his fortunate natural gifts. Now, however, let him ask whether his maxim of neglecting his gifts, besides agreeing with his pro-pensity to idle amusement, agrees also with what is called duty. He sees that a system of nature could indeed exist in accordance with such a law, even though man (like the inhabitants of the South Sea Islands) should let his talents rust and resolve to devote his life merely to idleness, indulgence, and propagation—in a word, to pleasure. But he cannot possibly will that this should become a universal law of nature or that it should be implanted in us by a natural instinct. For, as a rational being, he necessarily wills that all his faculties should be developed, inasmuch as they are given to him for all sorts of possible purposes.

4 A fourth man, for whom things are going well, sees that others (whom he could help) have to struggle with great hardships, and he asks, "What concern of mine is it? Let each one be as happy as heaven wills, or as he can make himself; I will not take anything from him or even envy him; but to his welfare or to his assistance in time of need I have no desire to contribute." If such a way of thinking were a universal law of nature, certainly the human race could exist, and without doubt even better than in a state where everyone talks of sympathy and good will, or even exerts himself occasionally to practice them while, on the other hand, he cheats when he can and betrays or otherwise violates the rights of man. Now although it is possible that a universal law of nature according to that maxim could exist, it is nevertheless impossible to will that such a principle should hold everywhere as a law of nature. For a will which resolved this would conflict with itself, since instances can often arise in which he would need the love and sympathy of others, and in which he would have robbed himself, by such a law of nature springing from his own will, of all hope of the aid he desires.

The will is thought of as a faculty of determining itself to action in accordance with the conception of certain laws. Such a faculty can be found only in rational beings. That which serves the will as the objective ground of its self-determination is an end, and, if it is given by reason alone, it must hold alike for all rational beings. On the other hand, that which contains the ground of the possibility of the action, whose result is an end, is called the means. The subjective ground of desire is the incentive,[5] while the objective ground of volition is the motive. Thus arises the distinction between subjective ends, which rest on incentives, and the objective ends, which depend on motives valid for every rational being. Practical principles are formal when they disregard all subjective ends; they are material when they have subjective ends, and thus certain incentives, as their basis. The ends which a rational being arbitrarily proposes to himself as consequences of his action are material ends and are without exception only relative, for only their relation to a particularly constituted faculty of desire in the subject gives them their worth. And this worth cannot, therefore, afford any universal principles for all rational beings or valid and necessary principles for every volition. That is, they cannot give rise to any practical laws. All these relative ends, therefore, are grounds for hypothetical imperatives only.

But suppose that there were something the existence of which in itself had absolute worth, something which, as an end in itself, could be a ground of definite laws. In it and only in it could lie the ground of a possible categorical imperative, i.e., of a practical law.

Now, I say, man and, in general, every rational being exists as an end in himself and not merely as a means to be arbitrarily used by this or that will. In all his actions, whether they are directed to himself or to other rational beings, he must always be regarded at the same time as an end. All objects of inclinations have only a conditional worth, for if the inclinations and the needs founded on them did not exist, their object would be without worth. The inclinations themselves as the sources of needs, however, are so lacking in absolute worth that the universal wish of every rational being must be indeed to free himself completely from them. Therefore, the worth of any objects to be obtained by our actions is at all times conditional. Beings whose existence does not depend on our will but on nature, if they are not rational beings, have only a relative worth as means and are therefore called "things"; on the other hand, rational beings are designated "persons" because their nature indicates that they are ends in themselves, i.e., things which may not be used merely as means. Such a being is thus an object of respect and, so far, restricts all [arbitrary] choice. Such beings are not merely subjective ends whose existence as a result of our action has a worth for us, but are objective ends, i.e., beings whose existence in itself is an end. Such an end is one for which no other end can be substituted, to which these beings should serve merely as means. For, without them, nothing of absolute worth could be found, and if all worth is conditional and thus contingent, no supreme practical principle for reason could be found anywhere.

---

[5][*Triebfeder* in contrast to *Bewegungsgrund*. Abbott translates the former as "spring," but "urge" might better convey the meaning. I follow Greene and Hudson's excellent usage in their translation of the *Religion Within the Limits of Reason Alone*.]

Thus if there is to be a supreme practical principle and a categorical imperative for the human will, it must be one that forms an objective principle of the will from the conception of that which is necessarily an end for everyone because it is an end in itself. Hence this objective principle can serve as a universal practical law. The ground of this principle is: rational nature exists as an end in itself. Man necessarily thinks of his own existence in this way; thus far it is a subjective principle of human actions. Also every other rational being thinks of his existence by means of the same rational ground which holds also for myself; thus it is at the same time an objective principle from which, as a supreme practical ground, it must be possible to derive all laws of the will. The practical imperative, therefore, is the following: Act so that you treat humanity, whether in your own person or in that of another, always as an end and never as a means only.

Utilitarianism

John Stuart Mill

WHAT UTILITARIANISM IS

The creed which accepts as the foundation of morals *utility*, or the *greatest happiness principle*, holds that actions are right in proportion as they tend to promote happiness, wrong as they tend to produce the reverse of happiness. By 'happiness' is intended pleasure, and the absence of pain; by 'unhappiness,' pain, and the privation of pleasure. To give a clear view of the moral standard set up by the theory, much more requires to be said; in particular, what things it includes in the ideas of pain and pleasure; and to what extent this is left an open question. But these supplementary explanations do not affect the theory of life on which this theory of morality is grounded—namely, that pleasure, and freedom from pain, are the only things desirable as ends; and that all desirable things (which are as numerous in the utilitarian as in any other scheme) are desirable either for the pleasure inherent in themselves, or as means to the promotion of pleasure and the prevention of pain.

Now such a theory of life excites in many minds, and among them in some of the most estimable in feeling and purpose, inveterate dislike. To suppose that life has (as they express it) no higher end than pleasure—no better and nobler object of desire and pursuit—they designate utterly as mean and groveling; as a doctrine worthy only of swine, to whom the followers of Epicurus were, at a

From John Stuart Mill, *Utilitarianism*, Chapters 2, 3, and 4 with omissions. Abridged by the editor.

very early period, contemptuously likened; and modern holders of the doctrine are occasionally made the subject of equally polite comparisons by its German, French, and English assailants.

When thus attacked, the Epicureans have always answered that it is not they but their accusers who represent human nature in a degrading light; since the accusation supposes human beings to be capable of no pleasures except those of which swine are capable. If this supposition were true, the charge could not be gainsaid, but would then be no longer an imputation; for if the sources of pleasure were precisely the same to human beings and to swine, the rule of life which is good enough for the one would be good enough for the other. The comparison of the Epicurean life to that of beasts is felt as degrading, precisely because a beast's pleasures do not satisfy a human being's conceptions of happiness. Human beings have faculties more elevated than the animal appetites, and when once made conscious of them, do not regard anything as happiness which does not include their gratification. I do not, indeed, consider the Epicureans to have been by any means faultless in drawing out their scheme of consequences from the utilitarian principle. To do this in any sufficient manner, many Stoic, as well as Christian elements require to be included. But there is no known Epicurean theory of life which does not assign to the pleasures of the intellect, of the feelings and imagination, and of the moral sentiments, a much higher value as pleasures than to those of mere sensation. It must be admitted, however, that utilitarian writers in general have placed the superiority of mental over bodily pleasures chiefly in the greater permanency, safety, uncostliness, etc., of the former—that is, in their circumstantial advantages rather than in their intrinsic nature. And on all these points utilitarians have fully proved their case; but they might have taken the other, and, as it may be called, higher ground, with entire consistency. It is quite compatible with the principle of utility to recognize the fact, that some *kinds* of pleasure are more desirable and more valuable than others. It would be absurd that while, in estimating all other things, quality is considered as well as quantity, the estimation of pleasures should be supposed to depend on quantity alone.

If I am asked what I mean by difference of quality in pleasures, or what makes one pleasure more valuable than another merely as a pleasure, except its being greater in amount, there is but one possible answer. Of two pleasures, if there be one to which all or almost all who have experience of both give a decided preference, irrespective of any feeling of moral obligation to prefer it, that is the more desirable pleasure. If one of the two is, by those who are competently acquainted with both, placed so far above the other that they prefer it, even though knowing it to be attended with a greater amount of discontent, and would not resign it for any quantity of the other pleasure which their nature is capable of, we are justified in ascribing to the preferred enjoyment a superiority in quality, so far outweighing quantity as to render it, in comparison, of small account.

Now it is an unquestionable fact that those who are equally acquainted with, and equally capable of appreciating and enjoying, both, do give a most marked preference to the manner of existence which employs their higher faculties. Few human creatures would consent to be changed into any of the lower animals, for a promise of the fullest allowance of a beast's pleasures; no intelligent human being would consent to be a fool, no instructed person would be an ignoramus, no person of feeling and conscience would be selfish and base, even though they should be persuaded that the fool, the dunce, or the rascal is better satisfied with his lot than they are with theirs. They would not resign what they possess more than he for the most complete satisfaction of all the desires which they have in common with him. If they ever fancy they would, it is only in cases of unhappiness so extreme, that to escape from it they would exchange their lot for almost any other, however undesirable in their own eyes. A being of higher faculties requires more to make him happy, is capable probably of more acute suffering, and certainly accessible to it at more points, than one of an inferior type; but in spite of these liabilities, he can never really wish to sink into what he feels to be a lower grade of existence. We may give what explanation we please of this unwillingness: we may attribute it to pride, a name which is given indiscriminately to some of the most and to some of the least estimable feelings of which mankind are capable; we may refer it to the love of liberty and personal independence, an appeal to which was with the Stoics one of the most effective means for the inculcation of it; to the love of power, or to the love of excitement, both of which do really enter into and contribute to it: but its most appropriate appellation is a sense of dignity, which all human beings possess in one form or other, and in some, though by no means in exact, proportion to their higher faculties, and which is so essential a part of the happiness of those in whom it is strong, that nothing which conflicts with it could be, otherwise than momentarily, an object of desire to them. Whoever supposes that this preference takes place at a sacrifice of happiness—that the superior being, in anything like equal circumstances, is not happier than the inferior—confounds the two very different ideas, of *happiness* and *content*. It is indisputable that the being whose capacities of enjoyment are low, has the greatest chance of having them fully satisfied; and a highly endowed being will always feel that any happiness which he can look for, as the world is constituted, is imperfect. But he can learn to bear its imperfections, if they are at all bearable; and they will not make him envy the being who is indeed unconscious of the imperfections, but only because he feels not at all the good which those imperfections qualify. It is better to be a human being dissatisfied than a pig satisfied; better to be Socrates dissatisfied than a fool satisfied. And if the fool, or the pig, are of a different opinion, it is because they only know their own side of the question. The other party to the comparison knows both sides.

It may be objected that many who are capable of the higher pleasures, occasionally, under the influence of temptation, postpone them to the lower. But this is quite compatible with a full appreciation of the intrinsic superiority of the higher. Men often, from infirmity of character, make their election for the nearer good, though they know it to be the less valuable; and this no less when the choice is between two bodily pleasures, than when it is between bodily and mental. They pursue sensual indulgences to the injury of health, though perfectly aware that health is the greater good. It may be further objected that many who begin with youthful enthusiasm for everything noble, as they advance in years sink into indolence and selfishness. But I do not believe that those who undergo this very common change, voluntarily choose the lower description of pleasures in preference to the higher. I believe that before they devote themselves exclusively to the one, they have already become incapable of the other. Capacity for the nobler feelings is in most natures a very tender plant, easily killed, not only by hostile Influences, but by mere want of sustenance; and in the majority of young persons it speedily dies away if the occupations to which their position in life has devoted them, and the society into which it has thrown them, are not favorable to keeping that higher capacity in exercise. Men lose their high aspirations as they lose their intellectual tastes, because they have not time or opportunity for indulging them; and they addict themselves to inferior pleasures not because they deliberately prefer them, but because they are either the only ones to which they have access or the only ones which they are any longer capable of enjoying. It may be questioned whether anyone who has remained equally susceptible to both classes of pleasures, ever knowingly and calmly preferred the lower; though many, in all ages, have broken down in an ineffectual attempt to combine both.

From this verdict of the only competent judges I apprehend there can be no appeal. On a question which is the best worth having of two pleasures, or which of two modes of existence is the most grateful to the feelings, apart from its moral attributes and from its consequences, the judgment of those who are qualified by knowledge of both, or, if they differ, that of the majority among them, must be admitted as final. And there need be the less hesitation to accept this judgment respecting the quality of pleasures, since there is no other tribunal to be referred to even on the question of quantity. What means are there of determining which is the acutest of two pains, or the intensest of two pleasurable sensations, except the general suffrage of those who are familiar with both? Neither pains nor pleasures are homogeneous, and pain is always heterogeneous with pleasure. What is there to decide whether a particular pleasure is worth purchasing at the cost of a particular pain, except the feelings and judgment of the experienced? When, therefore, those feelings and judgment declare the pleasures derived from the higher faculties to be preferable *in kind*, apart from the question of intensity, to those of which the animal nature, disjoined from the higher faculties, is susceptible, they are entitled on this subject to the same regard.

I have dwelt on this point, as being a necessary part of a perfectly just conception of utility, or happiness, considered as the directive rule of human conduct. But it is by no means an indispensable condition to the acceptance of the utilitarian standard; for that standard is not the agent's own greatest happiness, but the greatest amount of happiness altogether; and if it may possibly be doubted whether a noble character is always the happier for its nobleness, there can be no doubt that it makes other people happier, and that the world in general is immensely a gainer by it. Utilitarianism, therefore, could only attain its end by the general cultivation of nobleness of character, even if each individual were only benefited by the nobleness of others, and his own, so far as happiness is concerned, were a sheer deduction from the benefit. But the bare enunciation of such an absurdity as this last renders refutation superfluous.

According to the 'greatest happiness principle,' as above explained, the ultimate end, with reference to and for the sake of which all other things are desirable (whether we are considering our own good or that of other people), is an existence exempt as far as possible from pain, and as rich as possible in enjoyments, both in point of quantity and quality; the test of quality, and the rule for measuring it against quantity, being the preference felt by those who in their opportunities of experience, to which must be added their habits of self-consciousness and self-observation, are best furnished with the means of comparison. This, being, according to the utilitarian opinion, the end of human action, is necessarily also the standard of morality; which may accordingly be defined, the rules and precepts for human conduct, by the observance of which an existence such as has been described might be, to the greatest extent possible, secured to all mankind; and not to them only, but, so far as the nature of things admits, to the whole sentient creation.

A state of exalted pleasure lasts only moments, or in some cases, and with some intermissions, hours or days, and is the occasional brilliant flash of enjoyment, not its permanent and steady flame. Of this the philosophers who have taught that happiness is the end of life were as fully aware as those who taunt them. The happiness which they meant was not a life of rapture; but moments of such, in an existence made up of few and transitory pains, many and various pleasures, with a decided predominance of the active over the passive, and having as the foundation of the whole, not to expect more from life than it is capable of bestowing. A life thus composed, to those who have been fortunate enough to obtain it, has always appeared worthy of the name of happiness. And such an existence is even now the lot of many, during some considerable portion of their lives. The present wretched education, and wretched social arrangements, are the only real hindrance to its being attainable by almost all.

The objectors perhaps may doubt whether human beings, if taught to consider happiness as the end of life, would be satisfied with such a moderate share of it. But great numbers of mankind have been satisfied with much less. The main constitutents of a satisfied life appear to be two, either of which by itself is often found sufficient for the purpose: tranquillity and excitement. With much tranquillity, many find that they can be content with very little pleasure; with much excitement, many can reconcile themselves to a considerable quantity of pain. There is assuredly no inherent impossibility in enabling even the mass of mankind to unite both; since the two are so far from being incompatible that they are in natural alliance, the prolongation of either being a preparation for, and exciting a wish for, the other. It is only those in whom indolence amounts to a vice, that do not desire excitement after an interval of repose; it is only those in whom the need of excitement is a disease, that feel the tranquillity which follows excitement dull and insipid, instead of pleasurable in direct proportion to the excitement which preceded it. When people who are tolerably fortunate in their outward lot do not find in life sufficient enjoyment to make it valuable to them, the cause generally is, caring for nobody but themselves. To those who have neither public nor private affections, the excitements of life are much curtailed, and in any case dwindle in value as the time approaches when all selfish interests must be terminated by death; while those who leave after them objects of personal affection, and especially those who have also cultivated a fellow-feeling with the collective interests of mankind, retain as lively an interest in life on the eve of death as in the vigor of youth and health. Next to selfishness, the principal cause which makes life unsatisfactory is want of mental cultivation. A cultivated mind (I do not mean that of a philosopher, but any mind to which the fountains of knowledge have been opened, and which has been taught, in any tolerable degree, to exercise its faculties) finds sources of inexhaustible interest in all that surrounds it; in the objects of nature, the achievements of art, the imaginations of poetry, the incidents of history, the ways of mankind, past and present, and their prospects in the future. It is possible, indeed, to become indifferent to all this, and that too without having exhausted a thousandth part of it; but only when one has had from the beginning no moral or human interest in these things, and has sought in them only the gratification of curiosity.

Meanwhile, let utilitarians never cease to claim the morality of self-devotion as a possession which belongs by as good a right to them, as either to the Stoic or to the Transcendentalist. The utilitarian morality does recognize in human beings the power of sacrificing their own greatest good for the good of others. It only refuses to admit that the sacrifice is itself a good. A sacrifice which does not increase, or tend to increase, the sum total of happiness, it considers as wasted. The only self-renunciation which it applauds, is devotion to the happiness, or to some of the means of happiness, of others; either of mankind collectively, or of individuals within the limits imposed by the collective interests of mankind.

I must again repeat, what the assailants of utilitarianism seldom have the justice to acknowledge, that the happiness which forms the utilitarian standard of what is right in conduct, is not the agent's own happiness, but that of all concerned. As between his own happiness and that of others, utilitarianism requires him to be as strictly impartial as a disinterested and benevolent spectator. In the golden rule of Jesus of Nazareth, we read the complete spirit of the ethics of utility. To do as you would be done by, and to love your neighbor as yourself, constitute the ideal perfection of utilitarian morality. As the means of making the nearest approach to this ideal, utility would enjoin, first, that laws and social arrangements should place the happiness, or (as speaking practically it may be called) the interest, of every individual, as nearly as possible in harmony with the interest of the whole and secondly, that education and opinion, which have so vast a power over human character, should so use that power as to establish in the mind of every individual an indissoluble association between his own happiness and the good of the whole—especially between his own happiness and the practice of such modes of conduct, negative and positive, as regard for the universal happiness pre-scribes; so that not only he may be unable to conceive the possibility of happiness to himself, consistently with conduct opposed to the general good, but also that a direct impulse to promote the general good may be in every individual one of the habitual motives of action, and the sentiments connected therewith may fill a large and prominent place in every human being's sentient existence. If the impugners of the utilitarian morality represented it to their own minds in this its true character, I know not what recommendation possessed by any other morality they could possibly affirm to be wanting to it; what more beautiful or more exalted developments of human nature any other ethical system can be supposed to foster, or what springs of action, not accessible to the utilitarian, such systems rely on for giving effect to their mandates.

The objectors to utilitarianism cannot always be charged with representing it in a discreditable light. On the contrary, those among them who entertain anything like a just idea of its disinterested character sometimes find fault with its standard as being too high for humanity. They say it is exacting too much to require that people shall always act from the inducement of promoting the general interests of society. But this is to mistake the very meaning of a standard of morals, and confound the rule of action with the motive of it. It is the business of ethics to tell us what are our duties, or by what test we may know them; but no system of ethics requires that the sole motive of all we do shall be a feeling of duty; on the contrary, ninety-nine hundredths of all our actions are done from other motives, and rightly so done, if the rule of duty does not condemn them. It is the more unjust to utilitarianism that this particular misapprehension should be made a ground of objection to it, inas-much as utilitarian moralists have gone beyond almost all others in affirming that the motive has nothing to do with the morality of the action, though much with the worth of the agent. He who saves a fellow creature from drowning does what is morally right, whether his motive be duty, or the hope of being paid for his trouble; he who betrays the friend that trusts him, is guilty of a crime, even if his object be to serve another friend to whom he is under greater obligations. But to speak only of actions done from the motive of duty, and in direct obedience to principle: it is a misapprehension of the utilitarian mode of thought, to conceive it as implying that people should fix their minds upon so wide a generality as the world, or society at large. The great majority of good actions are intended not for the benefit of the world, but for that of individuals, of which the good of the world is made up; and the thoughts of the most virtuous man need not on these occasions travel beyond the particular persons concerned, except so far as is necessary to assure himself that in benefiting them he is not violating the rights, that is, the legitimate and authorized expectations, of anyone else. The multiplication of happiness is, according to the utilitarian ethics, the object of virtue: the occasions on which any person (except one in a thousand) has it in his power to do this on an extended scale, in other words to be a public benefactor, are but exceptional, and on these occasions alone is he called on to consider public utility; in every other case, private utility, the interest or happiness of some few persons, is all he has to attend to. Those alone the influence of whose actions extends to society in general, need concern themselves habitually about so large an object. In the case of abstinences indeed—of things which people forbear to do from moral considerations, though the consequences in the particular case might be beneficial—it would be unworthy of an intelligent agent not to be consciously aware that the action is of a class which, if practiced generally, would be generally injurious, and that this is the ground of the obligation to abstain from it. The amount of regard for the public interest implied in this recognition is no greater than is demanded by every system of morals, for they all enjoin to abstain from whatever is manifestly pernicious to society.

OF THE ULTIMATE SANCTION OF THE PRINCIPLE OF UTILITY

The question is often asked, and properly so, in regard to any supposed moral standard—What is its sanction? what are the motives to obey it? or more specifically, what is the source of its obligation? whence does it derive its binding force? It is a necessary part of moral philosophy to provide the answer to this question; which, though frequently assuming the shape of an objection to the utilitarian morality, as if it had some special applicability to that above others, really arises in regard to all standards. It arises, in fact, whenever a person is called on to *adopt* a standard, or refer morality to any basis on which he has not been accustomed to rest in. For the customary morality, that which education and opinion have consecrated, is the only one which presents itself to the mind with the feeling of being *in itself* obligatory; and when a person is asked to believe that this morality *derives* its obligation from some general principle round which custom has not thrown the same halo, the assertion is to him a paradox; the supposed corollaries seem to have a more binding force then the original theorem; the superstructure seems to stand better without, than with, what is represented as its foundation. He says to himself, I feel that I am bound not to rob or murder, betray or deceive; but why am I bound to promote the general happiness? If my own happiness lies in something else, why may I not give that the preference?

The principle of utility either has, or there is no reason why it might not have, all the sanctions which belong to any other system of morals. Those sanctions are either external or internal. Of the external sanctions it is not necessary to speak at any length. They are, the hope of favor and the fear of displeasure, from our fellow-creatures or from the Ruler of the Universe, along with whatever we may have of sympathy or affection for them, or of love and awe of Him, inclining us to do His will independently of selfish consequences. There is evidently no reason why all these motives for observance should not attach themselves to the utilitarian morality, as completely and as powerfully as to any other. Indeed, those of them which refer to our fellow-creatures are sure to do so, in proportion to the amount of general intelligence; for whether there be any other ground of moral obligation than the general happiness or not, men do desire happiness; and however imperfect may be their own practice, they desire and commend all conduct in others towards themselves, by which they think their happiness is promoted. With regard to the religious motive, if men believe, as most profess to do, in the goodness of God, those who think that conduciveness to the general happiness is the essence, or even only the criterion of good, must necessarily believe that it is also that which God approves. The whole force therefore of external reward and punishment, whether physical or moral, and whether proceeding from God or from our fellow men, together with all that the capacities of human nature admit of disinterested devotion to either, become available to enforce the utilitarian morality, in proportion as that morality is recognized; and the more powerfully, the more the appliances of education and general cultivation are bent to the purpose.

So far as to external sanctions. The internal sanction of duty, whatever our standard of duty may be, is one and the same—a feeling in our own mind: a pain, more or less intense, attendant on violation of duty, which in properly cultivated moral natures rises, in the more serious cases, into shrinking from it as an impossibility. This feeling, when disinterested, and connecting itself with the pure idea of duty, and not with some particular form of it, or with any of the merely accessory circumstances, is the essence of conscience; though in that complex phenomenon as it actually exists, the simple fact is in general all encrusted over with collateral associations, derived from sympathy, from love, and still more from fear; from all the forms of religious feeling; from the recollections of childhood and of all our past life; from self-esteem, desire of the esteem of others, and occasionally even self-abasement. This extreme complication is, I apprehend, the origin of the sort of mystical character which, by a tendency of the human mind of which there are many other examples, is apt to be attributed to the idea of moral obligation, and which leads people to believe that the idea cannot possibly attach itself to any other objects than those which, by a supposed mysterious law, are found in our present experience to excite it. Its binding force, however, consists in the existence of a mass of feeling which must be broken through in order to do what violates our standard of right, and which, if we do nevertheless violate the standard, will probably have to be encountered afterwards in the form of remorse. Whatever theory we have of the nature or origin of conscience, this is what essentially constitutes it.

The ultimate sanction, therefore, of all morality (external motives apart) being a subjective feeling in our own minds, I see nothing embarrassing to those whose standard is utility, in the question, what is the sanction of that particular standard? We may answer, the same as of all other moral standards— the conscientious feelings of mankind. Undoubtedly this sanction has no binding efficacy on those who do not possess the feelings it appeals to; but neither will these persons be more obedient to any other moral principle than to the utilitarian one. On them morality of any kind has no hold but through the external sanctions. Meanwhile the feelings exist, a fact in human nature, the reality of which, and the great power with which they are capable of acting on those in whom they have been duly cultivated, are proved by experience. No reason has ever been shown why they may not be cultivated to as great intensity in connection with the utilitarian, as with any other rule of morals.

It is not necessary, for the present purpose, to decide whether the feeling of duty is innate or implanted. Assuming it to be innate, it is an open question to what objects it naturally attaches itself; for the philosophic supporters of that theory are now agreed that the intuitive perception is of principles of morality and not of the details. If there be anything innate in the matter, I see no reason why the feeling which is innate should not be that of regard to the pleasures and pains of others. If there is any principle of morals which is intuitively obligatory, I should say it must be that. If so, the intuitive ethics would coincide with the utilitarian, and there would be no further quarrel between them. Even as it is, the intuitive moralists, though they believe that there are other intuitive moral obligations, do already believe this to be one; for they unanimously hold that a large *portion* of morality turns upon the consideration due to the interests of our fellow-creatures. Therefore, if the belief in the transcendental origin of moral obligation gives any additional efficacy to the internal sanction, it appears to me that the utilitarian principle has already the benefit of it.

On the other hand, if, as is my own belief, the moral feelings are not innate, but acquired, they are not for that reason the less natural. It is natural to man to speak, to reason, to build cities, to cultivate the ground, though these are acquired faculties. The moral feelings are not indeed a part of our nature, in the sense of being in any perceptible degree present in all of us; but this, unhappily, is a fact admitted by those who believe the most strenuously in their transcendental origin. Like the other acquired capacities above referred to, the moral faculty, if not a part of our nature, is a natural outgrowth from it; capable, like them, in a certain small degree, of springing up spontaneously; and susceptible of being brought by cultivation to a high degree of development. Unhappily it is also susceptible, by a sufficient use of the external sanctions and of the force of early impressions, of being cultivated in almost any direction; so that there is hardly anything so absurd or so mischievous that it may not, by means of these influences, be made to act on the human mind with all the authority of conscience. To doubt that the same potency might be given by the same means to the principle of utility, even if it had no foundation in human nature, would be flying in the face of all experience.

But moral associations which are wholly of artificial creation, when intellectual culture goes on, yield by degrees to the dissolving force of analysis: and if the feeling of duty, when associated with utility, would appear equally arbitrary; if there were no leading department of our nature, no powerful class of sentiments, with which that association would harmonize, which would make us feel it congenial, and incline us not only to foster it in others (for which we have abundant interested motives), but also to cherish it in ourselves; if there were not, in short, a natural basis of sentiment for utilitarian morality, it might well happen that this association also, even after it had been implanted by education, might be analyzed away.

But there *is* this basis of powerful natural sentiment; and this it is which, when once the general happiness is recognized as the ethical standard, will constitute the strength of the utilitarian morality. This firm foundation is that of the social feelings of mankind; the desire to be in unity with our fellow-creatures, which is already a powerful principle in human nature, and happily one of those which tend to become stronger, even without express inculcation, from the influences of advancing civilization.

Neither is it necessary to the feeling which constitutes the binding force of the utilitarian morality on those who recognize it, to wait for those social influences which would make its obligation felt by mankind at large. In the comparatively early state of human advancement in which we now live, a person cannot indeed feel that entireness of sympathy with all others, which would make any real discordance in the general direction of their conduct in life impossible; but already a person in whom the social feeling is at all developed, cannot bring himself to think of the rest of his fellow-creatures as struggling rivals with him for the means of happiness, whom he must desire to see defeated in their object in order that he may succeed in his. The deeply rooted conception which every individual even now has of himself as a social being, tends to make him feel it one of his natural wants that there should be harmony between his feelings and aims and those of his fellow-creatures. If differences of opinion and of mental culture make it impossible for him to share many of their actual feelings—perhaps make him denounce and defy those feelings—he still needs to be conscious that his real aim and theirs do not conflict; that he is not opposing himself to what they really wish for, namely their own good, but is, on the contrary, promoting it. This feeling in most individuals is much inferior in strength to their selfish feelings, and is often wanting altogether. But to those who have it, it possesses all the characters of a natural feeling. It does not present itself to their minds as a superstition of education, or a law despotically imposed by the power of society, but as an attribute which it would not be well for them to be without. This conviction is the ultimate sanction of the greatest happiness morality. This it is which makes any mind, of well-developed feelings, work with, and not against, the outward motives to care for others, afforded by what I have called the external sanctions; and when those sanctions are wanting, or act in an opposite direction, constitutes in itself a powerful internal binding force, in proportion to the sensitiveness and thoughtfulness of the character; since few but those whose mind is a moral blank, could bear to lay out their course of life on the plan of paying no regard to others except so far as their own private interest compels.

OF WHAT SORT OF PROOF THE PRINCIPLE OF UTILITY IS SUSCEPTIBLE

Questions [about] ends are ... questions about what things are desirable. The utilitarian doctrine is that happiness is desirable, and the only thing desirable, as an end; all other things being only desirable as means to that end. What ought to be required of this doctrine—what conditions is it requisite that the doctrine should fulfill—to make good its claim to be believed?

The only proof capable of being given that an object is visible, is that people actually see it. The only proof that a sound is audible, is that people hear it: and so of the other sources of our experience. In like manner, I apprehend, the sole evidence it is possible to produce that anything is desirable, is that people do actually desire it. If the end which the utilitarian doctrine proposes to itself were not, in theory and in practice, acknowledged to be an end, nothing could ever convince any person that it was so. No reason can be given why the general happiness is desirable except that each person, so far as he believes it to be attainable, desires his own happiness. This, however, being a fact, we have not only all the proof which the case admits of, but all which it is possible to require, that happiness is a good: that each person's happiness is a good to that person, and the general happiness, therefore, a good to the aggregate of all persons.

It results from the preceding considerations, that there is in reality nothing desired except happiness. Whatever is desired otherwise than *as a means* to some end beyond itself, and ultimately to happiness, is desired as itself a part of happiness, and is not desired for itself until it has become so. Those who desire virtue for its own sake, desire it either because the consciousness of it is a pleasure, or because the consciousness of being without it is a pain, or for both reasons united; as in truth the pleasure and pain seldom exist separately, but almost always together, the same person feeling pleasure in the degree of virtue attained, and pain in not having attained more. If one of these gave him no pleasure, and the other no pain, he would not love or desire virtue, or would desire it only for the other benefits which it might produce to himself or to persons whom he cared for.

We have now, then, an answer to the question, of what sort of proof the principle of utility is susceptible. If the opinion which I have now stated is psychologically true—if human nature is so constituted as to desire nothing which is not either a part of happiness or a means of happiness, we can have no other proof, and we require no other, that these are the only things desirable. If so, happiness is the sole end of human action, and the promotion of it the test by which to judge of all human conduct; from whence it necessarily follows that it must be the criterion of morality, since a part is included in the whole.

JUSTICE

Distributive Justice

John Rawls

We may think of a human society as a more or less self-sufficient association regulated by a common conception of justice and aimed at advancing the good of its members.[1] As a co-operative venture for mutual advantage, it is characterized by a conflict as well as an identity of interests. There is an identity of interests since social co-operation makes possible a better life for all than any would have if everyone were to try to live by his own efforts; yet at the same time men are not indifferent as to how the greater benefits produced by their joint labours are distributed, for in order to further their own aims each prefers a larger to a lesser share. A conception of justice is a set of principles for choosing between the social arrangements which determine this division and for underwriting a consensus as to the proper distributive shares.

Now at first sight the most rational conception of justice would seem to be utilitarian. For consider: each man in realizing his own good can certainly balance his own losses against his own gains. We can impose a sacrifice on ourselves now for the sake of a greater advantage later. A man quite properly acts, as long as others are not affected, to achieve his own greatest good, to advance his ends as far as possible. Now, why should not a society act on precisely the same principle? Why is not that which is rational in the case of one man right in the case of a group of men? Surely the simplest and most direct conception of the right, and so of justice, is that of maximizing the good. This assumes a prior understanding of what is good, but we can think of the good as already given by the interests of rational individuals. Thus just as the principle of individual choice is to achieve one's greatest good, to advance so far as possible one's own system of rational desires, so the principle of social choice is to realize the greatest good (similarly defined) summed over all the

From *Philosophy, Politics, and Society*, ed. by Peter Laslett and W. G. Runciman (Basil Blackwell, Oxford: Barnes and Noble Books, Totowa, N.J., 1967). Reprinted by permission of Basil Blackwell, Oxford; Barnes and Noble Books, Totowa, New Jersey.

[1] In this essay I try to work out some of the implications of the two principles of justice discussed in 'Justice as Fairness' which first appeared in the *Philosophical Review*, 1958, and which is reprinted in *Philosophy, Politics and Society*, Series II, pp. 132–57.

members of society. We arrive at the principle of utility in a natural way: by this principle a society is rightly ordered, and hence just, when its institutions are arranged so as to realize the greatest sum of satisfactions.

The striking feature of the principle of utility is that it does not matter, except indirectly, how this sum of satisfactions is distributed among individuals, any more than it matters, except indirectly, how one man distributes his satisfactions over time. Since certain ways of distributing things affect the total sum of satisfactions, this fact must be taken into account in arranging social institutions; but according to this principle the explanation of common-sense precepts of justice and their seemingly stringent character is that they are those rules which experience shows must be strictly respected and departed from only under exceptional circumstances if the sum of advantages is to be maximized. The precepts of justice are derivative from the one end of attaining the greatest net balance of satisfactions. There is no reason in principle why the greater gains of some should not compensate for the lesser losses of others; or why the violation of the liberty of a few might not be made right by a greater good shared by many. It simply happens, at least under most conditions, that the greatest sum of advantages is not generally achieved in this way. From the standpoint of utility the strictness of common-sense notions of justice has a certain usefulness, but as a philosophical doctrine it is irrational.

If, then, we believe that as a matter of principle each member of society has an inviolability founded on justice which even the welfare of everyone else cannot overrride, and that a loss of freedom for some is not made right by a greater sum of satisfactions enjoyed by many, we shall have to look for another account of the principles of justice. The principle of utility is incapable of explaining the fact that in a just society the liberties of equal citizenship are taken for granted, and the rights secured by justice are not subject to political bargaining nor to the calculus of social interests. Now, the most natural alternative to the principle of utility is its traditional rival, the theory of the social contract. The aim of the contract doctrine is precisely to account for the strictness of justice by supposing that its principles arise from an agreement among free and independent persons in an original position of equality and hence reflect the integrity and equal sovereignty of the rational persons who are the contractees. Instead of supposing that a conception of right, and so a conception of justice, is simply an extension of the principle of choice for one man to society as a whole, the contract doctrine assumes that the rational individuals who belong to society must choose together, in one joint act, what is to count among them as just and unjust. They are to decide among themselves once and for all what is to be their conception of justice. This decision is thought of as being made in a suitably defined initial situation one of the significant features of which is that no one knows his position in society, nor even his place in the distribution of natural talents and abilities. The principles of justice to which all are forever bound are chosen in the absence of this sort of specific information. A veil of ignorance prevents anyone from being advantaged or disadvantaged by the contingencies of social class and fortune; and hence the bargaining problems which arise in everyday life from the possession of this knowledge do not affect the choice of principles. On the contract doctrine, then, the theory of justice, and indeed ethics itself, is part of the general theory of rational choice, a fact perfectly clear in its Kantian formulation.

Once justice is thought of as arising from an original agreement of this kind, it is evident that the principle of utility is problematical. For why should rational individuals who have a system of ends they wish to advance agree to a violation of their liberty for the sake of a greater balance of satisfactions enjoyed by others? It seems more plausible to suppose that, when situated in an original position of equal right, they would insist upon institutions which returned compensating advantages for any sacrifices required. A rational man would not accept an institution merely because it maximized the sum of advantages irrespective of its effect on his own interests. It appears, then, that the principle of utility would be rejected as a principle of justice, although we shall not try to argue this important question here. Rather, our aim is to give a brief sketch of the conception of distributive shares implicit in the principles of justice which, it seems, would be chosen in the original position. The philosophical appeal of utilitarianism is that it seems to offer a single principle on the basis of which a consistent and complete conception of right can be developed. The problem is to work out a contractarian alternative in such a way that it has comparable if not all the same virtues.

In our discussion we shall make no attempt to derive the two principles of justice which we shall examine; that is, we shall not try to show that they would be chosen in the original position.[2] It must suffice that it is plausible that they would be, at least in preference to the standard forms of traditional theories. Instead we shall be mainly concerned with three questions: first, how to interpret these principles so that they define a consistent and complete conception of justice; second, whether it is possible to arrange the institutions of a constitutional democracy so that these principles are satisfied, at least approximately; and third, whether the conception of distributive shares which they define is compatible with common-sense notions of justice. The significance of these principles is that they allow for the strictness of the claims

---

[2]This question is discussed very briefly in 'Justice as Fairness,' see pp. 138–41. The intuitive idea is as follows. Given the circumstances of the original position, it is rational for a man to choose as if he were designing a society in which his enemy is to assign him his place. Thus, in particular, given the complete lack of knowledge (which makes the choice one under uncertainty), the fact that the decision involves one's life-prospects as a whole and is constrained by obligations to third parties (e.g., one's descendants) and duties to certain values (e.g., to religious truth), it is rational to be conservative and so to choose in accordance with an analogue of the maximum principle. Viewing the situation in this way, the interpretation given to the principles of justice earlier is perhaps natural enough. Moreover, it seems clear how the principle of utility can be interpreted; it is the analogue of the Laplacean principle for choice uncertainty. (For a discussion of these choice criteria, see R. D. Luce and H. Raiffa, *Games and Decisions* (1957), pp. 275–98).

of justice; and if they can be understood so as to yield a consistent and complete conception, the contractarian alternative would seem all the more attractive.

The two principles of justice which we shall discuss may be formulated as follows: first, each person engaged in an institution or affected by it has an equal right to the most extensive liberty compatible with a like liberty for all; and second, inequalities as defined by the institutional structure or fostered by it are arbitrary unless it is reasonable to expect that they will work out to everyone's advantage and provided that the positions and offices to which they attach or from which they may be gained are open to all. These principles regulate the distributive aspects of institutions by controlling the assignment of rights and duties throughout the whole social structure, beginning with the adoption of a political constitution in accordance with which they are then to be applied to legislation. It is upon a correct choice of a basic structure of society, its fundamental system of rights and duties, that the justice of distributive shares depends.

The two principles of justice apply in the first instance to this basic structure, that is, to the main institutions of the social system and their arrangement, how they are combined together. Thus, this structure includes the political constitution and the principal economic and social institutions which together define a person's liberties and rights and affect his life-prospects, what he may expect to be and how well he may expect to fare. The intuitive idea here is that those born into the social system at different positions, say in different social classes, have varying life-prospects determined, in part, by the system of political liberties and personal rights, and by the economic and social opportunities which are made available to these positions. In this way the basic structure of society favours certain men over others, and these are the basic inequalities, the ones which affect their whole life-prospects. It is inequalities of this kind, presumably inevitable in any society, with which the two principles of justice are primarily designed to deal.

Now the second principle holds that an inequality is allowed only if there is reason to believe that the institution with the inequality, or permitting it, will work out for the advantage of every person engaged in it. In the case of the basic structure this means that all inequalities which affect life-prospects, say the inequalities of income and wealth which exist between social classes, must be to the advantage of everyone. Since the principle applies to institutions, we interpret this to mean that inequalities must be to the advantage of the representative man for each relevant social position; they should improve each such man's expectation. Here we assume that it is possible to attach to each position an expectation, and that this expectation is a function of the whole institutional structure: it can be raised and lowered by reassigning rights and duties throughout the system. Thus the expectation of any position depends upon the expectations of the others, and these in turn depend upon the pattern of rights and duties established by the basic structure. But it is not clear what is meant by saying that inequalities must be to the advantage of every representative man....[One]...interpretation [of what is meant by saying that inequalities must be to the advantage of every representative man]...is to choose some social position by reference to which the pattern of expectations as a whole is to be judged, and then to maximize with respect to the expectations of this representative man consistent with the demands of equal liberty and equality of opportunity. Now, the one obvious candidate is the representative man of those who are least favoured by the system of institutional inequalities. Thus we arrive at the following idea: the basic structure of the social system affects the life-prospects of typical individuals according to their initial places in society, say the various income classes into which they are born, or depending upon certain natural attributes, as when institutions make discriminations between men and women or allow certain advantages to be gained by those with greater natural abilities. The fundamental problem of distributive justice concerns the differences in life-prospects which come about in this way. We interpret the second principle to hold that these differences are just if and only if the greater expectations of the more advantaged, when playing a part in the working of the whole social system, improve the expectations of the least advantaged. The basic structure is just throughout when the advantages of the more fortunate promote the well-being of the least fortunate, that is, when a decrease in their advantages would make the least fortunate even worse off than they are. The basic structure is perfectly just when the prospects of the least fortunate are as great as they can be.

In interpreting the second principle (or rather the first part of it which we may, for obvious reasons, refer to as the difference principle), we assume that the first principle requires a basic equal liberty for all, and that the resulting political system, when circumstances permit, is that of a constitutional democracy in some form. There must be liberty of the person and political equality as well as liberty of conscience and freedom of thought. There is one class of equal citizens which defines a common status for all. We also assume that there is equality of opportunity and a fair competition for the available positions on the basis of reasonable qualifications. Now, given this background, the differences to be justified are the various economic and social inequalities in the basic structure which must inevitably arise in such a scheme. These are the inequalities in the distribution of income and wealth and the distinctions in social prestige and status which attach to the various positions and classes. The difference principle says that these inequalities are just if and only if they are part of a larger system in which they work out to the advantage of the most unfortunate representative man. The just distributive shares determined by the basic structure are those specified by this constrained maximum principle.

Thus, consider the chief problem of distributive justice, that concerning the distribution of wealth as it affects the life-prospects of those starting out in the various income groups. These income classes define the relevant representative men from which the social system is to be judged. Now, a son of a member of the entrepreneurial class (in a capitalist society) has a better prospect than that of the son of an unskilled labourer. This will be true, it seems, even when the social injustices which presently exist are removed and the two men are of equal talent and ability; the inequality cannot be done away with as long as something like the family is maintained. What, then, can justify this inequality in life-prospects? According to the second principle it is justified only if it is to the advantage of the representative man who is worst off, in this case the representative unskilled labourer. The inequality is permissible because lowering it would, let's suppose, make the working man even worse off than he is. Presumably, given the principle of open offices (the second part of the second principle), the greater expectations allowed to entrepreneurs has the effect in the longer run of raising the life-prospects of the labouring class. The inequality in expectation provides an incentive so that the economy is more efficient, industrial advance proceeds at a quicker pace, and so on, the end result of which is that greater material and other benefits are distributed throughout the system. Of course, all of this is familiar, and whether true or not in particular cases, it is the sort of thing which must be argued if the inequality in income and wealth is to be acceptable by the difference principle.

We should now verify that this interpretation of the second principle gives a natural sense in which everyone may be said to be made better off. Let us suppose that inequalities are chain-connected: that is, if an inequality raises the expectations of the lowest position, it raises the expectations of all positions in between. For example, if the greater expectations of the representative entrepreneur raises that of the unskilled labourer, it also raises that of the semi-skilled. Let us further assume that inequalities are close-knit: that is, it is impossible to raise (or lower) the expectations of any representative man without raising (or lowering) the expectations of every other representative man, and in particular, without affecting one way or the other that of the least fortunate. There is no loose-jointedness, so to speak, in the way in which expectations depend upon one another. Now, with these assumptions, everyone does benefit from an inequality which satisfies the difference principle, and the second principle as we have formulated it reads correctly. For the representative man who is better off in any pair-wise comparison gains by being allowed to have his advantage, and the man who is worse off benefits from the contribution which all inequalities make to each position below. Of course, chain-connection and close-knitness may not obtain; but in this case those who are better off should not have a veto over the advantages available for the least advantaged. The stricter interpretation of the difference principle should be followed, and all inequalities should be arranged for the advantage of the most unfortunate even if some inequalities are not to the advantage of those in middle positions. Should these conditions fail, then, the second principle would have to be stated in another way.

It may be observed that the difference principle represents, in effect, an original agreement to share in the benefits of the distribution of natural talents and abilities, whatever this distribution turns out to be, in order to alleviate as far as possible the arbitrary handicaps resulting from our initial starting places in society. Those who have been favoured by nature, whoever they are, may gain from their good fortune only on terms that improve the well-being of those who have lost out. The naturally advantaged are not to gain simply because they are more gifted, but only to cover the costs of training and cultivating their endowments and for putting them to use in a way which improves the position of the less fortunate. We are led to the difference principle if we wish to arrange the basic social structure so that no one gains (or loses) from his luck in the natural lottery of talent and ability, or from his initial place in society, without giving (or receiving) compensating advantages in return. (The parties in the original position are not said to be attracted by this idea and so agree to it; rather, given the symmetries of their situation, and particularly their lack of knowledge, and so on, they will find it to their interest to agree to a principle which can be understood in this way.) And we should note also that when the difference principle is perfectly satisfied, the basic structure is optimal by the efficiency principle. There is no way to make anyone better off without making someone worse off, namely, the least fortunate representative man. Thus the two principles of justice define distributive shares in a way compatible with efficiency, at least as long as we move on this highly abstract level. If we want to say (as we do, although it cannot be argued here) that the demands of justice have an absolute weight with respect to efficiency, this claim may seem less paradoxical when it is kept in mind that perfectly just institutions are also efficient.

Our second question is whether it is possible to arrange the institutions of a constitutional democracy so that the two principles are satisfied, at least approximately. We shall try to show that this can be done provided the government regulates a free economy in a certain way. More fully, if law and government act effectively to keep markets competitive, resources fully employed, property and wealth widely distributed over time, and to maintain the appropriate social minimum, then if there is equality of opportunity underwritten by education for all, the resulting distribution will be just. Of course, all of these arrangements and policies are familiar. The only novelty in the following remarks, if there is any novelty at all, is that this framework of institutions can be made to satisfy the difference principle. To argue this, we must sketch the relations of these institutions and how they work together.

First of all, we assume that the basic social structure is controlled by a just constitution which secures the various liberties of equal citizenship. Thus the legal order is administered in accordance with the principle of legality, and liberty of conscience and freedom of thought are taken for granted. The political process is conducted, so far as possible, as a just procedure for choosing between governments and for enacting just legislation. From the standpoint of distributive justice, it is also essential that there be equality of opportunity in several senses. Thus, we suppose that, in addition to maintaining the usual social overhead capital, government provides for equal educational opportunities for all either by subsidizing private schools or by operating a public school system. It also enforces and underwrites equality of opportunity in commercial ventures and in the free choice of occupation. This result is achieved by policing business behaviour and by preventing the establishment of barriers and restriction to the desirable positions and markets. Lastly, there is a guarantee of a social minimum which the government meets by family allowances and special payments in times of unemployment, or by a negative income tax.

In maintaining this system of institutions the government may be thought of as divided into four branches. Each branch is represented by various agencies (or activities thereof) charged with preserving certain social and economic conditions. These branches do not necessarily overlap with the usual organization of government, but should be understood as purely conceptual. Thus the allocation branch is to keep the economy feasibly competitive, that is, to prevent the formation of unreasonable market power. Markets are competitive in this sense when they cannot be made more so consistent with the requirements of efficiency and the acceptance of the facts of consumer preferences and geography. The allocation branch is also charged with identifying and correcting, say by suitable taxes and subsidies wherever possible, the more obvious departures from efficiency caused by the failure of prices to measure accurately social benefits and costs. The stabilization branch strives to maintain reasonably full employment so that there is no waste through failure to use resources and the free choice of occupation and the deployment of finance is supported by strong effective demand. These two branches together are to preserve the efficiency of the market economy generally.

The social minimum is established through the operations of the transfer branch. Later on we shall consider at what level this minimum should be set, since this is a crucial matter; but for the moment, a few general remarks will suffice. The main idea is that the workings of the transfer branch take into account the precept of need and assign it an appropriate weight with respect to the other common-sense precepts of justice. A market economy ignores the claims of need altogether. Hence there is a division of labour between the parts of the social system as different institutions answer to different common-sense precepts. Competitive markets (properly supplemented by government operations) handle the problem of the efficient allocation of labour and resources and set a weight to the conventional precepts associated with wages and earnings (the precepts of each according to his work and experience, or responsibility and the hazards of the job, and so on), whereas the transfer branch guarantees a certain level of well-being and meets the claims of need. Thus it is obvious that the justice of distributive shares depends upon the whole social system and how it distributes total income, wages plus transfers. There is with reason strong objection to the competitive determination of total income, since this would leave out of account the claims of need and of a decent standard of life. From the standpoint of the original position it is clearly rational to insure oneself against these contingencies. But now, if the appropriate minimum is provided by transfers, it may be perfectly fair that the other part of total income is competitively determined. Moreover, this way of dealing with the claims of need is doubtless more efficient, at least from a theoretical point of view, than trying to regulate prices by minimum wage standards and so on. It is preferable to handle these claims by a separate branch which supports a social minimum. Henceforth, in considering whether the second principle of justice is satisfied, the answer turns on whether the total income of the least advantaged, that is, wages plus transfers, is such as to maximize their long-term expectations consistent with the demands of liberty.

Finally, the distribution branch is to preserve an approximately just distribution of income and wealth over time by affecting the background conditions of the market from period to period. Two aspects of this branch may be distinguished. First of all, it operates a system of inheritance and gift taxes. The aim of these levies is not to raise revenue, but gradually and continually to correct the distribution of wealth and to prevent the concentrations of power to the detriment of liberty and equality of opportunity. It is perfectly true, as some have said,[3] that unequal inheritance of wealth is no more inherently unjust than unequal inheritance of intelligence; as far as possible the inequalities founded on either should satisfy the difference principle. Thus, the inheritance of greater wealth is just as long as it is to the advantage of the worst off and consistent with liberty, including equality of opportunity. Now by the latter we do not mean, of course, the equality of expectations between classes, since differences in life-prospects arising from the basic structure are inevitable, and it is precisely the aim of the second principle to say when these differences are just. Indeed, equality of opportunity is a certain set of institutions which assures equally good education and changes of culture for all and which keeps open the competition for positions on the basis of qualities reasonably related to performance, and so on. It is these institutions which are put in jeopardy when inequalities and concentrations of wealth reach a certain limit; and the taxes imposed by the distribution branch are to prevent this limit from being exceeded. Naturally enough where this limit lies is a matter for political judgment guided by theory, practical experience, and plain hunch; on this question the theory of justice has nothing to say.

The second part of the distribution branch is a scheme of taxation for raising revenue to cover the costs of public goods, to make transfer payments, and the like. This scheme belongs to the distribution branch since the burden of taxation must be justly shared. Although we cannot examine the legal and economic complications involved, there are several points in favour of proportional expenditure taxes as part of an ideally just arrangement. For one thing, they are preferable to income taxes at the level of common-sense precepts of justice, since they impose a levy according to how much a man takes out of the common store of goods and not according to how much he contributes (assuming that income is fairly earned in return for productive efforts). On the other hand, proportional taxes treat everyone in a clearly

---

[3]Example F. von Hayek, *The Constitution of Liberty* (1960), p. 90.

defined uniform way (again assuming that income is fairly earned) and hence it is preferable to use progressive rates only when they are necessary to preserve the justice of the system as a whole, that is, to prevent large fortunes hazardous to liberty and equality of opportunity, and the like. If proportional expenditure taxes should also prove more efficient, say because they interfere with incentives, or whatever, this would make the case for them decisive provided a feasible scheme could be worked out.[4] Yet these are questions of political judgment which are not our concern; and, in any case, a proportional expenditure tax is part of an idealized scheme which we are describing. It does not follow that even steeply progressive income taxes, given the injustice of existing systems, do not improve justice and efficiency all things considered. In practice we must usually choose between unjust arrangements and then it is a matter of finding the lesser injustice.

Whatever form the distribution branch assumes, the argument for it is to be based on justice: we must hold that once it is accepted the social system as a whole—the competitive economy surrounded by a just constitutional and legal framework—can be made to satisfy the principles of justice with the smallest loss in efficiency. The long-term expectations of the least advantaged are raised to the highest level consistent with the demands of equal liberty. In discussing the choice of a distribution scheme we have made no reference to the traditional criteria of taxation according to ability to pay or benefits received; nor have we mentioned any of the variants of the sacrifice principle. These standards are subordinate to the two principles of justice; once the problem is seen as that of designing a whole social system, they assume the status of secondary precepts with no more independent force than the precepts of common sense in regard to wages. To suppose otherwise is not to take a sufficiently comprehensive point of view. In setting up a just distribution branch these precepts may or may not have a place depending upon the demands of the two principles of justice when applied to the entire system....

The sketch of the system of institutions satisfying the two principles of justice is now complete....

In order...to establish just distributive shares a just total system of institutions must be set up and impartially administered. Given a just constitution and the smooth working of the four branches of government, and so on, there exists a procedure such that the actual distribution of wealth, whatever it turns out to be, is just. It will have come about as a consequence of a just system of institutions satisfying the principles to which everyone would agree and against which no one can complain. The situation is one of pure procedural justice, since there is no independent criterion by which the outcome can be judged. Nor can we say that a particular distribution of wealth is just because it is one which could have resulted from just institutions although it has not, as this would be to allow too much. Clearly there are many distributions which may

[4]See N. Kaldor, *An Expenditure Tax* (1955).

be reached by just institutions, and this is true whether we count patterns of distributions among social classes or whether we count distributions of particular goods and services among particular individuals. There are indefinitely many outcomes and what makes one of these just is that it has been achieved by actually carrying out a just scheme of co-operation as it is publicly understood. It is the result which has arisen when everyone receives that to which he is entitled given his and others' actions guided by their legitimate expectations and their obligations to one another. We can no more arrive at a just distribution of wealth except by working together within the framework of a just system of institutions than we can win or lose fairly without actually betting.

This account of distributive shares is simply an elaboration of the familiar idea that economic rewards will be just once a perfectly competitive price system is organized as a fair game. But in order to do this we have to begin with the choice of a social system as a whole, for the basic structure of the entire arrangement must be just. The economy must be surrounded with the appropriate framework of institutions, since even a perfectly efficient price system has no tendency to determine just distributive shares when left to itself. Not only must economic activity be regulated by a just constitution and controlled by the four branches of government, but a just saving-function must be adopted to estimate the provision to be made for future generations....

Justice as Entitlement

Robert Nozick

The term "distributive justice" is not a neutral one. Hearing the term "distribution," most people presume that some thing or mechanism uses some principle or criterion to give out a supply of things. Into this process of distributing shares some error may have crept. So it is an open question, at least, whether redistribution should take place; whether we should do again what has already been done once, though poorly. However, we are not in the position of children who have been given portions of pie by someone who now makes last minute adjustments to rectify careless cutting. There is no *central* distribution, no person or group entitled to control all the resources, jointly deciding how they are to be doled out. What each person gets, he gets from others who give to him in exchange for something, or as a gift. In a free society, diverse persons control different resources, and new holdings arise out of the voluntary exchanges and actions of persons. There is no more a distributing or distribution of shares than there is a distributing of mates in a society in which persons choose whom they shall marry....

THE ENTITLEMENT THEORY

The subject of justice in holdings consists of three major topics. The first is the *original acquisition of holdings,* the appropriation of unheld things. This includes the issues of how unheld things may come to be held, the process, or processes, by which unheld things may come to be held, the things that may come to be held by these processes, the extent of what comes to be held by a particular process, and so on. We shall refer to the complicated truth about this topic, which we shall not formulate here, as the principle of justice in acquisition. The second topic concerns the *transfer of holdings* from one person to another. By what processes may a person transfer holdings to another? How may a person acquire a holding from another who holds it? Under this topic come general descriptions of voluntary exchange, and gift and (on the other hand) fraud, as well as reference to particular conventional details fixed upon in a given society. The complicated truth about this subject (with placeholders for conventional details) we shall call the principle of justice in transfer. (And we shall suppose it also includes principles governing how a person may divest himself of a holding, passing it into an unheld state.)

If the world were wholly just, the following inductive definition would exhaustively cover the subject of justice in holdings.

1 A person who acquires a holding in accordance with the principle of justice in acquisition is entitled to that holding.

2 A person who acquires a holding in accordance with the principle of justice in transfer, from someone else entitled to the holding, is entitled to the holding.

3 No one is entitled to a holding except by (repeated) applications of 1 and 2.

The complete principle of distributive justice would say simply that a distribution is just if [all are] entitled to the holdings they possess under the distribution.

A distribution is just if it arises from another just distribution by legitimate means. The legitimate means of moving from one distribution to another are specified by the principle of justice in transfer. The legitimate first "moves" are specified by the principle of justice in acquisition. Whatever arises from a just situation by just steps is itself just ... from a just situation a situation *could* have arisen via justice-preserving means does *not* suffice to show its justice. The fact that a thief's victims voluntarily *could* have presented him with gifts does not entitle the thief to his ill-gotten gains. Justice in holdings is historical; it depends upon what actually has happened. We shall return to this point later.

Not all actual situations are generated in accordance with the two principles of justice in holdings: the principle of justice in acquisition and the principle of justice in transfer. Some people steal from others, or defraud them, or enslave them, seizing their product and preventing them from living as they choose, or forcibly exclude others from competing in exchanges. None of these are forcibly exclude others from competing in exchanges. None of these are permissible modes of transition from one situation to another. And some persons acquire holdings by means not sanctioned by the principle of justice in acquisition. The existence of past injustice (previous violations of the first two principles of justice in holdings) raises the third major topic under justice in holdings: the rectification of injustice in holdings. If past injustice has shaped present holdings in various ways, some identifiable and some not, what now, if anything, ought to be done to rectify these injustices? What obligations do the performers of injustice have toward those whose position is worse than it would have been had the injustice not been done? Or, than it would have been had compensation been paid promptly? How, if at all, do things change if the beneficiaries and those made worse off are not the direct parties in the act of injustice, but, for example, their descendants? Is an injustice done to someone whose holding was itself based upon an unrectified injustice? How far back must one go in wiping clean the historical slate of injustices? What may victims of injustice permissibly do in order to rectify the injustices being done to them, including the many injustices done by persons acting through their government? I do not know of a thorough or theoretically sophisticated treatment of such issues. Idealizing greatly, let us suppose theoretical investigation will produce a principle of rectification. This principle uses historical information about previous situations and injustices done in them (as defined by the first two principles of justice and rights against interference), and information about the actual course of events that flowed from these injustices, until the present, and it yields a description (or descriptions) of holdings in the society. The principle of rectification presumably will make use of its best estimate of subjunctive information about what would have occurred (or a probability distribution over what might have occurred, using the expected value) if the injustice had not taken place. If the actual description of holdings turns out not to be one of the descriptions yielded by the principle, then one of the descriptions yielded must be realized...

HISTORICAL PRINCIPLES AND END-RESULT PRINCIPLES

The general outlines of the entitlement theory illuminate the nature and defects of other conceptions of distributive justice. The entitlement theory of justice in distribution is *historical*; whether a distribution is just depends upon how it came about. In contrast, *current time-slice principles* of justice hold that the justice of a distribution is determined by how things are distributed (who has what) as judged by some *structural* principle(s) of just distribution. A utilitarian who judges between any two distributions by seeing which has the greater sum of utility and, if the sum tie, applies some fixed equality criterion to choose the more equal distribution, would hold a current time-slice principle of justice....

Most persons do not accept current time-slice principles as constituting the whole story about distributive shares. They think it relevant in assessing the justice of a situation to consider not only the distribution it embodies, but also how that distribution came about. If some persons are in prison for murder or war crimes, we do not say that to assess the justice of the distribution in the society we must look only at what this person has, and that person has, and that person has,... at the current time. We think it relevant to ask whether someone did something so that he *deserved* to be punished, deserved to have a lower share. Most will agree to the relevance of further information with regard to punishments and penalties.

We construe the position we discuss too narrowly by speaking of *current time-slice principles*. Nothing is changed if structural principles operate upon a time sequence of current time-slice profiles and, for example, give someone more now to counterbalance the less he has had earlier. A utilitarian or an egalitarian or any mixture of the two over time will inherit the difficulties of his more myopic comrades. He is not helped by the fact that *some* of the information others consider relevant in assessing a distribution is reflected, unrecoverably, in past matrices. Henceforth, we shall refer to such unhistorical principles of distributive justice, including the current time-slice principles, as *end-result principles* or *end-state principles*.

In contrast to end-result principles of justice, *historical principles* of justice hold that past circumstances or actions of people can create differential entitlements or differential deserts to things. An injustice can be worked by moving from one distribution to another structurally identical one, for the second, in profile the same, may violate people's entitlements or deserts; it may not fit the actual history.

PATTERNING

The entitlement principles of justice in holdings that we have sketched are historical principles of justice. To better understand their precise character, we shall distinguish them from another subclass of the historical principles. Consider, as an example, the principle of distribution according to moral merit. This principle requires that total distributive shares vary directly with moral merit; no person should have a greater share than anyone whose moral merit is greater. (If moral merit could be not merely ordered but measured on an interval or ratio scale, stronger principles could be formulated.) Or consider the principle that results by substituting "usefulness to society" for "moral merit" in the previous principle. Or instead of "distribute according to moral merit," or "distribute according to usefulness to society," we might consider "distribute according to the weighted sum of moral merit, usefulness to society, and need," with the weights of the different dimensions equal. Let us call a principle of distribution *patterned* if it specifies that a distribution is to vary along with some natural dimension, weighted sum of natural dimensions, or lexicographic ordering of natural dimensions....

Almost every suggested principle of distributive justice is patterned: to each according to his moral merit, or needs, or marginal product, or how hard he tries, or the weighted sum of the foregoing, and so on. The principle of entitlement we have sketched is *not* patterned. There is no one natural dimension or weighted sum or combination of a small number of natural dimensions that yields the distributions generated in accordance with the principle of entitlement. The set of holdings that results when some persons receive their marginal products, others win at gambling, others receive a share of their mate's income, others receive gifts from foundations, others receive interest on loans, others receive gifts from admirers, others receive returns on investments, others make for themselves much of what they have, others find things, and so on, will not be patterned....

HOW LIBERTY UPSETS PATTERNS

It is not clear how those holding alternative conceptions of distributive justice can reject the entitlement conception of justice in holdings. For suppose a distribution favored by one of these non-entitlement conceptions is realized. Let us suppose it is your favorite one and let us call this distribution D_1; perhaps everyone has an equal share, perhaps shares vary in accordance with some dimension you treasure. Now suppose that Wilt Chamberlain is greatly in demand by basketball teams, being a great gate attraction. (Also suppose contracts run only for a year, with players being free agents.) He signs the following sort of contract with a team: In each home game, twenty-five cents from the price of each ticket of admission goes to him. (We ignore the question of whether he is "gouging" the owners, letting them look out for themselves.) The season starts, and people cheerfully attend his team's games; they buy their tickets, each time dropping a separate twenty-five cents of their admission price into a special box with Chamberlain's name on it. They are excited about seeing him play; it is worth the total admission price to them. Let us suppose that in one season one million persons attend his home games, and Wilt Chamberlain winds up with $250,000, a much larger sum than the average income and larger even than anyone else has. Is he entitled to this income? Is this new distribution, D_2, unjust? If so, why? There is *no* question about whether each of the people was entitled to the control over the resources they held in D_1, because that was the distribution (your favorite) that (for the purposes of argument) we assumed was acceptable. Each of these persons *chose* to give twenty-five cents of their money to Chamberlain. They could have spent it on going to the movies, or on candy bars, or on copies of *Dissent* magazine, or of *Monthly Review*. But they all, at least one million of them, converged on giving it to Wilt Chamberlain in exchange for watching him play basketball. If D_1 was a just distribution, and people voluntarily moved from it to D_2, transferring parts of their shares they were given under D_1 (what was it for if not to do something with?), isn't D_2 also just? If the people were entitled to dispose of the resources to which they were entitled (under D_1), didn't this include their being entitled to give it to, or exchange it with, Wilt Chamberlain? Can anyone else complain on grounds of justice? Each other person already has his legitimate share under D_1. Under D_1, there is nothing that anyone has that anyone else has a claim of justice against. After someone transfers something to Wilt Chamberlain, third parties *still* have their legitimate shares; *their* shares are not changed. By what process could such a transfer among two persons give rise to a legitimate claim of distributive justice on a portion of what was transferred, by a third party who had no claim of justice on any holding of the others *before* the transfer? To cut off objections irrelevant here, we might imagine the exchanges occurring in a socialist society, after hours. After playing whatever basketball he does in his daily work, or doing whatever other daily work he does, Wilt Chamberlain decides to put in *overtime* to earn additional money. (First his work quota is set; he works time over that.) Or imagine it is a skilled juggler people like to see, who puts on shows after hours.

Why might some [people] work overtime in a society in which it is assumed their needs are satisfied? Perhaps because they care about things other than needs. I like to write in books that I read, and to have easy access to books for browsing at odd hours. It would be very pleasant and convenient to have the resources of Widener Library in my back yard. No society, I assume, will provide such resources close to each person who would like them as part of his regular allotment (under D_1). Thus, persons either must do without some extra things that they want, or be allowed to do something extra to get some of these things. On what basis could the inequalities that would eventuate be forbidden? Notice also that small factories would spring up in a socialist society, unless forbidden. I melt down some of my personal possessions (under D_1) and build a machine out of the material. I offer you, and others, a philosophy lecture once a week in exchange for your cranking the handle on my machine, whose products I exchange for yet other things, and so on. (The raw materials used by the machine are given to me by others who possess them under D_1, in exchange for hearing lectures.) Each person might participate to gain things over and above their allotment under D_1. Some persons even might want to leave their job in socialist industry and work full time in this private sector.... Here I wish merely to note how private property even in means of production would occur in a socialist society that did not forbid people to use as they wished some of the resources they are given under the socialist distribution D_1. The socialist society would have to forbid capitalist acts between consenting adults.

REDISTRIBUTION AND PROPERTY RIGHTS

Patterned principles of distributive justice necessitate redistributive activities. The likelihood is small that any actual freely-arrived-at set of holdings fits a given pattern; and the likelihood is nil that it will continue to fit the pattern as people exchange and give. From the point of view of an entitlement theory, redistribution is a serious matter indeed, involving, as it does, the violation of people's rights. (An exception is those takings that fall under the principle of the rectification of injustices.) From other points of view, also, it is serious.

Taxation of earnings from labor is on a par with forced labor. Some persons find this claim obviously true: taking the earning of *n* hours labor is like taking *n* hours from the person; it is like forcing the person to work *n* hours for another's purpose. Others find the claim absurd. But even these, *if* they object to forced labor, would oppose forcing unemployed hippies to work for the benefit of the needy. And they would also object to forcing each person to work five extra hours each week for the benefit of the needy. But a system that takes five hours' wages in taxes does not seem to them like one that forces someone to work five hours, since it offers the person forced a wider range of choice in activities then does taxation in kind with the particular labor specified. (But we can imagine a gradation of systems of forced labor, from one that specifies a particular activity, to one that gives a choice among two activities, to ...; and so on up.) Furthermore, people envisage a system with something like a proportional tax on everything above the amount necessary for basic needs. Some think this does not force someone to work extra hours, since there is no fixed number of extra hours he is forced to work, and since he can avoid the tax entirely by earning only enough to cover his basic needs. This is a very uncharacteristic view of forcing for who *also* think people are forced to do something *whenever* the alternatives they face are considerably worse. However, *neither* view is correct. The fact that others intentionally intervene, in violation of a side constraint against aggression, to threaten force to limit the alternatives, in this case to paying taxes or (presumably the worse alternative) bare subsistence, makes the taxation system one of forced labor and distinguishes it from other cases of limited choices which are not forcings.

The man who chooses to work longer to gain an income more than sufficient for his basic needs prefers some extra goods or services to the leisure and activities he could perform during the possible nonworking hours; whereas the man who chooses not to work the extra time prefers the leisure activities to the extra goods or services he could acquire by working more. Given this, if it would be illegitimate for a tax system to seize some of a man's leisure (forced labor) for the purpose of serving the needy, how can it be legitimate for a tax system to seize some of a man's goods for that purpose? Why should we treat the man whose happiness requires certain material goods or services differently from the man whose preferences and desires make such goods unnecessary for his happiness? Why should the man who prefers seeing a movie (and who has to earn money for a ticket) be open to the required call to aid the needy, while the person who prefers looking at a sunset (and hence need earn no extra money) is not? Indeed, isn't it surprising that redistributionists choose to ignore the man whose pleasures are so easily attainable without extra labor, while adding yet another burden to the poor unfortunate who must work for his pleasures? ...

LOCKE'S THEORY OF ACQUISITION

Before we turn to consider other theories of justice in detail, we must introduce an additional bit of complexity into the structure of the entitlement theory. This is best approached by considering Locke's attempt to specify a principle of justice in acquisition. Locke views property rights in an unowned object as originating through someone's mixing his labor with it. This gives rise to many questions. What are the boundaries of what labor is mixed with? If a private astronaut clears a place on Mars, has he mixed his labor with (so that he comes to own) the whole planet, the whole uninhabited universe, or just a particular plot? Which plot does an act bring under ownership? The minimal (possibly disconnected) area such that an act decreases entropy in that area, and not elsewhere? Can virgin land (for the purposes of ecological investigation by high-flying airplane) come under ownership by a Lockean process? Building a fence around a territory presumably would make one the owner of only the fence (and the land immediately underneath it).

Why does mixing one's labor with something make one the owner of it? Perhaps because one owns one's labor, and so one comes to own a previously unowned thing that becomes permeated with what one owns. Ownership seeps over into the rest. But why isn't mixing what I own with what I don't own a way of losing what I own rather than a way of gaining what I don't? If I own a can of tomato juice and spill it in the sea so that its molecules (made radioactive, so I can check this) mingle evenly throughout the sea, do I thereby come to own the sea, or have I foolishly dissipated my tomato juice? Perhaps the idea, instead, is that laboring on something improves it and makes it more valuable....

It will be implausible to view improving an object as giving full ownership to it, if the stock of unowned objects that might be improved is limited. For an object's coming under one person's ownership changes the situation of all others. Whereas previously they were at liberty (in Hohfeld's sense) to use the object, they now no longer are. This change in the situation of others (by removing their liberty to act on a previously unowned object) need not worsen their situation. If I appropriate a grain of sand from Coney Island, no one else may now do as they will with *that* grain of sand. But there are plenty of other grains of sand left for them to do the same with. Or if not grains of sand, then other things. Alternatively, the things I do with the grain of sand I appropriate might improve the position of others, counterbalancing their loss of the liberty to use that grain. The crucial point is whether appropriation of an unowned object worsens the situation of others.

Locke's proviso that there be "enough and as good left in common for others" (sect. 27) is meant to ensure that the situation of others is not worsened....

Is the situation of persons who are unable to appropriate (there being no more accessible and useful unowned objects) worsened by a system allowing appropriation and permanent property? Here enter the various familiar social considerations favoring private property: it increases the social product by putting means of production in the hands of those who can use them most efficiently (profitably); experimentation is encouraged, because with separate persons controlling resources, there is no one person or small group whom someone with a new idea must convince to try it out; private property enables people to decide on the pattern and types of risks they wish to bear, leading to specialized types of risk bearing; private property protects future persons by leading some to hold back resources from current consumption for future markets; it provides alternate sources of employment for unpopular persons who don't have to convince any one person or small group to hire them, and so on. These considerations enter a Lockean theory to support the claim that appropriation of private property satisfies the intent behind the "enough and as good left over" proviso, *not* as a utilitarian justification of property. They enter to rebut the claim that because the proviso is violated no natural right to private property can arise by a Lockean process....

THE PROVISO

Whether or not Locke's particular theory of appropriation can be spelled out so as to handle various difficulties, I assume that any adequate theory of justice in acquisition will contain a proviso similar to the weaker of the ones we have attributed to Locke. A process normally giving rise to a permanent bequeathable property right in a previously unowned thing will not do so if the position of others no longer at liberty to use the thing is thereby worsened. It is important to specify *this* particular mode of worsening the situation of others, for the proviso does not encompass other modes. It does not include the worsening due to more limited opportunities to appropriate (the first way above, corresponding to the more stringent condition), and it does not include how I "worsen" a seller's position if I appropriate materials to make some of what he is selling, and then enter into competition with him. Someone whose appropriation otherwise would violate the proviso still may appropriate provided he compensates the others so that their situation is not thereby worsened; unless he does compensate these others, his appropriation will violate the proviso of the principle of justice in acquisition and will be an illegitimate one....

I believe that the free operation of a market system will not actually run afoul of the Lockean proviso.... If this is correct, the proviso will not play a very important role in the activities of protective agencies and will not provide a significant opportunity for future state action. Indeed, were it not for the effects of previous *illegitimate* state action, people would not think the possibility of the proviso's being violated as of more interest than any other logical possibility. (Here I make an empirical historical claim; as does someone who disagrees with this.) This completes our indication of the complication in the entitlement theory introduced by the Lockean proviso.

Morality and the Liberal Ideal

Michael J. Sandel

Liberals often take pride in defending what they oppose—pornography, for example, or unpopular views. They say the state should not impose on its citizens a preferred way of life, but should leave them as free as possible to choose their own values and ends, consistent with a similar liberty for others. This commitment to freedom of choice requires liberals constantly to distinguish between permission and praise, between allowing a practice and endorsing it. It is one thing to allow pornography, they argue, something else to affirm it.

Conservatives sometimes exploit this distinction by ignoring it. They charge that those who would allow abortions favor abortion, that opponents of school prayer oppose prayer, that those who defend the rights of Communists sympathize with their cause. And in a pattern of argument familiar in our politics, liberals reply by invoking higher principles; it is not that they dislike pornography less, but rather that they value toleration, or freedom of choice, or fair procedures more.

But in contemporary debate, the liberal rejoinder seems increasingly fragile, its moral basis increasingly unclear. Why should toleration and freedom of choice prevail when other important values are also at stake? Too often the answer implies some version of moral relativism, the idea that it is wrong to "legislate morality" because all morality is merely subjective. "Who is to say what is literature and what is filth? That is a value judgment, and whose values should decide?"

Relativism usually appears less as a claim than as a question. "Who is to judge?" But it is a question that can also be asked of the values that liberals defend. Toleration and freedom and fairness are values too, and they can hardly be defended by the claim that no values can be defended. So it is a mistake to affirm liberal values by arguing that all values are merely subjective. The relativist defense of liberalism is no defense at all.

What, then, can be the moral basis of the higher principles the liberal invokes? Recent political philosophy has offered two main alternatives—one utilitarian, the other Kantian. The utilitarian view, following John Stuart Mill, defends liberal principles in the name of maximizing the general welfare. The state should not impose on its citizens a preferred way of life, even for their own good, because doing so will reduce the sum of human happiness, at least in the long run; better that people choose for themselves, even if, on occasion, they get it wrong. "The only freedom which deserves the name," writes Mill in *On Liberty*, "is that of pursuing our own good in our own way, so long as we do not attempt to deprive others of theirs, or impede their efforts to obtain it." He adds that his argument does not depend on any notion of abstract right, only on the principle of the greatest good for the greatest number. "I regard utility as the ultimate appeal on all ethical questions; but it must be utility in the largest sense, grounded on the permanent interests of man as a progressive being."

Many objections have been raised against utilitarianism as a general doctrine of moral philosophy. Some have questioned the concept of utility, and the assumption that all human goods are in principle commensurable. Others have objected that by reducing all values to preferences and desires, utilitarians are unable to admit qualitative distinctions of worth, unable to distinguish noble desires from base ones. But most recent debate has focused on whether utilitarianism offers a convincing basis for liberal principles, including respect for individual rights.

In one respect, utilitarianism would seem well suited to liberal purposes. Seeking to maximize overall happiness does not require judging people's values, only aggregating them. And the willingness to aggregate preferences without judging them suggest a tolerant spirit, even a democratic one. When people go to the polls we count their votes, whatever they are.

But the utilitarian calculus is not always as liberal as it first appears. If enough cheering Romans pack the Colosseum to watch the lion devour the Christian, the collective pleasure of the Romans will surely outweigh the pain of the Christian, intense though it be. Or if a big majority abhors a small religion and wants it banned, the balance of preferences will favor suppression, not toleration. Utilitarians sometimes defend individual rights on the grounds that respecting them now will serve utility in the long run. But this calculation is precarious and contingent. It hardly secures the liberal promise not to impose on some the values of others. As the majority will is an inadequate instrument of liberal politics—by itself it fails to secure individual rights—so the utilitarian philosophy is an inadequate foundation for liberal principles.

The case against utilitarianism was made most powerfully by Immanuel Kant. He argued that empirical principles, such as utility, were unfit to serve as basis for the moral law. A wholly instrumental defense of freedom and rights not only leaves rights vulnerable, but fails to respect the inherent dignity of persons. The utilitarian calculus treats people as means to the happiness of others, not as ends in themselves, worthy of respect.

Contemporary liberals extend Kant's argument with the claim that utilitarianism fails to take seriously the distinction between persons. In seeking above all to maximize the general welfare, the utilitarian treats society as a whole as if it were a single person; it conflates our many, diverse desires into a single system of desires. It is indifferent to the distribution of satisfactions among persons, except insofar as this may affect the overall sum. But this fails to respect our plurality and distinctness. It uses some as means to the happiness of all, and so fails to respect each as an end in himself.

In the view of modern-day Kantians, certain rights are so fundamental that even the general welfare cannot override them. As John Rawls writes in his important work, *A Theory of Justice*, "Each person possesses an inviolability founded on justice that even the welfare of society as a whole cannot override.... The rights secured by justice are not subject to political bargaining or to the calculus of social interests."

So Kantian liberals need an account of rights that does not depend on utilitarian considerations. More than this, they need an account that does not depend on any particular conception of the good, that does not presuppose the superiority of one way of life over others. Only a justification neutral about ends could preserve the liberal resolve not to favor any particular ends, or to impose on its citizens a preferred way of life. But what sort of justification could this be? How is it possible to affirm certain liberties and rights as fundamental without embracing some vision of the good life, without endorsing some ends over others? It would seem we are back to the relativist predicament—to affirm liberal principles without embracing any particular ends.

The solution proposed by Kantian liberals is to draw a distinction between the "right" and the "good"—between a framework of basic rights and liberties, and the conceptions of the good that people may choose to pursue within the framework. It is one thing for the state to support a fair framework, they argue, something else to affirm some particular ends. For example, it is one thing to defend the right to free speech so that people may be free to form their own opinions and choose their own ends, but something else to support it on the grounds that a life of political discussion is inherently worthier than a life unconcerned with public affairs, or on the grounds that free speech will increase the general welfare. Only the first defense is available in the Kantian view, resting as it does on the ideal of a neutral framework.

Now, the commitment to a framework neutral with respect to ends can be seen as a kind of value—in this sense the Kantian liberal is no relativist—but its value consists precisely in its refusal to affirm a preferred way of life or conception of the good. For Kantian liberals, then, the right is prior to the good, and in two senses. First, individual rights cannot be sacrificed for the sake of the general good; and second, the principles of justice that specify these rights cannot be premised on any particular vision of the good life. What justifies the rights is not that they maximize the general welfare or otherwise promote the good, but rather that they comprise a fair framework within which individuals and groups can choose their own values and ends, consistent with a similar liberty for others.

Of course, proponents of the rights-based ethic notoriously disagree about what rights are fundamental, and about what political arrangements the ideal of the neutral framework requires. Egalitarian liberals support the welfare state, and favor a scheme of civil liberties together with certain social and economic rights—rights to welfare, education, health care, and so on. Libertarian liberals defend the market economy, and claim that redistributive policies violate peoples' rights; they favor a scheme of civil liberties combined with a strict regime of private property rights. But whether egalitarian or libertarian, rights-based liberalism begins with the claim that we are separate, individual persons, each with our own aims, interests, and conceptions of the good; it seeks a framework of rights that will enable us to realize our capacity as free moral agents, consistent with a similar liberty for others.

Within academic philosophy, the last decade or so has seen the ascendance of the rights-based ethic over the utilitarian one, due in large part to the influence of Rawls's *A Theory of Justice*. The legal philosopher H.L.A. Hart recently described the shift from "the old faith that some form of utilitarianism must capture the essence of political morality" to the new faith that "the truth must lie with a doctrine of basic human rights, protecting specific basic liberties and interests of individuals.... Whereas not so long ago great energy and much ingenuity of many philosophers were devoted to making some form of utilitarianism work, latterly such energies and ingenuity have been devoted to the articulation of theories of basic rights."

But in philosophy as in life, the new faith becomes the old orthodoxy before long. Even as it has come to prevail over its utilitarian rival, the rights-based ethic has recently faced a growing challenge from a different direction, from a view that gives fuller expression to the claims of citizenship and community than the liberal vision allows. The communitarian critics, unlike modern liberals, make the case for a politics of the common good. Recalling the arguments of Hegel against Kant, they question the liberal claim for the priority of the right over the good, and the picture of the freely choosing individual it embodies. Following Aristotle, they argue that we cannot justify political arrangements without reference to common purposes and ends, and that we cannot conceive of ourselves without reference to our role as citizens, as participants in a common life.

This debate reflects two contrasting pictures of the self. The rights-based ethic, and the conception of the person it embodies were shaped in large part in the encounter with utilitarianism. Where utilitarians conflate our many desires into a single system of desire, Kantians insist on the separateness of persons. Where the utilitarian self is simply defined as the sum of its desires, the Kantian self is choosing self, independent of the desires and ends it may have at any moment. As Rawls writes, "The self is prior to the ends which are affirmed by it; even a dominant end must be chosen from among numerous possibilities."

The priority of the self over its ends means I am never defined by my aims and attachments, but always capable of standing back to survey and assess and possibly to revise them. This is what it means to be a free and independent self, capable of choice. And this is the vision of the self that finds expression in the ideal of the state as a neutral framework. On the rights-based ethic, it is precisely because we are essentially separate, independent selves that we need a neutral framework, a framework of rights that refuses to choose among competing purposes and ends. If the self is prior to its ends, then the right must be prior to the good.

Communitarian critics of rights-based liberalism say we cannot conceive ourselves as independent in this way, as bearers of selves wholly detached from our aims and attachments. They say that certain of our roles are partly constitutive of the persons we are—as citizens of a country, or members of a movement, or partisans of a cause. But if we are partly defined by the communities we inhabit, then we must also be implicated in the purposes and ends characteristic of those communities. As Alasdair MacIntyre writes in his book, *After Virtue*, "What is good for me has to be the good for one who inhabits these roles." Open-ended though it be, the story of my life is always embedded in the story of those communities from which I derive my identity—whether family or city, tribe or nation, party or cause. In the communitarian view, these stories make a moral difference, not only a psychological one. They situate us in the world and give our lives their moral particularity.

What is at stake for a politics in the debate between unencumbered selves and situated ones? What are the practical differences between a politics of rights and a politics of the common good? On some issues, the two theories may produce different arguments for similar policies. For example, the civil rights movement of the 1960s might be justified by liberals in the name of human dignity and respect for persons, and by communitarians in the name of recognizing the full membership of fellow citizens wrongly excluded from the common life of the nation. And where liberals might support public education in hopes of equipping students to become autonomous individuals, capable of choosing their own ends and pursuing them effectively, communitarians might support public education in hopes of equipping students to become good citizens, capable of contributing meaningfully to public deliberations and pursuits.

On other issues, the two ethics might lead to different policies. Communitarians would be more likely than liberals to allow a town to ban pornographic bookstores, on the grounds that pornography offends its way of life and the values that sustain it. But a politics of civic virtue does not always part company with liberalism in favor of conservative policies. For example, communitarians would be more willing than some rights-oriented liberals to see states enact laws regulating plant closings, to protect their communities from the disruptive effects of capital mobility and sudden industrial change. More generally, where the liberal regards the expansion of individual rights and entitlements as unqualified moral and political progress, the communitarian is troubled by the tendency of liberal programs to displace politics from smaller forms of association to more comprehensive ones. Where libertarian liberals defend the private economy and egalitarian liberals defend the welfare state, communitarians worry about the concentration of power in both the corporate economy and the bureaucratic state, and the erosion of those intermediate forms of community that have at times sustained a more vital public life.

Liberals often argue that a politics of the common good, drawing as it must on particular loyalties, obligations, and traditions, opens the way to prejudice and intolerance. The modern nation-state is not the Athenian polis, they point out; the scale and diversity of modern life have rendered the Aristotelian political ethic nostalgic at best and dangerous at worst. Any attempt to govern by a vision of the good is likely to lead to a slippery slope of totalitarian temptations.

Communitarians reply, rightly in my view, that intolerance flourishes most where forms of life are dislocated, roots unsettled, traditions undone. In our day, the totalitarian impulse has sprung less from the convictions of confidently situated selves than from the confusions of atomized, dislocated, frustrated selves, at sea in a world where common meanings have lost their force. As Hannah Arendt has written, "What makes mass society so difficult to bear is not the number of people involved, or at least not primarily, but the fact that the world between them has lost its power to gather them together, to relate and to separate them." Insofar as our public life has withered, our sense of common involvement diminished, we lie vulnerable to the mass politics of totalitarian solutions. So responds the party of the common good to the party of rights. If the party of the common good is right, our most pressing moral and political project is to revitalize those civic republican possibilities implicit in our tradition but fading in our time.

MORALITY AND THE LAW
Morality and the Criminal Law
Patrick Devlin

In jurisprudence, as I have said, everything is thrown open to discussion and, in the belief that they cover the whole field, I have framed three interrogatories addressed to myself to answer:

1 Has society the right to pass judgement at all on matters of morals? Ought there, in other words, to be a public morality, or are morals always a matter for private judgement?

2 If society has the right to pass judgement, has it also the right to use the weapon of the law to enforce it?

3 If so, ought it to use that weapon in all cases or only in some; and if only in some, on what principles should it distinguish?

I shall begin with the first interrogatory and consider what is meant by the right of society to pass a moral judgement, that is, a judgement about what is good and what is evil. The fact that a majority of people may disapprove of a practice does not of itself make it a matter for society as a whole. Nine men out of ten may disapprove of what the tenth man is doing and still say that it is not their business. There is a case for a collective judgement (as distinct from a large number of individual opinions which sensible people may even refrain from pronouncing at all if it is upon somebody else's private affairs) only if society is affected. Without a collective judgement there can be no case at all for intervention. Let me take as an illustration the Englishman's attitude to religion as it is now and as it has been in the past. His attitude now is that a man's religion is his private affair; he may think of another man's religion that it is right or wrong, true or untrue, but not that it is good or bad. In earlier times that was not so; a man was denied the right to practice what was thought of as heresy, and heresy was thought of as destructive of society.

The language used in the passages I have quoted from the Wolfenden Report suggests the view that there ought not to be a collective judgement about immorality *per se*. Is this what is meant by "private morality" and "individual freedom of choice and action"? Some people sincerely believe that homosexuality is neither immoral nor unnatural. Is the "freedom of choice and action" that is offered to the individual, freedom to decide for himself what is moral or immoral, society remaining neutral; or is it freedom to be immoral if he wants to be? The language of the Report may be open to question, but the conclusions at which the Committee arrive answer this question unambiguously. If society is not prepared to say that homosexuality is morally wrong, there would be no basis for a law protecting youth from "corruption" or punishing a man for living on the "immoral" earnings of a homosexual prostitute, as the Report recommends. This attitude the Committee make even clearer when they come to deal with prostitution. In truth, the Report takes it for granted that there is in existence a public morality which condemns homosexuality and prostitution. What the Report seems to mean by private morality might perhaps be better described as private behavior in matters of morals.

This view—that there is such a thing as public morality—can also be justified by a *priori* argument. What makes a society of any sort is community of ideas, not only political ideas but also ideas about the way its members should behave and govern their lives; these latter ideas are its morals. Every society has a moral structure as well as a political one: or rather, since that might suggest two independent systems, I should say that the structure of every society is made up both of politics and morals. Take, for example, the institution of marriage. Whether a man should be allowed to take more than one wife is something about which every society has to make up its mind one way or the other. In England we believe in the Christian idea of marriage and therefore adopt monogamy as a moral principle. Consequently the Christian institution of marriage has become the basis of family life and so part of the structure of our society. It is there not because it is Christian. It has got there because it is Christian, but it remains there because it is built into the house in which we live and could not be removed without bringing it down. The great majority of those who live in this country accept it because it is the Christian idea of marriage and for them the only true one. But a non-Christian is bound by it, not because it is part of Christianity but because, rightly or wrongly, it has been adopted by the society in which he lives. It would be useless for him to stage a debate designed to prove that polygamy was theologically more correct and socially preferable; if he wants to live in the house, he must accept it as built in the way in which it is.

We see this more clearly if we think of ideas or institutions that are purely political. Society cannot tolerate rebellion; it will not allow argument about the rightness of the cause. Historians a century later may say that the rebels were right and the Government was wrong and a percipient and conscientious subject of the state may think so at the time. But it is not a matter which can be left to individual judgement.

The institution of marriage is a good example for my purpose because it bridges the division, if there is one, between politics and morals. Marriage is part of the structure of our society and it is also the basis of a moral code which condemns fornication and adultery. The institution of marriage would be gravely threatened if individual judgements were permitted about the morality of adultery; on these points there must be a public morality. But public morality is not to be confined to those moral principles which support institutions such as marriage. People do not think of monogamy as something which has to be supported because our society has chosen to organize itself upon it; they think of it as something that is good in itself and offering a good way of life and that it is for that reason that our society has adopted it. I return to the statement that I have already made, that society means a community of ideas; without shared ideas on politics, morals, and ethics no society can exist. Each one of us has ideas about what is good and what is evil; they cannot be kept private from the society in which we live. If men and women try to create a society in which there is no fundamental agreement about good and evil they will fail; if, having based it on common agreement, the agreement goes, the society will disintegrate. For society is not something that is kept together physically; it is held by the invisible bonds of common thought. If the bonds were too far relaxed the members would drift apart. A common morality is part of the bondage. The bondage is part of the price of society; and mankind, which needs society, must pay its price.

Common lawyers used to say that Christianity was part of the law of the land. That was never more than a piece of rhetoric as Lord Sumner said in *Bowman* v. *The Secular Society*. What lay behind it was the notion which I have been seeking to expound, namely that morals—and up till a century or so ago no one thought it worth distinguishing between religion and morals—were necessary to the temporal order. In 1675 Chief Justice Hale said: "To say that religion is a cheat is to dissolve all those obligations whereby civil society is preserved." In 1797 Mr. Justice Ashurst said of blasphemy that it was "not only an offense against God but against all law and government from its tendency to dissolve all the bonds and obligations of civil society." By 1908 Mr. Justice Phillimore was able to say: "A man is free to think, to speak and to teach what he pleases as to religious matters, but not as to morals."

You may think that I have taken far too long in contending that there is such a thing as public morality, a proposition which most people would readily accept, and may have left myself too little time to discuss the next question which to many minds may cause greater difficulty: to what extent should society use the law to enforce its moral judgements? But I believe that the answer to the first question determines the way in which the second should be approached and may indeed very nearly dictate the answer to the second question. If society has no right to make judgements on morals, the law must find some special justification for entering the field of morality. If homosexuality and prostitution are not in themselves wrong then the onus is very clearly on the lawgiver who wants to frame a law against certain aspects of them to justify the exceptional treatment. But if society has the right to make a judgement and has it on the basis that a recognized morality is as necessary to society as, say, a recognized government, then society may use the law to preserve morality in the same way as it uses it to safeguard anything else that is essential to its existence. If therefore the first proposition is securely established with all its implications, society has a prima facie right to legislate against immorality as such.

The Wolfenden Report, notwithstanding that it seems to admit the right of society to condemn homosexuality and prostitution as immoral, requires special circumstances to be shown to justify the intervention of the law. I think that this is wrong in principle and that any attempt to approach my second interrogatory on these lines is bound to break down. I think that the attempt by the Committee does break down and that this is shown by the fact that it has to define or describe its special circumstances so widely that they can be supported only if it is accepted that the law *is* concerned with immorality as such.

The widest of the special circumstances are described as the provision of "sufficient safeguards against exploitation and corruption of others, particularly those who are specially vulnerable because they are young, weak in body or mind, inexperienced, or in a state of special physical, official or economic dependence." The corruption of youth is a well-recognized ground for intervention by the State and for the purpose of any legislation the young can easily be defined. But if similar protection were to be extended to every other citizen, there would be no limit to the reach of the law. The "corruption and exploitation of others" is so wide that it could be used to cover any sort of immorality which involves, as most do, the co-operation of another person. Even if the phrase is taken as limited to the categories that are particularized as "specially vulnerable," it is so elastic as to be practically no restriction. This is not merely a matter of words. For if the words used are stretched almost beyond breaking-point, they still are not wide enough to cover the recommendations which the Committee make about prostitution.

Prostitution is not in itself illegal and the Committee do not think that it ought to be made so. If prostitution is private immorality and not the law's business, what concern has the law with the ponce or the brothel-keeper or the householder who permits habitual prostitution? The Report recommends that the laws which make these activities criminal offences should be maintained or strengthened and brings them (so far as it goes into principle; with regard to brothels it says simply that the law rightly frowns on them) under the head of exploitation. There may be cases of exploitation in this trade, as there are or used to be in many others, but in general a ponce exploits a prostitute no more than an impresario exploits an actress. The Report finds that "the great majority of prostitutes are women whose psychological makeup is such that they choose this life because they find in it a style of living which is to them easier, freer and more profitable than would be provided by any other occupation.... In the main the association between prostitute and ponce is voluntary and operates to mutual advantage." The Committee would agree that this could not be called exploitation in the ordinary sense. They say: "It is in our view an over-simplification to think that those who live on the earnings of prostitution are exploiting the prostitute as such. What they are really exploiting is the whole complex of the relationship between prostitute and customer; they are, in effect, exploiting the human weaknesses which cause the customer to seek the prostitute and the prostitute to meet the demand."

All sexual immorality involves the exploitation of human weaknesses. The prostitute exploits the lust of her customers and the customer the moral weakness of the prostitute. If the exploitation of human weaknesses is considered to create a special circumstance, there is virtually no field of morality which can be defined in such a way as to exclude the law.

I think, therefore, that it is not possible to set theoretical limits to the power of the State to legislate against immorality. It is not possible to settle in advance exceptions to the general rule or to define inflexibly areas of morality into which the law is in no circumstances to be allowed to enter. Society is entitled by means of its laws to protect itself from dangers, whether from within or without. Here again I think that the political parallel is legitimate. The law of treason is directed against aiding the king's enemies and against sedition from within. The justification for this is that established government is necessary for the existence of society and therefore its safety against violent overthrow must be secured. But an established morality is as necessary as good government to the welfare of society. Societies disintegrate from within more frequently than they are broken up by external pressures. There is disintegration when no common morality is observed and history shows that the loosening of moral bonds is often the first stage of disintegration, so that society is justified in taking the same steps to preserve its moral code as it does to preserve its government and other essential institutions. The suppression of vice is as much the law's business as the suppression of subversive activities; it is no more possible to define a sphere of private morality than it is to define one of private subversive activity. It is wrong to talk of private morality or of the law not being concerned with immorality as such or to try to set rigid bounds to the part which the law may play in the suppression of vice. There are no theoretical limits to the power of the State to legislate against treason and sedition, and likewise I think there can be no theoretical limits to legislation against immorality. You may argue that if a man's sins affect only himself it cannot be the concern of society. If he chooses to get drunk every night in the privacy of his own home, is any one except himself the worse for it? But suppose a quarter or a half of the population got drunk every night, what sort of society would it be? You cannot set a theoretical limit to the number of people who can get drunk before society is entitled to legislate against drunkenness. The same may be said of gambling. The Royal Commission on Betting, Lotteries, and Gaming took as their test the character of the citizen as a member of society. They said: "Our concern with the ethical significance of gambling is confined to the effect which it may have on the character of the gambler as a member of society. If we were convinced that whatever the degree of gambling this effect must be harmful we should be inclined to think that it was the duty of the state to restrict gambling to the greatest extent practicable."

In what circumstances the State should exercise its power is the third of the interrogatories I have framed. But before I get to it I must raise a point which might have been brought up in any one of the three. How are the moral judgements of society to be ascertained? By leaving it until now, I can ask it in the more limited form that is now sufficient for my purpose. How is the law-maker to ascertain the moral judgements of society? It is surely not enough that they should be reached by the opinion of the majority; it would be too much to require the individual assent of every citizen. English law has evolved and regularly uses a standard which does not depend on the counting of heads. It is that of the reasonable man. He is not to be confused with the rational man. He is not expected to reason about anything and his judgement may be largely a matter of feeling. It is the viewpoint of the man in the street—or to use an archaism familiar to all lawyers—the man in the Clapham omnibus. He might also be called the right-minded man. For my purpose I should like to call him the man in the jury box, for the moral judgement of society must be something about which any twelve men or women drawn at random might after discussion be expected to be unanimous. This was the standard the judges applied in the days before Parliament was as active as it is now and when they laid down rules of public policy. They did not think of themselves as making law but simply as stating principles which every right-minded person would accept as valid. It is what Pollock called "practical morality," which is based not on theological or philosophical foundations but "in the mass of continuous experience half-consciously or unconsciously accumulated and embodied in the morality of common sense." He called it also "a certain way of thinking on questions of morality which we expect to find in a reasonable civilized man or a reasonable Englishman, taken at random."

Immorality then, for the purpose of the law, is what every right-minded person is presumed to consider to immoral. Any immorality is capable of affecting society injuriously and in effect to a greater or lesser extent it usually does; this is what gives the law its *locus standi*. It cannot be shut out. But—and this brings me to the third question—the individual has a *locus standi* too; he cannot be expected to surrender to the judgement of society the whole conduct of his life. It is the old and familiar question of striking a balance between the rights and interests of society and those of the individual. This is something which the law is constantly doing in matters large and small. To take a very down-to-earth example, let me consider the right of the individual whose house adjoins the highway to have access to it; that means in these days the right to have vehicles stationary in the highway, sometimes for a considerable time if there is a lot of loading or unloading. There are many cases in which the courts have had to balance the private right of access against the public right to use the highway without obstruction. It cannot be done by carving up the highway into public and private areas. It is done by recognizing that each have rights over the whole; that if each were to exercise their rights to the full, they would come into conflict; and therefore that the rights of each must be curtailed so as to ensure as far as possible that the essential needs of each are safeguarded.

I do not think that one can talk sensibly of a public and private morality any more than one can of a public or private highway. Morality is a sphere in which there is a public interest and a private interest, often in conflict, and the problem is to reconcile the two. This does not mean that it is impossible to put forward any general statements about how in our society the balance ought to be struck. Such statements cannot of their nature be rigid or precise; they would not be designed to circumscribe the operation of the law-making power but to guide those who have to apply it. While every decision which a court of law makes when it balances the public against the private interest is an *ad hoc* decision, the cases contain statements of principle to which the court should have regard when it reaches its decision. In the same way it is possible to make general statements of principle which it may be thought the legislature should bear in mind when it is considering the enactment of laws enforcing morals.

I believe that most people would agree upon the chief of these elastic principles. There must be toleration of the maximum individual freedom that is consistent with the integrity of society. It cannot be said that this is a principle that runs all through the criminal law. Much of the criminal law that is regulatory in character—the part of it that deals with *malum prohibitum* rather than *malum in se*—is based upon the opposite principle, that is, that the choice of the individual must give way to the convenience of the many. But in all matters of conscience the principle I have stated is generally held to prevail. It is not confined to thought and speech; it extends to action, as is shown by the recognition of the right to conscientious objection in war-time; this example shows also that conscience will be respected even in times of national danger. The principle appears to me to be peculiarly approriate to all questions of morals. Nothing should be punished by the law that does not lie beyond the limits of tolerance. It is not nearly enough to say that a majority dislike a practice; there must be a real feeling of reprobation. Those who are dissatisfied with the present law on homosexuality often say that the opponents of reform are swayed simply by disgust. If that were so it would be wrong, but I do not think one can ignore disgust if it is deeply felt and not manufactured. Its presence is a good indication that the bounds of toleration are being reached. Not everything is to be tolerated. No society can do without intolerance, indignation, and disgust; they are the forces behind the moral law, and indeed it can be argued that if they or something like them are not present, the feelings of society cannot be weighty enough to deprive the individual of freedom of choice. I suppose that there is hardly anyone nowadays who would not be disgusted by the thought of deliberate cruelty to animals. No one proposes to relegate that or any other form of sadism to the realm of private morality or to allow it to be practiced in public or in private. It would be possible no doubt to point out that until a comparatively short while ago nobody thought very much of cruelty to animals and also that pity and kindliness and the unwillingness to inflict pain are virtues more generally esteemed now than they have ever been in the past. But matters of this sort are not determined by rational argument. Every moral judgement, unless it claims a divine source, is simply a feeling that no right-minded man could behave in any other way without admitting that he was doing wrong. It is the power of a common sense and not the power of reason that is behind the judgements of society. But before a society can put a practice beyond the limits of tolerance there must be a deliberate judgement that the practice is injurious to society. There is, for example, a general abhorrence of homosexuality. We should ask ourselves in the first instance whether, looking at it calmly and dispassionately, we regard it as a vice so abominable that its mere presence is an offence. If that is the genuine feeling of the society in which we live, I do not see how society can be denied the right to eradicate it. Our feeling may not be so intense as that. We may feel about it that, if confined, it is tolerable, but that if it spread it might be gravely injurious; it is in this way that most societies look upon fornication, seeing it as a natural weakness which must be kept within bounds but which cannot be rooted out. It becomes then a question of balance, the danger to society in one scale and the extent of the restriction in the other. On this sort of point the value of an investigation by such a body as the Wolfenden Committee and of its conclusions is manifest.

The limits of tolerance shift. This is supplementary to what I have been saying but of sufficient importance in itself to deserve statement as a separate principle which law-makers have to bear in mind. I suppose that moral standards do not shift; so far as they come from divine revelation they do not, and I am willing assume that the moral judgements made by a society always remain good for that society. But the extent to which society will tolerate—I mean tolerate, not approve—departures from moral standards varies from generation to generation. It may be that over-all tolerance is always increasing. The pressure of the human mind, always seeking greater freedom of thought, is outwards against the bonds of society forcing their gradual relaxation. It may be that history is a tale of contraction and expansion and that all developed societies are on their way to dissolution. I must not speak of things I do not know; and anyway as a practical matter no society is willing to make provision for its own decay. I return therefore to the simple and observable fact that in matters of morals the limits of tolerance shift. Laws, especially those which are based on morals, are less easily moved. It follows as another good working principle that in any new matter of morals the law should be slow to act. By the next generation the swell of indignation may have abated and law be left without the strong backing which it needs. But it is then difficult to alter the law without giving the impression that moral judgement is being weakened. This is now one of the factors that is strongly militating against any alteration to the law on homosexuality.

A third elastic principle must be advanced more tentatively. It is that as far as possible privacy should be respected. This is not an idea that has ever been made explicit in the criminal law. Acts or words done or said in public or in private are all brought within its scope without distinction in principle. But there goes with this a strong reluctance on the part of judges and legislators to sanction invasions of privacy in the detection of crime. The police have no more right to trespass than the ordinary citizen has; there is no general right of search; to this extent an Englishman's home is still his castle. The Government is extremely careful in the exercise even of those powers which it claims to be undisputed. Telephone tapping and interference with the mails afford a good illustration of this. A Committee of three Privy Councillors who recently inquired into these activities found that the Home Secretary and his predecessors had already formulated strict rules governing the exercise of these powers and the Committee were able to recommend that they should be continued to be exercised substantially on the same terms. But they reported that the power was "regarded with general disfavour."

This indicates a general sentiment that the right to privacy is something to be put in the balance against the enforcement of the law. Ought the same sort of consideration to play any part in the formation of the law? Clearly only in a very limited number of cases. When the help of the law is invoked by an injured citizen, privacy must be irrelevant; the individual cannot ask that his right to privacy should be measured against injury criminally done to another. But when all who are involved in the deed are consenting parties and the injury is done to morals, the public interest in the moral order can be balanced against the claims of privacy. The restriction on police powers of investigation goes further than the affording of a parallel; it means that the detection of crime committed in private and when there is no complaint is bound to be rather haphazard and this is an additional reason for moderation. These considerations do not justify the exclusion of all private immorality from the scope of the law. I think that, as I have already suggested, the test of "private behavior" should be substituted for "private morality" and the influence of the factor should be reduced from that of a definite limitation to that of a matter to be taken into account. Since the gravity of the crime is also a proper consideration, a distinction might well be made in the case of homosexuality between the lesser acts of indecency and the full offence, which on the principles of the Wolfenden Report it would be illogical to do.

The last and the biggest thing to be remembered is that the law is concerned with the minimum and not with the maximum; there is much in the Sermon on the Mount that would be out of place in the Ten Commandments. We all recognize the gap between the moral law and the law of the land. No man is worth much who regulates his conduct with the sole object of escaping punishment, and every worthy society sets for its members standards which are above those of the law. We recognize the existence of such higher standards when we use expressions such as "moral obligation" and "morally bound." The distinction was well put in the judgement of African elders in a family dispute: "We have power to make you divide the crops, for this is our law, and we will see this is done. But we have not power to make you behave like an upright man."

Immorality and Treason

H.L.A. Hart

The most remarkable feature of Sir Patrick's [i.e., Sir Patrick Devlin's] lecture is his view of the nature of morality—the morality which the criminal law may enforce. Most previous thinkers who have repudiated the liberal point of view have done so because they thought that morality consisted either of divine commands or of rational principles of human conduct discoverable by human reason. Since morality for them had this elevated divine or rational status as the law of God or reason, it seemed obvious that the state should enforce it, and that the function of human law should not be merely to provide men with the opportunity for leading a good life, but actually to see that they lead it. Sir Patrick does not rest his repudiation of the liberal point of view on these religious or rationalist conceptions. Indeed much that he writes reads like an abjuration of the notion that reasoning or thinking has much to do with morality. English popular morality has no doubt its historical connection with the Christian religion: 'That', says Sir Patrick, 'is how it got there'. But it does not owe its present status or social significance to religion any more than to reason.

What, then, is it? According to Sir Patrick it is primarily a matter of feeling. 'Every moral judgment', he says, 'is a feeling that no right-minded man could act in any other way without admitting that he was doing wrong.' Who then must feel this way if we are to have what Sir Patrick calls a public morality? He tells us that it is 'the man in the street', 'the man in the jury box', or (to use the

From *The Listener* (July 30, 1959), pp. 162–163. Copyright H.L.A. Hart, 1959. Reprinted by permission.

phrase so familiar to English lawyers) 'the man on the Clapham omnibus.' For the moral judgments of society so far as the law is concerned are to be ascertained by the standards of the reasonable man, and he is not to be confused with the rational man. Indeed, Sir Patrick says 'he is not expected to reason about anything and his judgment may be largely a matter of feeling.'

INTOLERANCE, INDIGNATION, AND DISGUST

But what precisely are the relevant feelings, the feelings which may justify use of the criminal law? Here the argument becomes a little complex. Widespread dislike of a practice is not enough. There must, says Sir Patrick, be 'a real feeling of reprobation'. Disgust is not enough either. What is crucial is a combination of intolerance, indignation, and disgust. These three are the forces behind the moral law, without which it is not 'weighty enough to deprive the individual of freedom of choice'. Hence there is, in Sir Patrick's outlook, a crucial difference between the mere adverse moral judgment of society and one which is inspired by feeling raised to the concert pitch of intolerance, indignation, and disgust.

This distinction is novel and also very important. For on it depends the weight to be given to the fact that when morality is enforced individual liberty is necessarily cut down. Though Sir Patrick's abstract formulation of his views on this point is hard to follow, his examples make his position fairly clear. We can see it best in the contrasting things he says about fornication and homosexuality. In regard to fornication, public feeling in most societies is not now of the concert-pitch intensity. We may feel that it is tolerable if confined: only its spread might be gravely injurious. In such cases the question whether individual liberty should be restricted is for Sir Patrick a question of balance between the danger to society in the one scale, and the restriction of the individual in the other. But if, as may be the case with homosexuality, public feeling is up to concert pitch, if it expresses a 'deliberate judgment' that a practice as such is injurious to society, if there is 'a genuine feeling that it is a vice so abominable that its mere presence is an offence', then it is beyond the limits of tolerance, and society may eradicate it. In this case, it seems, no further balancing of the claims of individual liberty is to be done, though as a matter of prudence the legislator should remember that the popular limits of tolerance may shift: the concert-pitch feeling may subside. This may produce a dilemma for the law; for the law may then be left without the full moral backing that it needs, yet it cannot be altered without giving the impression that the moral judgment is being weakened.

A SHARED MORALITY

If this is what morality is—a compound of indignation, intolerance, and disgust—we may well ask what justification there is for taking it, and turning it as such, into criminal law with all the misery which criminal punishment entails. Here Sir Patrick's answer is very clear and simple. A collection of individuals is not a society; what makes them into a society is among other things a shared or public morality. This is as necessary to its existence as an organized government. So society may use the law to preserve its morality like anything else essential to it. 'The suppression of vice is as much the law's business as the suppression of subversive activities'. The liberal point of view which denies this is guilty of 'an error in jurisprudence': for it is no more possible to define an area of private morality than an area of private subversive activity. There can be no 'theoretical limits' to legislation against immorality just as there are no such limits to the power of the state to legislate against treason and sedition.

Surely all this, ingenious as it is, is misleading. Mill's formulation of the liberal point of view may well be too simple. The grounds for interfering with human liberty are more various than the single criterion of 'harm to others' suggests: cruelty to animals or organizing prostitution for gain do not, as Mill himself saw, fall easily under the description of harm to others. Conversely, even where there is harm to others in the most literal sense, there may well be other principles limiting the extent to which harmful activities should be repressed by law. So there are multiple criteria, not a single criterion, determining when human liberty may be restricted. Perhaps this is what Sir Patrick means by a curious distinction which he often stresses between theoretical and practical limits. But with all its simplicities the liberal point of view is a better guide than Sir Patrick to clear thought on the proper relation of morality to the criminal law: for it stresses what he obscures—namely, the points at which thought is needed before we turn popular morality into criminal law.

SOCIETY AND MORAL OPINION

No doubt we would all agree that a consensus of moral opinion on certain matters is essential if society is to be worth living in. Laws against murder, theft, and much else would be of little use if they were not supported by a widely diffused conviction that what these laws forbid is also immoral. So much is obvious. But it does not follow that everything to which the moral vetoes of accepted morality attach is of equal importance to society; nor is there the slightest reason for thinking of morality as a seamless web: one which will fall to pieces carrying society with it, unless all its emphatic vetoes are enforced by law. Surely even in the face of the moral feeling that is up to concert pitch—the trio of intolerance, indignation, and disgust—we must pause to think. We must ask a question at two different levels which Sir Patrick never clearly enough identifies or separates. First, we must ask whether a practice which offends moral feeling is harmful, independently of its repercussion on the general moral code. Secondly, what about repercussion on the moral code? Is it really true that failure to translate this item of general morality into criminal law will jeopardize the whole fabric of morality and so of society?

We cannot escape thinking about these two different questions merely by repeating to ourselves the vague nostrum: 'This is part of public morality and public morality must be preserved if society is to exist.' Sometimes Sir Patrick seems to admit this, for he says in words which both Mill and the Wolfenden Report might have used, that there must be the maximum respect for individual liberty consistent with the integrity of society. Yet this, as his contrasting examples of fornication and homosexuality show, turns out to mean only that the immorality which the law may punish must be generally felt to be intolerable. This plainly is no adequate substitute for a reasoned estimate of the damage to the fabric of society likely to ensue if it is not suppressed.

Nothing perhaps shows more clearly the inadequacy of Sir Patrick's approach to this problem than his comparison between the suppression of sexual immorality and the suppression of treason or subversive activity. Private subversive activity is, of course, a contradiction in terms because 'subversion' means overthrowing government, which is a public thing. But it is grotesque, even where moral feeling against homosexuality is up to concert pitch, to think of the homosexual behaviour of two adults in private as in any way like treason or sedition either in intention or effect. We can make it *seem* like treason only if we assume that deviation from a general moral code is bound to affect that code, and to lead not merely to its modification but to its destruction. The analogy could begin to be plausible only if it was clear that offending against this item of morality was likely to jeopardize the whole structure. But we have ample evidence for believing that people will not abandon morality, will not think any better of murder, cruelty, and dishonesty, merely because some private sexual practice which they abominate is not punished by the law.

Because this is so the analogy with treason is absurd. Of course 'No man is an island': what one man does in private, if it is known, may affect others in many different ways. Indeed it may be that deviation from general sexual morality by those whose lives, like the lives of many homosexuals, are noble ones and in all other ways exemplary will lead to what Sir Patrick calls the shifting of the limits of tolerance. But if this has any analogy in the sphere of government it is not the overthrow of ordered government, but a peaceful change in its form. So we may listen to the promptings of common sense and of logic, and say that though there could not logically be a sphere of private treason there is a sphere of private morality and immorality.

Sir Patrick's doctrine is also open to a wider, perhaps a deeper, criticism. In his reaction against a rationalist morality and his stress on feeling, he has I think thrown out the baby and kept the bath water; and the bath water may turn out to be very dirty indeed. When Sir Patrick's lecture was first delivered *The Times* greeted it with these words: 'There is a moving and welcome humility in the conception that society should not be asked to give its reason for refusing to tolerate what in its heart it feels intolerable.' This drew from a correspondent in Cambridge the retort: 'I am afraid that we are less humble than we used to be. We once burnt old women because, without giving our reasons, we felt in our hearts that witchcraft was intolerable.'

This retort is a bitter one, yet its bitterness is salutary. We are not, I suppose, likely, in England, to take again to the burning of old women for witchcraft or to punishing people for associating with those of a different race or colour, or to punishing people again for adultery. Yet if these things were viewed with intolerance, indignation, and disgust, as the second of them still is in some countries, it seems that on Sir Patrick's principles no rational criticism could be opposed to the claim that they should be punished by law. We could only pray, in his words, that the limits of tolerance might shift.

CURIOUS LOGIC

It is impossible to see what curious logic has led Sir Patrick to this result. For him a practice is immoral if the thought of it makes the man on the Clapham omnibus sick. So be it. Still, why should we not summon all the resources of our reason, sympathetic understanding, as well as critical intelligence, and insist that before general moral feeling is turned into criminal law it is submitted to scrutiny of a different kind from Sir Patrick's? Surely, the legislator should ask whether the general morality is based on ignorance, superstition, or misunder-standing; whether there is a false conception that those who practice what it condemns are in other ways dangerous or hostile to society; and whether the misery to many parties, the blackmail and the other evil consequences of criminal punishment, especially for sexual offences, are well understood. It is surely extraordinary that among the things which Sir Patrick says are to be considered before we legislate against immorality these appear nowhere; not even as 'practical considerations', let alone 'theoretical limits'. To any theory which, like this one, asserts that the criminal law may be used on the vague ground that the preservation of morality is essential to society and yet omits to stress the need for critical scrutiny, our reply should be: 'Morality, what crimes may be committed in thy name!'

As Mill saw, and de Tocqueville showed in detail long ago in his critical but sympathetic study of democracy, it is fatally easy to confuse the democratic principle that power should be in the hands of the majority with the utterly different claim that the majority with power in their hands need respect no limits. Certainly there is a special risk in a democracy that the majority may dictate how all should live. This is the risk we run, and should gladly run; for it is the price of all that is so good in democratic rule. But loyalty to democratic principles does not require us to maximize this risk: yet this is what we shall do if we mount the man in the street on the top of the Clapham omnibus and tell him that if only he feels sick enough about what other people do in private to demand its suppression by law no theoretical criticism can be made of his demand.

SUGGESTED SUPPLEMENTARY READINGS TO PART ONE

Acton, Harry B.: *Kant's Moral Philosophy* (London: Macmillan and Co., Ltd., 1970).

Baier, Kurt: *The Moral Point of View: A Rational Basis for Ethics* (Ithaca, N.Y.: Cornell University Press, 1958).

Cooper, John M.: *Reason and the Human Good in Aristotle* (Cambridge, Mass.: Harvard University Press, 1975).

Dworkin, Ronald: "Lord Devlin and the Enforcement of Morals," *Yale Law Journal,* 75:986–1005, 1966.

Feinberg, Joel: *Doing and Deserving* (Princeton, N.J.: Princeton University Press, 1970).

Feinberg, Joel: *Social Philosophy* (Englewood Cliffs, N.J.: Prentice-Hall, Inc., 1973).

Held, Virginia: *Property, Profits, and Economic Justice* (Belmont, Calif.: Wadsworth Publishing Co., Inc., 1980).

MacIntyre, Alasdair C.: *After Virtue* (Notre Dame, Ind.: University of Notre Dame Press, 1981).

MacIntyre, Alasdair C.: *A Short History of Ethics* (New York: Macmillan Publishing Co., 1966).

Marx, Karl: *Economic and Philosophical Manuscripts* in T.B. Bottomore, ed., *Karl Marx: Early Writings* (London: C.A. Watts and Co., Ltd., 1963).

Paton, Herbert J.: *The Categorical Imperative* (Chicago: University of Chicago Press, 1948).

Plamenatz, John: *The English Utilitarians* (Oxford: Humanities Press, 1949).

Plato: *The Republic,* trans., Francis Cornford (New York: Oxford University Press, 1945).

Quinton, Anthony, ed.: *Utilitarian Ethics* (New York: St. Martin's Press, 1973).

Sterba, James: *The Demands of Justice* (Notre Dame, Ind.: University of Notre Dame Press, 1980).

Wolff, Robert Paul: *In Defense of Anarchism* (New York: Harper Torchbooks, 1970).

CENSORSHIP AND SEXUAL ETHICS

INTRODUCTION

People frequently argue over whether a book, movie, or play is sexually explicit to the point of being immoral. But the question of morality alone is not what makes the controversy over censorship and pornography so vexing. Indeed, it is not uncommon for *both* those condemning and advocating censorship to agree that a given book or movie is immoral. They agree, in other words, that intelligent, sensitive persons will be offended by it, but disagree about whether the law should prohibit its distribution. Again, we are faced with the issue of law and its relationship to morality discussed in Part One. Because of the legalistic fallacy, we cannot conclude that simply *because* something is immoral it should also be illegal. By banning a given book or movie, has the law placed an unacceptable limitation on personal liberty? Or, has it merely moved to protect the public's interest in maintaining moral standards and avoiding offensive materials?

In the Supreme Court case, *Paris Adult Theater I v. Slaton,* excerpts of which are reprinted in Part Two, the court established key principles that now regulate pornographic materials. Central to the case were two films shown by an Atlanta, Georgia, movie house entitled "It All Comes Out in the End" and "Magic Mirror," films that the Georgia Supreme Court found in violation of the state's pornography laws. The U.S. Supreme Court, in a split decision (5 to 4), upheld the lower court's decision, despite the fact that the films were not shown to minors and were exhibited in a private theater to consenting viewers. Chief Justice Burger, writing the majority opinion, argued that the state *had an interest in regulating the activity even of consenting adults.* Granting that no proof existed establishing a connection between the viewing of pornographic material and antisocial material, he nontheless insisted that the assumption of such a connection was a reasonable one.

Dissenting Justices, however, raised the issue of individual liberty in criticizing the majority opinion. The pressing question from their standpoint was whether a violation of the First Amendment to the Constitution (the "free speech" amendment) had occurred. They concluded that it had occurred insofar as the "state interest" that existed in the regulation of pornographic material was insufficient to override the right to freedom of speech guaranteed by the Constitution. In the case at hand, they insisted, the only viewers of the film were both non-minors and consenting adults. Given especially the problem of defining "obscenity" and the absence of proof connecting pornography with antisocial behavior, government should refrain from intruding into the private lives of individuals.

Two standard arguments against pornography reflect first a communitarian, and second an individualistic concern. In the first argument, the focus is on the welfare of the state and community, a focus that emphasizes effects of pornography upon criminal activity and the general standards of decency in a community. Chief Justice Burger's reference to "state interest" is communitarian in this sense. A similar argument, centuries old, was offered by Plato, who endorsed censorship as a necessary ingredient for the just state. In contrast, the second argument is personal in emphasis. It looks inward to the moral temper of the person affected by pornography. St. Paul, for example, appears to take this approach in the Bible.

In Walter Berns' "Democracy, Censorship and the Arts," we find Berns utilizing aspects of both the communitarian and personal approach in his justification of censorship. He grants that powerful and uplifting art has sometimes offended public tastes, but denies that society should abrogate its right to censor such art. Society has a stake in the moral quality of the books, plays, and movies it produces, and what is more, it has a right to protect that stake. In a democratic society, Berns reminds us, citizens have a right to express general preferences in a way that restricts the actions of a minority, even an elite minority. The regulation of obscene materials, thus, is viewed as an acceptable expression of majority rule.

In another condemnation of pornography, the philosopher, Ann Garry, argues that pornography degrades women. Pornography is bad because it tends to reduce women to sex objects, and thus fails to display respect for persons. Interestingly enough, while Garry's argument is aimed at pornography *in its present form*, she leaves the door open to the development of acceptable pornography in the future.

Yet even if Garry is right about the immorality of pornography, the question remains whether it should be regulated by law. Hence, we are brought full circle to the question at the beginning: if we prize personal liberty, then what in the context of sexually explicit materials constitutes a justified limitation on the exercise of that freedom? In the next article of this section, the philosopher,

Joel Feinberg, attempts to untangle the ways in which individual liberty can, and cannot, be acceptably restricted. Taking as his point of departure John Stuart Mill's "harm principle," which asserts that restrictions on liberty are justified only when failure to restrict would harm another, Feinberg goes on to ask whether any other justifications for restricting liberty exist. One might, for example, restrict liberty on the basis of harm to the very individual exercising that liberty. On this view, pornography should be restricted because it harms the viewer. Or one might restrict liberty on the basis of the mere immorality of material itself; hence, pornography should be restricted simply because it is immoral. In the end, however, Feinberg rejects such justifications. The only justification for censoring pornography, he believes, is that it is directly offensive. Furthermore it should be censored only when (1) others are not at liberty to avoid it (as in the case of a pornographic billboard); and (2) virtually everyone agrees that it is offensive.

The remaining articles of Part Two turn from the issue of censorship to confront sexual ethics directly. John Finnis sounds a theme already familiar from Part One when he adopts an Aristotelian posture to show why sexual practices such as premarital sex and homosexuality are genuinely immoral. Finnis uses the term "natural law" to characterize his argument, and his use of it reminds us of Aristotle's integration of moral knowledge with an understanding of the natural "telos" of human beings. The natural law approach to ethics, articulated in great detail by St. Thomas Aquinas, has special significance in the context of sexual ethics, for it is a cornerstone of much modern day Catholic teaching, teaching that has taken a strong stand on the immorality of a number of sexual practices, including premarital sex, homosexuality, and masturbation.

In "Homosexuality and Natural Law," Burton Leiser challenges the very notion that natural law can be used to condemn sexual behavior. How, for example, he asks, are we to determine the meaning of the terms "natural" and "unnatural"? The very vagueness of the terms, along with other problems of internal consistency, he concludes, add up to make natural law's condemnation of homosexuality in particular a philosophical failure.

Paris Adult Theater I. v. Slaton*

MR. CHIEF JUSTICE BURGER delivered the opinion of the Court.

Petitioners are two Atlanta, Georgia, movie theaters and their owners and managers, operating in the style of "adult" theaters. [T]he local state district attorney alleg[ed] that petitioners were exhibiting to the public for paid admission two allegedly obscene films, contrary to Georgia Code. The two films in question, "Magic Mirror" and "It All Comes Out in the End," depict sexual conduct characterized by the Georgia Supreme Court as "hard core pornography" leaving "little to the imagination."

After reviewing the films, the Georgia Supreme Court held that their exhibition should have been enjoined, stating:

> The films in this case leave little to the imagination. It is plain what they purport to depict, that is, conduct of the most salacious character. We hold that these films are also hard core pornography, and the showing of such films should have been enjoined since their exhibition is not protected by the first amendment.
>
> It should be clear from the outset that we do not undertake to tell the States what they must do, but rather to define the area in which they may chart their own course in dealing with obscene material. This Court has consistently held that obscene material is not protected by the First Amendment as a limitation on the state police power by virtue of the Fourteenth Amendment.

We categorically disapprove the theory, apparently adopted by the trial judge, that obscene, pornographic films acquire constitutional immunity from state regulation simply because they are exhibited for consenting adults only.

In particular, we hold that there are legitimate state interests at stake in stemming the tide of commercialized obscenity, even assuming that it is feasible to enforce effective safeguards against exposure to juveniles and to passersby. Rights and interests "other than those of the advocates are involved." These include the interest of the public in the quality of life and the total community environment, the tone of commerce in the great city centers, and, possibly, the public safety itself. The Hill-Link Minority Report of the Commission on Obscenity and Pornography indicates that there is at least an arguable correlation between obscene material and crime. Quite apart from sex crimes, however, there remains one problem of large proportions aptly described by Professor Bickel:

> It concerns the tone of the society, the mode, or to use terms that have perhaps greater currency, the style and quality of life, now and in the future. A man may be entitled to read an obscene book in his room or expose himself indecently there.... We should protect his privacy. But if he demands a right to obtain the books and pictures he wants in the market, and to foregather in public places—discreet, if you will, but accessible to all—with others who share his tastes, *then to grant him his right*

*413 U.S. 49, 93 S. Ct. 2628 (1973). Excerpts from the written opinions of Justices Burger, Douglas, and Brennan. References and footnotes omitted. Abridged by the editor.

is to affect the world about the rest of us, and to impinge on other privacies. Even supposing that each of us can, if he wishes, effectively avert the eye and stop the ear (which, in truth, we cannot), what is commonly read and seen and heard and done intrudes upon us all, want it or not.

But, it is argued, there are no scientific data which conclusively demonstrate that exposure to obscene material adversely affects men and women or their society. It is urged on behalf of the petitioners that, absent such a demonstration, any kind of state regulation is "impermissible." We reject this argument. It is not for us to resolve empirical uncertainties underlying state legislation, save the exceptional case where that legislation plainly impinges upon rights protected by the Constitution itself. Although there is no conclusive proof of a connection between antisocial behavior and obscene material, the legislature of Georgia could quite reasonably determine that such a connection does or might exist.

From the beginning of civilized societies, legislators and judges have acted on various unprovable assumptions. Such assumptions underlie much lawful state regulation of commercial and business affairs. The same is true of the federal securities and antitrust laws and a host of federal regulations. On the basis of these assumptions both Congress and state legislatures have, for example, drastically restricted associational rights by adopting antitrust laws, and have strictly regulated public expression by issuers of and dealers in securities, profit sharing "coupons," and "trading stamps," commanding what they must and must not publish and announce. Understandably those who entertain an absolutist view of the First Amendment find it uncomfortable to explain why rights of association, speech, and press should be severely restrained in the marketplace of goods and money, but not in the marketplace of pornography.

If we accept the unprovable assumption that a complete education requires certain books, and the well nigh universal belief that good books, plays, and art lift the spirit, improve the mind, enrich the human personality, and develop character, can we then say that a state legislature may not act on the corollary assumption that commerce in obscene books, or public exhibitions focused on obscene conduct, have a tendency to exert a corrupting and debasing impact leading to antisocial behavior? The sum of experience, including that of the past two decades, affords an ample basis for legislatures to conclude that a sensitive, key relationship of human existence, central to family life, community welfare, and the development of human personality, can be debased and distorted by crass commercial exploitation of sex. Nothing in the Constitution prohibits a State from reaching such a conclusion and acting on it legislatively simply because there is no conclusive evidence or empirical data.

It is argued that individual "free will" must govern, even in activities beyond the protection of the First Amendment and other constitutional guarantees of privacy, and that government cannot legitimately impede an individual's desire to see or acquire obscene plays, movies, and books. We do indeed base our society on certain assumptions that people have the capacity for free choice.

Most exercises of individual free choice—those in politics, religion, and expression of ideas—are explicitly protected by the Constitution. Totally unlimited play for free will, however, is not allowed in our or any other society. We have just noted, for example, that neither the First Amendment nor "free will" precludes States from having "blue sky" laws to regulate what sellers of securities may write or publish about their wares. Such laws are to protect the weak, the uninformed, the unsuspecting, and the gullible from the exercise of their own volition. Nor do modern societies leave disposal of garbage and sewage up to the individual "free will," but impose regulation to protect both public health and the appearance of public places. States are told by some that they must await a "laissez faire" market solution to the obscenity-pornography problem, paradoxically "by people who have never otherwise had a kind word to say for laissez-faire," particularly in solving urban, commercial, and environmental pollution problems.

Finally, petitioners argue that conduct which directly involves "consenting adults" only has, for that sole reason, a special claim to constitutional protection. Our Constitution establishes a broad range of conditions on the exercise of power by the States, but for us to say that our Constitution incorporates the proposition that conduct involving consenting adults only is always beyond state regulation, is a step we are unable to take. Commercial exploitation of depictions, descriptions, or exhibitions of obscene conduct on commercial premises open to the adult public falls within a State's broad power to regulate commerce and protect the public environment. The issue in this context goes beyond whether someone, or even the majority, considers the conduct depicted as "wrong" or "sinful." The States have the power to make a morally neutral judgment that public exhibition of obscene material, or commerce in such material, has a tendency to injure the community as a whole, to endanger the public safety, or to jeopardize, in Mr. Chief Justice Warren's words, the States' "right...to maintain a decent society."

To summarize, we have today reaffirmed the basic holding of *Roth v. United States* that obscene material has no protection under the First Amendment.

In this case we hold that the States have a legitimate interest in regulating commerce in obscene material and in regulating exhibition of obscene material in places of public accommodation.

In light of these holdings, nothing precludes the State of Georgia from the regulation of the allegedly obscene material exhibited in Paris Adult Theater I or II.

MR. JUSTICE DOUGLAS, dissenting.

I have expressed on numerous occasions my disagreement with the basic decision that held that "obscenity" was not protected by the First Amendment. I disagreed also with the definitions that evolved. Art and literature reflect tastes; and tastes, like musical appreciation, are hardly reducible to precise definitions. That is one reason I have always felt that "obscenity" was not an exception to the First Amendment. For matters of taste, like matters of belief, turn on the idiosyncrasies of individuals.

The other reason I could not bring myself to conclude that "obscenity" was not covered by the First Amendment was that prior to the adoption of our Constitution and Bill of Rights the Colonies had no law excluding "obscenity" from the regime of freedom of expression and press that then existed. I could find no such laws; and more important, our leading colonial expert, Julius Goebel, could find none.

People are, of course, offended by many offerings made by merchants in this area. They are also offended by political pronouncements, sociological themes, and by stories of official misconduct. The list of activities and publications and pronouncements that offend someone is endless. Some of it goes on in private; some of it is inescapably public, as when a government official generates crime, becomes a blatant offender of the moral sensibilities of the people, engages in burglary, or breaches the privacy of the telephone, the conference room, or the home. Life in this crowded modern technological world creates many offensive statements and many offensive deeds. There is no protection against offensive ideas, only against offensive conduct.

"Obscenity" at most is the expression of offensive ideas. There are regimes in the world where ideas "offensive" to the majority (or at least to those who control the majority) are suppressed. There life proceeds at a monotonous pace. Most of us would find that world offensive. One of the most offensive experiences in my life was a visit to a nation where bookstalls were filled only with books on mathematics and books on religion.

I am sure I would find offensive most of the books and movies charged with being obscene. But in a life that has not been short, I have yet to be trapped into seeing or reading something that would offend me. I never read or see the materials coming to the Court under charges of "obscenity," because I have thought the First Amendment made it unconstitutional for me to act as a censor. I see ads in book stores and neon lights over theaters that resemble bait for those who seek vicarious exhilaration. As a parent or a priest or as a teacher I would have no compunction in edging my children or wards away from the books and movies that did no more than excite man's base instincts. But I never supposed that government was permitted to sit in judgment on one's tastes or beliefs—save as they involved action within the reach of the police power of government.

When man was first in the jungle he took care of himself. When he entered a societal group, controls were necessarily imposed. But our society—unlike most in the world—presupposes that freedom and liberty are in a frame of reference that makes the individual, not government, the keeper of his tastes, beliefs, and ideas. That is the philosophy of the First Amendment; and it is the article of faith that sets us apart from most nations in the world.

MR. JUSTICE BRENNAN, with whom MR. JUSTICE STEWART and MR. JUSTICE MARSHALL join, dissenting.

Our experience since *Roth* requires us not only to abandon the effort to pick out obscene materials on a case-by-case basis, but also to reconsider a fundamental postulate of *Roth*: that there exists a definable class of sexually oriented expression that may be totally suppressed by the Federal and State Governments. Assuming that such a class of expression does in fact exist, I am forced to conclude that the concept of "obscenity" cannot be defined with sufficient specificity and clarity to provide fair notice to persons who create and distribute sexually oriented materials, to prevent substantial erosion of protected speech as a byproduct of the attempt to suppress unprotected speech, and to avoid very costly institutional harms. Given these inevitable side effects of state efforts to suppress what is assumed to be *unprotected* speech, we must scrutinize with care the state interest that is asserted to justify the suppression. For in the absence of some very substantial interest in suppressing such speech, we can hardly condone the ill effects that seem to flow inevitably from the effort.

In *Roe v. Wade*, we held constitutionally invalid a state abortion law, even though we were aware of

> the sensitive and emotional nature of the abortion controversy, of the vigorous opposing views, even among physicians, and of the deep and seemingly absolute convictions that the subject inspires. One's philosophy, one's experiences, one's exposure to the raw edges of human existence, one's religious training, one's attitudes toward life and family and their values, and the moral standards one establishes and seeks to observe, are all likely to influence and to color one's thinking and conclusions about abortion.

Like the proscription of abortions, the effort to suppress obscenity is predicated on unprovable, although strongly held, assumptions about human behavior, morality, sex, and religion. The existence of these assumptions cannot validate a statute that substantially undermines the guarantees of the First Amendment, any more than the existence of similar assumptions on the issue of abortion can validate a statute that infringes the constitutionally protected privacy interests of a pregnant woman.

If, as the Court today assumes, "a state legislature may...act on the...assumption that commerce in obscene books, or public exhibitions focused on obscene conduct, have a tendency to exert a corrupting and debasing impact leading to antisocial behavior," then it is hard to see how state-ordered regimentation of our minds can ever be forestalled. For if a State may, in an effort to maintain or create a particular moral tone, prescribe what its citizens cannot read or cannot see, then it would seem to follow that in pursuit of that same objective a State could decree that its citizens must read certain books or must view certain films.

In short, while I cannot say that the interests of the State—apart from the question of juveniles and unconsenting adults—are trivial or nonexistent, I am compelled to conclude that these interests cannot justify the substantial damage to constitutional rights and to the Nation's judicial machinery that inevitably results from state efforts to bar the distribution even of unprotected material to consenting adults.

Democracy, Censorship, and the Arts

Walter Berns

The case for censorship is at least as old as the case against it, and, contrary to what is usually thought today, has been made under decent and democratic auspices and by intelligent men. To the extent to which it is known today, however, it is thought to be pernicious or, at best, irrelevant to the enlightened conditions of the twentieth century. It begins from the premise that the laws cannot remain indifferent to the manner in which men amuse themselves, or to the kinds of amusements offered them. "The object of art," as Lessing put the case, "is pleasure, and pleasure is not indispensable. What kind and what degree of pleasure shall be permitted may justly depend on the law-giver."[1] Such a view, especially in this uncompromising form, appears excessively Spartan and illiberal to us; yet Lessing was one of the greatest lovers of art who ever lived and wrote.

We turn to the arts—to literature, films and the theatre, as well as to the graphic arts which were the special concern of Lessing—for the pleasure to be derived from them, and pleasure has the capacity to form our tastes and thereby to affect our lives, and the kind of people we become, and the lives of those with whom and among whom we live. Is it politically uninteresting whether men and women derive pleasure from performing their duties as citizens, parents, and spouses or, on the other hand, from watching their laws and customs and institutions ridiculed on the stage? Whether the passions are excited by, and the affections drawn to, what is noble or what is base? Whether the relations between men and women are depicted in terms of an eroticism wholly divorced from love and calculated to destroy the capacity for love and the institutions, such as the family, that depend on love? Whether a dramatist uses pleasure to attach man to what is beautiful or to what is ugly? We may not be accustomed to thinking of these things in this manner, but it is not strange that so much of the obscenity from which so many of us derive our pleasure today has an avowed political purpose.[2] It would seem that these pornographers know intuitively what liberals—for example, Morris Ernst—have forgotten, namely, that there is indeed a "causal relationship...between word or pictures and human behavior." At least they are not waiting for behavioral science to discover this fact.

The purpose is sometimes directly political and sometimes political in the sense that it will have political consequences intended or not. This latter purpose is to make us shameless, and it seems to be succeeding with astonishing speed. Activities that were once confined to the private scene—to the "ob-scene," to make an etymological assumption—are now presented for our

From Walter Berns, "Beyond the (Garbage) Pale or Democracy, Censorship and the Arts," in *Censorship and Freedom of Expression* ed. Harry M. Clor (Rand McNally, 1971). Pp. 56–63. Copyright 1971 by Rand McNally. Reprinted by permission.

[1] *Laocoön* (New York: Noonday Press), ch. 1, p. 10.

[2] *Che!* and *Hair*, for example, are political plays....

delectation and emulation in center stage. Nothing that is appropriate to one place is inappropriate to any other place. No act, we are to infer, no human possibility, no possible physical combination or connection, is shameful. Even our lawmakers now so declare. "However plebeian my tastes may be," Justice Douglas asked somewhat disingenuously in the *Ginzburg* case, "who am I to say that others' tastes must be so limited and that others' tastes have no 'social importance'?" Nothing prevents a dog from enjoying sexual intercourse in the marketplace, and it is unnatural to deprive man of the same pleasure, either actively or as voyeurs in the theater. Shame itself is unnatural, a convention devised by hypocrites to inhibit the pleasures of the body. We must get rid of our "hangups."

But what if, contrary to Freud and to what is generally assumed, shame is natural to man in the sense of being an original feature of human existence, and shamelessness unnatural in the sense of having to be acquired? What if the beauty that we are capable of knowing and achieving in our lives with each other derives from the fact that man is naturally a "blushing creature," the only creature capable of blushing? Consider the case of voyeurism, a case that, under the circumstances, comes quickly to mind. Some of us—I have even known students to confess to it—experience discomfort watching others on the stage or on the screen performing sexual acts, or even the acts preparatory to sexual acts, such as the disrobing of a woman by a man. This discomfort is caused by shame or is akin to shame. True, it could derive from the fear of being discovered enjoying what society still sees as a forbidden game. The voyeur who experiences shame in this sense is judging himself by the conventions of his society and, according to the usual modern account, the greater the distance separating him from his society in space or time, the less he will experience this kind of shame. This shame, which may be denoted as concealing shame, is a function of the fear of discovery by one's own group. The group may have its reasons for forbidding a particular act, and thereby leading those who engage in it to conceal it—to be ashamed of it—but these reasons have nothing to do with the nature of man. Voyeurism, according to this account, is a perversion only because society says it is, and a man guided only by nature would not be ashamed of it.

According to another view, however, not to be ashamed—to be a shameless voyeur—is more likely to require explanation, for voyeurism is by nature a perversion.

> Anyone who draws his sexual gratification from looking at another lives continuously at a distance. If it is normal to approach and unite with the partner, then it is precisely characteristic of the voyeur that he remains alone, without a partner, an outsider who acts in a stealthy and furtive manner. To keep his distance when it is essential to draw near is one of the paradoxes of his perversion. The looking of the voyeur is of course also a looking at and, as such, is as different from the looks exchanged by lovers as medical palpation from the gentle caress of the hand.[3]

---

[3]Erwin W. Straus, *Phenomenological Psychology* (Basic Books, New York, 1966), p. 219. I have no doubt that it is possible to want to observe sexual acts for reasons unrelated to voyeurism. Just as

From this point of view, voyeurism is perversion not merely because it is contrary to convention, but because it is contrary to nature. Convention here follows nature. Whereas sexual attraction brings man and woman together seeking a unity that culminates in the living being they together create, the voyeur maintains a distance; and because he maintains a distance he looks at, he does not communicate; and because he looks at he objectifies, he makes an object of that which is natural to join. Objectifying, he is incapable of uniting and therefore of love. The need to conceal voyeurism—the concealing shame—is corollary of the protective shame, the shame that impels lovers to search for privacy and for an experience protected from the profane and the eyes of the stranger. The stranger is "at odds with the shared unity of the [erotic couple] and his mere presence tends to introduce some objectification into every immediate relationship."[4] Shame, both concealing and protective, protects lovers and therefore love. And a polity without love—without the tenderness and the charming sentiments and the poetry and the beauty and the uniquely human things that depend on it and derive from it—a polity without love would be an unnatural monstrosity.[5]

To speak in a manner that is more obviously political, such a polity may even be impossible, except in a form unacceptable to free men. There is a connection between self-restraint and shame, and therefore a connection between shame and self-government or democracy. There is therefore a danger in promoting shamelessness and the fullest self-expression or indulgence. To live together requires rules and a governing of the passions, and those who are without shame will be unruly and unrulable; having lost the ability to restrain themselves by observing the rules they collectively give themselves, they will have to be ruled by others. Tyranny is the mode of government for the shameless and self-indulgent who have carried liberty beyond any restraint, natural and conventional.

Such was the argument made prior to the twentieth century, when it was generally understood that democracy, more than any other form of government, required self-restraint, which it would inculcate through moral education and impose on itself through laws, including laws governing the manner of public amusements. It was the tyrant who could usually allow the people to

---

a physician has a clinical interest in the parts of the body, philosophers will have an interest in the parts of the soul, or in the varieties of human things which are manifestations of the body and the soul. Such a "looking" would not be voyeurism and would be unaccompanied by shame; or the desire to see and to understand would require the "seer" to overcome shame. (Plato, *Republic*, 439c). In any event, the case of the philosopher is politically irrelevant, and aesthetically irrelevant as well.

[4]*Straus*, p. 221.

[5]It is easy to prove that shamefulness is not the only principle governing the question of what may properly be presented on the stage; shamefulness would not, for example, govern the case of a scene showing the copulating of a married couple who love each other very much. That is not intrinsically shameful—on the contrary—yet it ought not to be shown. The principle here is, I think, an aesthetic one: such a scene is dramatically weak because the response of the audience would be characterized by prurience and not by sympathy with what the scene is intended to portray, a beautiful love. This statement can be tested by joining a collegetown movie audience; it is confirmed unintentionally by a defender of nudity on the stage....

indulge themselves. Indulgence of the sort we are now witnessing did not threaten his rule, because his rule did not depend on a citizenry of good character. Anyone can be ruled by a tyrant, and the more debased his subjects the safer his rule. A case can be made for complete freedom of the arts among such people, whose pleasures are derived from activities divorced from their labors and any duties associated with citizenship. Among them a theatre, for example, can serve to divert the search for pleasure from what the tyrant regards as more dangerous or pernicious pursuits.[6]

Such an argument was not unknown among thoughtful men at the time modern democracies were being constituted. It is to be found in Jean-Jacques Rousseau's *Letter to M. d'Alembert on the Theatre.* Its principles were known by Washington and Jefferson, to say nothing of the antifederalists, and later on by Lincoln, all of whom insisted that democracy would not work without citizens of good character; and until recently no justice of the Supreme Court and no man in public life doubted the necessity for the law to make at least a modest effort to promote that good character, if only by protecting the effort of other institutions, such as the church and the family, to promote and maintain it. The case for censorship, at first glance, was made wholly with a view to the political good, and it had as its premise that what was good for the arts and sciences was *not* necessarily good for the polity....

It ought to be clear that this old and largely forgotten case for censorship was made by men who were not insensitive to the beauty of the arts and the noble role they can play in the lives of men. Rousseau admitted that he never willingly missed a performance of any of Molière's plays, and did so in the very context of arguing that all theatrical productions should be banned in the decent and self-governing polity. Like Plato he would banish the poets, yet he was himself a poet—a musician, opera composer, and novelist—and demonstrated his love for and knowledge of poetry, or as we would say, the arts, in his works and in his life. But he was above all a thinker of the highest rank, and as such he knew that the basic premise of the later liberalism is false. A century later John Stuart Mill could no longer conceive of a conflict between the intrinsic and therefore legitimate demands of the sciences and the intrinsic and therefore legitimate demands of the polity; whereas Rousseau had argued that the "restoration" of the arts and sciences did not tend to purify morals, but that, on the contrary, their restoration and popularization would be destructive of the possibility of a good civil society. His contemporaries were shocked and

---

[6]The modern tyrant does not encourage passivity among his subjects; on the contrary, they are expected by him to be public-spirited: to work for the State, to exceed production schedules, to be citizen soldiers in the huge armies, and to love Big Brother. Indeed, in Nazi Germany and the Soviet Union alike, the private life was and is discouraged, and with it erotic love and the private attachments it fosters. Censorship in a modern tyrannical state is designed to abolish the private life to the extent that this is possible. George Orwell understood this perfectly. This severe censorship that characterizes modern tyranny, and distinguishes it sharply from pre-modern tyranny, derives from the basis of modern tyrannical rule: both Nazism and Communism have roots in theory, and more precisely, a kind of utopian theory. The modern tyrant parades as a political philosopher, the heir of Nietzsche or Marx, with a historical mission to perform. He cannot leave his subjects alone.

angered by this teaching and excluded Rousseau from their society; if we were taught by them and more directly by Mill and his followers—Justice Douglas, for example—we might tend to dismiss it as the teaching of a madman or fool. Are we, however, still prepared to stand with Mill and his predecessors against Rousseau to argue that what is good for science is necessarily good for civil society? Or have certain terrible events and conditions prepared us to reconsider that issue? If so, and especially in the light of certain literary and theatrical events, we might be prepared to reconsider the issue of whether what is good for the arts is necessarily good for civil society.

Pornography and Respect for Women

Ann Garry

Pornography, like rape, is a male invention, designed to dehumanize women, to reduce the female to an object of sexual access, not to free sensuality from moralistic or parental inhibition.... Pornography is the undiluted essence of anti-female propaganda.

Susan Brownmiller
Against Our Will: Men, Women and Rape[1]

It is often asserted that a distinguishing characteristic of sexually explicit material is the degrading and demeaning portrayal of the role and status of the human female. It has been argued that erotic materials describe the female as a mere sexual object to be exploited and manipulated sexually.... A recent survey shows that 41 percent of American males and 46 percent of the females believe that "sexual materials lead people to lose respect for women."...Recent experiments suggest that such fears are probably unwarranted.

Presidential Commission on Obscenity and Pornography[2]

The kind of apparent conflict illustrated in these passages is easy to find in one's own thinking as well. For example, I have been inclined to think that pornography is innocuous and to dismiss "moral" arguments for censoring it because many such arguments rest on an assumption I do not share—that sex is an evil to be controlled. At the same time I believe that it is wrong to exploit or degrade human beings, particularly women and others who are especially

---

This article first appeared in *Social Theory and Practice*, 4 (Summer 1978). It is reprinted here as it appears in Sharon Bishop and Marjorie Weinzweig, eds. *Philosophy and Women* (Wadsworth, 1979). Reprinted by permission of the author.

[1](New York: Simon and Schuster, 1975), p. 394.

[2]*The Report of the Commission on Obscenity and Pornography* (Washington, D.C., 1970), p. 201. Hereinafter, *Report*.

susceptible. So if pornography degrades human beings, then even if I would oppose its censorship I surely cannot find it morally innocuous.

In an attempt to resolve this apparent conflict I discuss three questions: Does pornography degrade (or exploit or dehumanize) human beings? If so, does it degrade women in ways or to an extent that it does not degrade men? If so, must pornography degrade women, as Brownmiller thinks, or could genuinely innocuous, nonsexist pornography exist? Although much current pornography does degrade women, I will argue that it is possible to have nondegrading, nonsexist pornography. However, this possibility rests on our making certain fundamental changes in our conceptions of sex and sex roles....

The...argument I will consider is that pornography is morally objectionable, not because it leads people to show disrespect for women, but because pornography itself exemplifies and recommends behavior that violates the moral principle to respect persons. The content of pornography is what one objects to. It treats women as mere sex objects "to be exploited and manipulated" and degrades the role and status of women. In order to evaluate this argument, I will first clarify what it would mean for pornography itself to treat someone as a sex object in a degrading manner. I will then deal with three issues central to the discussion of pornography and respect for women: how "losing respect" for a woman is connected with treating her as a sex object; what is wrong with treating someone as a sex object; and why it is worse to treat women rather than men as sex objects. I will argue that the current content of pornography sometimes violates the moral principle to respect persons. Then...I will suggest that pornography need not violate this principle if certain fundamental changes were to occur in attitudes about sex.

To many people, including Brownmiller and some other feminists, it appears to be an obvious truth that pornography treats people, especially women, as sex objects in a degrading manner. And if we omit "in a degrading manner," the statement seems hard to dispute: How could pornography *not* treat people as sex objects?

First, is it permissible to say that either the content of pornography or pornography itself degrades people or treats people as sex objects? It is not difficult to find examples of degrading content in which women are treated as sex objects. Some pornographic films convey the message that all women really want to be raped, that their resisting struggle is not to be believed. By portraying women in this manner, the content of the movie degrades women. Degrading women is morally objectionable. While seeing the movie need not cause anyone to imitate the behavior shown, we can call the content degrading to women because of the character of the behavior and attitudes it recommends. The same kind of point can be made about films (or books or TV commercials) with other kinds of degrading, thus morally objectionable, content—for example, racist messages.[3]

---

[3]Two further points need to be mentioned here. Sharon Bishop pointed out to me one reason why we might object to either a racist or rapist mentality in film: it might be difficult for a Black or a

The next step in the argument is to infer that, because the content or message of pornography is morally objectionable, we can call pornography itself morally objectionable. Support for this step can be found in an analogy. If a person takes every opportunity to recommend that men rape women, we would think not only that his recommendation is immoral but that he is immoral too. In the case of pornography, the objection to making an inference from recommended behavior to the person who recommends is that we ascribe predicates such as "immoral" differently to people than to films or books. A film vehicle for an objectionable message is still an object independent of its message, its director, its producer, those who act in it, and those who respond to it. Hence one cannot make an unsupported inference from "the content of the film is morally objectionable" to "the film is morally objectionable." Because the central points in this paper do not depend on whether pornography itself (in addition to its content) is morally objectionable, I will not try to support this inference. (The question about the relation of content to the work itself is, of course, extremely interesting; but in part because I cannot decide which side of the argument is more persuasive, I will pass.[4]) Certainly one appropriate way to evaluate pornography is in terms of the moral features of its content. If a pornographic film exemplifies and recommends morally objectionable attitudes or behavior, then its content is morally objectionable.

Let us now turn to the first of our three questions about respect and sex objects: What is the connection between losing respect for a woman and treating her as a sex object? Some people who have lived through the era in which women were taught to worry about men "losing respect" for them if they engaged in sex in inappropriate circumstances find it troublesome (or at least amusing) that feminists—supposedly "liberated" women—are outraged at being treated as sex objects, either by pornography or in any other way. The apparent alignment between feminists and traditionally "proper" women need not surprise us when we look at it more closely.

The "respect" that men have traditionally believed they have for women— hence a respect they can lose—is not a general respect for persons as autonomous beings; nor is it respect that is earned because of one's personal merits or achievements. It is respect that is an outgrowth of the "double standard." Women are to be respected because they are more pure, delicate, and fragile than men, have more refined sensibilities, and so on. Because some women clearly do not have these qualities, thus do not deserve respect,

---

woman not to identify with the degraded person. A second point concerns different uses of the phrase "treats women as sex objects." A film treats a subject—the meaninglessness of contemporary life, women as sex objects, and so on—and this use of "treats" is unproblematic. But one should not suppose that this is the same use of "treats women as sex objects" that is found in the sentence "David treats women as sex objects." David is not treating the *subject* of women as sex objects.

[4]In order to help one determine which position one feels inclined to take, consider the following statement: It is morally objectionable to write, make, sell, act in, use, and enjoy pornography; in addition, the content of pornography is immoral; however, pornography itself is not morally objectionable. If this statement seems extremely problematic, then one might well be satisfied with the claim that pornography is degrading because its content is.

women must be divided into two groups—the good ones on the pedestal and the bad ones who have fallen from it. One's mother, grandmother, Sunday School teacher, and usually one's wife are "good" women. The appropriate behavior by which to express respect for good women would be, for example, not swearing or telling dirty jokes in front of them, giving them seats on buses, and other "chivalrous" acts. This kind of "respect" for good women is the same sort that adolescent boys in the back seats of cars used to "promise" not to lose. Note that men define, display, and lose this kind of respect. If women lose respect for women, it is not typically a loss of respect for (other) women as a class but a loss of self-respect.

It has now become commonplace to acknowledge that, although a place on the pedestal might have advantages over a place in the "gutter" beneath it, a place on the pedestal is not at all equal to the place occupied by other people (i.e., men). "Respect" for those on the pedestal was not respect for whole, full-fledged people but for a special class of inferior beings.

If a person makes two traditional assumptions—that (at least some) sex is dirty and that women fall into two classes, good and bad—it is easy to see how that person might think that pornography could lead people to lose respect for women or that pornography is itself disrespectful to women.[5] Pornography describes or shows women engaging in activities inappropriate for good women to engage in—or at least inappropriate for them to be seen by strangers engaging in. If one sees these women as symbolic representatives of all women, then all women fall from grace with these women. This fall is possible, I believe, because the traditional "respect" that men have had for women is not genuine, wholehearted respect for full-fledged human beings but half-hearted respect for lesser beings, some of whom they feel the need to glorify and purify.[6] It is easy to fall from a pedestal. Can we imagine 41 percent of men and 46 percent of women answering "yes" to the question, "Do movies showing men engaging in violent acts lead people to lose respect for men?"

Two interesting asymmetries appear. The first is that losing respect for men as a class (men with power, typically Anglo men) is more difficult than losing respect for women or ethnic minorities as a class. Anglo men whose behavior warrants disrespect are more likely to be seen as exceptional cases than are women or minorities (whose "transgressions" may be far less serious). Think of the following: women are temptresses; Blacks cheat the welfare system; Italians are gangsters; but the men of the Nixon administration are exceptions— Anglo men as a class did not lose respect because of Watergate and related scandals.

[5]The traditional meaning of "lose respect for women" was evidently the one assumed in the Abelson survey cited by the Presidential Commission. No explanation of its meaning is given in the report of the study. See H. Abelson et al., "National Survey of Public Attitudes Toward and Experience with Erotic Materials." *Tech. Report*, vol. 6, pp. 1–137.

[6]Many feminists point this out. One of the most accessible references is Shulamith Firestone, *The Dialectic of Sex: The Case for the Feminist Revolution* (New York: Bantam, 1970), especially pp. 128–32.

The second asymmetry concerns the active and passive roles of the sexes. Men are seen in the active role. If men lose respect for women because of something "evil" done by women (such as appearing in pornography), the fear is that men will then do harm to women—not that women will do harm to men. Whereas if women lose respect for male politicians because of Watergate, the fear is still that male politicians will do harm, not that women will do harm to male politicians. This asymmetry might be a result of one way in which our society thinks of sex as bad—as harm that men do to women (or to the person playing a female role, as in a homosexual rape)....Our slang words for sexual intercourse...or older words such as 'take' or 'have'—not only can mean harm but have traditionally taken a male subject and a female object. The active male screws (harms) the passive female. A "bad" woman only tempts men to hurt her further.

It is easy to understand why one's proper grandmother would not want men to see pornography or lose respect for women. But feminists reject these "proper" assumptions: good and bad classes of women do not exist; and sex is not dirty (though many people believe it is). Why then are feminists angry at the treatment of women as sex objects, and why are some feminists opposed to pornography?

The answer is that feminists as well as proper grandparents are concerned with respect. However, there are differences. A feminist's distinction between treating a woman as a full-fledged person and treating her as merely a sex object does not correspond to the good-bad woman distinction. In the latter distinction, "good" and "bad" are properties applicable to groups of women. In the feminist view, all women are full-fledged people—some, however, are treated as sex objects and perhaps think of themselves as sex objects. A further difference is that, although "bad" women correspond to those thought to deserve treatment as sex objects, good women have not corresponded to full-fledged people; only men have been full-fledged people. Given the feminist's distinction, she has no difficulty whatever in saying that pornography treats women as sex objects, not as full-fledged people. She can morally object to pornography or anything else that treats women as sex objects.

One might wonder whether any objection to treatment as a sex object implies that the person objecting still believes, deep down, that sex is dirty. I don't think so. Several other possibilities emerge. First, even if I believe intellectually and emotionally that sex is healthy, I might object to being treated *only* as a sex object. In the same spirit, I would object to being treated *only* as a maker of chocolate chip cookies or *only* as a tennis partner, because only one of my talents is being valued. Second, perhaps I feel that sex is healthy, but it is apparent to me that you think sex is dirty; so I don't want you to treat me as a sex object. Third, being treated as any kind of object, not just as a sex object, is unappealing. I would rather be a partner (sexual or otherwise) than an object. Fourth, and more plausible than the first three possibilities, is [the] view mentioned above [that sex is a harm men do to women]. Both (i) our traditional double standard of sexual behavior for men and women and (ii) the linguistic evidence that we connect the concept of sex with the concept of harm point to what is wrong with treating women as sex objects.... Because in our culture we connect sex with harm that men do to women, and because we think of the female role in sex as that of harmed object, we can see that to treat a woman as a sex object is automatically to treat her as less than fully human. To say this does not imply that no healthy sexual relationships exist; nor does it say anything about individual men's conscious intentions to degrade women by desiring them sexually (though no doubt some men have these intentions). It is merely to make a point about the concepts embodied in our language.

Psychoanalytic support for the connection between sex and harm comes from Robert J. Stoller. Stoller thinks that sexual excitement is linked with a wish to harm someone (and with at least a whisper of hostility). The key process of sexual excitement can be seen as dehumanization (fetishization) in fantasy of the desired person. He speculates that this is true in some degree of everyone, both men and women, with "normal" or "perverted" activities and fantasies.[7]

Thinking of sex objects as harmed objects enables us to explain some of the first three reasons why one wouldn't want to be treated as a sex object: (1) I may object to being treated only as a tennis partner, but being a tennis partner is not connected in our culture with being a harmed object; and (2) I may not think that sex is dirty and that I would be a harmed object; I may not know what your view is; but what bothers me is that this is the view embodied in our language and culture.

Awareness of the connection between sex and harm helps explain other interesting points. Women are angry about being treated as sex objects in situations or roles in which they do not intend to be regarded in that manner—for example, while serving on a committee or attending a discussion. It is not merely that a sexual role is inappropriate for the circumstances; it is thought to be a less fully human role than the one in which they intended to function.

Finally, the sex-harm connection makes clear why it is worse to treat women as sex objects than to treat men as sex objects, and why some men have had difficulty understanding women's anger about the matter. It is more difficult for heterosexual men than for women to assume the role of "harmed object" in sex; for men have the self-concept of sexual agents, not of passive objects. This is also related to my earlier point concerning the difference in the solidity of respect for men and for women; respect for women is more fragile. Despite exceptions, it is generally harder for people to degrade men, either sexually or nonsexually, than to degrade women. Men and women have grown up with

---

[7]"Sexual Excitement," *Archives of General Psychiatry* 33 (1976): 899–909, especially p. 903. The extent to which Stoller sees men and women in different positions with respect to harm and hostility is not clear. He often treats men and women alike, but in *Perversion: The Erotic Form of Hatred* (New York: Pantheon, 1975), pp. 89–91, he calls attention to differences between men and women especially regarding their responses to pornography and lack of understanding by men of women's sexuality. Given that Stoller finds hostility to be an essential element in male-oriented pornography, and given that women have not responded readily to such pornography, one can speculate about the possibilities for women's sexuality: their hostility might follow a different scenario; they might not be as hostile, and so on.

different patterns of self-respect and expectations regarding the extent to which they deserve and will receive respect or degradation. The man who doesn't understand why women do not want to be treated as sex objects (because he'd sure like to be) would not think of himself as being harmed by that treatment; a woman might.[8] Pornography, probably more than any other contemporary institution, succeeds in treating men as sex objects.

Having seen that the connection between sex and harm helps explain both what is wrong with treating someone as a sex object and why it is worse to treat a woman in this way, I want to use the sex-harm connection to try to resolve a dispute about pornography and women. Brownmiller's view, remember, was that pornography is "the undiluted essence of anti-female propaganda" whose purpose is to degrade women.[9] Some people object to Brownmiller's view by saying that, since pornography treats both men and women as sex objects for the purpose of arousing the viewer, it is neither sexist, antifemale, nor designed to degrade women; it just happens that degrading of women arouses some men. How can this dispute be resolved?

Suppose we were to rate the content of all pornography from most morally objectionable to least morally objectionable. Among the most objectionable would be the most degrading—for example, "snuff" films and movies which recommend that men rape women, molest children and puppies, and treat nonmasochists very sadistically.

Next we would find a large amount of material (probably most pornography) not quite so blatantly offensive. With this material it is relevant to use the analysis of sex objects given above. As long as sex is connected with harm done to women, it will be very difficult not to see pornography as degrading to women. We can agree with Brownmiller's opponent that pornography treats men as sex objects, too, but we maintain that this is only pseudoequality; such treatment is still more degrading to women.[10]

In addition, pornography often exemplifies the active/passive, harmer/harmed object roles in a very obvious way. Because pornography today is male-oriented and is supposed to make a profit, the content is designed to appeal to male fantasies. If we judge from the content of the most popular legally available pornography, male fantasies still run along the lines of stereotypical sex roles—and, if Stoller is right, include elements of hostility. In much

---

[8] Men seem to be developing more sensitivity to being treated as sex objects. Many homosexual men have long understood the problem. As women become more sexually aggressive, some heterosexual men I know are beginning to feel treated as sex objects. A man can feel that he is not being taken seriously if a woman looks lustfully at him while he is holding forth about the French judicial system or the failure of liberal politics. Some of his most important talents are not being properly valued.

[9] Brownmiller, *Against Our Will*, p. 394.

[10] I don't agree with Brownmiller that the purpose of pornography is to dehumanize women; rather it is to arouse the audience. The differences between our views can be explained, in part, by the points from which we begin. She is writing about rape; her views about pornography grow out of her views about rape. I begin by thinking of pornography as merely depicted sexual activity, though I am well aware of the male hostility and contempt for women that it often expresses. That pornography degrades women and excites men is an illustration of this contempt.

It would be impossible to demonstrate that freedom is good for its own sake, and indeed, this proposition is far from self-evident. Still, Stephen's analogy to fire seems an injustice to freedom. Fire has no constant and virtually invariant effects that tend to make it, on balance, a good thing whenever and wherever it occurs, and bad only when its subsequent remoter effects are so evil as to counterbalance its direct and immediate ones. Thus, a fire in one's bed while one is sleeping is dreadful because its effects are evil, but a fire under the pot on the stove is splendid because it makes possible a hot cup of coffee when one wants it. The direct effect of fire in these and all other cases is to oxidize material objects and raise the temperature in its immediate environment; but *these* effects, from the point of view of human interests, and considered just in themselves, are neither good nor bad.

Freedom has seemed to most writers quite different in this respect. When a free man violates his neighbor's interests, then his freedom, having been put to bad use, was, on balance, a bad thing, but unlike the fire in the bed, it was not an unalloyed evil. Whatever the harmful consequences of freedom in a given case, there is always a direct effect on the person of its possessor which must be counted a positive good. Coercion may prevent great evils, and be wholly justified on that account, but it always has its price. Coercion may be on balance a great gain, but its direct effects always, or nearly always, constitute a definite loss. If this is true, there is always a *presumption* in favor of freedom, even though it can in some cases be overriden by more powerful reasons on the other side.

The presumption in favor of freedom is usually said to rest on freedom's essential role in the development of traits of intellect and character which constitute the good of individuals and are centrally important means to the progress of societies. One consensus argument, attributable with minor variations to Von Humboldt, Mill, Hobhouse, and many others, goes roughly as follows. The highest good for man is neither enjoyment nor passive contentment, but rather a dynamic process of growth and self-realization. This can be called "happiness" if we mean by that term what the Greeks did, namely, "The exercise of vital powers along lines of excellence in a life affording them scope."[2] The highest social good is then the greatest possible amount of individual self-realization and (assuming that different persons are inclined by their natures in different ways) the resultant diversity and fullness of life. Self-realization consists in the actualization of certain uniquely human potentialities, the bringing to full development of certain powers and abilities. This in turn requires constant practice in making difficult choices among alternative hypotheses, policies, and actions—and the more difficult the better. John Stuart Mill explained why:

> The human faculties of perception, judgment, discriminative feeling, mental activity, and even moral preference are exercised only in making a choice. He who does

---

[2]See Edith Hamilton, *The Greek Way* (New York: W. W. Norton & Company, Inc., 1942), pp. 35ff.

anything because it is the custom makes no choice. He gains no practice either in discerning or in desiring what is best. The mental and moral, like the muscular, powers are improved only by being used.[3]

In short, one does not realize what is best in oneself when social pressures to conform to custom lead one mindlessly along. Even more clearly, one's growth will be stunted when one is given no choice in the first place, either because of being kept in ignorance or because one is terrorized by the wielders of bayonets.

Freedom to decide on one's own while fully informed of the facts thus tends to promote the good of the person who exercises it, even if it permits him to make foolish or dangerous mistakes. Mill added to this argument the citation of numerous social benefits that redound indirectly but uniformly to those who grant freedom as well as those who exercise it. We all profit from the fruits of genius, he maintained, and genius, since it often involves doggedness and eccentricity, is likely to flourish only where coercive pressures toward conformity are absent. Moreover, social progress is more likely to occur where there is free criticism of prevailing ways and adventurous experiments in living. Finally, true understanding of human nature requires freedom, since without liberty there will be little diversity, and without diversity *all* aspects of the human condition will be ascribed to fixed nature rather than to the workings of a particular culture....

LINES OF ATTACK ON MILL

Arguments against Mill's unsupplemented harm principle (his claim that the private and public harm principles state the *only* grounds for justified interference with liberty) have been mainly of two different kinds.[4] Many have argued that the harm principle justifies too much social and political interference in the affairs of individuals. Others allow that the prevention of individual and social harm is always a ground for interference, but insist that it is by no means the only ground.

(i) "No Man Is an Island"

Mill maintained in *On Liberty* that social interference is never justified in those of a man's affairs that concern himself only. But no man's affairs have effects on himself alone. There are a thousand subtle and indirect ways in which every individual act, no matter how private and solitary, affects others. It would therefore seem that society has a right, on Mill's own principles, to interfere in every department of human life. Mill anticipated this objection and took certain steps to disarm it. Let it be allowed that no human conduct is entirely, exclusively, and to the last degree self-regarding. Still, Mill, insisted, we can

[3]John Stuart Mill, *On Liberty* (New York: Liberal Arts Press, 1956), p. 71.
[4]Cf. H.L.A. Hart, *Law, Liberty, and Morality* (Stanford: Stanford University Press, 1963), p. 6.

distinguish between actions that are plainly other-regarding and those that are "directly," "chiefly," or "primarily" self-regarding. There will be a twilight area of cases difficult to classify, but that is true of many other workable distinctions, including that between night and day.

It is essential to Mill's theory that we make a distinction between two different kinds of consequences of human actions: the consequences *directly* affecting the interests of others, and those of primarily self-regarding behavior which only *indirectly* or *remotely* affect the interests of others. "No person ought to be punished simply for being drunk," Mill wrote, "but a soldier or policeman should be punished for being drunk on duty."[5] A drunk policeman directly harms the interests of others. His conduct gives opportunities to criminals and thus creates grave risk of harm to other citizens. It brings the police into disrepute, and makes the work of his colleagues more dangerous. Finally, it may lead to loss of the policeman's job, with serious consequences for his wife and children.

Consider, on the other hand, a hard working bachelor who habitually spends his evening hours drinking himself to stupor, which he then sleeps off, rising fresh in the morning to put in another hard day's work. His drinking does not *directly* affect others in any of the ways of the drunk policeman's conduct. He has no family; he drinks alone and sets no direct example; he is not prevented from discharging any of his public duties; he creates no substantial risk of harm to the interests of other individuals. Although even his private conduct will have some effects on the interests of others, these are precisely the sorts of effects Mill would call "indirect" and "remote." First, in spending his evenings the way he does, our solitary tippler is *not* doing any number of other things that might be of greater utility to others. In not earning and spending more money, he is failing to stimulate the economy (except for the liquor industry) as much as he might. Second, he fails to spend his evening time improving his talents and making himself a better person. Perhaps he has a considerable native talent for painting or poetry, and his wastefulness is depriving the world of some valuable art. Third, he may make those of his colleagues who like him sad on his behalf. Finally, to those who know of his habits, he is a "bad example."[6] All of these, "indirect harms" together, Mill maintained, do not outweigh the direct and serious harm that would result from social or legal coercion.

Mill's critics have never been entirely satisfied by this. Many have pointed out that Mill is concerned not only with political coercion and legal punishment but also with purely social coercion—moral pressure, social avoidance, ostracism. No responsible critic would wish the state to punish the solitary tippler, but social coercion is another matter. We can't prevent people from disap-

---

[5]Mill, *On Liberty*, pp. 99–100.

[6]Mill has a ready rejoinder to this last point: If the conduct in question is supposed to be greatly harmful to the actor himself, "the example on the whole must be more salutory" than harmful socially, since it is a warning lesson, rather than an alluring model to others. See Mill, *On Liberty*, p. 101.

proving of an individual for his self-regarding faults or from expressing that disapproval to others, without undue restriction on *their* freedom. Such expressions, in Mill's view, are inevitably coercive, constituting a "milder form of punishment." Hence "social punishment" of individuals for conduct that directly concerns only themselves—the argument concludes—is both inevitable and, according to Mill's own principles, proper.

Mill anticipated this objection, too, and tried to cope with it by making a distinction between types of social responses. We cannot help but lower in our estimation a person with serious self-regarding faults. We will think ill of him, judge him to be at fault, and make him the inevitable and proper object of our disapproval, distaste, even contempt. We may warn others about him, avoid his company, and withhold gratuitous benefits from him—"not to the oppression of his individuality but in the exercise of ours."[7] Mill concedes that all of these social responses can function as "penalties"—but they are suffered "only in so far as they are the natural and, as it were, the spontaneous consequences of the faults themselves, not because they are purposely inflicted on him for the sake of punishment."[8] Other responses, on the other hand, add something to the "natural penalties"—pointed snubbing, economic reprisals, gossip campaigns, and so on. The added penalties, according to Mill, are precisely the ones that are never justified as responses to merely self-regarding flaws—"if he displeases us, we may express our distaste; and we may stand aloof from a person as well as from a thing that displeases us, but we shall not therefore feel called on to make his life uncomfortable."[9]

(ii)   Other Proposed Grounds for Coercion

The distinction between self-regarding and other-regarding behavior, as Mill intended it to be understood, does seem at least roughly serviceable, and unlikely to invite massive social interference in private affairs. I think most critics of Mill would grant that, but reject the harm principle on the opposite ground that it doesn't permit enough interference. These writers would allow at least one, and as many as five or more, additional valid grounds for coercion. Each of these proposed grounds is stated in a principle listed below. One might hold that restriction of one person's liberty can be justified:

1 To prevent harm to others, either
   a injury to individual persons (The Private Harm Principle), or
   b impairment of institutional practices that are in the public interest (The Public Harm Principle);
2 To prevent offense to others (The Offense Principle);
3 To prevent harm to self (Legal Paternalism);

[7]Mill, *On Liberty*, p. 94.
[8]Mill, *On Liberty*, p. 95.
[9]Mill, *On Liberty*, p. 96.

4 To prevent or punish sin, i.e., to "enforce morality as such" *(Legal Moralism)*;

5 To benefit the self *(Extreme Paternalism)*;

6 To benefit others *(The Welfare Principle).*

The liberty-limiting principles on this list are best understood as stating neither necessary nor sufficient conditions for justified coercion, but rather specifications of the *kinds* of reasons that are always relevant or acceptable in support of proposed coercion, even though in a given case they may not be conclusive.[10] Each principle states that interference might be permissible *if* (but not *only if*) a certain condition is satisfied. Hence the principles are not mutually exclusive; it is possible to hold two or more of them at once, even all of them together, and it is possible to deny all of them. Moreover, the principles cannot be construed as stating sufficient conditions for legitimate interference with liberty, for even though the principle is satisfied in a given case, the general presumption against coercion might not be outweighed. The harm principle, for example, does not justify state interference to prevent a tiny bit of inconsequential harm. Prevention of minor harm always counts in favor of proposals (as in a legislature) to restrict liberty, but in a given instance it might not count *enough* to outweigh the general presumption against inter-ference, or it might be outweighed by the prospect of practical difficulties in enforcing the law, excessive costs, and forfeitures of privacy. A liberty-limiting principle states considerations that are always good reasons for coercion, though neither exclusively nor, in every case, decisively good reasons.

It will not be possible to examine each principle in detail here, and offer "proofs" and "refutations." The best way to defend one's selection of principles is to show to which positions they commit one on such issues as censorship of literature, "moral offenses," and compulsory social security programs. General principles arise in the course of deliberations over particular problems, espe-cially in the efforts to defend one's judgments by showing that they are consistent with what has gone before. If a principle commits one to an antece-dently unacceptable judgment, then one has to modify or supplement the principle in a way that does the least damage to the harmony of one's particular and general opinions taken as a group. On the other hand, when a solid, well-entrenched principle entails a change in a particular judgment, the over-riding claims of consistency may require that the judgment be adjusted.

OBSCENITY AND THE OFFENSE PRINCIPLE

Up to this point we have considered the harm and offense principles together in order to determine whether between them they are sufficient to regulate

---

[10] I owe this point to Professor Michael Bayles. See his contribution to *Issues in Law and Morality*, ed. Norman Care and Thomas Trelogan (Cleveland: The Press of Case Western Reserve University, 1973).

conventional immoralities, or whether they need help from a further independent principle, legal moralism. Morals offenses were treated as essentially private so that the offense principle could not be stretched to apply to them. Obscene literature and pornographic displays would appear to be quite different in this respect. Both are materials deliberately published for the eyes of others, and their existence can bring partisans of the unsupplemented harm principle into direct conflict with those who endorse *both* the harm and offense principles.

In its untechnical, prelegal sense, the word "obscenity" refers to material dealing with nudity, sex, or excretion in an offensive manner. Such material becomes obscene in the legal sense when, because of its offensiveness or for some other reason [this question had best be left open in the definition], it is or ought to be without legal protection. The legal definition then incorporates the everyday sense, and essential to both is the requirement that the material be *offensive*. An item may offend one person and not another. "Obscenity," if it is to avoid this subjective relativity, must involve an interpersonal objective sense of "offensive." Material must be offensive by prevailing community standards that are public and well known, or be such that it is apt to offend virtually everyone.

Not all material that is generally offensive need also be harmful in any sense recognized by the harm principle. It is partly an empirical question whether reading or witnessing obscene material causes social harm; reliable evidence, even of a statistical kind, of causal connections between obscenity and antisocial behavior is extremely hard to find.[11] In the absence of clear and decisive evidence of harmfulness, the American Civil Liberties Union insists that the offensiveness of obscene material cannot be a sufficient ground for its repression:

> ....the question in a case involving obscenity, just as in every case involving an attempted restriction upon free speech, is whether the words or pictures are used in such circumstances and are of such a nature as to create a clear and present danger that they will bring about a substantial evil that the state has a right to prevent. ... We believe that under the current state of knowledge, there is grossly insufficient evidence to show that obscenity brings about *any* substantive evil.[12]

The A.C.L.U. argument employs *only* the harm principle among liberty-limiting principles, and treats literature, drama, and painting as forms of expression subject to the same rules as expressions of opinion. In respect to both types of expression, "every act of deciding what should be barred carries with it a danger to the community."[13] The suppression itself is an evil to the author who

---

[11]There have been some studies made, but the results have been inconclusive. See the *Report of the Federal Commission on Obscenity and Pornography* (New York: Bantam Books, 1970), pp. 169–308.

[12]*Obscenity and Censorship* (Pamphlet published by the American Civil Liberties Union, New York, March, 1963), p. 7.

[13]*Obscenity and Censorship*, p. 4.

is squelched. The power to censor and punish involves risks that socially valuable material will be repressed along with the "filth." The overall effect of suppression, the A.C.L.U. concludes, is almost certainly to discourage nonconformist and eccentric expression generally. In order to override these serious risks, there must be in a given case an even more clear and present danger that the obscene material, if not squelched, will cause even greater harm; such countervailing evidence is never forthcoming. (If such evidence were to accumulate, the A.C.L.U. would be perfectly willing to change its position on obscenity.)

The A.C.L.U. stand on obscenity seems clearly to be the position dictated by the unsupplemented harm principle and its corollary, the clear and present danger test. Is there any reason at this point to introduce the offense principle into the discussion? Unhappily, we may be forced to if we are to do justice to all of our particular intuitions in the most harmonious way. Consider an example suggested by Professor Schwartz. By the provisions of the new Model Penal Code, he writes, "a rich homosexual may not use a billboard on Times Square to promulgate to the general populace the techniques and pleasures of sodomy."[14] If the notion of "harm" is restricted to its narrow sense, that is, contrasted with "offense," it will be hard to reconstruct a rationale for this prohibition based on the harm principle. There is unlikely to be evidence that a lurid and obscene public poster in Times Square would create a clear and present danger of injury to those who fail to avert their eyes in time as they come blinking out of the subway stations. Yet it will be surpassingly difficult for even the most dedicated liberal to advocate freedom of expression in a case of this kind. Hence, if we are to justify coercion in this case, we will likely be driven, however reluctantly, to the offense principle.

There is good reason to be "reluctant" to embrace the offense principle until driven to it by an example like the above. People take perfectly genuine offense at many socially useful or harmless activities, from commercial advertisements to insane chatter. Moreover, widespread irrational prejudices can lead people to be disgusted, shocked, even morally repelled by perfectly innocent activities, and we should be loath to permit their groundless repugnance to override the innocence. The offense principle, therefore, must be formulated very precisely and applied in accordance with carefully formulated standards so as not to open the door to wholesale and intuitively unwarranted repression. At the very least we should require that the prohibited conduct or material be of the sort apt to offend almost everybody, and not just some shifting majority or special interest group.

It is instructive to note that a strictly drawn offense principle would not only justify prohibition of conduct and pictured conduct that is in its inherent character repellent, but also conduct and pictured conduct that is inoffensive in itself but offensive in inappropriate circumstances. I have in mind so-called

---

[14]Schwartz, "Morals Offenses and the Penal Code," 680.

indecencies such as public nudity. One can imagine an advocate of the unsupplemented harm principle arguing against the public nudity prohibition on the grounds that the sight of a naked body does no one any harm, and the state has no right to impose standards of dress or undress on private citizens. How one chooses to dress, after all, is a form of self-expression. If we do not permit the state to bar clashing colors or bizarre hair styles, by what right does it prohibit total undress? Perhaps the sight of naked people could at first lead to riots or other forms of antisocial behavior, but that is precisely the sort of contingency for which we have police. If we don't take away a person's right of free speech for the reason that its exercise may lead others to misbehave, we cannot in consistency deny his right to dress or undress as he chooses for the same reason.

There may be no answering this challenge on its own ground, but the offense principle provides a ready rationale for the nudity prohibition. The sight of nude bodies in public places is for almost everyone acutely *embarrassing*. Part of the explanation no doubt rests on the fact that nudity has an irresistible power to draw the eye and focus the thoughts on matters that are normally repressed. The conflict between these attracting and repressing forces is exciting, upsetting, and anxiety-producing. In some persons it will create at best a kind of painful turmoil, and at worst that experience of exposure to oneself of "peculiarly sensitive, intimate, vulnerable aspects of the self"[15] which is called *shame*. "One's feeling is involuntarily exposed openly in one's face; one is uncovered...taken by surprise...made a fool of."[16] The result is not mere "offense," but a kind of psychic jolt that in many normal people can be a painful wound. Even those of us who are better able to control our feelings might well resent the *nuisance* of having to do so.

If we are to accept the offense principle as a supplement to the harm principle, we must accept two corollaries which stand in relation to it similarly to the way in which the clear and present danger test stands to the harm principle. The first, the *standard of unversality*, has already been touched upon. For the offensiveness (disgust, embarrassment, outraged sensibilities, or shame) to be sufficient to warrant coercion, it should be the reaction that could be expected from almost any person chosen at random from the nation as a whole, regardless of sect, faction, race, age, or sex. The second is the *standard of reasonable avoidability*. No one has a right to protection from the state against offensive experiences if he can effectively avoid those experiences with no unreasonable effort or inconvenience. If a nude person enters a public bus and takes a seat near the front, there may be no effective way for other patrons to avoid intensely shameful embarrassment (or other insupportable feelings) short of leaving the bus, which would be an unreasonable inconvenience. Similarly, obscene remarks over a loudspeaker, homosexual billboards

---

[15]Helen Merrill Lynd, *On Shame and the Search for Identity.* (New York: Science Editions, Inc., 1961), p. 33.

[16]Lynd, *On Shame and the Search for Identity*, p. 32.

in Times Square, and pornographic handbills thrust into the hands of passing pedestrians all fail to be reasonably avoidable.

On the other hand, the offense principle, properly qualified, can give no warrant to the suppression of *books* on the grounds of obscenity. When printed words hide decorously behind covers of books sitting passively on bookstore shelves, their offensiveness is easily avoided. The contrary view is no doubt encouraged by the common comparison of obscenity with "smut," "filth," or "dirt." This in turn suggests an analogy to nuisance law, which governs cases where certain activities create loud noises or terrible odors offensive to neighbors, and "the courts must weigh the gravity of the nuisance [substitute "offense" to the neighbors against the social utility [substitute "redeeming social value"] of the defendant's conduct." There is, however, one vitiating disanalogy in this comparison. In the case of "dirty books" the offense is easily avoidable. There is nothing like the evil smell of rancid garbage oozing right out through the covers of a book. When an "obscene" book sits on a shelf, who is there to be offended? Those who want to read it for the sake of erotic stimulation presumably will not be offended (or else they wouldn't read it), and those who choose not to read it will have no experience by which to be offended. If its covers are too decorous, some innocents may browse through it by mistake and be offended by what they find, but they need only close the book to escape the offense. Even this offense, minimal as it is, could be completely avoided by prior consultation of trusted book reviewers. I conclude that there are no sufficient grounds derived either from the harm or offense principles for suppressing obscene literature, unless that ground be the protection of children: but I can think of no reason why restrictions on sales to children cannot work as well for printed materials as they do for cigarettes and whiskey.

Natural Law and Unnatural Acts

John M. Finnis

Plato has situated the problem of sexual vice at the core of ethical speculation. In his great early dialogue, the *Gorgias,* in which he declares unequivocal 'war and battle' (cf. 447A) against the enlightened contemporary society, Plato has Socrates confront Callicles, the exponent of a pragmatic and egoistic hedonism. The crisis of their discussion, perhaps of the whole dialogue, is the question whether there are bad pleasures. Callicles maintains that the happy life consists in having many appetites which one can satisfy with enjoyment. Socrates asks whether a man is indeed happy who itches and wants to scratch, and can spend

From *The Heythrop Journal* II (1970): 365–66, 379–87. Copyright 1970 The Heythrop Journal. Reprinted by permission.

his life scratching. The question is vulgar and absurd, thinks Callicles; but he will not give way: a life of pleasurable scratching is a happy life. 'But suppose the itch were not confined to one's head. Must I go on with my question? Think what you will answer, Callicles, if you are asked the questions which naturally follow. To bring the matter to a head—take the life of one who wallows in unnatural vices.... Isn't that shocking and shameful and miserable?' (494E). The question makes Callicles squirm. Socrates presses him: 'Can it be, my good friend, that good is not identical with enjoyment of *whatever* kind? If it is, the shocking things I hinted at just now must obviously follow, and many other things as well' (495B). 'That's what you think, Socrates', retorts Callicles—it is the classical retort to all ethical speculation and teaching. But in fact the back of Callicles's resistance has been broken.

The appeal of Socrates-Plato has not been to any ethical doctrine of natural law. It has been to Callicles's, and the reader's, confused, submerged but real grasp of what is good and what is falling away, an aversion, a flight from good. Natural law is not a doctrine. It is one's permanent dynamic orientation towards an understanding grasp of the goods that can be realized by free choice, together with a bias (like the bias in one's 'speculation' towards raising questions that will lead one on from data to insight and from insight to judgement) towards actually making choices that are intelligibly (because intelligently) related to the goods which are understood to be attainable, or at stake, in one's situation. Now the jargon-laden sentence just uttered is a piece of speculation, theorizing, doctrine about natural law. But the point of all such theorizing can be little more than to uncover what is already available to everyone, submerged and confused, perhaps, but shaping everyone's practical attitudes and choices of what to do, what to love and what to respect....

... Human life-styles are malleable and plastic, yet not formless; the range of opportunities of flourishing that are open to one can be stated in principle (the statement being not so much a piece of speculation about 'human nature' as an appeal to the reader to reflect on his own experience and self-understanding and to agree that for him, too, these are the basic forms of flourishing). One might attempt a list (to cut a long story short) as follows:

> living, in health and some security; the acquisition of arts and skills to be cultivated for their own sake; the relishing of beauty; the seeking of knowledge and under-standing; the cultivation of friendships, immediate, communal and political; effective and intelligent freedom; a right relation in this passing life to the lasting principles of reality, 'the gods'; the procreation of children and their education so that they can attain for themselves, and in their own mode, the foregoing values....

Like any values, all these appear in practical discourse principally as principles of the form, 'Such-and-such is a good-to-be-pursued, and what threatens it avoided.' And certainly one can question the list I have offered, and suggest reformulations and additions. But I think it can be seen, both by observation and (more relevantly) by reflexion on one's own living, that these are the values which give sense and worth, in some immediate (and, as we shall see, questionable) measure, to the utterly varied and complex routines and projects in which we are engaged....

We talk easily, these days, about the 'significance', for example the 'unitive significance' (*significatio unitatis*) of sexual intercourse. Now the English, 'unitive significance', rather more than the Latin, suggests that this act of physical union of bodies in some way has the meaning of bringing about a uniting of the partners...[But] there seems no reason at all to accept that intercourse engaged in promiscuously, or as play or in sympathy or otherwise, need have any such effect. On the other hand, the Latin, *significatio unitatis*, rather suggests that intercourse expresses, is a symbol of, a union that already exists...[But] to say that intercourse 'has' this expressive sense or force obscures the fact that often intercourse actually expresses no more than a mutual taste for diversion, or a mutual *libido dominandi*.

What then is the source of the appeal and apparent plausibility of talk about the unitive significance of sexual intercourse? I think it is this: *granted* an ideal of a profound, life-long, exclusive, loving union between man and woman, then intercourse between these spouses is to be regarded as a very apt expression of their union, their common and exclusive project. And then one may wish to add...that this apt expression is somehow made less apt (or perhaps is impossible?) unless 'the partners bring to each other a complete offering of self-hood unspoiled by any liaison'—hence 'pre-marital intercourse can never be right'.[1]

But before one leaps with relief to this conclusion, let us raise a few questions, not so much about the all-too-questionable assertion that casual sexual play 'spoils one's self-hood'; but rather about the premise that intercourse is a peculiarly apt expression of the ideal of marriage. (*i*) Once more: What is it about intercourse, the union of bodies and members in *this way* (rather than that...), that makes it so apt an expression? (*ii*) Granted that this is the most apt expression of the ideal of marriage, does it follow that it is the only apt use of one's sexual powers? And even if it does follow, what is *morally* offensive about an inapt use of a physical capacity? (*iii*) More radically: What is the sense of the ideal of a profound, life-long, exclusive, loving union between one man and one woman?

This last question emerges, not out of a cheap cynicism, but from reflection on the meaning of friendship. It is self-evidently lovely for a person to go out from himself in friendship. *Bonum sui diffusivum* is the principle of a whole philosophical and theological civilization.[2] The mutual sharing of the good things of life is itself an unsurpassed good. So friendship does not rest satisfied with one friend, but seeks to extend itself to one's friend's friends, to widen the circle of love; it even dreams of a love of all men. For the union between one

[1]Report of the Committee on the Family in Contemporary Society. *The Lambeth Conference 1958* (London, 1958), 2, 156.

[2]Cf. Per Erik Persson, *Sacra Doctrina: Reason and Revelation in Aquinas* (Oxford, 1970), pp. 132–8, on the difference between the neo-Platonist and Thomist worlds of thought, and the corresponding treatments of the tag, *bonum sui diffusivum*.

man and another man is deepened and strengthened, not weakened and dissipated, by its extension to other persons, the friends of my friends, sharing an ever-greater good, namely the ever-extending sharing of the goods open to man. Into this meditation on friendship erupts the peremptory demand that *one* friendship be exclusive and share its highest good with no one. Or rather, to reverse the challenge: into contemporary Christian rhapsodies about 'the couple' *we* (married people) must inject the blunt question: Why is it not perhaps vice, rather than virtue, to cultivate the exclusive life of the couple, and to reserve certain good things for *one* other person? No amount of praise of unity or of acts signifying unity will be an adequate response to this question: indeed, it will only increase the urgency of the question.

The only eligible answer to the question, I think, is that given in the terse and masterly summary of the Christian ideal of marriage which prefaces the analysis of that ideal in the encyclical *Humanae Vitae*.[3] It runs: 'By means of the reciprocal personal gift of self, proper and exclusive to them, husband and wife tend towards the communion of their beings in view of mutual personal perfection'—so far, an inadequate response, an apparently senseless closing-in of the couple against the world—'*in order to* [my emphasis] collaborate with God in the generation and education of new lives'— and there's the solution, the challenge to 'the couple' to find their mutually fulfilling communion and friendship not in an inexplicably exclusive cultivation of each other, but in a common pursuit, the pursuit of a good that *de facto* cannot be adequately realized otherwise than by a single-minded devotion to that good, by the *only* two people who can be *the* mother and *the* father of *that* child. Now to say this is not to draw any further conclusions (which would in fact be unwarranted)— such as that marriage should be entered into primarily with the motive of having children, or that intercourse within marriage ought to be so motivated. No, the point is simply to issue a reminder about that dimension of sexuality which had not yet been mentioned, and to suggest in passing (because the emphasis of much modern catechetics seems to me profoundly awry) that what, in the last analysis, makes sense of the conditions of the marital enterprise, its stability and exclusiveness, is not the worthy and delightful sentiments of love and affection which invite one to marry, but the desire for and demands of a *procreative* community, a family.

However, to show that it is sensible to reserve a *complete and procreative self-giving* to the context of a stable and exclusive union is very far from showing that it is sensible to reserve *sexual intercourse* to that context. For a sexual movement, like any other bodily motion, has as a human action the meaning one gives it in context, and can be engaged in without any pretence that one is either establishing or expressing a stable and exclusive union.

The meaning one gives it—this meaning-giving is an act of choice. Now an intelligent choice to engage in sexual intercourse has to take into account a plain fact—not a 'meaning' so much as a biological fact of physical causality—*viz.*

[3]Para. 8.

that intercourse may bring about procreation; that a child may be conceived; that intercourse is procreative (cause and effect, nothing more). One can accept this fact and seek to capitalize on it, or one can ignore this fact and proceed regardless, or one can by simple means prevent the effect following from the cause. But in any case, one is willy nilly engaged, in sexual intercourse, with the basic human value of procreation. When I get into my car to drive home at night, I am not on a life-saving mission, but the causal potentialities of my activity bring me willy nilly within the range of the basic human value of life, and in terms of that value my actions can be characterized as sufficiently respectful of life, careless of life or wilfully violative of life, as the case may be. I am not bound to be always cultivating life, to be always cultivating God, or truth or social justice, or to be always procreating. But sometimes I find myself in (or bring myself within) situations which by their brute causal structure require of me an attention or a choice that will be adequately open to a basic value whose realization or violation is, by reason of that structure, at stake or in question in the situation. And the call of reason reaching up towards the source of all intelligible good is to remain fully open to that basic intelligible good which now immediately confronts me.

From this point, and from no other, unfolds naturally the whole Christian understanding of the morality of sexual activity. Certainly, the Christian grasp of this basic value, procreation, is distinctively intense—*genitum non factum*— and what is demanded in procreation is not just the *esse* but its *bene esse*, not a spawning, but the bringing of the child into a community of love which will provide the substance of his education into a loving ability to realize all the human values. But this peculiarly intense grasp of the basic natural value does not distort or render peculiar or non-natural the development of the norm of *prudentia* in response to the call of the value. As always, the question is: What actions, by their causal structure, involve a choice adequately open to the basic values, and what actions involve, by their causal structure, a choice immediately against a basic value?

The Christian weighting of the value of procreation, as the value of procreation and education within a *communio personarum*, means that fornication, in which procreation may follow but not within an assured *communio personarum*, involves an inadequate openness to procreation (so understood). Nor can this conclusion be avoided by pointing to the fact that it is easy to exclude the possibility of procreation from fornication. For the choice to exclude the possibility of procreation while engaging in intercourse is always, and in an obvious and unambiguous way (which it requires no Christian weighting of the value of procreation to see), a choice directly and immediately against a basic value. (To this last remark it is perhaps unneccessary to add that taking steps to prevent procreation when one has or is about to bring oneself within the range of the procreative value by engaging in sexual intercourse is obviously very different from the policy of *not* bringing oneself within the range of the value at times when procreation might follow, but engaging in intercourse at other times within the framework of the procreative *communio personarum*.)

And if a question is raised about solitary sexual acts or sexual intercourse *extra vas* (whether homo- or hetero-sexual), the Christian response, making explicit the confused natural sense of the question which Plato was able to appeal to even in a Callicles, turns on the fact that all sexual activity involves an inchoate version, or perhaps a kind of reminder, of the procreative causal potency of 'full' sexual intercourse; this reminder or inchoate version brings a sensitive man sufficiently within the range of the procreative value for that value to make its ordinary imperious claim (like the other basic values) to a sufficient openness and respect towards it. And it is this sense of the symbolic relation of sexual movements to the value of procreation (understood as the rich familial *communio personarum*)[4] that makes the fornication of even the 'naturally' sterile seem, to the Christian, an inadequate openness to a basic good.

So, since the value of procreation, like other basic values, is a permanent and irreducible part of the structure of our will, of our thirst for the intelligible good, and since, like other basic values, its realization or rejection are permanent possibilities always implicit in certain of our situations, it is possible to see (given the vertical perspective towards the Good that can confront us in the immediate form of our choice) that some sexual acts are (as types of choice) always wrong because an inadequate response, or direct closure, to the basic procreative value that they put in question. By a trick of certain European languages, we call the more visibly non-procreative of these acts 'unnatural'; but whether the opposition or indifference to procreation as a value be visible or merely causal, symbolic or effective, all such acts are morally of a kind. If someone wishes to distinguish within the class, we must ask him to reflect: 'Think what you will answer, Callicles, if you are asked the questions that naturally follow...the shocking things I hinted at just now must obviously follow, and many other things as well.'...

...If you do engage in a sexual act of conjugal love you cannot escape its *de facto* corollary: the act is also procreative, either actually, or very possibly, or only barely possibly or (though this does not matter where contraception is in question) only by way of a physical structure reminiscent of its procreative potentialities. And the effect of this is that willy nilly you are forced to choose directly (in a straightforward sense when contracepting, and in more or less symbolic senses in other forms of sexual vice) for or against procreation in that act.

Why, then, is it not 'licit' to break the nexus between the contextual intention of the act (which concerns the *significatio unitatis*) and its causal structure (which confers the *signification procreationis*)? There seems no sanctity in *de facto* connexions of this sort. I think the true reason why it can be said that *this* connexion should not be broken is that to attack either of the

---

[4]It is to this symbolic relation of intra-marital sexual acts to the value of procreation so understood that makes sense of marriage of the naturally sterile; their permanent and exclusive union honours the procreative community as a value they would wish to have devoted themselves to in common had they been able to effectively as well as symbolically.

significationes is wrong in itself. It is wrong to force sexual attentions on one's spouse, indifferent to her state or her wishes—not for any special sexual reason, but because that is contrary to the demands of the basic value of friendship. It is wrong to choose directly against procreation in a context where procreation is immediately in question—again for the general reason that it is wrong to choose against any basic value in such a way. Both basic values which together come in question in sexual intercourse must be respected, not because they are together, but because each is inescapably in question. One could only break the connexion by rejecting one in favour of the other, and that would be wrong; but it would equally be wrong to engage in sexual activity which involved one in rejecting both together.

Finally, there is a secondary and derivative sense in which there is an indissoluble nexus between friendship and procreation in one's sexual activity. Each value demands respect *through* the other. If you choose to reject the procreative value in your act, your act is morally vitiated and so a poor thing to share with your friend—an inadequate response to the fundamental call for friendship, which is to be worthy of your friend and seek true goods for him. Conversely, if you reject the demands of friendship in your act, your act is an inadequate response to the value of procreation, the value which makes sense of the peculiarly exclusive form of friendship that marriage is.

Homosexuality and Natural Law

Burton Leiser

...Theologians and other moralists have said homosexual acts violate the "natural law," and that they are therefore immoral and ought to be prohibited by the state.

The word *nature* has a built-in ambiguity that can lead to serious misunderstandings. When something is said to be "natural" or in conformity with "natural law" or the "law of nature," this may mean either (1) that it is in conformity with the descriptive laws of nature, or (2) that it is not artificial, that man has not imposed his will or his devices upon events or conditions as they exist or would have existed without such interference.

1 The Descriptive Laws of Nature The laws of nature, as these are understood by the scientist, differ from the laws of man. The former are purely descriptive, where the latter are prescriptive. When a scientist says that water

From *Liberty, Justice and Morals* copyright 1973, Burton Leiser. Reprinted by permission. Footnotes deleted.

boils at 212° Fahrenheit or that the volume of a gas varies directly with the heat that is applied to it and inversely with the pressure, he means merely that as a matter of recorded and observable fact, pure water under standard conditions always boils at precisely 212° Fahrenheit and that as a matter of observed fact, the volume of a gas rises as it is heated and falls as pressure is applied to it. These "laws" merely *describe* the manner in which physical substances *actually behave*. They differ from municipal and federal laws in that they *do not prescribe behavior*. Unlike man-made laws, natural laws are not passed by any legislator or group of legislators; they are not proclaimed or announced; they impose no obligation upon anyone or anything: their violation entails no penalty, and there is no reward for following them or abiding by them. When a scientist says that the air in a tire obeys the laws of nature that govern gases, he does *not* mean that the air, having been informed that it *ought* to behave in a certain way, behaves appropriately under the right conditions. He means, rather, that as a matter of fact, the air in a tire *will* behave like all other gases. In saying that Boyle's law governs the behavior of gases, he means merely that gases do, as a matter of fact, behave in accordance with Boyle's law, and that Boyle's law enables one to predict accurately what will happen to a given quantity of a gas as its pressure is raised; he does *not* mean to suggest that some heavenly voice has proclaimed that all gases should henceforth behave in accordance with the terms of Boyle's law and that a ghostly policeman patrols the world, ready to mete out punishments to any gases that violate the heavenly decree. In fact, according to the scientist, it does not make sense to speak of a natural law being violated. For if there were a true exception to a so-called law of nature, the exception would require a change in the description of those phenomena, and the law would have been shown to be no law at all. The laws of nature are revised as scientists discover new phenomena that require new refinements in their descriptions of the way things actually happen. In this respect they differ fundamentally from human laws, which are revised period-ically by legislators who are not so interested in *describing* human behavior as they are in *prescribing* what human behavior *should* be.

2   The Artificial as a Form of the Unnatural   On occasion when we say that something is not natural, we mean that it is a product of human artifice. A typewriter is not a natural object, in this sense, for the substances of which it is composed have been removed from their natural state—the state in which they existed before men came along—and have been transformed by a series of chemical and physical and mechanical processes into other substances. They have been rearranged into a whole that is quite different from anything found in nature. In short, a typewriter is an artificial object. In this sense, clothing is not natural, for it has been transformed considerably from the state in which it was found in nature; and wearing clothing is also unnatural, in this sense, for in one's natural state, before the application of anything artificial, before any human interference with things as they are, one is quite naked.

Human laws, being artificial conventions designed to exercise a degree of control over the natural inclinations and propensities of men, may in this sense be considered to be unnatural.

When theologians and moralists speak of homosexuality, contraception, abortion, and other forms of human behavior as being unnatural and say that for that reason such behavior must be considered to be wrong, in what sense are they using the word *unnatural*? Are they saying that homosexual behavior and the use of contraceptives are contrary to the scientific laws of nature, are they saying that they are artificial forms of behavior, or are they using the terms *natural* and *unnatural* in some third sense?

They cannot mean that homosexual behavior (to stick to the subject presently under discussion) violates the laws of nature in the first sense, for, as has been pointed out, in *that* sense it is impossible to violate the laws of nature. Those laws, being merely descriptive of what actually does happen, would have to *include* homosexual behavior if such behavior does actually take place. Even if the defenders of the theological view that homosexuality is unnatural were to appeal to a statistical analysis by pointing out that such behavior is not normal from a statistical point of view, and therefore not what the laws of nature require, it would be open to their critics to reply that any descriptive law of nature must account for and incorporate all statistical deviations, and that the laws of nature, in this sense, do not *require* anything. These critics might also note that the best statistics available reveal that about half of all American males engage in homosexual activity at some time in their lives, and that a very large percentage of American males have exclusively homosexual relations for a fairly extensive period of time; from which it would follow that such behavior is natural, for them, at any rate, in this sense of the word *natural*.

If those who say that homosexual behavior is unnatural are using the term *unnatural* in the second sense as artificial, it is difficult to understand their objection. That which is artificial is often far better than what is natural. Artificial homes seem, at any rate, to be more suited to human habitation and more conducive to longer life and better health than are caves and other natural shelters. There are distinct advantages to the use of such unnatural (artificial) amenities as clothes, furniture, and books. Although we may dream of an idyllic return to nature in our more wistful moments, we would soon discover, as Thoreau did in his attempt to escape from the artificiality of civilization, that needles and thread, knives and matches, ploughs and nails, and countless other products of human artifice are essential to human life. We would discover, as Plato pointed out in the *Republic,* that no man can be truly self-sufficient. Some of the by-products of industry are less than desirable, but neither industry nor the products of industry are intrinsically evil, even though both are unnatural in this sense of the word.

Interference with nature is not evil in itself. Nature, as some writers have put it, must be tamed. In some respects man must look upon it as an enemy to be conquered. If nature were left to its own devices, without the intervention of human artifice, men would be consumed by disease, they would be plagued by insects, they would be chained to the places where they were born with no means of swift communication or transport, and they would suffer the discomforts and the torments of wind and weather and flood and fire with no practical means of combating any of them. Interfering with nature, doing battle with nature, using human will and reason and skill to thwart what might otherwise follow from the conditions that prevail in the world is a peculiarly human enterprise, one that can hardly be condemned merely because it does what is not natural.

Homosexual behavior can hardly be considered to be unnatural in this sense. There is nothing artificial about such behavior. On the contrary, it is quite natural, in this sense, to those who engage in it. And even if it were not, even if it were quite artificial, this is not in itself a ground for condemning it.

It would seem, then, that those who condemn homosexuality as an unnatural form of behavior must mean something else by the word *unnatural,* something not covered by either of the preceding definitions. A third possibility is this:

3   Anything Uncommon or Abnormal Is Unnatural   If this is what is meant by those who condemn homosexuality on the ground that it is unnatural, it is quite obvious that their condemnation cannot be accepted without further argument. The fact that a given form of behavior is uncommon provides no justification for condemning it. Playing viola in a string quartet may be an uncommon form of human behavior. Yet there is no reason to suppose that such uncommon behavior is, by virtue of its uncommonness, deserving of condemnation or ethically or morally wrong. On the contrary, many forms of behavior are praised precisely because they are so uncommon. Great artists, poets, musicians, and scientists are uncommon in this sense; but clearly the world is better off for having them, and it would be absurd to condemn them or their activities for their failure to be common and normal. If homosexual behavior is wrong, then, it must be for some reason other than its unnaturalness in this sense of the word.

4   Any Use of an Organ or an Instrument That Is Contrary to Its Principal Purpose or Function Is Unnatural   Every organ and every instrument—perhaps even *every* creature—has a function to perform, one for which it is particularly designed. Any use of those instruments and organs that is consonant with their purposes is natural and proper, but any use that is inconsistent with their principal functions is unnatural and improper, and to that extent, evil or harmful. Human teeth, for example, are admirably designed for their principal functions—biting and chewing the kinds of food suitable for human consumption. But they are not particularly well suited for prying the caps from beer bottles. If they are used for that purpose, which is not natural to them, they are likely to crack or break under the strain. The abuse of one's teeth leads to their destruction and to a consequent deterioration in one's overall health. If they are used only for their proper function, however, they may continue to serve well for many years. Similarly, a given drug may have a proper function. If used in the furtherance of that end, it can preserve life and restore health. But if it is abused and employed for purposes for which it was never intended, it may cause serious harm and even death. The natural uses of things are good and proper, but their unnatural uses are bad and harmful.

What we must do, then, is to find the proper use, or the true purpose of each organ in our bodies. Once we have discovered that, we will know what constitutes the natural use of each organ and what constitutes an unnatural, abusive, and potentially harmful employment of the various parts of our bodies. If we are rational, we will be careful to confine behavior to the proper functions and to refrain from unnatural behavior. According to those philosophers who follow this line of reasoning, the way to discover the proper use of any organ is to determine what it is peculiarly suited to do. The eye is suited for seeing, the ear for hearing, the nerves for transmitting impulses from one part of the body to another, and so on.

What are the sex organs peculiarly suited to do? Obviously, they are peculiarly suited to enable men and women to reproduce their own kind. No other organ in the body is capable of fulfilling that function. It follows, according to those who follow the natural-law line, that the proper or natural function of the sex organs is reproduction, and that strictly speaking, any use of these organs for other purposes is unnatural, abusive, potentially harmful, and therefore wrong. The sex organs have been given to us in order to enable us to maintain the continued existence of mankind on this earth. All perversions— including masturbation, homosexual behavior, and heterosexual intercourse that deliberately frustrates the design of the sexual organs—are unnatural and bad. As Pope Pius XI once said, "Private individuals have no other power over the members of their bodies than that which pertains to their natural ends."

But the problem is not so easily resolved. Is it true that every organ has one and only one proper function? A hammer may have been designed to pound nails, and it may perform that particular job best. But it is not sinful to employ a hammer to crack nuts if you have no other more suitable tool immediately available. The hammer, being a relatively versatile tool, may be employed a number of ways. It has no one proper or natural function. A woman's eyes are well adapted to seeing, it is true. But they seem also to be well adapted to flirting. Is a woman's use of her eyes for the latter purpose sinful merely because she is not using them, at that moment, for their "primary" purpose of seeing? Our sexual organs are uniquely adapted for procreation, but that is obviously not the only function for which they are adapted. Human beings may—and do—use those organs for a great many other purposes, and it is difficult to see why any *one* use should be considered to be the only proper one. The sex organs seem to be particularly well adapted to give their owners and others intense sensations of pleasure. Unless one believes that pleasure itself is bad, there seems to be little reason to believe that the use of the sex organs for the production of pleasure in oneself or in others is evil. In view of the peculiar design of these organs, with their great concentration of nerve endings, it would seem that they were designed (if they *were* designed) with that very goal in mind, and that even use for such purposes would be no more unnatural than their use for the purpose of procreation.

Nor should we overlook the fact that human sex organs may be and are used to express, in the deepest and most intimate way open to man, the love of one person for another. Even the most ardent opponents of "unfruitful" intercourse admit that sex does serve this function. They have accordingly conceded that a man and his wife may have intercourse even though she is pregnant, or past the age of child bearing, or in the infertile period of her menstrual cycle.

Human beings are remarkably complex and adaptable creatures. Neither they nor their organs can properly be compared to hammers or to other tools. The analogy quickly breaks down. The generalization that a given organ or instrument has one and only one proper function does not hold up, even with regard to the simplest manufactured tools, for, as we have seen, a tool may be used for more than one purpose—less effectively than one especially designed for a given task, perhaps, but properly and certainly not *sinfully*. A woman may use her eyes not only to see and to flirt, but also to earn money—if she is, for example, an actress or a model. Though neither of the latter functions seems to have been a part of the original design, if one may speak sensibly of *design* in this context, of the eye, it is difficult to see why such a use of the eyes of a woman should be considered sinful, perverse, or unnatural. Her sex organs have the unique capacity of producing ova and nurturing human embryos, under the right conditions, but why should any other use of those organs, including their use to bring pleasure to their owner or to someone else, or to manifest love to another person, or even, perhaps, to earn money, be regarded as perverse, sinful, or unnatural? Similarly, a man's sexual organs possess the unique capacity of causing the generation of another human being, but if a man chooses to use them for pleasure, or for the expression of love, or for some other purpose—so long as he does not interfere with the rights of some other person—the fact that his sex organs do have their unique capabilities does not constitute a convincing justification for condemning their other uses as being perverse, sinful, unnatural, or criminal. If a man "perverts" himself by wiggling his ears for the entertainment of his neighbors instead of using them exclusively for their "natural" function of hearing, no one thinks of consigning him to prison. If he abuses his teeth by using them to pull staples from memos—a function for which teeth were clearly not designed—he is not accused of being immoral, degraded, and degenerate. The fact that people *are* condemned for using their sex organs for their own pleasure or profit, or for that of others, may be more revealing about the prejudices and taboos of our society than it is about our perception of the true nature or purpose of our bodies.

In this connection, it may be worthwhile to note that with the development of artificial means of reproduction (that is, test tube babies), the sex organs may become obsolete for reproductive purposes but would still contribute greatly to human pleasure. In addition, studies of animal behavior and anthropological reports indicate that such nonreproductive sex acts as masturbation, homosexual intercourse, and mutual fondling of genital organs are widespread, both among humans and among lower animals. Under suitable circumstances, many animals reverse their sex roles, males assuming the posture of females and presenting themselves to others for intercourse, and females mounting other females and going through all the actions of a male engaged in intercourse. Many peoples around the world have sanctioned and even ritualized homosexual relations. It would seem that an excessive readiness to insist that human sex organs are designed only for reproductive purposes and therefore ought to be used only for such purposes must be based upon a very narrow conception that is conditioned by our own society's peculiar history and taboos.

To sum up, then, the proposition that any use of an organ that is contrary to its principal purpose or function is unnatural assumes that organs *have* a principal purpose or function, but this may be denied on the ground that the purpose or function of a given organ may vary according to the needs or desires of its owner. It may be denied on the ground that a given organ may have more than one principal purpose or function, and any attempt to call one use or another the only natural one seems to be arbitrary, if not question-begging. Also, the proposition suggests that what is unnatural is evil or depraved. This goes beyond the pure description of things, and enters into the problem of the evaluation of human behavior, which leads us to the fifth meaning of *natural*.

5   That Which Is Natural Is Good, and Whatever Is Unnatural Is Bad   When one condemns homosexuality or masturbation or the use of contraceptives on the ground that it is unnatural, one implies that whatever is unnatural is bad, wrongful, or perverse. But as we have seen, in some sense of the word, the unnatural (the artificial) is often very good, whereas that which is natural (that which has not been subjected to human artifice or improvement) may be very bad indeed. Of course, interference with nature may be bad. Ecologists have made us more aware than we have ever been of the dangers of unplanned and uninformed interference with nature. But this is not say that *all* interference with nature is bad. Every time a man cuts down a tree to make room for a home for himself, or catches a fish to feed himself or his family, he is interfering with nature. If men did not interfere with nature, they would have no homes, they could eat no fish, and, in fact, they could not survive. What, then, can be meant by those who say that whatever is natural is good and whatever is unnatural is bad? Clearly, they cannot have intended merely to reduce the word *natural* to a synonym of *good, right,* and *proper,* and *unnatural* to a synonym of *evil, wrong, improper, corrupt,* and *depraved.* If that were all they had intended to do, there would be very little to discuss as to whether a given form of behavior might be proper even though it is not in strict conformity with someone's views of what is natural; for *good* and *natural* being synonyms, it would follow inevitably that whatever is good must be natural, and vice versa, by definition. This is certainly not what the opponents of homosexuality have been saying when they claim that homosexuality, being unnatural, is evil. For if it were, their claim would be quite empty. They would be saying merely that homosexuality, being evil, is evil—a redundancy that could easily be reduced to the simpler assertion that homosexuality is evil. This assertion, however, is not an argument. Those who oppose homosexuality and other sexual "perversions" on the ground that they are "unnatural" are saying that there is some objectively identifiable quality in such behavior that is unnatural; and that quality, once it has been identified by some kind of scientific observation, can be seen to be detrimental to those who engage in such behavior, or to those around them; and that *because* of the harm (physical, mental, moral, or spiritual) that results from engaging in any behavior possessing the attribute of unnaturalness, such behavior must be considered to be wrongful, and should be discouraged by society. "Unnaturalness" and "wrongfulness" are not synonyms, then, but different concepts. The problem with which we are wrestling is that we are unable to find a meaning for *unnatural* that enables us to arrive at the conclusion that homosexuality is unnatural or that if homosexuality is unnatural, it is therefore wrongful behavior. We have examined four common meanings of *natural* and *unnatural,* and have seen that none of them performs the task that it must perform if the advocates of this argument are to prevail. Without some more satisfactory explanation of the connection between the wrongfulness of homosexuality and its alleged unnaturalness, the argument...must be rejected.

SUGGESTED SUPPLEMENTARY READINGS TO PART TWO

Bogen, David S.: "The Supreme Court's Interpretation of the Guarantee of Free Speech," *Maryland Law Review* 35:555 ff., 1976.

Commager, Henry S.: *Freedom, Loyalty, Dissent* (New York: Oxford University Press, 1954).

Firestone, Shulamith: *The Dialectic of Sex: The Case for Feminist Revolution* (New York: Morrow, 1970).

Gerber, Albert: *Sex, Pornography, and the Law,* 2d rev. ed. (New York: Ballantine, 1964).

Hospers, John: *Libertarianism: A New Turn in Political Philosophy* (Los Angeles: Nash Publishing Co., 1970).

Jones, H.M.: "Censorship, State Secrets and Participatory Democracy," *Analysis* 33:143 ff., 1973.

Liston, Robert A.: *The Right to Know: Censorship in America* (New York: F. Watts, 1973).

Marnell, William H.: *The Right to Know: Media and the Common Good* (New York: Seabury Press, 1973).

Schauer, Frederick F.: *The Law of Obscenity* (Washington, D.C.: Bureau of National Affairs, 1976).

Tussman, Joseph: *Government and the Mind* (New York: Oxford University Press, 1977).

Vannoy, Russell: *Sex Without Love: A Philosophical Investigation* (Buffalo, N.Y.: Prometheus, 1980).

PART THREE

THREE

PREJUDICE AND EQUALITY

INTRODUCTION

Even critics of affirmative action programs agree that discrimination has been rampant in U.S. history. For most of the nineteenth century blacks were slaves. Women during the same period were prohibited from owning property, entering into contracts, serving on juries, becoming members of most professions, and voting. In 1950, Southern society remained strictly segregated by race with separate facilities for blacks and whites in libraries, schools, buses, and toilets. Moreover critics note that even today, over a century after the freeing of the slaves and decades after women were given the vote, the average income of black families is 57 percent that of white families, while working women earn on average only 63 percent as much as working males.

The history of the last few decades, however, has been a history of legislation designed to push society further towards the goal of racial and sexual equality. In 1963 and 1964 Congress passed two historic acts with lasting effects on blacks and women. In the Equal Pay Act (1963) Congress ruled that women must not be paid less than men for performing the same work, and in the Civil Rights Act (1964) Congress ruled through Titles VI and VII of the act that discrimination for reasons of race, sex, or national origin, whether by a public or private firm, was illegal.

Still more recently, the Equal Rights Amendment to the Constitution (known as the ERA) was presented to the separate states for ratification. The ERA, which appears in this section along with arguments from the U.S. Commission on Civil Liberties, was championed as a means of helping to ensure the equal treatment of men and women. But on June 30, 1982, the extended deadline set by Congress for passage of the ERA expired. The measure failed ratification by three states, and the future of additional reform-oriented racial or sexual legislation in the 1980s and 1990s is viewed skeptically by many.

This section considers two distinct issues: first, the moral relevance of the male-female relationship, and second, the fairness of programs designed to correct discrimination.

SEXUAL EQUALITY

Despite cries of "Long live the difference," the question of how differences between men and women affect, and should affect, their roles in society remains controversial. Some have answered it by turning to history and biology. The fact that women traditionally have filled certain roles reflects, they say, an underlying biological reality. In "The Inevitability of Patriarchy" Steven Goldberg argues that the natural aggressiveness of males, resulting from their hormonal structure, explains why they have dominated in positions of leadership in government, religion, and business, throughout history. The French writer, Simone de Beauvoir, on the other hand, rejects all approaches that see women as frozen by biology. For her, the nature of women, like human nature in general, is malleable rather than fixed, and ultimately is an artifact created by choice, history, and culture. Woman's past does not determine her future, and because she has invariably been the victim of history rather than its beneficiary, her first task is to mastermind her own historical liberation.

Even if one agrees with de Beauvoir that biology does not fix social roles or status, the challenge remains of discovering the particular shape that a sexually egalitarian society should take. What should such a society look like? Would it allow for sexual differences—in clothing, style, and professional focus? Some philosophers deny that it would, arguing that sexual liberation can happen only when sexual differences have the same relative significance as eye color; when, in other words, a person's sex, however apparent, is insignificant for predicting other personal characteristics. This ideal is rejected, however, by Bernard Boxill, who in his article, "Sexual Blindness and Sexual Equality," argues that society can be liberated without creating institutional sexlessness.

REMEDIES FOR DISCRIMINATION

Attempts to justify preferential treatment for women and minorities fall into two separate categories: the first is "forward looking"; the second "backward looking." Backward-looking solutions focus on the harm done to minorities and women by pervasive discrimination in the past and set out to remedy that harm through programs of compensation. These remedies may involve giving preference to women and minorities in hiring or in admission to professional schools, or it may involve more direct aid, such as improving schools in minority neighborhoods, or making grants to minority businesses. Forward-looking solutions, although they may recommend the same specific remedies, focus not on past harms but on the character of society in the future. A just racial/sexual mix, for example, is said to be a worthy goal for society to seek, and a goal, moreover, which is good in itself, apart from its tendency to compensate for past wrongs. Note, by the way, that these two attempts at justification fit neatly into the consequentialist-deontology dichotomy discussed in the basic theory section of Part One.

Using both forward- and backward-looking justifications, the United States judicial system, especially through a series of Supreme Court decisions, has defended a variety of corrective programs and societal changes. Beginning in the 1950s with the landmark, *Brown v. Topeka Board of Education* ruling, the Court struck down the "separate but equal" doctrine that allowed segregation in education. And in a series of decisions in the 1960s and early 1970s, most of which dealt with education issues, the Court affirmed the use of color as a factor in hiring (thus striking down the traditional "color-blind" doctrine), and in some cases insisted that hiring and promotion quotas be used to rectify the effects of past discrimination.

But in the mid-1970s the Supreme Court was confronted with a challenge of a different sort. Many observers thought that things had gone too far, and that the very programs designed to end discrimination, especially programs of preferential treatment in schools and professional programs, were practicing a new discrimination—namely, "reverse discrimination." It was then that an aspiring entrant to medical school sued the University of California at Davis for illegally barring him from medical school on the basis of race. Alan Bakke, a white, had been refused admission despite the fact that his qualifications and test scores were higher than many of the minority students admitted. Sixteen of 100 places in the University of California at Davis entering class had been reserved for minorities, and Bakke charged that this violated the equal protection clause of the Fourteenth Amendment as well as Title VI of the 1964 Civil Rights Act. In the landmark decision of *Bakke v. The University of California*, the Court agreed, objecting especially to the University's establishment of a quota for minorities that effectively barred whites from competing for the minority spots. Nonetheless, the Court's accompanying explanation of the decision was as important as the decision itself. Here, the Court affirmed the right of public institutions to use race as a "plus" in admissions. Thus while striking down quotas, the Court opened the door to programs of preferential treatment.

A few years later another white, Brian Weber, sued the Kaiser Corporation on similar grounds. Kaiser, in conjunction with the United Steelworkers Union, had instituted a training program designed to bring blacks into the traditionally segregated professional crafts. The program admitted candidates on the basis of seniority, but reserved 50 percent of the places for blacks. Weber, with more seniority than most of the blacks admitted, argued that his rejection violated

Title VII of the Civil Rights Act. Here, however, the Court denied that discrimination was a factor, arguing first that the 50 percent quota created no "absolute bar" to the admission of whites, and also that the spirit of Title VII encouraged programs to correct for past discrimination.

Some legal theorists find it difficult to reconcile the Weber and Bakke decisions, and whether reconcilable or not, the cases leave unsettled the extent to which the law will tolerate "quota-based" affirmative action plans, especially in private industry. But this much is certain: the Supreme Court has left many of the most important moral questions to the individual managers and school administrators who must design and implement affirmative action plans. Hence, the present law clearly allows the implementation of certain kinds of preferential treatment programs, but the question remains: Are such plans morally acceptable?

The most obvious objection to any race- or sex-conscious plans is that they are unfair because they treat people unequally. Critics of affirmative action point to the principle cited in the past when blacks and women were denied admittance to key social positions; namely, that persons should be hired, fired, promoted, or demoted on the basis of qualifications only, not on the basis of irrelevant characteristics such as race or sex. This is the approach taken by the contemporary philosopher, Lisa Newton, who condemns preferential treatment even when used in programs attempting to rectify the effects of discrimination. Appealing to a notion of justice that assigns equal worth to all human beings, Newton argues that preferential treatment is inconsistent with human equality.

Programs designed to compensate minorities or women for past discrimination are also often attacked for their arbitrariness, that is, for not compensating the right parties to the right extent. Critics ask whether *all* women have been the victims of discrimination? Moreover, is the young black who today is given preferential treatment in law school admissions the person who most deserves compensation? Or is it his father? The criticism relies on the fact that affirmative programs tend to compensate only those persons within range of the program's scope, and to compensate them in exactly equal amounts.

In sharp contrast to such arguments, the philosopher Richard Wasserstrom, who himself participated in the civil rights struggles of the 1960s, argues that modern programs of preferential treatment do not repeat the mistakes of the past. In the past the social hierarchy was dominated by white males who intentionally excluded minorities and women. This, Wasserstrom writes, is why society came to implement affirmative action plans in the first place. Today, even in the presence of such plans, the basic structure of the social hierarchy remains unchanged and discriminatory: white males continue to dominate positions of power and prestige. Furthermore, he argues, a rigid insistence on the use of qualifications alone in hiring and admittance decisions is hypocritical since we frequently accept decisions not based on qualifications. Seniority is often a factor in setting pay scales, and judges are often appointed on the basis not of their qualifications, but of their political party.

CASE STUDY—Prejudice and Equality

FREIDA MAE JONES

Freida Mae Jones was born in her grandmother's Georgia farm house on June 1, 1949. She was the sixth of George and Ella Jones's ten children. Mr. and Mrs. Jones moved to New York City when Freida was four because they felt that the educational and career opportunities for their children would be better in the north. With the help of some cousins, they settled in a five-room apartment in the Bronx. George worked as a janitor at Lincoln Memorial Hospital and Ella was a part-time housekeeper in a nearby neighborhood. The Joneses were conservative and strict parents. They kept a close watch on their children's activities and demanded they be home by a certain hour. The Joneses believed that because they were black, the children would have to perform and behave better than their peers to be successful. They believed that their children's education would be the most important factor in their success as adults.

Freida entered Memorial High School, a racially integrated public school, in September 1963. Seventy percent of the student body was caucasian, twenty percent black, and ten percent hispanic. About sixty percent of the graduates went on to college. Of this sixty percent, four percent were black and hispanic and all were male. In the middle of her senior year Freida was academically the top student in her class. Following school regulations, Freida met with her Guidance Counselor to discuss her plans upon graduation. The counselor advised her to consider training in a "practical" field such as housekeeping, cooking or sewing, so that she could find a job.

George and Ella Jones were furious when Freida told them what the counselor had advised. Ella said, "Don't they see what they are doing? Freida is the top rated student in her whole class and they are telling her to become a manual worker. She showed that she has a fine mind and can work better than any of her classmates and still she is told not to become anybody in this world. It's really not any different in the north than back home in Georgia, except that they don't try to hide it down south. They want her to throw away her fine mind because she is a black girl and not a white boy. I'm going to go up to her school tomorrow and talk to the Principal."

As a result of Mrs. Jones' visit to the Principal, Freida was assisted in applying to ten fine eastern colleges, each of which offered her full scholarships. In September 1966, Freida entered Werbley College, an exclusive private women's college in Massachusetts. In 1970, Freida graduated Summa Cum Laude in History. She decided to return to New York to teach grade school in the City's Public School system. Freida was unable to obtain a full-time position, so she substituted. She also enrolled as a part-time student in Columbia University's Graduate School of Education. By 1975 she had [attained] her Master of Arts degree in Teaching (MAT) from Columbia, but could not find a permanent

Prepared by Martin R. Moser, Ph.D., Assistant Professor of Management, The Graduate School of Management, Clark University, © 1980 by Martin R. Moser. Reprinted by permission.

teaching job. New York City was laying off teachers and had instituted a hiring freeze due to the City's financial problems.

Feeling frustrated about her future as a teacher, Freida decided to get an MBA. She thought that there was more opportunity in business than in education. Churchill Business School, a small, prestigious school located in upstate New York, accepted Freida into its MBA program.

Freida completed her MBA in 1977 and accepted an entry-level position at the Industrialist World Bank of Boston in a fast-track management development program. The three-year program introduced her to all facets of bank operations, from telling to loan training and operations management. She was rotated to branch offices throughout New England. After completing the program she became an Assistant Manager for Branch Operations in the West Springfield Branch Office.

During her second year in the program, Freida had met James Walker, a black doctoral student in Business Administration at the University of Massachusetts. Her assignment to West Springfield precipitated their decision to get married. They originally anticipated that they would marry when James finished his doctorate and he could move to Boston. Instead, they decided he would pursue a job in the Springfield-Hartford area.

Freida was not only the first black but also the first woman to hold an executive position in the West Springfield Branch Office. Throughout the training program Freida felt somewhat uneasy although she did very well. There were six other blacks in the training program, five men and one women and she found support and comfort in sharing her feelings with them. The group spent much of their free time together. Freida had hoped that she would be located near one or more of the group when she went out into the "real world." She felt that, although she was able to share her feelings about work with James, he did not have the full appreciation or understanding of her co-workers. However, the nearest group member was located one hundred miles away.

Freida's boss in Springfield was Stan Luboda, a fifty-five-year-old, native New Englander. Freida felt that he treated her differently than he did the other trainees. He always tried to help her and took a lot of time (too much according to Freida) explaining things to her. Freida felt that he was treating her like a child and not an intelligent and able professional.

"I'm really getting frustrated and angry about what is happening at the bank," Freida said to her husband. "The people don't even realize it, but their prejudice comes through all the time. I feel as if I have to fight all the time just to start off even. Luboda gives Paul Cohen more responsibility than me, and we both started at the same time with the same amount of training. He's meeting customers alone and Luboda has accompanied me to each meeting I've had with a customer."

"I run into the same thing at school," said James, "The people don't even know that they are doing it. The other day I met with a professor on my dissertation committee. I've known and worked with him for over three years.

He said he wanted to talk with me about a memo he had received. I asked him what it was about and he said that the records office wanted to know about my absence during the spring semester. He said that I had to sign some forms. He had me confused with Martin Jordan, another black student. Then he realized that it wasn't me, but Jordan, who he wanted. All I could think was that we all must look alike to him. I was angry. Maybe it was an honest mistake on his part, but whenever something like that happens, and it happens often, it gets me really angry."

"Something like that happened to me," said Freida. "I was using the copy machine, and Luboda's secretary was talking to someone in the hall. She had just gotten a haircut and was saying that her hair was now like Freida's—short and kinky, and that she would have to talk to me about how to take care of it. Luckily, my back was to her. I just bit my lip and went on with my business. Maybe she was trying to be cute, because I know she saw me standing there, but comments like that are not cute, they are racist."

"I don't know what to do," said James. "I try to keep things in perspective. Unless people interfere with my progress, I try to let it slide. I only have so much energy and it doesn't make any sense to waste it on people who don't matter. But that doesn't make it any easier to function in a racist environment. People don't realize that they are being racist. But a lot of times their expectations of black people or women, or whatever, are different because of skin color or gender. They expect you to be different, although if you were to ask them they would say that they don't. In fact, they would be highly offended if you implied that they were racist or sexist. They don't see themselves that way."

"Luboda is interfering with my progress," said Freida. "The kinds of experiences I have now will have a direct bearing on my career advancement. If decisions are being made because I am black or a woman, then they are racially and sexually biased. It's the same kind of attitude that the Guidance Counselor had when I was in high school, although not as blatant."

In September 1980, Freida decided to speak to Luboda about his treatment of her. She met with him in his office. "Mr. Luboda, there is something that I would like to discuss with you, and I feel a little uncomfortable because I'm not sure how you will respond to what I am going to say."

"I want you to feel that you can trust me," said Luboda. "I am anxious to help you in any way I can."

"I feel that you treat me differently than you treat the other people around here," said Freida. "I feel that you are over-cautious with me, that you always try to help me, and never let me do anything on my own."

"I always try to help the new people around here," answered Luboda. "I'm not treating you any differently than I treat any other person. I think that you are being a little too sensitive. Do you think that I treat you differently because you are black?"

"The thought had occurred to me," said Freida. "Paul Cohen started here the same time that I did and he has much more responsibility than I do."

Cohen had started at the bank at the same time as Freida and completed the management training program with Freida. Cohen was already handling accounts on his own, while Freida had not yet been given that responsibility.

"Freida, I know you are not a naive person," said Luboda. "You know the way the world works. There are some things which need to be taken more slowly than others. There are some assignments for which Cohen has been given more responsibility than you, and there are some assignments for which you are given more responsibility than Cohen. I try to put you where you do the most good."

"What you are saying is that Cohen gets the more visible, customer contact assignments and I get the behind-the-scenes running of the operations assignments," said Freida. "I'm not naive, but I'm also not stupid either. Your decisions are unfair. Cohen's career will advance more quickly than mine because of the assignments that he gets."

"Freida that is not true," said Luboda. "Your career will not be hurt because you are getting different responsibilities than Cohen. You both need the different kinds of experiences you are getting. And you have to face the reality of the banking business. We are in a conservative business. When we speak to customers we need to gain their confidence, and we put the best people for the job in the positions to achieve that end. If we don't get their confidence they can go down the street to our competitors and do business with them. Their services are no different than ours. It's a competitive business in which you need every edge you have. It's going to take time for people to change some of their attitudes about whom they borrow money from or where they put their money. I can't change the way people feel. I am running a business, but believe me I won't make any decisions that are detrimental to you or to the bank. There is an important place for you here at the bank. Remember, you have to use your skills to the best advantage of the bank as well as your career."

"So what you are saying is that all things being equal, except my gender and my race, Cohen will get different treatment than me in terms of assignments," said Freida.

"You're making it sound like I am making a racist and sexist decision," said Luboda. "I'm making a business decision utilizing the resources at my disposal and the market situation in which I must operate. You know exactly what I am talking about. What would you do if you were in my position?"

The Equal Rights Amendment

The proposed Equal Rights Amendment reads as follows:

Resolved by the Senate and House of Representatives of the United States of America in Congress assembled (two-thirds of each House concurring therein). That the following article is proposed as an amendment to the Constitution of the United States, which shall be valid to all intents and purposes as part of the Constitution when ratified by the legislatures of three-fourths of the several States within seven years from the date of its submission by the Congress:

"ARTICLE—

"Section 1. Equality of rights under the law shall not be denied or abridged by the United States or by any State on account of sex.

"Sec. 2. The Congress shall have the power to enforce, by appropriate legislation, the provisions of this article.

"Sec. 3. This amendment shall take effect two years after the date of ratification."

Statement on the Equal Rights Amendment

U.S. Commission on Civil Rights

FAMILY LAW

A woman's rights during marriage, as well as after—whether the marriage ends as a result of death or divorce—have traditionally been those of a second-class citizen. Many State laws still reflect their roots in the English common law view of the married woman as the property of her husband.

Some of the more oppressive aspects of this discrimination have been removed over the past century; so that a married woman can now own property, enter into contracts, be granted custody of her children, and, in most cases, keep her own earnings. However, laws covering marriage continue to deny women equal rights.

Marital property laws illustrate the persistence of sex bias against women. In Georgia, for example, a married couple's home belongs only to the husband, even when it has been paid for by the wife. In other States, the husband is given the right to manage and control marital property without the wife's consent, again, even if it was purchased with the wife's earnings. In Wisconsin, the earnings of a married woman "accruing from labor performed for her husband, or in his employ, or payable by him "are not considered her separate property and are subject to her husband's control.

From Senate Report #92-689 and the *Statement on the Equal Rights Amendment*, United States Commission on Civil Rights (1978) pp. 5–7.

The same bias is evident in laws that deny a woman the right to sue a third party who has injured her husband and thereby deprived her of his services. A husband, similarly deprived, can sue.

The married woman who chooses to be a full-time homemaker has the least legal and economic protection of all, since many States do not recognize her labor as having economic value. This is repugnant to the view of marriage as a partnership between the husband and the wife, with both performing different but equally important roles, each having economic significance.

The lack of economic value accorded a woman's contributions to a marriage is demonstrated in the case of a Nebraska farm couple who worked the land together for 33 years. When the husband died in 1974, his wife learned that in the Federal Government's eyes the farm belonged entirely to him. Unless she could prove that she helped to pay for its purchase or improvement, she would be liable for $25,000 inheritance tax. Her years of work, even the joint title, was no proof. Had the wife died first, her husband would have had to pay no tax.

In most States, when a marriage ends, distribution of the marital property follows a similar rule. Until a recent successful challenge under the Pennsylvania State ERA, a woman in that State was faced with the legal presumption that all the household articles acquired during the marriage—such as the stove, the TV, and even her jewelry—belonged to her husband, unless she could prove that she paid for them. While States like New York do not have such an explicit presumption, the result is often the same because one's legal rights to property generally are determined by proof of actual economic contribution or of receipt as gift. Most homemakers who earn no wages cannot establish such proof.

Sex-based roles and presumptions also affect a married woman's ability to get credit. This is true even under the Federal Equal Credit Opportunity Act (enacted to make credit available without discrimination on the basis of sex or marital status), since creditors may consider State marital property laws in determining creditworthiness.

Similar hardships face the homemaker under the social security program. Since she has no independent entitlement to benefits, if she becomes disabled, she and her dependents have no right to social security, even though her services are lost to her family. Because the program does not recognize the economic value of her contribution to the family, she will not receive benefits under her husband's coverage if she is widowed before the age of 50 unless she has minor or disabled children in her care. This is true even if she is disabled and cannot work.

The only economic "right" the married woman has traditionally had is the theoretical "right to support during a marriage." The significance of this "right" and the potential effect of the ERA on it have been primary targets of distortion by ERA opponents trying to argue that the amendment will strip away women's rights. In fact, the legal duty of a husband to support his wife is largely unenforceable. It is little more than myth, since courts will not interfere in an ongoing marriage to ensure adequate support either for the wife or for the children.

Laws governing support and alimony during separation and after divorce are similarly illusory in the benefits they appear to confer upon women. The reality is that only 14 percent of divorced wives were awarded alimony in 1975 and that fewer than half were able to collect their payments regularly. Similar enforcement problems exist for collecting child support. A study tracing child support payments over 10 years showed that 62 percent of male parents failed to comply fully with court-ordered child support payments in the first year after the order, and 42 percent did not make even a single payment. By the 10th year, 79 percent were making no payments at all....

WOMEN IN THE LABOR FORCE

Women who work outside the home continue to be disadvantaged by sex-role stereotypes and gender lines that affect employment opportunities and achievements. These women, too, stand to gain under the Equal Rights Amendment. Despite recent legislative reform and efforts to enforce Federal and State antidiscrimination laws, sex bias in employment persists.

While the labor market has provided increased job opportunities for women in recent years, most of the openings have been in clerical and service areas traditionally dominated by women. Indeed, occupational segregation by sex increased substantially between 1970 and 1976. Not only are the jobs held by women different from those held by men, but the evidence is that they are valued less by society.

In professional and technical fields, women are overrepresented in jobs that are lower on the career ladder than men in the same industries: women are teachers more often than principals, bookkeepers more often than comptrollers. Even within a traditional woman's field, clerical occupations, women are more likely to be employed in lower paying positions as typists, stenographers, secretaries, and file clerks, while men tend to be employed as administrative assistants, a higher paying clerical occupation. In general, the jobs in which women are concentrated pay lower salaries than those paid in traditionally male-dominated positions, even when these positions involve equivalent skill, effort, and responsibility.

Even when adjustments are made for education and occupation, women earn less than men. In 1976 a woman who attended 4 years of college was earning about as much as a man with 8 years of elementary school education. On the average, in 1976 women clerical workers earned $4,200 less than male clerical workers, and saleswomen earned $6,900 less than salesmen. In public employment, the median income for women working full time was $9,215 in 1975, while the median income for men was $13,118.

CRIMINAL LAW

Criminal law is another area in which women and men are treated differently because of their sex. This treatment has most often been disadvantageous to women, as both victims and offenders.

In some jurisdictions, definitions of criminal behavior and legal defenses reflect sex-based notions. In Alabama, for example, if a husband finds his wife in the act of adultery and immediately kills her he is not guilty of murder, but of the lesser crime of manslaughter. However, the same defense is not available to a wife.

This view that husbands have a special prerogative when it comes to their wives also is reflected in the laws of those States that do not recognize a charge of forcible rape as a crime when committed by a husband against his wife, regardless of the circumstances and degree of coercion involved.

Explicit sex lines similarly are found in prostitution laws. Traditionally, prostitution was defined as a "woman's act," with no attempt to penalize the men who paid or were paid for it. Although many jurisdictions have revised these laws to cover men as well as women, "less than half explicitly penalize the patrons of prostitution, and many of those that do impose less stringent penalties against patrons than prostitutes."

Sex-based definitions of criminal behavior also permeate the juvenile justice system which often subjects girls and boys to differing definitions of delinquent behavior and to different sentences. In general, more girls are detained for "status" offenses such as promiscuity or truancy; while boys are arrested for delinquent acts such as theft. On the average, girls are institutionalized for less serious conduct than boys and for longer periods of time.

Sentencing and parole statutes and practices further illustrate the persistent sex-based discrimination in criminal law. In some States, laws still mandate inderminate sentences for women, while men receive set minimum and maximum terms. This disparate treatment stems from the sex-based presumption that "women, including women offenders, are more malleable than men and thus more amenable to reform and rehabilitation. In practice, this means that a woman offender remains in custody until the prison administration finds she has been 'corrected' while a man who has been imprisoned 'does time' for some set period..." The result may be that the female offender is incarcerated far longer or far shorter than a man convicted of the same offense....

The Inevitability of Patriarchy

Steven Goldberg

Male dominance refers to the *feeling* acknowledged by the emotions of both men and women that the woman's will is somehow subordinate to the male's and that general authority in dyadic and familial relationships, in whatever terms a particular society defines authority, ultimately resides in the male. I

Abridged from pp. 33, 35, 49, 51, 105–112 in *The Inevitability of Patriarchy* by Steven Goldberg (New York: William Morrow and Company, 1973). Footnotes deleted. Copyright 1973 by Steven Goldberg. By permission of William Morrow and Company.

realize that this is not the most graceful way of defining male dominance, but it is the most accurate. As was the case with patriarchy, male dominance is universal; no society has ever failed to conform its expectations of men and women, and the social roles relevant to these expectations, to the feeling of men and women that it is the male who "takes the lead." [I shall] attempt to demonstrate that every society accepts the existence of these feelings, and conforms to their existence by socializing children accordingly, because every society must....

The voluminous writings of the feminists attest to the fact that, despite the virtual absence of customs of deference in American society, the feelings and emotional expectations that underpin the customs of every other society affect our behavior as surely as these feelings affect the behavior of the men and women of every other society. Thus the author of the feminist essay complains that she feels that she has somehow lost an argument with her husband, that somehow she was wrong, even when she knows intellectually that hers was the better argument, that she was right, and that her husband was being emotionally dishonest. Thus the feminist novelist objects to the fact that it is somehow the male who "takes the lead" in endless numbers of situations as varied as crossing streets and choosing friends. The husband tends to "tell" ("my husband told me to take the TV to the repair shop") while the wife tends to "ask" ("my wife asked me to take the TV to the repair shop"). To be sure, women do, as these novelists acknowledge, have a great deal of power in that they make decisions in many areas, but it is the *feeling* that the husband *lets* them make such decisions (that he delegates authority, that he "allows") that annoys the feminist and that is the evidence of the presence of male dominance....

The view of man and woman in society that implicitly underlies all of the arguments of the feminists is this: there is nothing inherent in the nature of human beings or of society that necessitates that any role or task (save those requiring great strength or the ability to give birth) be associated with one sex or the other; there is no natural order of things decreeing that dyadic and social authority must be associated with men, nor is there any reason why it must be men who rule in every society. Patriarchy, matriarchy, and "equiarchy" are all equally possible and—while every society may invoke "the natural order of things" to justify its particular system—all the expectations we have of men and women are culturally determined and have nothing to do with any sort of basic male or female nature.... I believe that in the past we have been looking in the wrong direction for the answer to the question of why every society rewards male roles with higher status than it does female roles (even when the male tasks in one society are the female tasks in another). While it is true that men are always in the positions of authority from which status tends to be defined, male roles are not given high status primarily *because* men fill these roles; men fill these roles because their biological aggression "advantage" can be manifested *in any non-child related area rewarded by high status in any society*.... As we shall see, this aggression "advantage" can be most manifested and can most enable men to reap status rewards *not* in those relatively homogeneous, collectivist primitive societies in which both male and female must play similar economic roles if the society is to survive or in the monarchy (which guarantees an occasional female leader); this biological factor will be given freest play in the complex, relatively individualistic, bureaucratic, democratic society which, of necessity, must emphasize organizational authority and in which social mobility is relatively free of traditional barrier to advancement. There were more female heads of state in the first two-thirds of the sixteenth century than in the first two-thirds of the twentieth.

The mechanisms involved here are easily seen if we examine any roles that males have attained by channeling their aggression toward such attainment. We will assume for now that equivalent women could *perform* the task of roles as well as men if they could attain the roles. Here we can speak of the corporation president, the union leader, the governor, the chairman of an association, or any other role or position for which aggression is a precondition for attainment. Now the environmentalist and the feminist will say that the fact that all such roles are nearly always filled by men is attributable not to male aggression but to the fact that women have not been allowed to enter the competitive race to attain these positions, that they have been told that these positions are in male areas, and that girls are socialized away from competing with boys in general. Women *are* socialized in this way, but again we must ask why. If innate male aggression has nothing to do with male attainment of positions of authority and status in the political, academic, scientific, or financial spheres, if aggression has nothing to do with the reasons why *every* society socializes girls away from those areas which are given high status and away from competition in general, then why is it never the *girls* in any society who are socialized toward these areas, why is it never the nonbiological roles played by women that have high status, why is it always boys who are told to compete, and why do women never "force" men into the low-status, nonmaternal roles that women play in every society?

These questions pose no problems if we acknowledge a male aggression that enables men to attain any nonbiological role given high status by any society. For one need merely consider the result of a society's *not* directing girls toward roles women are more capable of playing than are men or roles with status low enough that men will not strive for them. No doubt some women would be aggressive enough to succeed in competitions with men and there would be considerably more women in high-status positions than there are now. But most women would lose in such competitive struggles with men (because men have the aggression advantage) and so most women would be forced to live adult lives as failures in areas in which the society had *wanted them to succeed*. It is women, far more than men, who would never allow a situation in which girls are socialized in such a way that the vast majority of them were doomed to adult lifetimes of failure to live up to their own expectations. Now I have no doubt that there is a biological factor that gives women the desire to emphasize maternal and nurturance roles, but the point here is that we can accept the feminist assumption that there is no female propensity of this sort and still see that a society must socialize women away from roles that men will attain through their aggression. For if women did not develop an alternative set of criteria for success their sense of their own competence would suffer intolerably. It is undeniable that the resulting different values and expectations that are attached to men and women will tend to work against the aggressive woman while they work for the man who is not more aggressive. But this is the unavoidable result of the fact that most men are more aggressive than most women so that this woman, who is as aggressive as the average man, but more aggressive than most women, is an exception. Furthermore, even if the sense of competence of each sex did not necessitate society's attaching to each sex values and expectations based on those qualities possessed by each sex, observation of the majority of each sex by the population would "automatically" lead to these values and expectations being attached to men and women.

Socialization is the process by which society prepares children for adulthood. The way in which its goals conform to the reality of biology is seen quite clearly when we consider the method in which testosterone generates male aggression (testosterone's serially developing nature). Preadolescent boys and girls have roughly equal testosterone levels, yet young boys are far more aggressive than young girls. Eva Figes has used this observation to dismiss incorrectly the possibility of a hormone-aggression association. Now it is quite probable that the boy is more aggressive than the girl for a purely biological reason. We have seen that it is simplistic to speak simply in terms of hormone levels and that there is evidence of male-female differences in the behavior of infants shortly after birth (when differential socialization is not a plausible explanation of such differences). The fetal alteration of the boy's brain by the testosterone that was generated by his testes has probably left him far more sensitive to the aggression-related properties of the testosterone that is present during boyhood than the girl, who did not receive such alteration. But let us for the moment assume that this is not the case. This does not at all reduce the importance of the hormonal factor. For even if the boy is more aggressive than the girl only because the society allows him to be, the boy's socialization still flows from society's acknowledging biological reality. Let us consider what would happen if girls [had] the same innate aggression as boys and if a society did not socialize girls away from aggressive competitions. Perhaps half of the third-grade baseball team would be female. As many girls as boys would frame their expectations in masculine values and girls would develop not their feminine abilities but their masculine ones. During adolescence, however, the same assertion of the male chromosomal program that causes the boys to grow beards raises their testosterone level, and their potential for aggression, to a level far above that of the adolescent women. If society did not teach young girls that beating boys at competitions was unfeminine (behavior unappropriate for a woman), if it did not socialize them away from the political and economic areas in which aggression leads to attainment, these girls would grow into adulthood with self-images based not on succeeding in areas for which biology has left them better prepared than men, but on competitions that most women could not win. If women did not develop feminine qualities as girls (assuming that such qualities do not spring automatically from female biology) then they would be forced to deal with the world in the aggressive terms of men. They would lose every source of power their feminine abilities now give them and they would gain nothing. (Likewise, if there is a physiological difference between men and women which generates dimorphic behavior in the feelings elicited by an infant, social values and socialization will conform to this fact. They will conform both because observation by the population of men and women will preclude the development of values which ignore the physiological difference and because, even if such values could develop, they would make life intolerable for the vast majority of males, who would feel the tension between social expectation and the dearth of maternal feelings, and the vast majority of females, whose physiologically generated feelings toward the infant would be frustrated.)

If one is convinced that sexual biology gives the male an advantage in aggression, competitiveness, and dominance, but he does not believe that it engenders in men and women different propensities, cognitive aptitudes, and modes of perception, and if he considers it discrimination when male aggression leads to attainment of position even when aggression is not relevant to the task to be performed, then the unavoidable conclusion is that discrimination so defined is unavoidable. Even if one is convinced from the discussion in the following sections that the differing biological substrates that underlie the mental apparatus of men and women *do* engender different propensities, cognitive aptitudes, and modes of perception, he will probably agree that the relevance of this to male attainment of male roles is small when compared to the importance of male biological aggression to attainment. Innate tendencies to specific aptitudes *would* indicate that at any given level of competence there will be more men than women or vice versa (depending on the qualities relevant to the task) and that the very best will, in all probability, come from the sex whose potentials are relevant to the task. Nonetheless, drastic sexual differences in occupational and authority roles reflect male aggression and society's acknowledgment of it far more than they do differences in aptitudes, yet they are still inevitable.

In addition, even if artificial means were used to place large numbers of women in authority positions, it is doubtful that stability could be maintained. Even in our present male bureaucracies problems arise whenever a subordinate is more aggressive than his superior and, if the more aggressive executive is not allowed to rise in the bureaucracy, delicate psychological adjustments must be made. Such adjustments are also necessary when a male bureaucrat has a female superior. When such situations are rare exceptions adjustments can be made without any great instability occurring, particularly if the woman in the superior position complements her aggression with sensitivity and femininity. It would seem likely, however, that if women shared equally in power at each level of the bureaucracy, chaos would result for two reasons. Even if we consider the bureaucracy as a closed system, the excess of male aggression would soon manifest itself either in men moving quickly up the hierarchy or in a male refusal to acknowledge female authority. But a bureaucracy is not a closed system, and the discrepancy between male dominance in private life and bureaucratic female dominance (from the point of view of the male whose superior is a woman) would soon engender chaos. Consider that even the present minute minority of women in high authority positions expend enormous amounts of energy trying *not* to project the commanding authority that is seen as the mark of a good male executive. It is true that the manner in which aggression is manifested will be affected by the values of the society in general and the nature of the field of competition in particular; aggression in an academic environment is camouflaged far more than in the executive arena. While a desire for control and power and a single-mindedness of purpose are no doubt relevant, here aggression is not easily defined. One might inject the theoretical argument that women could attain positions of authority and leadership by countering the male's advantage in aggression with feminine abilities. Perhaps, but the equivalents of the executive positions in every area of suprafamilial life in every society have been attained by men, and there seems no reason to believe that, suddenly, feminine means will be capable of neutralizing male aggression in these areas. And, in any case, an emphasis on feminine abilities is hardly what the feminists desire. All of this can be seen in a considerably more optimistic light, from the point of view of most women, if one considers that the biological abilities possessed only by women are complemented by biologically generated propensities directing women to roles that can be filled only by women. But it is still the same picture.

On Being a Woman

Simone de Beauvoir

First we must ask: what is a woman? *"Tota mülier in utero,"* says one, "woman is a womb." But in speaking of certain women, connoisseurs declare that they are not women, although they are equipped with a uterus like the rest. All agree in recognizing the fact that females exist in the human species; today as always they make up about one half of humanity. And yet we are told that femininity is in danger; we are exhorted to be women, remain women, become women. It would appear, then, that every female human being is not necessarily a woman; to be so considered she must share in that mysterious and threatened reality known as femininity. Is this attribute something secreted by the ovaries? Or is it a Platonic essence, a product of the philosophic imagination? Is a rustling petticoat enough to bring it down to earth?...

If her functioning as a female is not enough to define a woman, if we decline also to explain her through "the eternal feminine," and if nevertheless we admit, provisionally, that women do exist, then we must face the question: what is a woman?

To state the question is, to me, to suggest, at once, a preliminary answer. The fact that I ask it is in itself significant. A man would never get the notion of writing a book on the peculiar situation of the human male.[1] But if I wish to define myself, I must first of all say: "I am a woman"; on this truth must be based all further discussion. A man never begins by presenting himself as an individual of a certain sex; it goes without saying that he is a man. The terms *masculine* and *feminine* are used symmetrically only as a matter of form, as on legal papers. In actuality the relation of the two sexes is not quite like that of two electrical poles, for man represents both the positive and the neutral, as is indicated by the common use of *man* to designate human beings in general; whereas woman represents only the negative, defined by limiting criteria, without reciprocity. In the midst of an abstract discussion it is vexing to hear a man say: "You think thus and so because you are a woman"; but I know that my only defense is to reply: "I think thus and so because it is true," thereby removing my subjective self from the argument. It would be out of the question to reply: "And you think the contrary because you are a man," for it is understood that the fact of being a man is no peculiarity. A man is in the right in being a man; it is the woman who is in the wrong. It amounts to this: just as for the ancients there was an absolute vertical with reference to which the oblique was defined, so there is an absolute human type, the masculine. Woman has ovaries, a uterus; these peculiarities imprison her in her subjectivity, circumscribe her within the limits of her own nature. It is often said that she thinks with her glands. Man superbly ignores the fact that his anatomy also includes glands, such as the testicles, and that they secrete hormones. He thinks of his body as a direct and normal connection with the world, which he believes he apprehends objectively, whereas he regards the body of woman as a hindrance, a prison, weighed down by everything peculiar to it. "The female is a female by virtue of a certain *lack* of qualities," said Aristotle; "we should regard the female nature as afflicted with a natural defectiveness." And St. Thomas for his part pronounced woman to be an "imperfect man," an "incidental" being. This is symbolized in Genesis where Eve is depicted as made from what Bossuet called "a supernumerary bone" of Adam.

---

[1]The Kinsey Report [Alfred C. Kinsey and others: *Sexual Behavior in the Human Male* (W. B. Saunders Co., 1948)] is no exception, for it is limited to describing the sexual characteristics of American men, which is quite a different matter.

Thus humanity is male and man defines woman not in herself but as relative to him; she is not regarded as an autonomous being. Michelet writes: "Woman, the relative being...." And Benda is most positive in his *Rapport d'Uriel*: "The body of man makes sense in itself quite apart from that of woman, whereas the latter seems wanting in significance by itself....Man can think of himself without woman. She cannot think of herself without man." And she is simply what man decrees; thus she is called "the sex," by which is meant that she appears essentially to the male as a sexual being. For him she is sex—absolute sex, no less. She is defined and differentiated with reference to man and not he with reference to her; she is incidental, the inessential as opposed to the essential. He is the Subject, he is the Absolute—she is the Other....[2]

It is only in the human perspective that we can compare the female and the male of the human species. But man is defined as a being who is not fixed, who makes himself what he is. As Merleau-Ponty very justly puts it, man is not a natural species: he is a historical idea. Woman is not a completed reality, but rather a becoming, and it is in her becoming that she should be compared with man: that is to say, her *possibilities* should be defined. What gives rise to much of the debate is the tendency to reduce her to what she has been, to what she is today, in raising the question of her capabilities; for the fact is that capabilities are clearly manifested only when they have been realized— but the fact is also that when we have to do with a being whose nature is transcendent action, we can never close the books....

We must not lose sight of those facts which make the question of a woman's labor a complex one. An important and thoughtful woman recently made a study of the women in the Renault factories; she states that they would prefer to stay in the home rather than work in the factory. There is no doubt that they get economic independence only as members of a class which is economically oppressed; and, on the other hand, their jobs at the factory do not relieve them of housekeeping burdens. If they had been asked to choose between forty hours of work a week in the factory or forty hours of work a week in the home, they would doubtless have furnished quite different answers. And perhaps they would cheerfully accept both jobs, if as factory workers they

---

[2]E. Lévinas expresses this idea most explicitly in his essay *Temps et l'Autre.* "Is there not a case in which otherness, alterity [*altérité*], unquestionably marks the nature of a being, as its essence, an instance of otherness not consisting purely and simply in the opposition of two species of the same genus? I think that the feminine represents the contrary in its absolute sense, this contrariness being in no wise affected by any relation between it and its specific difference...no more is the sexual difference a mere contradiction....Nor does this difference lie in the duality of two complementary terms, for two complementary terms imply a pre-existing whole....Otherness reaches its full flowering in the feminine, a term of the same rank as consciousness but of opposite meaning."

I suppose that Lévinas does not forget that woman, too, is aware of her own consciousness, or ego. But it is striking that he deliberately takes a man's point of view, disregarding the reciprocity of subject and object. When he writes that woman is mystery, he implies that she is mystery for man. Thus his description, which is intended to be objective, is in fact an assertion of masculine privilege.

were to be integrated in a world that would be theirs, in the development of which they would joyfully and proudly share. At the present time, peasants apart, the majority of women do not escape from the traditional feminine world; they get from neither society nor their husbands the assistance they would need to become in concrete fact the equals of the men. Only those women who have a political faith, who take militant action in the unions, who have confidence in their future, can give ethical meaning to thankless daily labor. But lacking leisure, inheriting a traditional submissiveness, women are naturally just beginning to develop a political and social sense. And not getting in exchange for their work the moral and social benefits they might rightfully count on, they naturally submit to its constraints without enthusiasm....

The advantage man enjoys, which makes itself felt from his childhood, is that his vocation as a human being in no way runs counter to his destiny as a male. Through the identification of phallus and transcendence, it turns out that his social and spiritual successes endow him with a virile prestige. He is not divided. Whereas it is required of woman that in order to realize her femininity she must make herself object and prey, which is to say that she must renounce her claims as sovereign subject. It is this conflict that especially marks the situation of the emancipated woman. She refuses to confine herself to her role as female, because she will not accept mutilation; but it would also be a mutilation to repudiate her sex. Man is a human being with sexuality; woman is a complete individual, equal to the male, only if she too is a human being with sexuality. To renounce her femininity is to renounce a part of her humanity. Misogynists have often reproached intellectual women for "neglecting them- selves"; but they have also preached this doctrine to them: if you wish to be our equals, stop using make-up and nail-polish.

This piece of advice is nonsensical. Precisely because the concept of femi- ninity is artifically shaped by custom and fashion, it is imposed upon each woman from without; she can be transformed gradually so that her canons of propriety approach those adopted by the males: at the seashore—and often elsewhere—trousers have become feminine. That changes nothing fundamental in the matter: the individual is still not free to do as she pleases in shaping the concept of femininity. The woman who does not conform devaluates herself sexually and hence socially, since sexual values are an integral feature of society....

Sexual Blindness and Sexual Equality

Bernard Boxill

In a recent important essay, Richard Wasserstrom describes what he thinks the "good or just society" would make of racial and sexual differences.[1] The good or just society, he argues, would exemplify the "assimilationist ideal."[2] That is, it would make of racial and sexual differences what present society makes of differences in eye color. In present society, no "basic political rights and obligations are determined on the basis of eye-color"; no "institutional benefits and burdens are connected with eye color"; and "except for the mildest sort of aesthetic preferences, a person would be thought odd who even made private, social decisions by taking eye-color into account."[3] In the good or just society, Wasserstrom contends, race and sex would be of no greater significance.[4] And, he continues, just as the typical adult in present society is "virtually oblivious to the eye color of other persons for all major inter-personal relationships," so the typical adult in the assimilationist society would be "indifferent to the sexual, physiological differences of other persons for all inter-personal relationships."[5]

The assimilationist vision of the sexually and racially ideal society springs, no doubt, from the most humane sentiments. We are seemingly so drawn to invidious discrimination against those of a different race or sex that it must be few who have not yearned for a society where people are blind to both their racial and sexual differences. Yet I shall argue that the assimilationist ideal is defective. The problem it attempts but fails to solve is the old one that has long troubled egalitarians: How are we to deal with the fact that, though we are undeniably equal, we are also undeniably different? In this essay I focus on the defects in the assimilationist argument that are due to the fact that though we are equal because we are human, we are also different because we are female and male. However my arguments should apply as well to the assimilationist position on racial differences. My conclusion is that we cannot plan that the good and just society be either "sex-blind" or "color-blind."

As Wasserstrom allows, there can be no important sex-role differentiations in the assimilationist society. If women are better than men at certain significant activities, or if men are better than women at certain significant activities,

---

From *Social Theory and Practice* Vol. 6, 3(Fall 1980), pp. 281–298. Copyright Social Theory and Practice. Reprinted by permission.

[1] Richard A. Wasserstrom, "Racism, Sexism and Preferential Treatment: An Approach to the Topics," *U.C.L.A. Law Review* 24(February 1977): 603.

[2] Ibid., p. 604.

[3] Ibid.

[4] Ibid., p. 605.

[5] Ibid., p. 606.

people will not likely be oblivious to their sexual differences. The correlation of sexual differences with activities that are significant would tend to make sexual differences themselves appear significant. Accordingly he proposes to break down all sex-activity correlations by designing activities so that women and men can succeed and excel equally at every activity. To use his illustration, if lifeguarding at the ocean as now practiced puts a premium on the kind of strength that gives men an advantage over women, the sexually ideal society would change the way lifeguarding is now practiced so that this advantage is nullified.[6]...

Wasserstrom is aware that his reform may have costs. But he seems to think that the only such cost is a possible loss in efficiency. The question whether to institute his reforms, he says, is simply "whether the increased cost (or loss of efficiency) was worth the gain in terms of equality and the avoidance of sex-role differentiation."[7] But I argue that he is mistaken. There are two major possible costs he does not consider: the loss of a whole province of our most significant activities, and a loss of opportunities to acquire self-esteem.

Significant Activities "It is likely," Wasserstrom writes, "that even in this ideal society, weightlifting contests and boxing matches would in fact be dominated, perhaps exclusively so, by men. But it is hard to find any *significant* activities or institutions that are analogous. And it is not clear that such insignificant activities would be worth continuing, especially since sports function in existing patriarchal societies to help maintain the dominance of males."[8] But surely this conclusion is hasty. Even if sports function in *existing* patriarchal societies to help maintain male dominance, it certainly does not follow that they will perform the same function in an *ideal* society. Consequently, the inference that they would not be "worth continuing" is invalid. But the deeper difficulties concern the claim that sports are *insignificant*.

What Wasserstrom may mean by this is suggested in the next paragraph where he allows that lifeguarding, which also requires considerable unaided strength, is "nontrivial."[9] Since lifeguarding is distinguished from say, weightlifting, because it performs a service, the implication is that sports are "trivial" and "insignificant" because they do not perform a service and (by extension) have no product. It is true that sports need not perform a service or have a product. Though "spectator sports" may be said to perform the service of entertaining the spectators, and sports in general may produce health, people can engage in sport without entertaining spectators or improving their health. But it is false that sports are for that reason "insignificant" and not worth continuing. There are many activities that, like sports, need have no product and need perform no service. But these activities are not "insignificant" or

[6]Ibid., p. 611, n. 59.
[7]Ibid.
[8]Ibid., italics in the original.
[9]Ibid.

"not worth continuing." On the contrary some of them are among our more significant activities and are well worth continuing. They are significant and well worth continuing because of what they are in themselves. These activities are unalienated activities. First I shall describe their nature. Then I shall show that sports are among them.

Alienated activity is not itself "the satisfaction of a need, but only a means to satisfy needs outside itself."[10] These needs are "outside" the activity in the sense that they can, at least conceivably, be satisfied "outside," that is, without the activity that usually provides for their satisfaction. As I understand it, what is really essential about labor's being alienated is that it is not in this sense itself the satisfaction of a need. Consequently, though Marx may be believed otherwise, I describe alienated activity as not essentially, though perhaps usually, involving the other man or capitalist who owns the alienated activity.[11] Now the products and services that happen to be demanded by society, as, for example, shoes, ships, and safe swimming are needs "outside" activities because they all can at least conceivably be satisfied without the usual human activities of shoemaking, shipbuilding and lifeguarding. Since alienated labor is "only a means" to satisfy such needs, the overwhelming consideration in its design is that it satisfy these needs efficiently. Hence, except inadvertently, that design will not allow the worker room to express himself or to "develop freely his mental and physical energies."[12] Further, if there is a need to engage in such activity, alienated labor cannot satisfy that need. Since such a need is for a particular kind of activity, and so can be satisfied only by engaging in that activity, it does not meet the condition of being "outside" the activity that satisfies it.

But if alienated labor is of this nature, unalienated activity must be activity that the worker has a need to engage in, and in particular, activity that is designed specifically to provide him with room to express and develop himself freely. This does not mean that it is unprincipled or undisciplined. As Marx wrote, "Really free labor, the composing of music, for example, is at the same time damned serious and requires the greatest effort."[13] That is to say, activity which is truly a form of self-expression and self-development is necessarily governed by the discipline of laws and principles. We can express ourselves in writing, music, painting and so on, and exercise our literary, musical, and in general our creative talents, only because there are laws governing literary, musical and artistic composition, and only if we submit ourselves to the discipline of these laws. As Marx put it most generally, in his free activity man "constructs in accordance with the laws of beauty."[14]

[10]Karl Marx, "Alienated Labour" in *Karl Marx Selected Writings*, edited by David McLellan (Oxford: Oxford University Press, 1977), p. 80.

[11]For further discussion of this see Richard Schact, *Alienation* (Garden City, NY: Anchor Books, 1971), pp. 100, 101.

[12]Karl Marx, "Alienated Labour" in *Karl Marx Selected Writings*, p. 80.

[13]Karl Marx, "Grundrisse" in *Karl Marx Selected Writings*, p. 368.

[14]Karl Marx, "Alienated Labour" in *Karl Marx Selected Writings*, p. 82.

My account of unalienated labor is independent of the controversy of whether, for Marx, unalienated activity includes economically productive activity.[15] Whether it does or not is irrelevant to the point I wish to make, which is that some activity that is not economically productive is unalienated. A second possible misunderstanding of my account is that painting, composing, and so on, have "products" and are significant, not in themselves but as a means to these "products." But this is a misunderstanding. Paintings and compositions are significant because of the activities they result from, not vice versa as in the usual case. As Marx noted, spiders or bees can do certain things better than an architect. However, their activities are quite different because the architect, unlike the bee or spider, had the idea in his imagination.[16] Thus, part of the activity in question is the working out of ideas.[17]

In elaborating his Aristotelian Principle, Rawls comes to relevantly similar conclusions. The Aristotelian Principle is a "principle of motivation" that "accounts for many of our major desires."[18] According to it "human beings enjoy the exercise of their realized capacities... and this enjoyment increases the more the capacity is realized, or the greater its complexity." Thus, "of two activities they do equally well [people] prefer the one calling on a larger repertoire of intricate and subtle discriminations."[19] Presumably such activities are more enjoyable because they "satisfy the desire for variety and novelty of experience" and permit or even require "individual style and personal expression."[20] This desire is, moreover, "relatively strong" and it must be reckoned with in the design of social institutions; for "otherwise human beings will find their culture and form of life dull and empty. Their vitality and zest will fail as their life becomes a tiresome routine."[21] Thus human beings have a need to engage in activities that call on the exercise of their abilities "simply for their own sakes."[22]

In sum, then, activities can be significant in themselves both in the sense that they are forms of self-expression in which excellence can be achieved, and in the sense that human beings have a profound need to engage in them. I now show that the assimilationist proposes to eliminate a considerable class of these activities.

Consider first, sport: We have seen that Wasserstrom proposes to eliminate it for the sake of sexual blindness. Now in practically all cultures and societies people engage in sport for its own sake. Assuming that people tend to recognise their own needs, it would seem that engaging in sport is in itself the satisfaction

[15]Karl Marx, *Capital*, Volume I in *Karl Marx Selected Writings*, p. 456.
[16]For a discussion of this see G. A. Cohen, "Marx's Dialectic of Labor," *Philosophy and Public Affairs*, 3 (1974): 235–62.
[17]See further Karl Marx, "Alienated Labour," in *Karl Marx Selected Writings*, p. 80.
[18]John Rawls, *A Theory of Justice* (Cambridge: Harvard University Press, 1971), p. 427.
[19]Ibid., p. 426.
[20]Ibid., p. 427.
[21]Ibid., p. 429.
[22]Ibid., p. 431.

of an important human need.[23] To forestall that this may be a "false need," I can show that sports can also be forms of self-expression in which excellence is achieved. Sports are not merely undisciplined, unprincipled explosions of physical energy. Though they are exercises of human energy that are freely engaged in because they are engaged in for themselves, they are governed by the most exacting rules. Moreover, since sport is not subservient to satisfying needs "outside" itself, in accordance with the Aristotelian Principle, its rules can be, and usually are, constructed to require the utmost in "intricate and subtle discriminations" that the players are capable of. Though Rawls allows that the Aristotelian Principle operates "even in games and pastimes,"[24] he unfortunately, but I think inadvertently, gives the notion of intricacy and subtlety involved an excessively intellectual interpretation. But anyone who has tried to describe a Dr. J stuff shot, or the fastidious shifts in balance and speed of the best high jumpers or shot-putters, and who also understands that what he or she would put into words is not the spontaneous perfection of the animal, but a deliberately acquired art, must acknowledge that sport, too, calls for "intricate and subtle discriminations." Further, as Rawls notes, since it is the very complexity of activities which makes them important avenues of self-expression—"for how could everyone do them in the same way?"[25]—being complex, sports too are important avenues of self-expression. And again, to prove this we need only take an educated look at the best practitioners of any sport. As infallibly as any maestro, they, too, put their personal stamp on their best performances. Finally, many sports are to a considerable extent art forms governed by the "laws of beauty." Few who have seen an accomplished performance of gymnastics or diving, or a perfect pole vault, or a well-run hurdles race, would care to deny this. In ancient Greece, Myron captured the beauty of the discus thrower in his famous discobolus.

An assimilationist might grant my argument that sports are significant, but deny my conclusion that assimilationism requires the suppression of sport. What he or she needs to show is that Wasserstrom allowed too easily that sports necessarily involve sex-activity correlations that subvert sexual blindness. Thus, a philosopher once argued to me that, even granting the physical differences between women and men, we could avoid sex-activity correlations in sport by classing competitors according to the physical talent that the particular sport called on, be it height, weight, oxygenation rate, or testosterone level. And he pointed out that we already do this in a rudimentary way, when we put competitors in age or weight classes. But this is too ingenious. It fails to see the forest for the trees. If one of the sexes has generally higher levels of the physical characteristic relevant to a particular sport, the other sex will simply not be represented, or well represented, in the classes of the sport that achieve real excellence. And this will do little for the cause of sex-blindness.

[23]Jan Boxill develops this theme in "Sport as unalienated activity," unpublished manuscript.
[24]Rawls, *A Theory of Justice*, p. 429.
[25]Ibid., p. 427.

Wasserstrom is correct, then, in saying that the assimilationist must eliminate sport. But it is only sport he must eliminate. The sexes do not differ only in strength. They differ also in physical appearance, flexibility, grace, and texture of voice, for example. Further, the exercise of these differences is central to many of our most aesthetically appealing and culturally important activities. The exercise of man's greater natural strength and woman's greater natural flexibility and grace is of course obvious in many forms of dance. Similarly, the importance of woman's naturally higher, and man's naturally deeper, voice is obvious in practically all forms of singing. Anyone who thinks of questioning the importance of the aesthetic value of the mix of soprano and bass voices should recall the lengths to which—including in particular the castration of little boys—the medievals went to secure it.

Finally, these losses of the assimilationist society cannot be "made up." Sport and the other activities the assimilationist would suppress have their own peculiar standards of excellence and beauty, and exercise different and peculiar sets of our abilities. Hence given the human need to engage in, and express the self in, all-around activity, though we could, for example, engage in the unalienated activity of philosophizing in the assimilationist society, we could not *replace* sport with philosophizing.

Self Esteem   Turning to the second cost of the assimilationist ideal, I now argue that in cutting off opportunities to engage in unalienated activity, the assimilationist society cuts off opportunities to acquire self-esteem.

Following Rawls, I take self-esteem as including "a person's sense of his own value, his secure conviction that his conception of his good, his plan of life, is worth carrying out."[26] As Rawls further notes, one of the two main sorts of curcumstances that support a person's self-esteem is finding his "person and deeds appreciated and confirmed by others who are likewise esteemed and their association enjoyed"..."unless our endeavors are appreciated by our associates it is impossible for us to maintain the conviction that they are worthwhile."[27] This theory that a person's self-esteem depends on his associates' appreciation of his endeavors has long been recognized by social theorists. Without denying that appreciation of any of our endeavors is likely to support self-esteem, I argue that appreciation of our unalienated activity is especially important.

If alienated activity is activity one feels to be somehow not one's own activity, that is, not activity which expresses one's own ideas and aspirations, the fact that others appreciate it is unlikely to give much support to one's self-esteem. Support for one's self-esteem would seem to come more surely from others' appreciation of activity one feels to be an expression of one's own ideas and aspirations, that is, activity which is truly an expression of oneself. But such activity is unalienated activity. Further, since unalienated activity is done

---

[26]Ibid., p. 440.
[27]Ibid., p. 441.

only for itself and for no ulterior motive, all other considerations can be set aside in order to achieve excellence and beauty. Consequently, there can be much for others to appreciate in one's unalienated activity. For these reasons, it would seem that an opportunity to engage in unalienated activity is also an important opportunity to acquire self-esteem. Hence in curtailing opportunities for unalienated activity, the assimilationists curtail opportunities to acquire self-esteem. And that is a serious cost.

However, it may seem that others' appreciation of one's endeavors, especially one's unalienated activity, is a chancy way to secure self-esteem. For what if one never achieves excellence or beauty? Must one lack self-esteem? This does not seem to be necessarily the case. If it is not, there must be another support for self-esteem that I have not mentioned. Further, if it flourishes in the assimilationist society, my present objection will seem less important.

What this other support for self-esteem could be may be suggested by Bernard Williams's distinction between regarding a person's life, and actions from a "technical point of view," and regarding them from "the human point of view."[28] It may be urged that what is important to persons' self-esteem is not so much that we appreciate their endeavors, which is only to see them from the technical point of view, but that we appreciate what it is for them to attempt what they attempted. Which is to see them from the human point of view. I agree that because appreciation from the human point of view can be accorded irrespective of the success or importance of our endeavors—and is to that extent unconditional—it probably offers a far more secure support for self-esteem than the appreciation accorded from the technical point of view. The question is whether the human point of view is likely to flourish in the assimilationist society. Though it is possible, I think there is reason to doubt it. To regard persons from the "human point of view," we must consider their endeavors important just because they are important to *them*. Thus, as Williams notes, from the human point of view, we regard the failed inventor, "not merely as failed inventor, but as a man who wanted to be a successful inventor," that is, as one to whom inventing was important.[29] But, as we have seen, whatever its ultimate significance many people find sport important. Hence the assimilationist's proposal to eliminate it casts doubt on the assumption that he or she views the members of the ideal society from the human point of view.

Finally, the fact that the costs of the assimilationist society involve essentially unalienated activity shows how inadequate Wasserstrom's reassurance is that the "occupational cases" that would have to be phased out are "infrequent and peripheral."[30] It is inadequate because the important costs of his reforms are not the elimination of the few "occupational cases" that the industrial

[28]Bernard Williams, "The Idea of Equality," in Joel Feinberg, editor, *Moral Concepts* (London: Oxford University Press, 1970), p. 159.
[29]Ibid.
[30]Wasserstrom, "Racism, Sexism, and Preferential Treatment," p. 611, n. 59.

revolution would have eliminated anyway. They are the elimination of the unalienated activity that the industrial revolution, by increasing our leisure time, has simultaneously made more possible and more important. Thus, perhaps what is most paradoxical is the assimilationist's belief that the industrial and technological revolution will reduce the significance of the differences between the sexes. For if I am right the very *opposite* is the truth.

At this point, critics may grant that I have pointed to some hitherto unnoticed costs of the sexually blind society, but maintain that I have not shown that society to be unjustified because I have not shown that it is not *worth* the costs. In particular, they may argue that the assimilationist society is worth the costs I mention because it gains so much for sexual equality.

To forestall any unjustified egalitarian sympathy for the assimilationist society, I stress that the sexual equality allegedly gained by the assimilationist society is not equality of income between the sexes. That equality is not an issue. I can propose a distribution of income between the sexes which is as radically egalitarian as the assimilationists can propose.

My first objection is that it is not necessary to incur the costs of the assimilationist society in order to have equality of opportunity between the sexes. These costs are the loss of opportunities to engage in unalienated activities and to achieve self-esteem, which are incurred by the elimination of all sex-activity correlations. But it is not necessary to eliminate correlations between sex and activity in order to have equality of opportunity between the sexes. Sex roles do subvert that equality, and perhaps human beings do tend to change sex-activity correlations into sex roles. Thus, the bare existence of correlations between sex and activities may engender a societal expectation that the sexes tend to excel at different activities, and this in turn can lead to societal factors that actively discourage women and men from pursuing certain activities.[31] When this occurs, sex roles exist and equality of opportunity ceases to exist. The point, however, is that sex-activity correlations need not thus develop into sex roles.[32] There is no reason [why] people cannot learn to successfully resist the tendency to move from a perception of sex-activity correlations to instituting sex roles....

It could be said that though abolishing sex-activity correlations is not necessary for sexual equality, it makes that equality more secure. If we do not notice our sexual differences we can hardly discriminate against each other on their basis. Further, it could be argued that the alternative arrangement I propose would leave society with a built-in potential for conflict between the sexes, and that the more harmonious society that sexual blindness would secure would be infinitely superior. But even this considerably weakened case for

---

[31]On this point see Joyce Trebilcot, "Sex Roles: The Argument from Nature," in *Sex Equality*, edited by Jane English (Englewood Cliffs, NJ: Prentice-Hall, 1977), p. 125. From *Ethics*, 85(1975): 249–55.

[32]Ibid.

sexual blindness collapses. Though sexual blindness may give us a safer enjoyment of sexual equality as equality of opportunity between the sexes, it does so at the expense of a more fundamental precept of egalitarianism, in terms of which equality of opportunity is itself justified.

That precept, which I refer to as equality of respect, is that each person has an equal right to the maximum opportunity, compatible with a like opportunity for others, to express himself or herself and to exercise and develop his or her talents as he or she sees fit. It is clearly a stronger requirement than equality of opportunity. As I defined it, and as it is commonly understood, equality of opportunity is equality of opportunity to gain available positions or careers. Hence, since we can express ourselves and exercise and develop our talents *outside* our positions and careers, equality of respect makes broader and stronger demands than equality of opportunity. More importantly—for the egalitarian at least—it is the precept in terms of which equality of opportunity is justified. Thus one reason why equality of opportunity is so important is that although careers are not the only avenues of self-expression and self-realization, they are major avenues of self-expression and self-realization.

Now the assimilationists do propose to sacrifice equality of respect for equality of opportunity. As we have seen, they propose to eliminate a substantial portion of our unalienated activities for the sake of sexual blindness. These activities are an especially rich medium of self-expression and self-realization, and probably for some people more than others. Consequently, to eliminate such activities for the sake of sexual blindness is to sacrifice equality of respect for sexual blindness. But the purpose of sexual blindness is that it secures equality of opportunity between the sexes. Hence the assimilationists propose to sacrifice equality of respect for equality of opportunity. Finally, since it is equality of respect which justifies equality of opportunity, their position is incoherent....

So the pursuit of sexual blindness is the pursuit of a chimera. The sexually blind or assimilationist society is either unequal in the most fundamental sense and incompatible with the autonomy of its members, or else it is impossible. The assimilationists fail to see these paradoxes because they try to describe the sexually ideal society in terms of equality of opportunity in abstraction from other values. But this is sure to lead to lopsided results. If we give due weight to all our values—in particular, to autonomy, to the uplifting use of our leisure time, to excellence and beauty in all its forms, as well as to equality of opportunity and equality of respect—we get a society that is saner, kinder, more equal, more familiar, and also more interesting and exciting that the bizarre and bleak world of the assimilationists.

For rather than requiring us to suppress opportunities, a true egalitarianism requires us to multiply and diversify them. For example, if men excel at firefighting and other activities requiring strength, we better use our ingenuity in the service of sex-equality to create activities women can excel at rather than to superannuate activities men excel at. Similarly, turning to activities we find valuable in themselves, if men dominate weightlifting, the way to sex equality is not to abolish weightlifting—that is only the way to a dreary sex-blind world—but to design activities women will dominate....

Reverse Discrimination as Unjustified

Lisa Newton

I have heard it argued that "simple justice" requires that we favor women and blacks in employment and educational opportunities, since women and blacks were "unjustly" excluded from such opportunities for so many years in the not so distant past. It is a strange argument, an example of a possible implication of a true proposition advanced to dispute the proposition itself, like an octopus absent-mindedly slicing off its head with a stray tentacle. A fatal confusion underlies this argument, a confusion fundamentally relevant to our under-standing of the notion of the rule of law.

Two senses of justice and equality are involved in this confusion. The root notion of justice, progenitor of the other, is the one that Aristotle (*Nicomachean Ethics* 5.6; *Politics* 1.2; 3.1) assumes to be the foundation and proper virtue of the political association. It is the condition which free men establish among themselves when they "share a common life in order that their association bring them self-sufficiency"—the regulation of their relationship by law, and the establishment, by law, of equality before the law. Rule of law is the name and pattern of this justice; its equality stands against the inequalities—of wealth, talent, etc.—otherwise obtaining among its participants, who by virtue of that equality are called "citizens." It is an achievement—complete, or more fre-quently, partial—of certain people in certain concrete situations. It is fragile and easily disrupted by powerful individuals who discover that the blind equality of rule of law is inconvenient for their interests. Despite its obvious instability, Aristotle assumed that the establishment of justice in this sense, the creation of citizenship, was a permanent possibility for men and that the resultant association of citizens was the natural home of the species. At levels below the political association, this rule-governed equality is easily found; it is exemplified by any group of children agreeing together to play a game. At the level of the political association, the attainment of this justice is more difficult, simply because the stakes are so much higher for each participant. The equality of citizenship is not something that happens of its own accord, and without the expenditure of a fair amount of effort it will collapse into the rule of a powerful few over an apathetic many. But at least it has been achieved, at some times in

From *Ethics* Vol. 83, No. 4 (1973), 308–312. Copyright 1973 by the University of Chicago Press. Reprinted by permission.

some places; it is always worth trying to achieve, and eminently worth trying to maintain, wherever and to whatever degree it has been brought into being.

Aristotle's parochialism is notorious; he really did not imagine that persons other than Greeks could associate freely in justice, and the only form of association he had in mind was the Greek *polis*. With the decline of the *polis* and the shift in the center of political thought, his notion of justice underwent a sea change. To be exact, it ceased to represent a political type and became a moral ideal: the ideal of equality as we know it. This ideal demands that all men be included in citizenship—that one Law govern all equally, that all men regard all other men as fellow citizens, with the same guarantees, rights, and protections. Briefly, it demands that the circle of citizenship achieved by any group be extended to include the entire human race. Properly understood, its effect on our associations can be excellent: it congratulates us on our achievement of rule of law as a process of government but refuses to let us remain complacent until we have expanded the associations to include others within the ambit of the rules, as often and as far as possible. While one man is a slave, none of us may feel truly free. We are constantly prodded by this ideal to look for possible unjustifiable discrimination, for inequalities not absolutely required for the functioning of the society and advantageous to all. And after twenty centuries of pressure, not at all constant, from this ideal, it might be said that some progress has been made. To take the cases in point for this problem, we are now prepared to assert, as Aristotle would never have been, the equality of sexes and of persons of different colors. The ambit of American citizenship, once restricted to white males of property, has been extended to include all adult free men, then all adult males including ex-slaves, then all women. The process of acquisition of full citizenship was for these groups a sporadic trail of half-measures, even now not complete; the steps on the road to full equality are marked by legislation and judicial decisions which are only recently concluded and still often not enforced. But the fact that we can now discuss the possibility of favoring such groups in hiring shows that over the area that concerns us, as least, full equality is presupposed as a basis for discussion. To that extent, they are full citizens, fully protected by the law of the land.

It is important for my argument that the moral ideal of equality be recognized as logically distinct from the condition (or virtue) of justice in the political sense. Justice in this sense exists *among* a citizenry, irrespective of the number of the populace included in that citizenry. Further, the moral ideal is parasitic upon the political virtue, for "equality" is unspecified—it means nothing until we are told in what respect that equality is to be realized. In a political context, "equality" is specified as "equal rights"—equal access to the public realm, public goods and offices, equal treatment under the law—in brief, the equality of citizenship. If citizenship is not a possibility, political equality is unintelligible. The ideal emerges as a generalization of the real condition and refers back to that condition for its content.

Now, if justice (Aristotle's justice in the political sense) is equal treatment under law for all citizens, what is justice? Clearly, injustice is the violation of that equality, discriminating for or against a group of citizens, favoring them with special immunities and privileges or depriving them of those guaranteed to the others. When the southern employer refuses to hire blacks in white-collar jobs, when Wall Street will only hire women as secretaries with new titles, when Mississippi high schools routinely flunk all black boys above ninth grade, we have examples of injustice, and we work to restore the equality of the public realm by ensuring that equal opportunity will be provided in such cases in the future. But of course, when the employers and the schools *favor* women and blacks, the same injustice is done. Just as the previous discrimination did, this reverse discrimination violates the public equality which defines citizenship and destroys the rule of law for the areas in which these favors are granted. To the extent that we adopt a program of discrimination, reverse or otherwise, justice in the political sense is destroyed, and none of us, specifically affected or not, is a citizen, a bearer of rights—we are all petitioners for favors. And to the same extent, the ideal of equality is undermined, for it has content only where justice obtains, and by destroying justice we render the ideal meaningless. It is, then, an ironic paradox, if not a contradiction in terms, to assert that the ideal of equality justifies the violation of justice; it is as if one should argue, with William Buckley, that an ideal of humanity can justify the destruction of the human race.

Logically, the conclusion is simple enough: all discrimination is wrong prima facie because it violates justice, and that goes for reverse discrimination too. No violation of justice among the citizens may be justified (may overcome prima facie objection) by appeal to the ideal of equality, for the ideal is logically dependent upon the notion of justice. Reverse discrimination, then, which attempts no other justification than an appeal to equality, is wrong. But let us try to make the conclusion more plausible by suggesting some of the implications of the suggested practice of reverse discrimination in employment and education. My argument will be that the problems raised there are insoluble, not only in practice but in principle.

We may argue, if we like, about what "discrimination" consists of. Do I discriminate against blacks if I admit none to my school when none of the black applicants are qualified by the tests I always give? How far must I go to root out cultural bias from my application forms and tests before I can say that I have not discriminated against those of different cultures? Can I assume that women are not strong enough to be roughnecks on my oil rigs, or must I test them individually? But this controversy, the most popular and well-argued aspect of the issue, is not as fatal as two others which cannot be avoided: if we are regarding the blacks as a "minority" victimized by discrimination, what is a "minority"? And for any group—blacks, women, whatever—that has been discriminated against, what amount of reverse discrimination wipes out the initial discrimination? Let us grant as true that women and blacks were discriminated against, even where laws forbade such discrimination, and grant for the sake of argument that a history of discrimination must be wiped out by reverse discrimination. What follows?

First, are there other groups which have been discriminated against? For they should have the same right of restitution. What about American Indians, Chicanos, Appalachian Mountain whites, Puerto Ricans, Jews, Cajuns, and Orientals? And if these are to be included, the principle according to which we specify a "minority" is simply the criterion of "ethnic (sub)group," and we're stuck with every hyphenated American in the lower-middle class clamoring for special privileges for *his* group—and with equal justification. For be it noted, when we run down the Harvard roster, we find not only a scarcity of blacks (in comparison with the proportion in the population) but an even more striking scarcity of those second-, third-, and fourth-generation ethnics who make up the loudest voice of Middle America. Shouldn't they demand *their* share? And eventually, the WASPs will have to form their own lobby, for they too are a minority. The point is simply this: there is no "majority" in America who will not mind giving up just a bit of their rights to make room for a favored minority. There are only other minorities, each of which is discriminated against by the favoring. The initial injustice is then repeated dozens of times, and if each minority is granted the same right of restitution as the others, an entire area of rule governance is dissolved into a pushing and shoving match between self-interested groups. Each works to catch the public eye and political popularity by whatever means of advertising and power politics lend themselves to the effort, to capitalize as much as possible on temporary popularity until the restless mob picks another group to feel sorry for. Hardly an edifying spectacle, and in the long run no one can benefit: the pie is no larger—it's just that instead of setting up and enforcing rules for getting a piece, we've turned the contest into a free-for-all, requiring much more effort for no larger a reward. It would be in the interests of all the participants to reestablish an objective rule to govern the process, carefully enforced and the same for all.

Second, supposing that we do manage to agree in general that women and blacks (and all the others) have some right of restitution, some right to a privileged place in the structure of opportunities for a while, how will we know when that while is up? How much privilege is enough? When will the guilt be gone, the price paid, the balance restored? What recompense is right for centuries of exclusion? What criterion tells us when we are done? Our experience with the Civil Rights movement shows us that agreement on these terms cannot be presupposed: a process that appears to some to be going at a mad gallop into a black takeover appears to the rest of us to be at a standstill. Should a practice of reverse discrimination be adopted, we may safely predict that just as some of us begin to see "a satisfactory start toward righting the balance," others of us will see that we "have already gone too far in the other direction" and will suggest that the discrimination ought to be reversed again. And such disagreement is inevitable, for the point is that we could not *possibly* have any criteria for evaluating the kind of recompense we have in mind. The context presumed by any discussion of restitution is the context of rule of law: law sets the rights of men and simultaneously sets the method for remedying the violation of those rights. You may exact suffering from others and/or damage payments for yourself if and only if the others have violated your rights; the suffering you have endured is not sufficient reason for them to suffer. And remedial rights exist only where there is law: primary human rights are useful guides to legislation but cannot stand as reasons for awarding remedies for injuries sustained. But then, the context presupposed by any discussion of restitution is the context of preexistent full citizenship. No remedial rights could exist for the excluded; neither in law nor in logic does there exist a right to *sue* for a standing to sue.

From these two considerations, then, the difficulties with reverse discrimination become evident. Restitution for a disadvantaged group whose rights under the law have been violated is possible by legal means, but restitution for a disadvantaged group whose grievance is that there was no law to protect them simply is not. First, outside of the area of justice defined by the law, no sense can be made of "the group's rights," for no law recognizes that group or individuals in it, qua members, as bearers of rights (hence *any* group can constitute itself as a disadvantaged minority in some sense and demand similar restitution). Second, outside of the area of protection of law, no sense can be made of the violation of rights (hence the amount of the recompense cannot be decided by any objective criterion). For both reasons, the practice of reverse discrimination undermines the foundation of the very ideal in whose name it is advocated; it destroys justice, law, equality, and citizenship itself, and replaces them with power struggles and popularity contests.

A Defense of Programs of Preferential Treatment

Richard Wasserstrom

Many justifications of programs of preferential treatment depend upon the claim that in one respect or another such programs have good consequences or that they are effective means by which to bring about some desirable end, e.g., an integrated, egalitarian society. I mean by "programs of preferential treatment" to refer to programs such as those at issue in the *Bakke* case—programs which set aside a certain number of places (for example, in a law school) as to which members of minority groups (for example, persons who are non-white or female) who possess certain minimum qualifications (in terms of grades and test scores) may be preferred for admission to those places

Originally published in 24 *UCLA Law Review* 581, Copyright 1977. The Regents of the University of California. All rights reserved. Reprinted by permission.

over some members of the majority group who possess higher qualifications (in terms of grades and test scores).

Many criticisms of programs of preferential treatment claim that such programs, even if effective, are unjustifiable because they are in some important sense unfair or unjust. In this paper I present a limited defense of such programs by showing that two of the chief arguments offered for the unfairness or injustice of these programs do not work in the way or to the degree supposed by critics of these programs.

The first argument is this. Opponents of preferential treatment programs sometimes assert that proponents of these programs are guilty of intellectual inconsistency, if not racism or sexism. For, as is now readily acknowledged, at times past employers, universities, and many other social institutions did have racial or sexual quotas (when they did not practice overt racial or sexual exclusion), and many of those who were most concerned to bring about the eradication of those racial quotas are now untroubled by the new programs which reinstitute them. And this, it is claimed, is inconsistent. If it was wrong to take race or sex into account when blacks and women were the objects of racial and sexual policies and practices of exclusion, then it is wrong to take race or sex into account when the objects of the policies have their race or sex reversed. Simple considerations of intellectual consistency—of what it means to give racism or sexism as a reason for condemning these social policies and practices—require that what was a good reason then is still a good reason now.

The problem with this argument is that despite appearances, there is no inconsistency involved in holding both views. Even if contemporary preferential treatment programs which contain quotas are wrong, they are not wrong for the reasons that made quotas against blacks and women pernicious. The reason why is that the social realities do make an enormous difference. The fundamental evil of programs that discriminated against blacks or women was that these programs were a part of a larger social universe which systematically maintained a network of institutions which unjustifiably concentrated power, authority, and goods in the hands of white male individuals, and which systematically consigned blacks and women to subordinate positions in the society.

Whatever may be wrong with today's affirmative action programs and quota systems, it should be clear that the evil, if any, is just not the same. Racial and sexual minorities do not constitute the dominant social group. Nor is the conception of who is a fully developed member of the moral and social community one of an individual who is either female or black. Quotas which prefer women or blacks do not add to an already relatively overabundant supply of resources and opportunities at the disposal of members of these groups in the way in which the quotas of the past did maintain and augment the overabundant supply of resources and opportunities already available to white males.

The same point can be made in a somewhat different way. Sometimes people say that what was wrong, for example, with the system of racial discrimination in the South was that it took an irrelevant characteristic, namely race, and used it systematically to allocate social benefits and burdens of various sorts. The defect was the irrelevance of the characteristic used—race—for that meant that individuals ended up being treated in a manner that was arbitrary and capricious.

I do not think that was the central flaw at all. Take, for instance, the most hideous of the practices, human slavery. The primary thing that was wrong with the institution was not that the particular individuals who were assigned the place of slaves were assigned there arbitrarily because the assignment was made in virtue of an irrelevant characteristic, their race. Rather, it seems to me that the primary thing that was and is wrong with slavery is the practice itself—the fact of some individuals being able to own other individuals and all that goes with that practice. It would not matter by what criterion individuals were assigned; human slavery would still be wrong. And the same can be said for most if not all of the other discrete practices and institutions which comprised the system of racial discrimination even after human slavery was abolished. The practices were unjustifiable—they were oppressive—and they would have been so no matter how the assignment of victims had been made. What made it worse, still, was that the institutions and the supporting ideology all interlocked to create a system of human oppression whose effects on those living under it were as devastating as they were unjustifiable.

Again, if there is anything wrong with the programs of preferential treatment that have begun to flourish within the past ten years, it should be evident that the social realities in respect to the distribution of resources and opportunities make the difference. Apart from everything else, there is simply no way in which all of these programs taken together could plausibly be viewed as capable of relegating white males to the kind of genuinely oppressive status characteristically bestowed upon women and blacks by the dominant social institutions and ideology.

The second objection is that preferential treatment programs are wrong because they take race or sex into account rather than the only thing that does matter—that is, an individual's qualifications. What all such programs have in common and what makes them all objectionable, so this argument goes, is that they ignore the persons who are more qualified by bestowing a preference on those who are less qualified in virtue of their being either black or female.

There are, I think, a number of things wrong with this objection based on qualifications, and not the least of them is that we do not live in a society in which there is even the serious pretense of a qualification requirement for many jobs of substantial power and authority. Would anyone claim, for example, that the persons who comprise the judiciary are there because they are the most qualified lawyers or the most qualified persons to be judges? Would anyone claim that Henry Ford II is the head of the Ford Motor Company because he is the most qualified person for the job? Part of what is wrong with even talking about qualifications and merit is that the argument derives some of its force from the erroneous notion that we would have a meritocracy were it not for programs of preferential treatment. In fact, the higher one goes in terms of prestige, power and the like, the less qualifications seem ever to be decisive. It is only for certain jobs and certain places that qualifications are used to do more than establish the possession of certain minimum competencies.

But difficulties such as these to one side, there are theoretical difficulties as well which cut much more deeply into the argument about qualifications. To begin with, it is important to see that there is a serious inconsistency present if the person who favors "pure qualifications" does so on the ground that the most qualified ought to be selected because this promotes maximum efficiency. Let us suppose that the argument is that if we have the most qualified performing the relevant tasks we will get those tasks done in the most economical and efficient manner. There is nothing wrong in principle with arguments based upon the good consequences that will flow from maintaining a social practice in a certain way. But it is inconsistent for the opponent of preferential treatment to attach much weight to qualifications on this ground, because it was an analogous appeal to the good consequences that the opponent of preferential treatment thought was wrong in the first place. That is to say, if the chief thing to be said in favor of strict qualifications and preferring the most qualified is that it is the most efficient way of getting things done, then we are right back to an assessment of the different consequences that will flow from different programs, and we are far removed from the considerations of justice or fairness that were thought to weigh so heavily against these programs.

It is important to note, too, that qualifications—at least in the educational context—are often not connected at all closely with any plausible conception of social effectiveness. To admit the most qualified students to law school, for example—given the way qualifications are now determined—is primarily to admit those who have the greatest chance of scoring the highest grades at law school. This says little about efficiency except perhaps that these students are the easiest for the faculty to teach. However, since we know so little about what constitutes being a good, or even successful lawyer, and even less about the correlation between being a very good law student and being a very good lawyer, we can hardly claim very confidently that the legal system will operate most effectively if we admit only the most qualified students to law school.

To be at all decisive, the argument for qualifications must be that those who are the most qualified deserve to receive the benefits (the job, the place in law school, etc.) because they are the most qualified. The introduction of the concept of desert now makes it an objection as to justice or fairness of the sort promised by the original criticism of the programs. But now the problem is that there is no reason to think that there is any strong sense of "desert" in which it is correct that the most qualified deserve anything.

Let us consider more closely one case, that of preferential treatment in respect to admission to college or graduate school. There is a logical gap in the inference from the claim that a person is most qualified to perform a task, e.g., to be a good student, to the conclusion that he or she deserves to be admitted as a student. Of course, those who deserve to be admitted should be admitted. But why do the most qualified deserve anything? There is simply no necessary connection between academic merit (in the sense of being most qualified) and deserving to be a member of a student body. Suppose, for instance, that there is only one tennis court in the community. Is it clear that the two best tennis players ought to be the ones permitted to use it? Why not those who were there first? Or those who will enjoy playing the most? Or those who are the worst and, therefore, need the greatest opportunity to practice? Or those who have the chance to play least frequently?

We might, of course, have a rule that says that the best tennis players get to use the court before the others. Under such a rule the best players would deserve the court more than the poorer ones. But that is just to push the inquiry back on stage. Is there any reason to think that we ought to have a rule giving good tennis players such a preference? Indeed, the arguments that might be given for or against such a rule are many and varied. And few if any of the arguments that might support the rule would depend upon a connection between ability and desert.

Someone might reply, however, that the most able students deserve to be admitted to the university because all of their earlier schooling was a kind of competition, with university admission being the prize awarded to the winners. They deserve to be admitted because that is what the rule of the competition provides. In addition, it might be argued, it would be unfair now to exclude them in favor of others, given the reasonable expectations they developed about the way in which their industry and performance would be rewarded. Minority-admission programs, which inevitably prefer some who are less qualified over some who are more qualified, all possess this flaw.

There are several problems with this argument. The most substantial of them is that it is an empirically implausible picture of our social world. Most of what are regarded as the decisive characteristics for higher education have a great deal to do with things over which the individual has neither control nor responsibility; such things as home environment, socioeconomic class of parents, and, of course, the quality of the primary and secondary schools attended. Since individuals do not deserve having had any of these things vis-à-vis other individuals, they do not, for the most part, deserve their qualifications. And since they do not deserve their abilities they do not in any strong sense deserve to be admitted because of their abilities.

To be sure, if there has been a rule which connects say, performance at high school with admission to college, then there is a weak sense in which those who do well in high school deserve, for that reason alone, to be admitted to college. In addition, if persons have built up or relied upon their reasonable expectations concerning performance and admission, they have a claim to be admitted on this ground as well. But it is certainly not obvious that these claims of desert are any stronger or more compelling than the competing claims based upon the needs of or advantages to women or blacks from programs of preferential treatment. And as I have indicated, all rule-based claims of desert are very weak unless and until the rule which creates the claim is itself shown to be a justified one. Unless one has a strong preference for the status quo, and unless one can defend that preference, the practice within a system of allocating places in a certain way does not go very far at all in showing that that is the right or the just way to allocate those places in the future.

A proponent of programs of preferential treatment is not at all committed to the view that qualifications ought to be wholly irrelevant. He or she can agree that, given the existing structure of any institution, there is probably some minimal set of qualifications without which one cannot participate meaningfully within the institution. In addition, it can be granted that the qualifications of those involved will affect the way the institution works and the way it affects others in the society. And the consequences will vary depending upon the particular institution. But all of this only establishes that qualifications, in this sense, are relevant, not that they are decisive. This is wholly consistent with the claim that race or sex should today also be relevant when it comes to matters such as admission to college or law school. And that is all that any preferential treatment program—even one with the kind of quota used in the *Bakke* case—has ever tried to do.

I have not attempted to establish that programs of preferential treatment are right and desirable. There are empirical issues concerning the consequences of these programs that I have not discussed, and certainly not settled. Nor, for that matter, have I considered the argument that justice may permit, if not require, these programs as a way to provide compensation or reparation for injuries suffered in the recent as well as distant past, or as a way to remove benefits that are undeservedly enjoyed by those of the dominant group. What I have tried to do is show that it is wrong to think that programs of preferential treatment are objectionable in the centrally important sense in which many past and present discriminatory features of our society have been and are racist and sexist. The social realities as to power and opportunity do make a fundamental difference. It is also wrong to think that programs of preferential treatment could, therefore, plausibly rest both on the view that such programs are not unfair to white males (except in the weak, rule-dependent sense described above) and on the view that it is unfair to continue the present set of unjust—often racist and sexist—institutions that comprise the social reality. And the case for these programs could rest as well on the proposition that, given the distribution of power and influence in the United States today, such programs may reasonably be viewed as potentially valuable, effective means by which to achieve admirable and significant social ideals of equality and integration.

SUGGESTED SUPPLEMENTARY READINGS TO PART THREE

Bayles, Michael D.: "Compensatory Reverse Discrimination in Hiring," *Social Theory and Practice* 2 (1973), 301ff. Bishop, Sharon and Marjorie Weinzweig, eds. *Philosophy and Women* (Belmont, Cal.: Wadsworth, 1979).

English, Jane, ed.: *Sex Equality* (Englewood Cliffs, N.J.: Prentice-Hall, Inc., 1977).

Feinberg, Joel: "Noncomparative Justice," *Philosophical Review* 83 (1974), 297ff.

Fullinwider, Robert K.: *The Reverse Discrimination Controversy* (Totowa, N.J.: Rowman and Littlefield, 1980).

Gilligan, Carol: *In a Different Voice* (Cambridge, Mass.: Harvard University Press, 1982).

Goldman, Alan H.: *Justice and Reverse Discrimination* (Princeton, N.J.: Princeton University Press, 1979).

Mill, John Stuart and Harriet Taylor Mill: *The Subjection of Women* (1969) in J. S. Mill and Harriet Taylor Mill, *Essays on Sex Equality* (Chicago: University of Chicago Press, 1970).

Nickel, James W.: "Classification by Race in Compensatory Programs," *Ethics* 84: 146ff., 1974.

———"Discrimination and Morally Relevant Characteristics," *Analysis* 32, 1972.

Sher, George: "Justifying Reverse Discrimination in Employment," *Philosophy and Public Affairs* (Winter 1975).

Wasserstrom, Richard: "The University and the Case for Preferential Treatment," *Philosophical Quarterly* 13: 165ff., 1976.

PART FOUR

FOUR

ABORTION

INTRODUCTION

For those opposing abortion in the United States, the world turned upside down in 1973. In that year the U.S. Supreme Court handed down its famous decision in *Roe v. Wade*. Until then states had the presumed right to regulate abortion, and they did so vigorously. Nontherapeutic abortions were illegal in virtually every state of the union and the states that did permit exceptions limited them to cases of rape or severe deformities of the fetus. After 1973, abortions became available to women throughout the U.S., and since then about 1.5 million abortions per year on average have been performed. Many hailed the decision as a victory for freedom and women's rights. But others, shocked by the failure of the court to regard the fetus as a person, saw it as a decision that legalized murder.

ROE V. WADE: **THE DECISION AND ITS AFTERMATH**

In *Roe v. Wade* the U.S. Supreme Court considered the claim of a Texas woman using the pseudonym "Jane Roe" that her constitutional right to privacy had been violated by Texas state laws forbidding all abortions save those designed to save the life of the mother. Her attorneys argued that their client was unable to secure a safe abortion in Texas and that she had inadequate funds to travel out of state to obtain a legal abortion. At issue were sections of the Texas penal code similar to those in many states. In the majority opinion (7-2) delivered by Judge Blackmun the justices found in favor of Roe, agreeing that she had been deprived of her constitutional rights. They affirmed a woman's right to privacy and, drawing an analogy between the right to privacy in abortion and in search and seizure, held that a woman's right included control over her own body.

The court declared that states could not regulate abortion prior to the beginning of the second trimester (that is, the second of three of the roughly three-month periods that make up a full-term pregnancy). After that time they could, but only on the condition that a compelling state interest could be demonstrated. During the second trimester, however, because the woman's right to privacy was held still to outweigh the interest of the state, only the *manner* of abortion, and presumably not the woman's right to *have* an abortion, could be regulated. The court conceded that in the third trimester when the fetus has reached "viability" (or the capacity to live outside the womb), the interest of the state in the "potential human life" represented by the fetus was "compelling" and thus justified state bans on abortion. The court denied that the fetus was a "legal person" and confessed its own inability to settle the deeper philosophical issues surrounding the moral status of the fetus. In the Constitution, it noted, the word "person" invariably refers to those who have already been born.

In a dissenting opinion, Justices White and Rehnquist argued that the final and unfortunate effect of the decision was to create an entirely new "right for pregnant mothers," one which had no basis in legal tradition and which had priority over the right of the potential life of the fetus. The word "privacy," Justice Rehnquist said, had nothing whatever to do with the right of a woman to have an abortion and was out of place in the present context. Finally, although it is true that certain liberties exist relating to abortion, states have been and should be granted the right to override such liberties in appropriate contexts.

From the perspective of law, *Roe v. Wade* left unanswered a swarm of key questions; and from the perspective of morality, it served only to fan the flames of a new public debate. Although the majority argued that the mother's right overrides that of the state to protect the potential life of the fetus, it did acknowledge that the *potential* life of the fetus was an important legal concern. Indeed, this is the basis for its allowing restrictions on abortion after the first trimester. How, then, if at all, should the value of a *potential* life weigh in legal disputes? Next, although denying that the fetus was a "legal person," at least under current law, the court expressly denied that it was offering the last word on the ultimate moral status of the fetus. Did the Court then mean to leave the door open to a constitutional amendment or other piece of legislation that would "define" a person in a way incompatible with abortion on demand? Furthermore, the concept of "privacy" is a complex one in the law, with competing definitions. The law has not spoken univocally with respect to what "privacy" means, as evidenced by the fact that a different definition was offered in the dissenting opinion of *Roe v. Wade* than in the majority one. Finally, what are we to make of the court's decision that the interest of the state becomes "compelling" after the second trimester insofar as that is the point after which the fetus is viable? Every day, it seems, improved medical techniques lower the age of viability another notch. And what will happen if ever a one-week-old fetus can be kept alive outside the womb?

In a 1983 Supreme Court case, *City of Akron v. Akron Center for Reproductive Health* (excerpts of which are included in this section), we find the court affirming its basic decision in *Roe v. Wade* and striking down a series of ordinances limiting abortions in Akron, Ohio. Because the Akron ordinances were designed neither to protect the life of the mother nor the state's legitimate interest in potential life, they were declared unconstitutional. But in an interesting minority opinion, the court's newest member, Justice Sandra Day O'Connor, expresses her doubt about whether the court can—as it attempted to do in *Roe v. Wade*—sidestep the ultimate question of whether the fetus is a person. Further, she raises the nagging question, mentioned earlier, of whether "viability" can be used as a rationale for settling abortion questions in an age where technology is constantly changing the boundary lines of the concept. We must recognize, she concludes, that the fetus possesses "potential life" every bit as much in the first weeks of pregnancy as when it is "viable."

POINTS OF VIEW

When thinking about abortion, we should keep in mind the distinction made in Part One between legal and moral permissibility. When debating *legal* permissibility, we are concerned with whether there should be laws on the books against abortion; when debating *moral* permissibility, we are concerned only with whether abortion can be justified in terms of moral concepts. Usually, what is morally impermissible is also legally impermissible, but not always. For example, some argue that abortion is morally wrong, but should be legally permitted. Their critics, also recognizing the law-morality distinction, respond that nonetheless in the instance of abortion legality must be subservient to morality. Since abortion violates the right to life, they ask, should not society outlaw abortion as it does murder?

It is tempting to think that the issue of abortion admits of only two views: for or against. In fact, people on both sides of the issue frequently qualify their views. For example, most who oppose abortion make an exception where the life of the mother is threatened. And most who defend it deny its *legal* permissibility after the first trimester and its *moral* permissibility when used as a mere method of birth control. The four short case studies that begin this section allow you to consider the abortion question against the background of specific variables sometimes said to affect the issue of permissibility. In doing so they raise specific questions. Is rape a valid reason for abortion? Is knowledge of a Down's Syndrome fetus? Is wanting a child of a different sex?

A distinction frequently drawn is that between a "human being" and a "moral person." Virtually everyone, including biologists and scientists, grants that a fetus is a human being. That is to say, the fetus is a member of the species Homo sapiens; it is not a tiger or a chimpanzee. But having said this, it remains to determine whether the fetus is a "moral person," that is, whether it is the bearer of rights in the same sense that you and I are the bearer of rights. It does not necessarily follow that because something is a human being it has a full complement of human rights. For example, incompetents and children do not have the right to own property, and murderers (at least according to some) do not have the right to life.

Those who oppose abortion do so largely out of concern for the value of the person they believe is constituted by, or potentially constituted by, the fetus. In "An Almost Absolute Value in History," John Noonan argues that moral personhood begins at conception. There simply is no other morally critical point in the spectrum between conception and birth that can be used to separate personhood from nonpersonhood. The remarkable and complex genetic code that marks something as a human being is passed from parents to fetus. Hence abortion, except in the unusual instance where the mother's life is at stake, is morally wrong.

Many of those who agree with Noonan's conclusion hope to outlaw abortion in the United States, and to overturn the effects of Roe v. Wade, through a new piece of legislation entitled "The Human Life Bill." This bill along with its supporting arguments is reprinted in the appendix at the end of this book (p. 473). If passed it would specify that human life begins at conception and that the Fourteenth Amendment applies to all humans. Two key claims are asserted in the supporting arguments: that informed scientists agree that life begins at conception, and that the U.S. Constitution defends the equal worth and inherent value of human life.

A strikingly different view is taken by the philosopher, Michael Tooley. Tooley argues that in order to have a right to something, one must be capable of desiring it. From this it follows that neither fetuses nor infants could have a right to life since they lack the desire to "continue to exist as a subject of experiences and other mental states." In turn, both abortion and infanticide are justified.

Both Tooley and Noonan are concerned with establishing a criterion of personhood. For Noonan, the criterion of personhood is satisfied at the moment of conception; for Tooley, it remains unsatisfied (surprisingly) until some time after birth. Still a third criterion of personhood, midway between Noonan and Tooley, is offered by the philosopher Larry Sumner in his article, "A Third Way." For him, what gives something moral status is "sentience," which he defines as the capacity for feeling or affect. Sentience, however, admits of degrees: in its more primitive form it includes only the ability to experience basic sensations of pleasure and pain, while in its more developed form, it includes the ability to want, plan, and desire. This, he argues, makes it possible to account for the fact that in moral terms "parmecia and horseflies count for nothing; dogs and cats count for something; chimpanzees and dolphins count for more; and human being count for most of all." With sentience as his criterion, Sumner proceeds to construct boundary lines for moral personhood in the fetus and hence for permissible versus impermissible abortion. First term fetuses clearly lack sentience, he argues, but third term fetuses clearly have it; hence, he concludes, the boundary line must be drawn at some point during the second trimester.

The focus so far has been on the issue of whether the fetus is or is not a moral person. Defenders of abortion, however, sometimes base their claims not on the counter-claim that the fetus is not a person, but on the claim that, whether a person or not, the mother's rights outweigh the right of the fetus to life. In the last article in this section, the late Jane English argues that although the issue of whether the fetus is a moral person cannot be finally resolved, the rights of the mother must be viewed as decidedly limited, especially in the instance of late-term pregnancy where the resemblance between the fetus and a newborn infant is striking. Nonetheless, she wants to insist that a mother has a right to her own self-defense and that this right makes a blanket policy against abortion unacceptable, even if one assumes the fetus is a moral person. Thus English, while taking a different theoretical route from Sumner's, arrives at a position which, like Sumner's, is not far from current practice.

CASE STUDIES—Abortion

SUSAN CRENSHAW

Susan Crenshaw was devastated when she put down the phone after speaking to a nurse at a local clinic. The laboratory tests were complete and she was pregnant. What was she to do? Although only about one month pregnant, she knew she must act quickly. As she considered the issue of having an abortion, she turned over in her mind the circumstances in which she found herself.

At nineteen Susan had just finished her freshman year of college at the nearby university. Brad Green, the father of her newly discovered fetus, was a fellow student at the university and they had been dating for two years. Three weeks ago, after months of what had been worse and worse arguing, the two had vowed never to see each other again. She wondered how much sympathy Brad would even have for her present situation.

Her parents had constantly warned about pregnancy, and she knew they would be angry. She also knew what they would recommend: an abortion. Susan herself, worried about pregnancy, had practiced birth control since her last year in high school—although she had known that any method of birth control failed to guarantee protection against pregnancy.

Her dream had been to become a business woman, perhaps even a corporate executive. With this in mind, she hoped to receive a Master's degree in business administration after finishing her undergraduate work. Having a child at this point would be a significant if not impossible detour between her and

The four case studies on abortion were prepared by the editor.

her goal. On the other hand, she had always planned on having children, and had believed that she would make a good mother.

What should she do?

KIMBERLY WILSON

Kimberly and Fred Wilson had been married for fifteen years. Fred was a manager in a local computer firm and Kimberly cared for their three boys at home. The news that she was pregnant did not surprise Kimberly, since she and her husband had hoped for another child, in particular, a girl. They had wanted a girl from the start, but three boys had followed. The oldest was now fourteen, and the other two were nine and five. At age thirty-five Kimberly knew that her own biological clock was running out, and though she was willing to expand the family from three to four to make room for a girl, she was simply not interested in another boy. Four was the limit she had placed on her family years ago, and she was determined that the next child would be a girl.

Recently she had learned about the medical procedure of amniocentesis which allows a physician to determine the sex of a child as well as other health related variables, e.g., Down's syndrome. As Kimberly considered what to say to her husband that evening, she was inclined to lobby hard for using the amniocentesis procedure as a way of ensuring the arrival of a girl. After all, she was only forty-five days pregnant; if the test revealed she was carrying a girl, there was no reason not to go through with the delivery. If on the other hand it was a boy, she could have an abortion. This would still allow them to try again for a girl.

What should the Wilsons do? If they decide to go ahead with Kimberly's strategy and explain it to the physician, should the physician go along?

SARAH FEINBERG

Sarah Feinberg had at first welcomed the news of her pregnancy. Happily married with a successful career she felt that she was ready for the child she had always wanted. At age thirty-seven Sarah remembered the many opportunities to become pregnant she had passed up for career reasons. Now, with a solid professional position in broadcasting, she knew that she could take six months away from work and return without harm. After six months she planned to hire a full-time babysitter to come into the Feinberg's home to care for the young child.

But all this was before she had learned the child had Down's syndrome. A routine amniocentesis test recommended by her physician for all patients over thirty-five had revealed the disease and had forced an agonizing decision on her and her husband. Two months pregnant she realized that she must either have the abortion soon or not at all. Although she knew that, despite serious problems, a Down's syndrome child could be very loving—and rewarding in many ways—she also knew that the special attention such children required would make it difficult, if not impossible, to leave the child with a babysitter.

What was she to do? The Down's syndrome itself frightened and depressed her. The thought of sacrificing the career she had worked so many years to achieve was another serious problem. After talking the matter over with her husband, David, she learned that he shared her fears and depression. David, however, made it clear that he would go along with whatever she wanted.

Should Sarah have an abortion?

DIANA LUDLOW

On August 9, at 10:20 p.m., while returning from a short trip to the local drugstore, Diana Ludlow was raped. She was attacked by two men, dragged into an alley where she was raped, and physically beaten. After the crime was reported to the local authorities, the police issued an all-points bulletin for the two criminals and an intensive search was instituted. The two criminals were apprehended by the police and conclusively identified by Diana.

Diana now knows that she must face her attackers in court in two months, although she wonders privately whether she can look at them again without crying. She has nightmares about the rape.

Shortly after it happened, Diana learned that she was pregnant. At eighteen, she is unmarried and works in a local department store. She has been dating the same boy for the last two years, and they have often spoken of marriage. Her boyfriend thinks that whatever the rapists get is too good for them, and has advised her to have an abortion.

What should Diana do?

Akron Center for Reproductive Health v. City of Akron

An Akron, Ohio, ordinance, (1) requires all abortions performed after the first trimester of pregnancy to be performed in a hospital (§ 1870.03); (2) prohibits a physician from performing an abortion on an unmarried minor under the age of 15 unless he obtains the consent of one of her parents or unless the minor obtains an order from a court having jurisdiction over her that the abortion be performed (§ 1870.05(B)); (3) requires that the attending physician inform his patient of the status of her pregnancy, the development of her fetus, the date of possible viability, the physical and emotional complications that may result from an abortion, and the availability of agencies to provide her with assistance and information with respect to birth control, adoption, and childbirth (§ 1870.06(B)), and also inform her of the particular risks associated with her pregnancy and the abortion technique to be employed (§ 1870.06(C)); (4) prohibits a physician from performing an abortion until 24 hours after the pregnant woman signs a consent form (§ 1870.07); and (5) requires physicians performing abortions to ensure that fetal remains are disposed of in a "humane and sanitary manner" (§ 1870.16). A violation of the ordinance is punishable as a misdemeanor.

*   *   *

Justice POWELL delivered the opinion of the Court.

In this litigation we must decide the constitutionality of several provisions of an ordinance enacted by the city of Akron, Ohio, to regulate the performance of abortions....

These cases come to us a decade after we held in *Roe v. Wade* (410 U.S. 113, 93 S.Ct. 705, 35, L.Ed.2d 147 (1973)), that the right to privacy, grounded in the concept of personal liberty guaranteed by the Constitution, encompasses a woman's right to decide whether to terminate her pregnancy. Legislative responses to the Court's decision have required us on several occasions, and again today, to define the limits of a State's authority to regulate the performance of abortions....

In *Roe v. Wade*, the Court held that the "right of privacy,...founded in the Fourteenth Amendment's concept of personal liberty and restrictions upon state action,...is broad enough to encompass a woman's decision whether or not to terminate her pregnancy." Although the Constitution does not specifically identify this right, the history of this Court's constitutional adjudication leaves no doubt that "the full scope of the liberty guaranteed by the Due

(No. 81-1172) 103 S. Ct. 2481 (1983) Argued November 30, 1982. Decided June 15, 1983. This case was edited by Professor Gregory Smith of the Philosophy Department at Loyola University of Chicago. The editor wishes to acknowledge and thank him.

Process Clause cannot be found in or limited by the precise terms of the specific guarantees elsewhere provided in the Constitution." Central among these protected liberties is an individual's "freedom of personal choice in matters of marriage and family life." The decision in Roe was based firmly on this long-recognized and essential element of personal liberty.

The Court also has recognized, because abortion is a medical procedure, that the full vindication of the woman's fundamental right necessarily requires that her physician be given "the room he needs to make his best medical judgment." The physician's exercise of this medical judgment encompasses both assisting the woman in the decision making process and implementing her decision should she choose abortion.

At the same time, the Court in Roe acknowledged that the woman's fundamental right "is not unqualified and must be considered against important state interests in abortion." But restrictive state regulation of the right to choose abortion, as with other fundamental rights subject to searching judicial examination, must be supported by a compelling state interest. [In Roe] we have recognized two such interests that may justify state regulation of abortions.

First, a State has an "important and legitimate interest in protecting the potentiality of human life." Although this interest exists "throughout the course of the woman's pregnancy," it becomes compelling only at viability, the point at which the fetus "has the capability of meaningful life outside the mother's womb." At viability this interest in protecting the potential life of the unborn child is so important that the State may proscribe abortions altogether, "except when it is necessary to preserve the life or health of the mother."

Second, because a State has a legitimate concern with the health of women who undergo abortions, "a State may properly assert important interests in safeguarding health [and] in maintaining medical standards." We held in Roe, however, that this health interest does not become compelling until "approximately the end of the first trimester" of pregnancy. Until that time, a pregnant woman must be permitted, in consultation with her physician, to decide to have an abortion and to effectuate that decision "free of interference by the State...."

We noted, for example, that States could establish requirements relating "to the facility in which the procedure is to be performed, that is whether it must be in a hospital or may be a clinic or some other place of less-than-hospital status...." We recognized the State's legitimate health interests in establishing, for second-trimester abortions, "standards for licensing all facilities where abortions may be performed." We found, however, that "the State must show more than [was shown in Roe] in order to prove that only the full resources of a licensed hospital, rather than those of some other appropriately licensed institution, satisfy these health interests...."

There can be no doubt that § 1870.03's second-trimester hospitalization requirement places a significant obstacle in the path of women seeking an abortion. A primary burden created by the requirement is additional cost to the woman....[A] second-trimester hospitalization requirement may force women to travel to find available facilities, resulting in both financial expense and additional health risk. It therefore is apparent that a second-trimester hospitalization requirement may significantly limit a woman's ability to obtain an abortion.... Since [Roe], however, the safety of second-trimester abortions has increased dramatically. The principal reason is that the D & E procedure (dilatation and evacuation) is now widely and successfully used for second-trimester abortions....

These developments, and the professional commentary supporting them, constitute impressive evidence that—at least during the early weeks of the second trimester—D & E abortions may be performed as safely in an outpatient clinic as in a full-service hospital. We conclude, therefore, that "present medical knowledge" convincingly undercuts Akron's justification for requiring that *all* second-trimester abortions be performed in a hospital....

The Akron ordinance provides that no abortion shall be performed except "with the informed written consent of the pregnant woman,...given freely and without coercion." (§ 1870.06(A)) Furthermore, "in order to ensure that the consent for an abortion is truly informed consent" the woman must be "orally informed by her attending physician" of the status of her pregnancy, the development of her fetus, the date of possible viability, the physical and emotional complications that may result from an abortion, and the availability of agencies to provide her with assistance and information with respect to birth control, adoption, and childbirth. (§ 1870.06(B)) In addition, the attending physician must inform her "of the particular risks associated with her own pregnancy and the abortion technique to be employed...[and] other information which in his own medical judgment is relevant to her decision as to whether to have an abortion or carry her pregnancy to term" § 1870.06(C)....

Viewing the city's regulations in this light, we believe that § 1870.06(B) attempts to extend the State's interest in ensuring "informed consent" beyond permissible limits. First, it is fair to say that much of the information required is designed not to inform the woman's consent but rather to persuade her to withhold it altogether. Subsection (3) requires the physician to inform his patient that "the unborn child is a human life from the moment of conception," a requirement inconsistent with the Court's holding in Roe v. Wade that a State may not adopt one theory of when life begins to justify its regulation of abortions. Moreover, much of the detailed description of "the anatomical and physiological characteristics of the particular unborn child" required by subsection (3) would involve at best speculation by the physician. And subsection (5), which begins with the dubious statement that "abortion is a major surgical procedure" and proceeds to describe numerous possible physical and psychological complications of abortion, is a "parade of horribles" intended to suggest that abortion is a particularly dangerous procedure.

An additional, and equally decisive, objection to § 1870.06(B) is its intrusion upon the *discretion* of the pregnant woman's physician. This provision specifies a litany of information that the physician must recite to each woman regardless of whether in his judgment the information is relevant to her personal decision....

The Akron ordinance prohibits a physician from performing an abortion until 24 hours after the pregnant woman signs a consent form. (§ 1870.07) The District Court upheld this provision on the ground that it furthered Akron's interest in ensuring "that a woman's abortion decision is made after careful consideration of all the facts applicable to her particular situation." The Court of Appeals reversed, finding that the inflexible waiting period had "no medical basis," and that careful consideration of the abortion decision by the woman "is beyond the state's power to require." We affirm the Court of Appeals' judgment....We find that Akron has failed to demonstrate that any legitimate state interest is furthered by an arbitrary and inflexible waiting period....

We affirm the judgment of the Court of Appeals invalidating those sections of Akron's "Regulations of Abortions" ordinance that deal with parental consent, informed consent, a 24-hour waiting period, and the disposal of fetal remains. The remaining portion of the judgment, sustaining Akron's requirement that all second-trimester abortions be performed in a hospital, is reversed. *It is so ordered.*

*　　*　　*

DISSENT

Justice O'Connor, with whom Justice White and Justice Rehnquist join.

In *Roe v. Wade*, the Court held that the "right of privacy...founded in the Fourteenth Amendment's concept of personal liberty and restrictions upon state action...is broad enough to encompass a woman's decision whether or not to terminate her pregnancy." The parties in these cases have not asked the Court to re-examine the validity of that holding and the court below did not address it. Accordingly, the Court does not re-examine its previous holding. Nonetheless, it is apparent from the Court's opinion that neither sound constitutional theory nor our need to decide cases based on the application of neutral principles can accommodate an analytical framework that varies according to the "stages" of pregnancy, where those stages, and their concomitant standards of review, differ according to the level of medical technology available when a particular challenge to state regulation occurs. The Court's analysis of the Akron regulations is inconsistent both with the methods of analysis employed in previous cases dealing with abortion, and with the Court's approach to fundamental rights in other areas.

Our recent cases indicate that a regulation imposed on "a lawful abortion 'is not unconstitutional unless it unduly burdens the right to seek an abortion.'" (*Maher v. Roe*, 432 U.S. 434 S.Ct. (1977)). In my view, this "unduly burdensome" standard should be applied to the challenged regulations throughout the entire pregnancy without reference to the particular "stage" of pregnancy involved. If the particular regulation does not "unduly burden" the fundamental right, then our evaluation of that regulation is limited to our determination that the regulation rationally relates to a legitimate state purpose....

The trimester or "three-stage" approach adopted by the Court in *Roe*, and, in a modified form, employed by the Court to analyze the state regulations in these cases, cannot be supported as a legitimate or useful framework for accommodating the woman's right and the State's interest. The decision of the court today graphically illustrates why the trimester approach is a completely nonworkable method of accommodating the conflicting personal rights and compelling state interests that are involved in the abortion context.

It is not difficult to see that despite the Court's purported adherence to the trimester approach adopted in *Roe*, the lines drawn in that decision have now been "blurred" because of what the Court accepts as technological advancement in the safety of abortion procedure. The State may no longer rely on a "bright line" that separates permissible from impermissible regulation, and it is no longer free to consider the second trimester as a unit and weigh the risks posed by all abortion procedures throughout that trimester. Rather, the State must continuously and conscientiously study contemporary medical and scientific literature in order to determine whether the effect of a particular regulation is to "depart from accepted medical practice" insofar as particular procedures and particular periods within the trimester are concerned. Assuming that legislative bodies are able to engage in this exacting task, it is difficult to believe that our Constitution *requires* that they do it as a prelude to protecting the health of their citizens. It is even more difficult to believe that this Court, without the resources available to those bodies entrusted with making legislative choices, believes itself competent to make these inquires and to revise these standards every time the American College of Obstetricians and Gynecologists (ACOG) or a similar group revises its views about what is and what is not appropriate medical procedure in this area. Indeed, the ACOG standards on which the Court relies were changed in 1982 after trial in the present cases. Before ACOG changed its standards in 1982, it recommended that all mid-trimester abortions be performed in a hospital. As today's decision indicates, medical technology is changing, and this change will necessitate our continued functioning as the nation's "ex officio medical board with powers to approve or disapprove medical and operative practices and standards throughout the United States." (*Planned Parenthood v. Danforth*, 420 U.S. 96 S.Ct. (1976))

Just as improvements in medical technology inevitably will move *forward* the point at which the State may regulate for reasons of maternal health, different technological improvements will move *backward* the point of viability at which the State may proscribe abortions except when necessary to preserve the life and health of the mother....

However, studies have demonstrated increasingly earlier fetal viability. It is certainly reasonable to believe that fetal viability in the first trimester of pregnancy may be possible in the not too distant future.

The *Roe* framework, then, is clearly on a collision course with itself. As the medical risks of various abortion procedures decrease, the point at which the State may regulate for reasons of maternal health is moved further forward to actual childbirth. As medical science becomes better able to provide for the separate existence of the fetus, the point of viability is moved further back toward conception....

The Court in *Roe* correctly realized that the State has important interests "in the areas of health and medical standards" and that "[t]he State has a legitimate interest in seeing to it that abortion, like any other medical procedure, is performed under circumstances that ensure maximum safety for the patient." The Court also recognized that the State has "*another* important and legitimate interest in protecting the potentiality of human life." I agree completely that the State has these interests, but in my view, the point at which these interests become compelling does not depend on the trimester of pregnancy. Rather, these interests are present *throughout* pregnancy....

In *Roe*, the Court held that although the State had an important and legitimate interest in protecting potential life, that interest could not become compelling until the point at which the fetus was viable. The difficulty with this analysis is clear: *potential* life is no less potential in the first weeks of pregnancy than it is at viability or afterward. At any stage in pregnancy, there is the *potential* for human life. Although the Court refused to "resolve the difficult question of when life begins," the Court chose the point of viability—when the fetus is *capable* of life independent of its mother—to permit the complete proscription of abortion. The choice of viability as the point at which the state interest in *potential* life becomes compelling is no less arbitrary than choosing any point before viability or any point afterward. Accordingly, I believe that the State's interest in protecting potential human life exists throughout the pregnancy....

The requirement that state interference "infringe substantially" or "heavily burden" a right before heightened scrutiny is applied is not novel in our fundamental-rights jurisprudence, or restricted to the abortion context. In *San Antonio Independent School District v. Rodriguez*, 411, U.S., 93 S.Ct. (1973) we observed that we apply "strict judicial scrutiny" only when legislation may be said to have "'deprived,' 'infringed,' or 'interfered' with the free exercise of some such fundamental personal right or liberty." If the impact of the regulation does not rise to the level appropriate for our strict scrutiny, then our inquiry is limited to whether the state law bears "some rational relationship to legitimate state purposes...."

Indeed, the Court today follows this approach. Although the Court does not use the expression "undue burden," the Court recognizes that even a "significant obstacle" can be justified by a "reasonable" regulation....

The "unduly burdensome" standard is particularly appropriate in the abortion context because of the *nature* and *scope* of the right that is involved. The privacy right involved in the abortion context "cannot be said to be absolute." "*Roe* did not declare an unqualified 'constitutional right to an abortion'." (*Maher* supra, 432, u.s., 97 S.Ct. 2382) Rather, the *Roe* right is intended to protect against state action "drastically limiting the availability and safety of the desired service," against the imposition of an "absolute obstacle" on the abortion decision, or against "official interference" and "coercive restraint" imposed on the abortion decision. That a state regulation may "inhibit" abortions to some degree does not require that we find that the regulation is invalid....

The Court invalidates the informed consent provisions of § 1870.06(B) and § 1870.06(C) of the Akron ordinance....We have approved informed consent provisions in the past even though the physician was required to deliver certain information to the patient. In *Danforth, supra*, the Court upheld a state informed consent requirement because "[t]he decision to abort, indeed, is an important, and often a stressful one, and it is desirable and imperative that it be made with full knowledge of its nature and consequences." In *H. L. v. Matheson*, (450 U.S. 398 S.Ct. (1981)) The Court noted that the state statute in the case required that the patient "be advised at a minimum about available adoption services, about fetal development, and about foreseeable complications and risks of an abortion....Indeed, we have held that an informed consent provision does not 'unduly burden the right to seek an abortion....'"

Section 1870.07 of the Akron ordinance requires a 24-hour waiting period between the signing of a consent form and the actual performance of the abortion, except in cases of [medical] emergency....

The Court's concern in this respect is simply misplaced. Although the waiting period may impose an additional cost on the abortion decision, this increased cost does not unduly burden the availability of abortions or impose an absolute obstacle to access to abortion. Further, the State is not required to "fine-tune" its abortion statutes so as to minimize the costs of abortions.

Assuming *arguendo* that any additional costs are such as to impose an undue burden on the abortion decision, the State's compelling interests in maternal physical and mental health and protection of fetal life clearly justify the waiting period. As we acknowledge in *Danforth*, the decision to abort is "a stressful one," and the waiting period reasonably relates to the State's interest in ensuring that a woman does not make this serious decision in undue haste. The decision also has grave consequences for the fetus, whose life the State has a compelling interest to protect and preserve. "No other [medical] procedure involves the purposeful termination of a potential life." The waiting period is surely a small cost to impose to ensure that the woman's decision is well considered in light of its certain and irreparable consequences on fetal life, and the possible effects on her own.

Finally, § 1870.16 of the Akron ordinance requires that "[a]ny physician who shall perform or induce an abortion upon a pregnant woman shall insure that the remains of the unborn child are disposed of in a humane and sanitary manner." The Court finds this provision void-for-vagueness. I disagree.

*   *   *

For the reasons set forth above, I dissent from the judgment of the Court in these cases.

An Almost Absolute Value in History

John T. Noonan, Jr.

The most fundamental question involved in the long history of thought on abortion is: How do you determine the humanity of a being? To phrase the question that way is to put in comprehensive humanistic terms what the theologians either dealt with as an explicitly theological question under the heading of "ensoulment" or dealt with implicitly in their treatment of abortion. The Christian position as it originated did not depend on a narrow theological or philosophical concept. It had no relation to theories of infant baptism. It appealed to no special theory of instantaneous ensoulment. It took the world's view on ensoulment as that view changed from Aristotle to Zacchia. There was, indeed, theological influence affecting the theory of ensoulment finally adopted, and, of course, ensoulment itself was a theological concept, so that the position was always explained in theological terms. But the theological notion of ensoulment could easily be translated into humanistic language by substituting "human" for "rational soul"; the problem of knowing when a man is a man is common to theology and humanism.

If one steps outside the specific categories used by the theologians, the answer they gave can be analyzed as a refusal to discriminate among human beings on the basis of their varying potentialities. Once conceived, the being was recognized as man because he had man's potential. The criterion for humanity, thus, was simple and all-embracing: If you are conceived by human parents, you are human.

The strength of this position may be tested by a review of some of the other distinctions offered in the contemporary controversy over legalizing abortion. Perhaps the most popular distinction is in terms of viability. Before any age of so many months, the fetus is not viable, that is, it cannot be removed from the mother's womb and live apart from her. To that extent, the life of the fetus is absolutely dependent on the life of the mother. This dependence is made the basis of denying recognition to its humanity.

There are difficulties with this distinction. One is that the perfection of artificial incubation may make the fetus viable at any time: It may be removed and artificially sustained. Experiments with animals already show that such a procedure is possible. This hypothetical extreme case relates to an actual difficulty: there is considerable elasticity to the idea of viability. Mere length of life is not an exact measure. The viability of the fetus depends on the extent of its anatomical and functional development. The weight and length of the fetus are better guides to the state of its development than age, but weight and length vary. Moreover, different racial groups have different ages at which their fetuses are viable. Some evidence, for example, suggests that Negro fetuses mature more quickly than white fetuses. If viability is the norm, the stand would vary with race and with many individual circumstances.

The most important objection to this approach is that dependence is not ended by viability. The fetus is still absolutely dependent on someone's care in order to continue existence; indeed a child of one or three or even five years of age is absolutely dependent on another's care for existence; uncared for, the older fetus or the younger child will die as surely as the early fetus detached from the mother. The unsubstantial lessening in dependence at viability does not seem to signify any special acquisition of humanity.

A second distinction has been attempted in terms of experience. A being who has had experience, has lived and suffered, who possesses memories, is more human than one who has not. Humanity depends on formation by experience. The fetus is thus "unformed" in the most basic human sense.

This distinction is not serviceable for the embryo which is already experiencing and reacting. The embryo is responsive to touch after eight weeks and at least at that point is experiencing. At an earlier stage the zygote is certainly alive and responding to its environment. The distinction may also be challenged by the rare case where aphasia has erased adult memory: Has it erased humanity? More fundamentally, this distinction leaves even the older fetus or the younger child to be treated as an unformed inhuman thing. Finally, it is not clear why experience as such confers humanity. It could be argued that certain central experiences such as loving or learning are necessary to make a man human. But then human beings who have failed to love or to learn might be excluded from the class called man.

A third distinction is made by appeal to the sentiments of adults. If a fetus dies, the grief of the parents is not the grief they would have for a living child. The fetus is an unnamed "it" till birth, and is not perceived as personality until at least the fourth month of existence when movements in the womb manifest a vigorous presence demanding joyful recognition by the parents.

Yet feeling is notoriously an unsure guide to the humanity of others. Many groups of humans have had difficulty in feeling that persons of another tongue, color, religion, sex, are as human as they. Apart from reactions to alien groups, we mourn the loss of a ten-year-old boy more than the loss of his one-day-old brother or his 90-year-old grandfather. The difference felt and the grief expressed vary with the potentialities extinguished, or the experience wiped out; they do not seem to point to any substantial difference in the humanity of baby, boy, or grandfather.

Distinctions are also made in terms of sensation by the parents. The embryo is felt within the womb only after about the fourth month. The embryo is seen only at birth. What can be neither seen nor felt is different from what is tangible. If the fetus cannot be seen or touched at all, it cannot be perceived as man.

Yet experience shows that sight is even more untrustworthy than feeling in determining humanity. By sight, color became an appropriate index for saying who was a man, and the evil of racial discrimination was given foundation. Nor can touch provide the test; a being confined by sickness, "out of touch" with others, does not thereby seem to lose his humanity. To the extent that touch still has appeal as a criterion, it appears to be a survival of the old English idea of "quickening"—a possible mistranslation of the Latin *animatus* used in the canon law. To that extent touch as a criterion seems to be dependent on the Aristotelian notion of ensoulment, and to fall when this notion is discarded.

Finally, a distinction is sought in social visibility. The fetus is not socially perceived as human. It cannot communicate with others. Thus, both subjectively and objectively, it is not a member of society. As moral rules are rules for the behavior of members of society to each other, they cannot be made for behavior toward what is not yet a member. Excluded from the society of men, the fetus is excluded from the humanity of men.

By force of the argument from the consequences, this distinction is to be rejected. It is more subtle than that founded on an appeal to physical sensation, but it is equally dangerous in its implications. If humanity depends on social recognition, individuals or whole groups may be dehumanized by being denied any status in their society. Such a fate is fictionally portrayed in *1984* and has actually been the lot of many men in many societies. In the Roman empire, for example, condemnation to slavery meant the practical denial of most human rights; in the Chinese Communist world, landlords have been classified as enemies of the people and so treated as nonpersons by the state. Humanity does not depend on social recognition, though often the failure of society to recognize the prisoner, the alien, the heterodox as human has led to the destruction of human beings. Anyone conceived by a man and a woman is human. Recognition of this condition by society follows a real event in the objective order, however imperfect and halting the recognition. Any attempt to limit humanity to exclude some group runs the risk of furnishing authority and precedent for excluding other groups in the name of the consciousness or perception of the controlling group in the society.

A philosopher may reject the appeal to the humanity of the fetus because he views "humanity" as a secular views of the soul and because he doubts the existence of anything real and objective which can be identified as humanity. One answer to such a philosopher is to ask how he reasons about moral questions without supposing that there is a sense in which he and the others of whom he speaks are human. Whatever group is taken as the society which determines who may be killed is thereby taken as human. A second answer is to ask if he does not believe that there is a right and wrong way of deciding moral questions. If there is such a difference, experience may be appealed to: To decide who is human on the basis of the sentiment of a given society has led to consequences which rational men would characterize as monstrous.

The rejection of the attempted distinctions based on viability and visibility, experience and feeling, may be buttressed by the following considerations: Moral judgments often rest on distinctions, but if the distinctions are not to appear arbitrary fiat, they should relate to some real difference in probabilities. There is a kind of continuity in all life, but the earlier stages of the elements of human life possess tiny probabilities of development. Consider for example, the spermatozoa in any normal ejaculate: there are about 200,000,000 in any single ejaculate, of which one has a chance of developing into a zygote. Consider the oocytes which may become ova: there are 100,000 to 1,000,000 oocytes in a female infant, of which a maximum of 390 are ovulated. But once spermatozoon and ovum meet and the conceptus is formed, such studies as have been made show that roughly in only 20 percent of the cases will spontaneous abortion occur. In other words, the chances are about 4 out of 5 that this new being will develop. At this stage in the life of the being there is a sharp shift in probabilities, an immense jump in potentialities. To make a distinction between the rights of spermatozoa and the rights of the fertilized ovum is to respond to an enormous shift in possibilities. For about twenty days after conception the egg may split to form twins or combine with another egg to form a chimera, but the probability of either event happening is very small.

It may be asked, What does a change in biological probabilities have to do with establishing humanity? The argument from probabilities is not aimed at establishing humanity but at establishing an objective discontinuity which may be taken into account in moral discourse. As life itself is a matter of probabilities, as most moral reasoning is an estimate of probabilities, so it seems in accord with the structure of reality and the nature of moral thought to be found a moral judgment on the change in probabilities at conception. The appeal to probabilities is the most commonsensical of arguments, to a greater or smaller degree all of us base our actions on probabilities, and in morals, as in law, prudence and negligence are often measured by the account one has taken of the probabilities. If the chance is 200,000,000 to 1 that the movement in the bushes into which you shoot is a man's, I doubt if many persons would hold you careless in shooting; but if the chances are 4 out of 5 that the movement is a human being's, few would acquit you of blame. Would the argument be different if only one out of ten children conceived came to term? Of course this argument would be different. This argument is an appeal to probabilities that actually exist, not to any and all states of affairs which may be imagined.

The probabilities as they do exist do not show the humanity of the embryo in the sense of a demonstration in logic any more than the probabilities of the movement in the bush being a man demonstrate beyond all doubt that the being is a man. The appeal is a "buttressing" consideration, showing the plausibility of the standard adopted. The argument focuses on the decisional factor in any moral judgment and assumes that part of the business of a moralist is drawing lines. One evidence of the nonarbitrary character of the line drawn is the difference of probabilities on either side of it. If a spermatozoon is destroyed, one destroys a being which had a chance of far less than 1 in 200 million of developing into a reasoning being, possessed of the genetic code, a heart and other organs, and capable of pain. If a fetus is destroyed, one destroys a being already possessed of the genetic code, organs, and sensitivity to pain, and one which had an 80 percent chance of developing further into a baby outside the womb who, in time, would reason.

The positive argument for conception as the decisive moment of humanization is that at conception the new being receives the genetic code. It is this genetic information which determines his characteristics, which is the biological carrier of the possibility of human wisdom, which makes him a self-evolving being. A being with a human genetic code is man.

This review of current controversy over the humanity of the fetus emphasizes what a fundamental question the theologians resolved in asserting the inviolability of the fetus. To regard the fetus as possessed of equal rights with other humans was not, however, to decide every case where abortion might be employed. It did decide the case where the argument was that the fetus should be aborted for its own good. To say a being was human was to say it had a destiny to decide for itself which could not be taken from it by another man's decision. But human beings with equal rights often come in conflict with each other, and some decision must be made as to whose claims are to prevail. Cases of conflict involving the fetus are different only in two respects: the total inability of the fetus to speak for itself and the fact that the right of the fetus regularly at stake is the right to life itself.

The approach taken by the theologians to these conflicts was articulated in terms of "direct" and "indirect." Again, to look at what they were doing from outside their categories, they may be said to have been drawing lines or "balancing values." "Direct" and "indirect" are spatial metaphors: "line-drawing" is another. "To weigh" or "to balance" values is a metaphor of a more complicated mathematical sort hinting at the process which goes on in moral judgments. All the metaphors suggest that, in the moral judgments made, comparisons were necessary, that no value completely controlled. The principle of double effect was no doctrine fallen from heaven, but a method of analysis appropriate where two relative values were being compared. In Catholic moral theology, as it developed, life even of the innocent was not taken as an absolute. Judgments on acts affecting life issued from a process of weighing. In the weighing, the fetus was always given a value greater than zero, always a value separate and independent from its parents. This valuation was crucial and fundamental in all Christian thought on the subject and marked it off from any approach which considered that only the parents' interests needed to be considered.

Even with the fetus weighed as human, one interest could be weighed as equal or superior: that of the mother in her own life The casuists between 1450 and 1895 were willing to weigh this interest as superior. Since 1895, that interest was given decisive weight only in the two special cases of the cancerous uterus and the ectopic pregnancy. In both of these cases the fetus itself had little chance of survival even if the abortion were not performed. As the balance was once struck in favor of the mother whenever her life was endangered, it could be so struck again. The balance reached between 1895 and 1930 attempted prudentially and pastorally to forestall a multitude of exceptions for interests less than life.

The perception of the humanity of the fetus and the weighing of fetal rights against other human rights constituted the work of the moral analysts. But what spirit animated their abstract judgments? For the Christian community it was the injunction of Scripture to love your neighbor as yourself. The fetus as human was a neighbor, his life had parity with one's own. The commandment gave life to what otherwise would have been only rational calculation.

The commandment could be put in humanistic as well as theological terms: Do not injure your fellow man without reason. In these terms, once the humanity of the fetus is perceived, abortion is never right except in self-defense. When life must be taken to save life, reason alone cannot say that a mother must prefer a child's life to her own. With this exception, now of great rarity, abortion violates the rational humanist tenet of the equality of human lives.

For Christians the commandment to love had received a special imprint in that the exemplar proposed of love was the love of the Lord for his disciples. In the light given by this example, self-sacrifice carried to the point of death seemed in the extreme situations not without meaning. In the less extreme cases, preference for one's own interests to the life of another seemed to express cruelty or selfishness irreconcilable with the demands of love.

Abortion and Infanticide

Michael Tooley

This essay deals with the question of the morality of abortion and infanticide. The fundamental ethical objection traditionally advanced against these practices rests on the contention that human fetuses and infants have a right to life. It is this claim which will be the focus of attention here. The basic issue to be discussed, then, is what properties a thing must possess in order to have a serious right to life. My approach will be to set out and defend a basic moral principle specifying a condition an organism must satisfy if it is to have a serious right to life. It will be seen that this condition is not satisfied by human fetuses and infants and thus that they do not have a right to life. So unless there are

Michael Tooley, "Abortion and Infanticide," *Philosophy and Public Affairs*, Vol. 2, 1 (Fall, 1972). Pp. 37–65. Copyright © Princeton University Press. Reprinted by permission of Princeton University Press.

other substantial objections to abortion and infanticide, one is forced to conclude that these practices are morally acceptable ones. In contrast, it may turn out that our treatment of adult members of other species—cats, dogs, polar bears—is morally indefensible. For it is quite possible that such animals do possess properties that endow them with a right to life.

ABORTION AND INFANTICIDE

One reason the question of the morality of infanticide is worth examining is that it seems very difficult to formulate a completely satisfactory liberal position on abortion without coming to grips with the infanticide issue. The problem the liberal encounters is essentially that of specifying a cutoff point which is not arbitrary: at what stage in the development of a human being does it cease to be morally permissible to destroy it? It is important to be clear about the difficulty here. The conservative's objection is not that since there is a continuous line of development from a zygote to a newborn baby, one must conclude that if it is seriously wrong to destroy a newborn baby it is also seriously wrong to destroy a zygote or any intermediate stage in the development of a human being. His point is rather that if one says it is wrong to destroy a newborn baby but not a zygote or some intermediate stage in the development of a human being, one should be prepared to point to a *morally relevant* difference between a newborn baby and the earlier stage in the development of a human being.

Precisely the same difficulty can, of course, be raised for a person who holds that infanticide is morally permissible. The conservative will ask what morally relevant differences there are between an adult human being and a newborn baby. What makes it morally permissible to destroy a baby, but wrong to kill an adult? So the challenge remains. But I will argue that in this case there is an extremely plausible answer.

Reflecting on the morality of infanticide forces one to face up to this challenge. In the case of abortion a number of events—quickening or viability, for instance—might be taken as cutoff points, and it is easy to overlook the fact that none of these events involves any morally significant change in the developing human. In contrast, if one is going to defend infanticide, one has to get very clear about what makes something a person, what gives something a right to life.

One of the interesting ways in which the abortion issue differs from most other moral issues is that the plausible positions on abortion appear to be extreme positions. For if a human fetus is a person, one is inclined to say that, in general, one would be justified in killing it only to save the life of the mother. Such is the extreme conservative position. On the other hand, if the fetus is not a person, how can it be seriously wrong to destroy it? Why would one need to point to special circumstances to justify such action? The upshot is that there is no room for a moderate position on the issue of abortion such as one finds, for example, in the Model Penal Code recommendations.

   Aside from the light it may shed on the abortion question, the issue of infanticide is both interesting and important in its own right. The theoretical interest has been mentioned: it forces one to face up to the question of what makes something a person. The practical importance need not be labored. Most people would prefer to raise children who do not suffer from gross deformities or from severe physical, emotional, or intellectual handicaps. If it could be shown that there is no moral objection to infanticide the happiness of society could be significantly and justifiably increased.

   Infanticide is also of interest because of the strong emotions it arouses. The typical reaction to infanticide is like the reaction to incest or cannibalism, or the reaction of previous generations to masturbation or oral sex. The response, rather than appealing to carefully formulated moral principles, is primarily visceral. When philosophers themselves respond in this way, offering no arguments, and dismissing infanticide out of hand, it is reasonable to suspect that one is dealing with a taboo rather than with a rational prohibition. I shall attempt to show that this is in fact the case.

TERMINOLOGY: "PERSON" VERSUS "HUMAN BEING"

How is the term "person" to be interpreted? I shall treat the concept of a person as a purely moral concept, free of all descriptive content. Specifically, in my usage the sentence "X is a person" will be synonymous with the sentence "X has a (serious) moral right to life."

   This usage diverges slightly from what is perhaps the more common way of interpreting the term "person" when it is employed as a purely moral term, where to say that X is a person is to say that X has rights. If everything that had rights had a right to life, these interpretations would be extensionally equivalent. But I am inclined to think that it does not follow from acceptable moral principles that whatever has any rights at all has a right to life. My reason is this. Given the choice between being killed and being tortured for an hour, most adult humans would surely choose the latter. So it seems plausible to say it is worse to kill an adult human being than it is to torture him for an hour. In contrast, it seems to me that while it is not seriously wrong to kill a newborn kitten, it is seriously wrong to torture one for an hour. This *suggests* that newborn kittens may have a right not to be tortured without having a serious right to life. For it seems to be true that an individual has a right to something whenever it is the case that, if he wants that thing, it would be wrong for others to deprive him of it. Then if it is wrong to inflict a certain sensation upon a kitten if it doesn't want to experience that sensation, it will follow that the kitten has a right not to have the sensation inflicted upon it. I shall return to this example later. My point here is merely that it provides some reason for holding that it does not follow from acceptable moral principles that if something has any rights at all, it has a serious right to life.

   There has been a tendency in recent discussions of abortion to use expressions such as "person" and "human being" interchangeably. B. A. Brody, for example, refers to the difficulty of determining "whether destroying the fetus constitutes the taking of a human life," and suggests it is very plausible that "the taking of a human life is an action that has bad consequences for him whose life is being taken." When Brody refers to something as a human life, he apparently construes this as entailing that the thing is a person. For if every living organism belonging to the species Homo sapiens counted as a human life, there would be no difficulty in determining whether a fetus inside a human mother was a human life.

The same tendency is found in Judith Jarvis Thomson's article, which opens with the statement: "Most opposition to abortion relies on the premise that the fetus is a human being, a person, from the moment of conception." The same is true of Roger Wertheimer, who explicitly says "First off I should note that the expression 'a human life,' 'a human being,' 'a person' are virtually interchangeable in this context."

The tendency to use expressions like "person" and "human being" interchangeably is an unfortunate one. For one thing, it tends to lend covert support to anti-abortionist positions. Given such usage, one who holds a liberal view of abortion is put in the position of maintaining that fetuses, at least up to a certain point, are not human beings. Even philosophers are led astray by this usage. Thus Wertheimer says that "except for monstrosities, every member of our species is indubitably a person, a human being, at the very latest at birth." Is it really *indubitable* that newborn babies are persons? Surely this is a wild contention. Wertheimer is falling prey to the confusion naturally engendered by the practice of using "person" and "human being" interchangeably. Another example of this is provided by Thomson: "I am inclined to think also that we shall probably have to agree that the fetus has already become a human person well before birth. Indeed, it comes as a surprise when one first learns how early in its life it begins to acquire human characteristics. By the tenth week, for example, it already has a face, arms and legs, fingers and toes; it has internal organs, and brain activity is detectable." But what do such physiological characteristics have to do with the question of whether the organism is a person? Thomson, partly, I think, because of the unfortunate use of terminology, does not even raise this question. As a result she virtually takes it for granted that there are some cases in which abortion is "positively indecent."

There is a second reason why using "person" and "human being" interchangeably is unhappy philosophically. If one says that the dispute between pro- and anti-abortionists centers on whether the fetus is a human, it is natural to conclude that it is essentially a disagreement about certain facts, a disagreement about what properties a fetus possesses. Thus Wertheimer says that "if one insists on using the raggy fact-value distinction, then one ought to say that the dispute is over a matter of fact in the sense in which it is a fact that the Negro slaves were human beings." I shall argue that the two cases are not parallel, and that in the case of abortion what is primarily at stake is what moral principles one should accept. If one says that the central issue between conservatives and liberals in the abortion question is whether the fetus is a person, it is clear that the dispute may be either about what properties a thing must have in order to be a person, in order to have a right to life—a moral question—or about whether a fetus at a given stage of development as a matter of fact possesses the properties in question. The temptation to suppose that the disagreement must be a factual one is removed.

It should now be clear why the common practice of using expressions such as "person" and "human being" interchangeably in discussions of abortion is unfortunate. It would perhaps be best to avoid the term "human" altogether, employing instead some expression that is more naturally interpreted as referring to a certain type of biological organism characterized in physiological terms, such as "member of the species Homo sapiens." My own approach will be to use the term "human" only in contexts where it is not philosophically dangerous.

THE BASIC ISSUE: WHEN IS A MEMBER OF THE SPECIES HOMO SAPIENS A PERSON?

Settling the issue of the morality of abortion and infanticide will involve answering the following questions. What properties must something have to be a person, i.e., to have a serious right to life? At what point in the development of a member of the species Homo sapiens does the organism possess the properties that make it a person? The first question raises a moral issue. To answer it is to decide what basic moral principles involving the ascription of a right to life one ought to accept. The second question raises a purely factual issue, since the properties in question are properties of a purely descriptive sort.

Some writers seem quite pessimistic about the possibility of resolving the question of the morality of abortion. Indeed, some have gone so far as to suggest that the question of whether the fetus is a person is in principle unanswerable: "we seem to be stuck with the indeterminateness of the fetus' humanity." An understanding of some of the sources of this pessimism will, I think, help us to tackle the problem. Let us begin by considering the similarity a number of people have noted between the issue of abortion and the issue of Negro slavery. The question here is why it should be more difficult to decide whether abortion and infanticide are acceptable than it was to decide whether slavery was acceptable. The answer seems to be that in the case of slavery there are moral principles of a quite uncontroversial sort that settle the issue. Thus most people would agree to some such principles as the following: No organism that has experiences, that is capable of thought and of using language, and that has harmed no one, should be made a slave. In the case of abortion, on the other hand, conditions that are generally agreed to be sufficient grounds for ascribing a right to life to something do not suffice to settle the issue. It is easy to specify other, purportedly sufficient conditions that will settle the issue, but no one has been successful in putting forward considerations that will convince others to accept those additional moral principles.

I do not share the general pessimism about the possibility of resolving the issue of abortion and infanticide because I believe it is possible to point to a very plausible moral principle dealing with the question of *necessary* conditions for something's having a right to life, where the conditions in question will provide an answer to the question of the permissibility of abortion and infanticide.

There is a second cause of pessimism that should be noted before proceeding. It is tied up with the fact that the development of an organism is one of gradual and continuous change. Given this continuity, how is one to draw a line at one point and declare it permissible to destroy a member of Homo sapiens up to, but not beyond, that point? Won't there be an arbitrariness about any point that is chosen? I will return to this worry shortly. It does not present a serious difficulty once the basic moral principles relevant to the ascription of a right to life to an individual are established.

Let us turn now to the first and most fundamental question: What properties must something have in order to be a person, i.e., to have a serious right to life? The claim I wish to defend is this: An organism possesses a serious right to life only if it possesses the concept of a self as a continuing subject of experiences and other mental states, and believes that it is itself such a continuing entity.

My basic argument in support of this claim, which I will call the self-consciousness requirement, will be clearest, I think, if I first offer a simplified version of the argument, and then consider a modification that seems desirable. The simplified version of my argument is this. To ascribe a right to an individual is to assert something about the prima facie obligations of other individuals to act, or to refrain from acting, in certain ways. However, the obligations in question are conditional ones, being dependent upon the existence of certain desires of the individual to whom the right is ascribed. Thus if an individual asks one to destroy something to which he has a right, one does not violate his right to that thing if one proceeds to destroy it. This suggests the following analysis: "A has a right to X" is roughly synonymous with "If A desires X, then others are under a prima facie obligation to refrain from actions that would deprive him of it."

Although this analysis is initially plausible, there are reasons for thinking it not entirely correct. I will consider these later. Even here, however, some expansion is necessary, since there are features of the concept of a right that are important in the present context, and that ought to be dealt with more explicitly. In particular, it seems to be a conceptual truth that things that lack consciousness, such as ordinary machines, cannot have rights. Does this conceptual truth follow from the above analysis of the concept of a right? The answer depends on how the term "desire" is interpreted. If one adopts a completely behavioristic interpretation of "desire," so that a machine that searches for an electrical outlet in order to get its batteries recharged is described as having a desire to be recharged, then it will not follow from this analysis that objects that lack consciousness cannot have rights. On the other hand, if "desire" is interpreted in such a way that desires are states necessarily standing in some sort of relationship to states of consciousness, it will follow from the analysis that a machine that is not capable of being conscious, and consequently of having desires, cannot have any rights. I think those who defend analyses of the concept of a right along the lines of this one do have in mind an interpretation of the term "desire" that involves reference to something more than behavioral dispositions. However, rather than relying on this, it seems preferable to make such an interpretation explicit. The following analysis is a natural way of doing that: "A has a right to X" is roughly synonymous with "A is the sort of thing that is a subject of experiences and other mental states. A is capable of desiring X, and if A does desire X, then others are under a prima facie obligation to refrain from actions that would deprive him of it."

The next step in the argument is basically a matter of applying this analysis to the concept of a right to life. Unfortunately the expression "right to life" is not entirely a happy one, since it suggests that the right in question concerns the continued existence of a biological organism. That this is incorrect can be brought out by considering possible ways of violating an individual's right to life. Suppose, for example, that by some technology of the future the brain of an adult human were to be completely reprogrammed, so that the organism would up with memories (or rather, apparent memories), beliefs, attitudes, and personality traits completely different from those associated with it before it was subjected to reprogramming. In such a case one would surely say that an individual had been destroyed, that an adult human's right to life had been violated, even though no biological organisms had been killed. This example shows that the expression "right to life" is misleading, since what one is really concerned about is not just the continued existence of a biological organism, but the right of a subject of experiences and other mental states to continue to exist.

Given this more precise description of the right with which we are here concerned, we are now in a position to apply the analysis of the concept of a right stated above. When we do so we find that the statement "A has a right to continue to exist as a subject of experiences and other mental states" is roughly synonymous with the statement "A is a subject of experiences and other mental states, A is capable of desiring to continue to exist as a subject of experiences and other mental states, and if A does desire to continue to exist as such an entity, then others are under a prima facie obligation not to prevent him from doing so."

The final stage in the argument is simply a matter of asking what must be the case if something is to be capable of having a desire to continue existing as a subject of experiences and other mental states. The basic point here is that the desires a thing can have are limited by the concepts it possesses. For the fundamental way of describing a given desire is as a desire that a certain proposition be true. Then, since one cannot desire that a certain proposition be true unless one understands it, and since one cannot understand it without possessing the concepts involved in it, it follows that the desires one can have are limited by the concepts one possesses. Applying this to the present case results in the conclusion that an entity cannot be the sort of thing that can desire that a subject of experiences and other mental states exist unless it possesses the concept of such a subject. Moreover, an entity cannot desire that it itself *continue* existing as a subject of experiences and other mental states unless it believes that it is now such a subject. This completes the justification of the claim that it is a necessary condition of something's having a serious right to life that it possess the concept of a self as a continuing subject of experiences, and that it believe that it is itself such an entity.

Let us now consider a modification in the above argument that seems desirable. This modification concerns the crucial conceptual claim advanced about the relationship between ascription of rights and ascription of the corresponding desires. Certain situations suggest that there may be exceptions to the claim that if a person doesn't desire something, one cannot violate his right to it. There are three types of situations that call this claim into question: (i) situations in which an individual's desires reflect a state of emotional disturbance; (ii) situations in which a previously conscious individual is temporarily unconscious; (iii) situations in which an individuals' desires have been distorted by conditioning or by indoctrination.

As an example of the first, consider a case in which an adult human falls into a state of depression which his psychiatrist recognizes as temporary. While in the state he tells people he wishes he were dead. His psychiatrist, accepting the view that there can be no violation of an individual's right to life unless the individual has a desire to live, decides to let his patient have his way and kills him. Or consider a related case in which one person gives another a drug that produces a state of temporary depression; the recipient expresses a wish that he were dead. The person who administered the drug then kills him. Doesn't one want to say in both these cases that the agent did something seriously wrong in killing the other person? And isn't the reason the action was seriously wrong in each case the fact that it violated the individual's right to life? If so, the right to life cannot be linked with a desire to live in the way claimed above.

The second set of situations are ones in which an individual is unconscious for some reason—that is, he is sleeping, or drugged, or in a temporary coma. Does an individual in such a state have any desires? People do sometimes say that an unconscious individual wants something, but it might be argued that if such talk is not to be simply false it must be interpreted as actually referring to the desires the individual *would* want if he were now conscious. Consequently, if the analysis of the concept of a right proposed above were correct, it would follow that one does not violate an individual's right if one takes his car, or kills him, while he is asleep.

Finally, consider situations in which an individual's desires have been distorted, either by inculcation of irrational beliefs or by direct conditioning. Thus an individual may permit someone to kill him because he has been convinced that if he allows himself to be sacrificed to the gods he will be gloriously rewarded in a life to come. Or an individual may be enslaved after first having been conditioned to desire a life of slavery. Doesn't one want to say that in the former case an individual's right to life has been violated, and in the latter his right to freedom?

Situations such as these strongly suggest that even if an individual doesn't want something, it is still possible to violate his right to it. Some modification of the earlier account of the concept of a right thus seems in order. The analysis given covers, I believe, the paradigmatic cases of violation of an individual's rights, but there are other, secondary cases where one also wants to say that someone's right has been violated which are not included.

Precisely how the revised analysis should be formulated is unclear. Here it will be sufficient merely to say that, in view of the above, an individual's right to X can be violated not only when he desires X, but also when he *would* now desire X were it not for one of the following: (i) he is in an emotionally unbalanced state; (ii) he is temporarily unconscious; (iii) he has been conditioned to desire the absence of X.

The critical point now is that, even given this extension of the conditions under which an individual's right to something can be violated, it is still true that one's right to something can be violated only when one has the conceptual capability of desiring the thing in question. For example, an individual who would now desire not to be a slave if he weren't emotionally unbalanced, or if he weren't temporarily unconscious, or if he hadn't previously been conditioned to want to be a slave, must possess the concepts involved in the desire not to be a slave. Since it is really only the conceptual capability presupposed by the desire to continue existing as a subject of experiences and other mental states, and not the desire itself, that enters into the above argument, the modification required in the account of the conditions under which an individual's rights can be violated does not undercut my defense of the self-consciousness requirement.

To sum up, my argument has been that having a right to life presupposes that one is capable of desiring to continue existing as a subject of experiences and other mental states. This in turn presupposes both that one has the concept of such a continuing entity and that one believes that one is oneself such an entity. So an entity that lacks such a consciousness of itself as a continuing subject of mental states does not have a right to life.

It would be natural to ask at this point whether satisfaction of this requirement is not only necessary but also sufficient to ensure that a thing has a right to life. I am inclined to an affirmative answer. However, the issue is not urgent in the present context, since as long as the requirement is in fact a necessary one we have the basis of an adequate defense of abortion and infanticide. If an organism must satisfy some other condition before it has a serious right to life, the result will merely be that the interval during which infanticide is morally permissible may be somewhat longer. Although the point at which an organism first achieves self-consciousness and hence the capacity of desiring to continue existing as a subject of experiences and other mental states may be a theoretically incorrect cutoff point, it is at least a morally safe one: any error it involves is on the side of caution.

SUMMARY AND CONCLUSIONS

Let us return now to my basic claim, the self-consciousness requirement: An organism possesses a serious right to life only if it possesses the concept of a self as a continuing subject of experiences and other mental states, and believes that it is itself such a continuing entity. My defense of this claim has been twofold. I have offered a direct argument in support of it, and I have tried to show that traditional conservative and liberal views on abortion and infanticide, which involve a rejection of it, are unsound. I now want to mention one final reason why my claim should be accepted. Consider the example mentioned in section II—that of killing, as opposed to torturing, newborn kittens. I suggested there that while in the case of adult humans most people would consider it worse to kill an individual than to torture him for an hour, we do not usually view the killing of a newborn kitten as morally outrageous, although we would regard someone who tortured a newborn kitten for an hour as heinously evil. I pointed out that a possible conclusion that might be drawn from this is that newborn kittens have a right not to be tortured, but do not have a serious right to life. If this is the correct conclusion, how is one to explain it? One merit of the self-consciousness requirement is that it provides an explanation of this situation. The reason a newborn kitten does not have a right to life is explained by the fact that it does not possess the concept of a self. But how is one to explain the kitten's having a right not to be tortured? The answer is that a desire not to suffer pain can be ascribed to something without assuming that it has any concept of a continuing self. For while something that lacks the concept of a self cannot desire that a self not suffer, it can desire that a given sensation not exist. The state desired—the absence of a particular sensation, or of sensations of a certain sort—can be described in a purely phenomenalistic language, and hence without the concept of a continuing self. So long as the newborn kitten possesses the relevant phenomenal concepts, it can truly be said to desire that a certain sensation not exist. So we can ascribe to it a right not to be tortured even though, since it lacks the concept of a continuing self, we cannot ascribe to it a right to life.

This completes my discussion of the basic moral principles involved in the issue of abortion and infanticide. But I want to comment upon an important factual question, namely, at what point an organism comes to possess the concept of a self as a continuing subject of experiences and other mental states, together with the belief that it is itself such a continuing entity. This is obviously a matter for detailed psychological investigation, but everyday observation makes it perfectly clear. I believe that a newborn baby does not possess the concept of a continuing self, any more than a newborn kitten possesses such a concept. If so, infanticide during a time interval shortly after birth must be morally acceptable.

But where is the line to be drawn? What is the cutoff point? If one maintained, as some philosophers have, that an individual possesses concepts only if he can express these concepts in language, it would be a matter of everyday observation whether or not a given organism possessed the concept of a continuing self. Infanticide would then be permissible up to the time an organism learned how to use certain expressions. However, I think the claim that acquisition of concepts is dependent on acquisition of language is mistaken. For example, one wants to ascribe mental states of a conceptual sort—such as beliefs and desires—to organisms that are incapable of learning a language. This issue of prelinguistic understanding is clearly outside the scope of this discussion. My point is simply that *if* an organism can acquire concepts without thereby acquiring a way of expressing those concepts linguistically, the question of whether a given organism possesses the concept of a self as a continuing subject of experiences and other mental states, together with the belief that it is itself such a continuing entity, may be a question that requires fairly subtle experimental techniques to answer.

If this view of the matter is roughly correct, there are two worries one is left with at the level of practical moral decisions, one of which may turn out to be deeply disturbing. The lesser worry is where the line is to be drawn in the case of infanticide. It is not troubling because there is no serious need to know the exact point at which a human infant acquires a right to life. For in the vast majority of cases in which infanticide is desirable, its desirability will be apparent within a short time after birth. Since it is virtually certain that an infant at such a stage of its development does not possess the concept of a continuing self, and thus does not possess a serious right to life, there is excellent reason to believe that infanticide is morally permissible in most cases where it is otherwise desirable. The practical moral problem can thus be satisfactorily handled by choosing some period of time, such as a week after birth, as the interval during which infanticide will be permitted. This interval could then be modified once psychologists have established the point at which a human organism comes to believe that it is a continuing subject of experiences and other mental states.

The troubling worry is whether adult animals belonging to species other than Homo sapiens may not also possess a serious right to life. For once one says that an organism can possess the concept of a continuing self, together with the belief that it is itself such an entity, without having any way of expressing that concept and that belief linguistically, one has to face up to the question of whether animals may not possess properties that bestow a serious right to life upon them. The suggestion itself is a familiar one, and one that most of us are accustomed to dismiss very casually. The line of thought advanced here suggests that this attitude may turn out to be tragically mistaken. Once one reflects upon the question of the *basic* moral principles involved in the ascription of a right to life to organisms, one may find himself driven to conclude that our everyday treatment of animals is morally indefensible, and that we are in fact murdering innocent persons.

A Third Way

Wayne Sumner

The practice of abortion confronts us with two different sets of moral questions belonging to two different decision contexts. The primary context is that in which a woman chooses whether to have an abortion and a physician chooses whether to perform it; here the focus is on the moral quality of abortion itself. Because this context is one of individual decision we will call the set of moral questions which it contains the *personal* problem of abortion. The secondary context is that in which a society chooses how, or whether, to regulate abortions; here the focus is on the merits of alternative abortion policies. Because this context is one of social decision we will call the set of moral questions which it contains the *political* problem of abortion.

Although the two kinds of problem raised by abortion are distinct, they are also connected. A complete view of the morality of abortion will therefore offer connected solutions to them. In most countries in the West, public discussion of abortion has been distorted by the dominance of two such views. The liberal view, espoused by "pro-choice" groups, holds that (voluntary) abortion is always morally innocuous and (therefore) that the only acceptable abortion policy is one which treats abortion as another variety of minor elective surgery. The conservative view, espoused by "pro-life" groups, holds that abortion is always morally serious and (therefore) that the only acceptable abortion policy is one which treats abortion as another variety of homicide.

Because they define the extremities of the continuum of possible positions, and because each is sufficiently simple and forceful to be advocated by a powerful movement, these established views constitute the familiar reference points in our abortion landscape. Yet neither has managed to command the allegiance of more than a small minority of the public. For the rest of us who are unwilling to embrace either of the extreme options the problem has been the lack of a well-defined middle ground between them. In contrast to the power of the established views more moderate alternatives may appear both indistinct and indecisive.

Public distrust of the established views is well grounded: neither stands up under critical scrutiny.[1] If their demise is not to leave us without any credible view of abortion three tasks must be successfully completed. The first is to define a third way with abortion and to distinguish it from both of the views which it will supersede. The second is to give it an intuitive defense by showing that it coheres better than either of its predecessors with considered moral judgments both on abortion itself and on closely related issues. Then, finally,

L.W. Sumner, *Abortion and Moral Theory* (Princeton University Press, 1981), chapter 5. Copyright © Princeton University Press. Excerpt reprinted by permission of Princeton University Press.

[1]I will not be defending this assessment in the present paper. For the arguments see *Abortion and Moral Theory*, chs. 2 and 3.

the third way must be grounded in a moral theory. The first two of these tasks will be undertaken here; the more daunting theoretical challenge is confronted elsewhere.[2]

1 SPECIFICATIONS

Despite their opposition, the two established views suffer from similar defects. Collating their failures will provide us with some positive guidelines to follow in building a more satisfactory alternative. The central issue in the morality of abortion is the moral status of the fetus. Let us say that a creature has *moral standing* if, for the purpose of moral decisionmaking, it must be counted for something in its own right. To count for nothing is to have no moral standing; to count for as much as possible (as much, that is, as any creature does) is to have full moral standing. We may, for the purpose of the present discussion, make this rather vague notion more precise by adopting the rights vocabulary favored by both of the established views. We will suppose that having (some) moral standing is equivalent to having (some) right to life. The central issue in the morality of abortion is then whether fetuses have moral standing in this sense.[3]

The conservative view, and also the more naive versions of the liberal view, select a precise point (conception, birth, etc.) as the threshold of moral standing, implying that the transition from no standing to full standing occurs abruptly. In doing so they rest more weight on these sudden events than they are capable of bearing. A view that avoids this defect will allow full moral standing to be acquired gradually. It will therefore attempt to locate not a threshold point, but a threshold period or stage.

Both of the established views attribute a uniform moral status to all fetuses, regardless of their dissimilarities. Each, for example, counts a newly conceived zygote for precisely as much (or as little) as a full-term fetus, despite the enormous differences between them. A view that avoids this defect will assign moral status differentially, so that the threshold stage occurs sometime during pregnancy.

A consequence of the uniform approach adopted by both of the established views is that neither can attach any significance to the development of the fetus during gestation. Yet this development is the most obvious feature of gestation. A view that avoids this defect will base the (differential) moral standing of the fetus at least in part on its level of development. It will thus assign undeveloped fetuses a moral status akin to that of ova and spermatozoa, whereas it will assign developed fetuses a moral status akin to that of infants.

---

[2]*Abortion and Moral Theory*, chs. 5 and 6.

[3]The adoption of this working definition of moral standing should not be construed as a concession that rights are the appropriate category for dealing with the moral issues posed by abortion. But since both of the established views employ the rhetoric of rights, there is some point to showing how that rhetoric is equally available to a moderate view. For a generalized notion of moral standing freed from all connection with rights, see *Abortion and Moral Theory*, Section 23.

2 A CRITERION OF MORAL STANDING

We are assuming that for a creature to have moral standing is for it to have a right to life. Any such right imposes duties on moral agents; these duties may be either negative (not to deprive the creature of life) or positive (to support the creature's life). Possession of a right to life implies at least some immunity against attack by others, and possibly also some entitlement to the aid of others. As the duties may vary in strength, so may the corresponding rights. To have some moral standing is to have some right to life, whether or not it may be overridden by the rights of others. To have full moral standing is to have the strongest right to life possessed by anyone, the right to life of the paradigm person. Depending on one's moral theory, this right may or may not be inviolable and indefeasible and thus may or may not impose absolute duties on others.

To which creatures should we distribute (some degree of) moral standing? On which criterion should we base this distribution? It may be easier to answer these questions if we begin with the clear case and work outward to the unclear ones. If we can determine why we ascribe full standing to the paradigm case, we may learn what to look for in other creatures when deciding whether or not to include them in the moral sphere.

The paradigm bearer of moral standing is an adult human being with normal capacities of intellect, emotion, perception, sensation, decision, action, and the like. If we think of such a person as a complex bundle of natural properties, then in principle we could employ as a criterion any of the properties common to all normal and mature members of our species. Selecting a particular property or set of properties will define a class of creatures with moral standing, namely, all (and only) those who share that property. The extension of that class will depend on how widely the property in question is distributed. Some putative criteria will be obviously frivolous and will immediately fail the tests of generality or moral relevance. But even after excluding the silly candidates, we are left with a number of serious ones. There are four that appear to be the most serious: we might attribute full moral standing to the paradigm person on the ground that he/she is (a) intrinsically valuable, (b) alive, (c) sentient, or (d) rational. An intuitive test of the adequacy of any of these candidates will involve first enumerating the class of beings to whom it will distribute moral standing and then determining whether that class either excludes creatures that upon careful reflection we believe ought to be included or includes creatures that we believe ought to be excluded. In the former case the criterion draws the boundary of the moral sphere too narrowly and fails as a necessary condition of moral standing. In the latter case the criterion draws the boundary too broadly and fails as a sufficient condition. (A given criterion may, of course, be defective in both respects.)

Beings may depart from the paradigm along several different dimensions, each of which presents us with unclear cases that a criterion must resolve. These cases may be divided into seven categories: (1) inanimate objects (natural and artificial); (2) nonhuman terrestrial species of living things (animals and plants); (3) nonhuman extraterrestrial species of living things (should there be any); (4) artificial "life forms" (androids, robots, computers); (5) grossly defective human beings (the severely and permanently retarded or deranged); (6) human beings at the end of life (especially the severely and permanently senile or comatose); (7) human beings at the beginning of life (fetuses, infants, children). Since the last context is the one in which we wish to apply a criterion, it will here be set aside. This will enable us to settle on a criterion without tailoring it specially for the problem of abortion. Once a criterion has established its credentials in other domains, we will be able to trace out its implication for the case for the fetus.

The first candidate for a criterion takes a direction rather different from that of the remaining three. It is a commonplace in moral philosophy to attribute to (normal adult) human beings a special worth or value or dignity in virtue of which they possess (among other rights) a full right to life. This position implies that (some degree of) moral standing extends just as far as (some degree of) this intrinsic value, a higher degree of the latter entailing a higher degree of the former. We cannot know which things have moral standing without being told which things have intrinsic worth (and why)—without, that is, being offered a theory of intrinsic value. What is unique about this criterion, however, is that it is quite capable in principle of extending moral standing beyond the class of living beings, thus embracing such inanimate objects as rocks and lakes, entire landscapes (or indeed worlds), and artifacts. Of course, nonliving things cannot literally have a right to *life*, but it would be simple enough to generalize to a right to (continued) *existence*, where this might include both a right not to be destroyed and a right to such support as is necessary for that existence. A criterion that invokes intrinsic value is thus able to define a much more capacious moral sphere than is any of the other candidates.

Such a criterion is undeniably attractive in certain respects: how else are we to explain why it is wrong to destroy priceless icons or litter the moon even when doing so will never affect any living, sentient, or rational being? But it is clear that it cannot serve our present purpose. A criterion must connect moral standing with some property of things whose presence or absence can be confirmed by a settled, objective, and public method of investigation. The property of being intrinsically valuable is not subject to such verification. A criterion based on intrinsic value cannot be applied without a theory of intrinsic value. Such a theory will supply a criterion of intrinsic value by specifying the natural properties of things in virtue of which they possess such value. But if things have moral standing in virtue of having intrinsic value, and if they have intrinsic value in virtue of having some natural property, then it is that natural property which is serving as the real criterion of moral standing, and the middle term of intrinsic value is eliminable without loss. A theory of intrinsic value may thus entail a criterion of moral standing, but intrinsic value cannot itself serve as that criterion....

The remaining three candidates for a criterion of moral standing (life, sentience, rationality) all satisfy the verification requirement since they all rest standing on empirical properties of things. They may be ordered in terms of the breadth of the moral spheres they define. Since rational beings are a proper subset of sentient beings, which are a proper subset of living beings, the first candidate is the weakest and will define the broadest sphere, whereas the third is the strongest and will define the narrowest sphere.[4] In an interesting recent discussion, Kenneth Goodpaster has urged that moral standing be accorded to all living beings, simply in virtue of the fact that they are alive.[5] Although much of his argument is negative, being directed against more restrictive criteria, he does provide a positive case for including all forms of life within the moral sphere.[6]

Let us assume that the usual signs of life—nutrition, metabolism, spontaneous growth, reproduction—enable us to draw a tolerably sharp distinction between animate and inanimate beings, so that all plant and animal species, however primitive, are collected together in the former category. All such creatures share the property of being *teleological systems*: they have functions, ends, directions, natural tendencies, and so forth. In virtue of their teleology such creatures have needs, in a nonmetaphorical sense—conditions that must be satisfied if they are to thrive or flourish. Creatures with needs can be benefited or harmed; they are benefited when their essential needs are satisfied and harmed when they are not. It also makes sense to say that such creatures have a good: the conditions that promote their life and health are good for them, whereas those that impair their normal functioning are bad for them. But it is common to construe morality as having essentially to do with benefits and harms or with the good of creatures. So doing will lead us to extend moral standing to all creatures capable of being benefited and harmed, that is, all creatures with a good. But this condition will include all organisms (and systems of organisms), and so life is the only reasonable criterion of moral standing.

This extension of moral standing to plants and to the simpler animals is of course highly counterintuitive, since most of us accord the lives of such creatures no weight whatever in our practical deliberations. How could we conduct our affairs if we were to grant protection of life to every plant and animal species? Some of the more extreme implications of this view are, however, forestalled by Goodpaster's distinction between a criterion of inclusion and a criterion of comparison.[7] The former determines which creatures

---

[4]Or so we shall assume, though it is certainly possible that some (natural or artificial) entity might display signs of intelligence but no signs of either sentience or life. We might, for instance, create forms of artificial intelligence before creating forms of artificial life.

[5]Kenneth E. Goodpaster, "On Being Morally Considerable," *Journal of Philosophy* 75, 6 (June 1978). Goodpaster speaks of "moral considerability" where we are speaking of moral standing. The notions are identical, except for the fact that Goodpaster explicitly refrains from restricting moral considerability to possession of rights, let along the right to life. Nothing in my assessment of Goodpaster's view will hang on this issue of rights.

[6]In the paragraph to follow I have stated that case in my own words.

[7]These are my terms; Goodpaster distinguishes between a criterion of moral considerability and a criterion of moral significance (p. 311). It is odd that when Goodpaster addresses the

have (some) moral standing and thus locates the boundary of the moral sphere; it is Goodpaster's contention that life is the proper inclusion criterion. The latter is operative entirely within the moral sphere and enables us to assign different grades of moral standing to different creatures in virtue of some natural property that they may possess in different degrees. Since all living beings are (it seems) equally alive, life cannot serve as a comparison criterion. Goodpaster does not provide such a criterion, though he recognizes its necessity. Thus his view enables him to affirm that all living creatures have (some) moral standing but to deny that all such creatures have equal standing. Though the lives of all animate beings deserve consideration, some deserve more than others. Thus, for instance, higher animals might count for more than lower ones, and all animals might count for more than plants.

In the absence of a criterion of comparison, it is difficult to ascertain just what reforms Goodpaster's view would require in our moral practice. How much weight must human beings accord to the lives of lichen or grass or bacteria or insects? When are such lives more important than some benefit for a higher form of life? How should we modify our eating habits, for example? There is a problem here that extends beyond the incompleteness and indeterminacy of Goodpaster's position. Suppose that we have settled on a comparison criterion; let it be sentience (assuming that sentience admits of degrees in some relevant respect). Then a creature's ranking in the hierarchy of moral standing will be determined by the extent of its sentience: nonsentient (living) beings will have minimal standing, whereas the most sentient beings (human beings, perhaps) will have maximal standing. But then we are faced with the obvious question: if sentience is to serve as the comparison criterion, why should it not also serve as the inclusion criterion? Conversely, if life is the inclusion criterion, does it not follow that nothing else can serve as the comparison criterion, in which case all living beings have equal standing? It is difficult to imagine an argument in favor of sentience as a comparison criterion that would not also be an argument in favor of it as an inclusion criterion.[8] Since the same will hold for any other comparison criterion, Goodpaster's view can avoid its extreme implications only at the price of inconsistency.

practical problems created by treating life as an inclusion criterion (p. 324) he does not appeal to the inclusion/comparison distinction. Instead he invokes the quite different distinction between its being reasonable to attribute standing to a creature and its being (psychologically and causally) possible to act on that attribution. One would have thought the question is not what we *can* bring ourselves to do but what we *ought* to bring ourselves to do, and that the inclusion/comparison distinction is precisely designed to help us answer this question.

   [8]Goodpaster does not defend separating the two criteria but merely says "we should not expect that the criterion for having 'moral standing' at all will be the same as the criterion for adjudicating competing claims to priority among beings that merit that standing" (p. 311). Certainly inclusion and comparison criteria can be different, as in Mill's celebrated evaluation of pleasures. For Mill every pleasure has some value simply in virtue of being a pleasure (inclusion), but its relative value is partly determined by its quality or kind (comparison). All of this is quite consistent (despite claims to the contrary by some critics) because every pleasure has some quality or other. Goodpaster's comparison criterion threatens to be narrower than his inclusion criterion; it certainly will be if degrees of standing are based on sentience, since many living things have no

Goodpaster's view also faces consistency problems in its claim that life is necessary for moral standing. Beings need not be organisms in order to be teleological systems, and therefore to have needs, a good, and the capacity to be benefited and harmed. If these conditions are satisfied by a tree (as they surely are), then they are equally satisfied by a car. In order to function properly most machines need periodic maintenance; such maintenance is good for them, they are benefited by it, and they are harmed by its neglect. Why then is being alive a necessary condition of moral standing? Life is but an (imperfect) indicator of teleology and the capacity to be benefited and harmed. But Goodpaster's argument then commits him to treating these deeper characteristics as the criterion of moral standing, and thus to according standing to many (perhaps most) inanimate objects.

This inclusion of (at least some) nonliving things should incline us to reexamine Goodpaster's argument—if the inclusion of all living things has not already done so. The connection between morality and the capacity to be benefited and harmed appears plausible, so what has gone wrong? We may form a conjecture if we again consider our paradigm bearer of moral standing. In the case of a fully normal adult human being, it does appear that moral questions are pertinent whenever the actions of another agent promise to benefit or threaten to harm such a being. Both duties and rights are intimately connected with benefits and harms. The kinds of acts that we have a (strict) duty not to do are those that typically cause harm, whereas positive duties are duties to confer benefits. Liberty-rights protect autonomy, which is usually thought of as one of the chief goods for human beings, and the connection between welfare-rights and benefits is obvious. But if we ask what counts as a benefit or a harm for a human being, the usual answers take one or both of the following directions:

1 The Desire Model Human beings are benefited to the extent that their desires (or perhaps their considered and informed desires) are satisfied; they are harmed to the extent that these desires are frustrated.

2 The Experience Model Human beings (are) benefited to the extent that they are brought to have experiences that they like or find agreeable; they are harmed to the extent that they are brought to have experiences that they dislike or find disagreeable.

We need not worry at this stage whether one of these models is more satisfactory than the other. On both models benefits and harms for particular persons are interpreted in terms of the psychological states of those persons, in terms, that is, of their interests or welfare. Such states are possible only for beings who are conscious or sentient. Thus, if morality has to do with the

sentience at all. It is inconsistent to base degrees of standing on (variations) in a property and also to extend (some) standing to beings who lack that property entirely.

promotion and protection of interests or welfare, morality can concern itself only with beings who are conscious or sentient.[9] No other beings can be beneficiaries or victims *in the morally relevant way*. Goodpaster is not mistaken in suggesting that nonsentient beings can be benefited and harmed. But he is mistaken in suggesting that morality has to do with benefits and harms as such, rather than with a particular category of them. And that can be seen the more clearly when we realize that the broadest capacity to be benefited and harmed extends not only out to but beyond the frontier of life. Leaving my lawn mower out in the rain is bad for the mower, pulling weeds is bad for the weeds, and swatting mosquitoes is bad for the mosquitoes; but there are no moral dimensions to any of these acts unless the interests or welfare of some sentient creature is at stake. Morality requires the existence of sentience in order to obtain a purchase on our actions.

The failure of Goodpaster's view has thus given us some reason to look to sentience as a criterion of moral standing. Before considering this possibility directly, it will be helpful to turn to the much narrower criterion of rationality. The rational/nonrational boundary is more difficult to locate with certainty than the animate/inanimate boundary, since rationality (or intelligence) embraces a number of distinct but related capacities for thought, memory, foresight, language, self-consciousness, objectivity, planning, reasoning, judgment, deliberation, and the like.[10] It is perhaps possible for a being to possess some of these capacities and entirely lack others, but for simplicity we will assume that the higher-order cognitive processes are typically owned as a bundle.[11] The bundle is possessed to one extent or another by normal adult human beings, by adolescents and older children, by persons suffering from the milder cognitive disorders, and by some other animal species (some primates and cetaceans for example). It is not possessed to any appreciable extent by fetuses and infants, by the severely retarded or disordered, by the

---

[9]Goodpaster does not shrink from attributing interests to nonsentient organisms since he assumes that if a being has needs, a good, and a capacity to be benefited and harmed, then that being has interests. There is much support for this assumption in the dictionary definitions of both "interest" and "welfare," though talk of protecting the interests or welfare of plants seems contrived and strained. But philosophers and economists have evolved technical definitions of "interest" and welfare" that clearly tie these notions to the psychological states of sentient beings. It is the existence of beings with interests or welfare *in this sense* that is a necessary condition of the existence of moral issues.

[10]Possession of a capacity at a given time does not entail that the capacity is being manifested or displayed at that time. A person does not lose the capacity to use language, for instance, in virtue of remaining silent or being asleep. The capacity remains as long as the appropriate performance could be elicited by the appropriate stimuli. It is lost only when this performance can no longer be evoked (as when the person has become catatonic or comatose). Basing moral standing on the possession of some capacity or set of capacities does not therefore entail silly results, such as that persons lose their rights when they fall asleep. This applies, of course, not only to rationality but also to other capacities, such as sentience.

[11]The practical impact of basing moral standing on rationality will, however, depend on which particular capacities are treated as central. Practical rationality (the ability to adjust means to ends, and vice versa) is, for instance, much more widely distributed through the animal kingdom than is the use of language.

irreversibly comatose, and by most other animal species. To base moral standing on rationality is thus to deny it alike to most nonhuman beings and to many human beings. Since the implications for fetuses and infants have already been examined, they will be ignored in the present discussion. Instead we will focus on why one might settle on rationality as a criterion in the first place.

That rationality is sufficient for moral standing is not controversial (though there are some interesting questions to be explored here about forms of artificial intelligence). As a necessary condition, however, rationality will exclude a good many sentient beings—just how many, and which ones, to be determined by the kind and the stringency of the standards employed. Many will find objectionable this constriction of the sphere of moral concern. Because moral standing has been defined in terms of the right to life, to lack moral standing is not necessarily to lack all rights. Thus one could hold that, although we have no duty to (nonrational) animals to respect their lives, we do have a duty to them not to cause them suffering. For the right not to suffer, one might choose a different (and broader) criterion—sentience, for example. (However, if this is the criterion appropriate for that right, why is it not also the criterion appropriate for the right to life?) But even if we focus strictly on the (painless) killing of animals, the implications of the criterion are harsh. Certainly we regularly kill nonhuman animals to satisfy our own needs or desires. But the justification usually offered for these practices is either that the satisfaction of those needs and desires outweighs the costs to the animals (livestock farming, hunting, fishing, trapping, experimentation) or that no decent life would have been available for them anyway (the killing of stray dogs and cats). Although some of these arguments doubtless are rationalizations, their common theme is that the lives of animals do have some weight (however slight) in the moral scales, which is why the practice of killing animals is one that requires moral justification (raises moral issues). If rationality is the criterion of moral standing, and if (most) nonhuman animals are nonrational, killing such creatures could be morally questionable only when it impinges on the interests of rational beings (as where animals are items of property). In no case could killing an animal be a wrong against it. However callous and chauvinistic the common run of our treatment of animals may be, still the view that killing a dog or a horse is morally no more serious (ceteris paribus) than weeding a garden can be the considered judgment of only a small minority.

The standard that we apply to other species we must in consistency apply to our own. The greater the number of animals who are excluded by that standard, the greater the number of human beings who will also be excluded. In the absence of a determinate criterion it is unclear just where the moral line will be drawn on the normal/abnormal spectrum: will a right to life be withheld from mongoloids, psychotics, the autistic, the senile, the profoundly retarded? If so, killing such persons will again be no wrong to them. Needless to say, most such persons (in company with many animals) are sentient and capable to some extent of enjoyable and satisfying lives. To kill them is to deprive them of lives that are of value to them. If such creatures are denied standing, this loss will be entirely discounted in our moral reasoning. Their lack of rationality may ensure that their lives are less full and rich than ours, that they consist of simpler pleasures and more basic enjoyments. But what could be the justification for treating their deaths as though they cost them nothing at all?

There is a tradition, extending back at least to Kant, that attempts just such a justification. One of its modern spokesmen is A.I. Melden, who treats the capacity for moral agency as the criterion of moral standing.[12] This capacity is manifested by participation in a moral community—a set of beings sharing allegiance to moral rules and recognition of one another's integrity. Rights can be attributed only to beings with whom we can have such moral intercourse, thus only to beings who have interests similar to ours, who show concern for the well-being of others, who are capable of uniting in cooperative endeavors, who regulate their activities by a sense of right and wrong, and who display the characteristically moral emotions of indignation, remorse, and guilt.[13] Rationality is a necessary condition (though not a sufficient one) for possessing this bundle of capacities. Melden believes that of all living creatures known to us only human beings are capable of moral agency.[14] Natural rights, including the right to life, are thus human rights.

We may pass over the obvious difficulty of extending moral standing to all human beings on this basis (including the immature and abnormal) and focus on the question of why the capacity for moral agency should be thought necessary for possession of a right to life. The notion of a moral community to which Melden appeals contains a crucial ambiguity. On the one hand it can be thought of as a community of moral agents—the bearers of moral duties. Clearly to be a member of such a community one must be capable of moral agency. On the other hand a moral community can be thought of as embracing all beings to whom moral agents owe duties—the bearers of moral rights. It cannot simply be assumed that the class of moral agents (duty-bearers) is coextensive with the class of moral patients (right-bearers). It is quite conceivable that some beings (infants, nonhuman animals) might have rights though they lack duties (because incapable of moral agency). The capacity for moral agency is (trivially) a condition of having moral duties. It is not obviously also a condition of having moral rights. The claim that the criterion for rights is the same as the criterion for duties is substantive and controversial. The necessity of defending this claim is merely concealed by equivocating on the notion of a moral community.

---

[12]A.I. Melden, *Rights and Persons* (Oxford: Basil Blackwell, 1977).

[13]Melden rejects rationality as a criterion of standing (p. 187), but only on the ground that a being's rationality does not ensure its possessing a sense of morality. Clearly rationality is a necessary condition of moral agency. Thus a criterion of moral agency will not extend standing beyond the class of rational beings.

[14]Whether or not this is so will depend on how strong the conditions of moral agency are. Certainly many nonhuman species display altruism, if we mean by this a concern for the well-being of conspecifics and a willingness to accept personal sacrifices for their good. On p. 199 Melden enumerates a number of features of our lives that are to serve as the basis of our possession of rights; virtually all mammals display all of these features.

Beings who acknowledge one another as moral agents can also acknowledge that (some) creatures who are not themselves capable of moral agency nonetheless merit (some) protection of life. The more we reflect on the function of rights, the stronger becomes the inclination to extend them to such creatures. Rights are securities for beings who are sufficiently autonomous to conduct their own lives but who are also vulnerable to the aggression of others and dependent upon these others for some of the necessaries of life. Rights protect the goods of their owners and shield them from evils. We ascribe rights to one another because we all alike satisfy these minimal conditions of autonomy, vulnerability, and dependence. In order to satisfy these conditions a creature need not itself be capable of morality: it need only possess interests that can be protected by rights. A higher standard thus seems appropriate for possession of moral duties than for possession of moral rights. Rationality appears to be the right sort of criterion for the former, but something less demanding (such as sentience) is better suited to the latter.

A criterion of life (or teleology) is too weak, admitting classes of beings (animate and inanimate) who are not suitable loci for moral rights; being alive is necessary for having standing, but it is not sufficient. A criterion of rationality (or moral agency) is too strong, excluding classes of beings (human and nonhuman) who are suitable loci for rights; being rational is sufficient for having standing, but it is not necessary. A criterion of sentience (or consciousness) is a promising middle path between these extremes. Sentience is the capacity for feeling or affect. In its most primitive form it is the ability to experience sensations of pleasure and pain, and thus the ability to enjoy and suffer. Its more developed forms include wants, aims, and desires (and thus the ability to be satisfied and frustrated); attitudes, tastes, and values; and moods, emotions, sentiments, and passions. Consciousness is a necessary condition of sentience, for feelings are states of mind of which their owner is aware. But it is not sufficient; it is at least possible in principle for beings to be conscious (percipient, for instance, or even rational) while utterly lacking feelings. If rationality embraces a set of cognitive capacities, then sentience is rooted in a being's affective and conative life. It is in virtue of being sentient that creatures have interests, which are compounded either out of their desires or out of the experiences they find agreeable (or both). If morality has to do with the protection and promotion of interests, it is a plausible conjecture that we owe moral duties to all those beings capable of having interests. But this will include all sentient creatures.

Like rationality, and unlike life, it makes sense to think of sentience as admitting of degrees. Within any given mode, such as the perception of pain, one creature may be more or less sensitive than another. But there is a further sense in which more developed (more rational) creatures possess a higher degree of sentience. The expansion of consciousness and of intelligence opens up new ways of experiencing the world, and therefore new ways of being affected by the world. More rational beings are capable of finding either fulfillment or frustration in activities and states of affairs to which less developed creatures are, both cognitively and affectively, blind. It is in this sense of a broader and deeper sensibility that a higher being is capable of a richer, fuller, and more varied existence. The fact that sentience admits of degrees (whether of sensitivity or sensibility) enables us to employ it both as an inclusion criterion and as a comparison criterion of moral standing. The animal kingdom presents us with a hierarchy of sentience. Nonsentient beings have no moral standing; among sentient beings the more developed have greater standing than the less developed, the upper limit being occupied by the paradigm of a normal adult human being. Although sentience is the criterion of moral standing, it is also possible to explain the relevance of rationality. The evolutionary order is one of ascending intelligence. Since rationality expands a creature's interests, it is a reliable indicator of the degree of moral standing which that creature possesses. Creatures less rational than human beings do not altogether lack standing, but they do lack full standing.

An analysis of degrees of standing would require a graded right to life, in which the strength of the right varied inversely with the range of considerations capable of overriding it. The details of any such analysis will be complex and need not be worked out here. However, it seems that we are committed to extending (some) moral standing at least to all vertebrate animals, and also to counting higher animals for more than lower.[15] Thus we should expect the higher vertebrates (mammals) to merit greater protection of life than the lower (fish, reptiles, amphibians, birds) and we should also expect the higher mammals (primates, cetaceans) to merit greater protection of life than the lower (canines, felines, etc.). Crude as this division may be, it seems to accord reasonably well with most people's intuitions that in our moral reasoning paramecia and horseflies count for nothing, dogs and cats count for something, chimpanzees and dolphins count for more, and human beings count for most of all.

A criterion of sentience can thus allow for the gradual emergence of moral standing in the order of nature. It can explain why no moral issues arise (directly) in our dealings with inanimate objects, plants, and the simpler forms of animal life. It can also function as a moral guideline in our encounters with novel life forms on other planets. If the creatures we meet have interests and are capable of enjoyment and suffering, we must grant them some moral standing. We thereby constrain ourselves not to exploit them ruthlessly for our own advantage. The kind of standing that they deserve may be determined by the range and depth of their sensibility, and in ordinary circumstances this will vary with their intelligence. We should therefore recognize as equals beings who are as rational and sensitive as ourselves. The criterion also implies that if we encounter creatures who are rational but nonsentient—who utterly lack affect and desire—nothing we can do will adversely affect such creatures (in morally relevant ways). We would be entitled, for instance, to treat them as a

---

[15]It is unclear at present whether invertebrates are capable of feeling pain, though the discovery of endorphins (opiates manufactured by the body) even in very simple organisms suggests that they may be. If so, then we are committed to extending (some) moral standing to invertebrates as well.

species of organic computer. The same obviously holds for forms of artificial intelligence; in deciding whether to extend moral standing to sophisticated machines, the question (as Bentham put it) is not whether they can reason but whether they can suffer.

A criterion of sentience also requires gentle usage of the severely abnormal. Cognitive disabilities and disorders may impair a person's range of sensibility, but they do not generally reduce that person to the level of a nonsentient being. Even the grossly retarded or deranged will still be capable of some forms of enjoyment and suffering and thus will still possess (some) moral standing in their own right. This standing diminishes to the vanishing point only when sentience is entirely lost or never gained in the first place. If all affect and responsivity are absent, and if they cannot be engendered, then (but only then) are we no longer dealing with a sentient creature. This verdict accords well with the contemporary trend toward defining death in terms of the permanent loss of cerebral functioning. Although such patients are in one obvious sense still alive (their blood circulates and is oxygenated), in the morally relevant sense they are now beyond our reach, for we can cause them neither good nor ill. A criterion of life would require us to continue treating them as beings with (full?) moral standing, whereas a criterion of rationality would withdraw that standing when reason was lost even though sensibility should remain. Again a criterion of sentience enables us to find a middle way.

Fastening upon sentience as the criterion for possession of a right to life thus opens up the possibility of a reasonable and moderate treatment of moral problems other than abortion, problems pertaining to the treatment of non-human animals, extraterrestrial life, artificial intelligence, "defective" human beings, and persons at the end of life. We need now to trace out its implications for the fetus.

3   THE MORALITY OF ABORTION

The adoption of sentience as a criterion determines the location of a threshold of moral standing. Since sentience admits of degrees, we can in principle construct a continuum ranging from fully sentient creatures at one extreme to completely nonsentient creatures at the other. The threshold of moral standing is that area of the continuum through which sentience fades into nonsentience. In phylogenesis the continuum extends from Homo sapiens to the simple animals and plants, and the threshold area is the boundary between vertebrates and invertebrates. In pathology the continuum extends from the fully normal to the totally incapacitated, and the threshold area is the transition from consciousness to unconsciousness. Human ontogenesis also presents us with a continuum from adult to zygote. The threshold area will be the stage at which sentience first emerges, but where is that to be located?

A mental life is built upon a physical base. The capacity for sentience is present only when the necessary physiological structures are present. Physiology, and in particular neurophysiology, is our principal guide in locating a threshold in the phylogenetic continuum. Like a stereo system, the brain of our paradigm sentient being is a set of connected components. These components may be roughly sorted into three groups: forebrain (cerebral hemispheres, thalamus, hypothalamus, amygdala), midbrain (cerebellum), and brainstem (upper part of the spinal cord, pineal and pituitary glands). The brainstem and midbrain play no direct role in the individual's conscious life; their various parts regulate homeostasis (temperature, respiration, heartbeat, etc.), secrete hormones, make reflex connections, route nerves, coordinate motor activities, and so on. All of these functions can be carried on in the total absence of consciousness. Cognitive, perceptual, and voluntary motor functions are all localized in the forebrain, more particularly in the cerebral cortex. Sensation (pleasure/pain), emotion, and basic drives (hunger, thirst, sex, etc.) are controlled by subcortical areas in the forebrain. Although the nerves that transmit pleasure/pain impulses are routed through the cortex, their ultimate destination is the limbic system (amygdala, hypothalamus). The most primitive forms of sentience are thus possible in the absence of cortical activity.

Possession of particular neural structures cannot serve as a criterion of moral standing, for we cannot rule out encounters with sentient beings whose structures are quite different from ours. But in all of the species with which we are familiar, the components of the forebrain (or some analogues) are the minimal conditions of sentience. Thus the evolution of the forebrain serves as an indicator of the kind and degree of sentience possessed by a particular animal species. When we turn to human ontogenesis we may rely on the same indicator.

The normal gestation period for our species is 280 days from the onset of the last menstrual period to birth. This duration is usually divided into three equal trimesters of approximately thirteen weeks each. A zygote has no central nervous system of any sort. The spinal cord makes its first appearance early in the embryonic period (third week), and the major divisions between forebrain, midbrain, and brainstem are evident by the end of the eighth week. At the conclusion of the first trimester virtually all of the major neural components can be clearly differentiated and EEG activity is detectable. The months to follow are marked chiefly by the growth and elaboration of the cerebral hemispheres, especially the cortex. The brain of a seven-month fetus is indistinguishable, at least in its gross anatomy, from that of a newborn infant. Furthermore, by the seventh month most of the neurons that the individual brain will contain during its entire lifetime are already in existence. In the newborn the brain is closer than any other organ to its mature level of development.

There is no doubt that a newborn infant is sentient—that it feels hunger, thirst, physical pain, the pleasure of sucking, and other agreeable and disagreeable sensations. There is also no doubt that a zygote, and also an embryo, are presentient. It is difficult to locate with accuracy the stage during which feeling first emerges in fetal development. The structure of the fetal brain, including the cortex, is well laid down by the end of the second trimester. But there is reason to expect the more primitive and ancient parts of that brain to function before the rest. The needs of the fetus dictate the order of appearance of neural functions. Thus the brainstem is established and functioning first, since it is required for the regulation of heartbeat and other metabolic processes. Since the mammalian fetus develops in an enclosed and protected environment, cognition and perception are not essential for survival and their advent is delayed. It is therefore not surprising that the cortex, the most complex part of the brain and the least important to the fetus, is the last to develop to an operational level.

Simple pleasure/pain sensations would seem to occupy a medial position in this priority ranking. They are localized in a part of the brain that is more primitive than the cortex, but they could have little practical role for a being that is by and large unable either to seek pleasurable stimuli or to avoid painful ones. Behavioral evidence is by its very nature ambiguous. Before the end of the first trimester, the fetus will react to unpleasant stimuli by flinching and withdrawing. However, this reaction is probably a reflex that is entirely automatic. How are we to tell when mere reflex has crossed over into consciousness? The information we now possess does not enable us to date with accuracy the emergence of fetal sentience. Of some judgments, however, we can be reasonably confident. First-trimester fetuses are clearly not yet sentient. Third-trimester fetuses probably possess some degree of sentience, however minimal. The threshold of sentience thus appears to fall in the second trimester. More ancient and primitive than cognition, the ability to discriminate simple sensations of pleasure and pain is probably the first form of consciousness to appear in the ontogenetic order. Further, when sentience emerges it does not do so suddenly. The best we can hope for is to locate a threshold stage or period in the second trimester. It is at present unclear just how far into that trimester this stage occurs.

The phylogenetic and pathological continua yield us clear cases at the extremes and unclear cases in the middle. The ontogenetic continuum does the same. Because there is no quantum leap into consciousness during fetal development, there is no clean and sharp boundary between sentient and nonsentient fetuses. There is therefore no precise point at which a fetus acquires moral standing. More and better information may enable us to locate the threshold stage ever more accurately, but it will never collapse that stage into a point. We are therefore inevitably confronted with a class of fetuses around the threshold stage whose sentience, and therefore whose moral status, is indeterminate.

A criterion based on sentience enables us to explain the status of other putative thresholds. Neither conception nor birth marks the transition from a presentient to a sentient being. A zygote has not one whit more consciousness than the gametes out of which it is formed. Likewise, although a neonate has more opportunity to employ its powers, it also has no greater capacity for sensation than a full-term fetus. Of thresholds located during gestation, quickening is the perception of fetal movement that is probably reflex and therefore preconscious. Only viability has some relevance, though at one remove. A fetus is viable when it is equipped to survive in the outside world. A being that is aware of, and can respond to, its own inner states is able to communicate its needs to others. This ability is of no use in utero but may aid survival in an extrauterine environment. A fetus is therefore probably sentient by the conventional stage of viability (around the end of the second trimester). Viability can therefore serve as a (rough) indicator of moral standing.

Our common moral consciousness locates contraception and infanticide in quite different moral categories. This fact suggests implicit recognition of a basic asymmetry between choosing not to create a new life in the first place and choosing to destroy a new life once it has been created. The boundary between the two kinds of act is the threshold at which that life gains moral protection. Since gametes lack moral standing, contraception (however it is carried out) merely prevents the creation of a new person. Since an infant has moral standing, infanticide (however it is carried out) destroys a new person. A second-trimester threshold of moral standing introduces this asymmetry into the moral assessment of abortion. We may define an early abortion as one performed sometime during the first trimester or early in the second, and a late abortion as one performed sometime late in the second trimester or during the third. An early abortion belongs in the same moral category as contraception: it prevents the emergence of a new being with moral standing. A late abortion belongs in the same moral category as infanticide: it terminates the life of a new being with moral standing. The threshold of sentience thus extends the morality of contraception forward to cover early abortion and extends the morality of infanticide backward to cover late abortion. One of the sentiments voiced by many people who contemplate the problem of abortion is that early abortions are importantly different from late ones. The abortion techniques of the first trimester (the IUD, menstrual extraction, vacuum aspiration) are not to be treated as cases of homicide. Those employed later in pregnancy (saline induction, hysterotomy) may, however, have a moral quality approaching that of infanticide. For most people, qualms about abortion are qualms about late abortion. It is a virtue of the sentience criterion that it explains and supports this differential approach.

The moral issues raised by early abortion are precisely those raised by contraception. It is for early abortions that the liberal view is appropriate. Since the fetus at this stage has no right to life, early abortion (like contraception) cannot violate its rights. But if it violates no one's rights, early abortion (like contraception) is a private act. There are of course significant differences between contraception and early abortion, since the former is generally less hazardous, less arduous, and less expensive. A woman has, therefore, good prudential reasons for relying on contraception as her primary means of birth control. But if she elects an early abortion, then, whatever the circumstances and whatever her reasons, she does nothing immoral.[16]

---

[16]Unless there are circumstances (such as extreme underpopulation) in which contraception would also be immoral.

The moral issues raised by late abortion are similar to those raised by infanticide. It is for late abortions that (a weakened form of) the conservative view is appropriate. Since the fetus at this stage has a right to life, late abortion (like infanticide) may violate its rights. But if it may violate the fetus' rights, then late abortion (like infanticide) is a public act. There is, however, a morally significant difference between late abortion and infanticide. A fetus is parasitic upon a unique individual in a manner in which a newborn infant is not. That parasitic relation will justify late abortion more liberally than infanticide, for they do not occur under the same circumstances.

Since we have already explored the morality of abortion for those cases in which the fetus has moral standing, the general approach to late abortions is clear enough. Unlike the simple and uniform treatment of early abortion, only a case-by-case analysis will here suffice. We should expect a serious threat to the woman's life or health (physical or mental) to justify abortion, especially if that threat becomes apparent only late in pregnancy. We should also expect a risk of serious fetal deformity to justify abortion, again especially if that risk becomes apparent (as it usually does) only late in pregnancy. On the other hand, it should not be necessary to justify abortion on the ground that pregnancy was not consented to, since a woman will have ample opportunity to seek an abortion before the threshold stage. If a woman freely elects to continue a pregnancy past that stage, she will thereafter need a serious reason to end it.

A differential view of abortion is therefore liberal concerning early abortion and conservative (in an extended sense) concerning late abortion. The status of the borderline cases in the middle weeks of the second trimester is simply indeterminate. We cannot say of them with certainty either that the fetus has a right to life or that it does not. Therefore we also cannot say either that a liberal approach to these abortions is suitable or that a conservative treatment of them is required. What we can say is that, from the moral point of view, the earlier an abortion is performed the better. There are thus good moral reasons, as well as good prudential ones, for women not to delay their abortions.

A liberal view of early abortion in effect extends a woman's deadline for deciding whether to have a child. If all abortion is immoral, her sovereignty over that decision ends at conception. Given the vicissitudes of contraception, a deadline drawn that early is an enormous practical burden. A deadline in the second trimester allows a woman enough time to discover that she is pregnant and to decide whether to continue the pregnancy. If she chooses not to continue it, her decision violates neither her duties nor any other being's rights. From the point of view of the fetus, the upshot of this treatment of early abortion is that its life is for a period merely probationary; only when it has passed the threshold will that life be accorded protection. If an abortion is elected before the threshold, it is as though from the moral point of view that individual had never existed.

Settling on sentience as a criterion of moral standing thus leads us to a view of the moral status of the fetus, and of the morality of abortion, which satisfies the constraints set out in Section 1. It is gradual, since it locates a threshold stage rather than a point and allows moral standing to be acquired incrementally.

It is differential, since it locates the threshold stage during gestation and thus distinguishes the moral status of newly conceived and full-term fetuses. It is developmental, since it grounds the acquisition of moral standing in one aspect of the normal development of the fetus. And it is moderate, since it distinguishes the moral status of early and late abortions and applies each of the established views to that range of cases for which it is appropriate....

Abortion and the Concept of a Person

Jane English

The abortion debate rages on. Yet the two most popular positions seem to be clearly mistaken. Conservatives maintain that a human life begins at conception and that therefore abortion must be wrong because it is murder. But not all killings of humans are murders. Most notably, self defense may justify even the killing of an innocent person.

Liberals, on the other hand, are just as mistaken in their argument that since a fetus does not become a person until birth, a woman may do whatever she pleases in and to her own body. First, you cannot do to as you please with your own body if it affects other people adversely.[1] Second, if a fetus is not a person, that does not imply that you can do to it anything you wish. Animals, for example, are not persons, yet to kill or torture them for no reason at all is wrong.

At the center of the storm has been the issue of just when it is between ovulation and adulthood that a person appears on the scene. Conservatives draw the line at conception, liberals at birth. In this paper I first examine our concept of a person and conclude that no single criterion can capture the concept of a person and no sharp line can be drawn. Next I argue that if a fetus is a person, abortion is still justifiable in many cases; and if a fetus is not a person, killing it is still wrong in many cases. To a large extent, these two solutions are in agreement. I conclude that our concept of a person cannot and need not bear the weight that the abortion controversy has thrust upon it.

The several factions in the abortion argument have drawn battle lines around various proposed criteria for determining what is and what is not a person. For example, Mary Anne Warren[2] lists five features (capacities for reasoning, self-awareness, complex communication, etc.) as her criteria for

Jane English, "Abortion and the Concept of a Person," *Canadian Journal of Philosophy*, Vol. V, 2, (October, 1975), pp. 233–243. Reprinted by permission.
[1]We also have paternalistic laws which keep us from harming our own bodies even when no one else is affected. Ironically, anti-abortion laws were originally designed to protect pregnant women from a dangerous but tempting procedure.

[2]Mary Anne Warren, "On the Moral and Legal Status of Abortion," *Monist* 57 (1973), p. 55.

personhood and argues for the permissibility of abortion because a fetus falls outside this concept. Baruch Brody[3] uses brain waves. Michael Tooley[4] picks having-a-concept-of-self as his criterion and concludes that infanticide and abortion are justifiable, while the killing of adult animals is not. On the other side, Paul Ramsey[5] claims a certain gene structure is the defining characteristic. John Noonan[6] prefers conceived-of-humans and presents counterexamples to various other candidate criteria. For instance, he argues against viability as the criterion because the newborn and infirm would then be non-persons, since they cannot live without the aid of others. He rejects any criterion that calls upon the sorts of sentiments a being can evoke in adults on the grounds that this would allow us to exclude other races as non-persons if we could just view them sufficiently unsentimentally.

These approaches are typical: foes of abortion propose sufficient conditions for personhood which fetuses satisfy, while friends of abortion counter with necessary conditions for personhood which fetuses lack. But these both presuppose that the concept of a person can be captured in a strait jacket of necessary and/or sufficient conditions.[7] Rather, "person" is a cluster of features, of which rationality, having a self concept and being conceived of humans are only part.

What is typical of persons? Within our concept of a person we include, first, certain biological factors: descended from humans, having a certain genetic makeup, having a head, hands, arms, eyes, capable of locomotion, breathing, eating, sleeping. There are psychological factors: sentience, perception, having a concept of self and of one's own interests and desires, the ability to use tools, the ability to use language or symbol systems, the ability to joke, to be angry, to doubt. There are rationality factors: the ability to reason and draw conclusions, the ability to generalize and to learn from past experience, the ability to sacrifice present interests for greater gains in the future. There are social factors: the ability to work in groups and respond to peer pressures, the ability to recognize and consider as valuable the interests of others, seeing oneself as one among "other minds," the ability to sympathize, encourage, love, the ability to evoke from others the responses of sympathy, encouragement, love, the ability to work with others for mutual advantage. Then there are legal factors: being subject to the law and protected by it, having the ability to sue and enter contracts, being counted in the census, having a name and citizenship, the ability to own property, inherit, and so forth.

---

[3]Baruch Brody, "Fetal Humanity and the Theory of Essentialism," in Robert Baker and Frederick Elliston, eds., *Philosophy and Sex* (Buffalo, N.Y., 1975).

[4]Michael Tolley, "Abortion and Infanticide," *Philosophy and Public Affairs* 2 (1982).

[5]Paul Ramsey, "The Morality of Abortion," in James Rachels, ed., *Moral Problems* (New York, 1971).

[6]John Noonan, "Abortion and the Catholic Church. A Summary History," *Natural Law Forum* 12 (1967), pp. 125–131.

[7]Wittgenstein has argued against the possibility of so capturing the concept of a game, *Philosophical Investigations* (New York, 1958), § 66.

Now the point is not that this list is incomplete, or that you can find counterinstances to each of its points. People typically exhibit rationality, for instance, but someone who was irrational would not thereby fail to qualify as a person. On the other hand, something could exhibit the majority of these features and still fail to be a person, as an advanced robot might. There is no single core of necessary and sufficient features which we can draw upon with the assurance that they constitute what really makes a person; there are only features that are more or less typical.

This is not to say that no necessary or sufficient conditions can be given. Being alive is a necessary condition for being a person, and being a U.S. Senator is sufficient. But rather than falling inside a sufficient condition or outside a necessary one, a fetus lies in the penumbra region where our concept of a person is not so simple. For this reason I think a conclusive answer to the question whether a fetus is a person is unattainable.

Here we might note a family of simple fallacies that proceed by stating a necessary condition for personhood and showing that a fetus has that characteristic. This is a form of the fallacy of affirming the consequent. For example, some have mistakenly reasoned from the premise that a fetus is human (after all, it is a human fetus rather than, say, a canine fetus), to the conclusion that it is a human. Adding an equivocation on "being," we get the fallacious argument that since a fetus is something both living and human, it is a human being.

Nonetheless, it does seem clear that a fetus has very few of the above family of characteristics, whereas a new born baby exhibits a much larger proportion of them—and a two-year old has even more. Note that one traditional anti-abortion argument has centered on pointing out the many ways in which a fetus resembles a baby. They emphasize its development ("It already has ten fingers...") without mentioning its dissimilarities to adults (it still has gills and a tail). They also try to evoke the sort of sympathy on our part that we only feel toward other persons ("Never to laugh...or feel the sunshine?"). This all seems to be a relevant way to argue, since its purpose is to persuade us that a fetus satisfies so many of the important features on the list that it ought to be treated as a person. Also note that a fetus near the time of birth satisfies many more of these factors than a fetus in the early months of development. This could provide reason for making distinctions among the different stages of pregnancy, as the U.S. Supreme Court has done.[8]

Historically, the time at which a person has been said to come into existence has varied widely. Muslims date personhood from fourteen days after conception. Some medievals followed Aristotle in placing ensoulment at forty days after conception for a male fetus and eighty days for a female fetus.[9] In

---

[8]Not because the fetus is partly a person and so has some of the rights of persons, but rather because of the rights of person-like non-persons. This I discuss...below.

[9]Aristotle himself was concerned, however, with the different question of when the soul takes form. For historical data, see Jimmye Kimmey, "How the Abortion Laws Happened," Ms. 1 (April, 1973), pp. 48ff, and John Noonan, *loc. cit*

European common law since the seventeenth century, abortion was considered the killing of a person only after quickening, the time when a pregnant woman first feels the fetus move on its own. Nor is this variety of opinions surprising. Biologically, a human being develops gradually. We shouldn't expect there to be any specific time or sharp dividing point when a person appears on the scene.

For these reasons I believe our concept of a person is not sharp or decisive enough to bear the weight of a solution to the abortion controversy. To use it to solve that problem is to clarify *obscurum per obscurius*.

Next let us consider what follows if a fetus is a person after all. Judith Jarvis Thomson's landmark article, "A Defense of Abortion,"[10] correctly points out that some additional argumentation is needed at this point in the conservative argument to bridge the gap between the premise that a fetus is an innocent person and the conclusion that killing it is always wrong. To arrive at this conclusion, we would need the additional premise that killing an innocent person is always wrong. But killing an innocent person is sometimes permissible, most notably in self defense. Some examples may help draw out our intuitions or ordinary judgments about self defense.

Suppose a mad scientist, for instance, hypnotized innocent people to jump out of the bushes and attack innocent passers-by with knives. If you are so attacked, we agree you have a right to kill the attacker in self defense, if killing him is the only way to protect your life or to save yourself from serious injury. It does not seem to matter here that the attacker is not malicious but himself an innocent pawn, for your killing of him is not done in a spirit of retribution but only in self defense.

How severe an injury may you inflict in self defense? In part this depends upon the severity of the injury to be avoided: you may not shoot someone merely to avoid having your clothes torn. This might lead one to the mistaken conclusion that the defense may only equal the threatened injury in severity; that to avoid death you may kill, but to avoid a black eye you may only inflict a black eye or the equivalent. Rather, our laws and customs seem to say that you may create an injury somewhat, but not enormously, greater than the injury to be avoided. To fend off an attack whose outcome would be as serious as rape, a severe beating or the loss of a finger, you may shoot; to avoid having your clothes torn, you may blacken an eye.

Aside from this, the injury you may inflict should only be the minimum necessary to deter or incapacitate the attacker. Even if you know he intends to kill you, you are not justified in shooting him if you could equally well save yourself by the simple expedient of running away. Self defense is for the purpose of avoiding harms rather than equalizing harms.

Some cases of pregnancy present a parallel situation. Though the fetus is itself innocent, it may pose a threat to the pregnant woman's well-being, life

---

[10]J.J. Thomson, "A Defense of Abortion," *Philosophy and Public Affairs* 1 (1971).

prospects or health, mental or physical. If the pregnancy presents a slight threat to her interests, it seems self defense cannot justify abortion. But if the threat is on a par with a serious beating or the loss of a finger, she may kill the fetus that poses such a threat, even if it is an innocent person. If a lesser harm to the fetus could have the same defensive effect, killing it would not be justified. It is unfortunate that the only way to free the woman from the pregnancy entails the death of the fetus (except in very late stages of pregnancy). Thus a self defense model supports Thomson's point that the woman has a right only to be freed from the fetus, not a right to demand its death.[11]

The self defense model is most helpful when we take the pregnant woman's point of view. In the pre-Thomson literature, abortion is often framed as a question of a third party: do you, a doctor, have a right to choose between the life of the woman and that of the fetus? Some have claimed that if you were a passer-by who witnessed a struggle between the innocent hypnotized attacker and his equally innocent victim, you would have no reason to kill either in defense of the other. They have concluded that the self defense model implies that a woman may attempt to abort herself, but that a doctor should not assist her. I think the position of the third party is somewhat more complex. We do feel some inclination to intervene on behalf of the victim rather than the attacker, other things equal. But if both parties are innocent, other factors come into consideration. You would rush to the aid of your husband whether he was attacker or attackee. If a hypnotized famous violinist were attacking a skid row bum, we would try to save the individual who is of more value to society. These considerations tend to support abortion in some cases.

But suppose you are a frail senior citizen who wishes to avoid being knifed by one of these innocent hypnotics, so you have hired a bodyguard to accompany you. If you are attacked, it is clear we believe that the bodyguard, acting as your agent, has a right to kill the attacker to save you from a serious beating. Your rights of self defense are transferred to your agent. I suggest that we should similarly view the doctor as the pregnant woman's agent in carrying out a defense she is physically incapable of accomplishing herself.

Thanks to modern technology, the cases are rare in which pregnancy poses as a clear a threat to a woman's bodily health as an attacker brandishing a switchblade. How does self defense fare when more subtle, complex and long-range harms are involved?

To consider a somewhat fanciful example, suppose you are a highly trained surgeon when you are kidnapped by the hypnotic attacker. He says he does not intend to harm you but to take you back to the mad scientist who, it turns out, plans to hypnotize you to have a permanent mental block against all your knowledge of medicine. This would automatically destroy your career which would in turn have a serious adverse impact on your family, your personal relationships and your happiness. It seems to me that if the only way you can avoid this outcome is to shoot the innocent attacker, you are justified in so

[11]*Ibid.*, p. 62.

doing. You are defending yourself from a drastic injury to your life prospects. I think it is no exaggeration to claim that unwanted pregnancies (most obviously among teenagers) often have such adverse life-long consequences as the surgeon's loss of livelihood.

Several parallels arise between various views on abortion and the self defense model. Let's suppose further that these hypnotized attackers only operate at night, so that it is well known that they can be avoided completely by the considerable inconvenience of never leaving your house after dark. One view is that since you could stay home at night, therefore if you go out and are selected by one of these hypnotized people, you have no right to defend yourself. This parallels the view that abstinence is the only acceptable way to avoid pregnancy. Others might hold that you ought to take along some defense such as Mace which will deter the hypnotized person without killing him, but that if this defense fails, you are obliged to submit to the resulting injury, no matter how severe it is. This parallels the view that contraception is all right but abortion is always wrong, even in cases of contraceptive failure.

A third view is that you may kill the hypnotized person only if he will actually kill you, but not if he will only injure you. This is like the position that abortion is permissible only if it is required to save a woman's life. Finally we have the view that it is all right to kill the attacker, even if only to avoid a very slight inconvenience to yourself and even if you knowingly walked down the very street where all these incidents have been taking place without taking along any Mace or protective escort. If we assume that a fetus is a person, this is the analogue of the view that abortion is always justifiable, "on demand."

The self defense model allows us to see an important difference that exists between abortion and infanticide, even if a fetus is a person from conception. Many have argued that the only way to justify abortion without justifying infanticide would be to find some characteristic of personhood that is acquired at birth. Michael Tooley, for one, claims infanticide is justifiable because the really significant characteristics of person[hood] are acquired some time after birth. But all such approaches look to characteristics of the developing human and ignore the relation between the fetus and the woman. What if, after birth, the presence of an infant or the need to support it posed a grave threat to the woman's sanity or life prospects? She could escape this threat by the simple expedient of running away. So a solution that does not entail the death of the infant is available. Before birth, such solutions are not available because of the biological dependence of the fetus on the woman. Birth is the crucial point not because of any characteristics the fetus gains, but because after birth the woman can defend herself by a means less drastic than killing the infant. Hence self defense can only be used to justify abortion without necessarily thereby justifying infanticide.

On the other hand, supposing a fetus is not after all a person, would abortion always be morally permissible? Some opponents of abortion seem worried that if a fetus is not a full-fledged person, then we are justified in treating it in any way at all. However, this does not follow. Non-persons do get some consideration in our moral code, though of course they do not have the same rights as persons have (and in general they do not have moral responsibilities), and though their interests may be overriden by the interests of persons. Still, we cannot just treat them in any way at all.

Treatment of animals is a case in point. It is wrong to torture dogs for fun or to kill wild birds for no reason at all. It is wrong Period, even though dogs and birds to not have the same rights persons do. However, few people think it is wrong to use dogs as experimental animals, causing them considerable suffering in some cases, provided that the resulting research will probably bring discoveries of great benefit to people. And most of us think it all right to kill birds for food or to protect our crops. People's rights are different from the consideration we give to animals, then, for it is wrong to experiment on people, even if others might later benefit a great deal as a result of their suffering. You might volunteer to be a subject, but this would be supererogatory; you certainly have a right to refuse to be a medical guinea pig.

But how do we decide what you may or may not do to non-persons? This is a difficult problem, one for which I believe no adequate account exists. You do not want to say, for instance, that torturing dogs is all right whenever the sum of its effects on people is good—when it doesn't warp the sensibilities of the torturer so much that he mistreats people. If that were the case, it would be all right to torture dogs if you did it in private, or if the torturer lived on a desert island or died soon afterward, so that his actions had no effect on people. This is an inadequate account, because whatever moral consideration animals get, it has to be indefeasible, too. It will have to be a general proscription of certain actions, not merely a weighing of the impact on people on a case-by-case basis.

Rather, we need to distinguish two levels on which consequences of actions can be taken into account in moral reasoning. The traditional objections to Utilitarianism focus on the fact that it operates solely on the first level, taking all the consequences into account in particular cases only. Thus Utilitarianism is open to "desert island" and "lifeboat" counterexamples because these cases are rigged to make the consequences of actions severely limited.

Rawls' theory could be described as a teleological sort of theory, but with teleology operating on a higher level.[12] In choosing the principles to regulate society from the original position, his hypothetical choosers make their decision on the basis of the total consequences of various systems. Furthermore, they are constrained to choose a general set of rules which people can readily learn and apply. An ethical theory must operate by generating a set of sympathies and attitudes toward others which reinforces the functioning of that set of moral principles. Our prohibition against killing people operates by means of certain moral sentiments including sympathy, compassion and guilt. But if these attitudes are to form a coherent set, they carry us further; we tend to

[12]John Rawls, *A Theory of Justice* (Cambridge, Mass., 1971) § 3–4.

perform supererogatory actions, and we tend to feel similar compassion toward person-like non-persons.

It is crucial that psychological facts play a role here. Our psychological constitution makes it the case that for our ethical theory to work, it must prohibit certain treatment of non-persons which are significantly person-like. If our moral rules allowed people to treat some person-like non-persons in ways we do not want people to be treated, this would undermine the system of sympathies and attitudes that makes the ethical system work. For this reason, we would choose in the original position to make mistreatment of some sorts of animals wrong in general (not just wrong in the cases with public impact), even though animals are not themselves parties in the original position. Thus it makes sense that it is those animals whose appearance and behavior are most like those people that get the most consideration in our moral scheme.

It is because of "coherence of attitudes," I think, that the similarity of a fetus to a baby is very significant. A fetus one week before birth is so much like a newborn baby in our psychological space that we cannot allow any cavalier treatment of the former while expecting full sympathy and nurturative support for the latter. Thus, I think that anti-abortion forces are indeed giving their strongest arguments when they point to the similarities between a fetus and a baby, and when they try to evoke our emotional attachment to and sympathy for the fetus. An early horror story from New York about nurses who were expected to alternate between caring for six-week premature infants and disposing of viable 24-week aborted fetuses is just that—a horror story. These beings are so much alike that no one can be asked to draw a distinction and treat them so very differently.

Remember, however, that in the early weeks after conception, a fetus is very much unlike a person. It is hard to develop these feelings for a set of genes which doesn't yet have a head, hands, beating heart, response to touch or the ability to move by itself. Thus it seems to me that the alleged "slippery slope" between conception and birth is not so very slippery. In the early stages of pregnancy, abortion can hardly be compared to murder for psychological reasons, but in the latest stages it is psychologically akin to murder.

Another source of similarity is the bodily continuity between fetus and adult. Bodies play a surprisingly central role in our attitudes toward persons. One has only to think of the philosophical literature on how far physical identity suffices for personal identity or Wittgenstein's remark that the best picture of the human soul is the human body. Even after death, when all agree the body is no longer a person, we still observe elaborate customs of respect for the human body; like people who torture dogs, necrophiliacs are not to be trusted with people.[13] So it is appropriate that we show respect to a fetus as the body continuous with the body of the person. This is a degree of resemblance to persons that animals cannot rival.

[13]On the other hand, if they can be trusted with people, then our moral customs are mistaken. It all depends on the facts of psychology.

Michael Tooley also utilizes a parallel with animals. He claims that it is always permissible to drown newborn kittens and draws conclusions about infanticide.[14] But it is only permissible to drown kittens when their survival would cause some hardship. Perhaps it would be a burden to feed and house six more or to find other homes for them. The alternative of letting them starve produces even more suffering than the drowning. Since the kittens get their rights second-hand, so to speak, *via* the need for coherence in our attitudes, their interests are often overriden by the interests of full-fledged persons. But if their survival would be no inconvenience to people at all, then it is wrong to drown them, *contra* Tooley.

Tooley's conclusions about abortion are wrong for the same reason. Even if a fetus is not a person, abortion is not always permissible, because of the resemblance of a fetus to a person. I agree with Thomson that it would be wrong for a woman who is seven months pregnant to have an abortion just to avoid having to postpone a trip to Europe. In the early months of pregnancy when the fetus hardly resembles a baby at all, then, abortion is permissible whenever it is in the interests of the pregnant woman or her family. The reasons would only need to outweigh the pain and inconvenience of the abortion itself. In the middle months, when the fetus comes to resemble a person, abortion would be justifiable only when the continuation of the pregnancy or the birth of the child would cause harms—physical, psychological, economic or social—to the woman. In the late months of pregnancy, even on our current assumption that a fetus is not a person, abortion seems to be wrong except to save a woman from significant injury or death.

The Supreme Court has recognized similar gradations in the alleged slippery slope stretching between conception and birth. To this point, the present paper has been a discussion of the moral status of abortion only, not its legal status. In view of the great physical, financial and sometimes psychological costs of abortion, perhaps the legal arrangement most compatible with the proposed moral solution would be the absence of restrictions, that is, so-called abortion "on demand."

So I include, first, that application of our concept of a person will not suffice to settle the abortion issue. After all, the biological development of a human being is gradual. Second, whether a fetus is a person or not, abortion is justifiable early in pregnancy to avoid modest harms and seldom justifiable late in pregnancy except to avoid significant injury or death.[15]

SUGGESTED SUPPLEMENTARY READINGS TO PART FOUR

Callahan, Daniel: *Abortion: Law, Choice and Morality* (London: Collier-Macmillan, 1970).

Cohen, Marshall, Nagel, Thomas, and Scanlon, Thomas, eds.: *Rights and Wrongs of Abortion* (Princeton: Princeton University Press, 1974).

---

[14]*Op. cit.,* pp. 40, 60–61.
[15]I am deeply indebted to Larry Crocker and Arthur Kuflik for their constructive comments.

Englehardt, H. Tristram, Jr.: "The Ontology of Abortion," in *Ethics*, 8, 1974.

Feinberg, Joel, ed.: *The Problem of Abortion* (Belmont, Calif.: Wadsworth, 1984).

Finnis, John: "The Rights and Wrongs of Abortion: A Reply to Judith Thomson," in *Philosophy and Public Affairs*, 2:117–145, 1973.

Glover, Jonathan: *Causing Death and Saving Lives* (Harmondsworth, Middlesex: Penguin Books, 1977).

Noonan, John T., Jr.: *How to Argue About Abortion* (New York: The Free Press, 1979).

Perkins, Robert, ed.: *Abortion* (Cambridge, Mass.: Schenkman Publishing Co., 1974).

Thomson, Judith Jarvis: "A Defense of Abortion," in *Philosophy and Public Affairs*, vol. 1, no. 1:47–66, 1971.

PART FIVE

EUTHANASIA

INTRODUCTION

In ancient Greece, the word "euthanasia" meant a good or easy death. Today, however, it is popularly taken to mean either "mercy killing," where someone takes positive action to bring about someone's death for the purpose of relieving suffering, or a decision to withhold treatment in a context where doing so will result in death. Can there be situations where the pain of a disease is so intense or the effects of the disease so debilitating and dehumanizing that the moral solution is to bring about a "good death"? Can there be situations where, because people have no hope of recovery, no hope of having relief from pain, or no capacity for speech and voluntary movement, it is best to "ease" them into death? According to some pro-euthanasia theorists, we are more merciful to suffering dogs and horses than we are to our suffering friends and relatives. Society's traditional view is that all forms of mercy killing are wrong; yet society, which frequently changes its mind, is looking harder at the issue than ever before. We are reminded that only twenty years ago abortion was almost a taboo subject. Today it is said to be every woman's constitutional right.

Euthanasia has come increasingly into the public eye because of modern medicine's success in preserving and extending life. In 1900, sixty percent of all deaths in the U.S. occurred as the result of infectious disease. Today the figure is less than five percent. Respirators, transplants, dialysis, and infant incubators are saving lives in a strikingly wide spectrum of cases, but they have raised, in turn, the question of the quality of the lives being saved.

For present purposes it will help to distinguish four separate types of cases in which euthanasia is at issue. First, there are those cases involving comatose patients who are unable to communicate in even a minimal manner, and for whom there is little or no hope of recovery. One of the case studies in this section, "Tyson Faulks," spells out the details of such a situation. Second, there are persons who, although conscious and capable of communicating, are suffering to such an extent—and from a malady from which there is little or no hope of recovery—that they desire to be helped to die. In the case study, "Donald Cowart" (sometimes called the "Texas Burn Case"), we read of an actual situation in which the pain from a burn disaster prompts a man to seek his own death. Third, there are persons suffering both from a severely deterio-rated personality and from a painful, incurable (and perhaps expensive) disease. The summary of a much-discussed court case, *Belchertown v. Saikewicz*, tells of a man aged 67 with a mental age of two-and-a-half, suffering from a fatal form of leukemia, the only treatment for which is painful, debilitating, and temporary. Finally, there is the class of cases involving defective newborns whose abnormalities range from Down's syndrome to partial or total brain loss. James Rachels' article, "Active and Passive Euthanasia," considers the most controversial class of such cases; namely, those in which a child is born both with a serious malady such as Down's syndrome, and also with an easily correctable but fatal problem such as an intestinal blockage. Is it permissible for the parents, not wanting to raise a Down's syndrome child, to refuse surgery for the intestinal blockage and let the child die?

Such cases underscore important distinctions in discussions of euthanasia: for example, between active and passive euthanasia, and between voluntary and involuntary euthanasia. Voluntary euthanasia is distinguished from invol-untary euthanasia by way of the locus of the decision for euthanasia. Insofar as the decision is made by the patient, that is, insofar as the patient gives his or her informed consent, then the euthanasia is said to be voluntary, in contrast to instances involving, for example, a comatose patient whose consent is impos-sible (unless obtained in advance through a "living will"). The distinction between active and passive euthanasia, on the other hand, concerns not the locus of decision but the nature of what is decided. It relies, ultimately, on the distinction between killing and letting die. Active euthanasia thus covers cases in which someone (typically the physician) takes active step to bring about the patient's death (e.g., by administering a lethal dose of morphine). Passive euthanasia, in contrast, involves at most the withholding of treatment, and thus relies on the disease to bring about death directly.

Whether the latter distinction can stand up to rigorous scrutiny is a subject of controversy. In his article, James Rachels challenges the "active-passive" distinction, pointing out that doing "nothing" in the right kind of case clearly counts as doing something. When one pulls the plug on a respirator, or refuses dialysis to a kidney damaged patient, has one done nothing? Then there are cases of conflicting effects. If a doctor knows that administering a pain killer will successfully relieve her patient's pain, but will shorten the patient's life, is she guilty of active euthanasia?

A distinction commonly made in the context of so-called passive euthanasia is that between "ordinary" and "extraordinary" means of treatment. Here the emphasis is on the kind of treatment being administered—and being considered for withdrawal—and the extent to which it is burdensome. Extraordinary treatments tend to be painful and expensive, and result merely in retardation or temporary nullification of the disease. Mechanical respirators and radiation therapy have been labeled "extraordinary" in this sense. The status quo is reflected in the code of the American Medical Association, which appears to recognize both the "active-passive" and the "ordinary-extraordinary" distinction. The code allows the withholding or withdrawing of extraordinary means of life supports under certain conditions, but absolutely disallows mercy killing.

Those who support euthanasia tend to emphasize the right of the patient to choose, the evil of pain, and the demoralizing, dehumanizing character of many diseases. All of these arguments, for example, are offered by Glanville Williams in his article defending certain forms of euthanasia. Critics of euthanasia, on the other hand, tend to emphasize the "edge-of-the-wedge" or "slippery slope" potentialities of euthanasia. Yale Kamisar in his piece, "Some Nonreligious Views against Proposed 'Mercy-Killing'," argues that allowing the practice of euthanasia in some cases could open the floodgates to its practice in other cases. Was not a moral justification for euthanasia, he asks, offered by Hitler to justify the wholesale killing of deformed and "unfit" persons in Nazi Germany? He and other critics also raise the matter of two crucial uncertainties, namely, that of flawed diagnosis and of the discovery of a new cure. Is it unimaginable, he asks, that we should "ease into death" someone suffering from a painful, "fatal" disease, only to discover a few weeks later either a cure for the disease or that our original diagnosis was wrong? Even doctors make mistakes, and with euthanasia the decision is final.

In "Euthanasia," the last article in the section, the English philosopher, Philippa Foot, defends a complex but intriguing position which relies on an analysis of what it could mean to say that bringing about someone's death was a "good" for him or her. After denying that a life in which pain outweighed pleasure would thereby be a life not worth living, she proceeds to establish her own position, which relies in part on understanding the special characteristics of human nature. In the end, she argues, all nonvoluntary forms of active euthanasia (i.e., killing someone against his or her will or without his or her consent) are wrong. However, all the other forms—nonvoluntary-passive, voluntary-active, and voluntary-passive—may at least *sometimes* be compatible with both justice and charity. Nonetheless, she opposes any attempt to weaken current prohibitions against euthanasia on the grounds that it might encourage abuse and impoverish our collective moral spirit.

CASE STUDIES—Euthanasia

DONALD COWART

Donald Cowart was the victim of one of the most painful and excruciating accidents ever. In 1972 he was burned as the result of a propane explosion so severely that he came to want nothing more than a speedy death.

Donald Cowart had been an athletic, outdoor type. After finishing high school he served in the military as a jet pilot and had plans to become either a professional pilot or a lawyer. With his military career behind him, he went to work temporarily with his father in the real estate business. One day, while examining a piece of real estate, he and his father parked unknowingly near a leaking propane line and, on returning to their car, were victims of a powerful gas explosion. His father died shortly after. Donald was kept alive thanks only to modern techniques of burn treatment.

Most of his body was ravaged by second and third degree burns. His ears were virtually gone, one eye had to be extracted, and the other had to be sewn shut in order to avoid infection. He had to be given daily baths—baths which fought infection but, because they contained a salt solution, were extraordinarily painful.

Donald Cowart longed for death. On one occasion, he crawled from his bed a few paces in an attempt to leap from a six-story window, and was prevented only by his own inability to reach the window. He consistently asked for the treatments to end, knowing that once the treatments stopped his death would be inevitable. The medical professionals in charge of his case refused.

Mr. Cowart was the subject of a psychiatric examination by professional psychologists from a nearby university. The report concluded that he was rational in all relevant respects. Nonetheless, the report disagreed with his conclusion that he should be allowed to terminate treatment, and recommended that a guardian be appointed for him who would make the correct decisions on his behalf. Nine months after the original accident, Mr. Cowart still insisted that he be allowed to die.

Should Mr. Cowart's treatment be terminated?

This case, prepared by the editor, is a summation of an actually occurring incident. The case was adapted from "A Demand to Die," by Robert B. White and H. Tristram Engelhardt, Jr., *Hastings Center Report* 5 (June 1975).

TYSON FAULKS

On Saturday, Tyson Faulks, age 61, celebrated his daughter's twentieth birthday with a game of tennis and a bottle of good wine. By Tuesday, after having suffered a stroke on Sunday, he looked very little like his former self. He was on a respirator, unconscious, with EEG readings that indicated possible brain damage.

Prepared by the editor.

Later, nearly a month after the stroke, the acting physician was forced to tell his wife, Jean, and their two children, that it was highly unlikely that Mr. Faulks would ever regain consciousness. The two children, although heartbroken by the news, seemed ready to accept its reality. Mrs. Faulks, on the other hand, resisted. She seemed more angry than sad, and said curtly, "Tyson has always been healthy; he has never missed a day of work. Why are you so negative about all this?"

At this point, the daily charge for the intensive care Mr. Faulks was receiving exceeded $400 a day. The family's insurance covered most but not all of the expense and if allowed to continue, the charges would surely eat up the family's hard-earned nest egg.

What should the physician do?

Summary: *Superintendent of Belchertown State School* v. *Saikewicz*

LIACOS, JUSTICE

On April 26, 1976, William E. Jones, superintendent of the Belchertown State School (a facility of the Massachusetts Department of Mental Health), and Paul R. Rogers, a staff attorney at the school, petitioned the Probate Court for Hampshire County for the appointment of a guardian of Joseph Saikewicz, a resident of the State school. Simultaneously they filed a motion for the immediate appointment of a [legal] guardian...with authority to make the necessary decisions concerning the care and treatment of Saikewicz, who was suffering with acute myeloblastic monocytic leukemia....

On May 5, 1976, the probate judge appointed a guardian....The guardian['s]...report indicated that Saikewicz's illness was an incurable one, and that although chemotherapy was the medically indicated course of treatment it would cause Saikewicz significant adverse side effects and discomfort. The guardian...concluded that these factors, as well as the inability of the ward to understand the treatment to which he would be subjected and the fear and pain he would suffer as a result, outweighed the limited prospect of any benefit from such treatment, namely, the possibility of some uncertain but limited extension of life. He therefore recommended "that not treating Mr. Saikewicz would be in his best interests."

A hearing on the report was held on May 13, 1976. Present were the petitioners and the guardian....After hearing the evidence, the judge entered findings of fact and an order that in essence agreed with the recommendation of the guardian....

From 370 *North Eastern Reporter*, 2nd Series 417, pp. 420–423, 428–432, and 435. Decided November 28, 1977.

Some Nonreligious Views Against Proposed "Mercy-Killing" Legislation

Yale Kamisar

A recent book, Glanville Williams' *The Sanctity of Life and the Criminal Law*,[1] once again brings to the fore the controversial topic of euthanasia, more popularly known as "mercy killing." In keeping with the trend of the euthanasia movement over the past generation, Williams concentrates his efforts for

Yale Kamisar, "Some Nonreligious Views Against Proposed 'Mercy-Killing' Legislation," *Minnesota Law Review*, Vol. 42, 6 (1958). Some footnotes deleted. Excerpts reprinted by permission.
[1](1957) (This book is hereinafter referred to as "Williams").
The book is an expanded and revised version of the James C. Carpentier lectures delivered by Professor Williams at Columbia University and at the Association of the Bar of the City of New York

reform on the *voluntary* type of euthanasia, for example, the cancer victim begging for death; as opposed to the *involuntary variety*, that is, the case of the congenital idiot, the permanently insane or the senile....

The Law On The Books condemns all mercy-killings. That this has a substantial deterrent effect, even its harshest critics admit. Of course, it does not stamp out all mercy-killings, just as murder and rape provisions do not stamp out all murder and rape, but presumably it does impose a substantially greater responsibility on physicians and relatives in a euthanasia situation and turns them away from significantly more doubtful cases than would otherwise be the practice under any proposed euthanasia legislation to date. When a mercy-killing occurs, however, The Law In Action is as malleable as The Law On The Books is uncompromising. The high incidence of failures to indict, acquittals, suspended sentences and reprieves lend considerable support to the view that—

> If the circumstances are so compelling that the defendant ought to violate the law, then they are compelling enough for the jury to violate their oaths. The law does well to declare these homicides unlawful. It does equally well to put no more than the sanction of an oath in the way of an acquittal....

As an ultimate philosophical proposition, the case for voluntary euthanasia is strong. Whatever may be said for and against suicide generally, the appeal of death is immeasurably greater when it is sought not for a poor reason or just any reason, but for "good cause," so to speak; when it is invoked not on behalf of a "socially useful" person, but on behalf of, for example, the pain-racked "hopelessly incurable" cancer victim. If a person is *in fact* (1) presently incurable, (2) beyond the aid of any respite which may come along in his life expectancy, suffering (3) intolerable and (4) unmitigable pain and of a (5) fixed and (6) rational desire to die, I would hate to have to argue that the hand of death should be stayed. But abstract propositions and carefully formed hypotheticals are one thing; specific proposals designed to cover everyday situations are something else again.

In essence, Williams' specific proposal is that death be authorized for a person in the above situation "by giving the medical practitioner a wide discretion and trusting to his good sense." This, I submit, raises too great a risk of abuse and mistake to warrant a change in the existing law. That a proposal entails risk of mistake is hardly a conclusive reason against it. But neither is it irrelevant. Under any euthanasia program the consequences of mistake, of

in the Spring of 1956. "The connecting thread," observes the author, "is the extent to which human life, actual or potential, is or ought to be protected under the criminal law of the English-speaking peoples," Preface, p. vii. The product of his dexterous needlework, one might add, is a coat of many colors: philosophical, medical, ethical, religious, social, as well as legal. *The Un-Sanctity of Life* would seem to be a more descriptive title, however, since the author presents cogent reasons for de-criminalizing infanticide and abortion at one end of man's span, and "unselfish abetment of suicide and the unselfish homicide upon request," *id.* at 310, at the other.

The book was recently lauded by Bertrand Russell, 10 Stan. L. Rev. 382 (1958). For most restrained receptions see the interesting and incisive reviews by Professor William J. Curran, 71 Harv. L. Rev. 585 (1958) and Professor Richard C. Donnelly, 67 Yale L.J. 753 (1958).

course, are always fatal. As I shall endeavor to show, the incidence of mistake of one kind or another is likely to be quite appreciable. If this indeed be the case, unless the need for the authorized conduct is compelling enough to override it, I take it the risk of mistake *is* a conclusive reason against such authorization. I submit too, that the possible radiations from the proposed legislation, e.g., involuntary euthanasia of idiots and imbeciles (the typical "mercy-killings" reported by the press) and the emergence of the legal precedent that there are lives not "worth living," give additional cause to pause.

I see the issue, then, as the need for voluntary euthanasia versus (1) the incidence of mistake and abuse; and (2) the danger that legal machinery initially designed to kill those who are a nuisance to themselves may someday engulf those who are a nuisance to others.

The "freedom to choose a merciful death by euthanasia" may well be regarded, as does Professor Harry Kalven in a carefully measured review of another recent book urging a similar proposal, as "a special area of civil liberties far removed from the familiar concerns with criminal procedures, race discrimination and freedom of speech and religion." The civil liberties angle is definitely a part of Professor Williams' approach:

> If the law were to remove its ban on euthanasia, the effect would merely be to leave this subject to the individual conscience. This proposal would...be easy to defend, as restoring personal liberty in a field in which men differ on the question of conscience....
>
> On a question like this there is surely everything to be said for the liberty of the individual.

I am perfectly willing to accept civil liberties as the battlefield, but issues of "liberty" and "freedom" mean little until we begin to pin down *whose* "liberty" and "freedom" and for *what* need and at *what* price. This paper is concerned largely with such questions....I am...concerned about the life and liberty of those who would needlessly be killed in the process or who would irrationally choose to partake of the process. Williams' price on behalf of those who are *in fact* "hopeless incurables" and *in fact* of a fixed and rational desire to die is the sacrifice of (1) some few, who, though they know it not, because their physicians know it not, need not and should not die; (2) others, probably not so few, who, though they go through the motions of "volunteering," are casualties of strain, pain, or narcotics to such an extent that they really know not what they do. My price on behalf of those who, despite appearances to the contrary, have some relatively normal and reasonably useful life left in them, or who are incapable of making the choice, is the lingering on for awhile of those who, if you will, *in fact* have no desire and no reason to linger on.

A CLOSE-UP VIEW OF VOLUNTARY EUTHANASIA

The Euthanasiast's Dilemma and Williams' Proposed Solution

As if the general principle they advocate did not raise enough difficulties in itself, euthanasiasts have learned only too bitterly that specific plans of enforcement are often much less palatable than the abstract notions they are designed to effectuate. In the case of voluntary euthanasia, the means of implementation vary from (1) the simple proposal that mercy-killings by anyone, typically relatives, be immunized from the criminal law; to (2) the elaborate legal machinery contained in the bills of the Voluntary Euthanasia Legalisation Society (England) and the Euthanasia Society of American for carrying out euthanasia.

The English Society would require the eligible patient, *i.e.*, one over twenty-one and "suffering from a disease involving severe pain and of an incurable and fatal character," to forward a specially prescribed application—along with two medical certificates, one signed by the attending physician, and the other by a specially qualified physician—to a specially appointed Euthanasia Referee "who shall satisfy himself by means of a personal interview with the patient and otherwise that the said conditions shall have been fulfilled and that the patient fully understands the nature and purpose of the application"; and, if so satisfied, shall then send a euthanasia permit to the patient; which permit shall, seven days after receipt, become " operative" in the presence of an official witness; unless the nearest relative manages to cancel the permit by persuading a court of appropriate jurisdiction that the requisite conditions have not been met.

The American Society would have the eligible patient, *i.e.*, one over twenty-one "suffering from severe physical pain caused by a disease for which no remedy affording lasting relief or recovery is at the time known to medical science," petition for euthanasia in the presence of two witnesses and file same, along with the certificate of an attending physician, in a court of appropriate jurisdiction; said court to then appoint a committee of three, of whom at least two must be physicians, "who shall forthwith examine the patient and such other persons as they deem advisable or as the court may direct and within five days after their appointment, shall report to the court whether or not the patient understands the nature and purpose of the petition and comes within the [act's] provisions"; whereupon, if the report is in the affirmative, the court shall—"unless there is some reason to believe that the report is erroneous or untrue"—grant the petition; in which event euthanasia is to be administered in the presence of the committee, or any two members thereof....

Nothing rouses Professor Williams' ire more than the fact that opponents of the euthanasia movement argue that euthanasia proposals offer either inadequate protection or overelaborate safeguards. Williams appears to meet this dilemma with the insinuation that because arguments are made in the antithesis *they must each be invalid, each be obstructionist, and each be made in bad faith*....He makes a brave try to break through the dilemma:

> [T]he reformers might be well advised, in their next proposal, to abandon all their cumbrous safeguards and to do as their opponents wish, giving the medical practitioner a wide discretion and trusting to his good sense.
>
> [T]he essence of the bill would then be simple. It would provide that no medical practitioner should be guilty of an offense in respect of an act done intentionally to accelerate the death of a patient who is seriously ill, unless it is proved that the act

was not done in good faith with the consent of the patient and for the purpose of saving him from severe pain in an illness believed to be of an incurable and fatal character. Under this formula it would be for the physician, if charged, to show that the patient was seriously ill, but for the prosecution to prove that the physician acted from some motive other than the humanitarian one allowed to him by law....

The "Choice"

Under current proposals to establish legal machinery, elaborate or otherwise, for the administration of a quick and easy death, it is not enough that those authorized to pass on the question decide that the patient, in effect, is "better off dead." The patient must concur in this opinion. Much of the appeal in the current proposal lies in this so-called "voluntary" attribute.

But is the adult patient really in a position to concur? Is he truly able to make euthanasia a "voluntary" act? There is a good deal to be said, is there not, for Dr. Frohman's pithy comment that the "voluntary" plan is supposed to be carried out "only if the victim is both sane and crazed by pain."

By hypothesis, voluntary euthanasia is not to be resorted to until narcotics have long since been administered and the patient has developed a tolerance to them. When, then, does the patient make the choice? While heavily drugged? Or is narcotic relief to be withdrawn for the time of decision? But if heavy dosage no longer deadens pain, indeed, no longer makes it bearable, how overwhelming is it when whatever relief narcotics offer is taken away, too?...

"Hypersensitivity to pain after analgesia has worn off is nearly always noted." Moreover, "the mental side-effects of narcotics, unfortunately for anyone wishing to suspend them temporarily without unduly tormenting the patient, appear to outlast the analgesic effect" and "by many hours." The situation is further complicated by the fact that "a person in terminal stages of cancer who had been given morphine steadily for a matter of weeks would certainly be dependent upon it physically and would probably be addicted to it and react with the addict's response."

The narcotics problem aside, Dr. Benjamin Miller, who probably has personally experienced more pain than any other commentator on the euthanasia scene, observes:

> Anyone who has been severely ill knows how distorted his judgment became during the worst moments of the illness. Pain and the toxic effect of disease, or the violent reaction to certain surgical procedures may change our capacity for rational and courageous thought.

If, say, a man in this plight were a criminal defendant and he were to decline the assistance of counsel would the courts hold that he had "intelligently and understandingly waived the benefit of counsel"?

Undoubtedly, some euthanasia candidates will have their lucid moments. How they are to be distinguished from fellow-sufferers who do not, or how these instances are to be distinguished from others when the patient is exercising an irrational judgment is not an easy matter. Particularly is this so under

Williams' proposal, where no specially qualified persons, psychiatrically trained or otherwise, are to assist in the process.

Assuming, for purposes of argument, that the occasion when a euthanasia candidate possesses a sufficiently clear mind can be ascertained and that a request for euthanasia is then made, there remain other problems. The mind of the pain-racked may occasionally be clear, but is it not also likely to be uncertain and variable? This point was pressed hard by the great physician, Lord Horder, in the House of Lords debates:

> During the morning depression he [the patient] will be found to favour the application under this Bill, later in the day he will think quite differently, or will have forgotten all about it. The mental clarity with which noble Lords who present this Bill are able to think and to speak must not be thought to have any counterpart in the alternating moods and confused judgments of the sick man.

The concept of "voluntary" in voluntary euthanasia would have a great deal more substance to it if, as is the case with voluntary admission statutes for the mentally ill, the patient retained the right to reverse the process with a specified number of days after he gives written notice of his desire to do so—but unfortunately this cannot be. The choice here, of course, is an irrevocable one....

Professor Williams states that where a pre-pain desire for "ultimate euthanasia" is "reaffirmed" under pain, "there is the best possible proof of full consent." Perhaps. But what if it is alternately renounced and reaffirmed under pain? What if it is neither affirmed nor renounced? What if it is only renounced? Will a physician be free to go ahead on the ground that the prior desire was "rational," but the present desire "irrational"? Under Williams' plan, will not the physician frequently "be walking in the margin of the law"—just as he is now? Do we really accomplish much more under this proposal than to put the euthanasia principle on the books?

Even if the patient's choice could be said to be "clear and incontrovertible," do not other difficulties remain? Is this the kind of choice, assuming that it can be made in a fixed and rational manner, that we want to offer a gravely ill person? Will we not sweep up, in the process, some who are not really tired of life, but think others are tired of them; some who do not really want to die, but who feel they should not live on, because to do so when there looms the legal alternative of euthanasia is to do a selfish or a cowardly act? Will not some feel an obligation to have themselves "eliminated" in order that funds allocated for their terminal care might be better used by their families or, financial worries aside, in order to relieve their families of the emotional strain involved?

It would not be surprising for the gravely ill person to seek to inquire of those close to him whether he should avail himself of the legal alternative of euthanasia. Certainly, he is likely to wonder about their attitude in the matter. It is quite possible, is it not, that he will not exactly be gratified by any inclination on their part—however noble their motives may be in fact—that he resort to the new procedure?

At such a time,... members of the family are not likely to be in the best state of mind, either, to make this kind of decision. Financial stress and conscious or unconscious competition for the family's estate aside:

> The chronic illness and persistent pain in terminal carcinoma may place strong and excessive stresses upon the family's emotional ties with the patient. The family members who have strong emotional attachment to start with are most likely to take the patient's fears, pains and fate personally. Panic often strikes them. Whatever guilt feelings they may have toward the patient emerge to plague them.
>
> If the patient is maintained at home, many frustrations and physical demands may be imposed on the family by the advanced illness. There may develop extreme weakness, incontinence and bad odors. The pressure of caring for the individual under these circumstances is likely to arouse a resentment and, in turn, guilt feelings on the part of those who have to do the nursing.

Nor should it be overlooked that while Professor Williams would remove the various procedural steps and the various personnel contemplated in the American and English Bills and bank his all on the "good sense" of the general practitioner, no man is immune to the fear, anxieties and frustrations engendered by the apparently helpless, hopeless patient. Not even the general practitioner:

> Working with a patient suffering from a malignancy causes special problems for the physician. First of all, the patient with a malignancy is most likely to engender anxiety concerning death, even in the doctor. And at the same time, this type of patient constitutes a serious threat or frustration to medical ambition. As a result, a doctor may react more emotionally and less objectively than in any other area of medical practice.... His deep concern may make him more pessimistic than is necessary. As a result of the feeling of frustration in his wish to help, the doctor may have moments of annoyance with the patient. He may even feel almost inclined to want to avoid this type of patient.

The only Anglo-American prosecution involving an alleged mercy-killing physician seems to be the case of Dr. Herman Sander. The state's testimony was to the effect that, as Sander had admitted on various occasions, he finally yielded to the persistent pleas of his patient's husband and pumped air into her veins "in a weak moment." Sander's version was that he finally "snapped" under the strain of caring for the cancer victim, bungled simple tasks, and became "obsessed" with the need to "do something" for her—if only to inject air into her *already* dead body. Whichever side one believes—and the jury evidently believed Dr. Sander—the case well demonstrates that at the moment of decision the tired practitioner's "good sense" may not be as good as it might be....

The "Hopelessly Incurable" Patient and the Fallible Doctor

Professor Williams notes as "standard argument" the plea that "no sufferer from an apparently fatal illness should be deprived of his life because there is always the possibility that the diagnosis is wrong, or else that some remarkable cure will be discovered in time."

Dr. Benjamin Miller is another who is unlikely to harbor an ulterior theological motive. His interest is more personal. He himself was left to die the death of a "hopeless" tuberculosis victim only to discover that he was suffering from a rare malady which affects the lungs in much the same manner but seldom kills. Five years and sixteen hospitalizations later, Dr. Miller dramatized his point by recalling the last diagnostic clinic of the brilliant Richard Cabot, on the occasion of his official retirement:

> He was given the case records [complete medical histories and results of careful examinations] of two patients and asked to diagnose their illnesses.... The patients had died and only the hospital pathologist knew the exact diagnosis beyond doubt, for he had seen the descriptions of the postmortem findings. Dr. Cabot, usually very accurate in his diagnosis, that day missed both.
>
> The chief pathologist who had selected the cases was a wise person. He had purposely chosen two of the most deceptive to remind the medical students and young physicians that even at the end of a long and rich experience one of the greatest diagnosticians of our time was still not infallible.

A generation ago, Dr. Haven Emerson, then President of the American Public Health Association, made the point that "no one can say today what will be incurable tomorrow. No one can predict what disease will be fatal or permanently incurable until medicine becomes stationary and sterile." Dr. Emerson went so far as to say that "to be at all accurate we must drop altogether the term 'incurables' and substitute for it some such term as 'chronic illness'."

That was a generation ago. Dr. Emerson did not have to go back more than a decade to document his contention. Before Banting and Best's insulin discovery, many a diabetic had been doomed. Before the Whipple-Minot-Murphy liver treatment made it a relatively minor malady, many a pernicious anemia sufferer had been branded "hopeless." Before the uses of sulfanilimide were disclosed, a patient with widespread streptococcal blood poisoning was a condemned man.

Today, we may take even that most resolute disease, cancer, and we need look back no further than the last decade of research in this field to document the same contention....

Voluntary v. Involuntary Euthanasia

Ever since the 1870s, when what was probably the first euthanasia debate of the modern era took place, most proponents of the movement—at least when they are pressed—have taken considerable pains to restrict the question to the plight of the unbearably suffering incurable who *voluntarily seeks* death while most of their opponents have striven equally hard to frame the issue in terms which would encompass certain involuntary situations as well, e.g., the "congenital idiots," the "permanently insane," and the senile....

The boldness and daring which characterizes most of Glanville Williams' book dims perceptibly when he comes to involuntary euthanasia proposals. As to the senile, he states:

> At present the problem has certainly not reached the degree of seriousness that would warrant an effort being made to change traditional attitudes toward the sanctity of life of the aged. Only the grimmest necessity could bring about a change that, however cautious in its approach, would probably cause apprehension and deep distress to many people, and inflict a traumatic injury upon the accepted code of behaviour built up by two thousand years of the Christian religion. It may be however, that as the problem becomes more acute it will itself cause a reversal of generally accepted values.

To me, this passage is the most startling one in the book. On page 348 Williams invokes "traditional attitudes towards the sanctity of life" and "the accepted code of behaviour built up by two thousand years of the Christian religion" to check the extension of euthanasia to the senile, but for 347 pages he had been merrily rolling along debunking both. Substitute "cancer victim" for "the aged" and Williams' passage is essentially the argument of many of his *opponents* on the voluntary euthanasia question.

The unsupported comment that "the problem [of senility] has certainly not reached the degree of seriousness" to warrant euthanasia is also rather puzzling, particularly coming as it does after an observation by Williams on the immediately preceding page that "it is increasingly common for men and women to reach an age of 'second childishness and mere oblivion,' with a loss of almost all adult faculties except that of digestion."

How "serious" does a problem have to be to warrant a change in these "traditional attitudes"? If, as the statement seems to indicate, "seriousness" of a problem is to be determined numerically, the problem of the cancer victim does not appear to be as substantial as the problem of the senile. For example, [out of] just the 95,837 first admissions to "public prolonged-care hospitals" for mental diseases in the United States in 1955, 23,561—or one fourth—were cerebral arteriosclerosis or senile brain disease cases. I am not at all sure that there are 20,000 cancer victims per year who die *unbearably painful* deaths. Even if there were, I cannot believe that among their ranks are some 20,000 per year who, when still in a rational state, so long for a quick and easy death that they would avail themselves of legal machinery for euthanasia.

If the problem of the incurable cancer victim "has reached the degree of seriousness that would warrant an effort being made to change traditional attitudes toward the sanctity of life," as Williams obviously thinks it has, then so has the problem of senility. In any event, the senility problem will undoubtedly soon reach even Williams' requisite degree of seriousness:

> A decision concerning the senile may have to be taken within the next twenty years. The number of old people are increasing by leaps and bounds. Pneumonia, 'the old man's friend' is now checked by antibiotics. The effects of hardship, exposure, starvation and accident are now minimized. Where is this leading us? . . . What of the

drooling, helpless, disoriented old man or the doubly incontinent old woman lying log-like in bed? Is it here that the real need for euthanasia exists?

If, as Williams indicates, "seriousness" of the problem is a major criterion for euthanatizing a category of unfortunates, the sum total of mentally deficient persons would appear to warrant high priority, indeed.

When Williams turns to the plight of the "hopelessly defective infants," his characteristic vim and vigor are, as in the senility discussion, conspicuously absent:

> While the Euthanasia Society of England has never advocated this, the Euthanasia Society of America did include it in its original program. The proposal certainly escapes the chief objection to the similar proposal for senile dementia: it does not create a sense of insecurity in society, because infants cannot, like adults, feel anticipatory dread of being done to death if their condition should worsen. Moreover, the proposal receives some support on eugenic grounds, and more importantly on humanitarian grounds—both on account of the parents, to whom the child will be a burden all their lives, and on account of the handicapped child itself. (It is not, however, proposed that any child should be destroyed against the wishes of its parents.) Finally, the legalization of euthanasia for handicapped children would bring the law into closer relation to its practical administration, because juries do not regard parental mercy-killing as murder. For these various reasons the proposal to legalize humanitarian infanticide is put forward from time to time by individuals. They remain in a very small minority, and the proposal may at present be dismissed as politically insignificant.

It is understandable for a reformer to limit his present proposals for change to those with a real prospect of success. But it is hardly reassuring for Williams to cite the fact that only "a very small minority" has urged euthanasia for "hopelessly defective infants" as the *only* reason for not pressing for such legislation now. If, as Williams sees it, the only advantage voluntary euthanasia has over the involuntary variety lies in the organized movements on its behalf, that advantage can readily be wiped out.

In any event, I do not think that such "a very small minority" has advocated "humanitarian infanticide." Until the organization of the English and American societies led to a concentration on the voluntary type, and until the by-products of the Nazi euthanasia program somewhat embarrassed, if only temporarily, most proponents of involuntary euthanasia, about as many writers urged one type as another. Indeed, some euthanasiasts have taken considerable pains to demonstrate the superiority of defective infant euthanasia over incurably ill euthanasia.

> As for dismissing euthanasia of defective infants as "politically insignificant," the only poll that I know of which measured the public response to both types of euthanasia revealed that *45 percent favored euthanasia for defective infants under certain conditions while only 37.3 percent approved euthanasia for the incurably and painfully ill under any conditions.* Furthermore, of those who favored the mercy-killing cure for incurable adults, some 40 percent would require only family permission or medical board approval, but not the patient's permission.

Nor do I think it irrelevant that while public resistance caused Hitler to yield on the adult euthanasia front, the killing of malformed and idiot children continued unhindered to the end of the war, the definition of "children" expanding all the while. Is it the embarrassing experience of the Nazi euthanasia program which has rendered destruction of defective infants presently "politically insignificant"? If so, is it any more of a jump from the incurably and painfully ill to the unorthodox political thinker than it is from the hopelessly defective infant to the same "unsavory character"? Or is it not so much that the euthanasiasts are troubled by the Nazi experience as it is that they are troubled that the public is troubled by the Nazi experience?...

> Look, when the messenger cometh, shut the door, and hold him fast at the door; is not the sound of his master's feet behind him?

This is the "wedge principle," the "parade of horrors" objection, if you will, to voluntary euthanasia. Glanville Williams' preemptory retort is:

> This use of the 'wedge' objection evidently involves a particular determination as to the meaning of words, namely the words 'if raised to a general line of conduct.' The author supposes, for the sake of argument, that the merciful extinction of life in a suffering patient is not in itself immoral. Still it is immoral, because if it were permitted this would admit 'a most dangerous wedge that might eventually put all life in a precarious condition.' It seems a sufficient reply to say that this type of reasoning could be used to condemn any act whatever, because there is no human conduct from which evil cannot be imagined to follow if it is persisted in when some of the circumstances are changed. All moral questions involve the drawing of a line, but the 'wedge principle' would make it impossible to draw a line, because the line would have to be pushed farther and farther back until all action became vetoed.

I agree with Williams that if a first step is "moral" it is moral wherever a second step may take us. The real point, however, the point that Williams sloughs, is that whether or not the first step is precarious, is perilous, is worth taking, rests in part on what the second step is likely to be.

It is true that the "wedge" objection can always be advanced, the horrors can always be paraded. But it is no less true that on some occasions the objection is much more valid than it is on others. One reason why the "parade of horrors" cannot be too lightly dismissed in this particular instance is that Miss Voluntary Euthanasia is not likely to be going it alone for very long. Many of her admirers, as I have endeavored to show in the preceding section, would be neither surprised nor distressed to see her joined by Miss Euthanatize the Congenital Idiots and Miss Euthanatize the Permanently Insane and Miss Euthanatize the Senile Dementia. And these lasses—whether or not they themselves constitute a "parade of horrors"—certainly make excellent majorettes for such a parade:

> Some are proposing what is called euthanasia; at present only a proposal for killing those who are a nuisance to themselves; but soon to be applied to those who are a nuisance to other people.

Another reason why the "parade of horrors" argument cannot be too lightly dismissed in this particular instance, it seems to me, is that the parade *has* taken place in our time and the order of procession has been headed by the killing of the "incurables" and the "useless":

> Even before the Nazis took open charge in Germany, a propaganda barrage was directed against the traditional compassionate nineteenth-century attitudes toward the chronically ill, and for the adoption of a utilitarian, Hegelian point of view. . . . Lay opinion was not neglected in this campaign. Adults were propagandized by motion pictures, one of which, entitled 'I Accuse', deals entirely with euthanasia. This film depicts the life history of a woman suffering from multiple sclerosis; in it her husband, a doctor, finally kills her to the accompaniment of soft piano music rendered by a sympathetic colleague in an adjoining room. Acceptance of this ideology was implanted even in the children. A widely used high-school mathematics text...included problems stated in distorted terms of the cost of caring for and rehabilitating the chronically sick and crippled. One of the problems asked, for instance, how many new housing units could be built and how many marriage-allowance loans could be given to newly wedded couples for the amount of money it cost the state to care for 'the crippled, the criminal and the insane....' The beginnings at first were merely a subtle shift in emphasis in the basic attitude of the physicians. *It started with the acceptance of the attitude, basic in the euthanasia movement, that there is such a thing as life not worthy to be lived.* This attitude in its early stages concerned itself merely with the severely and chronically sick. Gradually the sphere of those to be included in this category was enlarged to encompass the socially unproductive, the ideologically unwanted, the racially unwanted and finally all non-Germans. But it is important to realize that the infinitely small wedged-in lever from which this entire trend of mind received its impetus was the attitude toward the nonrehabilitatable sick.

The apparent innocuousness of Germany's "small beginnings" is perhaps best shown by the fact that German Jews were at first excluded from the program. For it was originally conceived that "the blessing of euthanasia should be granted only to [true] Germans."

Relatively early in the German program, Pastor Braune, Chairman of the Executive Committee of the Domestic Welfare Council of the German Protestant Church, called for a halt to euthanasia measures "since they strike sharply at the moral foundations of the nation as a whole. The inviolability of human life is a pillar of any social order." And the pastor raised the same question which euthanasia opponents ask today, as well they might, considering the disinclination of many in the movement to stop at voluntary "mercy killings": Where do we, how do we, draw the line? The good pastor asked:

> How far is the destruction of socially unfit life to go? The mass methods used so far have quite evidently taken in many people who are to a considerable degree of sound mind. . . . Is it intended to strike only at the utterly hopeless cases—the idiots and imbeciles? The instruction sheet, as already mentioned, also lists senile diseases. The latest decree by the same authorities requires that children with serious congenital disease and malformation of every kind be registered, to be collected and processed

in special institutions. This necessarily gives rise to grave apprehensions. Will a line be drawn at the tubercular? In the case of persons in custody by court order euthanasia measures have evidently already been initiated. Are other abnormal or antisocial persons likewise to be included? Where is the borderline? Who is abnormal, antisocial, hopelessly sick?

Williams makes no attempt to distinguish or minimize the Nazi Germany experience. Apparently he does not consider it worthy of mention in a euthanasia discussion....

A FINAL REFLECTION

There have been and there will continue to be compelling circumstances when a doctor or relative or friend will violate The Law On The Books and, more often than not, receive protection from The Law In Action. But this is not to deny that there are other occasions when The Law On The Books operates to stay the hand of all concerned, among them situations where the patient is in fact (1) presently incurable, (2) beyond the aid of any respite which may come along in his life expectancy, suffering (3) intolerable and (4) unmitigable pain and of a (5) fixed and (6) rational desire to die. That any euthanasia program may only be the opening wedge for far more objectionable practices, and that even within the bounds of a "voluntary" plan such as Williams' the incidence of mistake or abuse is likely to be substantial, are not much solace to one in the above plight.

It may be conceded that in a narrow sense it is an "evil" for such a patient to have to continue to suffer—if only for a little while. But in a narrow sense, long-term sentences and capital punishment are "evils," too. If we can justify the infliction of imprisonment and death by the state "on the ground of the social interests to be protected" then surely we can similarly justify the postponement of death by the state. The objection that the individual is thereby treated not as an "end" in himself but only as a "means" to further the common good was, I think, aptly disposed of by Holmes long ago. "If a man lives in society, he is likely to find himself so treated."

"Mercy-Killing" Legislation—A Rejoinder
Glanville Williams

I welcome Professor Kamisar's reply to my argument for voluntary euthanasia, because it is on the whole a careful, scholarly work, keeping to knowable facts and accepted human values. It is, therefore, the sort of reply that can be rationally considered and dealt with. In this short rejoinder I shall accept most of Professor Kamisar's valuable footnotes, and merely submit that they do not bear out his conclusion.

The argument in favour of voluntary euthanasia in the terminal stages of painful diseases is quite a simple one, and is an application of two values that are widely recognized. The first value is the prevention of cruelty. Much as men differ in their ethical assessments, all agree that cruelty is an evil—the only difference of opinion residing in what is meant by cruelty. Those who plead for the legalization of euthanasia think that it is cruel to allow a human being to linger for months in the last stages of agony, weakness, and decay, and to refuse him his demand for merciful release. There is also a second cruelty involved—not perhaps quite so compelling, but still worth consideration: the agony of the relatives in seeing their loved one in his desperate plight. Opponents of euthanasia are apt to take a cynical view of the desires of relatives, and this may sometimes be justified. But it cannot be denied that a wife who has to nurse her husband through the last stages of some terrible disease may herself be so deeply affected by the experience that her health is ruined, either mentally or physically. Whether the situation can be eased for such a person by voluntary euthanasia I do not know; probably it depends very much on the individuals concerned, which is as much as to say that no solution in terms of a general regulatory law can be satisfactory. The conclusions should be in favour of individual discretion.

The second value involved is that of liberty. The criminal law should not be invoked to repress conduct unless this is demonstrably necessary on social grounds. What social interest is there in preventing the sufferer from choosing to accelerate his death by a few months? What positive value does his life still possess for society, that he is to be retained in it by the terrors of the criminal law?

And, of course, the liberty involved is that of the doctor as well as that of the patient. It is the doctor's responsibility to do all he can to prolong worthwhile life, or, in the last resort, to ease his patient's passage. If the doctor honestly and sincerely believes that the best service he can perform for his suffering patient is to accede to his request for euthanasia, it is a grave thing that the law should forbid him to do so.

Glanville Williams, "'Mercy-Killing' Legislation—A Rejoinder," *Minnesota Law Review*, Vol. 43, 1 (1958). Reprinted by permission.

This is the short and simple case for voluntary euthanasia, and, as Kamisar admits, it cannot be attacked directly on utilitarian grounds. Such an attack can only be by finding possible evils of an indirect nature. These evils, in the view of Professor Kamisar, are (1) the difficulty of ascertaining consent, and arising out of that the danger of abuse; (2) the risk of an incorrect diagnosis; (3) the risk of administering euthanasia to a person who could later have been cured by developments in medical knowledge; (4) the "wedge" argument.

Before considering these matters, one preliminary comment may be made. In some parts of his Article Kamisar hints at recognition of the fact that a practice of mercy-killing exists among the most reputable of medical practitioners. Some of the evidence for this will be found in my book. [The Sanctity of Life and the Criminal Law 334–39 (1957).] In the first debate in the House of Lords, Lord Dawson admitted the fact, and claimed that it did away with the need for legislation. In other words, the attitude of conservatives is this: let medical men do mercy-killing, but let it continue to be called murder, and be treated as such if the legal machinery is by some unlucky mischance made to work: let us, in other words, take no steps to translate the new morality into the concepts of the law. I find this attitude equally incomprehensible in a doctor, as Lord Dawson was, and in a lawyer, as Professor Kamisar is. Still more baffling does it become when Professor Kamisar seems to claim as a virtue of the system that the jury can give a merciful acquittal in breach of their oaths. The result is that the law frightens some doctors from interposing, while not frightening others—though subjecting the braver group to the risk of prosecution and possible loss of liberty and livelihood. Apparently, in Kamisar's view, it is a good thing if the law is broken in a proper case, because that relieves suffering, but also a good thing that the law is there as a threat in order to prevent too much mercy being administered: thus, whichever result the law has is perfectly right and proper. It is hard to understand on what moral principle this type of ethical ambivalence is to be maintained. If Kamisar does approve of doctors administering euthanasia in some clear cases, and of juries acquitting them if they are prosecuted for murder, how does he maintain that it is an insuperable objection to euthanasia that diagnosis may be wrong and medical knowledge subsequently extended?

However, the references to merciful acquittals disappear after the first few pages of the article, and thenceforward the argument develops as a straight attack on euthanasia. So although at the beginning Kamisar says that he would have to have to argue against mercy-killing in a clear case, in fact he does proceed to argue against it with some zest....

Kamisar's first objection, under the heading of "The Choice," is that there can be no such thing as truly voluntary euthanasia in painful and killing diseases. He seeks to impale the advocates of euthanasia on an old dilemma. Either the victim is not yet suffering pain, in which case his consent is merely an uninformed and anticipatory one—and he cannot bind himself by contract to be killed in the future—or he is crazed by pain and stupefied by drugs, in which case he is not of sound mind. I have dealt with this problem in my book. Kamisar has quoted generously from it, and I leave the reader to decide. As I understand Kamisar's position, he does not really persist in the objection. With the laconic "Perhaps," he seems to grant me, though unwillingly, that there are cases where one can be sure of the patient's consent. But having thus abandoned his own point, he then goes off to a different horror, that the patient may give his consent only in order to relieve his relatives of the trouble of looking after him.

On this new issue, I will return Kamisar the compliment and say "Perhaps." We are certainly in an area where no solution is going to make things quite easy and happy for everybody, and all sorts of embarrassments may be conjectured. But these embarrassments are not avoided by keeping to the present law; we suffer from them already. If a patient, suffering pain in a terminal illness, wishes for euthanasia partly because of this pain and partly because he sees his beloved ones breaking under the strain of caring for him, I do not see how this decision on his part, agonizing though it may be, is necessarily a matter of discredit either to the patient himself or to his relatives. The fact is that, whether we are considering the patient or his relatives, there are limits to human endurance.

The author's next objection rests on the possibility of mistaken diagnosis. . . . I agree with him that, before deciding on euthanasia in any particular case, the risk of mistaken diagnosis would have to be considered. Everything that is said in the article would, therefore, be most relevant when the two doctors whom I propose in my suggested measure come to consult on the question of euthanasia; and the possibility of mistake might most forcefully be brought before the patient himself. But have these medical questions any real relevance to the legal discussion?

Kamisar, I take it, notwithstanding his wide reading in medical literature, is by training a lawyer. He has consulted much medical opinion in order to find arguments against changing the law. I ought not to object to this, since I have consulted the same opinion for the opposite purpose. But what we may well ask ourselves is this: is it not a trifle bizarre that we should be doing it at all? Our profession is the law, not medicine: how does it come about that lawyers have to examine medical literature to assess the advantages and disadvantages of a medical practice?

If the import of this question is not immediately clear, let me return to my imaginary State of Ruritania. Many years ago, in Ruritania as elsewhere, surgical operations were attended with great risk. Pasteur had not made his discoveries, and surgeons killed as often as they cured. In this state of things, the legislature of Ruritania passed a law declaring all surgical operations to be unlawful in principle but providing that each specific type of operation might be legalized by a statute specially passed for the purpose. The result is that, in Ruritania, as expert medical opinion sees the possibility of some new medical advance, a pressure group has to be formed in order to obtain legislative approval for it. Since there is little public interest in these technical questions, and since, moreover, surgical operations are thought in general to be inimical to the established religion, the pressure group has to work for many years before it gets a hearing. When at last a proposal for legalization is seriously mooted, the lawyers and politicians get to work upon it, considering what possible dangers are inherent in the new operation. Lawyers and politicians are careful people, and they are perhaps more prone to see the dangers than the advantages in a new departure. Naturally they find allies among some of the more timid or traditional or less knowledgeable members of the medical profession, as well as among the priesthood and the faithful. Thus it is small wonder that whereas appendicectomy has been practised in civilised countries since the beginning of the present century, a proposal to legalize it has still not passed the legislative assembly of Ruritania.

It must be confessed that on this particular matter the legal prohibition has not been an unmixed evil for the Ruritanians. During the great popularity of the appendix operation in much of the civilised world during the twenties and thirties of this century, large numbers of these organs were removed without adequate cause, and the citizens on Ruritania have been spared this inconvenience. On the other hand, many citizens of that country have died of appendicitis who would have been saved if they had lived elsewhere. And whereas in other countries the medical profession has now learned enough to be able to perform this operation with wisdom and restraint, in Ruritania it is still not being performed at all. Moreover, the law has destroyed scientific inventiveness in that country in the forbidden fields.

Now, in the United States and England we have no such absurd general law on the subject of surgical operations as they have in Ruritania. In principle, medical men are left free to exercise their best judgment, and the result has been a brilliant advance in knowledge and technique. But there are just two—or possibly three—operations which are subject to the Ruritanian principle. These are abortion, euthanasia, and possibly sterilization of convenience. In these fields we, too, must have pressure groups, with lawyers and politicians warning us of the possibility of inexpert practitioners and mistaken diagnosis, and canvassing medical opinion on the risk of an operation not yielding the expected results in terms of human happiness and the health of the body politic. In these fields we, too, are forbidden to experiment to see if the foretold dangers actually come to pass. Instead of that, we are required to make a social judgment on the probabilities of good and evil before the medical profession is allowed to start on its empirical tests.

This anomaly is perhaps more obvious with abortion than it is with euthanasia. Indeed, I am prepared for ridicule when I describe euthanasia as a medical operation. Regarded as surgery it is unique, since its object is not to save or prolong life but the reverse. But euthanasia has another object which it shares with many surgical operations—the saving of pain. And it is now widely recognised, as Lord Dawson said in the debate in the House of Lords, that the saving of pain is a legitimate aim of medical practice. The question whether euthanasia will effect a net saving of pain and distress is, perhaps, one that can be only finally answered by trying it. But it is obscurantist to forbid the experiment on the ground that until it is performed we cannot certainly know its results. Such an attitude, in any other field of medical endeavour, would save inhibited progress.

The argument based on mistaken diagnosis leads into the argument based on the possibility of dramatic medical discoveries. Of course, a new medical discovery which gives me opportunity of remission or cure will almost at once put an end to mercy-killings in the particular group of cases for which the discovery is made. On the other hand, the discovery cannot affect patients who have already died from their disease. The argument based on mistaken diagnosis is therefore concerned only with those patients who have been mercifully killed just before the discovery becomes available for use. The argument is that such persons may turn out to have been "mercy-killed" unnecessarily, because if the physician had waited a bit longer they would have been cured. Because of this risk for this tiny fraction of the total number of patients, patients who are dying in pain must be left to do so, year after year, against their entreaty to have it ended.

Just how real is the risk? When a new medical discovery is claimed, some time commonly elapses before it becomes tested sufficiently to justify large-scale production of the drug, or training in the techniques involved. This is a warning period when euthanasia in the particular class of case would probably be halted anyway. Thus it is quite probable that when the new discovery becomes available, the euthanasia process would not in fact show any mistakes in this regard.

Kamisar says that in my book I "did not deign this objection to euthanasia more than a passing reference." I still do not think it is worth any more than that.

The author advances the familiar but hardly convincing argument that the quantitative need for euthanasia is not large. As one reason for this argument, he suggests that not many patients would wish to benefit from euthanasia, even if it were allowed. I am not impressed by the argument. It may be true, but it is irrelevant. So long as there are *any* persons dying in weakness and grief who are refused their request for a speeding of their end, the argument for legalizing euthanasia remains. Next, the Article suggests that there is no great need for euthanasia because of the advances made with pain-killing drugs....In my book, recognising that medical science does manage to save many dying patients from the extreme of physical pain, I pointed out that it often fails to save them from an artificial, twilight existence, with nausea, giddiness, and extreme restlessness, as well as the long hours of consciousness of a hopeless condition. A dear friend of mine, who died of cancer of the bowel, spent his last months in just this state, under the influence of morphine, which deadened pain, but vomiting incessantly, day in and day out. The question that we have to face is whether the unintelligent brutality of such an existence is to be imposed on one who wished to end it.

The last part of the Article is devoted to the ancient "wedge" argument which I have already examined in my book. It is the trump card of the traditionalist, because no proposal for reform, however strong the arguments in favour, is immune from the wedge objection. In fact, the stronger the arguments in favour of a reform, the more likely it is that the traditionalist will take the wedge objection—it is then the only one he has. C.M. Cornford put the argument in its proper place when he said that the wedge objection means this, that you should not act justly today, for fear that you may be asked to act still more justly tomorrow.

We heard a great deal of this type of argument in England in the nineteenth century, when it was used to resist almost every social and economic change. In the present century we have had less of it, but (if I may claim the hospitality of these columns to say so) it seems still to be accorded an exaggerated importance in American thought. When lecturing on the law of torts in an American university a few years ago, I suggested that just as compulsory liability insurance for automobiles had spread practically through the civilised world, so we should in time see the law of tort superseded in this field by a system of state insurance for traffic accidents, administered independently of proof of fault. The suggestion was immediately met by one student with a horrified reference to "creeping socialism." That is the standard objection made by many people to any proposal for a new department of state activity. The implication is that you must resist every proposal, however admirable in itself, because otherwise you will never be able to draw the line. On the particular question of socialism, the fear is belied by the experience of a number of countries which have extended state control of the economy without going the whole way to socialistic state regimentation.

Kamisar's particular bogey, the racial laws of Nazi Germany, is an effective one in the democratic countries. Any reference to the Nazis is a powerful weapon to prevent change in the traditional taboo on sterilization as well as euthanasia. The case of sterilization is particularly interesting on this; I dealt with it at length in my book, though Kamisar does not mention its bearing on the argument. When proposals are made for promoting voluntary sterilization on eugenic and other grounds, they are immediately condemned by most people as the thin end of a wedge leading to involuntary sterilization; and then they point to the practices of the Nazis. Yet a more persuasive argument pointing in the other direction can easily be found. Several American states have sterilization laws, which for the most part were originally drafted in very wide terms, to cover desexualisation as well as sterilization, and authorizing involuntary as well as voluntary operations. This legislation goes back long before the Nazis; the earliest statute was in Indiana in 1907. What has been its practical effect? In several states it has hardly been used. A few have used it, but in practice they have progressively restricted it until now it is virtually confined to voluntary sterilization. This is so, at least, in North Carolina, as Mrs. Woodside's study strikingly shows. In my book I summed up the position as follows:

> The American experience is of great interest because it shows how remote from reality in a democratic community is the fear—frequently voiced by Americans themselves—that voluntary sterilization may be the "thin end of the wedge," leading to a large-scale violation of human rights as happened in Nazi Germany. In fact, the American experience is the precise opposite—starting with compulsory sterilization, administrative practice has come to put the operation on a voluntary footing.

But it is insufficient to answer the "wedge" objection in general terms; we must consider the particular fears to which it gives rise. Kamisar professes to fear certain other measures that the euthanasia societies may bring up if their present measure is conceded to them. Surely, these other measures, if any, will be debated on their merits? Does he seriously fear that anyone in the United States is going to propose the extermination of people of a minority race or religion? Let us put aside such ridiculous fancies and discuss practical politics.

The author is quite right in thinking that a body of opinion would favour the legalization of the involuntary euthanasia of hopelessly defective infants, and some day a proposal of this kind may be put forward. The proposal would have distinct limits, just as the proposal for voluntary euthanasia of incurable sufferers has limits. I do not think that any responsible body of opinion would now propose the euthanasia of insane adults, for the perfectly clear reason that any such practice would greatly increase the sense of insecurity felt by the borderline insane and by the large number of insane persons who have sufficient understanding on this particular matter.

Kamisar expresses distress at a concluding remark in my book in which I advert to the possibility of old people becoming an overwhelming burden on mankind. I share his feeling that there are profoundly disturbing possibilities here; and if I had been merely a propagandist, intent upon securing agreement for a specific measure of law reform, I should have done wisely to have omitted all reference to this subject. Since, however, I am merely an academic writer, trying to bring such intelligence as I have to bear on moral and social issues, I deemed the topic too important and threatening to leave without a word. I think I have made it clear, in the passages cited, that I am not for one moment proposing any euthanasia of the aged in present society; such an idea would shock me as much as it shocks Kamisar and would shock everybody else. Still, the fact that we may one day have to face is that medical science is more successful in preserving the body than in preserving the mind. It is not impossible that, in the foreseeable future, medical men will be able to preserve the mindless body until the age, say, of 1000, while the mind itself will have lasted only a tenth of that time. What will mankind do then? It is hardly possible to imagine that we shall establish huge hospital-mausolea where the aged are kept in a kind of living death. Even if it is desired to do this, the cost of the undertaking may make it impossible.

This is not an immediately practical problem, and we need not yet face it. The problem of maintaining persons afflicted with senile dementia is well within our economic resources as the matter stands at present. Perhaps some barrier will be found to medical advance which will prevent the problem becoming more acute. Perhaps, as time goes on, and as the alternatives become more clearly realised, men will become more resigned to human control over the mode of termination of life. Or the solution may be that after the individual has reached a certain age, or a certain degree of decay, medical science will hold its hand, and allow him to be carried off by natural causes. But what if these natural causes are themselves painful? Would it not be better kindness to substitute human agency?

In general, it is enough to say that we do not have to know the solutions to these problems. The only doubtful moral question on which we have to make an immediate decision in relation to involuntary euthanasia is whether we owe a moral duty to terminate the life of an insane person who is suffering from a painful and incurable disease. Such a person is left unprovided for under the legislative proposal formulated in my book. The objection to any system of involuntary euthanasia of the insane is that it may cause a sense of insecurity. It is because I think that the risk of this fear is a serious one that a proposal for the reform of the law must leave the insane out.

Active and Passive Euthanasia

James Rachels

The distinction between active and passive euthanasia is thought to be crucial for medical ethics. The idea is that it is permissible, at least in some cases, to withhold treatment and allow a patient to die, but it is never permissible to take any direct action designed to kill the patient. This doctrine seems to be accepted by most doctors, and it is endorsed in a statement adopted by the House of Delegates of the American Medical Association on December 4, 1973:

> The intentional termination of the life of one human being by another—mercy killing—is contrary to that for which the medical profession stands and is contrary to the policy of the American Medical Association.
>
> The cessation of the employment of extraordinary means to prolong the life of the body when there is irrefutable evidence that biological death is imminent is the decision of the patient and/or his immediate family. The advice and judgment of the physician should be freely available to the patient and/or his immediate family.

James Rachels, "Active and Passive Euthanasia," *The New England Journal of Medicine* 292, No. 2 (Jan. 9, 1975), pp. 78–80. Reprinted by permission.

However, a strong case can be made against this doctrine. In what follows I will set out some of the relevant arguments, and urge doctors to reconsider their views on this matter.

To begin with a familiar type of situation, a patient who is dying of incurable cancer of the throat is in terrible pain, which can no longer be satisfactorily alleviated. He is certain to die within a few days, even if present treatment is continued, but he does not want to go on living for those days since the pain is unbearable. So he asks the doctor for an end to it, and his family joins in the request.

Suppose the doctor agrees to withhold treatment, as the conventional doctrines says he may. The justification for his doing so is that the patient is in terrible agony, and since he is going to die anyway, it would be wrong to prolong his suffering needlessly. But now notice this. If one simply withholds treatment, it may take the patient longer to die, and so he may suffer more than he would if more direct action were taken and a lethal injection given. This fact provides strong reason for thinking that, once the initial decision not to prolong his agony has been made, active euthanasia is actually preferable to passive euthanasia, rather than the reverse. To say otherwise is to endorse the option that leads to more suffering rather than less, and is contrary to the humanitarian impulse that prompts the decision not to prolong his life in the first place.

Part of my point is that the process of being "allowed to die" can be relatively slow and painful, whereas being given a lethal injection is relatively quick and painless. Let me give a different sort of example. In the United States about one in 600 babies is born with Down's syndrome. Most of these babies are otherwise healthy—that is, with only the usual pediatric care, they will proceed to an otherwise normal infancy. Some, however, are born with congenital defects such as intestinal obstructions that require operations if they are to live. Sometimes, the parents and the doctor will decide not to operate, and let the infant die. Anthony Shaw describes what happens then:

> ...When surgery is denied [the doctor] must try to keep the infant from suffering while natural forces sap the baby's life away. As a surgeon whose natural inclination is to use the scalpel to fight off death, standing by and watching a salvageable baby die is the most emotionally exhausting experience I know. It is easy at a conference, in a theoretical discussion, to decide that such infants should be allowed to die. It is altogether different to stand by in the nursery and watch as dehydration and infection wither a tiny being over hours and days. This is a terrible ordeal for me and the hospital staff—much more so than for the parents who never set foot in the nursery.[1]

I can understand why some people are opposed to all euthanasia, and insist that such infants must be allowed to live. I think I can also understand why

---

[1]A. Shaw, "Doctor, Do We Have a Choice?" *The New York Times Magazine*, January 30, 1972, p. 59.

other people favor destroying these babies quickly and painlessly. But why should anyone favor letting "dehydration and infection wither a tiny being over hours and days"? The doctrine that says that a baby may be allowed to dehydrate and wither, but may not be given an injection that would end its life without suffering seems so patently cruel as to require no further refutation. The strong language is not intended to offend, but only to put the point in the clearest possible way.

My second argument is that the conventional doctrine leads to decisions concerning life and death made on irrelevant grounds.

Consider again the case of the infants with Down's syndrome who need operations for congenital defects unrelated to the syndrome to live. Sometimes, there is no operation, and the baby dies, but when there is no such defect, the baby lives on. Now, an operation such as that to remove an intestinal obstruction is not prohibitively difficult. The reason why such operations are not performed in these cases is, clearly, that the child has Down's syndrome and the parents and the doctor judge that because of that fact it is better for the child to die.

But notice that this situation is absurd, no matter what view one takes of the lives and potentials of such babies. If the life of such an infant is worth preserving, what does it matter if it needs a simple operation? Or, if one thinks it better that such a baby should not live on, what difference does it make that it happens to have an obstructed intestinal tract? In either case, the matter of life and death is being decided on irrelevant grounds. It is the Down's syndrome, and not the intestines, that is the issue. The matter should be decided, if at all, on that basis, and not be allowed to depend on the essentially irrelevant question of whether the intestinal tract is blocked.

What makes this situation possible, of course, is the idea that when there is an intestinal blockage, one can "let the baby die," but when there is no such defect there is nothing that can be done, for one must not "kill" it. The fact that this idea leads to such results as deciding life or death on irrelevant grounds is another good reason why the doctrine should be rejected.

One reason why so many people think that there is an important moral difference between active and passive euthanasia is that they think killing someone is morally worse than letting someone die. But is it? Is killing, in itself, worse than letting die? To investigate this issue, two cases may be considered that are exactly alike except that one involves killing whereas the other involves letting someone die. Then, it can be asked whether this difference makes any difference to the moral assessments. It is important that the cases be exactly alike, except for this one difference, since otherwise one cannot be confident that it is this difference and not some other that accounts for any variation in the assessment of the two cases. So, let us consider this pair of cases.

In the first, Smith stands to gain a large inheritance if anything should happen to his six-year-old cousin. One evening while the child is taking his bath, Smith sneaks into the bathroom and drowns the child, and then arranges things so that it will look like an accident.

In the second, Jones also stands to gain if anything should happen to his six-year-old cousin. Like Smith, Jones sneaks in planning to drown the child in his bath. However, just as he enters the bathroom Jones sees the child slip and hit his head, and fall face down in the water. Jones is delighted; he stands by, ready to push the child's head back under if it is necessary, but it is not necessary. With only a little thrashing about, the child drowns all by himself, "accidentally," as Jones watches and does nothing.

Now Smith killed the child, whereas Jones "merely" let the child die. That is the only difference between them. Did either man behave better, from a moral point of view? If the difference between killing and letting die were in itself a morally important matter, one should say that Jones's behavior was less reprehensible than Smith's. But does one really want to say that? I think not. In the first place, both men acted from the same motive, personal gain, and both had exactly the same end in view when they acted. It may be inferred from Smith's conduct that he is a bad man, although that judgment may be withdrawn or modified if certain further facts are learned about him—for example, that he is mentally deranged. But would not the very same thing be inferred about Jones from his conduct? And would not the same further considerations also be relevant to any modification of this judgment? Moreover, suppose Jones pleaded, in his own defense, "After all, I didn't do anything except just stand there and watch the child drown. I didn't kill him; I only let him die." Again, if letting die were in itself less bad than killing, this defense should have at least some weight. But it does not. Such a "defense" can only be regarded as a grotesque perversion of moral reasoning. Morally speaking, it is no defense at all.

Now, it may be pointed out, quite properly, that the cases of euthanasia with which doctors are concerned are not like this at all. They do not involve personal gain or the destruction of normal healthy children. Doctors are concerned only with cases in which the patient's life is of no further use to him, or in which the patient's life has become or will soon become a terrible burden. However, the point is the same in these cases: the bare difference between killing and letting die does not, in itself, make a moral difference. If a doctor lets a patient die, for humane reasons, he is in the same moral position as if he had given the patient a lethal injection for humane reasons. If his decision was wrong—if, for example, the patient's illness was in fact curable—the decision would be equally regrettable no matter which method was used to carry it out. And if the doctor's decision was the right one, the method used is not in itself important.

The AMA policy statement isolates the crucial issue very well: the crucial issue is "the intentional termination of the life of one human being by another." But after identifying this issue, and forbidding "mercy-killing," the statement goes on to deny that the cessation of treatment is the intentional termination of a life. This is where the mistake comes in, for what is the cessation of treatment, in these circumstances, if it is not "the intentional termination of the life of one human being by another"? Of course it is exactly that, and if it were not, there would be no point to it.

Many people will find this judgment hard to accept. One reason, I think, is that it is very easy to conflate the question of whether killing is, in itself, worse than letting die, and with the very different question of whether most actual cases of killing are more reprehensible than most actual cases of letting die. Most actual cases of killing are clearly terrible (think, for example, of all the murders reported in the newspapers), and one hears of such cases every day. On the other hand, one hardly ever hears of a case of letting die, except for the action of doctors who are motivated by humanitarian reasons. So one learns to think of killing in a much worse light than of letting die. But this does not mean that there is something about killing that makes it in itself worse than letting die, for it is not the bare difference between killing and letting die that makes the difference in these cases. Rather, the other factors—the murderer's motive of personal gain, for example, contrasted with the doctor's humanitarian motivation—account for different reactions to the different cases.

I have argued that killing is not in itself any worse than letting die; if my contention is right, it follows that active euthanasia is not any worse than passive euthanasia. What arguments can be given on the other side? The most common, I believe, is the following:

"The important difference between active and passive euthanasia is that, in passive euthanasia, the doctor does not do anything to bring about the patient's death. The doctor does nothing, and the patient dies of whatever ills already afflict him. In active euthanasia, however, the doctor does something to bring about the patient's death: he kills him. The doctor who gives the patient with cancer a lethal injection has himself caused his patient's death; whereas if he merely ceases treatment, the cancer is the cause of the death."

A number of points need to be made here. The first is that it is not exactly correct to say that in passive euthanasia the doctor does nothing, for he does do one thing that is very important: he lets the patient die. "Letting someone die" is certainly different, in some respects, from other types of action—mainly in that it is a kind of action that one may perform by way of not performing certain other actions. For example, one may let a patient die by way of not giving medication, just as one may insult someone by way of not shaking his hand. But for any purpose of moral assessment, it is a type of action nonetheless. The decision to let a patient die is subject to moral appraisal in the same way that a decision to kill him would be subject to moral appraisal: it may be assessed as wise or unwise, compassionate or sadistic, right or wrong. If a doctor deliberately let a patient die who was suffering from a routinely curable illness, the doctor would certainly be to blame for what he had done, just as he would be to blame if he had needlessly killed the patient. Charges against him would then be appropriate. It would be no defense at all for him to insist that he didn't "do anything." He would have done something very serious, indeed, for he let his patient die.

Fixing the cause of death may be very important from a legal point of view, for it may determine whether criminal charges are brought against the doctor. But I do not think that this notion can be used to show a moral difference between active and passive euthanasia. The reason why it is considered bad to be the cause of someone's death is that death is regarded as a great evil—and so it is. However, if it has been decided that euthanasia—even passive euthanasia—is desirable in a given case, it has also been decided that in this instance death is no greater an evil than the patient's continued existence. And if this is true, the usual reason for not wanting to be the cause of someone's death simply does not apply.

Finally, doctors may think that all of this is only of academic interest—the sort of thing that philosophers may worry about but that has no practical bearing on their own work. After all, doctors must be concerned about the legal consequences of what they do, and active euthanasia is clearly forbidden by the law. But even so doctors should also be concerned with the fact that the law is forcing upon them a moral doctrine that may well be indefensible, and has a considerable effect on their practices. Of course, most doctors are not now in the position of being coerced in this matter, for they do not regard themselves as merely going along with what the law requires. Rather, in statements such as the AMA policy statement that I have quoted, they are endorsing this doctrine as a central point of medical ethics. In that statement, active euthanasia is condemned not merely as illegal but as "contrary to that for which the medical profession stands," whereas passive euthanasia is approved. However, the preceding considerations suggest that there is really no moral difference between the two, considered in themselves (there may be important moral differences in some cases in their *consequences*, but, as I pointed out, these differences may make active euthanasia, and not passive euthanasia, the morally preferable option). So, whereas doctors may have to discriminate between active and passive euthanasia to satisfy the law, they should not do any more than that. In particular, they should not give the distinction any added authority and weight by writing it into official statements of medical ethics.

Euthanasia*

Philippa Foot

The widely used *Shorter Oxford English Dictionary* gives three meanings for the word "euthanasia": the first, "a quiet and easy death"; the second, "the means of procuring this"; and the third, "the action of inducing a quiet and easy death." It is a curious fact that no one of the three gives an adequate definition of the word as it is usually understood. For "euthanasia" means much more than a quiet and easy death, or the means of procuring it, or the action of inducing it. The definition specifies only the manner of the death, and if this were all that was implied a murderer, careful to drug his victim, could claim that his act was an act of euthanasia. We find this ridiculous because we take it for granted that in euthanasia it is death itself, not just the manner of death, that must be kind to the one who dies.

To see how important it is that "euthanasia" should not be used as the dictionary definition allows it to be used, merely to signify that a death was quiet and easy, one has only to remember that Hitler's "euthanasia" program traded on this ambiguity. Under this program, planned before the War but brought into full operation by a decree of 1 September 1939, some 275,000 people were gassed in centers which were to be a model for those in which Jews were later exterminated. Anyone in a state institution could be sent to the gas chambers if it was considered that he could not be "rehabilitated" for useful work. As Dr. Leo Alexander reports, relying on the testimony of a neuropathologist who received 500 brains from one of the killing centers,

> In Germany the exterminations included the mentally defective, psychotics (particularly schizophrenics), epileptics and patients suffering from infirmities of old age and from various organic neurological disorders such as infantile paralysis, Parkinsonism, multiple sclerosis and brain tumors....In truth, all those unable to work and considered nonrehabilitatable were killed.[1]

These people were killed because they were "useless" and "a burden on society"; only the manner of their deaths could be thought of as relatively easy and quiet.

Let us insist, then, that when we talk about euthanasia we are talking about a death understood as a good or happy event for the one who dies. This stipulation follows etymology, but is itself not exactly in line with current usage, which would be captured by the condition that the death should *not* be

Excerpted by the author especially for this volume from "Euthanasia," by Philippa Foot, *Philosophy and Public Affairs* Vol. 6, No. 2, 1977. Reprinted by permission of the author.

*I would like to thank Derek Parfit and the editors of *Philosophy & Public Affairs* for their very helpful comments.

[1]Leo Alexander, "Medical Science under Dictatorship," *New England Journal of Medicine*, 14 July 1949, 49.

an evil rather than that it *should* be a good. That this is how people talk is shown by the fact that the case of Karen Ann Quinlan and others in a state of permanent coma is often discussed under the heading of "euthanasia." Perhaps it is not too late to object to the use of the word "euthanasia" in this sense. Apart from the break with the Greek origins of the word there are other unfortunate aspects of this extension of the term. For if we say that the death must be supposed to be a good to the subject we can also specify that it shall be for his sake that an act of euthanasia is performed. If we say merely that death shall not be an evil to him we cannot stipulate that benefiting him shall be the motive where euthanasia is in question. Given the importance of the question, For whose sake are we acting? it is good to have a definition of euthanasia which brings under this heading only cases of opting for death for the sake of the one who dies. Perhaps what is most important is to say either that euthanasia is to be for the good of the subject or at least that death is to be no evil to him, thus refusing to talk Hitler's language. However, in this paper it is the first condition that will be understood, with the additional proviso that by an act of euthanasia we mean one of inducing or otherwise opting for death for the sake of the one who is to die.

A problem that is dauntingly difficult must now be faced. It is easy to say, as if this raised no problems, that an act of euthanasia is by definition one aiming at the *good* of the one whose death is in question, and that it is *for his sake* that his death is desired. But how is this to be explained? Presumably we are thinking of some evil already with him or to come on him if he continues to live, and death is thought of as a release from this evil. But this cannot be enough. Most people's lives contain evils such as grief or pain, but we do not therefore think that death would be a blessing to them. On the contrary life is generally supposed to be a good even for someone who is unusually unhappy or frustrated. How is it that one can ever wish for death for the sake of the one who is to die? This difficult question is central to the discussion of euthanasia, and we shall literally not know what we are talking about if we ask whether acts of euthanasia defined as we have defined them are ever morally permissible without first understanding better the reason for saying that life is a good, and the possibility that it is not always so.

If a man should save my life he would be my benefactor. In normal circumstances this is plainly true; but does one always benefit another in saving his life? It seems certain that he does not. Suppose, for instance, that a man were being tortured to death and was given a drug that lengthened his sufferings; this would not be a benefit but the reverse. Or suppose that in a ghetto in Nazi Germany a doctor saved the life of someone threatened by disease, but that the man once cured was transported to an extermination camp; the doctor might wish for the sake of the patient that he had died of the disease. Nor would a longer stretch of life always be a benefit to the person who was given it. Comparing Hitler's camps with those of Stalin, Dmitri Panin observes that in the latter the method of extermination was made worse by agonies that could stretch out over months.

Death from a bullet would have been bliss compared with what many millions had to endure while dying of hunger. The kind of death to which they were condemned has nothing to equal it in treachery and sadism.[2]

These examples show that to save or prolong a man's life is not always to do him a service: it may be better for him if he dies earlier rather than later. It must therefore be agreed that while life is normally a benefit to the one who has it, this is not always so.

The judgment is often fairly easy to make—that life is or is not a good to someone—but the basis for it is very hard to find. When life is said to be a benefit or a good, on what grounds is the assertion made?

The difficulty is underestimated if it is supposed that the problem arises from the fact that one who is dead has nothing, so that the good someone gets from being alive cannot be compared with the amount he would otherwise have had. For why should this particular comparison be necessary? Surely it would be enough if one could say whether or not someone whose life was prolonged had more good than evil in the extra stretch of time. Such estimates are not always possible, but frequently they are; we say, for example, "He was very happy in those last years," or, "He had little but unhappiness then." If the balance of good and evil determined whether life was a good to someone we would expect to find a correlation in the judgments. In fact, of course, we find nothing of the kind. First, a man who has no doubt that existence is a good to him may have no idea about the balance of happiness and unhappiness in his life, or of any other positive and negative factors that may be suggested. So the supposed criteria are not always operating where the judgment is made. And secondly the application of the criteria gives an answer that is often wrong. Many people have more evil than good in their lives; we do not, however, conclude that we would do these people no service by rescuing them from death.

To get around this last difficulty Thomas Nagel has suggested that experience itself is a good which must be brought in to balance accounts.

> ...life is worth living even when the bad elements of experience are plentiful, and the good ones too meager to outweigh the bad ones on their own. The additional positive weight is supplied by experience itself, rather than by any of its contents.[3]

This seems implausible because if experience itself is a good it must be so even when what we experience is wholly bad, as in being tortured to death. How should one decide how much to count for this experiencing; and why count anything at all?

Others have tried to solve the problem by arguing that it is a man's desire for life that makes us call life a good: if he wants to live then anyone who prolongs his life does him a benefit. Yet someone may cling to life where we would say confidently that it would be better for him if he died, and he may admit it too.

---

[2]Dmitri Panin, *The Notebooks of Sologdin* (London, 1976), 66–7.
[3]Thomas Nagel, "Death," in James Rachels, ed., *Moral Problems* (New York, 1971), 362.

Speaking of those same conditions in which, as he said, a bullet would have been merciful, Panin writes,

> I should like to pass on my observations concerning the absence of suicides under the extremely severe conditions of our concentration camps. The more that life became desperate, the more a prisoner seemed determined to hold onto it.[4]

One might try to explain this by saying that hope was the ground of this wish to survive for further days and months in the camp. But there is nothing unintelligible in the idea that a man might cling to life though he knew those facts about his future which would make any charitable man wish that he might die.

The problem remains, and it is hard to know where to look for a solution. Is there a conceptual connection between *life* and *good*? Because life is not always a good we are apt to reject this idea, and to think that it must be a contingent fact that life is usually a good, as it is a contingent matter that legacies [inheritances] are usually a benefit, if they are. Yet it seems not to be a contingent matter that to save someone's life is ordinarily to benefit him. The problem is to find where the conceptual connection lies.

When are we to say that life is a good or a benefit to a man? The dilemma that faces us is this. If we say that life as such is a good we find ourselves refuted by the examples given.... We therefore incline to think that it is as bringing good things that life is a good, where it is a good. But if life is a good only because it is the condition of good things why is it not equally an evil when it brings bad things? And how can it be a good even when it brings more evil than good?

It should be noted that the problem has here been formulated in terms of the balance of good and evil, not that of happiness and unhappiness, and that it is not to be solved by the denial (which may be reasonable enough) that unhappiness is the only evil or happiness the only good. In this paper no view has been expressed about the nature of goods other than life itself. The point is that on any view of the goods and evils that life can contain, it seems that a life with more evil than good could still itself be a good.

It may be useful to review the judgments with which our theory must square. Do we think that life can be a good to one who suffers a lot of pain? Clearly we do. What about severely handicapped people; can life be a good to them? Clearly it can be, for even if someone is almost completely paralyzed, perhaps living in an iron lung, perhaps able to move things only by means of a tube held between his lips, we do not rule him out of order if he says that some benefactor saved his life. Nor is it different with mental handicap. There are many fairly severely handicapped people—such as those with Down's syndrome (mongolism)—for whom a simple affectionate life is possible. What about senility? Does this break the normal connection between life and good? Here we must surely distinguish between forms of senility. Some forms leave a life

---

[4]Panin, *Sologdin*, 85.

which we count someone as better off having than not having, so that a doctor who prolonged it would benefit the person concerned. With some kinds of senility this is however no longer true. There are some in geriatric wards who are barely conscious, though they can move a little and swallow food put into their mouths. To prolong such a state, whether in the old or in the very severely mentally handicapped, is not to do them a service or confer a benefit. But of course it need not be the reverse: only if there is suffering would one wish for the sake of the patient that he should die.

It seems, therefore, that merely being alive even without suffering is not a good.... But how is the line to be drawn?... What is to count as ordinary human life in the relevant sense? If it were only the very senile or very ill who were to be said not to have this life it might seem right to describe it in terms of *operation*. But it will be hard to find the sense in which the men described by Panin were not operating, given that they dragged themselves out of the forest to work. What is it about the life that the prisoners were living that makes us put it on the other side of the dividing line from that of most of the physically or mentally handicapped and of some severely ill or suffering patients? It is not that they were in captivity, for life in captivity can certainly be a good. Nor is it merely the unusual nature of their life. In some ways the prisoners were living more as other men do than the patient in an iron lung.

The idea we need seems to be that of life which is ordinary human life in the following respect—that it contains a minimum of basic human goods. What is ordinary in human life—even in very hard lives—is that a man is not driven to work far beyond his capacity; that he has the support of a family or community; that he can more or less satisfy his hunger; that he has hopes for the future; that he can lie down to rest at night. Such things were denied to the men in the Vyatlag camps described by Panin; not even rest at night was allowed them when they were tormented by bed-bugs, by noise and stench, and by routines such as body-searches and bath-parades—arranged for the night time so that work norms would not be reduced. Disease too can so take over a man's life that the normal human goods disappear. When a patient is so overwhelmed by pain or nausea that he cannot eat with pleasure, if he can eat at all, and is out of the reach of even the most loving voice, he no longer has ordinary human life in the sense in which the words are used here. And we may now pick up a thread from an earlier part of the discussion by remarking that crippling depression can destroy the enjoyment of ordinary goods as effectively as external circumstances can remove them.

The suggested solution to the problem is, then, that there is a certain conceptual connection between *life* and *good*.... However, it is not the mere state of being alive that can determine, or itself count as, a good, but rather life coming up to some standard of normality. It was argued that it is as part of ordinary life that the elements of good that a man may have are relevant to the question of whether saving his life counts as benefiting him. Ordinary human lives, even very hard lives, contain a minimum of basic goods, but when these are absent the idea of life is no longer linked to that of good. And since it is in this way that the elements of good contained in a man's life are relevant to the question of whether he is benefited if his life is preserved, there is no reason why it should be the balance of good and evil that counts.

It should be added that evils are relevant in one way when, as in the examples discussed above, they destroy the possibility of ordinary goods, but in a different way when they invade a life from which the goods are already absent for a different reason. So, for instance, the connection between *life* and *good* may be broken because consciousness has sunk to a very low level, as in extreme senility or severe brain damage. In itself this kind of life seems to be neither good nor evil, but if suffering sets in one would hope for a speedy end.

This, admittedly inadequate, discussion of the sense in which life is normally a good, and of the reasons why it may not be so in some particular case, completes the account of what euthanasia is here taken to be. An act of euthanasia, whether literally act or rather omission, is attributed to an agent who opts for the death of another because in his case life seems to be an evil rather than a good. The question now to be asked is whether acts of euthanasia are ever justifiable. But there are two topics here rather than one. For it is one thing to say that some acts of euthanasia considered only in themselves and their results are morally unobjectionable, and another to say that it would be all right to legalize them. Perhaps the practice of euthanasia would allow too many abuses, and perhaps there would be too many mistakes. Moreover the practice might have very important and highly undesirable side-effects, because it is unlikely that we could change our principles about the treatment of the old and the ill without changing fundamental emotional attitudes and social relations. The topics must, therefore, be treated separately. In the next part of the discussion, nothing will be said about the social consequences and possible abuses of the practice of euthanasia, but only about acts of euthanasia considered in themselves.

What we want to know is whether acts of euthanasia, defined as we have defined them, are ever morally permissible. To be more accurate, we want to know whether it is ever sufficient justification of the choice of death for another that death can be counted a benefit rather than harm, and that this is why the choice is made.

It will be impossible to get a clear view of the area to which this topic belongs without first marking the distinct grounds on which objection may lie when one man opts for the death of another. There are two different virtues whose requirements are, in general, contrary to such actions. An unjustified act of killing, or allowing to die, is contrary to justice or to charity, or to both virtues, and the moral failings are distinct. Justice has to do with what men owe each other in the way of noninterference and positive service. When used in this wide sense, which has its history in the doctrine of the cardinal virtues, justice is not especially connected with, for instance, law courts but with the whole area of rights, and duties corresponding to rights. Thus murder is one form of injustice, dishonesty another, and wrongful failure to keep contracts a third; chicanery in a law court or defrauding someone of his inheritance are simply other cases of injustice. Justice as such is not directly linked to the good of another, and may require that something be rendered to him even where it will do him harm, as Hume pointed out when he remarked that a debt must be paid even to a profligate debauchee who "would rather receive harm than benefit from large possessions."[5] Charity, on the other hand, is the virtue which attaches us to the good of others. An act of charity is in question only where something is not demanded by justice, but a lack of charity and of justice can be shown where a man is denied something which he both needs and has a right to; both charity and justice demand that widows and orphans are not defrauded, and the man who cheats them is neither charitable nor just.

It is easy to see that the two grounds of objection to inducing death are distinct. A murder is an act of injustice. A culpable failure to come to the aid of someone whose life is threatened is normally contrary, not to justice, but to charity. But where one man is under contract, explicit or implicit, to come to the aid of another injustice too will be shown. Thus injustice may be involved either in an act or an omission, and the same is true of a lack of charity; charity may demand that someone be aided, but also that an unkind word not be spoken.

The distinction between charity and justice will turn out to be of the first importance when voluntary and involuntary euthanasia are distinguished later on. This is because of the connection between justice and rights, and something should now be said about this. I believe it is true to say that wherever a man acts unjustly he has infringed a right, since justice has to do with whatever a man is owed, and whatever he is owed is his as a matter of right. Something should therefore be said about the different kinds of rights. The distinction commonly made is between having a right in the sense of having a liberty, and having a "claim-right" or "right of recipience."[6] The best way to understand such a distinction seems to be as follows. To say that a man has a right in the sense of a liberty is to say that no one can demand that he not do the thing which he has a right to do. The fact that he has a right to do it consists in the fact that a certain kind of objection does not lie against his doing it. Thus a man has a right in this sense to walk down a public street or park his car in a public parking space. It does not follow that no one else may prevent him from doing so. If for some reason I want a certain man not to park in a certain place I may lawfully park there myself or get my friends to do so, thus preventing him from doing what he has a right (in the sense of a liberty) to do. It is different, however, with a claim-right. This is the kind of right which I have in addition to a liberty when, for example, I have a private parking space; now others have duties in the way of noninterference, as in this case, or of service, as in the case where my claim-right is to goods or services promised to me....

[5]David Hume, *Treatise*, Book III, Part II, Section I.
[6]See, for example, D. D. Raphael, "Human Rights Old and New," in D. D. Raphael, ed., *Political Theory and the Rights of Man* (London, 1967), and Joel Feinberg, "The Nature and Value of Rights," *The Journal of Value Inquiry* 4, no. 4 (Winter 1970), 243–57. Reprinted in Samuel Gorovitz, ed., *Moral Problems in Medicine* (Englewood Cliffs, N.J., 1976).

Where in this picture does the right to life belong? No doubt people have the right to live in the sense of a liberty, but what is important is the cluster of claim-rights brought together under the title of the right to life. The chief of these is, of course, the right to be free from interferences that threaten life. If other people aim their guns at us or try to pour poison into our drink we can, to put it mildly, demand that they desist. And then there are the services we can claim from doctors, health officers, bodyguards, and firemen; the rights that depend on contract or public arrangement. Perhaps there is no particular point in saying that the duties these people owe us belong to the right to life; we might as well say that all the services owed to anyone by tailors, dressmakers, and couturiers belong to a right called the right to be elegant. But contracts such as those understood in the patient-doctor relationship come in in an important way when we are discussing the rights and wrong of euthanasia, and are therefore mentioned here.

Let us now ask how the right to life affects the morality of acts of euthanasia. Are such acts sometimes or always ruled out by the right to life? This is certainly a possibility; for although an act of euthanasia is, by our definition, a matter of opting for death for the good of the one who is to die, there is, as we noted earlier, no simple connection between that to which a man has a right and that which is for his good. It is true that men have the right only to the kind of thing that is, in general, a good: we do not think that people have the right to garbage or polluted air. Nevertheless, a man may have the right to something which he himself would be better off without; where rights exist it is a man's will that counts not his or anyone else's estimate of benefit or harm. So the duties complementary to the right to life—the general duty of noninterference and the duty of service incurred by certain persons—are not affected by the quality of a man's life or by his prospects. Even if it is true that he would be, as we say, "better off dead," so long as he wants to live this does not justify us in killing him and may not justify us in deliberately allowing him to die. All of us have the duty of noninterference, and some of us may have the duty to sustain his life. Suppose, for example, that a retreating army has to leave behind wounded or exhausted soldiers in the wastes of an arid or snowbound land where the only prospect is death by starvation or at the hands of an enemy notoriously cruel. It has often been the practice to accord a merciful bullet to men in such desperate straits. But suppose that one of them demands that he should be left alive? It seems clear that his comrades have no right to kill him, though it is a quite different question as to whether they should give him a life-prolonging drug. The right to life can sometimes give a duty of positive service, but does not do so here. What it does give is the right to be left alone.

Interestingly enough we have arrived by way of a consideration of the right to life at the distinction normally labeled "active" versus "passive" euthanasia, and often thought to be irrelevant to the moral issue.[7] Once it is seen that the

---

[7]See, for example, James Rachels, "Active and Passive Euthanasia," *New England Journal of Medicine*, 292, no. 2 (9 January 1975), 78–80.

right to life is a distinct ground of objection to certain acts of euthanasia, and that this right creates a duty of noninterference more widespread than the duties of care there can be no doubt about the relevance of the distinction between passive and active euthanasia. Where everyone may have the duty to leave someone alone, it may be that no one has the duty to maintain his life, or that only some people do.

Where then do the boundaries of the "active" and "passive" lie? In some ways the words are themselves misleading, because they suggest the difference between act and omission which is not quite what we want. Certainly the act of shooting someone is the kind of thing we were talking about under the heading of "interference," and omitting to give him a drug a case of refusing care. But the act of turning off a respirator should surely be thought of as no different from the decision not to start it; if doctors had decided that a patient should be allowed to die, either course of action might follow, and both should be counted as passive rather than active euthanasia if euthanasia were in question. The point seems to be that interference in a course of treatment is not the same as other interference in a man's life, and particularly if the same body of people are responsible for the treatment and for its discontinuance. In such a case we could speak of the disconnecting of the apparatus as killing the man, or the hospital as allowing him to die. By and large, it is the act of killing that is ruled out under the heading of noninterference, but not in every case.

Doctors commonly recognize this distinction, and the grounds on which some philosophers have denied it seem untenable. James Rachels, for instance, believes that if the difference between active and passive is relevant anywhere, it should be relevant everywhere, and he has pointed to an example in which it seems to make no difference which is done. If someone saw a child drowning in a bath it would seem just as bad to let it drown as to push its head under water.[8] If "it makes no difference" means that one act would be as iniquitous as the other this is true. It is not that killing is *worse* than allowing to die, but that the two are contrary to distinct virtues, which gives the possibility that in some circumstances one is impermissible and the other permissible. In the circumstances invented by Rachels, both are wicked: it is contrary to justice to push the child's head under the water—something one has no right to do. To leave it to drown is not contrary to justice, but it is a particularly glaring example of lack of charity. Here it makes no practical difference because the requirements of justice and charity coincide; but in the case of the retreating army they did not: charity would have required that the wounded soldier be killed had not justice required that he be left alive.[9] In such a case it makes all the difference whether a man opts for the death of another in a positive action, or whether he allows him to die. An analogy with the right to property will make the point clear. If a man owns something he has the right to it even when its possession does him

---

[8] *Ibid.*

[9] It is not, however, that justice and charity conflict. A man does not lack charity because he refrains from an act of injustice which would have been for someone's good.

harm, and we normally have no right to take it from him. But if one day it should blow away, maybe nothing requires us to get it back for him; we could not deprive him of it, but we may allow it to go. This is not to deny that it will often be an unfriendly act or one based on an arrogant judgment when we refuse to do what he wants. Nevertheless, we would be within our rights, and it might be that no moral objection of any kind would lie against our refusal.

It is important to emphasize that a man's rights may stand between us and the action we would dearly like to take for his sake. They may, of course, also prevent action which we would like to take for the sake of others, as when it might be tempting to kill one man to save several. But it is interesting that the limits of allowable interference, however uncertain, seem stricter in the first case than the second. Perhaps there are no cases in which it would be all right to kill a man against his will *for his own sake* unless they could equally well be described as cases of allowing him to die, as in the example of turning off the respirator. However, there are circumstances, even if these are very rare, in which one man's life would justifiably be sacrificed to save others, and "killing" would be the only description of what was being done. For instance, a vehicle which had gone out of control might be steered from a path on which it would kill more than one man to a path on which it would kill one.[10] But it would not be permissible to steer a vehicle toward someone in order to kill him, against his will, for his own good. An analogy with property rights again illustrates the point. One may not destroy a man's property against his will on the grounds that he would be better off without it; there are however circumstances in which it could be destroyed for the sake of others. If his house is liable to fall and kill him that is his affair; it might, however, without injustice be destroyed to stop the spread of a fire.

We see then that the distinction between active and passive, important as it is elsewhere, has a special importance in the area of euthanasia. It should also be clear why James Rachels' other argument, that it is often "more humane" to kill than to allow to die, does not show that the distinction between active and passive euthanasia is morally irrelevant. It might be "more humane" in this sense to deprive a man of the property that brings evils on him, or to refuse to pay what is owed to Hume's profligate debauchee; but if we say this we must admit that an act which is "more humane" than its alternative may be morally objectionable because it infringes rights.

So far we have said very little about the right to service as opposed to the right to noninterference, though it was agreed that both might be brought under the heading of "the right to life." What about the duty to preserve life that may belong to special classes of persons such as bodyguards, firemen, or doctors? Unlike the general public they are not within their rights if they merely refrain from interfering and do not try to sustain life. The subject's

---

[10]For a discussion of such questions, see my article "The Problem of Abortion and the Doctrine of Double Effect," *Oxford Review*, no. 5 (1967); reprinted in Rachels, *Moral Problems*, and Gorovitz, *Moral Problems in Medicine*.

claim-rights are two-fold as far as they are concerned and passive as well as active euthanasia may be ruled out here if it is against his will. This is not to say that he has the right to any and every service needed to save or prolong his life: the rights of other people set limits to what may be demanded, both because they have the right not to be interfered with and because they may have a competing right to services. Furthermore one must inquire just what the contract or implicit agreement amounts to in each case. Firemen and body-guards presumably have a duty which is simply to preserve life, within the limits of justice to others and of reasonableness to themselves. With doctors it may however be different, since their duty relates not only to preserving life but also to the relief of suffering. It is not clear what a doctor's duties are to his patient if life can be prolonged only at the cost of suffering or suffering relieved only by measures that shorten life. George Fletcher has argued that what the doctor is under contract to do depends on what is generally done, because this is what a patient will reasonably expect.[11] This seems right. If procedures are part of normal medical practice then it seems that the patient can demand them however much it may be against his interest to do so. Once again it is not a matter of what is "most humane."

That the patient's right to life may set limits to permissible acts of euthanasia seems undeniable. If he does not want to die no one has the right to practice active euthanasia on him, and passive euthanasia may also be ruled out where he has a right to the services of doctors or others.

Perhaps few will deny what has so far been said about the impermissibility of acts of euthanasia, simply because we have so far spoken about the case of one who positively wants to live, and about his rights, whereas those who advocate euthanasia are usually thinking either about those who wish to die or about those whose wishes cannot be ascertained either because they cannot properly be said to have wishes or because, for one reason or another, we are unable to form a reliable estimate of what they are. The question that must now be asked is whether the latter type of case, where euthanasia though not *in*voluntary would again be *non*voluntary, is different from the one discussed so far. Would we have the right to kill someone for his own good so long as we had no idea that he positively wished to live? And what about the life-prolonging duties of doctors in the same circumstances? This is a very difficult problem. On the other hand, it seems ridiculous to suppose that a man's right to life is something which generates duties only where he has signaled that he wants to live; as a borrower does indeed have a duty to return something lent on indefinite loan only if the lender indicates that he wants it back. On the other hand, it might be argued that there is something illogical about the idea that a right has been infringed if someone incapable of saying whether he wants it or not is deprived of something that is doing him harm rather than good. Yet on the analogy of property we would say that a right has been infringed. Only if

[11]George Fletcher, "Legal Aspects of the Decision Not to Prolong Life," *Journal of the American Medical Association* 203, no. 1 (1 January 1968), 119–22. Reprinted in Gorovitz.

someone had earlier told us that in such circumstances he would not want to keep the thing could we think that his right had been waived. Perhaps if we could make confident judgments about what anyone in such circumstances would wish, or what he would have wished beforehand had he considered the matter, we could agree to consider the right to life as "dormant," needing to be asserted if the normal duties were to remain. But as things are we cannot make any such assumption; we simply do not know what most people would want, or would have wanted, us to do unless they tell us. This is certainly the case so far as active measures to end life are concerned. Possibly it is different, or will become different, in the matter of being kept alive, so general is the feeling against using sophisticated procedures on moribund patients, and so much is this dreaded by people who are old or terminally ill. Once again the distinction between active and passive euthanasia has come on the scene, but this time because most people's attitudes to the two are so different. It is just possible that we might presume, in the absence of specific evidence, that someone would not wish, beyond a certain point, to be kept alive; it is certainly not possible to assume that he would wish to be killed.

In the last paragraph we have begun to broach the topic of voluntary euthanasia, and this we must now discuss. What is to be said about the case in which there is no doubt about someone's wish to die: either he has told us beforehand that he would wish it in circumstances such as he is now in, and has shown no sign of a change of mind, or else he tells us now, being in possession of his faculties and of a steady mind. We should surely say that the objections previously urged against acts of euthanasia, which it must be remembered were all on the ground of rights, had disappeared. It does not seem that one would infringe someone's right to life in killing him with his permission and in fact at his request. Why should someone not be able to waive his right to life, or rather, as would be more likely to happen, to cancel some of the duties of noninterference that this right entails? (He is more likely to say that he should be killed by this man at this time in this manner, than to say that anyone may kill him at any time and in any way.) Similarly someone may give permission for the destruction of his property, and request it. The important thing is that he gives a critical permission, and it seems that this is enough to cancel the duty normally associated with the right. If someone gives you permission to destroy his property it can no longer be said that you have no right to do so, and I do not see why it should not be the same with taking a man's life. An objection might be made on the ground that only God has the right to take life, but in this paper religious as opposed to moral arguments are being left aside. Religion apart, there seems to be no case to be made out for an infringement of rights if a man who wishes to die is allowed to die or even killed. But of course it does not follow that there is no moral objection to it. Even with property, which is after all a relatively small matter, one might be wrong to destroy what one had the right to destroy. For, apart from its value to other people, it might be valuable to the man who wanted it destroyed, and charity might require us to hold our hand where justice did not.

Let us review the conclusion of this part of the argument, which has been about nonvoluntary and voluntary euthanasia and the right to life. It has been argued that from this side come stringent restrictions on the acts of euthanasia that could be morally permissible. Active nonvoluntary euthanasia is ruled out by that part of the right to life which creates the duty of noninterference though passive nonvoluntary euthanasia is not ruled out, except where the right to life-preserving action has been created by some special condition such as a contract between a man and his doctor. Voluntary euthanasia is another matter: as the preceding paragraph suggested, no right is infringed if a man is allowed to die or even killed at his own request.

Turning now to the other objection that normally holds against inducing the death of another, that it is against charity, or benevolence, we must tell a very different story. Charity is the virtue that gives attachment to the good of others, and because life is normally a good, charity normally demands that it should be saved or prolonged. But as we so defined an act of euthanasia that it seeks a man's death for his own sake—for his good—charity will normally speak in favor of it. This is not, of course, to say that charity can require an act of euthanasia which justice forbids, but if an act of euthanasia is not contrary to justice—that is, it does not infringe rights—charity will rather be in its favor than against.

Once more the distinction between nonvoluntary and voluntary euthanasia must be considered. Could it ever be compatible with charity to seek a man's death although he wanted to live, or at least had not let us know that he wanted to die? I have argued that in such circumstances active euthanasia would infringe his right to life, but passive euthanasia would not do so, unless he had some special right to life-preserving service from the one who allowed him to die. What would charity dictate? Obviously when a man wants to live there is a presumption that he will be benefited if his life is prolonged, and if it is so the question of euthanasia does not arise. But it is, on the other hand, possible that he wants to live where it would be better for him to die; perhaps he does not realize the desperate situation he is in, or perhaps he is afraid of dying. So, in spite of a very proper resistance to refusing to go along with a man's own wishes in the matter of life and death, someone might justifiably refuse to prolong the life even of someone who asked him to prolong it, as in the case of refusing to give the wounded soldier a drug that would keep him alive to meet a terrible end. And it is even more obvious that charity does not always dictate that life should be prolonged where a man's own wishes, hypothetical or actual, are not known.

So much for the relation of charity to nonvoluntary passive euthanasia, which was not, like nonvoluntary active euthanasia, ruled out by the right to life. Let us now ask what charity has to say about voluntary euthanasia both active and passive. It was suggested in the discussion of justice that if of sound mind and steady desire a man might give others the *right* to allow him to die or even to kill him, where otherwise this would be ruled out. But it was pointed out that this would not settle the question of whether the act was morally permissible, and it is this that we must now consider. Could not charity speak against what justice allowed? Indeed it might do so. For while the fact that a man wants to die suggests that his life is wretched, and while his rejection of life may itself tend to take the good out of the things he might have enjoyed, nevertheless his wish to die might here be opposed for his own sake just as it might be if suicide were in question. Perhaps there is hope that his mental condition will improve. Perhaps he is mistaken in thinking his disease incurable. Perhaps he wants to die for the sake of someone else on whom he feels he is a burden, and we are not ready to accept this sacrifice whether for ourselves or others. In such cases, and there will surely be many of them, it could not be for his own sake that we kill him or allow him to die, and therefore euthanasia as defined in this paper would not be in question. But this is not to deny that there could be acts of voluntary euthanasia both passive and active against which neither justice nor charity would speak.

We have now considered the morality of euthanasia both voluntary and nonvoluntary, and active and passive. The conclusion has been that nonvoluntary active euthanasia (roughly, killing a man against his will or without his consent) is never justified; that is to say, that a man's being killed for his own good never justifies the act unless he himself has consented to it. A man's rights are infringed by such an action, and it is therefore contrary to justice. However, all the other combinations, nonvoluntary passive euthanasia, voluntary active euthanasia, and voluntary passive euthanasia are sometimes compatible with both justice and charity. But the strong condition carried in the definition of euthanasia adopted in this paper must not be forgotten; an act of euthanasia as here understood is one whose purpose is to benefit the one who dies.

In the light of this discussion let us look at our present practices. Are they good or are they bad? And what changes might be made, thinking now not only of the morality of particular acts of euthanasia but also of the indirect effects of instituting different practices, of the abuses to which they might be subject and of the changes that might come about if euthanasia became a recognized part of the social scene.

The first thing to notice is that it is wrong to ask whether we should introduce the practice of euthanasia as if it were not something we already had. In fact we do have it. For instance it is common, where the medical prognosis is very bad, for doctors to recommend against measures to prolong life, and particularly where a process of degeneration producing one medical emergency after another has already set in. If these doctors are not certainly within their legal rights this is something that is apt to come as a surprise to them as to the general public. It is also obvious that euthanasia is often practiced where old people are concerned. If someone very old and soon to die is attacked by a disease that makes his life wretched, doctors do not always come in with life-prolonging drugs. Perhaps poor patients are more fortunate in this respect than rich patients, being more often left to die in peace; but it is in any case a well-recognized piece of medical practice, which is a form of euthanasia.

No doubt the case of infants with mental or physical defects will be suggested as another example of the practice of euthanasia as we already have it, since such infants are sometimes deliberately allowed to die. That they are deliberately allowed to die is certain: children with severe spina bifida malformations are not always operated on even where it is thought that without the operation they will die; and even in the case of children with Down's syndrome who have intestinal obstructions the relatively simple operation that would make it possible to feed them is sometimes not performed.[12] Whether this is euthanasia in our sense or only as the Nazis understood it is another matter. We must ask the crucial question, "Is it for the sake of the child himself that the doctors and parents choose his death?" In some cases the answer may really be yes, and what is more important it may really be true that the kind of life which is a good is not possible or likely for this child, and that there is little but suffering and frustration in store for him.[13] But this must presuppose that the medical prognosis is wretchedly bad, as it may be for some spina bifida children. With children who are born with Down's syndrome it is, however, quite different. Most of these are able to live on for quite a time in a reasonably contented way, remaining like children all their lives but capable of affectionate relationships and able to play games and perform simple tasks. The fact is, of course, that the doctors who recommend against life-saving procedures for handicapped infants are usually thinking not of them but rather of their parents and of other children in the family or of the "burden on society" if the children survive. So it is not for their sake but to avoid trouble to others that they are allowed to die. When brought out into the open this seems unacceptable: at least we do not easily accept the principle that adults who need special care should be counted too burdensome to be kept alive. It must in any case be insisted that if children with Down's syndrome are deliberately allowed to die this is not a matter of euthanasia except in Hitler's sense. And for our children, since we scruple to gas them, not even the manner of their death is "quiet and easy"; when not treated for an intestinal obstruction a baby simply starves to death. Perhaps some will take this as an argument for allowing active euthanasia, in which case they will be in the company of an S.S. man stationed in the Warthgenau who sent Eichmann a memorandum telling him that "Jews in the coming winter could no longer be fed" and submitting for his consideration a proposal as to whether "it would not be the most humane solution to kill those Jews who were incapable of work through some quicker means."[14] If we say we are

---

[12] I have been told this by a pediatrician in a well-known medical centre in the United States. It is confirmed by Anthony M. Shaw and Iris A. Shaw, "Dilemma of Informed Consent in Children," *New England Journal of Medicine* 289, no. 17 (25 October 1973), 885–90. Reprinted in Gorovitz.

[13] It must be remembered, however, that many of the social miseries of spina bifida children could be avoided. Professor R.B. Zachary is surely right to insist on this. See, for example, "Ethical and Social Aspects of Spina Bifida," *The Lancet*, 3 August 1968, 274–6. Reprinted in Gorovitz.

[14] Quoted by Hannah Arendt, *Eichmann in Jerusalem* (London, 1963), 90.

unable to look after children with handicaps we are no more telling the truth than was the S.S. man who said that the Jews could not be fed.

Nevertheless if it is ever right to allow deformed children to die because life will be a misery to them, or not to take measures to prolong for a little the life of a newborn baby whose life cannot extend beyond a few months of intense medical intervention, there is a genuine problem about active as opposed to passive euthanasia. There are well-known cases in which the medical staff has looked on wretchedly while an infant died slowly from starvation and dehydration because they did not feel able to give a lethal injection. According to the principles discussed in the earlier part of this paper they would indeed have had no right to give it, since an infant cannot ask that it should be done. The only possible solution—supposing that voluntary active euthanasia were to be legalized—would be to appoint guardians to act on the infant's behalf. In a different climate of opinion this might not be dangerous, but at present, when people so readily assume that the life of a handicapped baby is of no value, one would be loath to support it.

Finally, on the subject of handicapped children, another word should be said about those with severe mental defects. For them too it might sometimes be right to say that one would wish for death for their sake. But not even severe mental handicap automatically brings a child within the scope even of a possible act of euthanasia. If the level of consciousness is low enough it could not be said that life is a good to them, any more than in the case of those suffering from extreme senility. Nevertheless if they do not suffer it will not be an act of euthanasia by which someone opts for their death. Perhaps charity does not demand that strenuous measures are taken to keep people in this state alive, but euthanasia does not come into the matter, any more than it does when someone is, like Karen Ann Quinlan, in a state of permanent coma. Much could be said about this last case. It might even be suggested that in the case of unconsciousness this "life" is not the life to which "the right to life" refers. But that is not our topic here.

What we must consider, even if only briefly, is the possibility that euthanasia, genuine euthanasia, and not contrary to the requirements of justice or charity, should be legalized over a wider area. Here we are up against the really serious problem of abuse. Many people want, and want very badly, to be rid of their elderly relatives and even of their ailing husbands or wives. Would any safeguards ever be able to stop them describing as euthanasia what was really for their own benefit? And would it be possible to prevent the occurrence of acts which were genuinely acts of euthanasia but morally impermissible because infringing the rights of a patient who wished to live, or whose wishes were unknown?

Perhaps the furthest we should go is to encourage patients to make their own contracts with a doctor by making it known whether they wish him to prolong their life in case of painful terminal illness or of incapacity. A document such as the Living Will seems eminently sensible, and should surely be allowed to give a doctor following the previously expressed wishes of the patient immunity from legal proceedings by relatives.[15] Legalizing active euthanasia is, however, another matter. Apart from the special repugnance doctors feel towards the idea of a lethal injection, it may be of the very greatest importance to keep a psychological barrier up against killing. Moreover it is active euthanasia which is the most liable to abuse. Hitler would not have been able to kill 275,000 people in his "euthanasia" program if he had had to wait for them to need life-saving treatment. But there are other objections to active euthanasia, even voluntary active euthanasia. In the first place it would be hard to devise procedures that would protect people from being persuaded into giving their consent. And secondly the possibility of active voluntary euthanasia might change the social scene in ways that would be very bad. As things are, people do, by and large, expect to be looked after when they are old or ill. This is one of the good things that we have, but we might lose it, and be much worse off without it. It might come to be expected that someone likely to need a lot of looking after should call for the doctor and demand his own death. Something comparable could be good in an extremely poverty-stricken community where the children genuinely suffered from lack of food; but in rich societies such as ours it would surely be a spiritual disaster. Such possibilities should make us very wary of supporting large measures of euthanasia, even where moral principle applied to the individual act does not rule it out.

SUGGESTED SUPPLEMENTARY READINGS TO PART FIVE

Battin, Margaret Pabst: *Ethical Issues in Suicide* (Englewood Cliffs, N.J.: Prentice-Hall, Inc., 1982).

Battin, Margaret Pabst, and Mayo, David, eds.: *Suicide: The Philosophical Issues* (New York: St. Martin's Press, 1980).

Downing, A.B.: *Euthanasia and the Right to Die* (Los Angeles: Nash Publishing Co., 1969).

Fletcher, Joseph: *Morals and Medicine* (Boston: Beacon Press, 1960).

Ladd, John, ed.: *Ethical Issues Relating to Life and Death* (New York: Oxford University Press, 1979).

Lecky, W.E.H.: *History of European Morals* (New York: G. Brazziler, 1955).

Perlin, Seymour, ed.: *A Handbook for the Study of Suicide* (New York: Oxford University Press, 1975).

Quinlan, Joseph, and Julia: *Karen Ann: The Quinlans Tell Their Story* (New York: Doubleday, 1977).

Williams, Glanville: *The Sanctity of Life and the Criminal Law* (New York: Alfred Knopf, 1957).

[15]Details of this document are to be found in J.A. Behnke and Sissela Bok, eds., *The Dilemmas of Euthanasia* (New York, 1975), and in A.B. Downing, ed. *Euthanasia and the Right to Life: The Case for Voluntary Euthanasia* (London, 1969).

PUNISHMENT AND THE
DEATH PENALTY

INTRODUCTION

Crime and punishment, recurrent events in any society, are highly variable in specific form and extent. Law in the early Roman Empire required that if a slave owner was murdered by one of his slaves, then *all* of his slaves, not only those responsible, be executed; and this law was carried out to the letter in households of even three and four hundred slaves. One need only to recall the prevalence at different times in history of punishments such as the rack, the cross, the wheel, the stocks, and burning at the stake to realize that our modern habit in the Western, non-Moslem world of substituting in the place of these various punishments a single punishment, deprivation of liberty for varying amounts of time, reflects a culturally specific approach and, no doubt, our preoccupation with individual liberty as an overriding value.

THEORIES OF PUNISHMENT:
UTILITARIAN AND RETRIBUTIVIST

Disciplined inquiry into the morality of punishment is relatively new, and in the two hundred or so years in which it has flourished, two particular theories about the justification of punishment have dominated the scene: *retributive* and *utilitarian*. This polarization of moral vision stems from the same basic bifurcation already noticed between deontology and consequentialism; deontological philosophers usually adopt retributivist theories of punishment, and consequentialists utilitarian ones.

   Utilitarian views of punishment are forward-looking; they are unconcerned with the past apart from its ability to inform decisions about the future, and they focus instead on the goods and evils likely to be brought about by imposing different punishments. The emphasis is not so much on what the criminal "deserves" as on what effects the punishment will have; not so much on whether the punishment fits the crime as on whether it will reform the criminal or deter other would-be criminals. Utilitarians thus justify punishment through its capacity to bring about three kinds of effects:

1 Rehabilitation
2 Prevention
3 Deterrence

Rehabilitation concerns the ability of the punishment to reform the criminal and to make him a law-abiding citizen. Hence utilitarian theories are concerned with the details of punishment in application: Does solitary confinement discourage or encourage recidivism (the return to crime by punished criminals)? How about psychological counseling? The answers to these and similar questions will determine for the utilitarian which forms of punishment are appropriate. Prevention, closely associated with rehabilitation, concerns not the effect of punishment on the welfare of the criminal, but on society, and deals with the extent to which a given punishment succeeds in preventing the criminal from harming society by committing further crimes. Imprisonment clearly helps prevent crime by locking the criminal away from his would-be victims. Rehabilitation, similarly, is a crime preventive, and works not by preventing access to crime but by encouraging dispositional changes. One form of punishment, of course, trumps all others in terms of its preventive ability: the death penalty. It undeniably forecloses all possibility of its victim's committing future crimes, but, as we shall see, it also forecloses all possibility of correcting any judicial error. The last category, deterrence, concerns the effect, great or small, a punishment will have on discouraging crime by others. The extent to which punishment, and especially the death penalty, deters others is a matter of hot dispute, but the principle underlying deterrence is obvious enough: the more a person worries about the punishment he or she may receive, the more that individual will include it as a factor in calculating whether to commit a crime. These three factors taken together and each weighed for its proper contribution to overall welfare constitute the final verdict for the morality of a given punishment from a utilitarian perspective.

Retributivist theories, in contrast to utilitarian ones, are backward-looking. It is the crime itself, its nature, motive, and extent, that matters for the retributivist. Considerations of future consequences are at best irrelevant distractions, and at worst an excuse to treat the criminal as a mere tool for the purposes of others. Some have spoken of retribution as an instantiation of "an eye for an eye, a tooth for a tooth," and others as a proper pain to counteract the (presumably) illicit pleasure gained by the crime. Still others have defined retribution through its capacity to satisfy the right of the criminal to be punished or to annul the evil committed through the crime. But all these views represent decided tangents in the explanation of retributive theory; by far the most prevalent and best accepted definition of retribution is mirrored in R.S. Downie's remark, made in "Justifying Punishment," included in this section, that retribution has as its underlying principle the notion that "punishment is justified insofar as it is a morally fitting response to the violation of law." Or, to use the argument of Hugo Bedau (whose article is also reprinted in this section), retribution relies on two fundamental principles: that crimes should be punished, and that the severity of the punishment should be proportionate to the gravity of the offense. It is this latter emphasis on the proportionality of punishment that people have in mind when they characterize retributive theory through the line from the Gilbert and Sullivan operetta, The Mikado, "Let the punishment fit the crime."[1]

On closer inspection, each theory reveals a sufficient number of ambiguities or failings to keep its critics complaining. As might be guessed from the discussion in Part One, consequentialism's perennial problem with justice reappears in utilitarian theories of punishment, this time in the form of complaints about violations of fairness and of human rights. Our intuitions about punishment imply that graver crimes deserve graver punishments and that the innocent ought not to be punished, but it is precisely here that critics of utilitarianism assert that the theory fails. If it could be shown that the consequences would be better, then is not utilitarianism bound to recommend disproportionate punishments or, in exceptional cases, the punishment of the innocent? Was this not the claim—that giving a lesser crime a greater penalty would nonetheless have offsetting benefits by way of deterrence—that justified the imposition of the death sentence in sixteenth-century England for sheep stealing? The excerpt from the American Friends Service Committee included below brings the issue of the fairness of utilitarian theories into sharp relief, especially through its critique of the concept central to the application of such theories, that is, rehabilitation. John Stuart Mill's classic response to the claim that utilitarianism requires disproportionate punishments and the punishment of the innocent is that such practices would weaken the overall system of justice, and thus generate clear disutility. Whether the response is fully adequate, however, remains to be seen.[2]

---

[1] Two other theories of punishment, less in the mainstream than the utilitarian and retributivist theories, are articulated by J.D. Mabbott and Herbert Morris. For Mabbott, there is only one reason for punishment: that someone has broken the law where the law prescribes punishment. See J.D. Mabbott, "Punishment," Mind, Vol. 48 (1939). For Morris, punishment should be seen as a way of rectifying an unfair distribution of burdens and benefits in society which was brought about by the crime itself. See Herbert Morris, "Persons and Punishment," The Monist, Vol. 52 (1968), 475–501.

[2] Further ramifications of the consequence-fairness problem emerge. Insofar as the need for deterrence varies according to the prevalence of a given type of lawbreaking, it appears that utilitarianism should endorse stricter punishment when a crime is on the increase. But why should the general level of bad check writing affect my level of punishment? Others have wondered whether utilitarianism can even successfully distinguish between, say, imprisonment and quarantine. What, they ask, is the difference in principle between forcing a person to remain apart from society in order to prevent harming it by communicating a disease and doing the same to prevent harming it by crime? And yet we think of the criminal and the quarantined victim of a disease in

Defenders of utilitarianism, in addition to making counter-claims to these objections, offer their own list of weaknesses for retributivist theory. It is well and good, they note, to speak of proportionality in punishment, but if punishment is to be proportionate, it must be proportionate to some absolute level, and how is this to be determined? The notion of an "eye for an eye" might, of course, be employed in setting this level but it allows marked ambiguities in application. It may work for murder, as Kant suggests when he argues that death is the only appropriate response to murder, but how about other crimes? What is the proper response to rape? Furthermore, by cutting the logical connection between punishment and social consequences, retributivist theories seem condemned to disallow the repetition of offense as a factor in sentencing. And yet most people agree with the current practice of imposing lesser penalties for first offenders, even though the gravity of the crime committed by a second or third offender may be as great.

Hence critics of retributivist theory charge it with the theoretical neglect of important variables. More than the abstract severity of the crime, they assert, is at stake. Crime, as the psychiatrist Carl Menninger argues in this section, is often the indirect product of poverty, psychosis, and social immaturity; hence to neglect these variables is to impose moral blindness upon oneself and to treat people by reference to an abstract concept that leaves out essential human factors. Menninger concludes that we must rely more on creative parole, counseling, education, and outpatient treatment.

Other critics of retribution assert that the dangerousness of a criminal to society may not be a simple function of the moral gravity of the crime, and when it is not, sentencing must proceed accordingly. Partial insanity may reduce the legal or moral guilt of a killer, but society may need to lock the person up for an equal or longer period than it does the non-insane killer.

In his article, "Justifying Punishment," R.S. Downie struggles with the question of what finally separates retributivist from utilitarian theories of punishment, and he elaborates the alleged weaknesses to which each is prone. Downie shows how adopting one or another of the theories will force concrete changes in the structuring of our judicial and penal systems.

THE DEATH PENALTY

A critic of capital punishment once remarked that anyone in the Judeo-Christian tradition who violates the commandment, "Thou shalt not kill," has a lot of

---

radically different moral modes. Finally, the utilitarian's rejection of the notion of deserts in punishment (what one deserves in light of the crime committed) is subject to the complaint that negative deserts are linked to positive deserts, and that the rejection of one implies the rejection of the other. That is, we seem unwilling to give up the notion that someone's moral excellence is ground for reward, for example, that a hero's rescue of a drowning child is the ground of public reward; but if not, are we free to give up the idea that someone's immorality is the ground for punishment?

explaining to do. Yet, while we may agree that any killing requires explanation, it is equally clear that a significant number of exceptions have been justified historically, with war and capital punishment being the outstanding instances. Indeed, it is only in the last three hundred years that serious public doubts about the death penalty have arisen. Russia in 1750 was the first country to abolish the death penalty for all crimes except treason, and in Great Britain during the nineteenth century religious and nonreligious forces finally united to reduce the number of crimes punishable by death from over 200 to two: treason and premeditated murder.

In the United States, the dispute over the death penalty came to a head in 1972 with the Supreme Court case of *Furman v. Georgia. Furman* extended a de facto moratorium on the death penalty which had been in place for a decade. In a split decision the court ruled that capital punishment was unconstitutional at least *in its existing form.* Two justices argued that it violated the Eighth Amendment's proscription of "cruel and unusual" punishment, while three other justices left aside the Eighth Amendment and focused instead on the Fourteenth, saying that it was in conflict with that amendment's call for "equal treatment under the law." These three justices, then, held that although the death penalty may be constitutional in itself, it had been applied in an arbitrary and inconsistent manner. They pointed to the fact that many more blacks than whites were executed, and this was true even after figures were adjusted to account for the disproportionate number of blacks who were found guilty of murder. In other words, they noted that the average black convicted of murder was more liable to receive the death penalty than the average white. Furthermore, states appeared to inflict capital punishment without the benefit of any guiding principles: similar cases appeared to have differing results.[3]

In the wake of *Furman* many states adjusted their judicial procedures, some making the death penalty mandatory for certain crimes and others establishing specific standards for applying the penalty. Making the death penalty mandatory for certain crimes, however, was struck down as unconstitutional in 1976 by the Supreme Court in *Woodson v. North Carolina.* Hence states were pressed to take into account aggravating and mitigating factors affecting each case. Some states, such as Georgia, responded by establishing a two-step process in which a defendant is found guilty or innocent in the first, and the determination of proper penalty is made in the second. It is this two-step process which was in effect as the case of *Gregg v. Georgia* (excerpted below) unfolded. In *Gregg,* the High Court acknowledged the constitutionality of a death sentence imposed by a Georgia court in order to comply with the emerging requirement of nonarbitrary treatment.

Since *Gregg,* the number of executions has skyrocketed. In 1977 there was one execution in the United States; in 1984, twenty-two. Indeed, in 1984 the

---

[3] Another important Supreme Court decision, *Coker v. Georgia* (1977), declared that the death penalty for rape was "grossly disproportionate" and hence unconstitutional.

number of executions exceeded the total number of executions for the past two decades.

The issue of discrimination still looms in capital contexts. As of December 1984, more than 40 percent of the prisoners on death row were black, and recent studies indicate that the application of the death penalty has not only been disproportionately focused on blacks, but that blacks convicted of killing a white were more likely to receive the death penalty than those convicted of killing a black.

Two writers included in this section, Immanuel Kant and Sidney Hook, defend the death penalty, and one, Hugo Bedau, criticizes it. All three extracts reflect two of the critical and unresolved issues surrounding the death penalty; namely, its proportionality and its deterrent effect. Kant stresses what for him is the perfect proportionality of the penalty, the justified taking of a life in response to an unjustified taking of a life by a criminal. Bedau, in turn, suggests that the general and overriding value of a human life should make us condemn not only murder, but its counterpart by the state. Both sides agree that the facts are murky about the value of deterrence of capital punishment in contrast to life imprisonment. In 1975, a University of Chicago econometrician concluded that each additional execution from 1933 to 1967 might have prevented at least one and as many as eight murders. Yet this often cited study is widely challenged, and even defenders of the death penalty confess that the available statistical evidence alone is not conclusive.

Gregg v. Georgia (1976)*

MAJORITY OPINION: Written by Justices Stewart, Powell, and Stevens

The history of the prohibition of "cruel and unusual" punishment already has been reviewed at length. The phrase first appeared in the English Bill of Rights of 1689, which was drafted by Parliament at the accession of William and Mary. The English version appears to have been directed against punishments unauthorized by statute and beyond the jurisdiction of the sentencing court, as well as those disproportionate to the offense involved. The American draftsmen, who adopted the English phrasing in drafting the Eighth Amendment, were primarily concerned, however, with proscribing "tortures" and other "barbarous" methods of punishment....

It is clear from the foregoing precedents that the Eighth Amendment has not been regarded as a static concept. As Mr. Chief Justice Warren said, in an oftquoted phrase, "[t]he Amendment must draw its meaning from the evolving standards of decency that mark the progress of a maturing society." Thus, an assessment of contemporary values concerning the infliction of a challenged sanction is relevant to the application of the Eighth Amendment. As we develop below more fully, this assessment does not call for a subjective judgment. It requires, rather, that we look to objective indicia that reflect the public attitude toward a given sanction.

But our cases also make clear that public perceptions of standards of decency with respect to criminal sanctions are not conclusive. A penalty also must accord with "the dignity of man," which is the "basic concept underlying the Eighth Amendment." This means, at least, that the punishment not be "excessive." When a form of punishment in the abstract (in this case, whether capital punishment may ever be imposed as a sanction for murder) rather than in the particular (the propriety of death as a penalty to be applied to a specific defendant for a specific crime) is under consideration, the inquiry into "excessiveness" has two aspects. First, the punishment must not involve the unnecessary and wanton infliction of pain. Second, the punishment must not be grossly out of proportion to the severity of the crime.

...[I]n assessing a punishment selected by a democratically elected legislature against the constitutional measure, we presume its validity. We may not require

United States Supreme Court, 428 U.S. 153 (1976). Footnotes deleted.

Editor's note: The key issue in this case is the constitutionality of Georgia's application of the death penalty to Troy Gregg. Georgia's procedure in capital cases specified a two-stage trial, one to determine guilt, and the other the appropriate punishment. At the first, a jury found Gregg guilty of armed robbery and murder. At the second, a jury (the same jury) recommended the punishment of death. Later, the Georgia Supreme Court upheld the imposition of the death sentence.

At the time, Georgia's statutes, amended in response to the U.S. Supreme Court's *Furman v. Georgia* decision (1972), retained the death penalty for six categories of crime: murder, kidnapping for ransom or where the victim is harmed, armed robbery, rape, treason, and aircraft hijacking.

the legislature to select the least severe penalty possible so long as the penalty selected is not cruelly inhumane or disproportionate to the crime involved. And a heavy burden rests on those who would attack the judgment of the representatives of the people.

This is true in part because the constitutional test is intertwined with an assessment of contemporary standards and the legislative judgment weighs heavily in ascertaining such standards. "[I]n a democratic society legislatures, not courts, are constituted to respond to the will and consequently the moral values of the people."

The deference we owe to the decisions of the state legislatures under our federal system is enhanced where the specification of punishments is concerned, for "these are peculiarly questions of legislative policy." Caution is necessary lest this Court become, "under the aegis of the Cruel and Unusual Punishment Clause, the ultimate arbiter of the standards of criminal responsibility...throughout the country."...

Four years ago, the petitioners in *Furman* and its companion cases predicated their argument primarily upon the asserted proposition that standards of decency had evolved to the point where capital punishment no longer could be tolerated. The petitioners in those cases said, in effect, that the evolutionary process had come to an end, and that standards of decency required that the Eighth Amendment be construed finally as prohibiting capital punishment for any crime regardless of its depravity and impact on society. This view was accepted by two Justices. Three other Justices were unwilling to go so far; focusing on the procedures by which convicted defendants were selected for the death penalty rather than on the actual punishment inflicted, they joined in the conclusion that the statutes before the Court were constitutionally invalid.

The petitioners in the capital cases before the Court today renew the "standards of decency" argument, but developments during the four years since *Furman* have undercut substantially the assumptions upon which their argument rested. Despite the continuing debate, dating back to the 19th century, over the morality and utility of capital punishment, it is now evident that a large proportion of American society continues to regard it as an appropriate and necessary criminal sanction.

The most marked indication of society's endorsement of the death penalty for murder is the legislative response to *Furman*. The legislatures of at least 35 States have enacted new statutes that provide for the death penalty for at least some crimes that result in the death of another person. And the Congress of the United States, in 1974, enacted a statute providing the death penalty for aircraft piracy that results in death....

As we have seen, however, the Eighth Amendment demands more than that a challenged punishment be acceptable to contemporary society. The Court also must ask whether it comports with the basic concept of human dignity at the core of the Amendment. Although we cannot "invalidate a category of penalties because we deem less severe penalties adequate to serve the ends of penology," the sanction imposed cannot be so totally without penological justification that it results in the gratuitous infliction of suffering.

The death penalty is said to serve two principal social purposes: retribution and deterrence of capital crimes by prospective offenders.

In part, capital punishment is an expression of society's moral outrage at particularly offensive conduct. This function may be unappealing to many, but it is essential in an ordered society that asks its citizens to rely on legal processes rather than self-help to vindicate their wrongs.

> The instinct for retribution is part of the nature of man, and channeling that instinct in the administration of criminal justice serves an important purpose in promoting the stability of a society governed by law. When people begin to believe that organized society is unwilling or unable to impose upon criminal offenders the punishment they "deserve," then there are sown the seeds of anarchy—of self-help, vigilante justice, and lynch law. *Furman v. Georgia* (STEWART, J., concurring).

"Retribution is no longer the dominant objective of the criminal law," but neither is it a forbidden objective nor one inconsistent with our respect for the dignity of men. Indeed, the decision that capital punishment may be the appropriate sanction in extreme cases is an expression of the community's belief that certain crimes are themselves so grievous an affront to humanity that the only adequate response may be the penalty of death.

Statistical attempts to evaluate the worth of the death penalty as a deterrent to crimes by potential offenders have occasioned a great deal of debate. The results simply have been inconclusive....

Although some of the studies suggest that the death penalty may not function as a significantly greater deterrent than lesser penalties, there is no convincing empirical evidence either supporting or refuting this view. We may nevertheless assume safely that there are murderers, such as those who act in passion, for whom the threat of death has little or no deterrent effect. But for many others, the death penalty undoubtedly is a significant deterrent. There are carefully contemplated murders, such as murder for hire, where the possible penalty of death may well enter into the cold calculus that precedes the decision to act. And there are some categories of murder, such as murder by a life prisoner, where other sanctions may not be adequate.

The value of capital punishment as a deterrent of crime is a complex factual issue the resolution of which properly rests with the legislatures, which can evaluate the results of statistical studies in terms of their own local conditions and with a flexibility of approach that is not available to the courts. Indeed, many of the post-*Furman* statutes reflect just such a responsible effort to define those crimes and those criminals for which capital punishment is most probably an effective deterrent.

In sum, we cannot say that the judgment of the Georgia Legislature that capital punishment may be necessary in some cases is clearly wrong....

We now consider whether Georgia may impose the death penalty on the petitioner in this case....

316 PART 6: PUNISHMENT AND THE DEATH PENALTY

In the wake of *Furman,* Georgia amended its capital punishment statute, but chose not to narrow the scope of its murder provisions. Thus, now as before *Furman,* in Georgia "[a] person commits murder when he unlawfully and with malice aforethought, either express or implied, causes the death of another human being." All persons convicted of murder "shall be punished by death or by imprisonment for life."

Georgia did act, however, to narrow the class of murderers subject to capital punishment by specifying 10 statutory aggravating circumstances, one of which must be found by the jury to exist beyond a reasonable doubt before a death sentence can ever be imposed. In addition, the jury is authorized to consider any other appropriate aggravating or mitigating circumstances. The jury is not required to find any mitigating circumstance in order to make a recommendation of mercy that is binding on the trial court, but it must find a *statutory* aggravating circumstance before recommending a sentence of death.

These procedures require the jury to consider the circumstances of the crime and the criminal before it recommends sentence. No longer can a Georgia jury do as Furman's jury did: reach a finding of the defendant's guilt and then, without guidance or direction, decide whether he should live or die. Instead, the jury's attention is directed to the specific circumstances of the crime: Was it committed in the course of another capital felony? Was it committed for money? Was it committed upon a peace officer or judicial officer? Was it committed in a particularly heinous way or in a manner that endangered the lives of many persons? In addition, the jury's attention is focused on the characteristics of the person who committed the crime: Does he have a record of prior convictions for capital offenses? Are there any special facts about this defendant that mitigate against imposing capital punishment (e.g., his youth, the extent of his cooperation with the police, his emotional state at the time of the crime). As a result, while some jury discretion still exists, "the discretion to be exercised is controlled by clear and objective standards so as to produce non-discriminatory application."

As an important additional safeguard against arbitrariness and caprice, the Georgia statutory scheme provides for automatic appeal of all death sentences to the State's Supreme Court. That court is required by statute to review each sentence of death and determine whether it was imposed under the influence of passion or prejudice, whether the evidence supports the jury's finding of a statutory aggravating circumstance, and whether the sentence is disproportionate compared to those sentences imposed in similar cases.

In short, Georgia's new sentencing procedures require as a prerequisite to the imposition of the death penalty, specific jury findings as to the circumstances of the crime or the character of the defendant. Moreover, to guard further against a situation comparable to that presented in *Furman,* the Supreme Court of Georgia compares each death sentence with the sentences imposed on similarly situated defendants to ensure that the sentence of death in a particular case is not disproportionate. On their face these procedures seem to satisfy the concerns of *Furman.* No longer should there be "no meaningful basis for distinguishing the few cases in which [the death penalty] is imposed from the many cases in which it is not."...

The basic concern of *Furman* centered on those defendants who were being condemned to death capriciously and arbitrarily. Under the procedures before the Court in that case, sentencing authorities were not directed to give attention to the nature or circumstances of the crime committed or to the character or record of the defendant. Left unguided, juries imposed the death sentence in a way that could only be called freakish. The new Georgia sentencing procedures, by contrast, focus the jury's attention on the particularized nature of the crime and the particularized characteristics of the individual defendant. While the jury is permitted to consider any aggravating or mitigating circumstances, it must find and identify at least one statutory aggravating factor before it may impose a penalty of death. In this way the jury's discretion is channeled. No longer can a jury wantonly and freakishly impose the death sentence; it is always circumscribed by the legislative guidelines. In addition, the review function of the Supreme Court of Georgia affords additional assurance that the concerns that prompted our decision in *Furman* are not present to any significant degree in the Georgia procedure applied here.

For the reasons expressed in this opinion, we hold that the statutory system under which Gregg was sentenced to death does not violate the Constitution. Accordingly, the judgment of the Georgia Supreme Court is affirmed....

DISSENTING: JUSTICE THURGOOD MARSHALL

In *Furman v. Georgia* (1972) (concurring opinion), I set forth at some length my views on the basic issue presented to the Court in [this case]. The death penalty, I concluded, is a cruel and unusual punishment prohibited by the Eighth and Fourteenth Amendments. That continues to be my view.

I have no intention of retracing the "long and tedious journey" that led to my conclusion in *Furman*. My sole purposes here are to consider the suggestion that my conclusion in *Furman* has been undercut by developments since then, and briefly to evaluate the basis for my Brethren's holding that the extinction of life is a permissible form of punishment under the Cruel and Unusual Punishments Clause.

In *Furman* I concluded that the death penalty is constitutionally invalid for two reasons. First, the death penalty is excessive. And second, the American people, fully informed as to the purposes of the death penalty and its liabilities, would in my view reject it as morally unacceptable.

Since the decision in *Furman*, the legislatures of 35 States have enacted new statutes authorizing the imposition of the death sentence for certain crimes, and Congress has enacted a law providing the death penalty for air piracy resulting in death. I would be less than candid if I did not acknowledge that these developments have a significant bearing on a realistic assessment of the moral acceptability of the death penalty to the American people. But if the constitutionality of the death penalty turns, as I have urged, on the opinion of an *informed* citizenry, then even the enactment of new death statutes cannot be viewed as conclusive. In *Furman,* I observed that the American people are largely unaware of the information critical to a judgment on the morality of the death penalty, and concluded that if they were better informed they would consider it shocking, unjust, and unacceptable. A recent study, conducted after the enactment of the post-*Furman* statutes, has confirmed that the American people know little about the death penalty, and that the opinions of an informed public would differ significantly from those of a public unaware of the consequences and effects of the death penalty.

Even assuming, however, that the post-*Furman* enactment of statutes authorizing the death penalty renders the prediction of the views of an informed citizenry an uncertain basis for a constitutional decision, the enactment of those statutes has no bearing whatsoever on the conclusion that the death penalty is unconstitutional because it is excessive. An excessive penalty is invalid under the Cruel and Unusual Punishments Clause "even though popular sentiment may favor" it. The inquiry here, then, is simply whether the death penalty is necessary to accomplish the legitimate legislative purposes in punishment, or whether a less severe penalty—life imprisonment—would do as well.

The two purposes that sustain the death penalty as nonexcessive in the Court's view are general deterrence and retribution. In *Furman,* I canvassed the relevant data on the deterrent effect of capital punishment. The state of knowledge at that point, after literally centuries of debate, was summarized as follows by a United Nations Committee:

> It is generally agreed between the retentionists and abolitionists, whatever their opinions about the validity of comparative studies of deterrence, that the data which now exist show no correlation between the existence of capital punishment and lower rates of capital crime.

The available evidence, I concluded in *Furman,* was convincing that "capital punishment is not necessary as a deterrent to crime in our society." ...

... The evidence I reviewed in *Furman* remains convincing, in my view, that "capital punishment is not necessary as a deterrent to crime in our society." The justification for the death penalty must be found elsewhere.

The other principal purpose said to be served by the death penalty is retribution. The notion that retribution can serve as a moral justification for the sanction of death finds credence in the opinion of my Brothers STEWART, POWELL, and STEVENS.... It is this notion that I find to be the most disturbing aspect of today's unfortunate [decision].

The concept of retribution is a multifaceted one, and any discussion of its role in the criminal law must be undertaken with caution. On one level, it can be said that the notion of retribution or reprobation is the basis of our insistence that only those who have broken the law be punished, and in this sense the notion is quite obviously central to a just system of criminal sanctions. But our recognition that retribution plays a crucial role in determining who may be punished by no means requires approval of retribution as a general justification for punishment. It is the question whether retribution can provide a moral justification for punishment—in particular, capital punishment—that we must consider.

My Brothers STEWART, POWELL, and STEVENS offer the following explanation of the retributive justification for capital punishment:

> The instinct for retribution is part of the nature of man, and channeling that instinct in the administration of criminal justice serves an important purpose in promoting the stability of a society governed by law. When people begin to believe that organized society is unwilling or unable to impose upon criminal offenders the punishment they "deserve," then there are sown the seeds of anarchy—of self-help, vigilante justice, and lynch law.

This statement is wholly inadequate to justify the death penalty. As my Brother BRENNAN stated in *Furman*, "[t]here is no evidence whatever that utilization of imprisonment rather than death encourages private blood feuds and other disorders." It simply defies belief to suggest that the death penalty is necessary to prevent the American people from taking the law into their own hands.

In a related vein, it may be suggested that the expression of moral outrage through the imposition of the death penalty serves to reinforce basic moral values—that it marks some crimes as particularly offensive and therefore to be avoided. The argument is akin to a deterrence argument, but differs in that it contemplates the individual's shrinking from antisocial conduct, not because he fears punishment, but because he has been told in the strongest possible way that the conduct is wrong. This contention, like the previous one, provides no support for the death penalty. It is inconceivable that any individual concerned about conforming his conduct to what society says is "right" would fail to realize that murder is "wrong" if the penalty were simply life imprisonment.

The foregoing contentions—that society's expression of moral outrage through the imposition of the death penalty pre-empts the citizenry from taking the law into its own hands and reinforces moral values—are not retributive in the purest sense. They are essentially utilitarian in that they portray the death penalty as valuable because of its beneficial results. These justifications for the death penalty are inadequate because the penalty is, quite clearly I think, not necessary to the accomplishment of those results.

There remains for consideration, however, what might be termed the purely retributive justification for the death penalty—that the death penalty is appropriate, not because of its beneficial effect on society, but because the taking of the murderer's life is itself morally good. Some of the language of the opinion of my Brothers STEWART, POWELL, and STEVENS...appears positively to embrace this notion of retribution for its own sake as a justification for capital punishment. They state:

> [T]he decision that capital punishment may be the appropriate sanction in extreme cases is an expression of the community's belief that certain crimes are themselves so grievous an affront to humanity that the only adequate response may be the penalty of death.

They then quote with approval from Lord Justice Denning's remarks before the British Royal Commission on Capital Punishment:

> The truth is that some crimes are so outrageous that society insists on adequate punishment, because the wrong-doer deserves it, irrespective of whether it is a deterrent or not.

Of course, it may be that these statements are intended as no more than observations as to the popular demands that it is thought must be responded to in order to prevent anarchy. But the implication of the statements appears to me to be quite different—namely, that society's judgment that the murderer "deserves" death must be respected not simply because the preservation of order requires it, but because it is appropriate that society make the judgment and carry it out. It is this latter notion, in particular, that I consider to be fundamentally at odds with the Eighth Amendment. The mere fact that the community demands the murderer's life in return for the evil he has done cannot sustain the death penalty, for as JUSTICES STEWART, POWELL, and STEVENS remind us, "the Eighth Amendment demands more than that a challenged punishment be acceptable to contemporary society." To be sustained under the Eighth Amendment, the death penalty must "compor[t] with the basic concept of human dignity at the core of the amendment;" the objective in imposing it must be "[consistent] with our respect for the dignity of [other] men." Under these standards, the taking of life "because the wrongdoer deserves it" surely must fail, for such a punishment has as its very basis the total denial of the wrongdoer's dignity and worth.

The death penalty, unnecessary to promote the goal of deterrence or to further any legitimate notion of retribution, is an excessive penalty forbidden by the Eighth and Fourteenth Amendments. I respectfully dissent.

The Crime of Punishment

Karl Menninger

Few words in our language arrest our attention as do "crime," "violence," "revenge," and "injustice." We abhor crime; we adore justice; we boast that we live by the rule of law. Violence and vengefulness we repudiate as unworthy of our civilization, and we assume this sentiment to be unanimous among all human beings.

Yet crime continues to be a national disgrace and world-wide problem. It is threatening, alarming, wasteful, expensive, abundant, and apparently increasing! In actuality it is decreasing in frequency of occurrence, but it is certainly increasing in visibility and the reactions of the public to it.

Our system for controlling crime is ineffective, unjust, expensive. Prisons seem to operate with revolving doors—the same people going in and out and in and out. *Who cares?*

Our city jails and inhuman reformatories and wretched prisons are jammed. They are known to be unhealthy, dangerous, immoral, indecent, crime-breeding dens of iniquity. Not everyone has smelled them, as some of us have. Not many have heard the groans and the curses. Not everyone has seen the hate and despair in a thousand blank, hollow faces. But, in a way, we all know how miserable prisons are. *We want them to be that way.* And they are. *Who cares?*

Professional and big-time criminals prosper as never before. Gambling syndicates flourish. White-collar crime may even exceed all others, but goes undetected in the majority of cases. We are all being robbed and we know who the robbers are. They live nearby. *Who cares?*

The public filches millions of dollars worth of food and clothing from stores, towels and sheets from hotels, jewelry and knick-knacks from shops. The public steals, and the same public pays it back in higher prices. *Who cares?*

Time and time again somebody shouts about this state of affairs, just as I am shouting now. The magazines shout. The newspapers shout. The television and radio commentators shout (or at least they "deplore"). Psychologists, sociologists, leading jurists, wardens, and intelligent police chiefs join the chorus. Governors and mayors and Congressmen are sometimes heard. They shout that the situation is bad, bad, bad, and getting worse. Some suggest that we immediately replace obsolete procedures with scientific methods. A few shout contrary sentiments. Do the clear indications derived from scientific discovery for appropriate changes continue to fall on deaf ears? Why is the public so long-suffering, so apathetic and thereby so continuingly self-destructive? How many Presidents (and other citizens) do we have to lose before we do something?

The public behaves as a sick patient does when a dreaded treatment is proposed for his ailment. We all know how the aching tooth may suddenly quiet down in the dentist's office, or the abdominal pain disappear in the surgeon's examining room. Why should a sufferer seek relief and shun it? Is it merely the fear of pain of the treatment? Is it the fear of unknown complications? Is it distrust of the doctor's ability? All of these, no doubt.

But, as Freud made so incontestably clear, the sufferer is always somewhat deterred by a kind of subversive, internal opposition to the work of cure. He suffers on the one hand from the pains of his affliction and yearns to get well. But he suffers at the same time from traitorous impulses that fight against the accomplishment of any change in himself, even recovery! Like Hamlet, he wonders whether it may be better after all to suffer the familiar pains and aches associated with the old method than to face the complications of a new and strange, even though possibly better way of handling things.

The inescapable conclusion is that society secretly *wants* crime, *needs* crime, and gains definite satisfactions from the present mishandling of it! We condemn crime; we punish offenders for it; but we need it. The crime and punishment ritual is a part of our lives. We need crimes to wonder at, to enjoy vicariously, to discuss and speculate about, and to publicly deplore. We need criminals to identify ourselves with, to envy secretly, and to punish stoutly. They do for us the forbidden, illegal things we *wish* to do and, like scapegoats of old, they bear the burdens of our displaced guilt and punishment—"the iniquities of us all."

We have to confess that there is something fascinating for us all about violence. That most crime is not violent we know but we forget, because crime is a breaking, a rupturing, a tearing—even when it is quietly done. To all of us crime seems like violence.

The very word "violence" has a disturbing, menacing quality.... In meaning it implies something dreaded, powerful, destructive, or eruptive. It is something we abhor—or do we? Its first effect is to startle, frighten—even to horrify us. But we do not always run away from it. For violence also intrigues us. It is exciting. It is dramatic. Observing it and sometimes even participating in it gives us acute pleasure.

The newspapers constantly supply us with tidbits of violence going on in the world. They exploit its dramatic essence often to the neglect of conservative reporting of more extensive but less violent damage—the flood disaster in Florence, Italy, for example. Such words as crash, explosion, wreck, assault, raid, murder, avalanche, rape, and seizure evoke pictures of eruptive devastation from which we cannot turn away. The headlines often impute violence metaphorically even to peaceful activities. Relations are "ruptured," a tie is "broken," arbitration "collapses," a proposal is "killed."

Meanwhile on the television and movie screens there constantly appear for our amusement scenes of fighting, slugging, beating, torturing, clubbing, shooting, and the like which surpass in effect anything that the newspapers can describe. Much of this violence is portrayed dishonestly; the scenes are only semirealistic; they are "faked" and romanticized.

Pain cannot be photographed; grimaces indicate but do not convey its intensity. And wounds—unlike violence—are rarely shown. This phony quality of television violence in its mentally unhealthy aspect encourages irrationality by giving the impression to the observer that being beaten, kicked, cut, and stomped, while very unpleasant, are not very painful or serious. For after being slugged and beaten the hero rolls over, opens his eyes, hops up, rubs his cheek, grins, and staggers on. The *suffering* of violence is a part both the TV and movie producers *and* their audience tend to repress.

Although most of us *say* we deplore cruelty and destructiveness, we are partially deceiving ourselves. We disown violence, ascribing the love of it to other people. But the facts speak for themselves. We do love violence, all of us, and we all feel secretly guilty for it, which is another clue to public resistance to crime-control reform.

The great sin by which we all are tempted is the wish to hurt others, and this sin must be avoided if we are to live and let live. If our destructive energies can be mastered, directed, and sublimated, we can survive. If we can love, we can live. Our destructive energies, if they cannot be controlled, may destroy our best friends, as in the case of Alexander the Great, or they may destroy supposed "enemies" or innocent strangers. Worst of all—from the standpoint of the individual—they may destroy us.

Over the centuries of man's existence, many devices have been employed in the effort to control these innate suicidal and criminal propensities. The earliest of these undoubtedly depended upon fear—fear of the unknown, fear of magical retribution, fear of social retaliation. These external devices were replaced gradually with the law and all its machinery, religion and its rituals, and the conventions of the social order.

The routine of life formerly required every individual to direct much of his aggressive energy against the environment. There were trees to cut down, wild animals to fend off, heavy obstacles to remove, great burdens to lift. But the machine has gradually changed all of this. Today, the routine of life, for most people, requires no violence, no fighting, no killing, no life-risking, no sudden supreme exertion: occasionally, perhaps, a hard pull or a strong push, but no tearing, crushing, breaking, forcing.

And because violence no longer has legitimate and useful vents or purposes, it must *all* be controlled today. In earlier times its expression was often a virtue, today its control is the virtue. The control involves symbolic, vicarious expressions of our violence—violence modified; "sublimated," as Freud called it; "neutralized," as Hartmann described it. Civilized substitutes for direct violence are the objects of daily search by all of us. The common law and the Ten Commandments, traffic signals and property deeds, fences and front doors, sermons and concerts, Christmas trees and jazz bands—these and a thousand other things exist today to help in the control of violence.

My colleague, Bruno Bettelheim, thinks we do not properly educate our youth to deal with their violent urges. He reminds us that nothing fascinated our forefathers more. The *Iliad* is a poem of violence. Much of the Bible is a record of violence. One penal system and many methods of child-rearing express violence—"violence to suppress violence." And, he concludes [in the article "Violence: A Neglected Mode of Behavior"]: "We shall not be able to deal intelligently with violence unless we are first ready to see it as a part of human nature, and then we shall come to realize the chances of discharging violent tendencies are now so severely curtailed that their regular and safe draining-off is not possible anymore."

Why aren't we all criminals? We all have the impulses; we all have the provocations. But becoming civilized, which is repeated ontologically in the process of social education, teaches us what we may do with impunity. What then evokes or permits the breakthrough? Why is it necessary for some to bribe their consciences and do what they do not approve of doing? Why does all sublimation sometimes fail and overt breakdown occur in the controlling and managing machinery of the personality? Why do we sometimes lose self-control? Why do we "go to pieces"? Why do we explode?

These questions point up a central problem in psychiatry. Why do some people do things they do not want to do? Or things we do not want them to do? Sometimes crimes are motivated by a desperate need to act, to do *something* to break out of a state of passivity, frustration, and helplessness too long endured, like a child who shoots a parent or a teacher after some apparently reasonable act. Granting the universal presence of violence within us all, controlled by will power, conscience, fear of punishment, and other devices, granting the tensions and the temptations that are also common to us all, why do the mechanisms of self-control fail so completely in some individuals? Is there not some pre-existing defect, some moral or cerebral weakness, some gross deficiency of common sense that lets some people tumble or kick or strike or explode, while the rest of us just stagger or sway?

When a psychiatrist examines many prisoners, writes [Seymour] Halleck [in *Psychiatry and the Dilemmas of Crime*], he soon discovers how important in the genesis of the criminal outbreak is the offender's previous *sense of help-lessness or hopelessness.* All of us suffer more or less from infringement of our personal freedom. We fuss about it all the time; we strive to correct it, extend it, and free ourselves from various oppressive or retentive forces. We do not want others to push us around, to control us, to dominate us. We realize this is bound to happen to some extent in an interlocking, interrelated society such as ours. No one truly has complete freedom. But restriction irks us.

The offender feels this way, too. He does not want to be pushed around, controlled, or dominated. And because he often feels that he is thus op-pressed (and actually is) and because he does lack facility in improving his situation without violence, he suffers more intensely from feelings of help-lessness.

Violence and crime are often attempts to escape from madness; and there can be no doubt that some mental illness is a flight from the wish to do the violence or commit the act. Is it hard for the reader to believe that suicides are sometimes committed to forestall the committing of murder? There is no doubt of it. Nor is there any doubt that murder is sometimes committed to avert suicide.

Strange as it may sound, many murderers do not realize whom they are killing, or, to put it another way, that they are killing the wrong people. To be sure, killing anybody is reprehensible enough, but the worst of it is that the person who the killer thinks should die (and he has reasons) is not the person he attacks. Sometimes the victim himself is partly responsible for the crime that is committed against him. It is this unconscious (perhaps sometimes conscious) participation in the crime by the victim that has long held up the very humani-tarian and progressive-sounding program of giving compensation to victims. The public often judges the victim as well as the attacker.

Rape and other sexual offenses are acts of violence so repulsive to our sense of decency and order that it is easy to think of rapists in general as raging, oversexed, ruthless brutes (unless they are conquering heroes). Some rapists are. But most sex crimes are committed by undersexed rather than oversexed individuals, often undersized rather than oversized, and impelled less by lust than by a need for reassurance regarding an impaired masculinity. The unconscious fear of women goads some men with a compulsive urge to conquer, humiliate, hurt, or render powerless some available sample of womanhood. Men who are violently afraid of their repressed but nearly emergent homosexual desires, and men who are afraid of the humiliation of impotence, often try to overcome these fears by violent demonstrations.

The need to deny something in oneself is frequently an underlying motive for certain odd behavior—even up to and including crime. Bravado crimes, often done with particular brutality and ruthlessness, seem to prove *to the doer* that "I am no weakling! I am no sissy! I am no coward. I am no homosexual! I am a tough man who fears nothing." The Nazi storm troopers, many of them mere boys, were systematically trained to stifle all tender emotions and force themselves to be heartlessly brutal.

Man perennially seeks to recover the magic of his childhood days—the control of the mighty by the meek. The flick of an electric light switch, the response of an automobile throttle, the click of a camera, the touch of a match to a skyrocket—these are keys to a sudden and magical display of great power induced by the merest gesture. Is anyone already so blasé that he is no longer thrilled at the opening of a door specially for him by a magic-eye signal? Yet for a few pennies one can purchase a far more deadly piece of magic—a stored explosive and missile encased within a shell which can be ejected from a machine at the touch of a finger so swiftly that no eye can follow. A thousand yards away something falls dead—a rabbit, a deer, a beautiful mountain sheep, a sleeping child, or the President of the United States. Magic! Magnified, projected power. "Look what I can do. I am the greatest!"

It must have come to every thoughtful person, at one time or another, in looking at the revolvers on the policemen's hips, or the guns soldiers and hunters carry so proudly, that these are instruments made for the express purpose of delivering death to someone. The easy availability of these engines of destruction, even to children, mentally disturbed people, professional criminals, gangsters, and even high school girls is something to give one pause. The National Rifle Association and its allies have been able to kill scores of bills that have been introduced into Congress and state legislatures for corrective gun control since the death of President Kennedy. Americans still spend about $2 billion on guns each year.

Fifty years ago, Winston Churchill declared that the mood and temper of the public in regard to crime and criminals is one of the unfailing tests of the civilization of any country. Judged by this standard, how civilized are we?

The chairman of the President's National Crime Commission, Nicholas de B. Katzenbach, declared...that organized crime flourishes in America because enough of the public wants its services, and most citizens are apathetic about its impact. It will continue uncurbed as long as Americans accept it as inevitable and, in some instances, desirable.

Are there steps that we can take which will reduce the aggressive stabs and self-destructive lurches of our less well-managing fellow men? Are there ways to prevent and control the grosser violations, other than the clumsy traditional maneuvers which we have inherited? These depend basically upon intimidation and slow-motion torture. We call it punishment, and justify it with our "feeling." We know it doesn't work.

Yes, there *are* better ways. There are steps that could be taken; some *are* taken. But we move too slowly. Much better use, it seems to me, could be made of the members of my profession and other behavioral scientists than having them deliver courtroom pronunciamentos. The consistent use of a diagnostic clinic would enable trained workers to lay what they can learn about an offender before the judge who would know best how to implement the recommendation.

This would no doubt lead to a transformation of prisons, if not to their total disappearance in their present form and function. Temporary and permanent detention will perhaps always be necessary for a few, especially the professionals, but this could be more effectively and economically performed with new types of "facility" (that strange, awkward word for institution).

I assume it to be a matter of common and general agreement that our object in all this is to protect the community from a repetition of the offense by the most economical method consonant with our other purposes. Our "other purposes" include the desire to prevent these offenses from occurring, to reclaim offenders for social usefulness, if possible, and to detain them in protective custody, if reclamation is *not* possible. But how?

The treatment of human failure or dereliction by the infliction of pain is still used and believed in by many nonmedical people. "Spare the rod and spoil the child" is still considered wise counsel by many.

Whipping is still used by many secondary schoolmasters in England, I am informed, to stimulate study, attention, and the love of learning. Whipping was long a traditional treatment of the "crime" of disobedience on the part of children, pupils, servants, apprentices, employees. And slaves were treated for centuries by flogging for such offenses as weariness, confusion, stupidity, exhaustion, fear, grief, and even overcheerfulness. It was assumed and stoutly defended that these "treatments" cured conditions for which they were administered.

Meanwhile, scientific medicine was acquiring many new healing methods and devices. Doctors can now transplant organs and limbs; they can remove brain tumors and cure incipient cancers; they can halt pneumonia, meningitis, and other infections; they can correct deformities and repair breaks and tears and scars. But these wonderful achievements are accomplished on *willing* subjects, people who voluntarily ask for help by even heroic measures. And the reader will be wondering, no doubt, whether doctors can do anything with or for people who *do not want* to be treated at all, in any way! Can doctors cure willful aberrant behavior? Are we to believe that crime is a *disease* that can be reached by scientific measures? Isn't it merely "natural meanness" that makes all of us do wrong things at times even when we "know better"? And are not self-control, moral stamina, and will power the things needed? Surely there is no medical treatment for the lack of those!

Let me answer this carefully, for much misunderstanding accumulates here. I would say that according to the prevalent understanding of the words, crime is *not* a disease. Neither is it an illness, although I think it *should* be! It *should* be treated, and it could be; but it mostly isn't.

These enigmatic statements are simply explained. Diseases are undesired states of being which have been described and defined by doctors, usually given Greek or Latin appellations, and treated by long-established physical and pharmacological formulae. Illness, on the other hand, is best defined as a state of impaired functioning of such a nature that the public expects the sufferer to repair to the physician for help. The illness may prove to be a disease; more often it is only vague and nameless misery, but something which doctors, not lawyers, teachers, or preachers, are supposed to be able and willing to help.

When the community begins to look upon the expression of aggressive violence as the symptom of an illness or as indicative of illness, it will be because it believes doctors can do something to correct such a condition. At present, some better-informed individuals do believe and expect this. However angry at or sorry for the offender, they want him "treated" in an effective way so that he will cease to be a danger to them. And they know that the traditional punishment, "treatment-punishment," will not effect this.

What *will?* What effective treatment is there for such violence? It will surely have to begin with motivating or stimulating or arousing in a cornered individual the wish and hope and intention to change his methods of dealing with the realities of life. Can this be done by education, medication, counseling, training? I would answer *yes.* It can be done successfully in a majority of cases, if undertaken in time.

The present penal system and the existing legal philosophy do not stimulate or even expect such a change to take place in the criminal. Yet change is what medical science always aims for. The prisoner, like the doctor's other patients, should emerge from his treatment experience a different person, differently equipped, differently functioning, and headed in a different direction than when he began the treatment.

It is natural for the public to doubt that this can be accomplished with criminals. But remember that the public *used* to doubt that change could be effected in the mentally ill. No one a hundred years ago believed mental illness to be curable. Today *all* people know (or should know) that *mental illness is curable* in the great majority of instances and that the prospects and rapidity of cure are directly related to the availability and intensity of proper treatment.

The forms and techniques of psychiatric treatment used today number in the hundreds. No one patient requires or receives all forms, but each patient is studied with respect to his particular needs, his basic assets, his interests, and his special difficulties. A therapeutic team may embrace a dozen workers—as in a hospital setting—or it may narrow down to the doctor and the spouse. Clergymen, teachers, relatives, friends, and even fellow patients often participate informally but helpfully in the process of readaptation.

All of the participants in this effort to bring about a favorable change in the patient—i.e., in his vital balance and life program—are imbued with what we may call a *therapeutic attitude.* This is one in direct antithesis to attitudes of avoidance, ridicule, scorn, or punitiveness. Hostile feelings toward the subject, however justified by his unpleasant and even destructive behavior, are not in the curriculum of therapy or in the therapist. This does not mean that therapists approve of the offensive and obnoxious behavior of the patient; they distinctly disapprove of it. But they recognize it as symptomatic of continued imbalance and disorganization, which is what they are seeking to change. They distinguish between disapproval, penalty, price, and punishment.

Doctors charge fees; they impose certain "penalties" or prices, but they have long since put aside primitive attitudes of retaliation toward offensive patients. A patient may cough in the doctor's face or may vomit on the office rug; a patient may curse or scream or even struggle in the extremity of his pain. But these acts are not "punished." Doctors and nurses have no time or thought for inflicting unnecessary pain even upon patients who may be difficult, disagreeable, provocative, and even dangerous. It is their duty to care for them, to try to make them well, and to prevent them from doing themselves or others harm. This requires love, not hate. This is the deepest meaning of the therapeutic attitude. Every doctor knows this; every worker in a hospital or clinic knows it (or should).

There is another element in the therapeutic attitude. It is the quality of hopefulness. If no one believes that the patient can get well, if no one—not even the doctor—has any hope, there probably won't be any recovery. Hope is just as important as love in the therapeutic attitude.

"But you were talking about the mentally ill," readers may interject, "those poor, confused, bereft, frightened individuals who yearn for help from you doctors and nurses. Do you mean to imply that willfully perverse individuals, our criminals, can be similarly reached and rehabilitated? Do you really believe that effective treatment of the sort you visualize can be applied to people *who do not want any help,* who are so willfully vicious, so well aware of the wrongs they are doing, so lacking in penitence or even common decency that punishment seems to be the only thing left?"

Do I believe there is effective treatment for offenders, and that they *can* be changed? *Most certainly and definitely I do.* Not all cases, to be sure; there are also some physical afflictions which we cannot cure at the moment. Some provision has to be made for incurables—pending new knowledge—and these will include some offenders. But I believe the majority of them would prove to be curable. The willfulness and the viciousness of offenders are part of the thing for which they have to be treated. These must not thwart the therapeutic attitude.

It is simply not true that most of them are "fully aware" of what they are doing, nor is it true that they want no help from anyone, although some of them say so. Prisoners are individuals: some want treatment, some do not. Some don't know what treatment is. Many are utterly despairing and hopeless. Where treatment is made available in institutions, many prisoners seek it even with the full knowledge that doing so will not lessen their sentences. In some prisons, seeking treatment by prisoners is frowned upon by the officials.

Various forms of treatment are even now being tried in some progressive courts and prisons over the country—educational, social, industrial, religious, recreational, and psychological treatments. Socially acceptable behavior, new work-play opportunities, new identity and companion patterns all help toward community reacceptance. Some parole officers and some wardens have been extremely ingenious in developing these modalities of rehabilitation and reconstruction—more than I could list here even if I knew them all. But some are trying. The secret of success in all programs, however, is the replacement of the punitive attitude with a therapeutic attitude.

Offenders with propensities for impulsive and predatory aggression should not be permitted to live among us unrestrained by some kind of social control. *But the great majority of offenders, even "criminals," should never become prisoners if we want to "cure" them.*

There are now throughout the country many citizens' action groups and programs for the prevention and control of crime and delinquency. With such attitudes of inquiry and concern, the public could acquire information (and incentive) leading to a change of feeling about crime and criminals. It will discover how unjust is much so-called "justice," how baffled and frustrated many judges are by the ossified rigidity of old-fashioned, obsolete laws and state constitutions which effectively prevent the introduction of sensible procedures to replace useless, harmful ones.

I want to proclaim to the public that things are not what it wishes them to be, and will only become so if it will take an interest in the matter and assume some responsibility for its own self-protection.

Will the public listen?

If the public does become interested, it will realize that we must have more facts, more trial projects, more checked results. It will share the dismay of the President's Commission in finding that no one knows much about even the incidence of crime with any definiteness or statistical accuracy.

The average citizen finds it difficult to see how any research would in any way change his mind about a man who brutally murders his children. But just such inconceivably awful acts most dramatically point up the need for research. Why should—how can—a man become so dreadful as that in our culture? How is such a man made? Is it comprehensible that he can be born to become so depraved?

There are thousands of questions regarding crime and public protection which deserve scientific study. What makes some individuals maintain their interior equilibrium by one kind of disturbance of the social structure rather than by another kind, one that would have landed him in a hospital? Why do some individuals specialize in certain types of crime? Why do so many young people reared in areas of delinquency and poverty and bad example never become habitual delinquents? (Perhaps this is a more important question than why some of them do.)

The public has a fascination for violence, and clings tenaciously to its yen for vengeance, blind and deaf to the expense, futility, and dangerousness of the resulting penal system. But we are bound to hope that this will yield in time to the persistent, penetrating light of intelligence and accumulating scientific knowledge. The public will grow increasingly ashamed of its cry for retaliation, its persistent demand to punish. This is its crime, *our* crime against criminals— and, incidentally, our crime against ourselves. For before we can diminish our sufferings from the ill-controlled aggressive assaults of fellow citizens, we must renounce the philosophy of punishment, the obsolete, vengeful penal attitude. In its place we would seek a comprehensive constructive social attitude— therapeutic in some instances, restraining in some instances, but preventive in its total social impact.

In the last analysis this becomes a question of personal morals and values. No matter how glorified or how piously disguised, vengeance as a human motive must be personally repudiated by each and every one of us. This is the message of old religions and new psychiatries. Unless this message is heard, unless we, the people—the man on the street, the housewife in the home—can give up our delicious satisfactions in opportunities for vengeful retaliation on scapegoats, we cannot expect to preserve our peace, our public safety, or our mental health.

The Problem with Rehabilitation

American Friends Service Committee

Prior to the latter part of the eighteenth century, imprisonment in the Western world was usually used only for pretrial detention or short jail terms. Instead, the usual sanctions imposed after conviction were capital punishment (even for trivial offenses), dismemberment, banishment, flogging, and monetary fines. One of the gentlest punishments was public humiliation in the stocks.

The transformation from imprisonment as an exceptional measure to its use as the typical sanction for crime was the product of the complex economic, political, intellectual, social, and humanitarian changes that pervaded nine-teenth-century life. The revolution against indiscriminate use of the death penalty demanded the development of alternative measures. Abandoned ships were pressed into service and at least one prison (California's San Quentin) was built where it was because that was the point at which a prison hulk was swept ashore during a storm. Transportation of criminals, as from England to Australia, proved to be a short-term expedient both because of the predictable opposition of the receiving colonies and because colonization at government expense ultimately proved more of an inducement than a deterrent to crime.

From "The Fallacy of the Individualized Treatment Model" in *Struggle for Justice: A Report on Crime and Punishment in America*. Prepared for the American Friends Service Committee. Copyright 1971, by Hill and Wang, Inc., a division of Farrar, Straus and Giroux, Inc. Reprinted by permission.

The prison as we now know it is perhaps most of all the product of the Industrial Revolution, which created a need for cheap labor and for a time made the criminal as much an asset as a liability. Before business and union pressures curbed such "unfair competition," the exploitation of convict labor often enabled penal institutions to break even or perhaps show a profit.

Concomitant with these economic determinants of a productive penology were the burgeoning concepts of democracy and the inalienable rights of man. Democratic theory required the assimilation of deviance into the dominant culture and provided a new view of the criminal as someone to be reformed as well as punished. The new concept of the prison was rationalized both by the English utilitarian theorists and, on this side of the Atlantic, by the humanitarian reformers exemplified by the Pennsylvania Quakers. The utilitarians perceived crime as a natural phenomenon flowing directly from humanity's self-seeking nature. Since human beings are motivated to maximize pleasure and minimize pain, they can be expected to transgress when they see it is to their advantage to do so. To ensure public safety, punishment for a criminal act needed only to offer sufficiently more pain than the transgression was worth, thereby deterring the offender from further crime and warning other potential offenders.

The Quakers in Pennsylvania differed largely by placing increased emphasis on reformation. They developed a solitary confinement system that, by holding the convict in total isolation and thus quarantining him from other prisoners, was supposed to encourage his meditation, reflection, and penitence. Though the expensiveness of this system never allowed it to be given a thorough trial, an attempt was made to perpetuate the isolation of convicts through such devices as the Auburn (silent) system.

The concept of a prison centered on forced convict labor was an apparently happy marriage of reformism and practicality. To view labor as therapy and idleness as the root of crime was an appealing notion for an economically expanding America with its Puritan moral heritage. The fact that the prisoner insofar as feasible paid the costs of his own imprisonment with his labor made long-term imprisonment economically and politically practicable. From the outset, however, there was an inherent dilemma in this approach. If prison was to reform, it had to provide incentives for conformity and hard work. But if it was to deter criminality, it must threaten a regime more unpleasant than that of the worst-off segments in the free society outside. This practical dilemma confined penal administration within narrow limits, for the rewards it could offer, whether monetary or psychological, were necessarily petty.

In the latter part of the nineteenth century and increasingly in the twentieth century, the decline of the prison as a productive economic institution has vitiated most of the purported therapy of "hard labor." Idleness or meaningless made-work is today the characteristic regime of many, perhaps most, inmates. More important, the concept of reformation as something achieved through penitence or the acquisition of working skills and habits has been deemphasized because of developments in social and behavioral science. Varying scientific or pseudoscientific approaches to crime, although in conflict with one another and unconfirmed by hard scientific data, view criminals as distinct biological, psychological, or social-cultural types.

Such theories all share a more or less deterministic premise, holding that man's behavior is caused by social or psychological forces located outside his consciousness and therefore beyond his control. Rehabilitation, therefore, is deemed to require expert help so as to provide the inmate with the understanding and guidance that it is assumed he cannot achieve on his own.

The individualized treatment model, the outcome of this historical process, has for nearly a century been the ideological spring from which almost all actual and proposed reform in criminal justice has been derived. It would be hard to exaggerate the power of this idea or the extent of its influence. In recent years it has been the conceptual foundation of such widely divergent approaches to criminal justice as the President's Crime Commission Report, the British *Why Prison?—A Quaker View of Imprisonment and Some Alternatives,* and the American Law Institute's Model Penal Code. Like other conceptions that become so entrenched that they slip imperceptibly into dogma, the treatment model has been assumed rather than analyzed, preached rather than evaluated.

The underlying rationale of this treatment model is deceptively simple. It rejects inherited concepts of criminal punishment as the payment of a debt owed to society, a debt proportioned to the magnitude of the offender's wrong. Instead it would save the offender through constructive measures of reformation, protect society by keeping the offender locked up until that reformation is accomplished, and reduce the crime rate not only by using cure-or-detention to eliminate recidivism, but hopefully also by the identification of potential criminals in advance so that they can be rendered harmless by preventive treatment. Thus the dispassionate behavioral expert displaces judge the theologian. The particular criminal act becomes irrelevant except insofar as it has diagnostic significance in classifying and treating the actor's particular criminal typology. Carried to an extreme, the sentence for all crimes would be the same: an indeterminate commitment to imprisonment, probation, or parole, whichever was dictated at any particular time by the treatment program. Any sentence would be the time required by the treatment program....to bring about rehabilitation, a period which might be a few weeks or a lifetime.

The treatment model's judicious blend of humanitarian, practical welfare, and scientific ancestry was nicely illustrated sixty years ago by the Elmira Reformatory's Zebulon R. Brockway:

> The common notion of a moral responsibility based on freedom should no longer be made a foundation principle for criminal laws, court procedure, and prison treatment. The claim of such responsibility need neither be denied nor affirmed, but put aside as being out of place in a system of treatment of offenders for the purpose of public protection. Together with abrogation of this responsibility goes, too, any awesome regard for individual liberty of choice and action by imprisoned criminals.

Their habitual conduct and indeed their related character must needs be directed
and really determined by their legalized custodians....

The perfected reformatory will be the receptacle and refinery of antisocial
humans who are held in custody under discretional indeterminateness for the
purpose of the public protection. Legal and sentimental inhibitions of necessary
coercion for the obdurate, intractable element of the institution population will be
removed and freedom given for the wide use of unimpassioned useful, forceful
measures. Frequent relapses to crime of prisoners discharged from these reformatories will be visited upon the management as are penalties for official malfeasance.
The change will be, in short, a change from the reign of sentiment swerved by the
feelings to a passionless scientific procedure pursuing welfare.[1]

As with any model, of course, its implementation has been uneven, often
halting, and seldom complete. Perhaps the closest approximation to the ideal
is in certain so-called sexual psychopath statutes under which an indeterminate
and potentially lifelong incarceration can be ordered as a civil commitment
without conviction of any crime. Judicial power is yielded grudgingly, however,
and legislators cling to the notion that maximum penalties should be graded
according to their ideas of relative blameworthiness, so that the result is a
patchwork quilt of inconsistent rationales. Overall, however, the movement
toward the individualized treatment model is unmistakable. Every state has
some form of parole, which provides a core indeterminacy. Compared to the
median time served, the maximum possible sentence for most crimes is so
excessive that the disposition of almost any conviction utilizes the treatment
process in some manner.

While opposition to "mollycoddling" prisoners still exists, the basic thrust
of the model has been accepted by almost all liberals, reformers of all persua-
sions, the scientific community, probably a majority of judges, and those of
law-and-order persuasion who perceive the model's repressive potential.

How has the model united such a motley collection of supporters? Its
conceptual simplicity and scientific aura appeal to the pragmatism of a society
confident that American know-how can reduce any social problem to manageable proportions. Its professed repudiation of retribution adds moral uplift
and an inspirational aura. At the same time, the treatment model is sufficiently
vague in concept and flexible in practice to accommodate both the traditional
and utilitarian objectives of criminal law administration. It claims to protect
society by incapacitating the prisoner in an institution until pronounced sufficiently reformed. This prospect is unpalatable enough and sufficiently threatening in its uncertainty to provide at least as effective a deterrent to potential
offenders as that of the traditional eye-for-an-eye model. Maximum flexibility
is required to achieve the model's goal, that of treatment individualized to
each offender's unique needs, so the system's administrators are granted
broad discretionary powers. Whatever the effect on offenders, these powers
have secured the support of a growing body of administrators, prosecutors,

[1]Zebulon R. Brockway, *Fifty Years of Prison Service* (New York, 1912).

and judges, for it facilitates the discharge of their managerial duties and frees them from irksome legal controls. Even the proponents of retribution, although denied entry through the front door, soon discovered that harsh sentences could be accommodated within the treatment model as long as they are rationalized in terms of public protection or the necessity for prolonged regimes of reeducation.

The treatment model tends to be all things to all people. This partially accounts for the paradox that while the model's ideological command has become ever more secure, its implementation has tended to form rather than substance. In fact, the model has never commanded more than lip service from most of its more powerful adherents. The authority given those who manage the system, a power more absolute than that found in any other sphere of law, has concealed the practices carried on in the name of the treatment model. At every level—from prosecutor to parole-board member—the concept of individualization has been used to justify secret procedures, unreviewable decision making, and an unwillingness to formulate anything other than the most general rules or policy. Whatever else may be credited to a century of individualized-treatment reform effort, there has been a steady expansion of the scope of the criminal justice system and a consolidation of the state's absolute power over the lives of those caught in the net.

The irony of this outcome emphasizes the importance of a searching examination of the assumptions underlying the individualized treatment model. Hopefully such an analysis will illuminate efforts to delineate the proper role of criminal justice in a free and democratic society. It may also help us to understand what factors have perpetuated our present criminal judicial system decade after decade in the face of compelling evidence of its systematic malfunctioning.

UNEXAMINED ASSUMPTIONS

When one probes beneath the surface of the treatment model, one finds not only untenable factual assumptions, but also disturbing value judgments that pose serious policy questions for our society. Here are some of the more perplexing of these problems with which we will be concerned:

1 A model of criminal justice that rests on the proposition that at least in large measure *crime is a problem of individual pathology;* that is, the model assumes that crime rates can be reduced by the treatment and cure of individual criminals and that future crimes can be prevented by the incapacitation of those predicted to be dangerous until they are cured. The difficulty of identifying the characteristics of such a pathology, if indeed it exists at all, will be noted below. To the extent that it is also acknowledged that social and environmental factors, such as slums, poverty, unemployment, and parental guidance or the lack of it, also "cause" crime, a program of individualized treatment is inadequate. If social factors cannot be controlled or predicted, the relevance of

individualized treatment is decreased and may be negligible. If the social pathology assumed to encourage a criminal culture is not being changed, is there ethical justification for individualized preventive detention? A prisoner detained to prevent crimes that could be avoided by social reforms may bear a greater resemblance to a scapegoat than to either a patient or a public enemy. We do not and probably cannot know the relative contributions of individual and social pathology to criminality; to the extent that social causation is relevant, the rationale for individualization is undercut. To date, our society has largely ignored this dilemma.

2 At the level of individual pathology, treatment ideology *assumes that we know something about the individual causes of crime.* If it is to have any scientific basis, such knowledge must be based on the study of representative samples both of criminals and of control groups of noncriminals. Comparison of the two may reveal factors that distinguish the criminals from the control groups; whether such differences have any causal significance poses additional research problems which, in this context, we have no occasion to face. We have libraries full of criminological research on the etiology of crime, but most of it has been conducted without control groups and therefore tells us nothing about causation (and usually not much else, either). In all this research, moreover, the data about criminals are derived from those who have been subject to correctional regimes and therefore identified and made available for study. But only a small proportion of those who commit criminal acts are caught, convicted, and subjected to correctional treatment. The criminals who are the subjects of all our research are almost certainly not representative. Our available sample is heavily biased toward criminals from the poor and outcast classes and away from the white middle and upper classes. Bias is also introduced by selective enforcement of criminal law. Welfare fraud or manslaughter in a ghetto barroom brawl is likely to land the perpetrator on the rolls of diagnosed criminals; business fraud or manslaughter by automobile on the freeway goes largely unprosecuted and unstudied. Therefore, even if we had a body of adequately controlled research findings it would merely describe the kinds of persons subjected to criminal treatment in a society where race and poverty are major determinants for the application of the criminal label. Such data might afford revealing insights about the administration of criminal justice in such a society, but would hardly provide the basis for a usable science of individual criminal pathology. We think it is important to ask why treatment ideology was embraced with such enthusiasm without bothering to inquire about the validity of the science on which it depends.

3 Even if the existence, significance, and characteristics of an individual criminal pathology are unknown, one might in theory still evolve *treatment methods that turned criminals into noncriminals.* It has been a frequent occurrence in medicine to stumble upon treatments that worked despite ignorance about the cause of the disease or the reasons for the treatment's success. The minimum methodological standards for investigating this possibility as to any particular treatment are (a) comparison with control groups of similar

subjects who are not treated; (b) control of other variables, such as maturation or changed environmental or social conditions, to negate the possibility that factors other than the treatment process were responsible for the outcome; and (c) reasonably reliable criteria for determining success or failure. Most research fails the first and second tests. Control groups are conspicuous by their rarity in treatment evaluation investigations. But the apparently insoluble problem of such research is the third requirement: the necessity of establishing indicators to distinguish success from failure. This is true even if one proceeds at the most superficial level, defining failure as recidivism, the commission of another crime following treatment. *We have no way of determining the real rate of recidivism because most criminals are undetected and most suspected criminals do not end up being convicted.* Recidivism rates are also subject to both deliberate manipulation and unconscious bias. Parole revocation (failure) rates can be manipulated for public relations or other purposes. Documented examples of such research falsification are known and the practice is probably not uncommon. Unconscious bias is introduced by the tendency of predictive and diagnostic judgments to become self-fulfilling prophecies. For example, those released on parole from a treatment program are likely to be formally or informally classified for the purpose of parole supervision into good risks (responded favorably to treatment) and poor risks (resisted treatment). The "poor risks" are likely to be subjected to tighter surveillance; their violations are therefore much more likely to be detected; their parole is more likely to be revoked; and the resulting differences in recidivism rates emerge as a "research finding" validating the efficacy of the particular treatment program.

4 In the absence of credible scientific data on the causation or treatment of crime, *the content of the correctional treatment program rests largely on speculation or on assumptions unrelated to criminality.* Thus one finds that accepted correctional practice is dominated by indoctrination in white Anglo-Saxon middle-class values. In institutions this means learning a trade, establishing work habits through the therapy of labor, keeping clean and clean-shaven, minding your own business, and acquiring such basic or supplemental educational skills and religious training as the institution might provide and the parole board might think relevant. On probation or parole, in addition to abstaining from crime, the ingredients for success are similar: sticking at a job, staying where you belong, supporting your family, avoiding bad companionship and bad habits, and abiding by the spoken ideals of conventional sexual morality. Without debating the merits of these ingredients of the good life— those of us not being corrected are free to take them or leave them—the fact that the correlation between such Puritan virtues and crime causation is speculative or nonexistent would, one might suppose, have raised some troubling questions. If the treatment has no proven (or likely) relationship to criminal pathology, what is its purpose? In the absence of such evidence, what is the propriety of coerced cultural indoctrination?

The closest parallel we can think of in American history, which developed at the same time as the correctional treatment model in response to the same kinds of reform pressures, was the policy of compulsory assimilation of American Indians, which the Indian Bureau attempted to carry out from 1849 through the end of the century. The deliberate discrediting of Indian cultural values, compulsory proselytizing, and the destruction of the tribal economic base were supplemented by government boarding schools, which Indian children were forced to attend throughout their formative years. The program and style of these schools bore striking resemblance to the correctional treatment model. There are other similarities as well. The correctional system also draws most of its clients from subcultures; perhaps half are from racial minorities (including some Indians on their second round of "treatment") and more than half from cultures of poverty or near-poverty. We do not suggest that the parallel is complete or that it follows that the motivation and purpose of the correctional system's treatment program is necessarily the same as the policy of the nineteenth-century Indian Bureau. But we are disturbed both by the similarities and by the absence of any probing dialogue that might explore the whole purpose and philosophy of correctional treatment.

5 Using rates of recidivism as the criterion for evaluating the success or failure of criminal justice programs poses more fundamental problems than the unreliability of the statistics. Surely it is ironic that although treatment ideology purports to look beyond the criminal's crime to the whole personality, and bases its claims to sweeping discretionary power on this rationale, *it measures its success against the single factor of an absence of reconviction for a criminal act.* Whether or not the subject of the treatment process has acquired greater self-understanding, a sense of purpose and power in his own destiny, or a new awareness of his relatedness to man and the universe is not subject to statistical study and so is omitted from the evaluation.

It will make a critical difference for the future of democracy whether our institutional and noninstitutional environments encourage the creation of morally autonomous, self-disciplined people who exercise independent judgment and purposefulness from their own inner strength, or whether instead they tend to stunt the human potential by training programs that, as with animals, condition their subjects to an unthinking conformity to inflexible, externally imposed rules. In studying the criminal justice system we have found few things to be thankful for, but the ineffectiveness of correctional treatment may well be one of those few. The only kind of morality the sticks-and-carrots regime of indeterminate treatment in correctional institutions can teach is the externally imposed variety. If such correctional methods really did work, it might be more success than a free society could endure.

6 *Remaking people is an educational function. What, then, of prison education?* We typically find an inadequate staff in a depressing environment with minimal facilities and equipment (no field studies here) operating an adult educational program across class, race, cultural, and status barriers for inmates whose chief motivation is to chalk up attendance marks so as to satisfy The Man on the Parole Board. From this soil we expect to reap the miracle—the maturation of a unique human being. At least that is what one would conclude from the uncritical acceptance of prison education as a "good thing" and a hallmark of society's humanity to prisoners.

7 The *discretionary power* granted to prosecutors, judges, and administrators in an individualized treatment system is unique in the legal system, awesome in scope and by its nature uncontrollable. If the theory posits that any one of many variables can be determinative of any individual decision, standards are necessarily nonexistent or so vague as to be meaningless, and review by any sort of court or appellate process is impossible. Yet it is evidently accepted without question that absolute power does not corrupt when exercised by government agents upon criminals. The chronicles of criminology and jurisprudence are filled with paeans celebrating the wise discretion of humble and contrite judges and administrative agencies. Their authors, however, would not for one moment surrender to the discretion of those same judges and agencies the assessment of their income and property taxes in accordance with the official's individualized determination of the subject's value to his country and his ability to pay. Indeed, the best antidote to being swept off one's feet by the claims made for the necessity and importance of the discretion that permeates criminal justice administration is to engage in a comparative examination of criminal law and the laws governing taxation, corporations, and commercial transactions. One will speedily discover that when it comes to matters concerning their vested interests, the men who have the power to write the law in this country give short shrift to discretion. They are not about to delegate the determination of the size of the oil depletion allowance to the discretion of the local internal revenue agent. If discretion is written into major law, it is because legislators are confident from the outset that they will be able to control its exercise.

Criminal justice is the surviving bastion of absolute legal discretion. The last of its colleagues, of which it is reputed to be the heir, was the Office for the Administration of Colonial Affairs.

8 In coming finally to the end of this preliminary enumeration of problem areas, we reach the area that is the most perplexing and the culmination of what has gone before. We have sketched a number of problematic features of a correctional treatment model of criminal justice. Most of the problems and defects that have been posed are not very difficult to understand; one might even categorize a number of them as obvious. How is one to account, then, for the enthusiastic and uncritical acceptance by most of the liberal and progressive elements in our society of reformative, indeterminate, individualized treatment as the ideal goal of a criminal justice system?

There is something about this phenomenon akin to religious conversion, an acceptance of what appears to be true and valuable, what we want to be true, even though it cannot be reduced to anything more precise than vague generalities. It seems obvious that extremely complex forces lie behind liberal treatment ideology's mission to control not just the crimes but the way of life of others. Guilt about the gulf that separates our material well-being from poverty and oppression may account for some of the prejudice against and irrational fear of the poor and the oppressed; or it may help to account for our eagerness to hand over the problem to specialists as a way of relieving our anxiety. Once you have delegated a problem to an expert, you are off the hook.

If we could make some sense out of this extraordinary willingness to believe unreasonable things about criminal justice and corrections, we might begin to have some understanding of the forces that perpetuate so unjust a system. We explore this problem further below; it is hardly necessary to state here, however, that we cannot provide a satisfactory solution to this major puzzle. We do, however, hope to promote its analysis and encourge its study. Such an inquiry seems to us to be prerequisite to effectuating basic changes in our concepts and practices of criminal justice. The most stubborn obstacles to such change are not, in our opinion, the growing problem of violent crime or the hard-line advocates of punitive law-and-order repression or the rigidity and increasingly conservative polarization of our law enforcement and correctional bureaucracies or the perversity of adverse public opinion. Serious as they are, such forces can be contained if adequate options are developed and promoted. We suspect that much of the current strength of these conservative forces derives from the fact that there is no tenable alternative model of a criminal justice system that affords accommodation of such competing vaflues as equality, respect for individual dignity and autonomy, encouragement of cultural diversity, and the need for a reasonably orderly society. The correctional treatment model does not begin to meet this need....

Justifying Punishment

R.S. Downie

Traditionally two very general sorts of justification have been offered for the practice of punishment: retributivist and utilitarian. According to the theory of retribution...guilt is a necessary and a sufficient condition of the infliction of punishment on an offender. Is the theory plausible?

It might be said against it that it does not reflect actual practice either in the law or in more informal normative orders such as schools or the family. In these institutions we find such practices as the relaxation of punishment for first offenders, warnings, pardons, and so on. Hence, it may seem that actual penal practice is at variance with the retributive theory if it is saying that guilt is a necessary and a sufficient condition of punishment. Only in games, it may be said, do we find a sphere where the infringement of rules is a necessary and a

From R.S. Downie, *Roles and Values* (London: Methuen and Co., Ltd., 1971). Copyright 1971, R.S. Downie. Reprinted by permission.

sufficient condition of the infliction of a penalty, and even in games there may be a 'playing the advantage' rule.

It is not clear, however, that the retributivist need be disturbed by this objection. He might take a high-handed line with the objection and say that if it is the case that actual penal practice does not reflect his theory then so much the (morally) worse for actual practice. Whatever people in fact do, he might argue, it is morally fitting that guilt be a necessary and a sufficient condition of the infliction of punishment.

A less high-handed line, and one more likely to conciliate the opponents of the retributivist theory, is to say that the statement of the theory so far provided is to be taken as a very general one. When it is said that guilt is a necessary and a sufficient condition of punishment it is not intended that punishment should in every case follow inexorably. There are cases where extenuating circumstances may be discovered and in such cases it would be legitimate to recommend mercy or even to issue a pardon. It is unfair to the retributivist to depict his theory as the inflexible application of rules. There is nothing in the theory which forbids it the use of all the devices in the law and in less formal institutions whereby punishment may in certain circumstances be mitigated. Even the sternest of retributivists can allow for the concept of mercy. Perhaps the objection may be avoided completely if the theory is stated more carefully as: guilt and nothing other than guilt may justify the infliction of punishment. To state the theory in this way is to enable it to accommodate the complex operation of extenuating factors which modify the execution of actual systems of law. But to say this is not yet to explain why guilt and nothing other than guilt may justify the infliction of punishment. Indeed, we might ask the retributivist to tell us why we should punish anyone at all.

Retributivists give a variety of answers to this question. One is that punishment annuls the evil which the offender has created. It is not easy to make sense of this claim. No amount of punishment can undo an offence that has been committed: what has been has been. Sometimes metaphors of punishment washing away sin are used to explain how punishment can annul evil. But such ideas can mislead. Certainly, the infliction of punishment may, as a matter of psychological fact, remove some people's *feelings* of guilt. But we may query whether this is necessarily a good thing. Whether or not it is, however, it is not the same as annulling the evil committed.

A second retributivist idea is that the offender has had some sort of illicit pleasure and that the infliction of pain will redress the moral balance. People speak of the criminal as 'paying for what he has done' or as 'reaping a harvest of bitterness'; the infliction of suffering is regarded as a fitting response to crime. But this view may be based on a confusion of the idea that 'the punishment must fit the crime', which is acceptable if it means only that punishment ought to be proportionate, with the idea that punishment is a fitting response to crime, which is not so obviously acceptable. It may be that the traditional *lex talionis* is based on a confusion of the two ideas. At any rate, it is the idea of punishment as the 'fitting response' which is essential to the retributivist position.

A third claim sometimes made by the retributivists is that an offender has a right to punishment. This claim is often mocked by the critics of retributivism on the grounds that it is an odd right that would gladly be waived by the holder! It might be thought that the view can be defended on the grounds that the criminal's right to punishment is merely the right correlative to the authority's duty to punish him. Such a defence is not plausible, however, for, even supposing there is a right correlative to a legal authority's duty to punish criminals, it is much more plausible to attribute this right to the society which is protected by the deterrent effect of punishment.

There are two arguments, more convincing than the first, which can be put forward in defence of the view that the offender has a right to punishment. One of these requires us to take the view in conjunction with the premise that punishment annuls evil. If punishment can somehow wash away the guilt of the offender then it is plausible to say that the offender has a right to be punished. The difficulty with this argument, however, is that it simply transfers the problems. It is now intelligible to say that the offender has a right to punishment, but, as we have already seen, it is not at all clear what it means to say that punishment annuls evil.

The other argument invites us to consider what the alternative is to punishing the criminal. The alternative, as we shall shortly see, may be to 'treat' him and attempt a 'cure' by means of various psychological techniques. Now this would be rejected as morally repugnant by many retributivists, on the grounds that an offender has freely decided to break the law and should be regarded as a self-determining rational being who knew what he was doing. An offender, so described, may be said to have a right to *punishment* (as distinct from psychological treatment, moral indoctrination, or brain-washing in the interests of the State). Such an argument produces a favourable response from many criminals who, when they have served their time in prison, feel that the matter is then over and that they ought to be protected from the attentions of moral doctors and the like. So stated, there may be some truth in the 'right to punishment' doctrine, however easy it is for the sophisticated to mock it.

So far we have been concerned to suggest detailed criticism of the retributivist theory. But there are two general criticisms which are commonly made of it at the moment (for it is a most unfashionable theory in philosophical and other circles). The first is that insofar as its claims are intelligible and prima facie acceptable, they are disguised utilitarian claims.

This criticism is valid against certain ways in which retributivists sometimes state their claims. For example, they have sometimes regarded the infliction of punishment as the 'emphatic denunciation by the community of a crime'. But we might well ask why society should bother to denounce crime unless it hopes by that means to do some good and diminish it. A second example of a retributivist claim which easily lends itself to utilitarian interpretation is that the infliction of punishment reforms the criminal by shocking him into a full awareness of his moral turpitude. The question here is not whether this claim is in fact plausible (criminologists do not find it so) but whether the justification of punishment it offers is esssentially retributivist. It seems rather to be utilitarian, and in this respect like the more familiar version of the reform theory we shall shortly examine.

It seems, then, that this criticism does have some force against certain retributivist claims, or against certain ways of stating retributivist claims. But the criticism does not do radical damage to retributivism. Provided the theory is stated in such a way that it is clear that the justification of punishment is necessarily only that it is a fitting response to an offender, then the fact that punishment may sometimes also do good need not count against retributivism. It is, however, an implication of retributivism that it must sometimes be obligatory to punish when punishment is not expected to do any good beyond itself.

It is precisely this implication which is used as the basis for the second criticism of retributivism. This criticism is a straightforward moral judgement, that the theory is morally objectionable in that it requires us to inflict punishment, which is by definition unpleasant and therefore as such evil, for no compensating greater good. The critics therefore invite us to reject the theory as a barbarous residue of old moral ideas.

In the context of philosophical analysis it is important to avoid taking sides in moral argument, as far as this can be done. But it may be worth pointing out that perhaps the great majority of ordinary people have sympathy with some form of retributivism. Contemporary philosophers often appeal to what the 'ordinary moral agent' would do or say in certain circumstances, or what the morality of 'common sense' would hold on certain topics, but if they make this appeal in settling questions of the justification of punishment they may find that the ordinary person adheres to some form of retributivism. Since there is generally something to be said for an appeal in moral matters to what people ordinarily think, let us consider whether the implication of retributivism is really so morally repugnant.

The implication is that on some occasions it will be obligatory to punish an offender even though this will do no good beyond itself, and that even when some further good is in fact accomplished by the punishment this is irrelevant to its justification. Now it may be that this implication is thought to be morally objectionable because the clause 'no good beyond itself' is equated with 'no good at all'. But a retributivist will claim that the mere fact of inflicting punishment on an offender is good in itself. It is not that a *further* good will result (although it may do so) but that the very fact of the punishment is fitting and to that extent good.

This argument may be made more convincing by an example. Let us suppose that a Nazi war criminal responsible for the cruel torture and deaths of many innocent people has taken refuge in South America where he is living *incognito*.

Let us suppose that he has become a useful and prosperous member of the community in which he is living. Let us suppose that the whereabouts of this criminal are discovered and it becomes possible to bring him to justice and punish him. It is very doubtful whether such punishment will have any utilitarian value at all; the criminal will not in any way be 'reformed' by treatment, and the deterrence of other war criminals seems an unrealistic aim. We can at least imagine that the punishment of such a criminal will have minimal utilitarian value and may even have disvalue in utilitarian terms. Nevertheless, many people might still feel that the criminal ought to be brought to justice and punished, that irrespective of any further good which may or may not result from the punishment, it is in itself good that such a man should be punished for his crimes. To see some force in this special pleading is to see that retributivism is not completely without moral justification although it can never on its own constitute a complete theory of the justification of punishment.

I have tried to find merits in the retributivist theory because it is frequently dismissed with contempt by philosophers and others at the present time, but we shall now consider theories of the justification of punishment with more obvious appeal. These are all different forms of utilitarianism and they therefore have in common the claim that the justification of punishment necessarily rests in the value of its consequences. There are two common forms of utilitarian justification: in terms of deterrence and in terms of reform.

According to the deterrence form of the utilitarian theory the justification of punishment lies in the fact that the threats of the criminal law will deter potential wrong-doers. But since threats are not efficacious unless they are carried out, proved wrong-doers must in fact have unpleasant consequences visited on them. The increase in the pain of the criminal, however, is balanced by the increase in the happiness of society, where crime has been checked. The theory is modified to account for two classes of people for whom the threats of the law cannot operate; the cases of infants and madmen on the one hand, and on the other hand cases in which accident, coercion and other 'excusing conditions' affected the action. In such cases the threats of the law would clearly have little effect and punishment would therefore do no social good.

A deterrent theory of this general sort has often been accepted by utilitarian philosophers from the time of Bentham, but it is frequently criticized. The most common criticism is that it does not rule out the infliction of 'punishment' or suffering on the innocent. Utilitarians, that is, argue that where excusing conditions exist punishment would be wasted or would be socially useless. But their argument shows only that the threat of punishment would not be effective in particular cases where there are excusing conditions; the infliction of 'punishment' in such cases would still have deterrent values on *others* who might be tempted to break the law. Moreover, people who have committed a crime may hope to escape by pleading excusing conditions and hence there would be social efficacy in punishing those with excuses. Presumably this is the point of 'strict liability' in the civil law. But if the deterrent theory commits us to such implications it is at variance with our ordinary views, for we do not accept that the punishment of the lunatic (say) is permissible whatever its social utility.

Utilitarians have sometimes tried to meet this objection by arguing that a system of laws which did not provide for excusing conditions might cause great misery to society. There would be widespread alarm in any society in which no excusing conditions were allowed to affect judicial decisions in criminal cases, and indeed (a utilitarian might argue) such a system might not receive the co-operation of society at large, without which no judicial system can long operate. The utilitarian reply, then, is that while punishment is justified by its deterrent value we must allow excusing conditions since they also have social utility.

It is doubtful, however, whether this reply is adequate. For if excusing conditions are allowed only insofar as they have social utility there remains the possibility that some unusual cases may crop up in which the infliction of suffering or 'punishment' on an innocent person would have social utility which would far outweigh the social utility of excusing him. This is not only a logical possibility on the deterrent theory but a very real possibility in communities in which the 'framing' of an innocent person might prevent rioting of a racial or religious kind. But this implication of the deterrent theory is at odds with widely accepted moral views. Rather it would be held that the rights of the individual must come before the good of society. This does not mean that the rights of the individual must never be sacrificed to the general good but only that there are certain basic rights, the rights of man, or rights which belong to persons as such, which must never be violated no matter what social good will accrue. It is the weakness of the deterrent version of the utilitarian justification of punishment that it cannot accommodate this truth. Here the deterrent theory contrasts adversely with the retributive theory which does stress the rights of the individual against those of society.

Despite this criticism, however, the deterrent theory cannot be entirely dismissed for it does have relevance at the level of legislation. Whereas it is a failure if it is regarded as an attempt to provide a complete justification of punishment it does succeed in bringing out one of the functions of punishment—that of acting as a deterrent to the potential criminal.

The second conception in terms of which utilitarians try to justify the infliction of punishment is that of 'reform'. They argue that when a criminal is in prison or in some other detention centre a unique opportunity is created for equipping him with a socially desirable set of skills and attitudes. The claim is that such a procedure will have a social utility which outweighs that of conventional punishment.[1] The theory is often based on a psychological or sociological

---

[1]This theory must be distinguished from that mentioned in the discussion of retributivism—that conventional punishment reforms by 'shocking' the criminal into an awareness of what he has done. Apart from the question of its consistency with the tenets of retributivism this claim does not seem to be supported by the facts; conventional punishment is said by criminologists in fact to increase the criminal's resentment against society.

study of the effects of certain kinds of deprivation, cultural starvation, and general lack of education on the individual's outlook, and the hope is that these may be put right by re-education or psychological treatment in the period when there would otherwise be conventional punishment.

There are certain oddities about the reform theory if it is intended to be a justification for punishment. The first is that the processes of reform need not involve anything which is painful or unpleasant in the conventional sense. Some critics of the theory would rule it out on that ground alone. In reply, the advocates of the theory might say that insofar as the criminal is *compelled* to undergo reform the process can count as 'punishment' in the conventional sense; at least the criminal is deprived of his liberty and that is in itself unpleasant whatever else may happen to him during his period of enforced confinement. A different line of defence might be to concede that reform is not punishment in the conventional sense and to go on to point out that the reform theory is an attempt to replace punishment with a practice which has greater utilitarian justification. According to this line, punishment cannot be justified on utilitarian grounds and the utilitarian must therefore replace punishment with a practice which is justifiable.

There is a second respect in which the reform theory has consequences which are at variance with traditional ideas on punishment. The processes of reform may involve what might be called 'treatment'. It happens to be true that many advocates of the theory are influenced by psychological doctrines to the effect that the criminal is suffering from a disease of social maladjustment from which he should be cured. Hence, the processes of reform may include more than re-education in the conventional sense; they may involve what is nearer to brainwashing (and from a strictly utilitarian point of view there is everything to be said in favour of this if it is in fact effective). A merit of the retributive theory is to insist that persons as ends in themselves should be protected against undue exposure to the influence of moral 'doctors' no matter how socially effective their treatment may be.

The third respect in which the theory departs from traditional ideas is that it gives countenance to the suggestion that the criminal may legitimately be detained until he is reformed. But in some advanced cases of social disease the cure may take some time. And what of the incurables? Here again the retributive theory reminds us of the inhumanity of treating people simply as social units to be moulded into desirable patterns.

So far we have considered three oddities of the reform theory, but none of these, of course, invalidates it. The first point simply brings out the nature of the reform theory, and the second and third are hardly implications in the strict sense but merely probable consequences if the practice which the theory reflects is developed in a certain direction. The fatal defect of the theory is rather that it is inadequate as an account of the very many complex ways in which the sanctions of the criminal law are intended to affect society. The reform theory concentrates on only one kind of case, that of the person who has committed an offence or a number of offences and who might do so again.

Moreover, it is plausible only for a certain range of cases in this class; those requiring treatment rather than conventional punishment. But it must be remembered that the criminal law is also intended for those, such as murderers, traitors, and embezzlers, for whom the possibility of a second offence is limited. Moreover, the criminal law serves also to deter ordinary citizens who might occasionally be tempted to commit offences. The inadequacy of the reform theory lies in its irrelevance to such important types of cases.

It is clear, then, that no one of the accounts of punishment provides on its own an adequate justification of punishment. The retributive theory, which is often taken to be an expression of barbarism, in fact provides a safeguard against the inhumane sacrifice of the individual for the social good, which is the moral danger in the utilitarian theory. Bearing in mind this moral doctrine about the rights of the individual we can then incorporate elements from both the deterrent and the reform versions of utilitarian justification. Only by drawing from all three doctrines can we hope to reflect the wide range of cases to which the criminal law applies.

The Right to Punish

Immanuel Kant

The right to punish contained in the penal law … is the right that the magistrate has to inflict pain on a subject in consequence of his having committed a crime.

Judicial punishment … is entirely distinct from natural punishment.… In natural punishment, vice punishes itself, and this fact is not taken into consideration by the legislator. Judicial punishment can never be used merely as a means to promote some other good for the criminal himself or for civil society, but instead it must in all cases be imposed on him only on the ground that he has committed a crime; for a human being can never be manipulated merely as a means to the purposes of someone else.… If this is so, what should one think of the proposal to permit a criminal who has been condemned to death to remain alive, if, after consenting to allow dangerous experiments to be made on him, he happily survives such experiments and if doctors thereby obtain new information that benefits the community? Any court of justice would repudiate such a proposal with scorn if it were suggested by a medical college, for [legal] justice ceases to be justice if it can be bought for a price.

What kind and what degree of punishment does public legal justice adopt as its principle and standard? None other than the principle of equality (illustrated

From Immanuel Kant, *The Metaphysical Elements of Justice*, trans. John Ladd (Indianapolis, Ind.: Bobbs-Merrill, 1965), pp. 99–106. Footnotes omitted. Reprinted with permission of the publisher, Bobbs-Merrill Educational Publishing Company, Inc.

by the pointer on the scales of justice), that is, the principle of not treating one side more favorably than the other. Accordingly, any undeserved evil that you inflict on someone else among the people is one that you do to yourself. If you vilify him, you vilify yourself; if you steal from him, you steal from yourself; if you kill him, you kill yourself. Only the Law of retribution (*jus talionis*) can determine exactly the kind and degree of punishment; it must be well understood, however, that this determination [must be made] in the chambers of a court of justice (and not in your private judgment). All other standards fluctuate back and forth and, because extraneous considerations are mixed with them, they cannot be compatible with the principle of pure and strict legal justice.

Now, it might seem that the existence of class distinctions would not allow for the [application of the] retributive principle of returning like for like. Nevertheless, even though these class distinctions may not make it possible to apply this principle to the letter, it can still always remain applicable in its effects if regard is had to the special sensibilities of the higher classes. Thus, for example, the imposition of a fine for a verbal injury has no proportionality to the original injury, for someone who has a good deal of money can easily afford to make insults whenever he wishes. On the other hand, the humiliation of the pride of such an offender comes much closer to equaling an injury done to the honor of the person offended; thus the judgment and Law might require the offender, not only to make a public apology to the offended person, but also at the same time to kiss his hand, even though he be socially inferior. Similarly, if a man of a higher class has violently attacked an innocent citizen who is socially inferior to him, he may be condemned, not only to apologize, but to undergo solitary and painful confinement, because by this means, in addition to the discomfort suffered, the pride of the offender will be painfully affected, and thus his humiliation will compensate for the offense as like for like.

But what is meant by the statement: "If you steal from him, you steal from yourself"? Inasmuch as someone steals, he makes the ownership of everyone else insecure, and hence he robs himself (in accordance with the Law of retribution) of the security of any possible ownership. He has nothing and can also acquire nothing, but he still wants to live, and this is not possible unless others provide him with nourishment. But, because the state will not support him gratis, he must let the state have his labor at any kind of work it may wish to use him for (convict labor), and so he becomes a slave, either for a certain period of time or indefinitely, as the case may be.

If, however, he has committed a murder, he must die. In this case, there is no substitute that will satisfy the requirements of legal justice. There is no sameness of kind between death and remaining alive even under the most miserable conditions, and consequently there is also no equality between the crime and the retribution unless the criminal is judicially condemned and put to death. But the death of the criminal must be kept entirely free of any maltreatment that would make an abomination of the humanity residing in the person suffering it. Even if a civil society were to dissolve itself by common agreement of all its members (for example, if the people inhabiting an island decided to separate and disperse themselves around the world), the last murderer remaining in prison must first be executed, so that everyone will duly receive what his actions are worth and so that the bloodguilt thereof will not be fixed on the people because they failed to insist on carrying out the punishment; for if they fail to do so, they may be regarded as accomplices in this public violation of legal justice.

Furthermore, it is possible for punishment to be equal in accordance with the strict Law of retribution only if the judge pronounces the death sentence. This is clear because only in this way will the death sentence be pronounced on all criminals in proportion to their inner viciousness (even if the crime involved is not murder, but some other crime against the state that can be expiated only by death). To illustrate this point, let us consider a situation, like the last Scottish rebellion, in which the participants are motivated by varying purposes, just as in that rebellion some believed that they were only fulfilling their obligations to the house of Stuart (like Balmerino and others), and others, in contrast, were pursuing their own private interests. Suppose that the highest court were to pronounce as follows: Each person shall have the freedom to choose between death and penal servitude. I say that a man of honor would choose death and that the knave would choose servitude. This is implied by the nature of human character, because the first recognizes something that he prizes more highly than life itself, namely, honor, whereas the second thinks that a life covered with disgrace is still better than not being alive at all (*animam praeferre pudori*). The first is without doubt less deserving of punishment than the other, and so, if they are both condemned to die, they will be punished exactly in proportion [to their inner viciousness]; the first will be punished mildly in terms of his kind of sensibility, and the second will be punished severely in terms of his kind of sensibility. On the other hand, if both were condemned to penal servitude, the first would be punished too severely and the second too mildly for their baseness. Thus, even in sentences imposed on a number of criminals united in a plot, the best equalizer before the bar of public legal justice is death.

The Death Sentence

Sidney Hook

Since I am not a fanatic or absolutist, I do not wish to go on record as being categorically opposed to the death sentence in all circumstances. I should like to recognize two exceptions. A defendant convicted of murder and sentenced to life should be permitted to choose the death sentence instead. Not so long

From *The Death Penalty in America*, ed. Hugo Adam Bedau (Garden City, N.Y.: Doubleday, 1967). Copyright Sidney Hook, 1967. Reprinted by permission.

ago a defendant sentenced to life imprisonment made this request and was rebuked by the judge for his impertinence. I can see no valid grounds for denying such a request out of hand. It may sometimes be denied, particularly if a way can be found to make the defendant labor for the benefit of the dependents of his victim as is done in some European countries. Unless such considerations are present, I do not see on what reasonable ground the request can be denied, particularly by those who believe in capital punishment. Once they argue that life imprisonment is either a more effective deterrent or more justly punitive, they have abandoned their position.

In passing, I should state that I am in favor of permitting any criminal defendant, sentenced to life imprisonment, the right to choose death. I can understand why certain jurists, who believe that the defendant wants thereby to cheat the state out of its mode of punishment, should be indignant at the idea. They are usually the ones who believe that even the attempt at suicide should be deemed a crime—in effect saying to the unfortunate person that if he doesn't succeed in his act of suicide, the state will punish him for it. But I am baffled to understand why the absolute abolitionist, dripping with treacly humanitarianism, should oppose this proposal. I have heard some people actually oppose capital punishment in certain cases on the ground that: "Death is too good for the vile wretch! Let him live and suffer to the end of his days." But the absolute abolitionist should be the last person in the world to oppose the wish of the lifer, who regards this form of punishment as torture worse than death, to leave our world.

My second class of exceptions consists of those who having been sentenced once to prison for premeditated murder, murder again. In these particular cases we have evidence that imprisonment is not a sufficient deterrent for the individual in question. If the evidence shows that the prisoner is so psychologically constituted that, without being insane, the fact that he can kill again with impunity may lead to further murderous behavior, the court should have the discretionary power to pass the death sentence if the criminal is found guilty of a second murder.

In saying that the death sentence should be *discretionary* in cases where a man has killed more than once, I am *not* saying that a murderer who murders again is more deserving of death than the murderer who murders once. Bluebeard was not twelve times more deserving of death when he was finally caught. I am saying simply this: that in a sub-class of murderers, i.e., those who murder several times, there may be a special group of sane murderers who, knowing that they will not be executed, will not hesitate to kill again and again. For *them* the argument from deterrence is obviously valid. Those who say that there must be no exceptions to the abolition of capital punishment cannot rule out the existence of such cases on a priori grounds. If they admit that there is a reasonable probability that such murderers will murder again or attempt to murder again, a probability which usually grows with the number of repeated murders, and still insist they would *never* approve of capital punishment, I would conclude that they are indifferent to the lives of the human beings doomed, on their position, to be victims. What fancies itself as a humanitarian attitude is sometimes an expression of sentimentalism. The reverse coin of sentimentalism is often cruelty.

Our charity for all human beings must not deprive us of our common sense. Nor should our charity be less for the future or potential victims of the murderer than for the murderer himself. There are crimes in this world which are, like acts of nature, beyond the power of men to anticipate or control. But not all or most crimes are of this character. So long as human beings are responsible and educable, they will respond to praise and blame and punishment. It is hard to imagine it but even Hitler and Stalin were once infants. Once you *can* imagine them as infants, however, it is hard to believe that they were already monsters in their cradles. Every confirmed criminal was once an amateur. The existence of confirmed criminals testifies to the defects of our education—where they can be reformed—and of our penology—where they cannot. That is why we are under the moral obligation to be intelligent about crime and punishment. Intelligence should teach us that the best educational and penological system is the one which prevents crimes rather than punishes them; the next best is one which punishes crime in such a way as to prevent it from happening again.

Capital Punishment

Hugo Adam Bedau

The Death Penalty as a Crime Deterrent

...In general, our knowledge about how penalties deter crimes and whether in fact they do—whom they deter, from which crimes, and under what conditions—is distressingly inexact. Most people nevertheless are convinced that punishments do deter, and that the more severe a punishment is the better it will deter. For more than a generation, social scientists have studied the question of whether the death penalty is a deterrent and of whether it is a better deterrent than the alternative of imprisonment. Their verdict, while not unanimous, is fairly clear. Whatever may be true about the deterrence of lesser crimes by other penalties, the deterrence achieved by the death penalty for murder is not measurably greater than the deterrence achieved by long-term imprisonment. In the nature of the case, the evidence is quite indirect. No one can identify for certain any crimes that did not occur because the would-be offender was deterred by the threat of the death penalty and that would not have been deterred by a lesser threat. Likewise, no one can identify any crimes

Abridged from *Matters of Life and Death: New Introductory Essays in Moral Philosophy*, ed. by Tom Reagan (New York: Random House, Inc., 1980). Copyright, 1980, Random House, Inc. Reprinted by permission.

that did occur because the offender was not deterred by the threat of prison even though he would have been deterred by the threat of death. Nevertheless, such evidence as we have fails to show that the more severe penalty (death) is really a better deterrent than the less severe penalty (imprisonment) for such crimes as murder.

If the conclusion stated above is correct, and the death penalty and long-term imprisonment are equally effective (or ineffective) as deterrents to murder, then the argument for the death penalty on grounds of deterrence is seriously weakened. One of the moral principles identified earlier comes into play and requires us to reject the death penalty on moral grounds. This is the principle that unless there is a good reason for choosing a more rather than a less severe punishment for a crime, the less severe penalty is to be preferred. This principle obviously commends itself to anyone who values human life and who concedes that, all other things being equal, less pain and suffering is always better than more. Human life is valued in part to the degree that it is free of pain, suffering, misery, and frustration, and in particular that it is free of such experiences when they serve no purpose. If the death penalty is not a more effective deterrent than imprisonment, then its greater severity than imprisonment is gratuitous, purposeless suffering and deprivation.

A Cost/Benefit Analysis of the Death Penalty

A full study of the costs and benefits involved in the practice of capital punishment would not be confined solely to the question of whether it is a better deterrent or preventive of murder than imprisonment. Any thorough-going utilitarian approach to the death-penalty controversy would need to examine carefully other costs and benefits as well, because maximizing the balance of social benefits over social costs is the sole criterion of right and wrong according to utilitarianism. Let us consider, therefore, some of the other costs and benefits to be calculated. Clinical psychologists have presented evidence to suggest that the death penalty actually incites some persons of unstable mind to murder others, either because they are afraid to take their own lives and hope that society will punish them for murder by putting them to death, or because they fancy that they, too, are killing with justification analogously to the justified killing involved in capital punishment. If such evidence is sound, capital punishment can serve as a counter-preventive or an incitement to murder, and these incited murders become part of its social cost. Imprisonment, however, has not been known to incite any murders or other crimes of violence in a comparable fashion. (A possible exception might be found in the imprisonment of terrorists, which has inspired other terrorists to take hostages as part of a scheme to force the authorities to release their imprisoned comrades.) The risks of executing the innocent are also part of the social cost. The historical record is replete with innocent persons indicted, convicted, sentenced, and occasionally legally executed for crimes they did not commit, not to mention the guilty persons unfairly convicted, sentenced to death, and executed on the strength of perjured testimony, fraudulent evidence, subornation of jurors, and other violations of the civil rights and liberties of the accused. Nor is this all. The high costs of a capital trial, of the inevitable appeals, the costly methods of custody most prisons adopt for convicts on "death row," are among the straightforward economic costs that the death penalty incurs. No scientifically valid cost/benefit analysis of capital punishment has ever been conducted, and it is impossible to predict exactly what such a study would show. Nevertheless, based on such evidence as we do have, it is quite possible that a study of this sort would favor abolition of all death penalties rather than their retention.

What if Executions Did Deter?

From the moral point of view, it is quite important to determine what one should think about capital punishment if the evidence clearly showed that the death penalty is a distinctly superior method of social defense by comparison with less severe alternatives. Kantian moralists...would have no use for such knowledge, because their entire case for the morality of the death penalty rests on the way it is thought to provide just retribution, not on the way it is thought to provide social defense. For a utilitarian, however, such knowledge would be conclusive. Those who follow Locke's reasoning would also be gratified, because they defend the morality of the death penalty both on the ground that it is retributively just and on the ground that it provides needed social defense.

What about the opponents of the death penalty, however? To oppose the death penalty in the face of incontestable evidence that it is an effective method of social defense seems to violate the moral principle that where grave risks are to be run, it is better that they be run by the guilty than by the innocent. Consider in this connection an imaginary world in which by executing a murderer the victim is invariably restored to life, whole and intact, as though the murder had never occurred. In such a miraculous world, it is hard to see how anyone could oppose the death penalty on moral grounds. Why shouldn't a murderer die if that will infallibly bring the victim back to life? What could possibly be morally wrong with taking the murderer's life under such conditions? It would turn the death penalty into an instrument of perfect restitution, and it would give a new and better meaning to *lex talionis,* "a life for a life." The whole idea is fanciful, of course, but it shows better than anything else how opposition to the death penalty cannot be both moral and wholly unconditional. If opposition to the death penalty is to be morally responsible, then it must be conceded that there are conditions (however unlikely) under which that opposition should cease.

But even if the death penalty were known to be a uniquely effective social defense, we could still imagine conditions under which it would be reasonable to oppose it. Suppose that in addition to being a slightly better preventive and deterrent than imprisonment, executions also have a slight incitive effect (so that for every ten murders an execution prevents or deters, it also incites another murder). Suppose also that the administration of criminal justice in capital cases is inefficient, unequal, and tends to secure convictions of murderers who least "deserve" to be sentenced to death (including some death sentences and a few executions of the innocent). Under such conditions, it would still be reasonable to oppose the death penalty, because on the facts supposed more (or not fewer) innocent lives are being threatened and lost by using the death penalty than would be risked by abolishing it. It is important to remember throughout our evaluation of the deterrence controversy that we cannot ever apply the principle...that advises us to risk the lives of the guilty in order to save the lives of the innocent. Instead, the most we can do is weigh the risk for the general public against the execution of those who are *found* guilty by an imperfect system of criminal justice. These hypothetical factual assumptions illustrate the contingencies upon which the morality of opposition to the death penalty rests. And not only the morality of opposition; the morality of any defense of the death penalty rests on the same contingencies. This should help us understand why, in resolving the morality of capital punishment one way or the other, it is so important to know, as well as we can, whether the death penalty really does deter, prevent, or incite crime, whether the innocent really are ever executed, and whether any of these things are likely to occur in the future.

How Many Guilty Lives Is One Innocent Life Worth?

The great unanswered question that utilitarians must face concerns the level of social defense that executions should be expected to achieve before it is justifiable to carry them out. Consider three possible situations: (1) At the level of a hundred executions per year, each additional execution of a convicted murderer reduces the number of murder victims by ten. (2) Executing every convicted murderer reduces the number of murders to 5,000 victims annually, whereas executing only one out of ten reduces the number to 5,001. (3) Executing every convicted murderer reduces the murder rate no more than does executing one in a hundred and no more than a random pattern of executions does.

Many people contemplating situation (1) would regard this as a reasonable trade-off: The execution of each further guilty person saves the lives of ten innocent ones. (In fact, situation (1) or something like it may be taken as a description of what most of those who defend the death penalty on grounds of social defense believe is true.) But suppose that, instead of saving 10 lives, the number dropped to 0.5, i.e., one victim avoided for each two additional executions. Would that be a reasonable price to pay? We are on the road toward the situation described in situation (2), where a drastic 90 percent reduction in the number of persons executed causes the level of social defense to drop by only 0.0002 percent. Would it be worth it to execute so many more murderers at the cost of such a slight decrease in social defense? How many guilty lives is one innocent life worth? In situation (3), of course, there is no basis for executing all convicted murderers, since there is no gain in social defense to show for each additional murderer executed after the first out of each hundred murderers has been executed. How, then, should we determine which out of each hundred convicted murderers is the unlucky one to be put to death?

It may be possible, under a complete and thoroughgoing cost/benefit analysis of the death penalty, to answer such questions. But an appeal merely to the moral principle that if lives are to be risked then let it be the lives of the guilty rather than the lives of the innocent will not suffice. (We have already noticed...that this abstract principle is of little use in the actual administration of criminal justice, because the police and the courts do not deal with the guilty as such but only with those *judged* guilty.) Nor will it suffice to agree that society deserves all the crime prevention and deterrence it can get by inflicting severe punishments. These principles are consistent with too many different policies. They are too vague by themselves to resolve the choice on grounds of social defense when confronted with hypothetical situations like those proposed above.

Since no adequate cost/benefit analysis of the death penalty exists, there is no way to resolve these questions from this standpoint at the present time. Moreover, it can be argued that we cannot have such an analysis without already establishing in some way or other the relative value of innocent lives versus guilty lives. Far from being a product of a cost/benefit analysis, this comparative evalution of lives would have to be brought into any such analysis. Without it, no cost/benefit analysis can get off the ground. Finally, it must be noted that we have no knowledge at present that begins to approximate anything like the situation described above in (1), whereas it appears from the evidence we do have that we achieve about the same deterrent and preventive effects whether we punish murder by death or by imprisonment. Therefore, something like the situation in (2) or in (3) may be correct. If so, this shows that the choice between the two policies of capital punishment and life imprisonment for murder will probably have to be made on some basis other than social defense; on that basis the two policies are equivalent and therefore equally acceptable.

CAPITAL PUNISHMENT AND RETRIBUTIVE JUSTICE

...Two leading principles of retributive justice [are] relevant to the capital-punishment controversy. One is the principle that crimes should be punished. The other is the principle that the severity of a punishment should be proportional to the gravity of the offense. (A corollary to the latter principle is the judgment that nothing so fits the crime of murder as the punishment of death.) Although these principles do not seem to stem from any concern over the worth, value, dignity, or rights of persons, they are moral principles of recognized weight and no discussion of the morality of capital punishment would be complete without them. Leaving aside all questions of social defense, how strong a case for capital punishment can be made on the basis of these principles? How reliable and persuasive are these principles themselves?

Crime Must Be Punished

... [T]here cannot be any dispute over this principle. In embracing it, of course, we are not automatically making a fetish of "law and order," in the sense that we would be if we thought that the most important single thing society can do with its resources is to punish crimes. In addition, this principle is not likely to be in dispute between proponents and opponents of the death penalty. Only those who completely oppose punishment for murder and other erstwhile capital crimes would appear to disregard this principle. Even defenders of the death penalty must admit that putting a convicted murderer in prison for years is a punishment of that criminal. The principle that crime must be punished is neutral to our controversy, because both sides acknowledge it and comply with it.

It is the other principle of retributive justice that seems to be a decisive one. Under the principle of retaliation, *lex talionis*, it must always have seemed that murderers ought to be put to death. Proponents of the death penalty, with rare exceptions, have insisted on this point, and it seems that even opponents of the death penalty must give it grudging assent. The strategy for opponents of the death penalty is to show either (a) that this principle is not really a principle of justice after all, or (b) that although it is, other principles outweigh or cancel its dictates. As we shall see, both these objections have merit.

Is Murder Alone to Be Punished By Death?

Let us recall, first, that not even the Biblical world limited the death penalty to the punishment of murder. Many other nonhomicidal crimes also carried this penalty (e.g., kidnapping, witchcraft, cursing one's parents). In our own recent history, persons have been executed for aggravated assault, rape, kidnapping, armed robbery, sabotage, and espionage. It is not possible to defend any of these executions (not to mention some of the more bizarre capital statutes, like the one in Georgia that used to provide an optional death penalty for desecration of a grave) on grounds of just retribution. This entails that either such executions are not justified or that they are justified on some ground other than retribution. In actual practice, few if any defenders of the death penalty have ever been willing to rest their case entirely on the moral principle of just retribution as formulated in terms of "a life for a life." Kant seems to have been a conspicuous exception. Most defenders of the death penalty have implied by their willingness to use executions to defend limb and property, as well as life, that they did not place much value on the lives of criminals when compared to the value of both lives and things belonging to innocent citizens.

Are All Murders to Be Punished By Death?

Our society for several centuries has endeavored to confine the death penalty
to some criminal homicides. Even Kant took a casual attitude toward a mother's
killing of her illegitimate child. ("A child born into the world outside marriage
is outside the law..., and consequently it is also outside the protection of the
law.")[1] In our society, the development nearly 200 years ago of the distinction
between first- and second-degree murder was an attempt to narrow the class
of criminal homicides deserving of the death penalty. Yet those dead owing to
manslaughter, or to any kind of unintentional, accidental, unpremeditated,
unavoidable, unmalicious killing are just as dead as the victims of the most
ghastly murder. Both the law in practice and moral reflection show how
difficult it is to identify all and only the criminal homicides that are appropriately
punished by death (assuming that any are). Individual judges and juries differ
in the conclusions they reach. The history of capital punishment for homicides
reveals continual efforts, uniformly unsuccessful, to identify before the fact
those homicides for which the slayer should die. Benjamin Cardozo, a justice
of the United States Supreme Court fifty years ago, said of the distinction
between degrees of murder that it was

> ...so obscure that no jury hearing it for the first time can fairly be expected to
> assimilate and understand it. I am not at all sure that I understand it myself after
> trying to apply it for many years and after diligent study of what has been written in
> the books. Upon the basis of this fine distinction with its obscure and mystifying
> psychology, scores of men have gone to their death.[2]

Similar skepticism has been registered on the reliability and rationality of
death-penalty statutes that give the trial court the discretion to sentence to
prison or to death. As Justice John Marshall Harlan of the Supreme Court
observed a decade ago,

> Those who have come to grips with the hard task of actually attempting to draft
> means of channeling capital sentencing discretion have confirmed the lesson taught
> by history.... To identify before the fact those characteristics of criminal homicide
> and their perpetrators which call for the death penalty, and to express these charac-
> teristics in language which can be fairly understood and applied by the sentencing
> authority, appear to be tasks which are beyond present human ability.[3]

The abstract principle that the punishment of death best fits the crime of
murder turns out to be extremely difficult to interpret and apply.

If we look at the matter from the standpoint of the actual practice of criminal
justice, we can only conclude that "a life for a life" plays little or no role
whatever. Plea bargaining (by means of which one of the persons involved in a
crime agrees to accept a lesser sentence in exchange for testifying against the
others to enable the prosecutor to get them all convicted), even where murder

---

[1]Immanuel Kant, *The Metaphysical Elements of Justice* (1797), tr. John Ladd, p. 106.
[2]Benjamin Cardozo, "What Medicine Can Do for Law" (1928), reprinted in Margaret E. Hall,
ed., *Selected Writings of Benjamin Nathan Cardozo* (1947), p. 204.
[3]*McGautha* v. *California*, 402 U.S. 183 (1971), at p. 204.

is concerned, is widespread. Studies of criminal justice reveal that what the courts (trial or appellate) decide on a given day is first-degree murder suitably punished by death in a given jurisdiction could just as well be decided in a neighboring jurisdiction on another day either as second-degree murder or as first-degree murder but without the death penalty. The factors that influence prosecutors in determining the charge under which they will prosecute go far beyond the simple principle of "a life for a life." Nor can it be objected that these facts show that our society does not care about justice. To put it succinctly, either justice in punishment does not consist of retribution, because there are other principles of justice; or there are other moral considerations besides justice that must be honored; or retributive justice is not adequately expressed in the idea of "a life for a life."

Is Death Sufficiently Retributive?

Given the reality of horrible and vicious crimes, one must consider whether there is not a quality of unthinking arbitrariness in advocating capital punishment for murder as the retributively just punishment. Why does death in the electric chair or the gas chamber or before a firing squad or on a gallows meet the requirements of retributive justice? When one thinks of the savage, brutal, wanton character of so many murders, how can retributive justice be served by anything less than equally savage methods of execution for the murderer? From a retributive point of view, the oft-heard exclamation, "Death is too good for him!" has a certain truth. Yet few defenders of the death penalty are willing to embrace this consequence of their own doctrine.

The reason they do not and should not is that, if they did, they would be stooping to the methods and thus to the squalor of the murderer. Where criminals set the limits of just methods of punishment, as they will do if we attempt to give exact and literal implementation to *lex talionis,* society will find itself descending to the cruelties and savagery that criminals employ. But society would be deliberately authorizing such acts, in the cool light of reason, and not (as is often true of vicious criminals) impulsively or in hatred and anger or with an insane or unbalanced mind. Moral restraints, in short, prohibit us from trying to make executions perfectly retributive. Once we grant the role of these restraints, the principle of "a life for a life" itself has been qualified and no longer suffices to justify the execution of murderers.

Other considerations take us in a different direction. Few murders, outside television and movie scripts, involve anything like an execution. An execution, after all, begins with a solemn pronouncement of the death sentence from a judge, is followed by long detention in maximum security awaiting the date of execution, various appeals, perhaps a final sanity hearing, and then "the last mile" to the execution chamber itself. As the French writer Albert Camus remarked,

> For there to be an equivalence, the death penalty would have to punish a criminal who had warned his victim of the date at which he would inflict a horrible death on

him and who, from that moment onward, had confined him at his mercy for months. Such a monster is not encountered in private life.[4]

Differential Severity Does Not Require Executions

What, then, emerges from our examination of retributive justice and the death penalty? If retributive justice is thought to consist in *lex talionis,* all one can say is that this principle has never exercised more than a crude and indirect effect on the actual punishments meted out. Other principles interfere with a literal and single-minded application of this one. Some murders seem improperly punished by death at all; other murders would require methods of execution too horrible to inflict; in still other cases any possible execution is too deliberate and monstrous given the nature of the motivation culminating in the murder. Proponents of the death penalty rarely confine themselves to reliance on this principle of just retribution and nothing else, since they rarely confine themselves to supporting the death penalty only for all murders.

But retributive justice need not be thought to consist of *lex talionis.* One might reject that principle as too crude and still embrace the retributive principle that the severity of punishments should be graded according to the gravity of the offense. Even though one need not claim that life imprisonment (or any kind of punishment other than death) "fits" the crime of murder, one can claim that this punishment is the proper one for murder. To do this, the schedule of punishments accepted by society must be arranged so that this mode of imprisonment is the most severe penalty used. Opponents of the death penalty need not reject this principle of retributive justice, even though they must reject a literal *lex talionis.*

Equal Justice and Capital Punishment

During the past generation, the strongest practical objection to the death penalty has been the inequities with which it has been applied. As Supreme Court Justice William O. Douglas once observed, "One searches our chronicles in vain for the execution of any member of the affluent strata of this society."[5] One does not search our chronicles in vain for the crime of murder committed by the affluent. Every study of the death penalty for rape has confirmed that black male rapists (especially where the victim is a white female) are far more likely to be sentenced to death (and executed) than white male rapists. Half of all those under death sentence during 1976 and 1977 were black, and nearly half of all those executed since 1930 were black. All the sociological evidence points to the conclusion that the death penalty is the poor man's justice; as the current street saying has it, "Those without the capital get the punishment."

---

[4]Albert Camus, *Resistance, Rebellion, and Death* (1961), p. 199.
[5]*Furman* v. *Georgia,* 408 U.S. 238 (1972), at pp. 251–252.

Let us suppose that the factual basis for such a criticism is sound. What follows for the morality of capital punishment? Many defenders of the death penalty have been quick to point out that since there is nothing intrinsic about the crime of murder or rape that dictates that only the poor or racial-minority males will commit it, and since there is nothing overtly racist about the statutes that authorize the death penalty for murder or rape, it is hardly a fault in the idea of capital punishment if in practice it falls with unfair impact on the poor and the black. There is, in short, nothing in the death penalty that requires it to be applied unfairly and with arbitrary or discriminatory results. It is at worst a fault in the system of administering criminal justice (and some, who dispute the facts cited above, would deny even this).

Presumably, both proponents and opponents of capital punishment would concede that it is a fundamental dictate of justice that a punishment should not be unfairly—inequitably or unevenly—enforced and applied. They should also be able to agree that when the punishment in question is the extremely severe one of death, then the requirement to be fair in using such a punishment becomes even more stringent. Thus, there should be no dispute in the death penalty controversy over these principles of justice. The dispute begins as soon as one attempts to connect these principles with the actual use of this punishment.

In this country, many critics of the death penalty have argued, we would long ago have got rid of it entirely if it had been a condition of its use that it be applied equally and fairly. In the words of the attorneys who argued against the death penalty in the Supreme Court during 1972, "It is a freakish aberration, a random extreme act of violence, visibly arbitrary and discriminatory—a penalty reserved for unusual application because, if it were usually used, it would affront universally shared standards of public decency."[6] It is difficult to dispute this judgment, when one considers that there have been in the United States during the past fifty years about half a million criminal homicides but only about 4,000 executions (all but 50 of which were of men).

We can look at these statistics in another way to illustrate the same point. If we could be assured that the 4,000 persons executed were the worst of the worst, repeated offenders without exception, the most dangerous murderers in captivity—the ones who had killed more than once and were likely to kill again, and the least likely to be confined in prison without imminent danger to other inmates and the staff—then one might accept half a million murders and a few thousand executions with a sense that rough justice had been done. But the truth is otherwise. Persons are sentenced to death and executed not because they have been found to be uncontrollably violent, hopelessly poor parole and release risks, or for other reasons. Instead, they are executed for entirely different reasons. They have a poor defense at trial; they have no

---

[6]NAACP Legal Defense and Educational Fund, Brief for Petitioner in *Aikens* v. *California*, O.T. 1971, No. 68–5027, reprinted in Philip English Mackey, ed., *Voices Against Death: American Opposition to Capital Punishment, 1787–1975* (1975), p. 288.

funds to bring sympathetic witnesses to court; they are immigrants or strangers in the community where they were tried; the prosecuting attorney wants the publicity that goes with "sending a killer to the chair"; they have inexperienced or overworked counsel at trial; there are no funds for an appeal or for a transcript of the trial record; they are members of a despised racial minority. In short, the actual study of why particular persons have been sentenced to death and executed does not show any careful winnowing of the worst from the bad. It shows that the executed were usually the unlucky victims of prejudice and discrimination, the losers in an arbitrary lottery that could just as well have spared them as killed them, the victims of the disadvantages that almost always go with poverty. A system like this does not enhance respect for human life; it cheapens and degrades it. However heinous murder and other crimes are, the system of capital punishment does not compensate for or erase those crimes. It only tends to add new injuries of its own to the catalogue of our inhumanity to each other.

CONCLUSION

My own view of the controversy is that on balance, given the moral principles we have identified in the course of our discussion (including the overriding value of human life), and given the facts about capital punishment and crimes against the person, the side favoring abolition of the death penalty has the better of the argument. And there *is* an alternative to capital punishment: long-term imprisonment. Such a punishment is retributive and can be made appropriately severe to reflect the gravity of the crime for which it is the punishment. It gives adequate (though hardly perfect) protection to the public. It is free of the worst defect to which the death penalty is liable: execution of the innocent. It tacitly acknowledges that there is no way for a criminal, alive or dead, to make amends for murder or other grave crimes against the person. Finally, it has symbolic significance. The death penalty, more than any other kind of killing, is done in the name of society and on its behalf. Each of us has a hand in such a killing, and unless such killings are absolutely necessary they cannot really be justified. Thus, abolishing the death penalty represents extending the hand of life even to those who by their crimes have "forfeited" any right to live. It is a tacit admission that we must abandon the folly and pretence of attempting to secure perfect justice in an imperfect world.

   Searching for an epigram suitable for our times, in which governments have launched vast campaigns of war and suppression of internal dissent by means of methods that can only be described as savage and criminal, Camus was prompted to admonish: "Let us be neither victims nor executioners." Perhaps better than any other, this exhortation points the way between forbidden extremes if we are to respect the humanity in each of us without trespassing on the humanity of others.

SUGGESTED SUPPLEMENTARY READINGS TO PART SIX

Acton, H.B., ed.: *The Philosophy of Punishment* (London: Macmillan, 1969).

Bedau, Hugo A., ed.: *The Death Penalty in America* (Garden City, N.Y.: Doubleday, 1965).

Ezorsky, Gertrude, ed.: *Philosophical Perspectives on Punishment* (Albany, N.Y.: SUNY Press, 1972).

Flew, Anthony: *Crime or Disease* (London: Macmillan, 1973).

Goldinger, Milton, ed.: *Punishment and Human Rights* (Cambridge, Mass.: Schenkman, 1974).

Hobbes, Thomas: *Leviathan,* Chapters XXVII and XXVIII.

Honderich, Ted: *Punishment: The Supposed Justifications* (London: Hutchinson, 1969).

Menninger, Karl: *The Crime of Punishment* (New York: Viking Press, 1966).

Sellin, Thorstein, ed.: *Capital Punishment* (New York: Harper and Row, 1967).

Schedler, George: "Capital Punishment and Its Deterrent Effect," *Social Theory and Practice* 4:47ff., 1976.

PART SEVEN

ECONOMIC RESPONSIBILITIES: CORPORATE AND SOCIAL

INTRODUCTION

In the past decade philosophers have turned their attention increasingly to matters of ethics and economics, investigating a broad range of questions asking about the rights and duties of individuals, corporations, and political systems from an economic perspective. Two such questions have provoked extensive discussion and are examined in this section: What ethical responsibilities, if any, do corporations and individual businesspersons possess?; and What duties do we owe to the poor in other countries?

ETHICS IN BUSINESS

Profits, many say, are incompatible with ethics. Fostered by images from the late nineteenth century of bearded robber barons, the attitude of some people towards business is categorical: to succeed in business one must compromise one's ethics. Many successful business people, however, find nothing problematic about maintaining ethical standards. The Dean of the Graduate School of Business at the University of Chicago once argued that business executives have significantly *higher* ethical standards than those of the average person.[1] Whatever the true story, the man or woman in the street continues to have a poor impression of the ethics of business; studies regularly show that business

---

[1]Dean Rossette of the School of Business at the University of Chicago made this point during a public debate with Professor Thomas Donaldson on the subject of teaching ethics in schools of business, September, 1983, at the University of Chicago. The purpose of the remark was to indicate a lessened need for the formal teaching of ethics to business students.

executives rank near the bottom of the professional ladder in the perception of ethical conduct.

Plato, both in the *Republic* and the *Laws*, is skeptical of mercantile motives, arguing in the *Laws* that it is those with moderate, not great, wealth who are more virtuous. As he explains, there are two ways to make money: the honest and the dishonest way. And, he continues, it stands to reason that those who have the most money have utilized *both* ways. Aristotle, Cicero, Aquinas and, indeed, most moral philosophers until the eighteenth century were also suspicious of economic motives, insisting that the virtue necessary for high office was inconsistent with the pursuit of profit. Even the loaning of money at interest, referred to in the Middle Ages as "usury," was condemned on the grounds that it allowed profit hungry entrepreneurs to benefit without dint of honest toil and labor (although historians point out that the Church's ban on usury was circumvented frequently through the use of special arrangements involving reciprocal favors).

It was not until the eighteenth century that a young professor of moral philosophy at Glasgow, Scotland, suggested that self-interest in the marketplace might not be so damaging to the public welfare as philosophers and theologians supposed. The young philosophy professor was Adam Smith, and the book he wrote which shook the economic foundations of Western Civilization was *An Inquiry into the Nature and Causes of the Wealth of Nations*.[2]

The Wealth of Nations is of special importance to the contemporary study of business ethics because it sets the tone for the moral justification of the pursuit of profit which is popular today. Smith did not believe that the highest motive was profit; he reserved that honor for benevolence. But he believed that the pursuit of profit in the context of a free-market economy could have dramatic benefits for society. In particular, it ensured that even those with the most *non*benevolent of motives would be forced to work for the common good. The force that turned the vice of self-interest into a virtue Smith called the "invisible hand," and it was the existence of this force that he believed we must dutifully protect by instituting the proper market arrangements, namely, ones that were of a laissez-faire or "free-market" character and which would get the government off the back of business.

Here is how the invisible hand is supposed to work. In a free market there are by definition no forced transfers. That is, all exchanges between persons—of labor, goods, money or some combination thereof—are entirely voluntary on the part of the exchanging parties. No one tells you, for example, that you must work for Jones (i.e., sell your labor) for a certain wage. It follows, argued Adam Smith, that persons will undertake transfers *only* when both parties benefit, or at least believe they benefit. When the implications of this micro-situation are extended to apply to the entire society we have a vision of business working to

---

[2]1776; reprinted in the *Glasgow Edition of the Works and Correspondence of Adam Smith*, ed. R. H. Campbell (London: Oxford University Press, 1976).

benefit the common good. Every money maker, as a matter of self-interest, schemes to enhance the interests of others. How, he or she asks, can I make my product better or less expensive? Society is the winner, ending up with the best possible products at the lowest possible prices. And if that were not enough, the benefit is accomplished without the heavy hand of government and without an idealistic reliance on the benevolence of the average person.

Smith's vision of the good society, one in which social good is lifted up by the power of the invisible hand, is still very much with us today. Indeed, it is the cornerstone of modern Western economic theory (sometimes called neoclassical economic theory) and lies behind the views espoused by Milton Friedman in the article included in this section, "The Social Responsibility of Business Is to Increase Its Profits." It is a short step from the analysis of free transfers in the marketplace to the conclusion that business should, as a moral matter, increase its profits, since, as Adam Smith showed, the pursuit of profit maximization in a free market necessitates satisfying the interests of others. To this basic economic argument Friedman adds a straightforwardly deontological one; namely, because managers of corporations are hired by stockholders to maximize return on investment, it follows that managers have a fiduciary *duty* to live up to the terms of their agreement and pursue profits with single-minded devotion.

Much, however, has happened since the eighteenth century, and not everyone—even those squarely within the neoclassical tradition—believes that Smith's theory of the invisible hand is gospel. Smith, himself, of course never lived to see some of the tragic realities of the industrial revolution that were, whether rightly or wrongly, justified in his name. He did not live to see the grime and poverty of the London slums, or the seven- and eight-year-old children working fourteen hours a day in the woolen mills. We do not know what Smith would have thought had he lived, but it is undeniable that Western governments, while buying much of Smith's free market approach, have stopped short of truly laissez-faire economic systems. Today almost all Western democracies have child labor laws, federal banking laws, tariffs, embargoes, quotas, social security, welfare payments, unemployment insurance, federal regulatory agencies, national monetary systems, federally chartered corporations, and income tax—all of which deviate sharply from Smith's vision of the "government hands off" market.

Economists themselves were quick to notice seeming flaws in Smith's theory. If no transfers are forced, for example, it may be true that both parties will exchange only when each *believes* himself better off. But what if one party believes wrongly? What if a consumer believes that a certain drug will enhance fertility, whereas in truth, although enhancing fertility, the drug also brings on crippling birth defects? Or what if one person, through no fault of his or her own, has little or nothing to "transfer"? Suppose, for example, one is the victim of insular poverty and has no skills, or is crippled, or retarded? Or what if it becomes possible for a group of producers, utilizing economies of scale or brand-name loyalties, to charge prices *above* what a "fair" or "equilibrium" price would be, simply because it is too expensive for other producers to enter the market in competition? These and other problems have led some economists to speak not only of the "invisible hand," but also of the "invisible foot."

Even staunch defenders of capitalism now refer regularly to market "imperfections" and endorse the intervention of government in ways that Smith never imagined. And in the arena of corporate responsibility, theorists such as Kenneth Goodpaster and John Matthews (whose article is reprinted below) reject the assumption that the marketplace automatically ensures social welfare. In contrast, they argue, there is a crying need for the corporation to develop its "conscience." George C. Lodge, in a similar vein, asserts that the simplistic notion of property used by some to justify corporate and entrepreneurial amorality is both wrong-headed and out of date. A clear understanding of the notion of property, he concludes, reveals that ownership necessarily implies societal responsibilities.

DUTIES TO THE POOR ABROAD

In the basic theories of traditional morality, such as those of Mill and Kant, little reference is made to differences between duties owed to fellow citizens on the one hand, and to persons in foreign lands on the other. Neither the principle of the greatest happiness for the greatest number, nor of the categorical imperative, is limited to the inhabitants of the nation state. And yet in our daily lives we typically *feel* a stronger obligation to friends and fellow citizens—with whom we share a common culture and heritage—than to perfect strangers abroad. Nor do the theories of Adam Smith, Karl Marx, or Milton Friedman— theories that have economic issues as their special focus—have much to say about how to make the difficult trade-offs between duties to friends and to strangers. What, then, should moral theory say about our obligations to the poor in other countries? What should it say, in particular, about persons in other countries who are malnourished, ill-housed, and starving?

The three final readings attempt to answer this question in different ways. In "The Case Against Helping the Poor," Garrett Hardin argues that we have greatly exaggerated our duties to the poor abroad and have failed to face the grim realities of the modern world. For many it is a simple choice of starving now or later. Ironically, helping prevent starvation now, argues Hardin, many aggravate the starvation problem later. In sharp contrast to this view, Peter Singer argues in a utilitarian vein that refusing to come to the rescue of the world's starving poor is, if not outright murder, at least cruelly unjust. He considers a variety of possible objections that might be made to our having a duty to render aid abroad, including the arguments presented by Garrett Hardin, yet finds reasons to reject them all.

In the final article of this section, the political philosopher Henry Shue concludes, just as Singer does, that we must assume responsibilities toward those abroad. Yet he argues for this conclusion not on the basis of the utilitarian framework employed by Singer, but by appeal to the notion of a "basic right."

Defined as a right the preservation of which is necessary for the enjoyment of all other rights, a basic right is one which, according to Shue, imposes specific duties on persons and governments. Because persons in foreign countries possess the rights to security and subsistence, it follows for Shue that we in this country have correlative duties both to avoid the deprivation of such rights and to aid in their fulfillment.

CASE STUDY—Economic Responsibilities

PLASMA INTERNATIONAL

The Sunday headline in the Tampa, Florida, newspaper read:

Blood Sales Result in Exorbitant Profits for Local Firm

The story went on to relate how the Plasma International Company, headquartered in Tampa, Florida, purchased blood in underdeveloped countries for as little as 45[1] cents a pint and resold the blood to hospitals in the United States and South America. A recent disaster in Nicaragua produced scores of injured persons and the need for fresh blood. Plasma International had 10,000 pints of blood flown to Nicaragua from West Africa and charged the hospitals $75 per pint, netting the firm nearly three quarters of a million dollars.

As a result of the newspaper story, a group of irate citizens, led by prominent civic leaders, demanded that the City of Tampa, and the State of Florida, revoke Plasma International's licenses to practice business. Others protested to their congressmen to seek enactment of legislation designed to halt the sale of blood for profit. The spokesperson was reported as saying, "What kind of people are these—selling life and death? These men prey on the needs of dying people, buying blood from poor, ignorant Africans for 45 cents worth of beads and junk, and selling it to injured people for $75 a pint. Well, this company will soon find out that the people of our community won't stand for their kind around here."

"I just don't understand it. We run a business just like any other business; we pay taxes and we try to make an honest profit," said Sol Levin as he responded to reporters at the Tampa International Airport. He had just returned home from testifying before the House Subcommittee on Medical Standards. The recent publicity surrounding his firm's activities during the recent earthquakes had once again fanned the flames of public opinion. An election year was an unfortunate time for the publicity to occur. The politicians and the media were having a field day.

Case prepared by T.W. Zimmer and P.L. Preston, reprinted from *Business and Society: Cases and Text* ed., Robert D. Hay, Edmund R. Gray, and James E. Gates (Cincinnati: South-Western Publishing Co., 1976). Reprinted by permission.

[1]Prices have been adjusted in this article to allow for inflation occurring since the article was written (ed.).

Levin was a successful stockbroker when he founded Plasma International Company three years ago. Recognizing the world's need for safe, uncontaminated, and reasonably priced whole blood and blood plasma, Levin and several of his colleagues pooled their resources and went into business. Initially, most of the blood and plasma they sold was purchased through store-front operations in the southeast United States. Most of the donors were, unfortunately, men and women who used the money obtained from the sale of their blood to purchase wine. While sales increased dramatically on the base of an innovative marketing approach, several cases of hepatitis were reported in recipients. The company wisely began a search for new sources.

Recognizing their own limitations in the medical-biological side of the business they recruited a highly qualified team of medical consultants. The consulting team, after extensive testing, and a worldwide search, recommended that the blood profiles and donor characteristics of several rural West African tribes made them ideal prospective donors. After extensive negotiations with the State Department and the government of the nation of Burami, the company was able to sign an agreement with several of the tribal chieftains.

As Levin reviewed these facts, and the many costs involved in the sale of a commodity as fragile as blood, he concluded that the publicity was grossly unfair. His thoughts were interrupted by the reporter's question: "Mr. Levin, is it necessary to sell a vitally needed medical supply, like blood, at such high prices especially to poor people in such a critical situation?" "Our prices are determined on the basis of a lot of costs that we incur that the public isn't even aware of," Levin responded. However, when reporters pressed him for details of these "relevant" costs, Levin refused any further comment. He noted that such information was proprietary in nature and not for public consumption.

The Social Responsibility of Business Is to Increase Its Profits

Milton Friedman

When I hear businessmen speak eloquently about the "social responsibilities of business in a free-enterprise system," I am reminded of the wonderful line about the Frenchman who discovered at the age of 70 that he had been speaking prose all his life. The businessmen believe that they are defending free enterprise when they declaim that business is not concerned "merely" with profit but also with promoting desirable "social" ends; that business has a "social conscience" and takes seriously its responsibilities for providing employment, eliminating discrimination, avoiding pollution and whatever else may be the catchwords of the contemporary crop of reformers. In fact they are—or would be if they or anyone else took them seriously—preaching pure and unadulterated socialism. Businessmen who talk this way are unwitting puppets of the intellectual forces that have been undermining the basis of a free society these past decades.

The discussion of the "social responsibilities of business" are notable for their analytical looseness and lack of rigor. What does it mean to say that "business" has responsibilities? Only people can have responsibilities. A corporation is an artificial person and in this sense may have artificial responsibilities, but "business" as a whole cannot be said to have responsibilities, even in this vague sense. The first step toward clarity to examining the doctrine of the social responsibility of business is to ask precisely what it implies for whom.

Presumably, the individuals who are to be responsible are businessmen, which means individual proprietors or corporate executives. Most of the discussion of social responsibility is directed at corporations, so in what follows I shall mostly neglect the individual proprietors and speak of corporate executives.

In a free-enterprise, private-property system, a corporate executive is an employee of the owners of the business. He has direct responsibility to his employers. That responsibility is to conduct the business in accordance with their desires, which generally will be to make as much money as possible while conforming to the basic rules of the society, both those embodied in law and those embodied in ethical custom. Of course, in some cases his employers may have a different objective. A group of persons might establish a corporation for an eleemosynary purpose—for example, a hospital or a school. The manager of such a corporation will not have money profit as his objectives but the rendering of certain services.

In either case, the key point is that, in his capacity as a corporate executive, the manager is the agent of the individuals who own the corporation or establish the eleemosynary institution, and his primary responsibility is to them.

Needless to say, this does not mean that it is easy to judge how well he is performing his task. But at least the criterion of performance is straightforward, and the persons among whom a voluntary contractual arrangement exists are clearly defined.

Of course, the corporate executive is also a person in his own right. As a person, he may have many other responsibilities that he recognizes or assumes voluntarily—to his family, his conscience, his feelings of charity, his church, his clubs, his city, his country. He may feel impelled by these responsibilities to devote part of his income to causes he regards as worthy, to refuse to work for particular corporations, even to leave his job, for example, to join his country's armed forces. If we wish, we may refer to some of these responsibilities as "social responsibilities." But in these respects he is acting as a principal, not an agent; he is spending his own money or time or energy, not the money of his employers or the time or energy he has contracted to devote to their purposes. If these are "social responsibilities," they are the social responsibilities of individuals, not of business.

What does it mean to say that the corporate executive has a "social responsibility" in his capacity as businessman? If this statement is not pure rhetoric, it must mean that he is to act in some way that is not in the interest of his employers. For example, that he is to refrain from increasing the price of the product in order to contribute to the social objective of preventing inflation, even though a price increase would be in the best interests of the corporation. Or that he is to make expenditures on reducing pollution beyond the amount that is in the best interests of the corporation or that is required by law in order to contribute to the social objective of improving the environment. Or that, at the expense of corporate profits, he is to hire "hardcore" unemployed instead of better qualified available workmen to contribute to the social objective of reducing poverty.

In each of these cases, the corporate executive would be spending someone else's money for a general social interest. Insofar as his actions in accord with his "social responsibility" reduce returns to stockholders, he is spending their money. Insofar as his actions raise the price to customers, he is spending the customers' money. Insofar as his actions lower the wages of some employees, he is spending their money.

The stockholders or the customers or the employees could separately spend their own money on the particular action if they wished to do so. The executive is exercising a distinct "social responsibility," rather than serving as an agent of the stockholders or the customers or the employees, only if he spends the money in a different way than they would have spent it.

But if he does this, he is in effect imposing taxes, on the one hand, and deciding how the tax proceeds shall be spent, on the other.

This process raises political questions on two levels: principle and consequences. On the level of political principle, the imposition of taxes and the expenditure of tax proceeds are governmental functions. We have established elaborate constitutional, parliamentary and judicial provisions to control these functions, to assure that taxes are imposed so far as possible in accordance with the preferences and desires of the public—after all, "taxation without representation" was one of the battle cries of the American Revolution. We have a system of checks and balances to separate the legislative function of imposing taxes and enacting expenditures from the executive function of collecting taxes and administering expenditure programs and from the judicial function of mediating disputes and interpreting the law.

Here the businessman—self-selected or appointed directly or indirectly by stockholders—is to be simultaneously legislator, executive and jurist. He is to decide whom to tax by how much and for what purpose, and he is to spend the proceeds—all this guided only by general exhortations from on high to restrain inflation, improve the environment, fight poverty and so on and on.

The whole justification for permitting the corporate executive to be selected by the stockholders is that the executive is an agent serving the interests of his principal. This justification disappears when the corporate executive imposes taxes and spends the proceeds for "social" purposes. He becomes in effect a public employee, a civil servant, even though he remains in name an employee of a private enterprise. On grounds of political principle, it is intolerable that such civil servants—insofar as their actions in the name of social responsibility are real and not just window-dressing—should be selected as they are now. If they are to be civil servants, then they must be elected through a political process. If they are to impose taxes and make expenditures to foster "social" objectives, then political machinery must be set up to make the assessment of taxes and to determine through a political process the objectives to be served.

This is the basic reason why the doctrine of "social responsibility" involves the acceptance of the socialist view that political mechanisms, not market mechanisms, are the appropriate way to determine the allocation of scarce resources to alternative uses.

On the grounds of consequences, can the corporate executive in fact discharge his alleged "social responsibilities"? On the one hand, suppose he could get away with spending the stockholders' or customers' or employees' money. How is he to know how to spend it? He is told that he must contribute to fighting inflation. How is he to know what action of his will contribute to that end? He is presumably an expert in running his company—in producing a product or selling it or financing it. But nothing about his selection makes him an expert on inflation. Will his holding down the price of his product reduce inflationary pressure? Or, by leaving more spending power in the hands of his customers, simply divert it elsewhere? Or, by forcing him to produce less because of the lower price, will it simply contribute to shortages? Even if he could answer these questions, how much cost is he justified in imposing on his stockholders, customers, and employees for this social purpose? What is his appropriate share and what is the appropriate share of others?

And, whether he wants to or not, can he get away with spending his stockholders', customers' or employees' money? Will not the stockholders fire him? (Either the present ones or those who take over when his actions in the name of social responsibility have reduced the corporation's profits and the price of its stock.) His customers and his employees can desert him for other producers and employers less scrupulous in exercising their social responsibilities.

This facet of "social responsibility" doctrine is brought into sharp relief when the doctrine is used to justify wage restraint by trade unions. The conflict of interest is naked and clear when union officials are asked to subordinate the interest of their members to some more general purpose. If the union officials try to enforce wage restraint, the consequence is likely to be wildcat strikes, rank-and-file revolts and the emergence of strong competitors for their jobs. We thus have the ironic phenomenon that union leaders—at least in the U.S.—have objected to Government interference with the market far more consistently and courageously than have business leaders.

The difficulty of exercising "social responsibility" illustrates, of course, the great virtue of private competitive enterprise—it forces people to be responsible for their own actions and makes it difficult for them to "exploit" other people for either selfish or unselfish purposes. They can do good—but only at their own expense.

Many a reader who has followed the argument this far may be tempted to remonstrate that it is all well and good to speak of Government's having the responsibility to impose taxes and determine expenditures for such "social" purposes as controlling pollution or training the hard-core unemployed, but that the problems are too urgent to wait on the slow course of political processes, that the exercise of social responsibility by businessmen is a quicker and surer way to solve pressing current problems.

Aside from the question of fact—I share Adam Smith's skepticism about the benefits that can be expected from "those who affected to trade for the public good"—this argument must be rejected on grounds of principle. What it amounts to is an assertion that those who favor the taxes and expenditures in question have failed to persuade a majority of their fellow citizens to be of like mind and that they are seeking to attain by undemocratic procedures what they cannot attain by democratic procedures. In a free society, it is hard for "evil" people to do "evil," especially since one man's good is another's evil.

I have, for simplicity, concentrated on the special case of the corporate executive, except only for the brief digression on trade unions. But precisely the same argument applies to the newer phenomenon of calling upon stockholders to require corporations to exercise social responsibility (the recent G.M. crusade for example). In most of these cases, what is in effect involved is some stockholders trying to get other stockholders (or customers or employees) to contribute against their will to "social" causes favored by the activists. Insofar as they succeed, they are again imposing taxes and spending the proceeds.

The situation of the individual proprietor is somewhat different. If he acts to reduce the returns of his enterprise in order to exercise his "social responsibility," he is spending his own money, not someone else's. If he wishes to spend his money on such purposes, that is his right, and I cannot see that there is any objection to his doing so. In the process, he, too, may impose costs on employees and customers. However, because he is far less likely than a large corporation or union to have monopolistic power, any such side effects will tend to be minor.

Of course, in practice the doctrine of social responsibility is frequently a cloak for actions that are justified on other grounds rather than a reason for those actions.

To illustrate, it may well be in the long-run interest of a corporation that is a major employer in a small community to devote resources to providing amenities to that community or to improving its government. That may make it easier to attract desirable employees, it may reduce the wage bill or lessen losses from pilferage and sabotage or have other worthwhile effects. Or it may be that, given the laws about the deductibility of corporate charitable contributions, the stockholders can contribute more to charities they favor by having the corporation make the gift than by doing it themselves, since they can in that way contribute an amount that would otherwise have been paid as corporate taxes.

In each of these—and many similar—cases, there is a strong temptation to rationalize these actions as an exercise of "social responsibility." In the present climate of opinion, with its widespread aversion to "capitalism," "profits," and "soulless corporation" and so on, this is one way for a corporation to generate goodwill as a by-product of expenditures that are entirely justified in its own self-interest.

It would be inconsistent of me to call on corporate executives to refrain from this hypocritical window-dressing because it harms the foundations of a free society. That would be to call on them to exercise a "social responsibility"! If our institutions, and the attitudes of the public make it in their self-interest to cloak their actions in this way, I cannot summon much indignation to denounce them. At the same time, I can express admiration for those individual proprietors or owners of closely held corporations or stockholders of more broadly held corporations who disdain such tactics as approaching fraud.

Whether blameworthy or not, the use of the cloak of social responsibility, and the nonsense spoken in its name by influential and prestigious businessmen, does clearly harm the foundations of a free society. I have been impressed time and again by the schizophrenic character of many businessmen. They are capable of being extremely far-sighted and clear-headed in matters that are internal to their businesses. They are incredibly short-sighted and muddle-headed in matters that are outside their businesses but affect the possible survival of business in general. This short-sightedness is strikingly exemplified in the calls from many businessmen for wage and price guidelines or controls or income policies. There is nothing that could do more in a brief period to destroy a market system and replace it by a centrally controlled system than effective governmental control of prices and wages.

The short-sightedness is also exemplified in speeches by businessmen on social responsibility. This may gain them kudos in the short run. But it helps to strengthen the already too prevalent view that the pursuit of profits is wicked and immoral and must be curbed and controlled by external forces. Once this view is adopted, the external forces that curb the market will not be the social consciences, however highly developed, of the pontificating executives; it will be the iron fist of Government bureaucrats. Here, as with price and wage controls, businessmen seem to me to reveal a suicidal impulse.

The political principle that underlies the market mechanism is unanimity. In an ideal free market resting on private property, no individual can coerce any other, all cooperation is voluntary, all parties to such cooperation benefit or they need not participate. There are no values, no "social" responsibilities in any sense other than the shared values and responsibilities of individuals. Society is a collection of individuals and of the various groups they voluntarily form.

The political principle that underlies the political mechanism is conformity. The individual must serve a more general social interest—whether that be determined by a church or a dictator or a majority. The individual may have a vote and say in what is to be done, but if he is overruled, he must conform. It is appropriate for some to require others to contribute to a general social purpose whether they wish to or not.

Unfortunately, unanimity is not always feasible. There are some respects in which conformity appears unavoidable, so I do not see how one can avoid the use of the political mechanism altogether.

But the doctrine of "social responsibility" taken seriously would extend the scope of the political mechanism to every human activity. It does not differ in philosophy from the most explicitly collectivist doctrine. It differs only by professing to believe that collectivist ends can be attained without collectivist means. That is why, in my book *Capitalism and Freedom*, I have called it a "fundamentally subversive doctrine" in a free society, and have said that in such a society, "there is one and only one social responsibility of business—to use its resources and engage in activities designed to increase its profits so long as it stays within the rules of the game, which is to say, engages in open and free competition without deception or fraud."

Can a Corporation Have a Conscience?

Kenneth E. Goodpaster and John B. Matthews, Jr.

During the severe racial tensions of the 1960s, Southern Steel Company (actual case, disguised name) faced considerable pressure from government and the press to explain and modify its policies regarding discrimination both within its plants and in the major city where it was located. SSC was the largest employer in the area (it had nearly 15,000 workers, one-third of whom were black) and had made great strides toward removing barriers to equal job opportunity in its several plants. In addition, its top executives (especially its chief executive officer, James Weston) had distinguished themselves as private citizens for years in community programs for black housing, education, and small business as well as in attempts at desegregating all-white police and local government organizations.

SSC drew the line, however, at using its substantial economic influence in the local area to advance the cause of the civil rights movement by pressuring banks, suppliers, and the local government:

"As individuals we can exercise what influence we may have as citizens," James Weston said, "but for a corporation to attempt to exert any kind of economic compulsion to achieve a particular end in a social area seems to me to be quite beyond what a corporation should do and quite beyond what a corporation can do. I believe that while government may seek to compel social reforms, any attempt by a private organization like SSC to impose its views, its beliefs, and its will upon the community would be repugnant to our American constitutional concepts and that appropriate steps to correct this abuse of corporate power would be universally demanded by public opinion."

Weston could have been speaking in the early 1980s on any issue that corporations around the United States now face. Instead of social justice, his theme might be environmental protection, product safety, marketing practice, or international bribery. His statement for SSC raises the important issue of corporate responsibility. Can a corporation have a conscience?

Weston apparently felt comfortable saying it need not. The responsibilities of ordinary persons and of "artificial persons" like corporations are, in his view, separate. Persons' responsibilities go beyond those of corporations. Persons, he seems to have believed, ought to care not only about themselves but also about the dignity and well-being of those around them—ought not only to care but also to act. Organizations, he evidently thought, are creatures of, and to a degree prisoners of, the systems of economic incentive and political sanction that give them reality and therefore should not be expected to display the same moral attributes that we expect of persons.

Others inside business as well as outside share Weston's perception. One influential philosopher—John Ladd—carries Weston's view a step further:

"It is improper to expect organizational conduct to conform to the ordinary principles of morality," he says. "We cannot and must not expect formal organizations, or their representatives acting in their official capacities, to be honest, courageous, considerate, sympathetic, or to have any kind of moral integrity. Such concepts are not in the vocabulary, so to speak, of the organizational language game."[1]

In our opinion, this line of thought represents a tremendous barrier to the development of business ethics both as a field of inquiry and as a practical

---

[1]See John Ladd, "Morality and the Ideal of Rationality in Formal Organizations," *The Monist*, October 1970, p. 499.

force in managerial decision making. This is a matter about which executives must be philosophical and philosophers must be practical. A corporation can and should have a conscience. The language of ethics does have a place in the vocabulary of an organization. There need not be and there should not be a disjunction of the sort attributed to SSC's James Weston. Organizational agents such as corporations should be no more and no less morally responsible (rational, self-interested, altruistic) than ordinary persons.

We take this position because we think an analogy holds between the individual and the corporation. If we analyze the concept of moral responsibility as it applies to persons, we find that projecting it to corporations as agents in society is possible.

DEFINING THE RESPONSIBILITY OF PERSONS

When we speak of the responsibility of individuals, philosophers say that we mean three things: someone is to blame, something has to be done, or some kind of trustworthiness can be expected.

We apply the first meaning, what we shall call the *causal* sense, primarily to legal and moral contexts where what is at issue is praise or blame for a past action. We say of a person that he or she was responsible for what happened, is to blame for it, should be held accountable. In this sense of the word, *responsibility* has to do with tracing the causes of actions and events, of finding out who is answerable in a given situation. Our aim is to determine someone's intention, free will, degree of participation, and appropriate reward or punishment.

We apply the second meaning of *responsibility* to rule following, to contexts where individuals are subject to externally imposed norms often associated with some social role that people play. We speak of the responsibilities of parents to children, of doctors to patients, of lawyers to clients, of citizens to the law. What is socially expected and what the party involved is to answer for are at issue here.

We use the third meaning of *responsibility* for decision making. With this meaning of the term, we say that individuals are responsible if they are trustworthy and reliable, if they allow appropriate factors to affect their judgment; we refer primarily to a person's independent thought processes and decision making, processes that justify an attitude of trust from those who interact with him or her as a responsible individual.

The distinguishing characteristic of moral responsibility, it seems to us, lies in this third sense of the term. Here the focus is on the intellectual and emotional processes in the individual's moral reasoning. Philosophers call this "taking a moral point of view" and contrast it with such other processes as being financially prudent and attending to legal obligations.

To be sure, characterizing a person as "morally responsible" may seem rather vague. But vagueness is a contextual notion. Everything depends on how we fill in the blank in "vague for———purposes."

In some contexts the term "six o'clockish" is vague, while in others it is useful and informative. As a response to a space-shuttle pilot who wants to know when to fire the reentry rockets, it will not do, but it might do in response to a spouse who wants to know when one will arrive home at the end of the workday.

We maintain that the processes underlying moral responsibility can be defined and are not themselves vague, even though gaining consensus on specific moral norms and decisions is not always easy.

What, then, characterizes the processes underlying the judgment of a person we call morally responsible? Philosopher William K. Frankena offers the following answer:

"A morality is a normative system in which judgments are made, more or less consciously, [out of a] consideration of the effects of actions...on the lives of persons...including the lives of others besides the person acting....David Hume took a similar position when he argued that what speaks in a moral judgment is a kind of sympathy....A little later,...Kant put the matter somewhat better by characterizing morality as the business of respecting persons as ends and not as means or as things...."[2]

Frankena is pointing to two traits, both rooted in a long and diverse philosophical tradition:

1 *Rationality* Taking a moral point of view includes the features we usually attribute to rational decision making, that is, lack of impulsiveness, care in mapping out alternatives and consequences, clarity about goals and purposes, attention to details of implementation.

2 *Respect* The moral point of view also includes a special awareness of and concern for the effects of one's decisions and policies on others, special in the sense that it goes beyond the kind of awareness and concern that would ordinarily be part of rationality, that is, beyond seeing others merely as instrumental to accomplishing one's own purposes. This is respect for the lives of others and involves taking their needs and interests seriously, not simply as resources in one's own decision making but as limiting conditions which change the very definition of one's habitat from a self-centered to a shared environment. It is what philosopher Immanuel Kant meant by the "categorical imperative" to treat others as valuable in and for themselves.

It is this feature that permits us to trust the morally responsible person. We know that such a person takes our point of view into account not merely as a useful precaution (as in "honesty is the best policy") but as important in its own right.

These components of moral responsibility are not too vague to be useful. Rationality and respect affect the manner in which a person approaches practical decision making: they affect the way in which the individual processes

---

[2]See William K. Frankena, *Thinking About Morality* (Ann Arbor: University of Michigan Press, 1980), p. 26.

information and makes choices. A rational but not respectful Bill Jones will not lie to his friends *unless* he is reasonably sure he will not be found out. A rational but not respectful Mary Smith will defend an unjustly treated party *unless* she thinks it may be too costly to herself. A rational *and* respectful decision maker, however, notices—and cares—whether the consequences of his or her conduct lead to injuries or indignities to others.

Two individuals who take "the moral point of view" will not of course always agree on ethical matters, but they do at least have a basis for dialogue.

PROJECTING RESPONSIBILITY TO CORPORATIONS

Now that we have removed some of the vagueness from the notion of moral responsibility as it applies to persons, we can search for a frame of reference in which, by analogy with Bill Jones and Mary Smith, we can meaningfully and appropriately say that corporations are morally responsible. This is the issue reflected in the SSC case.

To deal with it, we must ask two questions: Is it meaningful to apply moral concepts to actors who are not persons but who are instead made up of persons? And even if meaningful, is it advisable to do so?

If a group can act like a person in some ways, then we can expect it to behave like a person in other ways. For one thing, we know that people organized into a group can act as a unit. As business people well know, legally a corporation is considered a unit. To approach unity, a group usually has some sort of internal decision structure, a system of rules that spell out authority relationships and specify the conditions under which certain individuals' actions become official actions of the group.[3]

If we can say that persons act responsibly only if they gather information about the impact of their actions on others and use it in making decisions, we can reasonably do the same for organizations. Our proposed frame of reference for thinking about and implementing corporate responsibility aims at spelling out the processes associated with the moral responsibility of individuals and projecting them to the level of organizations. This is similar to, though an inversion of, Plato's famous method in the *Republic*, in which justice in the community is used as a model for justice in the individual.

Hence, corporations that monitor their employment practices and the effects of their production processes and products on the environment and human health show the same kind of rationality and respect that morally responsible individuals do. Thus, attributing actions, strategies, decisions, and moral responsibilities to corporations as entities distinguishable from those who hold offices in them poses no problem.

And when we look about us, we can readily see differences in moral responsibility among corporations in much the same way that we see differences among persons. Some corporations have built features into their management

---

[3]See Peter French, "The Corporation as a Moral Person," *American Philosophical Quarterly*, July 1979, p. 207.

incentive systems, board structures, internal control systems, and research agendas that in a person we would call self-control, integrity, and conscientiousness. Some have institutionalized awareness and concern for consumers, employees, and the rest of the public in ways that others clearly have not.

As a matter of course, some corporations attend to the human impact of their operations and policies and reject operations and policies that are questionable. Whether the issue be the health effects of sugared cereal or cigarettes, the safety of tires or tampons, civil liberties in the corporation or the community, an organization reveals its character as surely as a person does.

Indeed, the parallel may be even more dramatic. For just as the moral responsibility displayed by an individual develops over time from infancy to adulthood,[4] so too we may expect to find stages of development in organizational character that show significant patterns.

EVALUATING THE IDEA OF MORAL PROJECTION

Concepts like moral responsibility not only make sense when applied to organizations but also provide touchstones for designing more effective models than we have for guiding corporate policy.

Now we can understand what it means to invite SSC as a corporation to be morally responsible both in-house and in its community, but *should* we issue the invitation? Here we turn to the question of advisability. Should we require the organizational agents in our society to have the same moral attributes we require of ourselves?

Our proposal to spell out the processes associated with moral responsibility for individuals and then to project them to their organizational counterparts takes on added meaning when we examine alternative frames of reference for corporate responsibility.

Two frames of reference that compete for the allegiance of people who ponder the question of corporate responsibility are emphatically opposed to this principle of moral projection—what we might refer to as the "invisible hand" view and the "hand of government" view.

The Invisible Hand

The most eloquent spokesman of the first view is Milton Friedman (echoing many philosophers and economists since Adam Smith). According to this pattern of thought, the true and only social responsibilities of business organizations are to make profits and obey the laws. The workings of the free and competitive marketplace will "moralize" corporate behavior quite independently of any attempts to expand or transform decision making via moral projection.

---

[4]A process that psychological researchers from Jean Piaget to Lawrence Kohlberg have examined carefully; see Jean Piaget, *The Moral Judgment of the Child* (New York: Free Press, 1965) and Lawrence Kohlberg, *The Philosophy of Moral Development* (New York: Harper & Row, 1981).

A deliberate amorality in the executive suite is encouraged in the name of systemic morality: the common good is best served when each of us and our economic institutions pursue not the common good or moral purpose, advocates say, but competitive advantage. Morality, responsibility, and conscience reside in the invisible hand of the free market system, not in the hands of the organizations within the system, much less the managers within the organizations.

To be sure, people of this opinion admit, there is a sense in which social or ethical issues can and should enter the corporate mind, but the filtering of such issues is thorough: they go through the screens of custom, public opinion, public relations, and the law. And, in any case, self-interest maintains primacy as an objective and a guiding star.

The reaction from this frame of reference to the suggestion that moral judgment be integrated with corporate strategy is clearly negative. Such an integration is seen as inefficient and arrogant, and in the end both an illegitimate use of corporate power and an abuse of the manager's fiduciary role. With respect to our SSC case, advocates of the invisible hand model would vigorously resist efforts, beyond legal requirements, to make SSC right the wrongs of racial injustice. SSC's responsibility would be to make steel of high quality at least cost, to deliver it on time, and to satisfy its customers and stockholders. Justice would not be part of SSC's corporate mandate.

The Hand of Government

Advocates of the second dissenting frame of reference abound, but John Kenneth Galbraith's work has counterpointed Milton Friedman's with insight and style. Under this view of corporate responsibility, corporations are to pursue objectives that are rational and purely economic. The regulatory hands of the law and the political process rather than the invisible hand of the marketplace turn these objectives to the common good.

Again, in this view, it is a system that provides the moral direction for corporate decision making—a system, though, that is guided by political managers, the custodians of the public purpose. In the case of SSC, proponents of this view would look to the state for moral direction and responsible management, both within SSC and in the community. The corporation would have no moral responsibility beyond political and legal obedience.

What is striking is not so much the radical difference between the economic and social philosophies that underlie these two views of the source of corporate responsibility but the conceptual similarities. Both views locate morality, ethics, responsibility, and conscience in the systems of rules and incentives in which the modern corporation finds itself embedded. Both views reject the exercise of independent moral judgment by corporations as actors in society.

Neither view trusts corporate leaders with stewardship over what are often called noneconomic values. Both require corporate responsibility to march to the beat of drums outside. In the jargon of moral philosophy, both views press for a rule-centered or a system-centered ethics instead of an agent-centered ethics. These frames of reference countenance corporate rule-following responsibility for corporations but not corporate decision-making responsibility.

The Hand of Management

To be sure, the two views under discussion differ in that one looks to an invisible moral force in the market while the other looks to a visible moral force in government. But both would advise against a principle of moral projection that permits or encourages corporations to exercise independent, noneconomic judgment over matters that face them in their short- and long-term plans and operations.

Accordingly, both would reject a third view of corporate responsibility that seeks to affect the thought processes of the organization itself—a sort of "hand of management" view—since neither seems willing or able to see the engines of profit regulate themselves to the degree that would be implied by taking the principle of moral projection seriously. Cries of inefficiency and moral imperialism from the right would be matched by cries of insensitivity and illegitimacy from the left, all in the name of preserving us from corporations and managers run morally amuck.

Better, critics would say, that moral philosophy be left to philosophers, philanthropists, and politicians than to business leaders. Better that corporate morality be kept to glossy annual reports, where it is safely insulated from policy and performance.

The two conventional frames of reference locate moral restraint in forces external to the person and the corporation. They deny moral reasoning and intent to the corporation in the name of either market competition or society's system of explicit legal constraints and presume that these have a better moral effect than that of rationality and respect.

Although the principle of moral projection, which underwrites the idea of a corporate conscience and patterns it on the thought and feeling processes of the person, is in our view compelling, we must acknowledge that it is neither part of the received wisdom, nor is its advisability beyond question or objection. Indeed, attributing the role of conscience to the corporation seems to carry with it new and disturbing implications for our usual ways of thinking about ethics and business.

Perhaps the best way to clarify and defend this frame of reference is to address the objections to the principle found in the last pages of this article. There we see a summary of the criticisms and counterarguments we have heard during hours of discussion with business executives and business school students. We believe that the replies to the objections about a corporation having a conscience are convincing.

LEAVING THE DOUBLE STANDARD BEHIND

We have come some distance from our opening reflection on Southern Steel Company and its role in its community. Our proposal—clarified, we hope, through these objections and replies—suggests that it is not sufficient to draw a sharp line between individuals' private ideas and efforts and a corporation's institutional efforts but that the latter can and should be built upon the former.

Does this frame of reference give us an unequivocal prescription for the behavior of SSC in its circumstances? No, it does not. Persuasive arguments might be made now and might have been made then that SSC should not have used its considerable economic clout to threaten the community into deseg-regation. A careful analysis of the realities of the environment might have disclosed that such a course would have been counterproductive, leading to more injustice than it would have alleviated.

The point is that some of the arguments and some of the analyses are or would have been moral arguments, and thereby the ultimate decision that of an ethically responsible organization. The significance of this point can hardly be overstated, for it represents the adoption of a new perspective on corporate policy and a new way of thinking about business ethics. We agree with one authority, who writes that "the business firm, as an organic entity intricately affected by and affecting its environment, is as appropriately adaptive...to demands for responsible behavior as for economic service."[5]

The frame of reference here developed does not offer a decision procedure for corporate managers. That has not been our purpose. It does, however, shed light on the conceptual foundations of business ethics by training attention on the corporation as a moral agent in society. Legal systems of rules and incentives are insufficient, even though they may be necessary, as frameworks for corporate responsibility. Taking conceptual cues from the features of moral responsibility normally expected of the person in our opinion deserves practicing managers' serious consideration.

The lack of congruence that James Weston saw between individual and corporate moral responsibility can be, and we think should be, overcome. In the process, what a number of writers have characterized as a double standard—a discrepancy between our personal lives and our lives in organiza-tional settings—might be dampened. The principle of moral projection not only helps us to conceptualize the kinds of demands that we might make of corporations and other organizations but also offers the prospect of harmoniz-ing those demands with the demands that we make of ourselves.

IS A CORPORATION A MORALLY RESPONSIBLE "PERSON"?

Objection 1 to the Analogy

Corporations are not persons. They are artificial legal constructions, machines for mobilizing economic investments toward the efficient production of goods and services. We cannot hold a corporation responsible. We can only hold individuals responsible.

---

[5]See Kenneth R. Andrews, *The Concept of Corporate Strategy*, revised edition (Homewood, Ill.: Dow Jones-Irwin, 1980), p. 99.

Reply

Our frame of reference does not imply that corporations are persons in a literal sense. It simply means that in certain respects concepts and functions normally attributed to persons can also be attributed to organizations made up of persons. Goals, economic values, strategies, and other such personal attributes are often usefully projected to the corporate level by managers and researchers. Why should we not project the functions of conscience in the same way? As for holding corporations responsible, recent criminal prosecutions such as the case of Ford Motor Company and its Pinto gas tanks suggest that society finds the idea both intelligible and useful.

Objection 2

A corporation cannot be held responsible at the sacrifice of profit. Profitability and financial health have always been and should continue to be the "categorical imperatives" of a business operation.

Reply

We must of course acknowledge the imperatives of survival, stability, and growth when we discuss corporations, as indeed we must acknowledge them when we discuss the life of an individual. Self-sacrifice has been identified with moral responsibility in only the most extreme cases. The pursuit of profit and self-interest need not be pitted against the demands of moral responsibility. Moral demands are best viewed as containments—not replacements—for self-interest.

This is not to say that profit maximization never conflicts with morality. But profit maximization conflicts with other managerial values as well. The point is to coordinate imperatives, not deny their validity.

Objection 3

Corporate executives are not elected representatives of the people, nor are they anointed or appointed as social guardians. They therefore lack the social mandate that a democratic society rightly demands of those who would pursue ethically or socially motivated policies. By keeping corporate policies confined to economic motivations, we keep the power of corporate executives in its proper place.

Reply

The objection betrays an oversimplified view of the relationship between the public and the private sector. Neither private individuals nor private corporations that guide their conduct by ethical or social values beyond the demands of law should be constrained merely because they are not elected to do so. The demands of moral responsibility are independent of the demands of political legitimacy and are in fact presupposed by them.

To be sure, the state and the political process will and must remain the primary mechanisms for protecting the public interest, but one might be forgiven the hope that the political process will not substitute for the moral judgment of the citizenry or other components of society such as corporations.

Objection 4

Our system of law carefully defines the role of agent or fiduciary and makes corporate managers accountable to shareholders and investors for the use of their assets. Management cannot, in the name of corporate moral responsibility, arrogate to itself the right to manage these assets by partially noneconomic criteria.

Reply

First, it is not so clear that investors insist on purely economic criteria in the management of their assets, especially if some of the shareholders' resolutions and board reforms of the last decade are any indication. For instance, companies doing business in South Africa have had stockholders question their activities, other companies have instituted audit committees for their boards before such auditing was mandated, and mutual funds for which "socially responsible behavior" is a major investment criterion now exist.

Second, the categories of "shareholder" and "investor" connote wider time spans than do immediate or short-term returns. As a practical matter, considerations of stability and long-term return on investment enlarge the class of principals to which managers bear a fiduciary relationship.

Third, the trust that managers hold does not and never has extended to "any means available" to advance the interests of the principals. Both legal and moral constraints must be understood to qualify that trust—even, perhaps, in the name of a larger trust and a more basic fiduciary relationship to the members of society at large.

Objection 5

The power, size, and scale of the modern corporation—domestic as well as international—are awesome. To unleash, even partially, such power from the discipline of the marketplace and the narrow or possibly nonexistent moral purpose implicit in that discipline would be socially dangerous. Had SSC acted in the community to further racial justice, its purposes might have been admirable, but those purposes could have led to a kind of moral imperialism or worse. Suppose SSC had thrown its power behind the Ku Klux Klan.

Reply

This is a very real and important objection. What seems not to be appreciated is the fact that power affects when it is used as well as when it is not used. A decision by SSC not to exercise its economic influence according to "noneconomic" criteria is inevitably a moral decision and just as inevitably affects the community. The issue in the end is not whether corporations (and other organizations) should be "unleashed" to exert moral force in our society but rather how critically and self-consciously they should choose to do so.

The degree of influence enjoyed by an agent, whether a person or an organization, is not so much a factor recommending moral disengagement as a factor demanding a high level of moral awareness. Imperialism is more to be feared when moral reasoning is absent than when it is present. Nor do we suggest that the "discipline of the marketplace" be diluted; rather, we call for it to be supplemented with the discipline of moral reflection.

Objection 6

The idea of moral projection is a useful device for structuring corporate responsibility only if our understanding of moral responsibility at the level of the person is in some sense richer than our understanding of moral responsibility on the level of the organization as a whole. If we are not clear about individual responsibility, the projection is fruitless.

Reply

The objection is well founded. The challenge offered by the idea of moral projection lies in our capacity to articulate criteria or frameworks of reasoning for the morally responsible person. And though such a challenge is formidable, it is not clear that it cannot be met, at least with sufficient consensus to be useful.

For centuries, the study and criticism of frameworks have gone on, carried forward by many disciplines, including psychology, the social sciences, and philosophy. And though it would be a mistake to suggest that any single framework (much less a decision mechanism) has emerged as the right one, it is true that recurrent patterns are discernible and well enough defined to structure moral discussion.

In the body of the article, we spoke of rationality and respect as components of individual responsibility. Further analysis of these components would translate them into social costs and benefits, justice in the distribution of goods and services, basic rights and duties, and fidelity to contracts. The view that pluralism in our society has undercut all possibility of moral agreement is anything but self-evident. Sincere moral disagreement is, of course, inevitable and not clearly lamentable. But a process and a vocabulary for articulating such values as we share is no small step forward when compared with the alternatives.

Perhaps in our exploration of the moral projection we might make some surprising and even reassuring discoveries about ourselves.

Objection 7

Why is it necessary to project moral responsibility to the level of the organization? Isn't the task of defining corporate responsibility and business ethics sufficiently discharged if we clarify the responsibilities of men and women in business as individuals? Doesn't ethics finally rest on the honesty and integrity of the individual in the business world?

Reply

Yes and no. Yes, in the sense that the control of large organizations does finally rest in the hands of managers, of men and women. No, in the sense that what is being controlled is a cooperative system for a cooperative purpose. The projection of responsibility to the organization is simply an acknowledgement of the fact that the whole is more than the sum of its parts. Many intelligent people do not an intelligent organization make. Intelligence needs to be structured, organized, divided, and recombined in complex processes for complex purposes.

Studies of management have long shown that the attributes, successes, and failures of organizations are phenomena that emerge from the coordination of persons' attributes and that explanations of such phenomena require categories of analysis and description beyond the level of the individual. Moral responsibility is an attribute that can manifest itself in organizations as surely as competence or efficiency.

Objection 8

Is the frame of reference here proposed intended to replace or undercut the relevance of the "invisible hand" and the "government hand" views, which depend on external controls?

Reply

No. Just as regulation and economic competition are not substitutes for corporate responsibility, so corporate responsibility is not a substitute for law and the market. The imperatives of ethics cannot be relied on—nor have they ever been relied on—without a context of external sanctions. And this is true as much for individuals as for organizations.

This frame of reference takes us beneath, but not beyond, the realm of external systems of rules and incentives and into the thought processes that interpret and respond to the corporation's environment. Morality is more than merely part of that environment. It aims at the projection of conscience, not the enthronement of it in either the state or the competitive process.

The rise of the modern large corporation and the concomitant rise of the professional manager demand a conceptual framework in which these phenomena can be accommodated to moral thought. The principle of moral projection furthers such accommodation by recognizing a new level of agency in society and thus a new level of responsibility.

Objection 9

Corporations have always taken the interests of those outside the corporation into account in the sense that customer relations and public relations generally are an integral part of rational economic decision making. Market signals and social signals that filter through the market mechanism inevitably represent the interests of parties affected by the behavior of the company. What, then, is the point of adding respect to rationality?

Reply

Representing the affected parties solely as economic variables in the environment of the company is treating them as means or resources and not as ends in themselves. It implies that the only voice which affected parties should have in organizational decision making is that of potential buyers, sellers, regulators, or boycotters. Besides, many affected parties may not occupy such roles, and those who do may not be able to signal the organization with messages that effectively represent their stakes in its actions.

To be sure, classical economic theory would have us believe that perfect competition in free markets (with modest adjustments from the state) will result in all relevant signals being "heard," but the abstractions from reality implicit in such theory make it insufficient as a frame of reference for moral responsibility. In a world in which strict self-interest was congruent with the common good, moral responsibility might be unnecessary. We do not, alas, live in such a world.

The element of respect in our analysis of responsibility plays an essential role in ensuring the recognition of unrepresented or underrepresented voices in the decision making of organizations as agents. Showing respect for persons as ends and not mere means to organizational purposes is central to the concept of corporate moral responsibility.

The New Property

George C. Lodge

The Lockean ideology attached supreme importance to property rights as a means to fulfilling the values of survival, justice, and self-respect. We have seen that by the term "property," Locke meant both body and estate, and that by "estate" he meant essentially land or clearly owned artifacts; and that he regarded the sole role of the state as being the protection of property, a man's body and estate. He was speaking for a clientele who owned property and were anxious to keep it from the king. For them, property was the means to political and economic independence, the guarantor of freedom. Those who did not own property, those who had sold even their bodies through wage labor, were so deprived of independence as to be incapable of voting freely and, therefore, were made ineligible to vote. In early America, property was widely diffused—nearly everyone had a reasonable chance to own some. (Slaves were, of course, excepted, being property themselves. In fact, slavery was justified in part because of the enormous power of property rights as an idea in America.)

After a period in which the corporation was seen as the creation of a legislature for the fulfillment of a specific community need, the idea of individual property rights came to make the corporation legitimate. Time and again this right was used to protect the corporation as an individual against the intervention of the state. And although the ownership of the corporation became more and more diffused until it was nothing but a myth, the idea of property was maintained, its unreality ignored in the name of efficiency and growth.[1] Today, the concept of private property when applied to the large public corporation is so obscure as to be nearly useless for legitimization. At the same time, uncertainty about the definition of efficiency and the acceptability of growth deprive these two notions of their old force.

The beginning of the disintegration of the idea of property rights in America can be set in the year 1877, when Chief Justice Morrison R. Waite found in *Munn v. Illinois*[2] that property "affected with a public interest" ceases to be purely private. Waite employed this concept to justify state regulation of rates charged by a private warehouse. The doctrine was taken further in 1934 in *Nebbia v. New York*,[3] when the Supreme Court found that the state could intervene whenever the public needed protection in the name of community need. It is hard to improve on the much earlier statement of the problem of private property rights versus the public interest made by Chief Justice Shaw in Massachusetts in 1839:

From *The New American Ideology* by George C. Lodge (Alfred A. Knopf, Inc., 1975). Copyright, 1975, George C. Lodge. Reprinted by permission.

[1]James Willard Hurst, *The Legitimacy of the Business Corporation in the Law of the United States, 1780–1970* (Charlottesville: The University Press of Virginia, 1970), pp. 234–53.

[2]*Munn v. Illinois*, 94 U.S. 113 (1877).

[3]*Nebbia v. New York*, 291 U.S. 502 (1934).

It is difficult, perhaps impossible, to lay down any general rule, that would precisely define the power of the government in the acknowledged right of eminent domain. It must be large and liberal, so as to meet the public exigencies, and it must be so limited and constrained, as to secure effectually the rights of citizens; and it must depend, in some instances, upon the nature of the exigencies as they arise, and the circumstances of individual cases.[4]

The continuing disintegration of property rights as a legitimizing idea today is rooted in two factors: the changes that have come about in the nature of the American community (Shaw's "public exigencies"), and the continued dispersion of "ownership" of some 2,000 large publicly held corporations which account for something like 70–80 percent of the nation's corporate assets.[5] As the right to property gives way, a new idea is taking its place—the communitarian right of all members to survival, to income, to health, education, green space, natural beauty, and so on. It is not that the right to property need be abolished or that it is evil. It can continue to be appropriate in some settings, including most of the nation's several million small and clearly proprietary enterprises. But it has lost its dominant place as the prime guarantor and arbiter of human rights. In particular, it has lost its utility with respect to the large nonproprietary corporation.

The transformation is observable in several key areas. In the first place, technology has opened access to new sectors of our universe in which the traditional notions of property rights and ownership are simply irrelevant. Outer space and the seabed, for example, are defined by international law as "the common province of mankind" and "the common heritage of mankind," respectively.[6] No person, no corporation, no state may own these areas. They belong to all; they are of "the commons."

In the second place, scarce resources are coming to be placed in the public domain. We are increasingly aware of the scarcity of vital commodities: clean air to breathe, pure water to drink, fertile soil, natural beauty, fuel for energy, and perhaps food to eat. In the name of survival, these resources are moving inexorably beyond property into a new cradle of legitimacy composed of two related ideas: community need, and harmony between man and nature.

---

[4]J. Shaw, per curiam, Boston Water Power Co. v. Boston and Worcester Railroad, 3 Pick, 360 (1839). Quoted in Harry N. Scheiber, "The Road to Munn: Eminent Domain and the Concept of Public Purpose in the State Courts," Perspectives in American History, vol. v, (1971): 399.

[5]In 1968, the United States contained about 1.6 million profit-seeking corporations. Forty-three % of those possessed assets of less than $50,000 and 94% had assets of less than $1 million. On the other hand, 1,900 companies, constituting 0.13% of the corporate population, had assets of $100 million or more and held about 60% of total corporate assets. This concentration of assets in large publicly owned firms whose shares are traded on the stock exchanges has been increasing steadily since World War II. Neil Jacoby has estimated that 10,000 of the 1.6 million corporations have stock which is publicly traded—Neil H. Jacoby, Corporate Power and Social Responsibility (New York: The Macmillan Co., 1973), pp. 28, 49, and 179. Jacoby used data from Statistics of Income: Corporation Returns 1965 (Washington D.C.: U.S. Government Printing Office, 1965), pp. 4–5; Betty Bock, Concentration, Oligopoly and Profit: Concept and Data (New York: The Conference Board, 1972).

[6]Elisabeth Mann Borgese, "The Promise of Self Management," The Center Magazine, June 1972.

Examples of this transformation in new law are abundant, none more dramatic than the National Environmental Protection Act and the Clean Air Act. In 1972, for example, a land developer began construction of a high-rise apartment building on a small plot of land near Mammoth Lake in the High Sierras of California. Residents sued to halt the construction even though it was on private land. It offended the environment, they said. The case worked its way to the California Supreme Court, and in a 6-1 decision the court ruled in favor of the residents. In consequence, state and local governments now must make environmental-impact studies and expose them to public scrutiny before they can approve private construction projects which may have a significant impact on the environment. The California decision meant that citizens can sue to halt any such project that is not accompanied by such a study. According to the attorneys who represented the Mammoth Lake residents, the California court decision was "the first time that any U.S. law has given citizens the right to participate directly in private land-use decisions before they are made." A number of land development and housing companies are in a quandary about what to do. "I think they want to put the builders out of business," said Gene Meyers, executive vice president of Levitt United.[7]

In much the same vein a federal task force on land use, headed by Laurance S. Rockefeller, advised President Nixon in 1973 that henceforth "development rights" on private property must be regarded as resting with the community rather than with property owners:

> There is a new mood in America. Increasingly, citizens are asking what urban growth will add to the quality of their lives. They are questioning the way relatively unconstrained piecemeal urbanization is changing their communities, and are rebelling against the traditional processes of government and the market place which they believe have inadequately guided development in the past....They are measuring new development proposals by the extent to which environmental criteria are satisfied.[8]

Even with declining fertility rates, the report said, the nation's population will keep growing until well into the twenty-first century. It put present growth at the rate of 27,000 new households a week. The Constitution guarantees these families the right to move about freely, a fact that caused the task force to raise some long-range questions. May not the "new mood" force this attribute of individualism to change, in the face of community need? May it not be necessary for every level of government, covering every locality, to plan its growth, to provide for open space, proper housing, and the rest? And may this not require that communities establish population ceilings? Specifically, the report urged that all levels of government engage in buying up land for public uses and adopt strict regulations governing the use of privately held land. It observed that the states have the power to do this, "but must overcome a tradition of inactivity."

---

[7]Earl C. Gottschalk, Jr., "Guarding the Land," *Wall Street Journal*, Oct. 9, 1972.
[8]Quoted in Gladwin Hill, "Authority to Develop Land Is Termed a Public Right," *The New York Times*, May 30, 1973.

The strength of this tradition cannot be underestimated. Colorado Springs, for example, is a heavenly place nestled beneath the majesty of the Rocky Mountains on the edge of the Great Plains. Recently, its population has been growing by leaps and bounds, with industrial sprawl marrings its perimeters. Youths abound, and there is insufficient work for them to do; vandalism is high. The community is running out of water and inversion makes the air foul on certain days. It is turning from heaven to hell before the stricken eyes of its business and civic leaders. I spoke to those leaders in 1972 about their ideology, which is as near to pure Lockeanism as one is likely to find in America today. They heard me out and shuffled silently from the hall. Later, in the hotel bar, I met the city manager who had heard the speech. He told me, "You're right. We have to plan as a community, but every time I suggest it, they call me a socialist or something worse." Others from the hall joined us in the bar. Relaxed, they lamented their plight, the waywardness of their children, the decline of what they had held dear. I made my speech again; this time the ideological barriers were more permeable. Since then, even Colorado Springs has begun to plan—its Lockeanism eroded by crisis.

In April 1974, the Environmental Protection Agency, acting under the National Environmental Protection Act, moved indirectly to limit the population size of Ocean County, New Jersey. An official of the EPA said, "We intend to do this all over the country." The EPA ruled that the national pollution standards set by the act required a total population of no more than 250,000 in sixteen municipalities of the county. It sought to enforce this ruling by refusing to grant the Ocean County Sewage Authority either the required discharge permit or federal funds to build a system which would serve a larger population.[9]

In the third place, mass urbanization has undermined the traditional theory of private domain. The old ideas simply fade, slowly but surely, as increasing numbers of people pay rent in vast complexes where ownership guarantees none of the political, social, and economic independence described by Locke and formerly provided by the family farm or business. The old idea of property is powerless to prevent the deterioration of low-cost housing blocks; already the federal government owns large tracts of faltering or abandoned inner-city housing. In 1972, for example, the Department of Housing and Urban Development found itself the reluctant owner of 5,000 single-family homes in Detroit's wasteland; the situation is as bad in other cities.[10] Cities and neighborhoods within cities are communities, and can only function if they are treated as such. But this requires entirely different ideological foundations, an entirely new collective consciousness.

In the fourth place, there has been a shift in the nature and function of work and in the means that workers have to fulfillment and self-respect. Of primary importance here is the fact that virtually all members of the American com-

---

[9]U.S. Environmental Protection Agency, Region II, "Conclusions and Recommendations on the Central Service Area Sewage Project of Ocean County, New Jersey," April 1974.

[10]John Herbers, "U.S. Now Big Landlord in Decaying Inner City," *The New York Times*, Jan. 2, 1972.

munity now have at least a theoretical right that would have been unthinkable as recently as fifty years ago: the right, in effect, to survive. Along with this go other rights of community membership—to a minimum income, to health services, even to entertainment as in public television. (And further rights derive from membership in certain communities, such as IBM or AT&T, Oregon or Los Angeles.) The definition of survival has now become disconnected from work, being guaranteed by the community.

This has several important implications for the idea of property rights. The right to survive as a right of membership is obviously more important than property rights. And the idea of one's body being one's property, which was so central to Lockean individualistic thought, loses force.

Other factors have eroded the old notion of labor as a man's use of his own body. Today, labor increasingly means skill, knowledge, education, and organization. These are not owned by anybody; they are the product of the community. Further, as Robert L. Heilbroner has put it: "In the advanced capitalist nations, new elites based on science and technology are gradually displacing the older elites based on wealth."[11] At the same time, other wealth-producing factors such as resources and capital are becoming less clearly "owned" and of decreasing importance compared with the intangibles of knowledge and organization.

The ascendancy of community-created labor resources, coupled with the communitarian guarantee of survival and the decline in the legitimacy of property rights—and thus in the old basis of managerial authority—is having profound organizational effects. There need be no top or bottom in the managerial hierarchy; there must merely be a gradient of different skills and roles. Authority can derive from a variety of sources, which may have nothing to do with property....And because the number, size, and importance of organizations (particularly the corporation) are growing, the terms of membership in those organizations are of increasing concern. Once, private ownership of his labor conferred a degree of individual independence upon a worker, even if it was only his body that he owned. But the worker today is increasingly compelled to function in a large organization in which any rights he may have depend upon his locus there and upon his dedication to the organization's goals.

Charles Reich has stated the dilemma well:

When status and relationships to organizations replace private property, the result is a change in the degree of independent sovereignty enjoyed by the individual. Private property gave each person a domain in which he could be independent, and it enabled him to tell the rest of the world to go fly a kite. But a person whose "property" consists of a position in an organization is tied to the fate of the organization; if the organization goes down he goes with it.[12]

---

[11]Robert L. Heilbroner in *The New York Times Magazine*, as quoted in John K. Galbraith, *Economics and the Public Purpose* (Boston: Houghton Mifflin Co., 1973), p. 81.

[12]Charles Reich, *The Greening of America* (New York: Random House, Inc., 1970), p. 111.

This redefinition of property plays havoc with some profoundly traditional notions of individual incentive and responsibility. As Aristotle wrote:

> that which is common to the greatest number has the least care bestowed upon it. Every one thinks chiefly of his own, hardly at all of the common interest, and only when he is himself concerned as an individual. For besides other considerations, everybody is more inclined to neglect the duty which he expects another to fulfill; as in families many attendants are often less useful than a few.[13]

Western man has seemed to husband best that which is his. Furthermore, we derive important psychological satisfaction from owning something, even though it be but a knick-knack. Surely this trait in our culture will not wither soon; nonetheless, we must adjust it to the new concept of place in the communitarian order.

Other cultures have succeeded in reaching a solution here. In Japan, for example, the common interest has always been placed above that of the individual. Indeed, the individual achieves fulfillment only insofar as he contributes to his family, to his village, to the greater Japan. Centuries of cultural development and environmental adaptation have created this ideology—if a break in the dike around your rice paddy causes a flood in mine, our individual interests become inseparable from our common interest and the latter must prevail. Tightly delimited in resources, the Japanese have consequently produced a radically different ideology and radically different institutions from the United States or the West in general. As we move into an era of communitarianism, we can see that these institutions are functioning in many ways more effectively than ours. The role of the state and its relationship to business, for example, have given Japan a substantial edge in its strategic planning in the world economy. But the difficulty of moving away from our Western bias is as great as the seeming inevitability of such a movement.

Finally, the 2,000 or so largest corporations in America, which control most of the nation's corporate assets, have over the years detached themselves from the old idea of property. Even when managers cling to it for legitimacy, what authority they have derives from their place in a hierarchy of uncertain legitimacy. Since large corporations have obvious potential power and influence, this uncertainty renders them vulnerable to charges of abuse and conspiracy. Whether or not their power and influence are in fact abusive or conspiratorial, their estrangement from the old bases of legitimacy makes them suspect. The problem is heightened when the community is unclear or inexplicit about what it expects of corporations.

Myth has it that a share of General Motors, for example, is philosophically as important as a share in the ownership of the corporation. The myth, however, is empty of reality. A share of GM is nothing more than a claim on income and is generally disposed of if a share of IBM pays more. The claim that the

---

[13]Aristotle, *Politics*, Book II, 1261b, in Benjamin Jowett, *The Politics of Aristotle* (Oxford, England: The Clarendon Press, 1885), p. 30.

shareholders elect the board of directors which in turn controls the "hired hands" of management is vapid. Myles Mace, in his study of corporate boards of directors, quotes one typical executive vice president:

> Management creates policies. We decide what course we are going to paddle our canoe in. We tell our directors the direction of the company and the reasons for it. Theoretically, the board has a right to veto, but they never exercise it....We communicate with them. But they are in no position to challenge what we propose to do.[14]

So management appoints the board and the board endorses management in a mystical, self-perpetuating process, which albeit efficient, is plainly illegitimate.[15] We were willing to live with the illegitimacy as long as efficiency and growth were of overriding importance, but now that other factors have called into question the previously uncounted costs of growth, our willingness is evaporating. The individual components of corporate America—what Galbraith calls the planning system—are too large and powerful to be left to themselves; and collectively, in the complexes these organizations have formed with each other and in the economic sectors they dominate, they have become political forces to be reckoned with on the very largest scale. No one can doubt that the intentions of the utility industry, the oil industry, the automobile industry, and the communications industry have become matters of national concern politically and socially, as well as economically. Yet although in fact these are vast industrial complexes, the terms in which they regard themselves are frequently individualistic and proprietary.

Even in the equity markets that serve these industries, the trend from the individual to the collective is apparent and sweeping. Investors in the equity markets, theoretically the owners of the corporations, are increasingly unidentifiable as individuals to whom the ownership of corporations could conceivably be attached. "Like the curator of the National Zoo," said G. Bradford Cook, when he retired as chairman of the Securities and Exchange Commission, "I feel constrained to warn: The individual investor has acquired the status of an endangered species."[16] The place of the individual investor has been taken by huge organizations whose ownership is also extremely obscure: mutual funds, insurance companies, pension funds, and bank trust departments. Whereas such groups accounted for only 35 percent of the dollar value of New York Stock Exchange trading volume in 1963, the percentage is well over 70 today. This development has changed and perhaps profoundly threatened capital market structures; John C. Whitehead, a Goldman, Sachs partner, asserts that institutional dominance has endangered the market's valuation capability and

[14]Myles L. Mace, "The Presidents and the Board of Directors," *Harvard Business Review*, March–April 1972, p. 41.

[15]The fact that the courts are holding directors increasingly liable for the sins of managers does not really help the legitimacy problem, even though it has probably increased the wariness of directors. The amount of liability insurance sold to directors and officers has increased from practically nothing to more than $1 billion—"The Law: Trouble for the Top," *Forbes*, Sept. 1, 1968, p. 23.

[16]*Business Week*, June 2, 1973, pp. 58 and 59.

demolished its liquidity: "We can look forward in another decade to complete dominance of our markets and of our corporations by a relatively small handful of institutions—the kind of industrial society that currently exists in Europe and Japan."[17]

This phenomenon of gigantism is having an interesting side effect on the innovation and enterprise which historically have been the handmaidens of the traditional ideology. Because the big institutions show market interest in relatively few stocks, newer and smaller companies are finding it increasingly difficult to go public at all. The vulnerability of our system to the acquisitiveness of the giants can be sensed in the example of Morgan Guaranty, which in 1972 owned more common stock than any other institution on earth—$2 billion worth of IBM, $1.1 billion of Kodak, and $500 million or more of Avon, Sears, and Xerox.[18] Taken together, all of these factors have thoroughly confused our original notions of the role of the publicly held corporation and eroded its legitimacy. Ideologically, it has become a mere collection of persons and matter with considerable potential power—political and social as well as economic—floating dangerously in a philosophic limbo. If it survives, as it probably will, it has to be made legitimate. The only questions are how and by whom. The issues surrounding these questions fall into two categories:

1 Those having to do with the external relationships between the corporate collective and the communities which it affects.

2 Those having to do with the internal structure of the organization and thus with managerial authority and collective discipline.

The Case Against Helping the Poor

Garrett Hardin

Environmentalists use the metaphor of the earth as a "spaceship" in trying to persuade countries, industries and people to stop wasting and polluting our natural resources. Since we all share life on this planet, they argue, no single person or institution has the right to destroy, waste, or use more than a fair share of its resources.

But does everyone on earth have an equal right to an equal share of its resources? The spaceship metaphor can be dangerous when used by misguided

From "Lifeboat Ethics: The Case Again Helping the Poor," *Psychology Today* (1974) Vol. 8, pp. 38–43, 123 126. Copyright Garrett Hardin, 1974. Reprinted by permission.

[17]In Japan, equity capital is rarely more than 25% of the corporation's total capitalization. Management controls companies with virtually no interference from stockholders. Ultimate control lies with the company's bank. The bank has no vote, but the company's dependence on the bank gives it what a Japanese manager once described as the "power of irresistible persuasion." Banks in turn are heavily influenced by government. See Peter F. Drucker, "Global Management," *Challenge to Leadership* (New York: The Free Press, 1973), p. 240.

[18]*Business Week*, June 2, 1973, p. 59.

idealists to justify suicidal policies for sharing our resources through uncon-
trolled immigration and foreign aid. In their enthusiastic but unrealistic generosity, they confuse the ethics of a spaceship with those of a lifeboat.

A true spaceship would have to be under the control of a captain, since no
ship could possibly survive if its course were determined by committee.
Spaceship Earth certainly has no captain; the United Nations is merely a
toothless tiger, with little power to enforce any policy upon its bickering
members.

If we divide the world crudely into rich nations and poor nations, two thirds
of them are desperately poor, and only one third comparatively rich, with the
United States the wealthiest of all. Metaphorically each rich nation can be seen
as a lifeboat full of comparatively rich people. In the ocean outside each
lifeboat swim the poor of the world, who would like to get in, or at least to
share some of the wealth. What should the lifeboat passengers do?

First, we must recognize the limited capacity of any lifeboat. For example, a
nation's land has a limited capacity to support a population and as the current
energy crisis has shown us, in some ways we have already exceeded the
carrying capacity of our land.

ADRIFT IN A MORAL SEA

So here we sit, say fifty people in our lifeboat. To be generous, let us assume it
has room for ten more, making a total capacity of sixty. Suppose the fifty of us
in the lifeboat see 100 others swimming in the water outside, begging for
admission to our boat or for handouts. We have several options: we may be
tempted to try to live by the Christian ideal of being "our brother's keeper," or
by the Marxist ideal of "to each according to his needs." Since the needs of all
in the water are the same, and since they can all be seen as "our brothers," we
could take them all into our boat, making a total of 150 in a boat designed for
sixty. The boat swamps, everyone drowns. Complete justice, complete
catastrophe.

Since the boat has an unused excess capacity of ten more passengers, we
could admit just ten more to it. But which ten do we let in? How do we choose?
Do we pick the best ten, the neediest ten, "first come, first served"? And what
do we say to the ninety we exclude? If we do let an extra ten into our lifeboat,
we will have lost our "safety factor," an engineering principle of critical
importance. For example, if we don't leave room for excess capacity as a safety
factor in our country's agriculture, a new plant disease or a bad change in the
weather could have disastrous consequences.

Suppose we decide to preserve our small safety factor and admit no more to
the lifeboat. Our survival is then possible, although we shall have to be
constantly on guard against boarding parties.

While this last solution clearly offers the only means of our survival, it is
morally abhorrent to many people. Some say they feel guilty about their good
luck. My reply is simple: "Get out and yield your place to others." This may
solve the problem of the guilt-ridden person's conscience, but it does not

change the ethics of the lifeboat. The needy person to whom the guilt-ridden person yields his place will not himself feel guilty about his good luck. If he did, he would not climb aboard. The net result of conscience-stricken people giving up their unjustly held seats is the elimination of that sort of conscience from the lifeboat.

This is the basic metaphor within which we must work out our solutions. Let us now enrich the image, step by step, with substantive additions from the real world, a world that must solve real and pressing problems of overpopulation and hunger.

The harsh ethics of the lifeboat become even harsher when we consider the reproductive differences between the rich nations and the poor nations. The people inside the lifeboats are doubling in numbers every eighty-seven years; those swimming around outside are doubling, on the average, every thirty-five years, more than twice as fast as the rich. And since the world's resources are dwindling, the difference in prosperity between the rich and the poor can only increase.

As of 1973, the U.S. had a population of 210 million people, who were increasing by 0.8 percent per year. Outside our lifeboat, let us imagine another 210 million people, (say the combined populations of Colombia, Ecuador, Venezuela, Morocco, Pakistan, Thailand, and the Philippines) who are increasing at a rate of 3.3 percent per year. Put differently, the doubling time for this aggregate population is twenty-one years, compared to eighty-seven years for the U.S.

MULTIPLYING THE RICH AND THE POOR

Now suppose the U.S. agreed to pool its resources with those seven countries, with everyone receiving an equal share. Initially the ratio of Americans to non-Americans in this model would be one-to-one. But consider what the ratio would be after eighty-seven years, by which time the Americans would have doubled to a population of 420 million. By then, doubling every twenty-one years, the other group would have swollen to 3.54 billion. Each American would have to share the available resources with more than eight people.

But, one could argue, this discussion assumes that current population trends will continue, and they may not. Quite so. Most likely the rate of population increase will decline much faster in the U.S. than it will in the other countries, and there does not seem to be much we can do about it. In sharing with "each according to his needs," we must recognize that needs are determined by population size, which is determined by the rate of reproduction, which at present is regarded as a sovereign right of every nation, poor or not. This being so, the philanthropic load created by the sharing ethic of the spaceship can only increase.

THE TRAGEDY OF THE COMMONS

The fundamental error of spaceship ethics, and the sharing it requires, is that it leads to what I call "the tragedy of the commons." Under a system of private property, the men who own property recognize their responsibility to care for it, for if they don't they will eventually suffer. A farmer, for instance, will allow no more cattle in a pasture than its carrying capacity justifies. If he overloads it, erosion sets in, weeds take over, and he loses the use of the pasture.

If a pasture becomes a commons open to all, the right of each to use it may not be matched by a corresponding responsibility to protect it. Asking everyone to use it with discretion will hardly do, for the considerate herdsman who refrains from overloading the commons suffers more than a selfish one who says his needs are greater. If everyone would restrain himself, all would be well; but it takes only one less than everyone to ruin a system of voluntary restraint. In a crowded world of less than perfect human beings, mutual ruin is inevitable if there are no controls. This is the tragedy of the commons.

One of the major tasks of education today should be the creation of such an acute awareness of the dangers of the commons that people will recognize its many varieties. For example, the air and water have become polluted because they are treated as commons. Further growth in the population or per capita conversion of natural resources into pollutants will only make the problem worse. The same holds true for the fish of the oceans. Fishing fleets have nearly disappeared in many parts of the world, technological improvements in the art of fishing are hastening the day of complete ruin. Only the replacement of the system of the commons with a responsible system of control will save the land, air, water and oceanic fisheries.

THE WORLD FOOD BANK

In recent years there has been a push to create a new commons called a World Food Bank, an international depository of food reserves to which nations would contribute according to their abilities and from which they would draw according to their needs. This humanitarian proposal has received support from many liberal international groups, and from such prominent citizens as Margaret Mead, U.N. Secretary General Kurt Waldheim, and Senators Edward Kennedy and George McGovern.

A world food bank appeals powerfully to our humanitarian impulses. But before we rush ahead with such a plan, let us recognize where the greatest political push comes from, lest we be disillusioned later. Our experience with the "Food for Peace program," or Public Law 480, gives us the answer. This program moved billions of dollars worth of U.S. surplus grain to food-short, population-long countries during the past two decades. But when P.L. 480 first became law, a headline in the business magazine *Forbes* revealed the real power behind it: "Feeding the World's Hungry Millions: How It Will Mean Billions for U.S. Business."

And indeed it did. In the years 1960 to 1970, U.S. taxpayers spent a total of $7.9 billion on the Food for Peace program. Between 1948 and 1970, they also paid an additional $50 billion for other economic-aid programs, some of which went for food and food-producing machinery and technology. Though all U.S. taxpayers were forced to contribute to the cost of P.L. 480, certain special interest groups gained handsomely under the program. Farmers did not have to contribute the grain; the Government, or rather the taxpayers, bought it from them at full market prices. The increased demand raised prices of farm products generally. The manufacturers of farm machinery, fertilizers and pesticides benefited by the farmers' extra efforts to grow more food. Grain elevators profited from storing the surplus until it could be shipped. Railroads made money hauling it to ports, and shipping lines profited from carrying it overseas. The implementation of P.L. 480 required the creation of a vast Government bureaucracy, which then acquired its own vested interest in continuing the program regardless of its merits.

EXTRACTING DOLLARS

Those who proposed and defended the Food for Peace program in public rarely mentioned its importance to any of these special interests. The public emphasis was always on its humanitarian effects. The combination of silent selfish interests and highly vocal humanitarian apologists made a powerful and successful lobby for extracting money from taxpayers. We can expect the same lobby to push now for the creation of a World Food Bank.

However great the potential benefit to selfish interests, it should not be a decisive argument against a truly humanitarian program. We must ask if such a program would actually do more good than harm, not only momentarily but also in the long run. Those who propose the food bank usually refer to a current "emergency" or "crisis" in terms of world food supply. But what is an emergency? Although they may be infrequent and sudden, everyone knows that emergencies will occur from time to time. A well-run family, company, organization or country prepares for the likelihood of accidents and emergencies. It expects them, it budgets for them, it saves for them.

LEARNING THE HARD WAY

What happens if some organizations or countries budget for accidents and others do not? If each country is solely responsible for its own well-being, poorly managed ones will suffer. But they can learn from experience. They may mend their ways, and learn to budget for infrequent but certain emergencies. For example, the weather varies from year to year, and periodic crop failures are certain. A wise and competent government saves out of the production of the good years in anticipation of bad years to come. Joseph taught this policy to Pharaoh in Egypt more than 2,000 years ago. Yet the great majority of the governments in the world today do not follow such a policy. They lack either the wisdom or the competence, or both. Should those nations that do manage to put something aside be forced to come to the rescue each time an emergency occurs among the poor nations?

"But it isn't their fault!" some kindhearted liberals argue. "How can we blame the poor people who are caught in an emergency? Why must they suffer for the sins of their governments?" The concept of blame is simply not relevant here. The real question is, what are the operational consequences of establishing a world food bank? If it is open to every country every time a need develops, slovenly rulers will not be motivated to take Joseph's advice. Someone will always come to their aid. Some countries will deposit food in the world food bank, and others will withdraw it. There will be almost no overlap. As a result of such solutions to food shortage emergencies, the poor countries will not learn to mend their ways, and will suffer progressively greater emergencies as their populations grow.

POPULATION CONTROL THE CRUDE WAY

On the average, poor countries undergo a 2.5 percent increase in population each year; rich countries, about 0.8 percent. Only rich countries have anything in the way of food reserves set aside, and even they do not have as much as they should. Poor countries have none. If poor countries received no food from the outside, the rate of their population growth would be periodically checked by crop failures and famines. But if they can always draw on a world food bank in time of need, their population can continue to grow unchecked, and so will their "need" for aid. In the short run, a world food bank may diminish that need, but in the long run it actually increases the need without limit.

Without some system of worldwide food sharing, the proportion of people in the rich and poor nations might eventually stabilize. The overpopulated poor countries would decrease in numbers, while the rich countries that had room for more people would increase. But with a well-meaning system of sharing, such as a world food bank, the growth differential between the rich and the poor countries will not only persist, it will increase. Because of the higher rate of population growth in the poor countries of the world, 88 percent of today's children are born poor, and only 12 percent rich. Year by year the ratio becomes worse, as the fast-reproducing poor outnumber the slow-reproducing rich.

A world food bank is thus a commons in disguise. People will have more motivation to draw from it than to add to any common store. The less provident and less able will multiply at the expense of the abler and more provident, bringing eventual ruin upon all who share in the commons. Besides, any system of "sharing" that amounts to foreign aid from the rich nations to the poor nations will carry the taint of charity, which will contribute little to the world peace so devoutly desired by those who support the idea of a world food bank.

As past U.S. foreign-aid programs have amply and depressingly demonstrated, international charity frequently inspires mistrust and antagonism rather than gratitude on the part of the recipient nation.

CHINESE FISH AND MIRACLE RICE

The modern approach to foreign aid stresses the export of technology and advice, rather than money and food. As an ancient Chinese proverb goes:

"Give a man a fish and he will eat for a day, teach him how to fish and he will eat for the rest of his days." Acting on this advice, the Rockefeller and Ford Foundations have financed a number of programs for improving agriculture in the hungry nations. Known as the "Green Revolution," these programs have led to the development of "miracle rice" and "miracle wheat," new strains that offer bigger harvests and greater resistance to crop damage. Norman Borlaug, the Nobel Prize winning agronomist who, supported by the Rockefeller Foundation, developed "miracle wheat," is one of the most prominent advocates of a world food bank.

Whether or not the Green Revolution can increase food production as much as its champions claim is a debatable but possibly irrelevant point. Those who support this well-intended humanitarian effort should first consider some of the fundamentals of human ecology. Ironically, one man who did was the late Alan Gregg, a vice president of the Rockefeller Foundation. Two decades ago he expressed strong doubts about the wisdom of such attempts to increase food production. He likened the growth and spread of humanity over the surface of the earth to the spread of cancer in the human body, remarking that "cancerous growths demand food; but, as far as I know, they have never been cured by getting it."

OVERLOADING THE ENVIRONMENT

Every human born constitutes a draft on all aspects of the environment: food, air, water, forests, beaches, wildlife, scenery and solitude. Food can, perhaps, be significantly increased to meet a growing demand. But what about clean beaches, unspoiled forests, and solitude? If we satisfy a growing population's need for food, we necessarily decrease its per capita supply of the other resources needed by men.

India, for example, now has a population of 600 million, which increases by 15 million each year. This population already puts a huge load on a relatively impoverished environment. The country's forests are now only a small fraction of what they were three centuries ago, and floods and erosion continually destroy the insufficient farmland that remains. Every one of the 15 million new lives added to India's population puts an additional burden on the environment, and increases the economic and social costs of crowding. However humanitarian our intent, every Indian life saved through medical or nutritional assistance from abroad diminishes the quality of life for those who remain, and for subsequent generations. If rich countries make it possible, through foreign aid, for 600 million Indians to swell to 1.2 billion in a mere twenty-eight years, as their current growth rate threatens, will future generations of Indians thank us for hastening the destruction of their environment? Will our good intentions be sufficient excuse for the consequences of our actions?

My final example of a commons in action is one for which the public has the least desire for rational discussion—immigration. Anyone who publicly questions the wisdom of current U.S. immigration policy is promptly charged with bigotry, prejudice, ethnocentrism, chauvinism, isolationism or selfishness.

Rather than encounter such accusations, one would rather talk about other matters, leaving immigration policy to wallow in the crosscurrents of special interests that take no account of the good of the whole, or the interests of posterity.

Perhaps we still feel guilty about things we said in the past. Two generations ago the popular press frequently referred to Dagos, Wops, Polacks, Chinks and Krauts, in articles about how America was being "overrun" by foreigners of supposedly inferior genetic stock. But because the implied inferiority of foreigners was used then as justification for keeping them out, people now assume that restrictive policies could only be based on such misguided notions. There are other grounds.

A NATION OF IMMIGRANTS

Just consider the numbers involved. Our Government acknowledges a net inflow of 400,000 immigrants a year. While we have no hard data on the extent of illegal entries, educated guesses put the figure at about 600,000 a year. Since the natural increase (excess of births over deaths) of the resident population now runs about 1.7 million per year, the yearly gain from immigration amounts to at least 19 percent of the total annual increase, and may be as much as 37 percent if we include the estimate for illegal immigrants. Considering the growing use of birth-control devices, the potential effect of educational campaigns by such organizations as Planned Parenthood Federation of America and Zero Population Growth, and the influence of inflation and the housing shortage, the fertility rate of American women may decline so much that immigration could account for all the yearly increase in population. Should we not at least ask if that is what we want?

For the sake of those who worry about whether the "quality" of the average immigrant compares favorably with the quality of the of the average resident, let us assume that immigrants and nativeborn citizens are of exactly equal quality, however one defines that term. We will focus here only on quantity; and since our conclusions will depend on nothing else, all charges of bigotry and chauvinism become irrelevant.

IMMIGRATION VS. FOOD SUPPLY

World food banks *move food to the people,* hastening the exhaustion of the environment of the poor countries. Unrestricted immigration, on the other hand, *moves people to the food,* thus speeding up the destruction of the environment of the rich countries. We can easily understand why poor people should want to make this latter transfer, but why should rich hosts encourage it?

As in the case of foreign-aid programs, immigration receives support from selfish interests and humanitarian impulses. The primary selfish interest in unimpeded immigration is the desire of employers for cheap labor, particularly in industries and trades that offer degrading work. In the past, one wave of foreigners after another was brought into the U.S. to work at wretched jobs for wretched wages. In recent years the Cubans, Puerto Ricans and Mexicans have had this dubious honor. The interests of the employers of cheap labor mesh well with the guilty silence of the country's liberal intelligentsia. White Anglo-Saxon Protestants are particularly reluctant to call for a closing of the doors to immigration for fear of being called bigots.

But not all countries have such reluctant leadership. Most educated Hawaiians, for example, are keenly aware of the limits of their environment, particularly in terms of population growth. There is only so much room on the islands, and the islanders know it. To Hawaiians, immigrants from the other forty-nine states present as great a threat to those from other nations. At a recent meeting of Hawaiian government officials in Honolulu, I had the ironic delight of hearing a speaker, who like most of his audience was of Japanese ancestry, ask how the country might practically and constitutionally close its doors to further immigration. One member of the audience countered: "How can we shut the door now! We have many friends and relatives in Japan that we'd like to bring here some day so that they can enjoy Hawaii too." The Japanese-American speaker smiled sympathetically and answered: "Yes, but we have children now, and someday we'll have grandchildren too. We can bring more people here from Japan only by giving away some of the land that we hope to pass on to our grandchildren some day. What right do we have to do that?"

At this point, I can hear U.S. liberals asking: "How can you justify slamming the door once you're inside? You say that immigrants should be kept out. But aren't we all immigrants, or the descendants of immigrants? If we insist on staying, must we not admit all others?" Our craving for intellectual order leads us to seek and prefer symmetrical rules and morals: a single rule for me and everybody else; the same rule yesterday, today, and tomorrow. Justice, we feel, should not change with time and place.

We Americans of non-Indian ancestry can look upon ourselves as the descendants of thieves who are guilty morally, if not legally, of stealing this land from its Indian owners. Should we then give back the land to the now living American descendants of those Indians? However morally or logically sound this proposal may be, I, for one, am unwilling to live by it and I know no one else who is. Besides, the logical consequence would be absurd. Suppose that, intoxicated with a sense of pure justice, we should decide to turn our land over to the Indians. Since all our wealth has also been derived from the land, wouldn't we be morally obliged to give that back to the Indians too?

PURE JUSTICE VS. REALITY

Clearly, the concept of pure justice produces an infinite regression to absurdity. Centuries ago, wise men invented statutes of limitations to justify the rejection of such pure justice, in the interest of preventing continual disorder. The law zealously defends property rights, but only relatively recent property rights. Drawing a line after an arbitrary time has elapsed may be unjust, but the alternatives are worse.

We are all the descendants of thieves, and the world's resources are inequitably distributed. But we must begin the journey to tomorrow from the point where we are today. We cannot remake the past. We cannot safely divide the wealth equitably among all peoples so long as people reproduce at different rates. To do so would guarantee that our grandchildren, and everyone else's grandchildren, would have only a ruined world to inherit.

To be generous with one's own possessions is quite different from being generous with those of posterity. We should call this point to the attention of those who, from a commendable love of justice and equality, would institute a system of the commons, either in the form of a world food bank, or of unrestricted immigration. We must convince them if we wish to save at least some parts of the world from environmental ruin.

Without a true world government to control reproduction and the use of available resources, the sharing ethic of the spaceship is impossible. For the foreseeable future, our survival demands that we govern our actions by the ethics of a lifeboat, harsh though they may be. Posterity will be satisfied with nothing else.

Rich and Poor

Peter Singer

Consider these facts: by the most cautious estimates, 400 million people lack the calories, protein, vitamins and minerals needed for a normally healthy life. Millions are constantly hungry; others suffer from deficiency diseases and from infections they would be able to resist on a better diet. Children are worst affected. According to one estimate, 15 million children under five die every year from the combined effects of malnutrition and infection. In some areas, half the children born can be expected to die before their fifth birthday....

Death and disease apart, absolute poverty remains a miserable condition of life, with inadequate food, shelter, clothing, sanitation, health services and education. According to World Bank estimates which define absolute poverty in terms of income levels insufficient to provide adequate nutrition, something like 800 million people—almost 40 percent of the people of developing countries—live in absolute poverty. Absolute poverty is probably the principal cause of human misery today.

This is the background situation, the situation that prevails on our planet all the time. It does not make headlines. People died from malnutrition and related diseases yesterday, and more will die tomorrow. The occasional droughts, cyclones, earthquakes and floods that take the lives of tens of thousands in one place and at one time are more newsworthy. They add greatly to the total amount of human suffering; but it is wrong to assume that when there are no major calamities reported, all is well.

The problem is not that the world cannot produce enough to feed and shelter its people. People in the poor countries consume, on average, 400 lbs of grain a year, while North Americans average more than 2000 lbs. The difference is caused by the fact that in the rich countries we feed most of our grain to animals, converting it into meat, milk and eggs. Because this is an inefficient process, wasting up to 95 percent of the food value of the animal feed, people in rich countries are responsible for the consumption of far more food than those in poor countries who eat few animal products. If we stopped feeding animals on grains, soybeans and fishmeal the amount of food saved would—if distributed to those who need it—be more than enough to end hunger throughout the world.

These facts about animal food do not mean that we can easily solve the world food problem by cutting down on animal products, but they show that the problem is essentially one of distribution rather than production. The world does produce enough food....

At present, very little is being transferred. Members of the Organization of Petroleum Exporting Countries lead the way, giving an average of 2.1 percent of their Gross National Product. Apart from them, only Sweden, The Netherlands and Norway have reached the modest UN target of 0.7 percent of GNP. Britain gives 0.38 percent of its GNP in official development assistance and a small additional amount in unofficial aid from voluntary organizations. The total comes to less than £1 per month per person, and compares with 5.5 percent of GNP spent on alcohol, and 3 percent on tobacco. Other, even wealthier nations, give still less: Germany gives 0.27 percent, the United States 0.22 percent and Japan 0.21 percent.

THE MORAL EQUIVALENT OF MURDER?

If these are the facts, we cannot avoid concluding that by not giving more than we do, people in rich countries are allowing those in poor countries to suffer from absolute poverty, with consequent malnutrition, ill health and death. This is not a conclusion which applies only to governments. It applies to each absolutely affluent individual, for each of us has the opportunity to do something about the situation; for instance, to give our time or money to voluntary organizations like Oxfam, War on Want, Freedom From Hunger, and so on. If, then, allowing someone to die is not intrinsically different from killing someone, it would seem that we are all murderers.

Is this verdict too harsh? Many will reject it as self-evidently absurd. They would sooner take it as showing that allowing to die cannot be equivalent to killing than as showing that living in an affluent style without contributing to Oxfam is ethically equivalent to going over to India and shooting a few peasants. And no doubt, put as bluntly as that, the verdict *is* too harsh.

There are several significant differences between spending money on luxuries instead of using it to save lives, and deliberately shooting people.

First, the motivation will normally be different. Those who deliberately shoot others go out of their way to kill; they presumably want their victims dead, from malice, sadism, or some equally unpleasant motive. A person who buys a colour television set presumably wants to watch television in colour—not in itself a terrible thing. At worst, spending money on luxuries instead of giving it away indicates selfishness and indifference to the sufferings of others, characteristics which may be undesirable but are not comparable with actual malice or similar motives.

Second, it is not difficult for most of us to act in accordance with a rule against killing people: it is, on the other hand, very difficult to obey a rule which commands us to save all the lives we can. To live a comfortable, or even luxurious life it is not necessary to kill anyone; but it is necessary to allow some to die whom we might have saved, for the money that we need to live comfortably could have been given away. Thus the duty to avoid killing is much easier to discharge completely than the duty to save. Saving every life we could would mean cutting our standard of living down to the bare essentials needed to keep us alive.[1] To discharge this duty completely would require a degree of moral heroism utterly different from what is required to mere avoidance of killing.

A third difference is the greater certainty of the outcome of shooting when compared with not giving aid. If I point a loaded gun at someone and pull the trigger, it is virtually certain that the person will be injured, if not killed; whereas the money that I could give might be spent on a project that turns out to be unsuccessful and helps no one.

Fourth, when people are shot there are identifiable individuals who have been harmed. We can point to them and to their grieving families. When I buy my colour television, I cannot know whom my money would have saved if I had given it away. In a time of famine I may see dead bodies and grieving families on my new television, and I might not doubt that my money would have saved some of them: even then it is impossible to point to a body and say that had I not bought the set, that person would have survived.

Fifth, it might be said that the plight of the hungry is not my doing, and so I cannot be held responsible for it. The starving would have been starving if I

---

[1]Strictly, we would need to cut down to the minimum level compatible with earning the income which, after providing for our needs, left us most to give away. Thus if my present position earns me, say, £10,000 a year, but requires me to spend £1,000 a year on dressing respectably and maintaining a car, I cannot save more people by giving away the car and clothes if that will mean taking a job which, although it does not involve me in these expenses, earns me only £5,000.

had never existed. If I kill, however, I am responsible for my victims' deaths, for those people would not have died if I had not killed them....

Do the five differences not only explain, but also justify, our attitudes? Let us consider them one by one:

1 Take the lack of an identifiable victim first. Suppose that I am a travelling salesman, selling tinned food, and I learn that a batch of tins contains a contaminant, the known effect of which when consumed is to double the risk that the consumer will die from stomach cancer. Suppose I continue to sell the tins. My decision may have no identifiable victims. Some of those who eat the food will die from cancer. The proportion of consumers dying in this way will be twice that of the community at large, but which among the consumers died because they ate what I sold, and which would have contracted the disease anyway? It is impossible to tell; but surely this impossibility makes my decision no less reprehensible than it would have been had the contaminant had more readily detectable, though equally fatal, effects.

2 The lack of certainty that by giving money I could save a life does reduce the wrongness of not giving, by comparison with deliberate killing: but it is insufficient to show that not giving is acceptable conduct. The motorist who speeds through pedestrian crossings, heedless of anyone who might be on them, is not a murderer. She may never actually hit a pedestrian; yet what she does is very wrong indeed.

3 The notion of responsibility for acts rather than omissions is more puzzling. On the one hand we feel ourselves to be under a greater obligation to help those whose misfortunes we have caused. (It is for this reason that advocates of overseas aid often argue that Western nations have created the poverty of Third World nations, through forms of economic exploitation which go back to the colonial system.) On the other hand any consequentialist would insist that we are responsible for all the consequences of our actions, and if a consequence of my spending money on a luxury item is that someone dies, I am responsible for that death. It is true that the person would have died even if I had never existed, but what is the relevance of that? The fact is that I do exist, and the consequentialist will say that our responsibilities derive from the world as it is, not as it might have been.

One way of making sense of the non-consequentialist view of responsibility is by basing it on a theory of rights of the kind proposed by John Locke or, more recently, Robert Nozick. If everyone has a right to life, and this right is a right *against* others who might threaten my life, but not a right to assistance from others when my life is in danger, then we can understand the feeling that we are responsible for acting to kill but not for omitting to save. The former violates the rights of others, the latter does not.

Should we accept such a theory of rights? If we build up our theory of rights by imagining, as Locke and Nozick do, individuals living independently from each other in a 'state of nature', it may seem natural to adopt a conception of rights in which as long as each leaves the other alone, no rights are violated. I might, on this view, quite properly have maintained my independent existence if I had wished to do so. So if I do not make you any worse off than you would have been if I had had nothing at all to do with you, how can I have violated your rights? But why start from such an unhistorical, abstract and ultimately inexplicable idea as an independent individual? We now know that our ancestors were social beings long before they were human beings, and could not have developed the abilities and capacities of human beings if they had not been social beings first. In any case we are not, now, isolated individuals. If we consider people living together in community, it is less easy to assume that rights must be restricted to rights against interference. We might, instead, adopt the view that taking rights to life seriously is incompatible with standing by and watching people die when one could easily save them.

   4 What of the difference in motivation? That a person does not positively wish for the death of another lessens the severity of the blame she deserves; but not by as much as our present attitudes to giving aid suggest. The behaviour of the speeding motorist is again comparable, for such motorists usually have no desire at all to kill anyone. They merely enjoy speeding and are indifferent to the consequences. Despite their lack of malice, those who kill with cars deserve not only blame but also severe punishment.

   5 Finally, the fact that to avoid killing people is normally not difficult, whereas to save all one possibly could save is heroic, must make an important difference to our attitude to failure to do what the respective principles demand. Not to kill is a minimum standard of acceptable conduct we can require of everyone; to save all one possibly could is not something that can realistically be required, especially not in societies accustomed to giving as little as ours do. Given the generally accepted standards, people who give, say, £100 a year to Oxfam are more aptly praised for above average generosity than blamed for giving less than they might. The appropriateness of praise and blame is, however, a separate issue from the rightness or wrongness of actions. The former evaluates the agent: the latter evaluates the action. Perhaps people who give £100 really ought to give at least £1,000, but to blame them for not giving more could be counterproductive. It might make them feel that what is required is too demanding, and if one is going to be blamed anyway, one might as well not give anything at all.

   (That an ethic which put saving all one possibly can on the same footing as not killing would be an ethic for saints or heroes should not lead us to assume that the alternative must be an ethic which makes it obligatory not to kill, but puts us under no obligation to save anyone. There are positions in between these extremes, as we shall soon see.)

   To summarize our discussion of the five differences which normally exist between killing and allowing to die, in the context of absolute poverty and overseas aid. The lack of an identifiable victim is of no moral significance, though it may play an important role in explaining our attitudes. The idea that we are directly responsible for those we kill, but not for those we do not help, depends on a questionable notion of responsibility, and may need to be based on a controversial theory of rights. Differences in certainty and motivation are ethically significant, and show that not aiding the poor is not to be condemned as murdering them; it could, however, be on a par with killing someone as a result of reckless driving, which is serious enough. Finally the difficulty of completely discharging the duty of saving all one possibly can makes it inappropriate to blame those who fall short of this target as we blame those who kill; but this does not show that the act itself is less serious. Nor does it indicate anything about those who, far from saving all they possibly can, make no effort to save anyone. . . .

OBJECTIONS TO THE ARGUMENT

Taking Care of Our Own

Anyone who has worked to increase overseas aid will have come across the argument that we should look after those near us, our families and then the poor in our own country, before we think about poverty in distant places.

No doubt we do instinctively prefer to help those who are close to us. Few could stand by and watch a child drown; many can ignore a famine in Africa. But the question is not what we usually do, but what we ought to do, and it is difficult to see any sound moral justification for the view that distance, or community membership, makes a crucial difference to our obligations.

Consider, for instance, racial affinities. Should whites help poor whites before helping poor blacks? Most of us would reject such a suggestion out of hand, and our discussion of the principle of equal consideration of interests . . . as shown why we should reject it: people's need for food has nothing to do with their race, and if blacks need food more than whites, it would be a violation of the principle of equal consideration to give preference to whites.

The same point applies to citizenship or nationhood. Every affluent nation has some relatively poor citizens, but absolute poverty is limited largely to the poor nations. Those living on the streets of Calcutta, or in a drought-stricken region of the Sahel, are experiencing poverty unknown in the West. Under these circumstances it would be wrong to decide that only those fortunate enough to be citizens of our own community will share our abundance.

We feel obligations of kinship more strongly than those of citizenship. Which parents could give away their last bowl of rice if their own children were starving? To do so would seem unnatural, contrary to our nature as biologically evolved beings—although whether it would be wrong is another question altogether. In any case, we are not faced with that situation, but with one in which our own children are well-fed, well-clothed, well-educated, and would now like new bikes, a stereo set, or their own car. In these circumstances any special obligations we might have to our children have been fulfilled, and the needs of strangers make a stronger claim upon us. . . .

Population and the Ethics of Triage

Perhaps the most serious objection to the argument that we have an obligation to assist is that since the major cause of absolute poverty is overpopulation, helping those now in poverty will only ensure that yet more people are born to live in poverty in the future....

In support of this view Garrett Hardin has offered a metaphor: we in the rich nations are like the occupants of a crowded lifeboat adrift in a sea full of drowning people. If we try to save the drowning by bringing them aboard our boat will be overloaded and we shall all drown. Since it is better that some survive than none, we should leave the others to drown. In the world today, according to Hardin, 'lifeboat ethics' apply. The rich should leave the poor to starve, for otherwise the poor will drag the rich down with them.

Against this view, some writers have argued that overpopulation is a myth. The world produces ample food to feed its population, and could, according to some estimates, feed ten times as many. People are hungry not because there are too many but because of inequitable land distribution, the manipulation of Third World economies by the developed nations, wastage of food in the West, and so on.

Putting aside the controversial issue of the extent to which food production might one day be increased, it is true, as we have already seen, that the world now produces enough to feed its inhabitants—the amount lost by being fed to animals itself being enough to meet existing grain shortages. Nevertheless population growth cannot be ignored. Bangladesh could, with land reform and using better techniques, feed its present population of 80 million; but by the year 2000, according to World Bank estimates, its population will be 146 million. The enormous effort that will have to go into feeding an extra 66 million people, all added to the population within a quarter of a century, means that Bangladesh must develop at full speed to stay where she is. Other low income countries are in similar situations. By the end of the century. Ethiopia's population is expected to rise from 29 to 54 million; Somalia's from 3 to 7 million, India's from 620 to 958 million, Zaire's from 25 to 47 million. What will happen then? Population cannot grow indefinitely. It will be checked by a decline in birth rates or a rise in death rates. Those who advocate triage are proposing that we allow the population growth of some countries to be checked by a rise in death rates—that is, by increased malnutrition, and related diseases; by widespread famines; by increased infant mortality; and by epidemics of infectious diseases....

If triage is to be rejected it must be tackled on its own ground, within the framework of consequentialist ethics. Here it is vulnerable. Any consequentialist ethics must take probability of outcome into account. A course of action that will certainly produce some benefit is to be preferred to an alternative course that may lead to a slightly larger benefit, but is equally likely to result in no benefit at all. Only if the greater magnitude of the uncertain benefit outweighs its uncertainty should we choose it. Better one certain unit of benefit than a 10 percent chance of 5 units; but better a 50 percent chance of 3 units than a single certain unit. The same principle applies when we are trying to avoid evils.

The policy of triage involves a certain, very great evil: population control by famine and disease. Tens of millions would die slowly. Hundreds of millions would continue to live in absolute poverty, at the very margin of existence. Against this prospect, advocates of the policy place a possible evil which is greater still: the same process of famine and disease, taking place in, say, fifty year's time, when the world's population may be three times its present level, and the number who will die from famine, or struggle on in absolute poverty, will be that much greater. The question is: how probable is this forecast that continued assistance now will lead to greater disasters in the future?

Forecasts of population growth are notoriously fallible, and theories about the factors which affect it remain speculative. One theory, at least as plausible as any other, is that countries pass through a 'demographic transition' as their standard of living rises. When people are very poor and have no access to modern medicine their fertility is high, but population is kept in check by high death rates. The introduction of sanitation, modern medical techniques and other improvements reduces the death rate, but initially has little effect on the birth rate. Then population grows rapidly. Most poor countries are now in this phase. If standards of living continue to rise, however, couples begin to realize that to have the same number of children surviving to maturity as in the past, they do not need to give birth to as many children as their parents did. The need for children to provide economic support in old age diminishes. Improved education and the emancipation and employment of women also reduce the birthrate, and so population growth begins to level off. Most rich nations have reached this stage, and their populations are growing only very slowly.

If this theory is right, there is an alternative to the disasters accepted as inevitable by supporters of triage. We can assist poor countries to raise the living standards of the poorest members of their population. We can encourage the governments of these countries to enact land reform measures, improve education, and liberate women from a purely child-bearing role....Success cannot be guaranteed; but the evidence that improved economic security and education reduce population growth is strong enough to make triage ethically unacceptable. We cannot allow millions to die from starvation and disease when there is a reasonable probability that population can be brought under control without such horrors....

Basic Rights

Henry Shue

...Unfortunately, for well over 1,000,000,000 human beings today the level of existence discussed here probably seems beyond reach, too far above them to be contemplated seriously. This need not be and must not continue....

BASIC RIGHTS

Nietzsche, who holds strong title to being the most misunderstood and most underrated philosopher of the last century, considered much of conventional morality—and not conceptions of rights only—to be an attempt by the powerless to restrain the powerful: an enormous net of fine mesh busily woven around the strong by the masses of the weak. And he was disgusted by it, as if fleas were pestering a magnificent leopard or ordinary ivy were weighing down a soaring oak. In recoiling from Nietzsche's *assessment* of morality, many have dismissed too quickly his insightful *analysis* of morality. Moral systems obviously serve more than one purpose, and different specific systems serve some purposes more fully or better than others, as of course Nietzsche himself also recognized. But one of the chief purposes of morality in general, and certainly of conceptions of rights, and of basic rights above all, is indeed to provide some minimal protection against utter helplessness to those too weak to protect themselves. Basic rights are a shield for the defenseless against at least some of the more devastating and more common of life's threats, which include, as we shall see, loss of security and loss of subsistence. Basic rights are a restraint upon economic and political forces that would otherwise be too strong to be resisted. They are social guarantees against actual and threatened deprivations of at least some basic needs. Basic rights are an attempt to give to the powerless a veto over some of the forces that would otherwise harm them the most.

Basic rights are the morality of the depths. They specify the line beneath which no one is to be allowed to sink. This is part of the reason that basic rights are tied as closely to self-respect as Feinberg indicates legal claim-rights are. And this helps to explain why Nietzsche found moral rights repugnant. His eye was on the heights, and he wanted to talk about how far some might soar, not about how to prevent the rest from sinking lower. It is not clear that we cannot do both.

And it is not surprising that what is in an important respect the essentially negative goal of preventing or alleviating helplessness is a central purpose of something as important as conceptions of basic rights. For everyone healthy adulthood is bordered on each side by helplessness, and it is vulnerable to interruption by helplessness, temporary or permanent, at any time. And many of the people in the world now have very little control over their fates, even over such urgent matters as whether their own children live through infancy. Nor is it surprising that although the goal is negative, the duties correlative to rights will turn out to include positive actions. The infant and the aged do not need to be assaulted in order to be deprived of health, life, or the capacity to enjoy active rights. The classic liberal's main prescription for the good life—do not interfere with thy neighbor—is the only poison they need. To be helpless they need only to be left alone....

Basic rights, then, are everyone's minimum reasonable demands upon the rest of humanity. They are the rational basis for justified demands the denial of which no self-respecting person can reasonably be expected to accept. Why should anything be so important? The reason is that rights are basic in the sense used here only if enjoyment of them is essential to the enjoyment of all other rights. This is what is distinctive about a basic right. When a right is genuinely basic, any attempt to enjoy any other right by sacrificing the basic right would be quite literally self-defeating, cutting the ground from beneath itself. Therefore, if a right is basic, other, non-basic rights may be sacrificed, if necessary, in order to secure the basic right. But the protection of a basic right may not be sacrificed in order to secure the enjoyment of a non-basic right. It may not be sacrificed because it cannot be sacrificed successfully. If the right sacrificed is indeed basic, then no right for which it might be sacrificed can actually be enjoyed in the absence of the basic right. The sacrifice would have proven self-defeating.

In practice, what this priority for basic rights usually means is that basic rights need to be established securely before other rights can be secured. The point is that people should be able to *enjoy*, or *exercise*, their other rights. The point is simple but vital. It is not merely that people should "have" their other rights in some merely legalistic or otherwise abstract sense compatible with being unable to make any use of the substance of the right. For example, if people have rights to free association, they ought not merely to "have" the rights to free association but also to enjoy their free association itself. Their freedom of association ought to be provided for by the relevant social institutions. This distinction between merely having a right and actually enjoying a right may seem a fine point, but it turns out later to be critical....

SECURITY RIGHTS

Our first project will be to see why people have a basic right to physical security—a right that is basic not to be subjected to murder, torture, mayhem, rape, or assault. The purpose in raising the questions why there are rights to physical security and why they are basic is not that very many people would seriously doubt either that there are rights to physical security or that they are basic. Although it is not unusual in practice for members of at least one ethnic group in a society to be physically insecure—to be, for example, much more likely than other people to be beaten by the police if arrested—few, if any, people would be prepared to defend in principle the contention that anyone lacks a basic right to physical security. Nevertheless, it can be valuable to formulate explicitly the presuppositions of even one's most firmly held beliefs, especially because these presuppositions may turn out to be general principles that will provide guidance in other areas where convictions are less firm. Precisely because we have no real doubt that rights to physical security are basic, it can be useful to see why we may properly think so.

If we had to justify our belief that people have a basic right to physical security to someone who challenged this fundamental conviction, we could in fact give a strong argument that shows that if there are any rights (basic or not basic) at all, there are basic rights to physical security. No one can fully enjoy any right that is supposedly protected by society if someone can credibly threaten him or her with murder, rape, beating, etc., when he or she tries to enjoy the alleged right. Such threats to physical security are among the most serious and—in much of the world—the most widespread hindrances to the enjoyment of any right. If any right is to be exercised except at great risk, physical security must be protected. In the absence of physical security people are unable to use any other rights that society may be said to be protecting without being liable to encounter many of the worst dangers they would encounter if society were not protecting the rights....

SUBSISTENCE RIGHTS

The main reason for discussing security rights, which are not very controversial, was to make explicit the basic assumptions that support the usual judgment that security rights are basic rights. Now that we have available an argument that supports them, we are in a position to consider whether matters other than physical security should, according to the same argument, also be basic rights. It will emerge that subsistence, or minimal economic security, which is more controversial than physical security, can also be shown to be as well justified for treatment as a basic right as physical security is—and for the same reasons.

By minimal economic security, or subsistence, I mean unpolluted air, unpolluted water, adequate food, adequate clothing, adequate shelter, and minimal preventive public health care. Many complications about exactly how to specify the boundaries of what is necessary for subsistence would be interesting to explore. But the basic idea is to have available for consumption what is needed for a decent chance at a reasonably healthy and active life of more or less normal length, barring tragic interventions. This central idea is clear enough to work with, even though disputes can occur over exactly where to draw its outer boundaries. A right to subsistence would not mean, at one extreme, that every baby born with a need for open-heart surgery has a right to have it, but it also would not count as adequate food a diet that produces a life expectancy of 35 years of fever-laden, parasite-ridden listlessness....

The same considerations that support the conclusion that physical security is a basic right support the conclusion that subsistence is a basic right. Since the argument is now familiar, it can be given fairly briefly.

It is quite obvious why, if we still assume that there are some rights that society ought to protect and still mean by this the removal of the most serious and general hindrances to the actual enjoyment of the rights, subsistence ought to be protected as a basic right. No one can fully, if at all, enjoy any right that is supposedly protected by society if he or she lack the essentials for a reasonably healthy and active life. Deficiencies in the means of subsistence can be just as fatal, incapacitating, or painful as violations of physical security. The resulting damage or death can at least as decisively prevent the enjoyment of any right as can the effects of security violations. Any form of malnutrition, or fever due to exposure, that causes severe and irreversible brain damage, for example, can effectively prevent the exercise of any right requiring clear thought and may, like brain injuries caused by assault, profoundly disturb personality. And, obviously, any fatal deficiencies end all possibility of the enjoyment of rights as firmly as an arbitrary execution.

Indeed, prevention of deficiencies in the essentials for survival is, if anything, more basic than prevention of violations of physical security. People who lack protection against violations of their physical security can, if they are free, fight back against their attackers or flee, but people who lack essentials, such as food, because of forces beyond their control, often can do nothing and are on their own utterly helpless.

The scope of subsistence rights must not be taken to be broader than it is. In particular, this step of the argument does not make the following absurd claim: since death and serious illness prevent or interfere with the enjoyment of rights, everyone has a basic right not to be allowed to die or to be seriously ill. Many causes of death and illness are outside the control of society, and many deaths and illnesses are the result of very particular conjunctions of circumstances that general social policies cannot control. But it is not impractical to expect some level of social organization to protect the minimal cleanliness of air and water and to oversee the adequate production, or import, and the proper distribution of minimal food, clothing, shelter, and elementary health care....

STANDARD THREATS

Before we turn over the coin of basic rights and consider the side with the duties, we need to establish two interrelated points about the rights side. One point... [is that] standard threats... [are] the targets of the social guarantees for the enjoyment of the substance of a right. The other point specifically concerns basic rights and the question whether the reasoning in favor of treating security and subsistence as the substances of basic rights does not generate an impractically and implausibly long list of things to which people will be said to have basic rights. The two points are interrelated because the clearest manner by which to establish that the list of basic rights must, on the contrary, be quite short is to invoke the fact that the social guarantees required by the structure of a right are guarantees, not against all possible threats, but only against what I will call standard threats....

CORRELATIVE DUTIES

Many Americans would probably be initially inclined to think that rights to subsistence are at least slightly less important than rights to physical security, even though subsistence is at least as essential to survival as security is and even though questions of security do not even arise when subsistence fails. Much official U.S. government rhetoric routinely treats all "economic rights," among which basic subsistence rights are buried amidst many non-basic rights, as secondary and deferrable.... Anyone familiar with the causes of malnutrition in underdeveloped countries today will recognize that the following hypothetical case is in no way unusual.

Suppose the largest tract of land in the village was the property of the descendant of a family that had held title to the land for as many generations back as anyone could remember. By absolute standards this peasant was by no means rich, but his land was the richest in the small area that constituted the universe for the inhabitants of this village. He grew, as his father and grandfather had, mainly the black beans that are the staple (and chief—and adequate—source of protein) in the regional diet. His crop usually constituted about a quarter of the black beans marketed in the village. Practically every family grew part of what they needed, and the six men he hired during the seasons requiring extra labor held the only paid jobs in the village—everyone else just worked his own little plot.

One day a man from the capital offered this peasant a contract that not only guaranteed him annual payments for a 10-year lease on his land but also guaranteed him a salary (regardless of how the weather, and therefore the crops, turned out—a great increase in his financial security) to be the foreman for a new kind of production on his land. The contract required him to grow flowers for export and also offered him the opportunity, which was highly recommended, to purchase through the company, with payments in installments, equipment that would enable him to need to hire only two men. The same contract was offered to, and accepted by, most of the other larger landowners in the general region to which the village belonged.

Soon, with the sharp reduction in supply, the price of black beans soared. Some people could grow all they needed (in years of good weather) on their own land, but the families that needed to supplement their own crop with purchases had to cut back their consumption. In particular, the children in the four families headed by the laborers who lost their seasonal employment suffered severe malnutrition, especially since the parents had originally worked as laborers only because their own land was too poor or too small to feed their families.

Now, the story contains no implication that the man from the capital or the peasants-turned-foremen were malicious or intended to do anything worse than single-mindedly pursue their own respective interests. But the outsider's offer of the contract was one causal factor, and the peasant's acceptance of the contract was another causal factor, in producing the malnutrition that would probably persist, barring protective intervention, for at least the decade the contract was to be honored. If the families in the village had rights to subsistence, their rights were being violated. Society, acting presumably by way of the government, ought to protect them from a severe type of active harm that eliminates their ability even to feed themselves....

TWO THESES ABOUT ECONOMIC DEPRIVATION

The thesis that particular deprivations are accidental often seems to be the explanation recommended by common sense, although we may not ordinarily think explicitly in terms of this distinction. Well-informed people are aware, for example, that the "Brazilian miracle" has left large numbers of the poorest Brazilians worse off then ever, that the Shah's "White Revolution" made relatively small inroads upon malnutrition and infant mortality, that President and Prime Minister Marcos's "New Society" is a similar failure, etc. But, especially if one assumes that those who dictate economic strategy are reasonable and well-intentioned people, one may infer that these repeated failures to deal with the basic needs of the most powerless are, in spite of the regularity with which they recur, unfortunate but unpredictable by-products of fundamentally benevolent, or anyhow enlightened, economic plans.

Alternatively one might infer that the continuing deprivations are inherent in the economic strategies being used, and that would lead to the second kind of thesis: that the continuance of the deprivations is essential to the economic strategies. Since this thesis may be less familiar. I would like to quote an example of it at some length. Because this particular formulation is intended by the analyst, Richard Fagen, to apply only to Latin America (with the exception of Cuba and, of course, to varying degrees in various different countries), a thesis concerning essential deprivation would naturally have to be formulated differently for Africa, Asia, and elsewhere. The following is intended, then, only as one good example, formulated in specifics to over only a single region, of the second type of thesis:

• Aggregate economic growth in Latin America over the past decade has been above world averages. The per capita income in the region now exceeds $1,000....

• The actual situation with respect to income distribution and social equity is, in general, appalling. Fifty percent of the region's citizens have incomes of less than $200 per year; one-third receive less than $100. The top five percent of the population controls one-third of the total income. The emphasis on industrialization and export-led growth almost everywhere reinforces and accelerates the neglect of agriculture—at least agriculture in basic foodstuffs for domestic consumption....

• Related to the income distribution and social equity issues is the problem of unemployment. In some countries as many as one out of three persons in the working-age population is unable to find a job of any sort....

• The kind of development that has taken place is reflected in the structure of external indebtedness. Current estimates are that the countries of the region now owe approximately $80 billion in public and publicly guaranteed debt alone....

• The Latin American state is everywhere involved in economic development and management. It is usually the prime borrower abroad, often an important investor at home, frequently a chief partner of foreign capital, and always a source of regulations on everything from wages to import quotas. State capitalism has come to Latin America with a vengeance, and even the governments that claim to give the freest play to market forces are in fact constantly intervening to establish the rules under which "free markets" will be allowed to operate.

The above sketch of Latin American development aids in understanding the nature of contemporary authoritarianism.... The linkages are complex, but very largely determine the public policies that will be followed. Creditors want to be paid in dollars or in other international currencies. The international financial institutions are critically concerned with the debtor country's balance of payments. A sharp increase in exports—acknowledged to be the best way to achieve a more favorable balance and repay the debt—is very difficult to achieve in the short run. Also difficult to accomplish is a dramatic increase in capital inflows—except by borrowing even more.

This leaves imports as a natural target for those who would save hard currency. But in order to cut imports—or at least that sector of imports that is least important to ruling elites, economic managers, and most national and international business—mass consumption must be restricted. Since quotas and tariffs are seen as inappropriate policy instruments, to a large extent consumer demand must be managed through restrictions on the real purchasing power of wage-earners—and increases in unemployment.

When coupled with cutbacks in government expenditures (typically in public works and welfare-enhancing subsidies), a huge proportion of the adjustment burden is thus transferred to the working class. In an inflationary economy, the proportional burden is even greater. Needless to say, where minimal possibilities of political expression exist, this kind of adjustment medicine does not go down easily. Repression of trade unions as effective organizations and workers as individuals is in this sense " necessary" for those in charge of managing the economy and for their friends and allies abroad....

....[I]t is now, I hope, quite clear that the honoring of subsistence rights may often in no way involve transferring commodities to people, but may instead involve preventing people's being deprived of the commodities or the means to grow, make, or buy the commodities. Preventing such deprivations will indeed require what can be called positive actions, especially protective and self-protective actions....

So I want to suggest that with every basic right, three types of duties correlate:

1 Duties to *avoid* depriving.
2 Duties to *protect* from deprivation.
3 Duties to *aid* the deprived.

This may be easier to see in the case of the more familiar basic right, the right to physical security (the right not to be tortured, executed, raped, assaulted, etc.). For every person's right to physical security, there are three correlative duties:

1 Duties not to eliminate a person's security—duties to *avoid* depriving.
2 Duties to protect people against deprivation of security by other people—duties to *protect* from deprivation.
3 Duties to provide for the security of those unable to provide for their own—duties to *aid* the deprived.

Similarly, for every right to subsistence there are:

1 Duties not to eliminate a person's only available means of subsistence—duties to *avoid* depriving.
2 Duties to protect people against deprivation of the only available means of subsistence by other people—duties to *protect* from deprivation.
3 Duties to provide for the subsistence of those unable to provide for their own—duties to *aid* the deprived.

If this suggestion is correct, the common notion that *rights* can be divided into rights to forbearance (so-called negative rights), as if some rights have correlative duties only to avoid depriving, and rights to aid (so-called positive rights), as if some rights have correlative duties only to aid, is thoroughly misguided. This misdirected simplification is virtually ubiquitous among contemporary North Atlantic theorists and is, I think, all the more pernicious for the degree of unquestioning acceptance it has now attained....

SUGGESTED SUPPLEMENTARY READINGS TO PART SEVEN

Bayles, Michael D.: *Morality and Population Policy* (University, Ala.: University of Alabama Press, 1980).

Bowie, Norman: *Business Ethics* (Englewood Cliffs, N.J.: Prentice-Hall, Inc., 1982).

Brown, Peter G., and Shue, Henry, eds.: *Food Policy: The Responsibility of the United States in the Life and Death Choices* (New York: Free Press, 1977).

Carr, Albert: "Is Business Bluffing Ethical?" *Harvard Business Review* (January–February, 1968), pp. 143ff.

Donaldson, Thomas: *Corporations and Morality* (Englewood Cliffs, N.J.: Prentice-Hall, Inc., 1982).

Donaldson, Thomas, ed.: *Case Studies in Business Ethics* (Englewood Cliffs, N.J.: Prentice-Hall, Inc., 1984).

Donaldson, Thomas, and Werhane, Patricia, eds.: *Ethical Issues in Business: A Philosophical Approach* (Englewood Cliffs, N.J.: Prentice-Hall, Inc., 1983).

Environmental Ethics: A journal devoted to environmental issues.

Ewing, David: *Freedom Inside the Organization* (New York: McGraw-Hill, 1977).

French, Peter: "The Corporation as Moral Person," in *American Philosophical Quarterly* 3 (1979), pp. 207–15.

Miller, Frank, and Sartorius, Rolf: "Population Policy and Public Goods," *Philosophy and Public Affairs* 8:148–74, 1979.

Passmore, John: *Man's Responsibility for Nature* (New York: Scribner's, 1974).

Pastin, Mark, and Hooker, Michael: "Ethics and the Foreign Corrupt Practices Act," *Business Horizons* (December, 1980), 43–47.

Velasquez, Manuel: *Business Ethics* (Englewood Cliffs, N.J.: Prentice-Hall, Inc., 1983).

PART EIGHT

NUCLEAR WAR

INTRODUCTION

More than ever today we are thinking the unthinkable. Perhaps because of its staggering potential consequences, nuclear war is a topic no one can avoid; indeed, many have called it *the* moral issue of the century.

As citizens of a democratic country, we are also faced with the need to register our opinion about political issues that have a direct bearing on the strategic decisions made by our government regarding nuclear arms. In the case study presented below, "The Freeze Referendum," we read about how California voters confronted a resolution on the state ballot endorsing a "mutual, verifiable freeze" on the production and deployment of nuclear arms. The language in the referendum, by the way, is almost identical to that in the national freeze resolution considered by the U.S. Congress in 1983.

To make a rational decision about so important an issue as the freeze, one must first tackle the theoretical, factual, and moral issues surrounding the issues of deterrence and nuclear strategy. The articles in Part Eight are designed to provoke thinking about these issues by providing a diverse spectrum of views regarding the use and threatened use of nuclear arms. Some key moral questions raised by these articles which must be at the forefront of any serious attempt to understand the nuclear issue include:

1 How, if at all, are nuclear weapons morally different from conventional ones?

2 Do principles exist that should govern the use of weapons—and the type of weapons used—in war? Or is it true that in war anything goes?

3 What are the morally relevant differences between evaluating the *use* of nuclear arms on the one hand, and the *threat* to use them on the other? Does it follow that whatever is wrong to use is also wrong to threaten to use?

4 What role does intention play in the acceptability of a strategy for fighting a war? If a nation intentionally targets only military installations with its missiles, but knows that if used they would also destroy the civilian population, is the government morally responsible for the civilian deaths in the event of war?

In addition to these straightforwardly moral questions there is a host of empirical questions relevant to the moral issue. For example, which nuclear arms are "destabilizing" (i.e., which make peace between rival powers more precarious) and which are not? What are the likely aftereffects of an all-out nuclear exchange? And, what are the likely consequences of various strategies, e.g., the freeze, unilateral disarmament, mutual disarmament, and mutual build-up?

Solly Zuckerman's article, "A Brief History of the Arms Race," provides many of the basic facts about nuclear arms in the context of the superpower rivalry, as well as a brief history of the arms race. It also offers a glimpse of the fundamental perspectives taken by the "hawks" and the "doves" in the nuclear issue, that is, by those eager to build up our nuclear defenses, and those wanting to freeze or phase them out.

Constance Holden's piece, "Scientists Describe 'Nuclear Winter'" discusses the effects of an all-out nuclear exchange. This article is a distillation of claims made by a small group of well-known scientists, including Carl Sagan, who popularized the term, "nuclear winter." The scientists argue that dust clouds created by the explosions from a nuclear exchange would create a "pall of darkness with sunlight about five percent of normal in the mid-latitudes of the Northern Hemisphere." Temperatures would drop to subfreezing for months with disastrous planetary consequences. Since the appearance of the notion of "nuclear winter" some scientists have questioned the extent of the predicted catastrophe, yet all have recognized the possibility of some form of "nuclear winter" and, of course, the generally catastrophic consequences of any full-scale nuclear exchange.

In "A Rational Approach to Disarmament," President Reagan's Secretary of Defense, Caspar Weinberger, uses an analysis of the present conflict between the superpowers to argue that effective deterrence demands more, not fewer, arms. The doctrine of "no first use," moreover, is one he insists would encourage dangerous Soviet adventurism. This is a luxury that the U.S., with its commitment to defending Europe from a Soviet land invasion, cannot afford. In contrast, Thomas Donaldson argues that any sincere threats to use nuclear arms are always immoral because they violate key limitations on the exercise of the right to self-defense. We understand the concept of national self-defense on analogy with self-defense in individual and family contexts, he suggests; and, if we pay attention to the limitations on self-defense appropriate to situations roughly analogous to national nuclear defense, we will realize that nuclear weapons transgress valid moral boundaries. In particular, nuclear deterrence as a strategy threatens noncombatants (children, political dissidents, the insane, and members of other, nonbelligerent countries) in a way that clashes with fundamental moral convictions.

In a strong reply to all those (such as Donaldson) who would condemn nuclear weapons on moral grounds, Christopher Morris asserts that in the event the U.S. is attacked by the Soviets with nuclear weapons, something approximating a Hobbesian state of nature would ensue, with the result that ordinary moral precepts such as the sanctity of innocents would not apply. We may recall from Part One that Hobbes believed that in the absence of a sovereign power, each person's natural self-interestedness would go unchecked, and that as a result such a state of nature is exempt from traditional moral rules. Thus according to Morris our threats to use nuclear weapons in the event of attack are not necessarily immoral.

The last article in the section is drawn from the U.S. Catholic Bishops' pastoral letter on nuclear arms, entitled "The Challenge of Peace: God's Promise and Our Response." Although directed to the Catholic community, the Bishops explicitly affirm that the arguments in the document are directed towards, and accessible to, the entire U.S. citizenry. In a categorical denunciation of nuclear arms, the Bishops draw on traditional "just war" theory to show that the use of nuclear arms can easily violate the principle of "discrimination" (i.e., the rule against intentionally killing noncombatants) and will certainly violate the principle of "proportionality" (i.e., the rule against using means the disvalue of which outweighs the value of the end). Nonetheless, the Bishops do not categorically condemn the present U.S. policy of deterrence, arguing that although immoral in the end, the policy may be an acceptable interim measure *along the road* to nuclear disarmament.

CASE STUDY—Nuclear War

THE FREEZE REFERENDUM

In November of 1982, some seven million Californians went to the polls to vote on the issue of a "mutual, verifiable Nuclear Freeze" as a matter of policy. If the resolution passed, it was to be forwarded to the U.S. Congress in an effort to influence the passage of national freeze legislation.

Prior to the California vote, newspapers and other media were filled with editorials and factual assertions relating to the freeze. Often the arguments were purely emotional. Freeze supporters, using tactics reminiscent of the 1960s, marched on behalf of their cause shouting slogans such as "Two, four, six, eight, we don't want to radiate." Freeze opponents countered that a vote

This case study was prepared by the editor.

for the resolution was a vote for communism. "Those people are the best friends the KGB ever had," snapped one disgruntled critic.

Freeze opponents included the Reagan Administration and the California Aerospace industry. Freeze defenders, on the other hand, were represented largely by small, activist, political organizations. All groups lobbied heavily.

The serious, well-intentioned California voter found himself confronted by one of the most difficult public policy issues ever to arise in the United States. Which side should he support?

How would *you* have voted on the resolution? Why?

Postscript

Although the early polls showed the freeze leading by as much as 40 percentage points (70%-30%), the results of the election were considerably closer:

For: 3,795,732 (52%)
Against: 3,439,082 (47.5%)

The closeness prompted many commentators to observe that the Reagan Administration along with the California aerospace industry were able to persuade large numbers of wavering voters that the freeze ran contrary to their interests. The White House hailed the vote as a moral victory for its views, despite the fact that the resolution passed by a slim majority.

A Brief History of the Arms Race

Solly Zuckerman

According to the O.E.D., to deter means to 'restrain from acting or proceeding by any consideration of danger or trouble', and a deterrent is something 'which deters'. In the popular mind, however, and, in the words of General Sir John Hackett,[1] in those of 'military dinosaurs' and 'airborne pterodactyls', the word 'deterrent' today means a nuclear weapon. As one who has read book after book, memoir after memoir on the subject, I can well appreciate that the nuclear [era] has become a golden age for writers who wish to obscure reality in a miasma of words, numbers and acronyms.

The concept of mutual deterrence is basically simple. In discharging its responsibility for the security, survival and welfare of the state, every sovereign government must try to deter another government from taking action which it judges to be contrary to the national interests which it is charged to promote and defend. Conversely, a sane government will be deterred from embarking on hostile acts against another country if, in its judgment, such action would entail either a certain or a significant risk that its own people, its economy and its apparatus of state control, would suffer disproportionately more than would be justified by the value of whatever prizes victory might bring. It is axiomatic that no sane government would initiate or permit acts which, in its opinion, might escalate to a level that would trigger 'unacceptable' nuclear retaliation.

That, in its simplest form, is what is implied by the state of mutual deterrence which characterizes the relations in the nuclear sphere between the NATO and Warsaw Pact countries. As Harold Macmillan, then the United Kingdom's Prime Minister, put it as far back as 1960[2] it is hardly likely 'that even the most ambitious or the most ruthless statesman would consciously enter upon so unrewarding an adventure' as the destruction of his own country by nuclear weapons. McGeorge Bundy, the Director of the US National Security Council at the beginning of the sixties, tells us[3] that, from the year he started his presidency, President Kennedy held that 'a general nuclear exchange, even at the levels of 1961, would be so great a disaster as to be an unexampled failure of statesmanship'.

But the concept of nuclear deterrence did not start in so simple a form, nor, the way events are moving, will it end like that. The story begins with the devastation of Hiroshima and Nagasaki in 1945. This final act of the Second World War revealed that the Americans could make weapons of destruction

From *Nuclear Illusion and Reality* by Solly Zuckerman (1983). Copyright 1982 by Solly Zuckerman. Reprinted by permission of Viking-Penguin, Inc.
[1]Sir John Hackett, "The Best Possible Defense for Britain," *Sunday Telegraph* (24 May), 1981.
[2]Harold Macmillan, *Pointing the Way* (London: Macmillan, 1972).
[3]McGeorge Bundy, 1989 (Keynote remarks at Annual Conference of International Institute for Strategic Studies, Villars, Switzerland).

that were thousands of times more fearful than any that had been known before. Then, three years before the United Kingdom exploded its own first atomic weapon, the Russians demonstrated that they, too, knew the secret of the 'The Bomb'. That was in 1949, just about the time when conditions in Europe, and particularly the extension of the sphere of Soviet domination, had led to the formation of NATO as a defensive alliance whose purpose was to prevent the USSR extending still further the geographical area over which it held political sway.

For a time the West believed that it enjoyed an advantage in nuclear weapons, and that its air forces were far more powerful than the Soviet Union's. So in 1954, John Foster Dulles,[4] then the American Secretary of State, proclaimed the doctrine of 'massive retaliation', that is, that in order to deter or counter aggression, the US would 'depend primarily upon a great capacity to retaliate instantly by means and at places of its own choosing'. These were bold words for, almost simultaneously, the grim threat of nuclear retaliation on the American homeland started to become apparent.

This was when the scene underwent a quantum-like transformation. The Soviet Union demonstrated that it could deliver nuclear warheads not only by aircraft, but also by means of inter-continental ballistic missiles. This gave a new twist to the arms race, as the United States accelerated its work in the same field of armaments. Slowly the realization grew that were the West, and in particular the United States, to use nuclear weapons against the Soviet homeland, the Russians would undoubtedly retaliate in kind, however much smaller in numerical terms their nuclear armoury was at the time. The concept of mutual strategic deterrence then became clear, and with it the belief that since neither side knew whether the other would be the first to unleash a nuclear war, it was essential that both developed the means whereby they could retaliate, whatever the damage they had suffered from what became known as 'a first strike' from the other side. A retaliatory nuclear force had to be 'invulnerable', a term probably first used in this connection by Sir Winston Churchill in 1955.[5] Various techniques were developed to achieve this end.

Paranoia then started to take over, masked by figures of numbers of warheads and delivery systems which, for most people, completely obscured the facts of the destruction that could already by wreaked by a just a few nuclear bombs. A few politicians recognized the danger. From 1959 onwards Harold Macmillan fought passionately and valiantly, but in vain, to bring the nuclear arms race to an end. He wanted a ban on all further nuclear testing. At the end of 1960 John F. Kennedy succeeded Eisenhower as President of the United States, and Robert McNamara, then head of the Ford motor company, overnight became his Secretary of Defense, taking over what for him was a new and vastly bigger responsibility. He quickly realized that if Soviet military units were to intrude into NATO territory, there was little sense in the idea of a massive nuclear attack on the Soviet homeland if the Russians could retaliate in kind by striking

---

[4]J.F. Dulles, 1954 Address to Council of Foreign Relations, 12 January.
[5]*Hansard,* House of Commons, March 1955, Cols. 2899–1900.

at America. The price in terms of the destruction which would result from nuclear retaliation would be too high. Instead, he formulated what he first called a 'full options' policy. This necessitated a build-up of NATO's conventional forces.

At the NATO conference held in Lisbon in 1952, force levels had been set for the alliance at 96 divisions, partly in order to obviate the danger of nuclear war by making it possible to offer a conventional defense to a Soviet attack. But by 1954 it had become apparent that these divisions were never going to materialize, and the NATO Council decided that 'tactical nuclear weapons' should be used to redress any disparity in numbers of men that might occur in a war between the West and the USSR. McNamara's 'full options' policy would comprehend 'graduated nuclear deterrence'.

Simultaneously the heavily-pressed Secretary of Defense had to go on adding flesh to the bones of the concept of mutual strategic nuclear deterrence. Each of the three armed Services wanted the honour of deterring the USSR. McNamara accordingly had to agree [to] a level for the size of the American nuclear forces that could be relied upon to constitute a sufficient threat to the USSR to deter the latter from any nuclear action which would be a direct threat to the USA....

But who it was who set the numerical criterion for 'assured nuclear destruction', later to become 'mutually assured destruction' or MAD, and who it was who persuaded McNamara to accept the criterion, I do not know. What was called for was the power to eliminate a quarter of the Soviet Union's population and to destroy half of its industrial capacity. This, it was estimated, could be done by wiping out the 200 largest cities of the USSR, which together are the home of a third of the country's population. By one of those fortunate coincidences, it transpired that this arbitrary measure of destruction accorded with the level of nuclear armaments whose production had already been planned. In other words, McNamara felt himself bound to put his stamp of approval on what was already in train, presumably in the hopes that by so doing America's nuclear build-up would come to an end. That it did not is clear from the figures for the present size of the nuclear armouries of the super-powers as published during the course of the SALT II negotiations. Between them, the two sides will be allowed to deploy more than 10,000 warheads which could be delivered in a 'strategic' nuclear exchange. In addition, they dispose three, four times as many 'tactical' and 'theatre' nuclear weapons.

Even though the SALT II Treaty that was signed by President Carter has not been ratified by the American Senate, there is no reason to suppose that either side has yet contravened what was agreed about these numbers. They are well in excess of what either side would need were it ever to initiate what has been called 'a spasm of mutual annihilation'....

A retaliatory force obviously has to look credible, has to look real. If only one side had nuclear weapons, an opponent would be at its mercy. For a state of mutual deterrence to be stable, there has to be some equality of degree of threat above some indefinable level. Clearly, too, to be credible, nuclear forces have to be, or have to seem to be, invulnerable to a 'first strike', by which one means that if one side were to decide to strike at the other without warning, it should not be able to destroy all of its opponent's retaliatory forces. In the framework of deterrent theory, enough should be certain to remain to deter even the idea of a first strike. That is the prescribed reason why both the United States and the USSR maintain a triad of forces: land-based missiles, a force of missile-carrying submarines, and long-range aircraft. If it were possible to eliminate any one of the three arms of strategic deterrence, a possibility to which I shall return, but which I would discount since it has only an illusory political significance, the remaining two, or even one, should be able to threaten 'unacceptable' retaliation.

In spite of the excessive strength of the nuclear armouries of the two sides, and because of the chronic climate of world-wide international unrest, and particularly of the enduring suspicion that prevails between the USA and the USSR, both sides are fearful lest the other gain some advantage in the nuclear arms race. Like their American opposite numbers, the Soviet leaders listened, for example, to the exaggerated claims of their research and development chiefs that an anti-ballistic missile (ABM) system could be devised which would destroy incoming enemy missiles either in outer space or after they had re-entered the earth's atmosphere. Khrushchev boasted that the Russians had it in their power 'to hit a fly in space'. Technical men on both sides have worked feverishly to develop such a system, with complicated radars linked to computer-communication networks and then to batteries of nuclear-armed missiles which would be launched instantaneously into automatically calculated ballistic paths to meet incoming enemy warheads. At the same time, other technical teams focused their efforts on means whereby ABM systems could be defeated. They designed decoys to be carried in the terminal stage of a ballistic missile to confuse the anti-ballistic missile radars. The decoys would be released at the same time as the nuclear warheads, making it difficult, or even impossible for the defending radar systems to differentiate the right objects to track and destroy in flight. But the whole thing was a mirage.

Because these matters are never kept completely secret in the United States, a spirited public debate was stimulated in the late sixties between those technical men who, in spite of one costly failure after another, still claimed that it was possible to devise an effective ABM system, and those who said it was not. Billions of dollars had been spent. In 1967, when ABM fever was at its most acute, and with strong pressure from many quarters for the continued development, and then deployment, of a system of defenses against missiles, President Johnson summoned not only Dr. Don Hornig, his chief Science Adviser, and the Joint Chiefs of Staff, but also the three past presidential Science Advisers, Dr. James Kilian, Dr. George Kistiakowsky, and Dr. Jerome Wiesner, as well as the last three Directors of Defense Research and Engineering in the Pentagon: Dr. Herbert York, Dr. Harold Brown, and Dr. John Foster. York describes[6] how the discussion led the President to put two simple questions

---

[6]H.F. York, *Race to Oblivion* (New York: Simon and Schuster, 1970).

about a defense system against a possible Russian missile attack: 'Will it work and should it be deployed?' All present agreed that the answers were No. For what the President wanted to know was whether it was possible to devise a defense which could be relied upon to destroy *all* incoming warheads. It was not sufficient to destroy, say, one in every two, since if only one warhead got through, it would be enough to destroy Washington.

Once both sides were ready to admit the technical and functional futility of work on ABMs, work which could only 'destabilize' the state of mutual deterrence, the first of the SALT talks was embarked upon. Agreement was reached in 1972, by which time Nixon was President and Kissinger in action. Work on the main ABM deployment programmes in the USA and the USSR was then halted. But R and D on ABMs nonetheless continued. It still continues....

Today the US strategy of assured or mutually assured destruction has, in theory, been supplanted by what the nuclear theorists know as PD 59— Presidential Directive 59. This was issued by President Carter in 1979, and it is the general understanding that in it he declared that instead of retaliating against a Soviet nuclear attack by an onslaught on Soviet cities, the Americans would destroy Soviet military targets—missile sites, submarine depots, armament stores, command centres and so on. PD 59, in short, proclaims what in the jargon is called 'counterforce' strategy, as opposed to a 'countervalue' strategy, the latter being a euphemism for a policy which defines cities as prime targets. PD 59 would therefore be a policy which in theory offered more 'options' than one which led immediately to the destruction of the Western world, including the USSR.

In this sense the new directive is a reflection of McNamara's transformation of 'massive retaliation' into a 'full options' and then 'flexible response' policy for NATO.

In view of the enormous size of the nuclear armouries of the USA and the USSR, one dare not lose sight of the fact that from the operational point of view there is practically no difference, apart from the verbal one, between what is now called counterforce and what is termed countervalue. Henry Kissinger justified the development of MIRVed* missiles by the United States because MIRVs were going to be accurate enough to 'take out' Soviet military targets, so that, on paper at least, cities would be spared. He therefore regarded the affirmation of a counterforce strategy as more 'humane' than one based upon 'assured destruction'. So, at the time of the SALT II talks, it was only 'logical' for the Americans to press on with the MIRV systems which they had already developed, and for which it was appropriate to formulate a different policy, especially as it was argued that the Russians were fairly advanced in the development of their own accurate MIRVed missiles. If the Russians were to develop the capacity to threaten or, worse, to embark upon, a first strike

---

Editor's note: "MIRV" stands for "Multiple, Independently-Targetable, Reentry Vehicles." A MIRVed missile is able to carry many nuclear warheads, each of which can be targeted to a separate destination.

against the American nuclear forces, the Americans clearly could not forgo what they had already achieved technically. Moreover, there was another consideration. For the total weight it could carry, a MIRVed ballistic missile could wreak more destruction than a ballistic missile carrying the same 'throw-weight' in one nuclear charge—for from this point of view, the greater the number of nuclear packets in the total explosive charge the better. From the Soviet point of view, the Americans were not going to abandon MIRV developments. Why should they? The fact that a 'counterforce' policy could not deprive either side of so much of its total retaliatory forces—for example, ballistic missile submarines would be immune to a counterforce strike—as to make any meaningful difference to the prospective levels of retribution, was immaterial in the context of a technological race.

The earlier views expressed by Henry Kissinger about 'counterforce' seem to be the conventional wisdom embodied in PD 59. The belief now is that were the state of deterrence to break down, a Soviet nuclear offensive would begin with an assault on American fixed missile sites, with the USA then striking at corresponding military targets in the USSR. Theoretically that would then leave both sides with their missile submarines and long-range aircraft intact.

But it is inevitable, too, that were military installations rather than cities to become the objectives of nuclear attack, millions, even tens of millions, of civilians would nonetheless be killed, whatever the number of missile sites, airfields, armament plants, ports, and so on that would be destroyed. As I have said, statements of the accuracy of missile strikes are given in terms of the acronym CEP (circular error probable), i.e. the radius of a circle within which fifty percent of strikes would fall. Even if one were to assume that navigational, homing and all the other devices worked perfectly, the fifty percent outside the magic circle would not necessarily have a normal distribution; that is to say, the strikes falling off in regular fashion with increasing distance from the pre-ordained target. Moreover, whatever the accuracy with which they could be delivered, nuclear weapons still have an enormous area of effect relative to the precise 'military' targets at which the supposed counterforce strikes would be aimed. And, were a nuclear exchange ever to be embarked upon, it seems inevitable that the side which felt it was losing would use elements of its nuclear armoury against the enemy's centres of population.

Scientists Describe "Nuclear Winter"

Constance Holden

First it was physicians telling the world that, in the event of a nuclear attack, there could be no adequate medical care for survivors. Now biologists and atmospheric physicists, bolstered by new calculations, say that the ecosystem itself would be gravely and permanently damaged by a full-scale nuclear war.

The findings were presented at a 2-day conference, "The World After Nuclear War," held in Washington at the end of October. The central figures were Cornell astronomer Carl Sagan and biologist Paul Ehrlich of Stanford.

Although policy questions were carefully avoided, there were at least two implications. One was that a single nuclear counterforce strike, even if unilateral, would be suicidal to the nation launching it. The other was that no one in the world would be unaffected by such an event. Some Third World nations would be compelled to abandon the idea that it would not be all bad to have the two great powers finish each other off.

Sagan, describing climatological effects, said things would be a lot worse than indicated by any prior calculation, including a 1975 report by the National Academy of Sciences. He and his colleagues, in a paper known as TTAPS[1], evaluated numerous scenarios of attacks ranging from 100 megatons (the equivalent of 8000 Hiroshimas) to 10,000 megatons. In the 5000 megaton case—approximately that required for a preemptive counterforce strike—they predicted that clouds of dust would create a pall of darkness with sunlight about 5 percent of normal in the mid-latitudes of the Northern Hemisphere. Temperatures would drop precipitously to as low as $-23°C$ and remain sub-freezing for months. Radioactivity would be more lethal than previously estimated, with up to 250 rads—half the human lethal dose—covering 30 percent of the area. The atmosphere would be further polluted by poisonous fumes emanating from urban fires. Depletion of ozone by oxides of nitrogen would raise the level of ultraviolet radiation, damaging immune systems and causing blindness.

One of the major findings was that effects would not be confined to the Northern Hemisphere. Disturbances in global circulation patterns would result in the interhemispheric transport of hundreds of tons of nuclear debris, resulting in light and temperature reductions as well as radioactive fallout in the Southern Hemisphere as well.

"Perhaps the most striking and unexpected consequence" of the studies said Sagan, is that even a small war could have devastating climatic effects if cities are targeted. If bombs totaling 100 megatons—0.8 percent of the combined

Constance Holden, "Scientists Describe 'Nuclear Winter,'" *Science*, Vol. 222 (19 Nov., 1983), pp. 822–823. Copyright 1983 by the AAAS. Reprinted by permission.
[1]R.P. Turco, et al., "Nuclear Winter: Global Consequences of Multiple Nuclear Explosions," *Science* 222 (1983): 1283–92.

strategic arsenals—were dropped on 100 cities, the smoke from firestorms consuming large stores of combustible materials would be pumped into the stratosphere, resulting in months of gloom and subfreezing temperatures. The threshold for dire long-term environmental effects, said Sagan, "is surprisingly low."

Ehrlich supplemented this picture with an accounting of biological consequences of a 5000-megaton exchange. Depicting most survivors in the Northern Hemisphere "starving to death in a dark, smoggy world," he said that the cooling alone would be "the worst catastrophe mankind has experienced." Livestock would die from the effects of radiation and cold; photosynthesis by plants would cease. Thick ice would cover bodies of standing water. Forest fires would rage through dead trees. Agriculture would be destroyed if the war occurred just before or during the growing season. Plagues of insect pests—the animal life best equipped to survive the disaster—would damage food and spread disease. Starvation would also afflict those in the Southern Hemisphere, not only in areas dependent on food imports, but because cold air would decimate delicate tropical growth and result in mass species extinction.

The conference was a result of a year of careful planning, and represented a remarkable consensus among more than 100 scientists involved. Sagan said it all began in 1971 when Mariner 9 arrived at Mars during a dust storm which created a significant warming of the martian atmosphere and took months to settle. He also observed that the worldwide effects of even a minimal lowering of temperature was demonstrated in 1815 when particulates from the eruption of a volcano in Indonesia lowered global temperatures 1°C, resulting in "the year without a summer" in 1816.

More recently, scientists were inspired by a 1982 issue of the Swedish journal *Ambio* which contained new estimates on the climatic effects of nuclear war by Paul J. Crutzen of the Max Planck Institute. This led to the TTAPS effort, which was reviewed by scientists from around the world at a meeting in Cambridge, Massachusetts, last spring.

Russian scientists, who have been doing their own calculations, are also believed to be in fundamental agreement. This was dramatically illustrated at the meeting by a satellite hookup which showed Ehrlich and Sagan exchanging conclusions with four high-ranking members of the Soviet Academy of Sciences.

To what degree, if any, might this new perspective on nuclear war affect the deliberations of strategic planners? The overall impression from the conference is that nuclear war on any scale would be worse than anything it was meant to avoid. As keynote speaker Donald Kennedy of Stanford said, "It is no longer acceptable to think of sequelae in minutes, days, or even months. What biologists are telling us today is that the proper time scale is years."

Science asked several government spokesmen for their reactions to the scientists' findings. The general response is summed up by a Department of Defense official who said, "So what?" The government already knows nuclear war would be absolutely devastating, and the real question is how to prevent it. A State Department official was asked what the meaning of deterrence—that is, the threat of using a weapon—would be if its actual use would be suicidal. He said it's still a deterrent if the Russians believe we would use it. He added that if the Russians believed that we believed a first strike would be suicidal, they might relax a little and not put so much into their own first strike capabilities.

The only agency that seems to have been affected by the findings is the Federal Emergency Management Agency. A FEMA spokesman said that while they were unmoved by the physicians's message, which they thought "exaggerated," they were worried about problems of food supply, which appear to be "even more profound than we had anticipated." He said the problems of cold and dark were for the long-term planners and part of FFMA's primary responsibility. In keeping with FEMA's job, which is to act as though every catastrophe is manageable, the spokesman pointed out that even in the worst case, only 5 percent of the nation's land area would be blown up; that 75 percent of what would be needed for a nuclear attack was already done for other assorted disasters; and that the United States has a much better transportation system than the Russians for pre-attack evacuation.

A National Academy of Sciences committee headed by George Carrier of Harvard University is currently winding up a 9-month study of the long-term atmospheric effects of nuclear war, commissioned by the Defense Nuclear Agency, which Sagan said is substantially in accord with his colleagues' findings.

Whether or not the government sees the information as significant, there is definitely an accelerating concern among scientists. The International Council of Scientific Unions is starting a 2-year study for which a series of meetings, starting this month, is being held in Stockholm. A scientific symposium is also planned in Tokyo.

It would appear that growing numbers are coming to agree with biologist Thomas Eisner of Cornell University who said at the meeting: "I no longer feel that a single biologist in this country or the world can be exempt from becoming involved in these issues."

A Rational Approach to Disarmament

Caspar W. Weinberger

I would like to talk about a matter which concerns all of us equally. That is the threat of nuclear war which all of us, to our dismay, have lived with now for some 34 years. This is a most disagreeable and difficult subject, But I am very concerned because some Americans are expressing doubts that our President and his Administration share their abhorrence for war and, in particular, nuclear war.

From *Defense* (August, 1982). Reprinted by permission.

This is a terrible misconception made even worse by various grim prognoses of the destruction nuclear weapons would wreak and by the pictures we see on television of old nuclear tests.

We have seen enough images of war lately, and indeed many of us have seen far too much of war itself in our lifetimes. I would, therefore, prefer to offer, here, the possibility of peace even though I offer it in an undeniably turbulent world, at a most dangerous period of our history.

In the early part of Homer's *Iliad*, Hector finds his wife, Andromache, with their child, Astyanax, on the walls above Troy. The little boy, frightened by his father's armor and helmet, cries out. Hector removes his helmet, and the two parents laugh as the son recognizes the father. Hector then lifts Astyanax in his arms, jostles him in the air over his head, and the family shares a moment of peace.

This is a picture of life as we want it, not the terrible carnage churning below on the plains of Troy, not even the glory of great soldiers which the *Iliad* also celebrates. The contrast intended by Homer between these scenes of war and peace is as vivid as the choice which every generation has had to face.

We choose peace, but not because we are Democrats or Republicans. We want peace because we are Americans and a civilized people. We reject war as a deliberate instrument of foreign policy because it is repugnant to our national morality. War prevents people from leading the kinds of lives which this country was fashioned to protect and to enhance. As civilized people, we reject war because it kills and maims soldiers and civilians alike and undermines the fabric of life.

But nuclear war is even more horrible than war in any other form. Its destructive power has been described at length in popular journals recently. The images are sufficiently terrible that the temptation is strong to turn our backs on the whole subject. But, grim as they are, those matters have to be thought about and dealt with. It is part of my task to do that and to know not only what we are faced with, but how we may best prevent such a catastrophe from happening.

Physicians, it seems to me, should adopt a similar attitude to their work. A physician who deals with the sick every day sees many unpleasant things: cancer, heart disease, disorders of the nervous system, the patient's pain and the family's anguish. The response to these manifestly is not to walk away. It is not to throw up one's hands in dismay and respond with sentiment and emotion alone. That will save no one's life. What is required is a mixture of the compassion we all feel for the sick, plus the most objective and informed judgment about a course of action, followed by an equally steady hand in restoring the patient's health and easing his pain.

Those of us who are charged with the responsibility for the health and strength of this nation's defense are in a somewhat parallel position. The prospect of nuclear war is ghastly in the extreme. But we cannot allow the dread with which we look upon it to obscure our judgment on how to prevent it. Obviously, this too would not save lives.

To the extent of our powers we must, using all the judgment and technical skills and latest knowledge available, arrive at an objective, rational policy which will accomplish what we all want. Of course, we take, as our starting point, that which everyone agrees to: that nuclear war is so terrible that it must not be allowed to happen. This, however, is not a policy. It is a national objective which all of us share, very much like the compassion one feels for the sick. The policy question is, how do we achieve our objective?

Our policy to prevent war since the age of nuclear weapons began has been one of deterrence. Our strategic nuclear weapons are only retaliatory. Their purpose is to provide us with a credible retaliatory capability in the event we are struck first. The idea on which this is based is quite simple: it is to make the cost of starting a nuclear war much higher than any possible benefit to an aggressor. This policy has been approved, through the political processes of the democratic nations it protects, since at least 1950. Most important, it works. It has worked in the face of major international tensions involving the great powers, and it has worked in the face of war itself.

But while the idea of deterrence has stood the test of time and usefulness beyond reproach, the things we must do to maintain that deterrence have changed substantially, as the Soviets' quest for nuclear superiority grew to fruition.

In the fifties, the requirements of deterrence were minimal. Our overwhelming nuclear superiority both in weapons and the means of their delivery made moot the question of whether an adversary would be deterred by unacceptable costs, if he attacked first. It also gave us the ability to deter conventional attacks on our allies. By the mid-sixties, however, the Soviets' nuclear force had grown greatly in strength. They had also achieved a major edge in conventional weapons in Europe. To discourage the prospect of conflict there, NATO decided that it would meet and answer force at whatever level it might be initiated, while retaining the option to use even greater force as the most effective preventative against aggression in the first place. It is important to remember here that the retention of this option is absolutely consistent with our nuclear weapons; that is, to deter aggression and to prevent other nuclear weapons being used against us or our allies. In simple language, we do not start fights—in Europe or anywhere.

We see disturbing evidence such as the Soviet's development of a refiring capability and major expenditures for civil defense shelters and air defense which indicates that they do think they can fight and win a nuclear war. We do not share this perception; we know nuclear war is unwinnable.

But we do not feel we can successfully deter attack from an adversary such as the USSR, if we relieve them of the necessity of all defensive planning. To do so would erode our deterrent by announcing that under no circumstances would we ever use our weapons first.

Recently it has been argued that we should adopt such a policy of "no first use" of nuclear force in the defense of Europe. While this sounds plausible enough, it lessens the effectiveness of deterrence. We must remember that

NATO has effectively prevented Soviet aggression against Europe. In no small part, this is because our policy makes clear to the Soviets the tremendous risks to them of aggression there. Also, a "no first use" policy might imply that the first use of conventional force is somehow acceptable.

We reject this entirely. And we do so because *our policy is to deter—not to encourage—the first use of force against us.*

The point is that we oppose the use of forces and arms as a means for anyone to secure his objectives. Force of arms is not the way to resolve international disputes.

I wish I could tell you that the Soviets shared this view. Unfortunately, history and all the facts we know stand in the way of such a policy by them.

For the past 21 years, the Soviets have concentrated tremendous efforts and resources on achieving a clear superiority in nuclear forces. The result has been the addition to their arsenal of new weapons systems such as the SS-17, SS-18, and SS-19 ICBMs, the Backfire bomber, the Typhoon submarine, several new types of cruise missiles, and the SS-20 intermediate range missile. These efforts dwarf our own. In fact, since 1970, they have out-vested us by about $400 billion in military armaments.

No less important is the fact that the Soviets do regard their nuclear forces as a means of coercion. Well over two-thirds of their nuclear force sits in land-based ICBM weapons whose speed, destructive power, and above all, accuracy give those who possess them the capability to aim with assurance at the military targets in the United States in a first strike or to aim at targets in Europe or Asia with their SS-20s.

By contrast, our own strategic weapons are apportioned among our submarines, land-based ICBMs, and bombers. The Soviets' clear advantage in land-based ICBMs gives them the ability to destroy segments of our relatively smaller and unfortunately less effective land-based missile force. We do not intend to match them missile for missile in land-based ICBMs. Our system of deterrence requires simply that we must be able to inflict damage so unacceptable that no one would attack us.

This does not mean, however, that we can allow any part of our Triad to become vulnerable. Our ongoing ability to maintain deterrence rests on the continued accuracy, power, communications structure, and survivability of all our nuclear forces. The point is that while the number of weapons is important, it is less so than the combination of capabilities, forces, and their survivability, along with the national resolve and will essential to convince an aggressor that he could not hope to gain from attacking first.

What then has deterrence done? Again, I must stress that it has worked and is working today. There have been 37 years of peace in Europe. Despite the threat of the Soviet Army; despite the threat of the Soviets' nuclear weapons, Western Europe has prospered. Its political freedoms have flourished, and its social institutions have grown stronger. Indeed, there has not been an equal period of uninterrupted peace on the European continent since the Roman

Empire fell. At the risk of stating the obvious, the United States and the rest of the world have also avoided the scourge of nuclear fire. Deterrence, thus, is and remains our best immediate hope of keeping peace.

However, it is not enough to assume that deterrence can be maintained simply by doing what we have done in the past. For the unavoidable fact is that even though the world remains at nuclear peace and nuclear threats do not appear on the horizon, still we do not feel safe. Many worry about the sophistication of modern delivery systems. Others fear the results of continuing to compete with the Soviets on this barren plain. Still more are alarmed at the destructive capability within the great powers' arsenals.

We are worried about all these matters too. That is why we are absolutely serious about the arms reductions negotiations currently underway in Geneva, and the President's new strategic arms reductions plans. But again, as with the policy of deterrence, the right approach to this process can only be one based on rational, prudent, and statesman-like determination of ends and means.

The one thing we must not expect from arms reductions negotiations is the kind of world that existed before nuclear weapons were tested. The forbidden fruit has been tasted, and in this case, the fruit is not the weapons, but the knowledge of them. As much as we would like to, we cannot erase that knowledge. Setting our sights on that object would be utterly unrealistic. The proper aim of arms reduction, therefore, should be first to reduce the probability of war. If possible, it should also aim to reduce the costs of maintaining deterrence and should reduce the possibilities of war through misinterpretation or misunderstanding.

The proposal to freeze current levels of nuclear weapons was born partly at least of deeply felt convictions which this Administration shares. A freeze, however, would not reduce the probability of war. It would go against the first and foremost aim of arms control because it would lock the United States and our allies into a position of permanent military disadvantage. And that disadvantage or imbalance, if you will, erodes deterrence which we believe has kept the peace. For if one side improves its forces, either by dint of its own efforts or through the other's inactivity, then the temptation will grow for the stronger to use its superior systems, or, at a minimum, to contemplate achieving domination by the threat of nuclear war—nuclear blackmail it is called. It is an understatement that we must not allow either of these things to happen, under any circumstances.

For similar reasons, a freeze would chill any hopes we have of convincing the Soviets to agree to any meaningful arms reductions. If a freeze went into effect now, the advantage the Soviets currently enjoy would be irreversibly sealed and stamped with the official imprimatur of an international agreement. Why, then, would they wish to change—that is to lower their forces together with us? Granting them but a thread of rationality, or even a normal supply, if we froze an imbalance in their favor, I cannot see that the Soviets would have the slightest incentive to achieve the major and bilateral reductions we must have if we are to lessen the danger now existing.

It is exactly those bilateral reductions which President Reagan's arms reduction proposals aim to achieve. In the past few months, our highest priority has been to lay the groundwork for the strategic arms negotiations with the Soviet Union. The President has now proposed major reductions in strategic arms to verifiable, equal, and agreed levels. We are also continuing our negotiations to reduce the intermediate range nuclear weapons that threaten Europe and Asia. In Geneva, we have put forward detailed proposals designed to limit those intermediate range nuclear forces and to eliminate entirely the missiles of greatest concern to each side. This approach, which has won the strong support of our allies, would go far towards lowering the threshold of risk which the Europeans feel so acutely today.

These proposals are not bargaining chips or ploys. Let all who doubt this know that President Reagan's greatest wish is for peace. I have heard him say more times than I can recall that if he could leave no other legacy, it would be that of having improved the prospects for peace. A meaningful reduction in nuclear arms would be a welcome first step in the arms control process and an historic step towards the peace which lowered tensions nurture. No one should doubt that this is what drives our efforts. No one should doubt that this is what we are pledged to—in hope, in word, and deed.

I wish that I could end by assuring you that our hopes and good faith could accomplish all that we want. But that I cannot do in all good conscience. Instead I must tell you what I see as the truth about our situation and not what I am sure all of us would prefer to hear: that is, there is no easy or royal road to peace, just as there is no easy road to anything really worthwhile. There is no miracle drug which will keep us and our allies safe and free while the nuclear threat is excised.

In the short term, we must remember that as health is not just the absence of sickness, neither is peace just the absence of war. Health requires care to ensure that it will continue, that disease will not occur. One needs the right diet, exercise, personal habits, and so on. So it is with peace. It cannot stand by itself. It needs care to ensure its continuance. A nation must conduct its own business, maintain its strength, and aided by alliances be prepared to resist those for whom peace is not the first priority. Peace without these steps will not be peace for long. Thus we dare not permit our abhorrence of war to keep us from the work which our love of peace demands.

We cannot blink in the face of our worst fears. The Soviets are aware that their buildup is frightening. I think it safe to say that one of the chief effects which it was designed to create is the natural horror which all feel who are willing to face that buildup with realism. We cannot, though, and we must not let this apprehension unstring us.

If we fail in the short term to reestablish the balance, the danger will surely increase. "If you make yourself into a sheep, you'll find a wolf nearby," says the Russian proverb. We don't want to be wolves or sheep. We only want to live in peace with freedom, and that means we must be able to deter any attack on us or our allies.

But if our immediate goal is to avoid war, our long-term goal is to reduce its probability. Here, too, in the area of arms control we have seen the frustrating paradox that the road to peace is marked with the preparations for war. But there is no rational solution. Who, for instance can believe that the Soviets would ever consent to reduce their forces if they thought that we lacked the national will or resolve to maintain a balance in the first place?

Thus we must draw deeply upon our national patience and fortitude in the future if we are to accomplish what all of us really agree we must do: protecting and strengthening the peace. For negotiations cannot succeed without patience—peace cannot succeed without fortitude.

I began with a story in the *Iliad*. There is, it seems to me, another metaphor in Astyanax's reaction to his helmeted father. And that is that the young and maybe even the not so young sometimes fail to recognize what it is that protects them. We are too old and, I hope, too wise to respond by crying out at the sight of our protectors. And we are too young to surrender our hopes in despair or our principles in fear.

The *Iliad* is the first book of great literature in a long tradition which reaches to us across the ages. It is a book about war, but it questions war and it questions politics and it questions life. This questioning is one of the noblest traits of our civilization and it is one enshrined at Harvard under the rubric of "healthy skepticism." Others call it freedom. We owe it to our ancestors and to "the age that is waiting before" to do all within our power to ensure that this civilization is preserved—and preserved in peace with freedom.

Nuclear Deterrence and Self-Defense*

Thomas Donaldson

It is often said in discussions of nuclear arms that consequences overwhelm principles, that considerations of ten or twenty or forty million human dead overwhelm those of abstract rights and principles. Hence, most discussions of the morality of U.S. nuclear deterrence policy have focused on the issue of whether deterrence does in fact deter. That is, they focus on whether deterrence discourages the awesome consequences of nuclear war.[1] But what if it could

From *Ethics* 95 (April 1985): 537–549. © 1985 by The University of Chicago. All rights reserved.

*This article is indebted to the participants in the Ethics, Politics and Arms Control Seminar at the University of Chicago, including Russell Hardin, Duncan Snidal, Gerald Dworkin, Robin Lovin, Ruth Adams, James Gustafson, Robert Sachs, Charles Lipson, and John Mearsheimer.

[1] Douglas Lackey has argued that unilateral nuclear disarmament is defensible both on conse-quentialist and on prudential grounds in "Missiles and Morals: A Utilitarian Look at Nuclear

be shown that nuclear deterrence is a moral failure apart from the sheer number of casualties resulting from a nuclear war? In this article I show that the structure of the moral argument for nuclear deterrence is flawed owing to straightforward considerations of the principle of self-defense. I analyze the concept of a right to self-defense by isolating a set of limiting conditions on its exercise; I then map individual analogues to a policy of national nuclear deterrence to show that deterrence fails to meet these conditions. Because the position I defend regards nuclear deterrence as morally unacceptable, it does not tolerate nuclear threats even when considered as an interim solution along the road to disarmament.

I want to define nuclear deterrence as a policy implemented for the purpose of avoiding enemy attack involving the maintenance of a strategic system of megaton-level, thermonuclear warheads and delivery vehicles targeted on the enemy, with the express intent to use such weapons in the event of enemy attack. I have in mind, then, the very sort of strategic nuclear weapons systems now possessed by the superpowers. For present purposes it makes no difference whether or not we limit the enemy attack to the nuclear kind, thus adopting a no-first-use policy.

One should distinguish between a policy that is a bluff and one that is not. For present purposes I am concerned with only "reliable threats," that is, ones backed by the sincere intent to use nuclear arms in the event of attack. As are most students of the arms race, I am convinced that considerations of technology, strategic policy, and counterintelligence make a bluff policy unworkable, but I shall not argue that here.

What is special about nuclear arms? Many weapons have been condemned as representing a qualitatively new, unacceptable stage of evil. Critics complained about the introduction of gattling and machine guns. Still earlier, the introduction of chariots, iron weapons, horse armor, stirrups, and gunpowder escalated war's capacity for destruction. Yet such advances have proven essential for the defense of civilized societies. Are not nuclear weapons the next step in a relatively smooth continuum of war's advancing destructiveness, regrettable in their awesome ability but necessary in their deterrent capability?

I think not. Indeed, one may grant—and I shall—that, when the earlier definition of deterrence is altered to refer to the maintenance of conventional

---

Deterrence," *Philosophy & Public Affairs* 11 (1982): 189–231; while Russell Hardin—disagreeing with Lackey—has mapped many important complexities inherent in game-theoretic analyses of nuclear strategy in "Unilateral versus Mutual Disarmament," *Philosophy & Public Affairs* 22 (1983): 236–54. For some classic and well-known discussions of the issue of nuclear deterrence, see Geoffrey Goodwin, *Ethics and Nuclear Deterrence* (New York: St Martin's Press, 1982); Philip Green, *Deadly Logic: The Theory of Nuclear Deterrence* (Columbus: Ohio State University Press, 1966); Harvard Nuclear Study Group, *Living with Nuclear Weapons* (New York: Bantam Books, 1983); Roy E. Jones, *Nuclear Deterrence: A Short Political Analysis* (London: Routledge & Kegan Paul, 1968); Patrick Morgan, *Deterrence: A Conceptual Analysis* (Beverly Hills, Calif.: Sage Publications, 1977); Emma Rothschild, "The Delusions of Deterrence," *New York Review of Books* 30 (April 14, 1983): 40–49; and U.S. Catholic Bishops, *The Challenge of Peace: God's Call and Our Response* (Washington, D.C.: Office of Publishing Services, U.S. Catholic Conference, 1983) (the final version of the pastoral letter).

rather than nuclear weapons, deterrence may be morally justified. This is not to say that any sort of deterrence policy involving conventional weapons is morally justified; it is only to say that certain forms of conventional deterrence can be. The shift to nuclear from nonnuclear weapons systems, however, rules out the possibility of justifying a deterrence strategy.

For most defenders of deterrence, it is primarily the enormity of the threat to human life posed by an enemy possessing nuclear weapons that justifies the risks inherent in a policy of deterrence. Conversely, it has been the enormity of the threat posed by the mere possession of nuclear weapons on both sides, including the possibility of fail-safe failures, that has been used to argue against the policy of deterrence. In this way, arguments pro and con tend to be consequentialist. Evils are weighed against evils in terms of their magnitude. We might phrase a simplistic consequential argument in a single proposition:

Adopting a policy of deterrence reduces the likelihood of enemy attack.

Let us assume that the damage inflicted on the enemy in the event of a nuclear counterattack in consequential terms is roughly equal to the damage inflicted by the enemy. (This assumption, by the way, seems reasonable in light of current knowledge.) Let us note with Douglas Lackey that, all other things being equal, and considering only the issue of total casualties, the probability of an enemy attack under a policy of deterrence must be half or less that of an attack under a policy of unilateral disarmament.[2] That is, since the policy of deterrence involves nuclear response in the event of attack, and since the damage in consequential terms would in this event be twice as great, it follows that, in order to be morally justifiable, the posture of deterrence must make the chance of attack twice as unlikely as it is with a policy of unilateral disarmament. The requirement that the likelihood of attack be halved places a substantial burden on defenders of deterrence who wish to use straightforward consequential arguments.

Indeed this is one reason why most sophisticated defenders of deterrence never adopt such straightforwardly consequential positions. Another is that simply adding up the amount of potential harm overlooks accepted moral priorities. In particular, because consequentialism typically assumes that each person counts for one and no more than one it discourages a nation's favoring its own safety over that of the enemy and, in turn, treating an aggressor with less sympathy than his victim.

A stronger argument for deterrence buttresses consequential considerations by reference to a right to self-defense. For present purposes let us assume that an individual is justified in killing in self-defense.[3] It seems to follow that nations too have such a right. Indeed, traditional justifications of the right to self-defense on the part of nations have turned on the so-called domestic

---

[2]Lackey

[3]It is worth noting that the existence of a right to kill another in self-defense is not an open-and-shut moral issue. Though the majority of humanity accepts such a right, many respected moral authorities do not. The very existence of the doctrine of pacifism implies disagreement.

analogy. As Michael Walzer puts it: "A man has certain rights in his home...because neither his life nor his liberty is secure unless there exists some physical space in which he is safe from intrusion. Similarly again, the right of a nation or people not be be invaded derives from the common life its members have made."[4]

To see the importance of the introduction of the right to self-defense in the deterrence argument, consider two hypothetical cases. Under the first, a country knows that a policy of nuclear deterrence that targets the enemy country will reduce the chances of nuclear enemy aggression by 50 percent. Under the second, the same country knows that targeting a completely innocent country will lessen the chances of enemy nuclear aggression by 70 percent. Clearly, the first case is morally preferable to the second despite the enhancement of deterrence. Here we are reminded of Paul Ramsey's point that, even if it turned out that one could eliminate fifty thousand annual holiday accident fatalities in the United States by tying babies to the bumpers of traveling automobiles, the practice is morally unacceptable. By augmenting consequential considerations by the notion of self-defense, supporters of deterrence are thus able to accommodate the presumption that, in exercising the right to self-defense, harm to an aggressor, but not harm to a nonaggressor, is justified.

There are further ramifications of the concept of self-defense. Michael Walzer's brief argument on behalf of deterrence in his *Just and Unjust Wars* concludes that the harm threatened by an enemy intending to use nuclear weapons is sufficiently severe that the threat justifies a counter-nuclear threat in order to prevent such harm. And we must agree with Walzer that, ceteris paribus, the greater the harm threatened, the greater the morally justified harm that may be threatened in response. Unarmed robbery is to be distinguished from armed robbery, and the justification for using a gun to deter an armed burglar is greater than is the justification for using a gun to deter an unarmed burglar. It seems to follow, then, that nuclear threats are justified against nuclear enemies.

Yet even assuming the domestic analogy is correct, specific limitations on the exercise of self-defense must be acknowledged. International covenants and treaties consistently affirm such limitations, as when article 22 of the Hague Regulations states that "the right of belligerents to adopt means of injuring the enemy is not unlimited."[5] Walzer himself grants that nothing but aggression can justify war: "There must," he says, "actually have been a wrong."[6] The point is worth emphasizing. Self-defense is distinct from self-preservation, and harming another in self-defense is not justified if the party harmed is innocent. Sentenced to die in the electric chair, John Gacy, the mass murderer, may posess the Hobbesian right to attempt to escape as an act of

---

[4]Michael Walzer, *Just and Unjust Wars* (New York: Basic Books, 1977), p. 55.

[5]For an account of the impact of international law on the arms race, see Milan Sahovic, "Disarmament and International Law," in *The Dynamics of the Arms Race*, ed. Carl Carlton and Carlo Schaerf (New York: John Wiley & Sons, 1975), pp. 160–170.

[6]Walzer, pp. 61–62.

self-preservation; but he does not have the right to kill his jailor. One may harm an attacker who is harming, or about to harm, oneself, but not unless that person is morally culpable or—at a minimum—insane.

Still further, the right of self-defense is limited by a principle of proportionality. Force must be proportional to its ends, and this means not only that no more force must be used than is necessary to achieve a given end but also that the value of the end must outweigh the disvalue of the means. Using a gun in self-defense is morally justified only if the gun is actually needed for self-defense and if the harm caused by the gun is roughly proportional to the harm avoided.

Thus three limiting conditions for the right to self-defense emerge.

1 One should avoid harming persons who are neither inflicting nor about to inflict harm.

2 The force one intends to use should be proportional to its ends.

3 One should avoid harming persons who are neither culpable nor insane.

The critical moral feature of nuclear weapons systems that frustrates the above conditions might be called "technological recalcitrance." That is to say, at present levels of technology, such weapons systems are recalcitrant to the intentions of their users: they are relatively uncontrollable, subject to accidents, and strikingly indiscriminate in the scope of their damage.

Let us sketch the outward shape of the problem of technological recalcitrance manifested in nuclear weapons systems. It is a feature of such systems that the time between decision and delivery is extremely short. The delivery time of the new Pershing missiles in Europe is about nine minutes. Countering such an immediately present danger means abandoning the luxury of even modest deliberation time. Defense strategists are driven to employ increasingly complex, hair-triggered control systems capable of launching hundreds of nuclear weapons at a moment's notice. Nuclear weapons systems, thus, become technologically "slippery."

Technologically slippery systems increase the risk of accidental attack and hence the risk of violating principles 1 and 3. The ever-present possibility of human error is aggravated by the use of independent automated delivery mechanisms. Almost every traditional weapons system lacked this feature. The sword, the spear, the cavalry, were relatively accident free. When Marcus Aurelius considered marching on Partha, he could be confident his attack was the result of human intention. A nuclear counterattack may occur as a consequence of technological accident, or it may occur in response to a limited, accidental launch by the other side. In neither case could the enemy be regarded as either culpable or insane.

Furthermore, the very character of nuclear weapons systems implies increased harm to noncombatants—to persons who are neither harming nor about to harm us. Nuclear weapons systems are quite different from single nuclear weapons. In such systems individual weapons occur as parts of complex attack plans designed to explode thousands of bombs in a given order and pattern. This, coupled with the indiscriminate character of the hydrogen nuclear explosion, means that civilian casualties in the event of a nuclear attack by the superpowers would be substantial. It explains why even theories designed to justify war, such as the *jus ad bellum* and *jus in bello* doctrines, have difficulty justifying the inevitable harm to noncombatants resulting from nuclear warfare.[7] A nuclear strike would bring about as a matter of certainty the deaths of thousands of persons who could in no way be regarded as culpable. Even if one includes the ordinary Soviet citizen along with Soviet leaders as culpable agents, thousands of children under the age of six would be killed. A nuclear exchange may also harm innocents living beyond the boundaries of targeted nations. Indeed, Jonathan Schell has argued that nuclear weapons are unique in threatening the very existence of the human species.[8]

Next, a nuclear weapons system tends to foreclose options to negotiate and thus to frustrate the principle of proportionality. A delivery time of seven or twenty minutes forecloses the possibility of allowing the other side to respond to the initiation of hostilities and consider peace negotiations. This drawback is critical since, whether in the resolution of strikes or war, compromise is more likely the closer one moves to the brink of disaster. With conventional warfare, the steady advance of pain and death tends to weaken the idealism of its participants and bring home the costs of the struggle. With nuclear warfare, there are no costs until the final terrible moment—and then everything becomes due at once. Again, traditional weapons were more accommodating. When Louis XIV began a march against the enemy, the enemy had days or weeks to reconsider the issue in contention; and so did Louis.[9]

Thus nuclear weapons systems are distinguished by the feature of technological recalcitrance. This recalcitrance to human intention, spawned by the technical properties of the weapon itself, means that the maintenance of such systems is an action with double effect. In addition to the (hoped-for) effect of decreasing the likelihood of enemy attack, there is the increased probability of accidental or unwanted destruction and, in turn, of a violation of the conditions limiting the right to self-defense.[10]

---

[7]The *jus ad bellum* and *jus in bello* doctrines were introduced by medieval writers. The former addresses the issue of whether a particular war or act of self-defense is justified, while the latter addresses the issue of whether a particular action in a given war is justified. For interpretations of just war theories, see Iris Claude, Jr., "Just Wars: Doctrines and Institutions," *Political Science Quarterly* 95 (1980): 83–96; James T. Johnson, *Just War Tradition and the Restraint of War(A Moral and Historical Inquiry* (Princeton, N.J.: Princeton University Press, 1981); William V. O'Brien, *The Conduct of Just and Limited War* (New York: Praeger Publishers, 1981); Thomas D. O'Connor, "A Reappraisal of the Just War Tradition," *Ethics* 85 (1974) 171–73; Paul Ramsey, *The Just War: Force and Political Responsibility* (New York: Charles Scribner's Sons, 1968); and James Childress, "Just War Theories," in *War or Peace? The Search for New Answers*, ed. Thomas A. Shannon (New York: Orbis Books, 1980).

[8]Jonathan Schell, *The Fate of the Earth* (New York: Alfred A. Knopf, Inc., 1982).

[9]Only with the beginning of World War I did humanity witness an erosion of the opportunity to negotiate at the brink of disaster, as mobilization systems became sufficiently elaborate that, once started, their reversal was almost impossible.

[10]This feature may, of course, be shared by other nonnuclear weapons, e.g., large conventional bombs, poison gases, and weapons of biological warfare.

But surely, critics will reply, the matter cannot be so simple. The issue of noncombatant immunity is the subject of a growing literature which reveals the difficulties of simplistic proscriptions against noncombatant harm in the context of modern warfare. The proscription against the killing of innocents, called the principle of "discrimination" in the *jus in bello* tradition, is a subject of vigorous controversy. For example, William O'Brien writes that "the literal application of noncombatant immunity is incompatible with modern war, wherein much of the hostilities are carried out by weapons of great ranges and destructive powers. If discrimination means no direct intentional killing of noncombatants in the sense that no such killing would be foreseeable in using the modern weapons of war, no warfare waged in an environment including noncombatants and civilian targets would be morally permissible."[11] O'Brien concludes that respect for the right of legitimate self-defense implies a rejection of what he calls the "pacifist position," that is, a strict interpretation of the principle of noncombatant immunity. Discrimination cannot be viewed as an ironclad principle; instead it must seen as a relative prescription enjoining us to concentrate our attacks on military objectives and to minimize our destruction of noncombatants and civilian targets.[12] The upper limit of damage to noncombatants should be established, O'Brien adds, by reference to the principle of proportionality.

Let us set aside for the moment the issue of whether O'Brien exaggerates the technological recalcitrance of modern, nonnuclear weaponry. His primary challenge is to a strict interpretation of what earlier were asserted to be two limiting conditions on the right to self-defense: (1) one should avoid harming persons who are neither inflicting nor about to inflict harm and (2) one should avoid harming agents who are neither culpable nor insane. Serious problems, however, arise for O'Brien's analysis.

To conclude that the principle of discrimination means merely a "minimization" of noncombatant deaths leaves open the question of what counts as an acceptable minimum. To answer the question by reference to the principle of proportionality has the effect of reducing the principle of discrimination to the principle of proportionality, and this is an effect which flies in the face of the traditional insight that noncombatant immunity is a prior and limiting principle governing any weighing of costs and benefits.

Worse, however, is the circularity that arises. Clearly, it is not an argument against a strict interpretation of noncombatant immunity to say that modern warfare as we know it would be impossible, for what is at stake is precisely the permissibility of certain aspects of modern warfare. Nor is it an argument against a strict interpretation to appeal to the right of self-defense, for, again, it is the character of the limiting conditions on the exercise of the right to self-defense that is at issue.

---

[11]William O'Brien, "Just War Doctrine in a Nuclear Context," *Theological Studies* 44 (1983): 191–220.
[12]Ibid., p. 211.

Instead of beginning with the complex realities of global arsenals and strategies, it helps to begin with the home territory of the self-defense analogy, namely, the right of individuals to defend themselves against harm from others. This is the basis of the domestic analogy and the basis, in turn, of the moral justification of threats by nations to use nuclear arms in self-defense. A bit of moral geometry, utilizing parameters drawn from instances of self-defense in ordinary moral life, will show that there is no instance of domestic self-defense in which the parameters resemble those of nuclear deterrence and in which one is justified in adopting the deterrence posture in question. It shows, in short, that the domestic analogy cannot provide a justification for nuclear deterrence because "domestic" situations are unambiguous with respect to the issue of harm to innocents.

Let us consider the parameters of domestic situations in more detail. If an individual, A, adopts a policy of deterrence that includes the sincere intent to harm B in the event B attempts to initiate harm, then the justifiability of A's policy of deterrence is a function of at least three variables: level of risk to A, probability of harm to innocents, and level of harm to B. As risk to A increases, ceteris paribus, so does the force of the moral argument on behalf of the policy of deterrence. For example, if B has not threatened A, or if B is not in a position to inflict significant harm on A, then A's justification for threatening harm to B loses force. As the probability of harm to innocents increases, however, the reverse is true, that is, the moral argument on behalf of the deterrent threat is weakened. For example, one's belief that adopting a policy of deterrence places no innocent persons at risk would be reason weighing heavily on behalf of the policy. Finally, as the level of sincerely threatened harm to the aggressor increases, the moral support for a policy of deterrence decreases. Since harm is a prima facie evil, and because greater harm implies greater evil, threatening more harm requires a stronger justification than threatening less does. Thus as A threatens to inflict increasing levels of harm to B, the justifiability of A's threat decreases; yet the point at which A is no longer justified in making the threat will be affected by the level of harm that B is threatening in turn.

Utilizing the three variables isolated above, it becomes possible to map analogues to a policy of nuclear deterrence in ordinary moral life. A policy of nuclear deterrence is analogous to domestic situations where the risk to A is extremely high, where the level of threatened harm to B is at least equally high, and where the probability not only of harming but also of killing innocents as a result of A's policy of deterrence is nonnegligible, that is, significant. Now the first factor speaks strongly on behalf of a deterrence policy, while the second and third speak against it. And yet—and here is the crucial point—the third factor is decisive in a manner which makes it impossible for us to imagine a relevantly similar case of self-defense drawn from domestic moral life in which the probability of killing innocents is significant and deterrence is justified. So low is the threshhold at which the probability of such killing triggers our moral indignation that we condemn sincere threats to kill aggressors made by individuals in everyday situations of self-defense when the probability of killing innocents rises above insignificance.

Let us clarify this point by constructing two hypothetical cases of persons adopting "deterrence" policies where the three relevant variables are the same as those operating at the level of national nuclear deterrence. In other words, let us construct cases on the level of individual or family self-defense that are analogous to that of national nuclear defense. It will be helpful in the following examples to assume the absence of police force or national government, that is, to assume a kind of state of nature, to mirror the absence of global authority at the international level.

Scenario 1   A undertakes to protect himself (or his family) against the threat of armed aggressors. A possesses a remarkable gun, one that kills when pointed in the general vicinity of an assailant and operates on the principle of identifying the assailant's chromosomal structure. Its drawback is that it also destroys all other persons with the same chromosomal structure within a one-hundred-mile radius.

Scenario 2   A has received a threat from Murder, Inc. A undertakes to protect himself (or his family) through the use of nitroglycerin stored in A's home. Signs are posted in A's window reading "Warning: High Explosives on Hair Trigger, Intruders will be destroyed!" Although the nitroglycerin can be triggered by moving one of the many trip wires positioned around the house, it can also be triggered by accident, for example, by an earthquake. The amount of nitroglycerin is sufficient also to destroy the homes of surrounding neighbors.

Scenario 1 reflects the indiscriminate effects of the use of a nuclear weapons system through the indiscriminate targeting effects of the chromosome gun. Scenario 2, on the other hand, reflects not only the indiscriminate effects of the use of such weapons but also their accident-prone tendencies. In both scenarios 1 and 2, three key variables are relevantly similar to those at the level of national nuclear deterrence: that is to say, risk to A is extremely high, level of threatened harm to B is at least equally high, and the probability of harm to innocents as a result of adoption of the policy of deterrence is significant. (When speaking of possible harm to innocents, we are focusing not on the actual carrying out of the threat—where the probability of harm to innocents, of course, would be close to 1.0—but on the adoption of the policy of deterrence. In scenarios 1 and 2 even the sincere adoption of the deterrence policies in question poses risk to innocents.)[13]

Would the rigging of one's home with nitroglycerin or the making of a sincere threat to use a chromosome gun be justified even if doing so had a stronger deterrent effect than alternate threats? Would either policy be justified even if the scruples of one's enemy allowed the use of such threats?[14] No one, I think, could make a convincing case for such policies of deterrence; and the

[13]The importance of separating the morality of the use of nuclear weapons from the morality of the threat to use nuclear weapons is underscored in Jeff McMahon's "Deterrence and Deontology," *Ethics* 95 (April 1985): 517-537.

[14]The fact that a man standing in a crowded elevator is about to shoot someone standing outside the elevator does not justify the person outside, however innocent, in throwing a grenade into the elevator.

difficulty of making a convincing case stems from more than the inherent power of the weapons in question or the sheer number of potential casualties. The problem, rather, is with whom the weapons might kill and under what conditions.

If A were protecting his family rather than himself, we might sympathize more with his desire to make such threats. But the threats themselves would not thereby become permissible. It is common when discussing fiduciary and managerial responsibility to point out that one's duties to serve the interests of others fail to excuse the violation of standard moral norms.[15] This point has special force, moreover, when the moral norms in question are relatively exceptionless, for example, the prohibition on the killing of innocents.

It follows that a national policy of nuclear deterrence cannot be justified by appeal to some type of domestic analogy. The domestic analogy fails to justify the exercise of self-defense through the use of nuclear weapons systems on the national level since relevantly similar analogues on the domestic level clash with common moral intuition. The limiting conditions for self-defense are not fulfilled. If there is some right of self-defense possessed by nations that does not derive from our more fundamental convictions about individual self-defense, then the conclusion of the foregoing analysis may be questioned. But I cannot imagine what such a right would look like.

Although the argument so far is deontological in form, it need not neglect morally relevant probabilities. For example, our condemnation of the threat in scenario 1 undoubtedly presumes that it is not the case that the surrounding area is sparsely populated and that only one in ten million persons shares the chromosomal structure targeted by the gun. Were this true, the chances of killing an innocent person would be negligible, and we might well retract our condemnation of the threat. Similarly, in the context of national policies of deterrence the critical value of deterring enemy attack establishes as a necessary condition for declaring a policy impermissible that both the number of innocents likely to be harmed and the risk of harming them be significant. This is nothing other than the application of the principle of proportionality identified earlier as a limiting condition on the exercise of self-defense.[16] Disputes over what should and and should not count as "significant" are inevitable, but it seems likely that even low numbers will count and that present policies of nuclear deterrence satisfy the condition. In its recognition of even low probabilities, the analysis of nuclear permissibility resembles that of recklessness in the law. If a person picks up a pistol from a table containing six pistols, one of

---

[15]For a discussion of this point, see Thomas Donaldson, *Corporations and Morality* (Englewood Cliffs, N.J.: Prentice-Hall, Inc., 1982), esp. chap. 5.

[16]Here the issue of national self-defense differs from that of individual self-defense. Since in individual self-defense only a single life is being defended from attack, any risk undertaken in the act of self-defense to a single additional innocent person is sufficient, ceteris paribus, to violate the proportionality criterion. But in the instance of national self-defense, millions of lives are typically being defended. Hence it does not follow that a risk undertaken in the act of national self-defense to a single innocent individual—or even a handful of individuals—will necessarily violate the principle of proportionality.

which he knows is loaded, then aims it at a total stranger and pulls the trigger, the person is guilty of recklessness. And the label of recklessness applies no less when the probabilities are much smaller and the table contains, not six, but sixty pistols.[17] Nonetheless, were it possible, owing to special empirical features of the deterrence context (involving, say, remarkably low yield nuclear weapons with pinpoint accuracy), to demonstrate that either the number of innocents to be harmed or the risk of harming them were truly insignificant, then one might successfully rebut charges of moral impermissibility.

That the present analysis includes an assessment of at least hypothetical probabilities does not render its form consequential rather than deontological. The emphasis remains with the principles limiting the exercise of self-defense. Rather, the application of the principles requires a healthy sense of realism. Consider again the analogy of recklessness. Recklessness is wrong on principle yet requires probabilistic assessments for its application. The answer to the question of whether it is reckless to carry about a dynamite cap in one's briefcase depends on the empirical characteristics of dynamite caps, their likelihood of exploding under certain conditions, and so on. Were threats by nations to use powerful weapons of indiscriminate destruction never fulfilled, then categorical denunciations of such threats would be harder to justify. Even Kant speaks of the "empirical spring" necessary to apply the Categorical Imperative.

The peculiarly deontological character of the present argument is reflected not only in its emphasis on principles but also in its insistence that in thinking about nuclear deterrence, more than consequences matter. Not only the predicted consequences of either intentionally adopting the policy or undertaking an eventual strike are evil—though these are awesome enough—but also the intentional performance of the actions themselves. Some actions ought not to be done; some risks ought not to be assumed; and they ought not to be done or assumed as a matter of principle.

If, as I have suggested, nuclear deterrence ultimately lacks a viable moral defense, either from a domestic analogy or elsewhere, is one forced to recommend surrender to the Soviets? No such recommendation is entailed by the impermissibility of making sincere threats to launch a nuclear strike. Even assuming the implausibility of some variation of the "bluff" strategy, the obvious alternatives to unilateral nuclear disarmament are multilateral or bilateral nuclear disarmament. There exists also the option of substituting

[17]Legal theorists acknowledge that the matter is different when the person's action is part of a practice that serves a valid human end and when the innocents placed at risk generally stand to benefit. When we step into our automobiles and confront the small but existing possibility that we will injure another motorist or pedestrian, the risks must be weighed against the general benefits of automobile transportation, benefits which accrue to the public at large. When drunk or driving an automobile with bad steering, the risks are too great; under normal conditions they are not. Nuclear deterrence is difficult to subsume under this exception, however, since it seems implausible that, e.g., our nuclear threat against the Soviet Union benefits innocent Soviet citizens. For a classical analysis of recklessness in the law, see Glanville L. Williams, *Criminal Law: The General Part* (London: Stevens & Sons, 1953), pp. 49–59.

conventional for nuclear weapons, which many believe would provide an adequate deterrence and one less dangerous than what we presently possess.[18] Even were this not the case, a unilateral decision by the United States to back out of the superpower rivalry would not entail the Soviet occupation of Detroit; indeed, it is a decision which some believe would enhance rather than harm the long-term self-interest of the U.S. citizenry.

This is not the place to defend or debate these empirical matters, and in the most important sense the outcome of such a debate is irrelevant to the article's conclusion. If risking the launch of nuclear missiles—a launch which would have as one of its foreseeable consequences the deaths of untold innocents—is impermissible, then it is impermissible whether national self-interest is enhanced or not. It is no surprise that morality sometimes requires the conscious assumption of risk. In the present context, however, it may help to recognize that even the existence of risk to ourselves from the abandonment of our present policies, much less its degree, is a matter of dispute.

Our conclusion, then, is in keeping with the spirit of *jus in bello* and *jus ad bello* doctrines insofar as it condemns nuclear deterrence by an appeal to moral principle; again, the problem is not only the enormity of the horror but also the kind of horror. In contrast to such theories, however, the conclusion has been reached through an analysis not of specific acts of war, for example, area bombing, but of moral analogues to policies of national nuclear deterrence on a domestic level. Nuclear deterrence finds its strongest rationale in arguments that supplement consequential considerations by an appeal to the right of self-defense. But the right of society to its self-defense, like its right to imprison lawbreakers, requires limiting conditions for its exercise. The very technological recalcitrance of nuclear weapons systems places the fulfillment of these conditions at significant risk. In this instance, the risks are too high, and they are too high as a matter of principle.

A Contractual Defense of Nuclear Deterrence*

Christopher Morris

It is a widely accepted moral principle that it is wrong to kill the innocent. Yet this is precisely what we threaten to do in the event of a nuclear attack. In fact, it is an essential part of nuclear deterrence. Is nuclear deterrence then immoral? Many people, both of the left and the right, believe this to be so.

From *Ethics: Theory and Practice* ed., Manuel Velasquez (Englewood Cliffs, N.J.: Prentice-Hall, Inc., 1985). Pp. 203–13. Copyright 1984 Christoper Morris. Reprinted by permission.
[18]For a discussion of this issue, see Richard H. Ullman, "Denuclearizing International Politics," *Ethics* 95 (April 2985): 567-588.
*This essay is essentially a simplified version of the position developed in "A Contractarian Defense of Nuclear Deterrence," forthcoming in a special issue of *Ethics*, vol. 95. I am grateful to Gregory Kavka, Alan Vick, and Manual Velasquez for comments and criticism, as well as to the

However, the principle prohibiting the killing of the innocent as stated above is implausible since it does not make allowances for accidental and unintended killings. Thus, many moral philosophers distinguish between direct and indirect killings and argue that indirect killings are not always wrong. One very influential way of making this distinction involves the traditional doctrine of double effect, according to which only acts of direct killing are morally prohibited, while acts of indirect killing may be morally permissible. The doctrine is usually stated as follows: in distinguishing between the good and the bad effects of an act of killing, the act is indirect and morally permissible if

1 the act in itself is not impermissible,
2 the bad effect is not the means to the good effect,
3 the good but not the bad effect is intended, and
4 the good effect is not outweighed by the bad effect.

Killing some civilians while bombing an enemy military installation might thus be permissible if the bad effect (killing the civilians) was neither intended nor the means to the good effect (destroying the installation) and if, say, the number of lives saved by the bombing is greater than the number of civilian casualties. The doctrine would justify such killings where the deaths were the unintended side effects of permissible acts.

An appeal to the doctrine of double effect may not, however, help the defender of nuclear deterrence, for the innocent civilians who are slaughtered by nuclear retaliation surely would not be killed indirectly. Consider what is called "countervalue" retaliation, the nuclear targeting of enemy centers of population. Such retaliation clearly would involve acts of direct killing since conditions 2 and 3 of the doctrine of double effect would not be satisfied. The bad effect (killing massive numbers of innocent civilians) would be both intended and a means to the good effect ("punishing" enemy aggression, deterring future aggression, or whatever).

In view of this, some moral philosophers counsel that we use only "counterforce" strategies, that is, strategies that aim our missiles solely at military targets and not at innocent civilians. However, given the huge numbers of Soviet casualties to be expected from counterforce retaliatory strikes, condition 4 of the doctrine of double effect surely is not satisfied. In terms of numbers of lives, the good effect is outweighed by the bad.

Threatening to kill, however, is not the same as actually killing. Perhaps we are justified in *threatening* nuclear retaliation, so long as we do not intend to carry out our threat. That is, perhaps the morally appropriate deterrent strategy is bluffing. Naturally, we should not expect such an insincere threat to be credible once our moral reluctance became known to our adversary. The effectiveness of such a bluff depends on our adversary's belief that we would (or might) launch a retaliatory second strike in the event of nuclear attack. I do

participants at the various lectures and conferences where earlier versions of the essay were presented. I am also grateful to David Gauthier and Gregory Kavka for the use they have allowed me to make of their unpublished writings.

not believe that a policy based on such a bluff is acceptable. First, it would depend on deception—or at least dissimulation—for its effectiveness, and this may be impossible to achieve in an open society. Second, a deceptive policy is inconsistent with the values of an open society like ours. Third, it seems incredible that the most effective means of national defense should depend on such deception. Thus it is my belief that this approach will not salvage our deterrence practices.

Faced with such a conclusion, some moral philosophers would recommend unilateral nuclear disarmament. Though I cannot argue here against this alternative, I should note that I find it unacceptable for a number of reasons. The claims of some proponents of disarmament to the effect that the dangers of Soviet domination or Soviet nuclear blackmail are small seem to me to lack credibility.[1] And many cases for unilateral nuclear disarmament depend on such claims. Further, disarmament proposals usually assume a simultaneous build-up of conventional military forces (to deter conventional attack). But citizens of the Western alliance are notoriously unwilling to shoulder the costs of such a rearmament program. Proponents of unilateral disarmament often forget that nuclear weapons are inexpensive in comparison to conventional weapons and forces.

Given the unacceptability of unilateral nuclear disarmament, how can we justify nuclear deterrence? Nuclear deterrence involves threatening to kill directly massive numbers of innocents in the event of an enemy nuclear attack, an act not justified by the traditional doctrine of double effect. Is nuclear deterrence then morally impermissible? I shall argue that this is not the case.

Let me begin by stating clearly the moral principle that is involved in this issue. Nuclear deterrence involves threatening to kill directly massive numbers of innocents. Directly killing the innocent is thought to be morally wrong, at least in normal circumstances. The relevant moral principle would thus seem to be the following, which I will call principle P: It is wrong directly to kill innocent persons.

The terms involved in this principle should be understood as follows. An act of direct killing is one that is not an act of indirect killing as defined by the doctrine of double effect. A person is any creature that is owed some moral consideration. An innocent person is a person who is not threatening another. (Sometimes this is called the "causal" sense of innocence, in contrast to the "moral" or "judicial" sense, according to which innocence is equivalent to absence of guilt.) Thus, principle P prohibits the killing of nonthreatening persons except in those cases of indirect or unintentional killing justified by the doctrine of double effect.

---

[1]See Douglas P. Lackey, "Missiles and Morals: A Utilitarian Look at Nuclear Deterrence," *Philosophy and Public Affairs*, vol. II (1980), pp. 189–231; Russell Hardin, "Unilateral Versus Mutual Disarmament," Gregory S. Kavka, "Doubts About Unilateral Nuclear Disarmament," and Douglas P. Lackey, "Disarmament Revisited: A Reply to Kavka and Hardin," *Philosophy and Public Affairs*, vol. 12 (1983), pp. 236–54, 255–60, 261–65.

According to the natural law tradition, killing the innocent directly is absolutely wrong, that is, it is impermissible whatever the consequences.[2] But I reject the interpretation of P as absolute. Interpreting P as absolute commits us to refrain from using (or threatening to use) nuclear weapons. Given what I have said above, interpreting the principle in this manner would commit us to bluffing or, more likely, to unilateral nuclear disarmament and that, I am assuming, is unacceptable in the present circumstances. Further, given that some deterrent strategies reduce considerably the likelihood of nuclear conflict[3] and that absolutist interpretations of P commit us to rejecting such strategies, then surely that is at least a partial reason for rejecting such interpretations.[4]

Does my rejection of the absolute interpretation of P commit me to interpreting P as *defeasible*? A moral principle is defeasible when it may be overridden by other moral considerations. Utilitarianism, for example, supposes that all our duties are derived from the principle of maximizing the total quantity of the good, where the good is identified with happiness, well-being, or utility. According to such a view, all of our duties are defeasible, since whatever maximizes happiness in one situation may very well not do so in another.

Utilitarian interpretations of P are, of course, only one way of rendering the principle defeasible; other moral theories may do this as well. But understanding the inappropriateness of utilitarian accounts will set the stage for the interpretation of P that I wish to defend.

Utilitarianism would have us consider in our moral deliberations the welfare of all individuals that could be affected by our actions. Further, not only are we to do this, we are also to count their well-being equally with ours. Utilitarianism has often been criticized as too flexible a moral theory; depending on the circumstances, it can be said to justify too much that we think is wrong. It is not always clear that such criticisms are correct, but they seem beside the point here. Rather, what is striking about utilitarianism as it is applied to matters of conflict and war is not how flexible but how demanding a theory it is. After all, it requires us to count our enemy's welfare equally with our own.

Utilitarianism, as has often been noted, is a moral theory that takes a certain ideal that is at best suited for close friends or family and applies it to all persons.

---

[2] See G.E.M. Anscombe, "Modern Moral Philosophy" and "War and Murder" in G.E.M. Anscombe, *Collected Philosophical Papers*, vol. 3 (Minneapolis: University of Minnesota Press, 1981), pp. 26–42, 51–61; Alan Donagan, *The Theory of Morality* (Chicago: University of Chicago Press, 1977); and Jeffrie G. Murphy, "The Killing of the Innocent," *The Monist*, vol. 57 (1973), pp. 527–50.

[3] See Lackey, "Missiles and Morals." See also Gregory S. Kavka, "Deterrence, Utility, and Rational Choice," *Theory and Decision*, vol. 12 (1980), pp. 41–60.

[4] If it is thought that the doctrine of double effect does not rule out counterforce retaliation, then the absolutist interpretation of P may commit us to counterforce deterrent strategies, and that would be most destabilizing in the current situation. (Such a move would in the present circumstances likely engender an arms race in space, something that does not appear to frighten the current United States administration.)

Countless critics have remarked on the inappropriateness of this transference. However, another point needs to be emphasized, and that is that utilitarianism is very irrational when applied to situations of major conflict, such as nuclear war. While most wars are not zero sum—that is, both sides have some interests in common—it is doubtful that any argument could be given for the rationality of accepting the principle of utility in all such situations, at least if we understand rationality as not requiring total self-sacrifice. After all, the interests in conflict may be too important to be compromised or abandoned easily. It is one thing to commit oneself to the principle of utility in situations when others are themselves willing to accept the same principle, but it is entirely another matter to commit oneself to the principle of utility in a nonutilitarian world. I conclude, therefore, that the utilitarian interpretation of principle P as defeasible is not acceptable.

Normally, in moral theory it is thought that "absolute" and "defeasible" are contradictory terms. That is, it is assumed that if a principle is not absolute, then it must be defeasible, and vice versa. However, I want to argue that there are circumstances in which P is neither defeasible nor absolute.

The position I wish to defend is this: In certain circumstances respecting P would be irrational. In such circumstances, P (and other principles of justice)[5] is no longer rationally binding.[6] Thus, in such circumstances directly killing the innocent would not be unjust because nothing would be unjust.[7] These circumstances, which I shall call Hobbesian states of nature, are, I believe, exceedingly rare in the modern world, the behavior of nation-states to the contrary. However, an enemy nuclear attack would bring about such circumstances, or so I shall argue. Therefore, massive nuclear retaliation would not, in those circumstances, be unjust because during an enemy nuclear attack nothing would be unjust. P, on this account, would not be absolute, for it would not be wrong to do what P prohibits. But neither would P be defeasible: since considerations of justice would no longer be binding, there would be no considerations of justice that could override it. Let me now turn to defending these claims.

Faced with the apparent choice between interpreting P as absolute (as recommended by many natural law and natural rights theories) and the demand to accord equal weight to the welfare of the enemy (as recommended by utilitarianism), some moral philosophers counsel retreat into moral nihilism: in war, anything goes; nothing is prohibited. In the social sciences and in

[5]My concern in this essay is with justice. I assuming that what is true of justice need not be true of the other virtues. For instance, the virtue of benevolence may be binding in situations where justice is not.

[6]The notion of rationality I am using here is basically that widely used in the social sciences, especially in economics and game theory, i.e., a person is rational insofar as he maximizes the satisfaction of his preferences. I would want, however, to amend this conception in the manner suggested by David P. Gauthier in "Reason and Maximization," *Canadian Journal of Philosophy*, vol. 4 (1975), pp. 411–33, so as to handle certain types of problems of strategic interaction (namely, prisoners' dilemmas, for those readers familiar with these issues).

[7]The "nothing" will be qualified later, with regard to uninvolved third parties.

politics, such a position often goes under the name of "realism." But such talk is dubious, as well as dangerous. For one, it contradicts seemingly entrenched patters of ordinary discourse.[8] In war, as well as at other times, most people attempt to justify their actions by reference to moral standards. It is extremely difficult to talk about war without using moral language; even slogans such as "war is hell" do not usually allow us to dispense with moral categories.

Equally important, however, is the danger of destabilization that comes from nihilism. Obviously, such a position reinforces mutual suspicion. At present the United States and the Soviet Union greatly distrust each other. Each appears to believe that the other is acquiring or already possesses offensive nuclear weapons. Should either party come to believe, or be reinforced in its belief, that the other thinks nothing is forbidden, then that party would find it difficult to trust the other to refrain from seeking a first-strike advantage. Assurance that the other side is capable and willing to impose constraints on its behavior is crucial to stabilization. Since abstaining from first-strike advantage is stabilizing, it is clear that a retreat to nihilism may have a significant destabilizing effect. In this context, the suspicion that the other side seeks to use allegedly defensive weapons for offensive, first-strike ends can only increase.

Nonetheless, the retreat to nihilism has an important grain of truth to it, and this is the truth expressed in Thomas Hobbes' account of the relations between nations. According to Hobbes, nations find themselves in a "state of nature" in which there are no binding moral obligations. Relations between nations thus are relations of power, unconstrained by moral rules. In a similar fashion, relations between individuals in a state of nature are also mere relations of power, unconstrained by moral considerations. The difference for Hobbes is that individuals have the possibility of establishing an enforcer or sovereign and thus of escaping from their plight, while no such escape is possible in the world of nations.[9]

But Hobbes' account may be defective in two ways. First, it may be possible to accept his analysis of the problem facing rational individuals in a state of nature without accepting his solution of absolute and unconstrained sovereignty, that is, without accepting his view that only the establishment of an all-powerful and indivisible ruler can end the state of nature.[10] Second, it is not clear that Hobbes' account of international relations must be accepted.[11] I shall not pronounce on the accuracy of Hobbes' account in terms of the nations with which he was familiar in the seventeenth century, but nations today are interdependent in ways that transform their situation. Let me explain these two points.

---

[8]Essentially this is the argument of Michael Walzer, *Just and Unjust Wars* (New York: Basic Books, 1977).

[9]Thomas Hobbes, *The Leviathan* (Harmondsworth: Penguin Books, 1968; 1651); see especially chapter 13.

[10]See, for example, David Gauthier, *The Logic of Leviathan* (Oxford: Clarendon Press, 1969), especially chapter 4, section 4.

[11]See H.L.A. Hart, *The Concept of Law* (Oxford: Clarendon Press, 1972), pp. 208–31.

According to contractarian ethics, relations of justice obtain only between parties that find themselves in certain situations. Following John Rawls, we may call these "circumstances of justice."[12] In this view, relations of justice exist only between parties that are interdependent in certain ways. Individuals in the circumstances of justice are roughly equal in physical and mental powers, and thus are unable to dominate one another and are vulnerable to attack; resources are moderately scarce (relative to needs and wants); needs and wants, although in conflict to some degree, are such as to allow for mutually beneficial interaction. The most important condition here for our purposes is that of mutual advantage: individuals find themselves in the circumstances of justice only if there exists the possibility of mutually beneficial interaction. But in the absence of possible mutual advantage, there is no place for justice since individuals have no reason to constrain their self-interested activity.

Cooperative interaction, as I shall define it, is mutually beneficial interaction made possible by constraints on self-interested behavior. Between interdependent nations today there appears to be at least some room for such interaction. Thus, contrary to Hobbes' account of international relations, modern nations meet one of the most important conditions for cooperative interaction. Assuming the remaining circumstances of justice obtain between nations, norms of cooperation such as Hobbes' first few laws of nature would be rationally binding on them.[13]

Such norms, however, would be binding on nations only insofar as others are willing to abide by them.[14] The problem in international relations, of course, is to obtain assurances that others are willing to abide by these norms of cooperation. Between nations, there is no absolute sovereign capable of impartial enforcement of agreements and some system of enforcement is necessary if cooperation is to be rational.

Hobbes assumed that the requisite international mechanism would have to be a supranational sovereign. Since no such international sovereign exists, he concluded that norms of cooperation could not be enforced between nations. But this is a mistake. In many relations between individuals where police protection is unavailable, norms of cooperation are often adequately enforced by the parties themselves. Indeed, the threat to retaliate can often provide adequate enforcement without recourse to other measures. In the same way, we may suppose that threats to retaliate when leveled among nations can also provide the requisite enforcement mechanism that makes cooperation possible. If such threats are morally permissible, then we need not search for an international sovereign to ensure international cooperation.

[13]See David Hume, "Enquiry Concerning the Principles of Morals," section 3, in *Enquiries*, 3rd ed., rev. by P.H. Nidditch (Oxford: Clarendon Press, 1975), and John Rawls, *A Theory of Justice* (Cambridge: Harvard University Press, 1971), pp. 126ff.

[13]These laws require that one pursue peace, be willing to give up an equal amount of natural liberty on the condition that others do so as well, and keep one's agreements. Hobbes believed that the laws of nature are summarized in the counsel "Do not that to another, which thou wouldest not have done to thy selfe." Hobbes, *Leviathan*, chapters 14–15.

[14]"Be willing when others are too..." Hobbes, *Leviathan*, chapter 14.

What strategies promise to stabilize the current situation and provide an enforcement mechanism that can make cooperative interaction between nations possible? Let us suppose that

> [i]n the long run, insofar as nuclear weapons are concerned, what each superpower needs for the deterrence of nuclear and conventional attacks on itself and its main allies is the capacity for assured destruction...and a limited capacity for actual warfare. A complete counter-force capability would be disastrous for crisis stability if it consisted of vulnerable forces; and even a complete invulnerable counter-force capability might incite the opponent to strike first in order to use his vulnerable weapons.[15]

Thus, we might suppose that the United States should renounce a first strike on the condition that the Soviet Union does so as well.[16] Adoption of the recommendations quoted above—maintaining the capacity for assured destruction— would convince each party that the other renounces striking first and would provide the threat that makes cooperative interaction possible.

But a threat to retaliate with massive strikes is an acceptable means of deterrence only if it does not violate a basic norm of justice like principle P. Such threats will not violate basic norms of justice when norms of justice no longer bind, i.e., when cooperation between the two parties no longer is possible. But in the event of an enemy nuclear attack, cooperative relations have in fact ended. In such circumstances the parties are back in a Hobbesian state of nature and norms of justice no longer bind.[17]

In such a state of nature, the prohibition on the direct killing of the innocent, like all other principles of justice, becomes a mere counsel of nonmoral prudence. Threatening an adversary with countervalue retaliation in the event of a nuclear attack is therefore permissible because in the circumstances in which such a threat would be carried out it would not be impermissible to do so. I am assuming here, of course, that a *threat* to do X in circumstances C is

[15]Albert Carnesale, Paul Doty, Stanley Hoffman, Samuel P. Huntington, Joseph S. Nye, Jr., and Scott Sagan, *living with Nuclear Weapons* (New York: Bantam Books, 1983), p. 250.

[16]See McGeorge Bundy, George Kennan, Robert McNamara, and Gerard Smith, "Nuclear Weapons and the Atlantic Alliance," *Foreign Affairs*, vol. 60 11992), pp. 753–68. Of course, renouncing a first strike would require a change in NATO defense policy and an unpopular rise in European conventional defense spending.

[17]In the event of an enemy nuclear attack, not only have cooperative relations in fact ended, but cooperative relations are no longer possible on terms acceptable to rational agents. This latter point is controversial and is not a feature of Hobbes' contractarian theory. Cooperative relations presuppose a baseline for determining terms of cooperation, and I am supposing that such a baseline precludes worsening the position of the other side prior to negotiating a cooperative agreement. This account is developed in David Gauthier, "Morals by Agreement" (manuscript, University of Pittsburgh, no date); see also Robert Nozick, *Anarchy, State and Utopia* (New York: Basic Books, 1974) for a noncontractarian account of such a condition on cooperation. Should another party first worsen one's position before endeavoring to cooperate, then cooperation is no longer possible on terms acceptable to rational agents. In other words, cooperation is rational only from a baseline of noncoercion.

Let me expand these remarks somewhat. Contractarian moralists suppose that principles of justice are rationally acceptable only if it is advantageous to live in a world where individuals constrain their self-interested behavior. Thus, to be acceptable to all members of a society, such principles must be mutually beneficial. Advantage here is to be determined in reference to some

morally permissible if *doing* X in those circumstances is not morally impermissible.[18]

In the account above I have assumed that the prohibition against killing the innocent directly is part of an acceptable contractarian morality. Rational agents, in a contractarian choice situation, would find such a prohibition mutually advantageous. Further, I am supposing that this prohibition is a basic principle, one that binds as long as contractarian morality is in force. A morality is "in force," I shall say, when rational agents are in the "circumstances of justice" and are not forced back into a state of nature; in those situations, such a morality is binding on rational agents.

Principle P, then, binds rational agents up until the point at which they are forced back to a state of nature. It is never permissible, I shall assume, to return unilaterally to a state of nature since this would violate Hobbes' first law of nature, which is to seek peace and follow it. But should another nation unilaterally return to a state of nature, e.g., by launching a nuclear attack, then P, and all other principles of justice, become mere counsels of nonmoral prudence. Thus, massive retaliation is not, under such circumstances, morally impermissible, and by extension a threat to retaliate massively is also morally permissible.

Such an account of P would not justify the killing of the innocent in any situation of conflict. The account that I have developed shows how it is suspended in certain situations, namely when an adversary unilaterally returns to a Hobbesian state of nature. In the event, say, of any enemy nuclear attack, the United States (or the Soviet Union) would no longer be bound by P. This does not mean, however, that P is suspended in all conflicts. For surely not all wars involve the complete return to a Hobbesian state of nature. In most wars,

---

nonmoral state; otherwise, no claim could be made about the nonmoral rationality of moral practices that was not begging the question. Hobbes supposes that the baseline from which contractarian moralities are determined is one in which individuals interact noncooperatively. Thus, if one party, holding a pistol to another's head, secures the latter's "consent" to enslavement, genuine moral obligations are created; the deal is mutually advantageous. Now we need not follow Hobbes here; we need not suppose that such a baseline is the proper starting point for the conventionalist's construction of morality. Would it in fact be rational to comply with an "agreement" that had been secured by coercion? Clearly not, at least once the means of coercion had been withdrawn. Thus we shall say that the proper baseline for adoption of principles of justice is one of noninteraction. Such a standpoint precludes one party worsening the position of another immediately prior to the agreement. I assume, then, that the baseline of contractarian cooperation precludes coercion.

[18]I am assuming merely that if an act is not impermissible, then neither is threatening that act. I also think that sincerely threatening an act is not impermissible if and only if the act itself is not impermissible. But this is a stronger and more controversial principle, and my argument in this paper does not require it. On this issue, see Gregory S. Kavka, "Some Paradoxes of Deterrence," *Journal of Philosophy*, vol. 75 (1978), pp. 285–302; David P. Gauthier, "Deterrence, Maximization, and Rationality" (manuscript, University of Pittsburgh, 1983); and Gregory S. Kavka, "Deterrent Intentions and Retaliatory Actions" (manuscript, University of California, Irvine, 1983). Note also the analogy with punishment: one may legitimately threaten another with some specified punishment should this person commit some action, if so punishing would not be impermissible in the event that individual commits the specified action.

there is an important residue of mutual interest, enough to generate binding rules of conduct—those prohibiting certain weapons, protecting noncombatants, governing the treatment of prisoners, and so on. Thus, this argument is not a justification of terror or obliteration bombing, to cite just two examples. For instance, it is doubtful that the Allies during the latter years of World War II were in a situation in which P was suspended.[19] Certainly the American bombings of Tokyo and Hiroshima and Nagasaki could not be justified by the account I offer here; nothing has been said about suspending P in the pursuit of the unconditional surrender of an enemy state. Mere expediency in the conduct of war would not suffice to justify suspending P.

Nevertheless, an important objection deserves to be considered. In the event of an enemy attack, I have argued that massive countervalue retaliation is not prohibited because P (and other principles of justice) no longer would be in force. Thus killing the innocent would not be wrong (or right). Now someone might grant that we would be in a state of nature with regard to the Soviet leaders and other officials involved in the decision to attack, but demur at the idea that innocent Soviet citizens would be in a similar position. After all, the inhabitants of uninvolved third countries would not be placed in a state of nature by Soviet aggression against us, so we would not be relieved of the prohibition against attacking them. Why should Soviet children, for example, be different?

Such an objection to my argument is difficult to meet. I do not wish to argue that all persons are plunged back into a state of nature by enemy aggression and that we would not be acting wrongly were we to use the occasion to drop bombs on other peoples. Yet I do want to hold that we would not be acting wrongly to retaliate against innocent Soviet citizens in the event of a Soviet attack.

May we deter, for instance, an enemy nuclear attack by threatening some third party about which enemy leaders happen to care? Would the inhabitants of this otherwise uninvolved nation also be in a state of nature with respect to us in the event of an enemy nuclear attack?

According to my reasoning, members of society A are not prohibited from deterring attack by society B by threatening to kill innocent members of that society. Is A, however, not prohibited from deterring B by threatening to kill members of C, where C is an uninvolved third country? Should I agree, then am I not supposing that members of B are in some way collectively responsible for the aggressive acts of their leaders? It is hard to conceive of a plausible account of collective responsibility that could hold Soviet children responsible for the aggressive acts of Kremlin officials. Yet I must be able to distinguish between innocent Soviets and innocent third parties since I wish to hold that

---

[19]Although it is possible that the British were in precisely such a situation in the early years of World War II and that they were only then justified in suspending P and initiating the bombing of German cities. This does not appear to have been the case with the atomic bombing of Hiroshima and Nagasaki. See Walzer, *Just and Unjust Wars*, pp. 255ff.

the latter are not placed in a state of nature by the aggressive actions of Soviet leaders. A reply to this objection requires further analysis of the nature of contractarian moral relations between individuals and groups.

Two individuals who find themselves in the contractarian circumstances of justice and who directly interact with one another are bound to one another by obligations of justice. This much is granted by all contractarian moral theories. What if the individuals are in the circumstances of justice yet do not directly interact with one another? Suppose two individuals, Ann and Boris, stand to benefit mutually from cooperative interaction yet do not interact directly because they live very far apart, Ann in the United States, Boris in the Soviet Union. Yet the two are in the circumstances of justice. While Ann and Boris do not stand to benefit mutually from direct cooperative interaction (until they directly interact), they do stand to benefit from indirect cooperative interaction as members of different societies.

Cooperative relations can be direct or indirect. Obligations of justice can thus bind individuals directly, as natural individuals, or indirectly, as members of a group. Ann and Boris each have obligations of the first sort to the individuals with which they directly interact, perhaps most members of their respective societies. They have only obligations of the second sort to one another. These latter obligations they have by virtue of their membership in societies that stand to benefit from cooperative interaction. Obligations of international justice thus bind individuals only as citizens of a society; obligations of individual justice bind natural individuals.

Suppose that cooperative relations between two countries break down due to a nuclear attack of one upon the other. Then Ann and Boris would find themselves in a Hobbesian state of nature with respect to one another. While it is possible that they could be able to return to civil society with greater ease than their aggressive leaders, nonetheless relations of justice no longer obtain between them.

Note, however, that if Boris were visiting Ann in the United States when his leaders launched an attack, then each would be bound by justice to one another as natural individuals, even though neither would be bound to one another as members of different societies. Ann, or any other American, would be bound by justice not to kill Boris, assuming that he is innocent in the relevant sense.

What distinguishes Soviet citizens from third parties is that we remain bound by justice to the latter even when our obligations to the former are dissolved. In the absence of aggressive behavior on their part, relations of justice continue between the United States and third party nations, thus rendering nuclear strikes against them morally impermissible.

I shall briefly note an implication of this reply to the objection just considered. If we remain bound by justice to uninvolved third parties, then the doctrine of double effect (which I accept) obligates us to minimize the adverse side effects of nuclear retaliation on third parties. Were a massive nuclear retaliation against the Soviet Union to destroy human life on the planet, then the fourth condition of the doctrine of double effect would prohibit it. Note, though, that our obligations, according to my account, would be to the third parties and not to the Soviet citizens. My argument thus places some moral restrictions on the nature of a permissible retaliatory strike against an enemy nuclear attack. Such retaliation could not directly kill innocent third parties.

I have sketched a contractarian account of the moral prohibition on the killing of the innocent. If my account should prove to be sound, then I shall have provided reason to believe that threatening massive slaughter of the innocent is not a morally prohibited response to an enemy nuclear threat. Insofar as such an account is necessary in order to justify nuclear deterrence, which is under attack from both the right and the left, then the argument may prove a useful contribution to current debates.

The Challenge of Peace: God's Promise and Our Response

SUMMARY

The Second Vatican Council opened its evaluation of modern warfare with the statement: "The whole human race faces a moment of supreme crisis in its advance toward maturity." We agree with the council's assessment; the crisis of the moment is embodied in the threat which nuclear weapons pose for the world and much that we hold dear in the world. We have seen and felt the effects of the crisis of the nuclear age in the lives of people we serve. Nuclear weaponry has drastically changed the nature of warfare, and the arms race poses a threat to human life and human civilization which is without precedent.

We write this letter from the perspective of Catholic faith. Faith does not insulate us from the daily challenges of life but intensifies our desire to address them precisely in light of the gospel which has come to us in the person of the risen Christ. Through the resources of faith and reason we desire in this letter to provide hope for people in our day and direction toward a world freed of the nuclear threat.

As Catholic bishops we write this letter as an exercise of our teaching ministry. The Catholic tradition on war and peace is a long and complex one; it stretches from the Sermon on the Mount to the statements of Pope John Paul II. We wish to explore and explain the resources of the moral religious teaching and to apply it to specific questions of our day. In doing this we realize, and we want readers of this letter to recognize, that not all statements in this letter have the same moral authority. At times we state universally binding moral principles found in the teaching of the Church; at other times the pastoral letter makes specific applications, observations and recommendations which allow for diversity of opinion on the part of those who assess the factual data of situations differently. However, we expect Catholics to give our moral judgments serious consideration when they are forming their own views on specific problems.

The experience of preparing this letter has manifested to us the range of strongly held opinion in the Catholic community on questions of fact and judgment concerning issues of war and peace. We urge mutual respect among individuals and groups in the Church as this letter is analyzed and discussed. Obviously, as bishops, we believe that such differences should be expressed within the framework of Catholic moral teaching. We need in the Church not only conviction and commitment but also civility and charity.

While this letter is addressed principally to the Catholic community, we want it to make a contribution to the wider public debate in our country on the dangers and dilemmas of the nuclear age. Our contribution will not be primarily technical or political, but we are convinced that there is no satisfactory answer to the human problems of the nuclear age which fails to consider the moral and religious dimensions of the questions we face.

Although we speak in our own name, as Catholic bishops of the Church in the United States, we have been conscious in the preparation of this letter of the consequences our teaching will have not only for the United States but for other nations as well. One important expression of this awareness has been the consultation we have had, by correspondence and in an important meeting held at the Vatican (January 18–19, 1983), with representatives of European bishops' conferences. This consultation with bishops of other countries, and, of course, with the Holy See, has been very helpful to us.

Catholic teaching has always understood peace in positive terms. In the words of Pope John Paul II: "Peace is not just the absence of war....Like a cathedral, peace must be constructed patiently and with unshakable faith." (Coventry, England, 1982.) Peace is the fruit of order. Order in human society must be shaped on the basis of respect for the transcendence of God and unique dignity of each person, understood in terms of freedom, justice, truth and love. To avoid war in our day we must be intent on building peace in an increasingly interdependent world. In Part III of this letter we set forth a positive vision of peace and the demands such a vision makes on diplomacy, national policy, and personal choices.

While pursuing peace incessantly, it is also necessary to limit the use of force in a world comprised of nation states, faced with common problems but devoid of an adequate international political authority. Keeping the peace in the nuclear age is a moral and political imperative. In Parts I and II of this letter we set forth both the principles of Catholic teaching on war and a series of judgments, based on these principles, about concrete policies. In making these judgments we speak as moral teachers, not as technical experts.

I. SOME PRINCIPLES, NORMS AND PREMISES OF CATHOLIC TEACHING

A. On War

1 Catholic teaching begins in every case with a presumption against war and for peaceful settlement of disputes. In exceptional cases, determined by the moral principles of the just-war tradition, some uses of force are permitted.

2 Every nation has a right and duty to defend itself against unjust aggression.

3 Offensive war of any kind is not morally justifiable.

4 It is never permitted to direct nuclear or conventional weapons to "the indiscriminate destruction of whole cities or vast areas with their populations...." (*Pastoral Constitution*, #80.) The intentional killing of innocent civilians or non-combatants is always wrong.

5 Even defensive response to unjust attack can cause destruction which violates the principle of proportionality, going far beyond the limits of legitimate defense. This judgment is particularly important when assessing planned use of nuclear weapons. No defensive strategy, nuclear or conventional, which exceeds the limits of proportionality is morally permissible.

B. On Deterrence

1 "In current conditions 'deterrence' based on balance, certainly not as an end in itself but as a step on the way toward a progressive disarmament, may still be judged morally acceptable. Nonetheless, in order to ensure peace, it is indispensable not to be satisfied with this minimum which is always susceptible to the real danger of explosion." (Pope John Paul II, "Message to U.N. Special Session on Disarmament," #8, June 1982)

2 No *use* of nuclear weapons which would violate the principles of discrimination or proportionality may be *intended* in a strategy of deterrence. The moral demands of Catholic teaching require resolute willingness not to intend or to do moral evil even to save our own lives or the lives of those we love.

3 Deterrence is not an adequate strategy as a long-term basis for peace; it is a transitional strategy justifiable only in conjunction with resolute determination to pursue arms control and disarmament. We are convinced that "the fundamental principle on which our present peace depends must be replaced by another, which declares that the true and solid peace of nations consists not in equality of arms but in mutual trust alone." (Pope John XXIII, *Peace on Earth*, #113.)

C. The Arms Race and Disarmament

1 The arms race is one of the greatest curses on the human race; it is to be condemned as a danger, an act of aggression against the poor, and a folly which does not provide the security it promises. (Cf: *Pastoral Constitution*, #81, *Statement of the Holy See to the United Nations*, 1976.)

2 Negotiations must be pursued in every reasonable form possible; they should be governed by the "demand that the arms race should cease; that the stockpiles which exist in various countries should be reduced equally and simultaneously by the parties concerned; that nuclear weapons should be banned; and that a general agreement should eventually be reached about progressive disarmament and an effective method of control." (Pope John XXIII, *Peace on Earth*, #112.)

D. On Personal Conscience

1 *Military Service*: "All those who enter the military service in loyalty to their country should look upon themselves as the custodians of the security and freedom of their fellow countrymen; and when they carry out their duty properly, they are contributing to the maintenance of peace." (*Pastoral Constitution*, #79.)

2 *Conscientious Objection*: "Moreover, it seems just that laws should make humane provision for the case of conscientious objectors who refuse to carry arms, provided they accept some other form of community service." (*Pastoral Constitution*, #79.)

3 *Non-violence*: "In this same spirit we cannot but express our admiration for all who forego the use of violence to vindicate their rights and resort to other means of defense which are available to weaker parties, provided it can be done without harm to the rights and duties of others and of the community." (*Pastoral Constitution*, #78.)

4 *Citizens and Conscience*: "Once again we deem it opportune to remind our children of their duty to take an active part in public life, and to contribute towards the attainment of the common good of the entire human family as well as to that of their own political community.... In other words, it is necessary that human beings, in the intimacy of their own consciences, should so live and act in their temporal lives as to create a synthesis between scientific, technical and professional elements on the one hand, and spiritual values on the other." (Pope John XXIII, *Peace on Earth*, #146, 150.)

II. MORAL PRINCIPLES AND POLICY CHOICES

As bishops in the United States, assessing the concrete circumstances of our society, we have made a number of observations and recommendations in the process of applying moral principles to specific policy choices.

A. On the Use of Nuclear Weapons

1 *Counter Population Use*: Under no circumstances may nuclear weapons or other instruments of mass slaughter be used for the purpose of destroying population centers or other predominantly civilian targets. Retaliatory action

which would indiscriminately and disproportionately take many wholly innocent lives, lives of people who are in no way responsible for reckless actions of
their government, must also be condemned.

2 *The Initiation of Nuclear War*: We do not perceive any situation in which
the deliberate initiation of nuclear war, on however restricted a scale, can be
morally justified. Non-nuclear attacks by another state must be resisted by
other than nuclear means. Therefore, a serious moral obligation exists to
develop non-nuclear defensive strategies as rapidly as possible. In this letter
we urge NATO to move rapidly toward the adoption of a "no first use" policy,
but we recognize this will take time to implement and will require the development of an adequate alternative defense posture.

3 *Limited Nuclear War*: Our examination of the various arguments on this
question makes us highly skeptical about the real meaning of "limited." One
of the criteria of the just-war teaching is that there must be a reasonable hope
of success in bringing about justice and peace. We must ask whether such a
reasonable hope can exist once nuclear weapons have been exchanged. The
burden of proof remains on those who assert that meaningful limitation is
possible. In our view the first imperative is to prevent any use of nuclear
weapons and we hope that leaders will resist the notion that nuclear conflict
can be limited, contained or won in any traditional sense.

B.   On Deterrence

In concert with the evaluation provided by Pope John Paul II, we have arrived
at a strictly conditional moral acceptance of deterrence. In this letter we have
outlined criteria and recommendations which indicate the meaning of conditional acceptance of deterrence policy. We cannot consider such a policy
adequate as a long-term basis for peace.

C.   On Promoting Peace

1 We support immediate, bilateral verifiable agreements to halt the testing,
production and deployment of new nuclear weapons systems. This recommendation is not to be identified with any specific political initiative.

2 We support efforts to achieve deep cuts in the arsenals of both superpowers; efforts should concentrate first on systems which threaten the retaliatory forces of either major power.

3 We support early and successful conclusion of negotiations of a comprehensive test ban treaty.

4 We urge new efforts to prevent the spread of nuclear weapons in the
world, and to control the conventional arms race, particularly the conventional
arms trade.

5 We support, in an increasingly interdependent world, political and economic policies designed to protect human dignity and to promote the human

rights of every person, especially the least among us. In this regard, we call for the establishment of some form of global authority adequate to the needs of the international common good.

This letter includes many judgments from the perspective of ethics, politics and strategy needed to speak concretely and correctly to the "moment of supreme crisis" identified by Vatican II. We stress again that readers should be aware, as we have been, of the distinction between our statement of moral principles and of official Church teaching and our application of these to concrete issues. We urge that special care be taken not to use passages out of context; neither should brief portions of this document be cited to support positions it does not intend to convey or which are not truly in accord with the spirit of its teaching.

In concluding this summary we respond to two key questions often asked about this pastoral letter:

Why do we address these matters fraught with such complexity, controversy and passion? We speak as pastors, not politicians. We are teachers, not technicians. We cannot avoid our responsibility to lift up the moral dimensions of the choices before our world and nation. The nuclear age is an era of moral as well as physical danger. We are the first generation since Genesis with the power to threaten the created order. We cannot remain silent in the face of such danger. Why do we address these issues? We are simply trying to live up to the call of Jesus to be peacemakers in our own time and situation.

What are we saying? Fundamentally, we are saying that the decisions about nuclear weapons are among the most pressing moral questions of our age. While these decisions have obvious military and political aspects, they involve fundamental moral choices. In simple terms, we are saying that good ends (defending one's country, protecting freedom, etc.) cannot justify immoral means (the use of weapons which kill indiscriminately and threaten whole societies). We fear that our world and nation are headed in the wrong direction. More weapons with greater destructive potential are produced every day. More and more nations are seeking to become nuclear powers. In our quest for more and more security we fear we are actually becoming less and less secure.

In the words of our Holy Father, we need a "moral about-face." The whole world must summon the moral courage and technical means to say no to nuclear conflict; no to weapons of mass destruction; no to an arms race which robs the poor and the vulnerable; and no to the moral danger of a nuclear age which places before humankind indefensible choices of constant terror or surrender. Peacemaking is not an optional commitment. It is a requirement of our faith. We are called to be peacemakers, not by some movement of the moment, but by our Lord Jesus. The content and context of our peacemaking is set not by some political agenda or ideological program, but by the teaching of his Church....

MORAL PRINCIPLES AND POLICY CHOICES
[EXPANDED VERSION]

178. Targeting doctrine raises significant moral questions because it is a significant determinant of what would occur if nuclear weapons were ever to be used. Although we acknowledge the need for deterrent, not all forms of deterrence are morally acceptable. There are moral limits to deterrence policy as well as to policy regarding use. Specifically, it is not morally acceptable to intend to kill the innocent as part of a strategy of deterring nuclear war. The question of whether U.S. policy involves an intention to strike civilian centers (directly targeting civilian populations) has been one of our factual concerns.

179. This complex question has always produced a variety of responses, official and unofficial in character. The NCCB Committee has received a series of statements of clarification of policy from U.S. government officials.[1] Essentially these statements declare that it is not U.S. strategic policy to target the Soviet civilian population as such or to use nuclear weapons deliberately for the purpose of destroying population centers. These statements respond, in principle at least, to one moral criterion for assessing deterrence policy: the immunity of non-combatants from direct attack either by conventional or nuclear weapons.

180. These statements do not address or resolve another very troublesome moral problem, namely, that an attack on military targets or militarily significant industrial targets could involve "indirect" (i.e., unintended) but massive civilian casualties. We are advised, for example, that the United States strategic nuclear targeting plan (SIOP—Single Integrated Operational Plan) has identified 60 "military" targets within the city of Moscow alone, and that 40,000 "military" targets for nuclear weapons have been identified in the whole of the Soviet Union.[2] It is important to recognize that Soviet policy is subject to the same moral judgment; attacks on several "industrial targets" or politically significant targets in the United States could produce massive civilian casualties. The number of civilians who would necessarily be killed by such strikes is horren-

---

[1] Particularly helpful was the letter of January 15, 1983 of Mr. William Clark, national security adviser, to Cardinal Bernardin. Mr. Clark stated, "For moral, political and military reasons, the United States does not target the Soviet civilian population as such. There is no deliberately opaque meaning conveyed in the last two words. We do not threaten the existence of Soviet civilization by threatening Soviet cities. Rather, we hold at risk the war-making capability of the Soviet Union—its armed forces, and the industrial capacity to sustain war. It would be irresponsible for us to issue policy statements which might suggest to the Soviets that it would be to their advantage to establish privileged sanctuaries within heavily populated areas, thus inducing them to locate much of their war-fighting capability within those urban sanctuaries." A reaffirmation of the administration's policy is also found in Secretary Weinberger's *Annual Report to the Congress* (Caspar Weinberger, *Annual Report to the Congress*, February 1, 1983, p. 55): "The Reagan Administration's policy is that under no circumstances may such weapons be used deliberately for the purpose of destroying populations." Also the letter of Mr. Weinberger to Bishop O'Connor of February 9, 1983, has a similiar statement.

[2] S. Zuckerman, *Nuclear Illusion and Reality* (New York: 1982): D. Ball, cited, p. 36; T. Powers, "Choosing a Strategy for World War III," *The Atlantic Monthly*, November 1982, pp. 82–110.

dous.[3] This problem is unavoidable because of the way modern military facilities and production centers are so thoroughly interspersed with civilian living and working areas. It is aggravated if one side deliberately positions military targets in the midst of a civilian population. In our consultations, administration officials readily admitted that, while they hoped any nuclear exchange could be kept limited, they were prepared to retaliate in a massive way if necessary. They also agreed that once any substantial numbers of weapons were used, the civilian casualty levels would quickly become truly catastrophic, and that even with attacks limited to "military" targets, the number of deaths in a substantial exchange would be almost indistinguishable from what might occur if civilian centers had been deliberately and directly struck. These possibilities pose a different moral question and are to be judged by a different moral criterion: the principle of proportionality.

181.   While any judgment of proportionality is always open to differing evaluations, there are actions which can be decisively judged to be disproportionate. A narrow adherence exclusively to the principle of noncombatant immunity as a criterion for policy is an inadequate moral posture for it ignores some evil and unacceptable consequences. Hence, we cannot be satisfied that the assertion of an intention not to strike civilians directly, or even the most honest effort to implement that intention, by itself constitutes a "moral policy" for the use of nuclear weapons.

182.   The location of industrial or militarily significant economic targets within heavily populated areas or in those areas affected by radioactive fallout could well involve such massive civilian casualties that, in our judgment, such a strike would be deemed morally disproportionate, even though not intentionally indiscriminate.

183.   The problem is not simply one of producing highly accurate weapons that might minimize civilian casualties in any single explosion, but one of increasing the likelihood of escalation at a level where many, even "discriminating," weapons would cumulatively kill very large numbers of civilians. Those civilian deaths would occur both immediately and from the long-term effects of social and economic devastation.

184.   A second issue of concern to us is the relationship of deterrence doctrine to war-fighting strategies. We are aware of the argument that war-fighting capabilities enhance the credibility of the deterrent, particularly the strategy of extended deterrence. But the development of such capabilities raises other strategic and moral questions. The relationship of war-fighting capabilities and targeting civilian populations would violate the principle of discrimination—one of the central moral principles of a Christian ethic of war. But "counterforce targeting," while preferable from the perspective of protecting civilians, is often joined with a declaratory policy which conveys the notion that nuclear war is subject to precise rational and moral limits. We have already expressed

---

[3]Cf. the comments in Pontifical Academy of Sciences, "Statement on the Consequences of the Use of Nuclear Weapons," cited.

our severe doubts about such a concept. Furthermore, a purely counterforce strategy may seem to threaten the viability of other nations' retaliatory forces, making deterrence unstable in a crisis and war more likely.

185.   While we welcome any effort to protect civilian populations, we do not want to legitimize or encourage moves which extend deterrence beyond the specific objective of preventing the use of nuclear weapons or other actions which could lead directly to a nuclear exchange.

186.   These considerations of concrete elements of nuclear deterrence policy, made in light of John Paul II's evaluation, but applied through our own prudential judgments, lead to us to a strictly conditioned moral acceptance of nuclear deterrence. We cannot consider it adequate as a long-term basis for peace.

187.   This strictly conditioned judgment yields criteria for morally assessing the elements of deterrence strategy. Clearly, these criteria demonstrate that we cannot approve of every weapons system, strategic doctrine, or policy initiative advanced in the name of strengthening deterrence. On the contrary, these criteria require continual public scrutiny of what our government pro-poses to do with the deterrent.

188.   *On the basis of these criteria we wish now to make some specific evaluations:*

  1 If nuclear deterrence exists only to prevent the *use* of nuclear weapons by others, then proposals to go beyond this to planning for prolonged periods of repeated nuclear strikes and counterstrikes, or "prevailing" in nuclear war, are not acceptable. They encourage notions that nuclear war can be engaged in with tolerable human and moral consequences. Rather, we must continually say "no" to the idea of nuclear war.

  2 If nuclear deterrence is our goal, "sufficiency" to deter is an adequate strategy; the quest for nuclear superiority must be rejected.

  3 Nuclear deterrence should be used as a step on the way toward progressive disarmament. Each proposed addition to our strategic system or change in strategic doctrine must be assessed precisely in light of whether it will render steps toward "progressive disarmament" more or less likely.

189.   Moreover, these criteria provide us with the means to make some judgments and recommendations about the present direction of U.S. strategic policy. Progress toward a world freed of dependence on nuclear deterrence must be carefully carried out. But it must not be delayed. There is an urgent moral and political responsibility to use the "peace of a sort" we have as a framework to move toward authentic peace through nuclear arms control, reductions, and disarmament. Of primary importance in this process is the need to prevent the development and deployment of destabilizing weapons systems on either side; a second requirement is to insure that the more sophisticated command and control systems do not become mere hair triggers for automatic launch on warning; a third is the need to prevent the proliferation of nuclear weapons in the international system.

190. In light of these general judgments *we oppose* some specific proposals in respect to our present deterrence posture:

1 The addition of weapons which are likely to be vulnerable to attack, yet also possess a "prompt hard-target kill" capability that threatens to make the other side's retaliatory forces vulnerable. Such weapons may seem to be useful primarily in a first strike;[4] we resist such weapons for this reason and we oppose Soviet deployment of such weapons which generate fear of a first strike against U.S. forces.

2 The willingness to foster strategic planning which seeks a nuclear war-fighting capability that goes beyond the limited function of deterrence outlined in this letter.

3 Proposals which have the effect of lowering the nuclear threshold and blurring the difference between nuclear and conventional weapons.

191. In support of the concept of "sufficiency" as an adequate deterrent, and in light of the present size and composition of both the U.S. and Soviet strategic arsenals, we *recommend*:

1 Support for immediate, bilateral, verifiable agreements to halt the testing, production, and deployment of new nuclear weapons systems.[5]

2 Support for negotiated bilateral deep cuts in the arsenals of both superpowers, particularly those weapons systems which have destabilizing characteristics; U.S. proposals like those for START (Strategic Arms Reduction Talks) and INF (Intermediate-range Nuclear Forces) negotiations in Geneva are said to be designed to achieve deep cuts.[6] Our hope is that they will be pursued in a manner which will realize these goals.

3 Support for early and successful conclusion of negotiations of a comprehensive test ban treaty.

4 Removal by all parties of short-range nuclear weapons which multiply dangers disproportionate to their deterrent value.

5 Removal by all parties of nuclear weapons from areas where they are likely to be overrun in the early stages of war, thus forcing rapid and uncontrollable decisions on their use.

6 Strengthening of command and control over nuclear weapons to prevent inadvertent and unauthorized use.

192. These judgments are meant to exemplify how a lack of unequivocal condemnation of deterrence is meant only to be an attempt to acknowledge the role attributed to deterrence, but not to support its extension beyond the

---

[4]Several experts in strategic theory would place both the MX missile and Pershing II missiles in this category.

[5]In each of the successive drafts of this letter we have tried to state a central moral imperative: that the arms race should be stopped and disarmament begun. The implementation of this imperative is open to a wide variety of approaches. Hence we have chosen our own language in this paragraph, not wanting either to be identified with one specific political initiative or to have our words used against specific political measures.

[6]Cf. President Reagan's "Speech to the National Press Club" (November 18, 1981) and "Address at Eureka College" (May 9, 1982), Department of State, *Current Policy* #346 and #387.

limited purpose discussed above. Some have urged us to condemn all aspects of nuclear deterrence. This urging has been based on a variety of reasons, but has emphasized particularly the high and terrible risk that either deliberate use or accidental detonation of nuclear weapons could quickly escalate to something utterly disproportionate to any acceptable moral purpose. That determination requires highly technical judgments about hypothetical events. Although reasons exist which move some to condemn reliance on nuclear weapons for deterrence, we have not reached this conclusion for the reasons outlined in this letter.

193.   Nevertheless, there must be no misunderstanding of our profound skepticism about the moral acceptability of any use of nuclear weapons. It is obvious that the use of any weapons which violate the principle of discrimination merits unequivocal condemnation. We are told that some weapons are designed for purely "counterforce" use against military forces and targets. The moral issue, however, is not resolved by the design of weapons or the planned intention for use; there are also consequences which must be assessed. It would be a perverted political policy or moral casuistry which tried to justify using a weapon which "indirectly" or "unintentionally" killed a million innocent people because they happened to live near a "militarily significant target."

194.   Even the "indirect effects" of initiating nuclear war are sufficient to make it an unjustifiable moral risk in any form. It is not sufficient, for example, to contend that "our" side has plans for "limited" or "discriminate" use. Modern warfare is not readily contained by good intentions or technological designs. The psychological climate of the world is such that mention of the term "nuclear" generates uneasiness. Many contend that the use of one tactical nuclear weapon could produce panic, with completely unpredictable consequences. It is precisely this mix of political, psychological, and technological uncertainty which has moved us in this letter to reinforce with moral prohibitions and prescriptions the prevailing political barrier against resort to nuclear weapons. Our support for enhanced command and control facilities, for major reductions in strategic and tactical nuclear forces, and for a "no first use" policy (as set forth in this letter) is meant to be seen as a complement to our desire to draw a moral line against nuclear war.

195.   Any claim by any government that it is pursuing a morally acceptable policy of deterrence must be scrutinized with the greatest care. We are prepared and eager to participate in our country in the ongoing public debate on moral grounds.

196.   The need to rethink the deterrence policy of our nation, to make the revisions necessary to reduce the possibility of nuclear war, and to move toward a more stable system of national and international security will demand a substantial intellectual, political, and moral effort. It also will require, we believe, the willingness to open ourselves to the providential care, power and word of God, which call us to recognize our common humanity and the bonds of mutual responsibility which exist in the international community in spite of political differences and nuclear arsenals.

197.   Indeed, we do acknowledge that there are many strong voices within our own episcopal ranks and within the wider Catholic community in the United States which challenge the strategy of deterrence as an adequate response to the arms race today. They highlight the historical evidence that deterrence has not, in fact, set in motion substantial processes of disarmament.
198.   Moreover, these voices rightly raise the concern that even the conditional acceptance of nuclear deterrence as laid out in a letter such as this might be inappropriately used by some to reinforce the policy of arms buildup. In its stead, they call us to raise a prophetic challenge to the community of faith—a challenge which goes beyond nuclear deterrence, toward more resolute steps to actual bilateral disarmament and peacemaking. We recognize the intellectual ground on which the argument is built and the religious sensibility which gives it its strong force.
199.   The dangers of the nuclear age and the enormous difficulties we face in moving toward a more adequate system of global security, stability and justice require steps beyond our present conceptions of security and defense policy. In the following section we propose a series of steps aimed at a more adequate policy for preserving peace in a nuclear world.

*   *   *

SUGGESTED SUPPLEMENTARY READINGS TO PART EIGHT

Cockburn, Andrew: *The Threat: Inside the Soviet Military Machine* (New York: Random House, 1983).
Ethics (April, 1985): A special edition of the journal devoted to the issue of nuclear deterrence.
Ground Zero: *Nuclear War: What's in It for You?* (New York: Pocket Books, 1982).
Harvard Study Group: *Living with Nuclear Weapons* (New York: Bantam Books, 1983).
Holmes, Arthur: *War and Christian Ethics* (Grand Rapids, Mich.: Baker Book House, 1971).
Johnson, James: *Just War Tradition and the Restraint of War* (Princeton, N.J.: Princeton University Press, 1981).
Kennan, George: *Nuclear Delusion* (New York: Pantheon, 1983).
Lefever, Ernest W., and Hunt, E. Stephan: *The Apocalyptic Premise* (Chicago: The University of Chicago Press, 1982).
Ramsey, Paul: *The Just War* (Lanham, Md.: University Press of America, 1983).
Sterba, James P., ed.: *The Ethics of War and Nuclear Deterrence* (Belmont, Calif.: Wadsworth Publishing Co., 1984).
Union of Concerned Scientists: *Beyond the Freeze* (Boston: Beacon Press, 1982).
U.S. Department of Defense: *Soviet Military Power* (Washington, D.C.: U.S. Government Printing Office, 1983).
U.S. Office of Technology: *The Effects of Nuclear War* (Washington, D.C.: U.S. Government Printing Office, 1979).
Walzer, Michael: *Just and Unjust Wars* (New York: Basic Books, 1977).

(See also the bibliography included in the footnotes of the article, "Nuclear Deterrence and Self-Defense," by Thomas Donaldson in this volume.)

APPENDIX

THE HUMAN LIFE BILL

Be it enacted by the Senate and House of Representatives of the United States of America in Congress assembled, *That title 42 of the United States Code shall be amended at the end thereof by adding the following new chapter:*

Chapter 101

SECTION 1. (a) The Congress finds that the life of each human being begins at conception.

(b) The Congress further finds that the fourteenth amendment to the Constitution of the United States protects all human beings.

PURPOSE OF THE PROPOSED ACT

The purpose of S. 158 is first, to recognize the biological fact that the life of each human being begins at conception; second, to affirm that every human life has intrinsic worth and equal value regardless of its stage or condition; and third, to enforce the fourteenth amendment by ensuring that its protection of life extends to all human beings.

NEED FOR THIS LEGISLATION

To protect the lives of human beings is the highest duty of government. Our nation's laws are founded on respect for the life of each and every human being. The Declaration of Independence holds that the right to life is a

475

self-evident, inalienable right of every human being. Embodied in the statement that "all men are created equal" is the idea of the intrinsic worth and equal value of every human life. The author of the Declaration, Thomas Jefferson explained in later years that "[t]he care of human life and happiness, and not their destruction, is the first and only legitimate object of good government."

Today there is a strong concern among many citizens that government is not fulfilling its duty to protect the lives of all human beings. Since 1973 abortion has been available on demand nationwide, resulting in more than one and one-half million abortions per year. Yet this abrupt and fundamental shift in policy occurred without any prior inquiry by any branch of the federal government to determine whether the unborn children being aborted are living human beings. Nor has any branch of the federal government forthrightly faced the question whether our law should continue to affirm the sanctity of human life—the intrinsic worth and equal value of all human life—or whether our law should now reject the sanctity of life in favor of some competing ethic. Only by determining whether unborn children are human beings, and deciding whether our law should and does accord intrinsic worth and equal value to their lives, can our government rationally address the issue of abortion.

The Subcommittee has taken pains to separate its consideration of the two questions. In this report we shall often refer to the "scientific question" and the "value question" as a convenient shorthand. We have analyzed the testimony of various witnesses and sources of public record as they relate to each question separately. And we report separately our conclusions on each question.

We emphasize that both questions must be answered by some branch of government before the abortion issue can be fully and rationally resolved. The need for Congress to investigate both questions stems partly from the self-professed institutional limitations of our federal judiciary. The Supreme Court, in its 1973 abortion decision, declared itself unable to resolve when the life of a human being begins: "When those trained in the respective disciplines of medicine, philosophy, and theology are unable to arrive at any consensus, the judiciary, at this point in the development of man's knowledge, is not in a position to speculate as to the answer." *Roe v. Wade*, (1973). The Court went on to explain that a "wide divergence of thinking" exists on the "sensitive and difficult" question of when a human life begins; hence, the judiciary is not competent to resolve the question.

As a result of its self-professed inability to decide when the life of a human being begins, the Supreme Court rendered its 1973 abortion decision without considering whether unborn children are living human beings. And because the Court did not consider whether unborn children are living human beings, it was able to avoid an explicit decision on whether our law accords intrinsic worth and equal value to the life of every human being regardless of stage or condition. The Court thus declined to address either of the crucial questions relevant to protecting unborn children under the law: the Court addressed neither the scientific question nor the value question. The Court's entire 1973 opinion concerning the power of states to protect unborn children—including the Court's ruling on personhood of the unborn—must be read in light of this failure to resolve the two fundamental questions concerning the existence and value of unborn human life.

That a judicial decision addressing neither of these fundamental questions has led to a national policy of abortion on demand throughout the term of pregnancy is a great anomaly in our constitutional system. It is important to examine the judicial reasoning that led to this result. The Court held that "the right of personal privacy includes the abortion decision," but added that "this right is not unqualified and must be considered against important state interests in regulation."...Because it did not resolve whether unborn children are human beings, the Court could not make an informed decision on whether abortions implicate the interest and duty of the states to protect living human beings. Still, without purporting to know whether unborn children are living human beings, the Court stated by fiat that they are not protected as persons under the fourteenth amendment.

Then the Court created judge-made rules governing abortions. During the first three months of an unborn child's life, the states may do nothing to regulate or prohibit the aborting of the child. In the next three months of the unborn child's life, the state may regulate only the manner in which the child is aborted; but abortion remains available on demand. In the final three months before the child is born, the states may prohibit abortions except when necessary to preserve the "life or health of the mother."...

The apparently restrictive standard for the third trimester has in fact proved no different from the standard of abortion on demand expressly allowed during the first six months of the unborn child's life. The exception for maternal health has been so broad in practice as to swallow the rule. The Supreme Court has defined "health" in this context to include "all factors—physical, emotional, psychological, familial, and the woman's age—relevant to the well-being of the patient." *Doe v. Bolton*, (1973). Since there is nothing to stop an abortionist from certifying that a third-trimester abortion is beneficial to the health of the mother—in this broad sense—the Supreme Court's decision has in fact made abortion available on demand throughout the pre-natal life of the child, from conception to birth....

A congressional determination that unborn children are human beings and that their lives have intrinsic worth and equal value will encourage the Court to reexamine the results and the reasoning of *Roe v. Wade*. In *Roe* the Court expressed a desire to decide the abortion issue "consistent with the relative weights of the respective interests involved...." The Court's view of the relative weight of the interests of the unborn child was necessarily influenced by the Court's professed inability to determine whether the unborn child was a living human being. It is difficult to believe that the Court would again balance the respective interests in such a way as to allow abortion on demand, if the Court were to recognize that one interest involved was the life of a human being.

THE SCIENTIFIC QUESTION: WHEN DOES A HUMAN LIFE BEGIN

During the course of eight days of hearings, fifty-seven witnesses testified on S. 158 before the Subcommittee. Of these witnesses, twenty-two, including world-renowned geneticists, biologists, and practicing physicians, addressed the medical and biological questions raised by the bill. Eleven testified in support of the bill and eleven in opposition.

The testimony of these witnesses and the voluminous submissions received by the Subcommittee demonstrate that contemporary scientific evidence points to a clear conclusion: the life of a human being begins at conception, the time when the process of fertilization is complete. Until the early nineteenth century science had not advanced sufficiently to be able to know that conception is the beginning of a human life; but today the facts are beyond dispute....

It may at first seem difficult to reconcile the existence of such a broad consensus with the testimony of some witnesses opposing S. 158 before this subcommittee who emphatically denied that it is possible to determine when a human life begins. If the facts are so clear, it is crucial to understand how, for example, one noted professor of genetics from Yale University School of Medicine could say that he knows of no scientific evidence that shows when actual human life exists.

Such statements appear on the surface to present a direct contradiction to the biological evidence discussed above. The explanation of this apparent contradiction lies in the existence of the two distinct questions identified above, the scientific question and the value question. We must consider not only whether unborn children are human beings but also whether to accord their lives intrinsic worth and value equal to those of other human beings. The two questions are separate and distinct. It is a scientific question whether an unborn child is a human being, in the sense of a living member of the human species. It is a value question whether the life of an unborn child has intrinsic worth and equal value with other human beings.

Those witnesses who testified that science cannot say whether unborn children are human beings were speaking in every instance to the value question rather than the scientific question. No witness raised any evidence to refute the biological fact that from the moment of human conception there exists a distinct individual being who is alive and is of the human species. No witness challenged the scientific consensus that unborn children are "human beings," insofar as the term is used to mean living beings of the human species....

THE VALUE QUESTION: SHOULD WE VALUE ALL HUMAN LIVES EQUALLY?

The answer to the scientific question casts the value question in clear relief. Unborn children are human beings. But should our nation value all human lives equally? Scientific evidence is not relevant to this question. The answer is a matter of ethical judgement.

Deeply engrained in American society and American constitutional history is the ethic of the sanctity of innocent human life. The sanctity-of-life ethic recognizes each human life as having intrinsic worth simply by virtue of its being human. If, as a society, we reject this ethic, we must inevitably adopt some other standard for deciding which human lives are of value and are worthy of protection. Because the standards some use to make such decisions turn on various qualities by which they define which lives are worthy of protection, the alternative to the sanctity-of-life ethic is often termed the "quality-of-life ethic." A sharp division exists today between those who affirm the sanctity-of-life ethic and those who reject it in favor of the quality-of-life ethic. The Supreme Court has never purported to decide which ethic our Constitution mandates for valuing the lives of human beings before birth. Nevertheless, deciding which ethic should apply is fundamental to resolving the abortion issue under the Constitution....

Advocates of a quality-of-life ethic vary in the qualities they choose as a standard for which human lives to value. The common element of every "quality of life" view, however, is a denial of the intrinsic worth of all human life, along with an attempt to define what qualities must be present in a human being before its life is to be valued.

Our constitutional history leaves no doubt which ethic is written into our fundamental law. The Declaration of Independence expressly affirms the sanctity of human life:

> We hold these truths to be self-evident, that all men are created equal, that they are endowed by their Creator with certain unalienable rights, that among these are life, liberty, and the pursuit of happiness.

The proponents of the fourteenth amendment argued for the amendment on the basis of these principles. Congressman John A. Bingham of Ohio, who drafted the first section of the fourteenth amendment, stated after the adoption of the Joint Resolution of Congress proposing this amendment:

> Before that great law [of the United States,] the only question to be asked of the creature claiming its protection is this: Is he a man? Every man is entitled to the protection of American law, because its divine spirit of equality declares that all men are created equal.

It is instructive to note that the highest court of West Germany accorded constitutional protection to unborn children precisely because the court affirmed the principle of the sanctity of human life. The "Basic Law," or the Bonn constitution, of West Germany guarantees the "right to life." The court explained this guarantee as a reaction against the Nazi regime's idea of "Destruction of Life Unworthy to Live" and as an "affirmation of the fundamental value of human life...."

Because it affirms the Constitution, the Subcommittee cannot accept any legal rule that would allow judges, scientists, or medical professors to decide that some human lives are not worth living. We must instead affirm the intrinsic worth of *all* human life. We find that the fourteenth amendment embodies the sanctity of human life and that today the government must affirm this ethic by recognizing the "personhood" of all human beings. Earlier we found, based upon scientific examination, that the life of each human being begins at conception. Now, basing our decision not upon science but upon the values embodied in our Constitution, we affirm the sanctity of all human life. Science can tell us whether a being is alive and a member of the human species. It cannot tell us whether to accord value to that being. The government of any society that accords intrinsic worth to all human life must make *both* factual determination recognizing the existence of all human beings *and* a value decision affirming the worth of human life.